AFRICAN VOICES ON SLAVERY AND THE SLAVE TRADE

Even though the history of slavery is a central topic for African, Atlantic world, and world history, most of the sources presenting research in this area are European in origin. To cast light on African perspectives, and on the point of view of enslaved men and women, this group of top Africanist scholars has examined both conventional historical sources (e.g., European travel accounts, colonial documents, court cases, and missionary records) and less-explored sources of information (e.g., folklore, oral traditions, songs and proverbs, life histories collected by missionaries and colonial officials, correspondence in Arabic, and consular and admiralty interviews with runaway slaves). Each source has a short introduction highlighting its significance and orienting the reader. This volume provides students and scholars with a trove of African sources for studying African slavery and the slave trade.

Alice Bellagamba is an associate professor of cultural anthropology and African studies at the University of Milan-Bicocca. She is the author of *Ethnographie, histoire et colonialism en Gambie* (2002) and *L'Africa e la stregoneria: Saggio di antropologia storica* (2008) and coeditor of *Beside the State: Emergent Powers in Contemporary Africa* (with Georg Klute, 2008). She has extensive fieldwork experience in the Senegambia and, since 2000, has directed MEBAO, a network of Italian and African scholars working on historical memory and heritage in West Africa. In 2004–05, she was Alexander Humboldt Fellow at the University of Bayreuth, and in 2011–12 a EURIAS senior Fellow at the Institute of Advanced Studies of Berlin.

Sandra E. Greene is a professor of African history at Cornell University. She has served as president and vice-president of the African Studies Association. Greene has written three books: *West African Narratives of Slavery: Texts from Late Nineteenth- and Early Twentieth-Century Ghana* (2011); *Sacred Sites and the Colonial Encounter: A History of Meaning and Memory in Ghana* (2002), which was a finalist for the 2003 Herskovits Award; and *Gender, Ethnicity and Social Change on the Upper Slave Coast: A History of the Anlo-Ewe* (1996), which earned an Honorable Mention from the 1997 Herskovits Award Committee.

Martin A. Klein is currently Professor Emeritus in the Department of History at the University of Toronto. Klein has taught African history for thirty-four years. He has served as president of both the African Studies Association (ASA) and the Canadian Association of African Studies. He has written or edited several books, including *Historical Dictionary of Slavery and Abolition* (2002); *Slavery and Colonial Rule in Africa* (Cambridge 1998), edited with Suzanne Miers; *Breaking the Chains: Slavery, Bondage, and Emancipation in Modern Africa and Asia* (1993); and *Women and Slavery in Africa* (1983), edited with Claire C. Robertson. His book *Slavery and Colonial Rule in French West Africa* earned an Honorable Mention from the Herskovits Award Committee. In 2001, Klein was awarded the ASA's Distinguished Africanist Award. He also edits Cambridge University Press's *New Perspectives in African History* series.

AFRICAN VOICES ON SLAVERY AND THE SLAVE TRADE

Edited by

ALICE BELLAGAMBA
University of Milan-Bicocca

SANDRA E. GREENE
Cornell University

MARTIN A. KLEIN
University of Toronto

With the assistance of Carolyn Brown

CAMBRIDGE
UNIVERSITY PRESS

CAMBRIDGE
UNIVERSITY PRESS

University Printing House, Cambridge CB2 8BS, United Kingdom

One Liberty Plaza, 20th Floor, New York, NY 10006, USA

477 Williamstown Road, Port Melbourne, VIC 3207, Australia

4843/24, 2nd Floor, Ansari Road, Daryaganj, Delhi - 110002, India

79 Anson Road, #06-04/06, Singapore 079906

Cambridge University Press is part of the University of Cambridge.

It furthers the University's mission by disseminating knowledge in the pursuit of education, learning and research at the highest international levels of excellence.

www.cambridge.org
Information on this title: www.cambridge.org/9780521145268

First published 2013
First paperback edition 2017

A catalogue record for this publication is available from the British Library

Library of Congress Cataloging in Publication data
Bellagamba, Alice.
    African voices on slavery and the slave trade / Alice Bellagamba, Sandra E. Greene, Martin A. Klein with the assistance of Carolyn Brown.
        p.   cm.
    Includes bibliographical references and index.
    ISBN 978-0-521-19470-9 (hardback)
    1. Slavery – Africa – History.   2. Slave trade – Africa – History.   3. Oral history – Africa.   I. Greene, Sandra E., 1952–   II. Klein, Martin A.   III. Title.
    HT1321.B39   2012
    306.362096–dc23   2012034316

ISBN 978-0-521-19470-9 Hardback
ISBN 978-0-521-14526-8 Paperback

CONTENTS

FIGURES

CONTRIBUTORS

Benjamin Acloque has focused on slavery in Mauritania since 1995 on which he has produced several academic works and articles. He is currently completing a PhD in social anthropology at the Ecole des Hautes Etudes en Sciences Sociales (EHESS) in Paris about the forms of hierarchy within a religious community (Ahl Barikalla) straddling Mauritania and Western Sahara.

Yacine Daddi Addoun is an assistant professor of African and African-American studies at the University of Kansas. He is interested in issues of slavery and its abolition in Algeria, the Sahara, the Maghreb, and the Islamic world more broadly, as well as the enslavement of Muslims in Europe and the New World.

Kofi Anyidoho is a professor of literature in the English Department and the first occupant of the Kwame Nkrumah Chair in African Studies at the University of Ghana-Legon. He has published numerous collections of poetry, the most recent of which include *Praise Song for the Land: Poems of Hope & Love & Care* (2002) and *The Place We Call Home* (2011). As a literary scholar, Anyidoho has also published many journal articles and book chapters, and he has edited a number of major books on African literature and culture. He is a past director of the CODESRIA African Humanities Institute Program and past president of the U.S.-based African Literature Association.

Felicitas Becker is a lecturer in African history at the University of Cambridge and a specialist in modern East African history with a particular focus on Islam. She has previously taught at Simon Fraser University, Vancouver, and SOAS, London. Her research interests include Muslim reform movements in trans-regional context, the aftermath of slavery and struggles for citizenship, women's history, political performance, and popular histories of "development."

Alice Bellagamba is an associate professor of social and cultural anthropology and African studies at the University of Milan-Bicocca. She has extensive fieldwork experience in the Gambia and neighboring Senegalese regions. Currently she is completing a research project that explores the history of the end of slavery in colonial Gambia. Using archival, oral, and ethnographic sources, she is also examining the impact that Gambia's internal slave-trading and slaveholding past has had on that country in more contemporary times.

Klara Boyer-Rossol is a PhD candidate in history of Africa at the University of Paris. She is studying the East African diaspora around the Indian Ocean, and more particularly the Makoa, who arrived on the west coast of Madagascar from continental Africa as slaves during the nineteenth century. She is interested in how they maintain and negotiate an original group identity, based on their recognition of ancestors who came from "overseas." Her research uses oral sources collected during fieldwork on the west coast of Madagascar.

Alessandra Brivio is an anthropologist. She holds a postdoctoral degree in anthropology from the University of Milan-Bicocca. Her research interests are African religions and memory of slavery in Africa. She has conducted field research in Benin, Togo, and Ghana.

Benjamin Claude Brower teaches history at the University of Texas at Austin. He is the author of *A Desert Named Peace: The Violence of France's Empire in the Algerian Sahara, 1844–1902* (2009).

Francesca Declich teaches social anthropology at the University of Urbino. She has written extensively about the Bantu speakers of southern Somalia and their origins in countries in East Africa, as well as about slavery in Somalia. Among her books and articles on these issues are "Gendered Narratives, History and Identity: Two Centuries along the Juba River among Zigula and Shanbara," in *History in Africa* (1995), and *I Bantu della Somalia. Etnogenesi e rituali mviko nella Somalia meridionale* (2002). She is currently engaged in a project concerning memories of slavery in northern Mozambique and, as a Fulbright Scholar at Stanford University, works on forced migrants from Somalia in Tanzania and the United States.

E. S. D. Fomin is currently teaching in the Department of History at the University of Yaounde-1, Cameroon. He has published several scholarly books and many articles in peer-reviewed journals, and he has a plethora of still-to-be-published conference papers. He was a 1997 NUFU grant beneficiary and a Ford Foundation Fellow at the University of Ghana-Legon in 1998, which have enabled him to coordinate many research projects on the legacy of slavery on Africa.

Paolo Gaibazzi is a lecturer in social anthropology at the University of Latvia. He works on the historical and contemporary dynamics of (im)mobility among the Gambian Soninke, with a specific focus on youth and on the relation between social stratification and migration.

Trevor Getz is a professor of African history at San Francisco State University. He is the author of *Slavery and Reform in West Africa* (2004) and *Abina and the Important Men* (2011). He is currently editing the new *Oxford African World Histories* series.

Sandra E. Greene is a professor of African history at Cornell University. She is the author of *Gender, Ethnicity and Social Change on the Upper Slave Coast* (1996); *Sacred Sites and the Colonial Encounter* (2002); *West African Narratives of Slavery* (2011); and numerous articles. She has also been president of the African Studies Association (United States).

Bruce S. Hall is an assistant professor in the Department of History at The Johns Hopkins University. He is the author of *A History of Race in Muslim West Africa, 1600–1960* (2011).

Bayo Holsey is an associate professor of African and African-American studies at Duke University, specializing in diaspora studies. In addition to her numerous articles in such journals as *Transition* and *Critique Internationale*, her book, *Routes of Remembrance* (2008), won the 2008 Amaury Talbot Prize for African Anthropology and the Association of Third World Studies 2008–2009 Toyin Falola Africa Book Award.

Hilary Jones is an assistant professor of history at the University of Maryland, College Park. She is the author of articles on marriage, urban society, and French republican politics in nineteenth-century Senegal. Her monograph, *The Métis of Senegal: Urban Life, Politics and French Colonialism in Nineteenth Century West Africa*, is forthcoming.

Martin A. Klein is Professor Emeritus at the University of Toronto, where he taught African history for twenty-nine years. He is the author of *Slavery and Colonial Rule in French West Africa* (1998) and has edited a number of books, including *Breaking the Chains: Slavery, Bondage and Emancipation in Modern Africa and Asia* (1993) and, with Claire Robertson, *Women and Slavery in Africa* (1983). He has served as president of the African Studies Association and the Canadian Association of African Studies.

George Michael La Rue is a professor of history at the Clarion University of Pennsylvania. He did his doctoral field research in Dar Fur, Sudan, and he continues to work on issues related to slavery in the Sudan and Egypt. His recent publications include "'My Ninth Master was a European': Enslaved Blacks in European Households in Egypt, 1798–1848," in Terence Walz and Kenneth Cuno, eds., *Race and Slavery in the Middle East: Histories of Trans-Saharan Africans in Nineteenth-Century Egypt, Sudan, and the Ottoman Mediterranean* (2010), and "The Brief Life of 'Ali, the Orphan of Kordofan," in Gwyn Campbell, ed., *Children in Slavery Through the Ages* (2009).

Ghislaine Lydon is an associate professor of African history at the University of California, Los Angeles. She has written articles and book chapters on a variety of topics, including caravan trade, slave transactions, and Muslim cultures. She is the author of *On Trans-Saharan Trails: Islamic Law, Trade Networks and Cross-Cultural Exchange in Nineteenth-Century Western Africa* (2009), winner of the Martin A. Klein Prize in African History.

Kristin Mann is a professor of history at Emory University. She is the author of *Marrying Well: Marriage, Status, and Social Change among the Educated Elite in Colonial Lagos* (1985) and *Slavery and the Birth of an African City: Lagos, 1760–1900* (2007) and the coeditor of *Law in Colonial Africa* (1991) and *Rethinking the African Diaspora: The Making of a Black Atlantic World in the Bight of Benin and Brazil* (2001). Kristin is currently working on a new research project, "Trans-Atlantic Lives: Slavery and Freedom in West Africa and Brazil."

Elisabeth McMahon is an assistant professor in the Department of History at Tulane University. Her current research examines the emotional lives of slaves in eastern Africa. She has published work in the *International Journal of African Historical Studies*, the *Journal of Women's History*, *Women's History Review*, and *Quaker History*.

Ismael M. Montana is an assistant professor of African history at Northern Illinois University. He specializes in the study of slavery and its abolition in eighteenth- and nineteenth-century Ottoman-Tunisia, and especially on the West African Hausa-speaking communities in Tunis. He coedited, with Paul E. Lovejoy and Behnaz A. Mirzai, *Slavery, Islam and Diaspora* (2009).

Bruce L. Mouser is Professor Emeritus of history from the University of Wisconsin–La Crosse. His principal research focus has been on the social and commercial transformation of the northern rivers of Sierra Leone between 1750 and 1860. His writings include *A Slaving Venture to Africa and Jamaica* (2002), three monographs in the University of Leipzig Papers on Africa series, and four in the University of Wisconsin African Studies Publications series. Mouser also publishes in African-American political history, *For Labor, Race, and Liberty* (2011), which the Society of Midland Authors awarded Second Best Biography written by a midwestern author for 2010/2011.

Olatunji Ojo teaches African history at Brock University, Ontario. His research interests, which include slavery, ethnicity, and identity formation, center on the history of social and economic change. His more recent publications include "'[I]n search of their relations, to set at liberty as many as they had the means': Ransoming Captives in Nineteenth Century Yorubaland," *Nordic Journal of African Studies* (2010), and "'Heepa' (Hail) Òrìsà: The Òrìsà Factor in the Birth of Yoruba Nation," *Journal of Religion in Africa* (2009).

Richard Roberts is the Frances and Charles Field Professor of History at Stanford University. He has written widely on the social history of French West Africa. His more recent books include *Litigants and Households: African Disputes and Colonial Courts in the French Soudan, 1895–1912* (2005). He has also coedited a number of volumes, including *Domestic Violence and the Law in Colonial and Postcolonial Africa*, with Emily Burrill and Elizabeth Thornberry (2010); *Muslim Family Law in Sub-Saharan Africa*, with Shamil Jeppie and Ebrahim Moosa (2010); and *Trafficking in Women and Children in Colonial and Postcolonial Africa*, with Benjamin Lawrance (2011).

Marie Rodet is a lecturer in African history in the School of Oriental and African Studies at the University of London. Her principal research interests lie in the field of migration history, gender studies, and history of slavery in West Africa in the nineteenth and twentieth centuries. Her most recent publications include *Les migrantes ignorées du Haut-Sénégal, 1900–1946* (2009) and an article, "Memories of Slavery in the Region of Kayes" in *Cahiers d'Études africaines* (2010).

Ute Röschenthaler teaches cultural anthropology at Goethe University, Frankfurt. She works on the history, culture, and economy of the Cross River region and on branded products in urban Mali and Cameroon. Her books include *Purchasing Culture: The Dissemination of Associations in the Cross River Region of Cameroon and Nigeria* (The Harriet Tubman Series of the African Diaspora).

Benedetta Rossi holds a Research Councils United Kingdom (RCUK) Fellowship in the Department of History of the University of Liverpool, where she teaches courses in African history and directs an MA program in International Slavery Studies. Her recent publications include the edited volume *Reconfiguring Slavery: West African Trajectories* (2009) and the coedited volume *Being and Becoming Hausa: Interdisciplinary Perspectives* (2010). She is currently finalizing a monograph on transformations of government in the Ader region of Niger over the late nineteenth and twentieth centuries.

Dana Rush is an assistant professor of African and African diaspora art history at the University of Illinois, Urbana. Her focus within the art history of Africa and its many diasporas is the arts and expressive cultures of the transatlantic religious system of Vodun, or Vodou as it is known in the Caribbean and the Americas. Her publications include articles in *African Arts* and *Journal Politique Africaine* and in a number of edited volumes. Her forthcoming book is entitled *Global Vodun: World Encounters with Coastal Bénin.* Her current research and next book project focus on histories and memories of domestic slavery in Bénin and Togo, which have been sustained to the present by the progeny of domestic slaves and their owners through multiform arts, religious performances, and oral histories.

Mohammed Bashir Salau is an assistant professor of history at the University of Mississippi. He is the author of *The West African Slave Plantation: A Case Study* (2011).

Ahmadou Sehou is a researcher at the University of Yaounde I (Cameroon), where he completed his PhD entitled L'esclavage dans les Lamidats de l'Adamaoua (Nord-Cameroun), du début du XIXᵉ à la fin du XXᵉ siècle (2010). He is the author of Cameroon's National Scientific Report for the UNESCO Slave Route Project, 2011. He is also a member of the Centre Africain de Recherches sur les Traites et les Esclavages (CARTE), Université Cheikh Anta Diop de Dakar (Sénégal).

Silke Strickrodt is a research Fellow at the German Historical Institute London. She is the author of *Those Wild Scenes: Africa in the Travel Writing of Sarah Lee (1791–1856)* (1998) and various articles on the history of the Slave Coast, Gold Coast, and Sierra Leone and editor (with Robin Law) of *Ports of the Slave Trade – Bights of Benin and Biafra* (1999).

Hideaki Suzuki is a postdoctoral Research Fellow at the Japan Society for the Promotion of Science and also research associate for the Indian Ocean World Centre, McGill University. As a historian, he focuses on the western Indian Ocean. His thesis is about slave traders in the nineteenth century in that region. He has published several articles in Japanese about the slave trade, slavery, and the Indian mercantile community, and his most recent interest is in redefining the Indian Ocean world.

Jeanne Maddox Toungara is an associate professor of history at Howard University. She is the author of more than a dozen articles on the history of women, family, education, economy, and politics of various West African communities. Her work has appeared in the *Journal of Modern African Studies, Journal of African Studies, Journal of Social History, Annales de l'Université d'Abidjian, African Studies Review, Les cahiers de la paix, West African Research Association Newsletter*, and others. She has contributed essays and chapters in *African Women: States of Crisis* (1996), *The Younger Brother in Mande* (1996), and *The Oxford Companion to the Politics of the World* (1993), and she is working on a book-length manuscript on political culture in the northwestern region of Côte d'Ivoire.

Pierluigi Valsecchi is a professor of African history in the Department of Political and Social Studies at the University of Pavia, Italy. He has worked on Ghanaian history and is the author of *Power and State Formation in West Africa: Appolonia from the 16th to the 18th Century* (2011) and coeditor (with Fabio Viti) of *Mondes Akan/Akan Worlds: Identity and Power in West Africa* (1999). His current research deals with the nineteenth- and twentieth-century history of the Ghana–Côte d'Ivoire border regions.

KOFI ANYIDOHO

African societies, by and large, remain predominantly oral in their modes of cultural production and transmission. It seems logical, therefore, that documentation and dissemination of knowledge in and about Africa must constantly strive to go beyond the printed word. At the University of Ghana, I was privileged to lead a 1997–1998 African Humanities Institute held under the theme *Memory & Vision: Africa and the Legacy of Slavery*. Our choice of theme was guided by a strong conviction that in order to make a more confident stride into the future, the continent of Africa – and indeed African peoples worldwide – needs to reexamine closely the full implications of what one scholar appropriately describes as "the single most traumatic body of experience in all our known history. Slavery is the living wound under the patchwork of scars."[1]

For slightly more than two weeks beginning on February 8, 1998, our team of African and African diaspora researchers was totally absorbed by an important field trip that put us on the trail of ancient slave routes. Our aim, quite simply, was to examine whatever traces there still might be of the legacy of slavery and the slave trade on the physical, cultural, and social landscape of certain communities known to have been most affected by the slave trade.

On our journey into the turbulent history of slavery and the slave trade in Africa, we as researchers discovered we had to reorder our thoughts. Above all, we had to revise our preferred notions of historical reconstruction and documentation. We had begun our program with a series of well-prepared lectures by eminent historians, literary scholars, and many others, almost all of whom had drawn heavily on archival records and countless written sources. Out there in the field, we discovered that some of the most challenging, the most engaging, and indeed the most compelling records and reminders of the experience of slavery and the slave trade were not to be located in the scripted and printed word, but deep in the minds and hearts of those for whom the experience of slavery must forever remain "a living wound." The people may or may not choose to talk about the experience and its pained recollection. But its traces are there in the landscape dominated by the silk cotton and the baobab trees – lonely giants stranded amid scenes of desolation – in the cryptic language of songs sung at play by a new generation of children, in the heavily encoded battle dress of the Sandema warrior dancers, in the closely guarded relics that

---

[1] Opoku-Agyemang, *Cape Coast Castle* (Accra, 1996), 1.

make up the mysterious wealth of Azagsuk, in the eternally vigilant ancestral deity of Fiisa, and in the dark recesses of those mysterious ancient caves at Sankana, which once served as the ultimate refuge against the constant menace of slave raiders.

The Ghanaian poet Kobena Eyi Acquah reminds us in his poem "Ol' Man River":

> For there are some things
> Which can only be said in song
> Only in the mother tongue[2]

We must add that there are also some things that can only be said through the deeply encoded language of the drum and the dance. This presents researchers into African history and culture with unresolved challenges. Among them is the challenge of developing a new kind of literacy, the ability and skills to read and interpret a range of sources: not only written texts, but also sources created by Africans themselves. For there are indeed some things that can only be said through the deeply encoded language of the drum and the dance. Even if we are able to read the drum and the dance, there is the other challenge of how to write and print these ancient modes of human communication. The challenge is real and perplexing, but it is not beyond a possible solution. However, it will require the combined skills and efforts of psychologists, linguists, historians, literary scholars, and musicologists. But even these specialists working together may not get very far without the crucial input of various experts within the oral, non-scribal tradition itself, experts such as Babalawo Akinwunmi, master teacher to Otis, the protagonist in Isidore Okpewho's novel, *Call Me by My Rightful Name*.[3] It is the drum that calls Otis again and again to return to ancestral time; and to do so he must go in style, he must dance his way back to a mythic memory of who he once was. And when in this same novel, the twin centenarian, Taiwo, wakes up one morning and is moved by "a certain feeling," she recognizes that it is something deeper than joy that moves her – a "Compulsion! To … dance" – and "she begins to wriggle her frail body, her arms swaying to a silent measure." As Kehinde, her twin sister, contemplates Taiwo's performance, she is also "touched by a tolerable lightness of being."[4] To understand the full significance and meaning of the dance and its accompanying ancestral chant, we, like Otis, must turn to Babalawo Akinwunmi, Ifa specialist, diviner, and healer, to guide our understanding through the maze of memory back to where things began to go wrong. Expert as well is the unnamed slave driver who effortlessly, almost casually, interprets the language of the drums to Ama, the enslaved protagonist in Manu Herbstein's novel *Ama*, as they approach the Asante royal palace in Kumasi.[5]

In the search for such experts, our greatest challenge and also our greatest hope is in finding the true owners of the story, the genuine guardians of the sacred word. For it is in their mouths and voices that the past is reborn; it is in their eyes that the darkness of the past once again transforms into the glowing light of knowledge and vision. And in their bodies, as revealed in dance, the frozen breath of history warms up once more into livid moments of memory as an energizing force.

---

[2]   Kobena Eyi Acquah, *Mystic of a Dream Dance* (Accra, 1989), 30.
[3]   Isidore Okpewho, *Call Me by My Rightful Name* (Trenton, NJ, 2004).
[4]   Okpewho, *Call Me*, 2.
[5]   Manu Herbstein, *Ama: A Story of the Atlantic Slave Trade* (Johannesburg, 2005).

MEMORY & VISION[6]

[for Children of *Musu*]

> We are Dancer and The Dance.
>
> Time before Memory.
> Memory beyond Time.
>
> We harvest Tears
> from laughter's Eyes.
> We even sow some Joy
> in sorrow's deepest Soul.
>
> We are Dancer and The Dance.
>
> In the space between the Drums & Us
> You'll feel unfold
> The endless saga of Ancestral Time.
>
> We are Dancer and The Dance.

There is a Journey we all must make into our Past
in order to come to terms with our Future.

For Five Hundred Years   and more   we have
journeyed into various spaces of the Earth.
And everywhere we go   we must confront
dimensions of ourselves we did not know were there.

There is something of Our-Story
something of our Mystery
carved into every TombStone
in all the Graveyards of the World
something of our History Enshrined
in every Monument and in every Anthem
ever erected in honour of the Spirit of Endurance.

Back home here   here in Africa
we perform our ResurrectionDance
in the company of Hyenas
pretending to be RoyalAncestors.

Some tell us ourSalvation
lies in a repudiation of ourSelves
a repudiation of ourHistory
of Pain   ourHistory
of Shame   ourHistory
of Endless Fragmentation

---

[6] Originally published in Kofi Anyidoho, *Praise Song for the Land* (Accra, 2002). It was composed at the invitation of choreographer F. Nii Yartey and performed as the opening and closing act of *Musu: Saga of the Slaves*, a dance drama written and directed by Nii Yartey.

But we must wander through History
into Myth and Memory
seeking Lost Landmarks
in a Geography of Scars
and of Tormented Remembrances.

It cannot   mustnot be
that the rest of the world came upon us
picked us up   used us to clean up their mess
dropped us off into trash   and moved on
into new eras of celebrative arrogance
hopeful   somehow hopeful that we shall forever
remain lost among shadows of our own doubts
lost forever among shadows of our own doubts.

Ours is the **IntroBlues**
the Forever Journey into **SoulTime**.

It is the quest for a Future
alive with the energy of Recovered
vision   a Future
released from the Trauma
of a Cyclonic Past
and from the Myopia
of a Stampeded Present.

With so much waiting to be undone
with so much left so long undone
to keep calling our situation a dilemma
is just a bad excuse for inaction.

Somehow   somehow   we must
recall that we are a People
who once rode the Dawn
with Civilization's Light
still glowing through our Mind.

And if today we seem lost among Shadows
we must probe the deep Night of our Blood
and seek out our Birth-Cord
from the garbage heap of History's crowded Lies.

A People once enSlaved   they say
are too often too willing
to be a People Self-enSlaved.

Always   we must recall the Fate
of those who fought to the Death
of the Last Warrior Fought
& Fought to the Death

& Resurrection
of the Final Hope.

> *So they wiped them out?*
> *Drowned their screams*
> *Burned their nerves and bones*
> *And scattered their ashes*
> *Across the intimidating splendour*
> *Of this young history of lies?*

The Asante   the Azande   and the Mande
the Madingo   and the Bakongo
the Basuto   the Dagaaba   and the Dogon
a people who once built Civilizations
of rare Glory
are now but Doubtful
memories on faded pages
of World History.

And
For Five Hundred Years – and more –
we've journeyed from Africa
through the Virgin Islands into Santo Domingo
from Havana in Cuba   to Savanna in Georgia
from Voudou Shores of Haiti   to Montego
Bay in Jamaica   from Ghana
to Guyana   from the Shanty-Towns
of Johanesburg   to the Favelas
in Rio de Janeiro
from Bukom   to Harlem   to Brixton
from Hamburg   to Moscow   to Kyoto –
and all we find   are a Dis-
possessed and Battered
people   still kneeling in a Sea
of Blood   lying Deep
in the Path of Hurricanes.

No matter how far away we try to hide away from ourSelves
we will have to come back
Home and find out   Where   and How   and Why
we lost
the Light in our Eyes.   How   and Why
we have become
Eternal Orphans living on Crumbs and LeftOvers.

We are the Dog who caught the Game
but now must sit under the table   Cracking
our Hopes over Bones
over Droppings from the Master's Hands.

In spite of all that pain   we can say Without a Doubt
that as a people   we do hold the World Record
for survival against the most Unreasonable Odds.

Yes   we hold the most spectacular Survival Record.
But we must hasten to remind ourSelves

> that just to survive
> simply to survive
> merely to survive
> barely to survive
> is not & can
> never be enough.

> *And so still we stand so tall among the cannonades*
> *We smell of mists   and of powdered memories.*

> *And those who took away our Voice*
> *They are now surprised*
> *They couldnt take away our Song.*

FINDING THE AFRICAN VOICE

ALICE BELLAGAMBA, SANDRA E. GREENE, AND MARTIN A. KLEIN

I t is always difficult to recover ordinary lives from the folds of history. This is especially true when it comes to slavery. For more than 400 years, men, women, and children from Africa were forcibly transported to other parts of the world. Most of their names have been lost. Their thoughts and feelings, their suffering and hopes, the little joys of their daily lives have disappeared from memory. New societies emerged and old ones were restructured as they absorbed enslaved African men, women, and children with a profound effect on the recipient societies and on those African communities that provided the slaves. Slavery and the slave trade also played a crucial role in the internal history of Africa, a past that post-abolition African societies recollect with even more difficulties than the relationships created by centuries of external slave trade between Africa and the rest of the world.

This volume of primary sources casts light on both the external and internal slave trade, and on the place of slavery in the political, economic, social, and cultural setup of Africa itself. The contributions are linked by the effort of giving voice to African perceptions and representations of one of the most tragic and sad aspects of African history.

Interest in the influence of slavery on human societies gripped the contemporary imagination in the United States, in part, as a result of the civil rights struggle. In finally acknowledging the rightful claims to full citizenship rights by peoples of African descent (most of whose ancestors had been enslaved), all Americans were forced to recognize the importance of slavery in shaping the history of the Americas. During this same period – that is, in the 1960s–1970s – social historians in Europe and the Americas were starting to challenge the elitist nature of the mainstream historiography. By examining the hidden histories of commoners, workers, women, and other historically subordinated groups, they brought to light the exploitation that many had suffered at the hands of the powerful and the prestigious. These were the contexts that saw the study of slavery and other injustices fire the historical imaginations of scholars far and wide but it took a bit longer for slavery and the slave trade within Africa to enter the picture. Colonial regimes, which held onto power up to the 1960s, saw these practices in Africa as a problem they had solved despite contrary evidence that they in fact continued to exist in places on the continent. African nationalists and the first generation of African scholars who had participated in efforts to free their countries from colonial domination also had no interest in exploring the heritage of slavery or the internal slave trade. They feared it would divide their new, fragile nations. Instead, they focused on histories that contributed to the establishment of a unifying pride in the pasts of their newly independent countries. That objective was shared also by scholars from the West who focused on reconstructing the histories and cultures in Africa's past. Instead of considering the ignoble past of internal slavery and slave trade, they concentrated on collecting formal oral traditions, historical narratives that served as the charters for existing political structures and that could be used to construct the kinds of academic histories that nationalists needed to foster the much sought-after pride in local institutions and practices undermined by European colonialists. When both African and Western scholars, under the influence of the changing political and intellectual trends in the Americas and Europe, began to turn their attention to slavery, they soon learned that this field of research was fraught with difficulties. There were silences in colonial archives, and informants of slave origin were generally reluctant to discuss their histories. Memories of slavery were unsettling for those whose ancestors owned slaves and for those who were the descendants of the enslaved. The children and grandchildren of the masters often did not want to talk about what their ancestors had done, and the descendants of slaves did not want to speak of a status from which they sought to escape. Many of the oral sources presented in this volume illustrate this restraint.

In 1969, Philip Curtin published *African Slave Trade: A Census*,[1] which critically examined estimates for the slave trade and tried to produce new ones. This spawned a major body of research on slave trade demography[2] that has made available a great deal of information about the slave trade and about slavery within Africa. We know not only about overall numbers, but about regional and ethnic distribution, male-female ratios, the number of children exported, and the organization of the trade. Yet, there are limitations. The demographic studies about the export trade –whether they focus on Africa or the Americas – are based on European and American shipping and customs records. It was clear that slavery and the vast military and commercial machine that supplied the labor needs of the Americas, of the Arabic Peninsula, and of the Indian Ocean also fed a demand for labor within Africa. Field research generated some material about the internal trade and slavery within Africa, but European sources were far more abundant. The earliest works on slavery within Africa – those of Claude Meillassoux, Suzanne Miers, Igor Kopytoff, Frederick Cooper, Paul Lovejoy, Claire Robertson, and Martin Klein[3] – focused less on quantitative analyses and more on qualitative descriptions. They did so using their own field observations and, for many, accounts produced by such European informants as slave traders, missionaries, and colonial administrators. But what of African perspectives? We need to hear how Africans understood and now remember that part of their own past associated with slavery and the slave trade. We need to listen to African voices.

Perhaps the earliest and most important effort to find African voices came once again from Philip Curtin, whose *Africa Remembered* culled a series of African narratives from

---

[1] From the University of Wisconsin Press.

[2] The culmination of almost forty years of research has been gathered together into the Transatlantic Slave Trade Database, which now contains data on about 35,000 of estimated 41,000 slave voyages across the Atlantic. See http://www.slavevoyages.org/tast/database/search

[3] Claude Meillassoux (ed.), *L'esclavage en Afrique precoloniale* (Paris, 1975); Suzanne Miers and Igor Kopytoff (eds.), *Slavery in Africa* (Madison, 1977); Frederick Cooper, *Plantation Slavery on the East Coast of Africa* (New Haven, 1977); Paul E. Lovejoy, *The Ideology of Slavery in Africa* (Beverly Hills, 1981); Claire Robertson and Martin A. Klein (eds.), *Women and Slavery in Africa* (Madison, 1983).

rare published literature.[4] This study was supplemented in the 1990s by Marcia Wright's *Strategies of Slaves and Women*. In that volume, Wright tapped the life histories of women caught in the maelstrom of the East African slave trade, which had been collected by missionaries. It produced a picture that focused on the strategies of enslaved women.[5] Then in the course of the 1990s, the United Nations Educational, Scientific and Cultural Organization (UNESCO) Slave Route project encouraged research on the causes, forms of operations, and consequences of the slave trade.[6] In 1998, the distinguished Ghanaian poet, Kofi Anyidoho, organized a seminar entitled 'Memory and Vision: Africa and the Legacy of Slavery,' which took a group of African and diaspora scholars through the hinterland of Ghana to explore African tales of slavery and the slave trade. In the process, Anyidoho developed a methodology that focused not on personal histories, but on memories of places and events. In the same year, the historian Djibril Tamsir Niane brought together a number of contributions on oral traditions and slavery in an online publication sponsored by UNESCO.[7] Scholars like Mamadou Diawara and Akosua Perbi were simultaneously finding ways to access memories of slavery by collecting songs, proverbs, and folktales,[8] while Ibrahima Thioub was chastising his colleagues for having downplayed the role of slavery in modern African history.[9] By making fresh materials available, this volume considers the ways Africans experienced slavery and the slave trade, and what followed in the course of abolition. Giving voice to slaves and the descendants of slaves has been our major concern. As our contributors make clear, this objective is not always achievable in the strict sense of finding sources articulated by slaves themselves. More often than not, their voices must be disentangled from narratives, texts, records, and an array of other evidence not originally meant to represent their perspective like missionary accounts, court records, and the historical narratives of master descendants.

The immediate genesis of this collaborative project was the organization in 2004 by Sandra Greene and Carolyn Brown of the African Slavery Oral Narratives Project. They believed that a lot of data on African slavery could be found in the field notes of scholars who were asking other questions and wanted to encourage scholars to take a deeper look at their data. A few years later, troubled particularly by the problem of finding slave voices, Alice Bellagamba suggested to Martin Klein that they organize a conference on the topic at the Rockefeller Foundation conference center at Bellagio, Italy. When it turned out that Brown and Greene had similar plans, we joined together. The conference took place in 2007. Much to our surprise, we received so many interesting proposals that we could not host them all at a conference center that had a capacity limit of twenty-three persons. As a result, we held a second and larger conference in Toronto in 2009.

---

[4] Philip Curtin (ed.), *Africa Remembered: Narratives by West Africans from the Era of the Atlantic Slave Trade* (Madison, 1967).

[5] Marcia Wright, *Strategies of Slaves and Women* (New York, 1993).

[6] http://portal.unesco.org/culture/en/ev.php-URL_ID=25659&URL_DO=DO_TOPIC&URL_SECTION=201.html

[7] Djibril Tamsir Niane, *Traditional Orale et Archives de la Traite Negrière* (Paris, 1998).

[8] Mamadou Diawara, *La Graine de la Parole.Dimension sociale et politique des traditions orales du royaume de Jaara (Mali) du XVeme au milieu du XIXeme siècle* (Stuttgart, 1989); Akosua Perbi, *A History of Indigenous Slavery in Ghana from the 15th to the 19th Century* (Accra, 2004).

[9] Ibrahima Thioub, "Regard critique sur les lectures africaines de l'esclavage et de la traite atlantique," in Issiaka Mande and Blandine Stefanson (eds.), *Les historiens africaines et la mondialisation* (Paris, 2005).

We found that many scholars – some established, but also a significant number of younger ones – were thinking about the same methodological problems that concerned us. Furthermore, some were interested in exploring different kinds of sources. We were interested in any kind of sources that cast light on how Africans experienced slavery, and in particular from the point of view of the enslaved. Much of what was presented at the conferences involved not new methodologies, but more critical and systematic ways of approaching older ones, although we were also interested in exploring new types of sources. We came to realize that there existed surprising potential in oral traditions, proverbs, and songs, but also in rituals and material culture. Kofi Anyidoho's foreword and poem invite us to pay attention to the living memories of slavery and the slave trade textured into the fabric of contemporary African societies. As they often require long-term acquaintance with people and contexts along with knowledge of the language in which they are performed and of the larger social and cultural background, such sources have often stymied researchers. This is one of the reasons why the selection of materials we present here opens with oral sources. The volume is divided into nine parts, each preceded by a short introduction. Each document has an introduction that comments on the way the sources were collected or identified and their value for the analysis of slavery. A list of questions helps the reader think critically about the source, and a short bibliography is provided for further reading.

The documents in Part One are not the formal state narratives that were the focus of research in the 1960s, but rather the oral traditions, historical tales, and interviews that present the perspectives of former slaves and their children as well as the descendants of the masters. They illustrate the diversity of traditions within Africa and the different kinds of information found in them. These documents give details on slave systems, life in slavery, and the struggles of ex-slaves for upward social mobility.

Part Two looks at a relatively unexplored set of sources: proverbs, songs, and material culture.[10] These sources present us with few facts, but rather with the way images have persisted, sometimes buried in fantastic folktales or religious rituals, at other times in songs and proverbs. These folk memories begin to give us a picture of the fears engendered by four centuries of slave-raiding and the ways those memories are perpetuated into the present.

Part Three focuses on African written accounts of slavery. It includes the defense of slavery by a slaveholding African chief, culled from the archives, the treatment of slavery in an African-authored text, and the effort of an African intellectual to understand the history of his own society. These documents suggest that more sources can be found illustrating diverse African attitudes and experiences. Some documents also display the ambiguous situations in which some Africans found themselves.[11]

The African voice is sometimes implicit in action and at other times is presented in the words of others. Part Four deals with European travelers' accounts. There are documents on slave flight in Tunisia, an account by a European travel writer of the poignant dilemma of the African concubine of a French pharmacist, a French description of a slave

---

[10] At the Toronto conference, Nicholas Argenti presented a paper of the memories of slavery buried in children's stories from Cameroon. It is being published as "Things that Don't Come by the Road: Folktales, Fosterage, and Memories of Slavery in the Cameroon Grassfields", *Comparative Studies in Society and History* 52 (2010), 224–254.

[11] Randy Sparks presented at Bellagio the letters of the sons of prominent slave traders from Calabar, who were enslaved in a local conflict but quickly freed and lionized while living in England, often by people hostile to slavery. We did not publish these because Sparks has written on the case. See Randy Sparks, *Two Princes of Calabar: An Eighteenth Century Atlantic Odyssey* (Cambridge, MA, 2004).

woman shipped north into Saharan slavery, and an account of a European sailor who at the beginning of the eighteenth century described the social inequalities and hierarchies of the Gold Coast.

Part Five suggests that in spite of the research already done, there is a lot of material to be found in colonial archives. The African voice is found in the letters and petitions Africans addressed to their colonial rulers and in the things Africans did. It is filtered through the reports and perceptions of colonial administrators and military officers who had to deal with slaves and sometimes reported their dealings. But a critical reading of these documents gives us a picture of the struggles of ordinary Africans.

One of the most important sources on the African experience is the courtroom. Part Six presents cases in which slaves appear either as litigants or as object of litigation. There are limitations to what we can get from judicial sources. African testimonies are shaped by their strategies and by the advice of prosecutors, defense attorneys, and judges. They do, however, provide examples of slaves speaking in their own voices. The cases presented here illustrate the trade in and exploitation of slave women, but one deals with slavery and inheritance and another involves the report of a slave trader brought in front of the court for his activities.

Part Seven involves missionary sources. Unlike administrators, missionaries stayed in one place and generally learned the languages of those they were trying to convert. Most of the early converts to Christianity were slaves. The missions often wrote up the experience of their converts in order to publicize what they were doing and to raise money to continue their efforts. Mission archives are thus often a rich source of the slave experience.[12] The cases presented here give a few of those stories, including two documents that raise the issue of human sacrifice.

The possibility of Muslim sources, written either in Arabic or in African languages using Arabic script, has recently come to light as scholars have begun working with documents preserved in private archives. The Ahmed Baba Institute in Timbuktu has 700,000 documents. There are more in other repositories. Many of these documents have not yet been studied, but Part Eight contains letters between a commercial family and a slave who traded on its behalf (Chapter 42). There is also a study of a court case involving a runaway slave in Mauritania (Chapter 43). Finally, Chapter 44 presents a totally unexpected source: slave wills from the island of Pemba in East Africa. This is particularly interesting because slaves were not supposed to be able to bequeath.

The last part of the volume focuses on the contemporary legacy of slavery, specifically the way in which the descendants of slaves and the descendants of masters shape their current relationships. In many parts of West Africa, the stigma associated with slave origins endures, but so too have slave descendants continued their struggle to gain respect and social recognition in the course of the twentieth and twenty-first centuries.[13]

* * *

Carolyn Brown was part of the team that initiated this project. She was valuable in the conceptualization of the conferences that led to this book, provided valuable contacts, and did

---

[12] Wright, *Strategies* Edward Alpers, "Suema."

[13] For more such cases, see Alice Bellagamba, Sandra Greene, Martin Klein, *The Bitter Legacy. African slavery past and present* (Princeton, 2013). For contemporary slavery, see Kevin Bales, *Disposable People: New Slavery in the Global Economy* (Berkeley and Los Angeles, 1999); Joel Quirk, *The Anti-Slavery Project. From the Slave Trade to Human Trafficking* (Philadelphia, 2011); Benjamin N. Lawrance and Richard L. Roberts, *Trafficking in Slavery's Wake. Law and the Experience of Women and Children in Africa* (Athens, 2012).

some editing. We valued her collaboration and regret that other commitments forced her to drop out of the editing of this volume.

We would like to thank those who have aided our work. For the 2007 workshop in Bellagio, we are indebted to the Rockefeller Foundation and the staff at Bellagio, who provided a welcoming environment conducive to debate and reflection. They also generously provided funds to bring four colleagues from Africa. For the Toronto conference, we are particularly indebted to the Jackman Humanities Institute, which provided financial support, and to Rick Halpern, then Principal of New College (University of Toronto), who provided advice, financial assistance, and a comfortable environment. Members of New College staff, particularly Krishnan Mehta, were also invaluable. Further, we thank Paul Lovejoy and the Harriet Tubman Institute for Research on the Global Migrations of African Peoples, the Connaught Foundation, and the Centre for Transnational and Diaspora Studies at the University of Toronto. We particularly appreciate the work of our webmaster, Yacine Daddi Addoun. The Italian Ethnological Mission in Bénin and West Africa (MEBAO) supported the fieldwork research and the travel expenses of Italian participants, while in various ways, the three universities of Cornell, Rutgers, and Milan-Bicocca aided the participation of Greene, Brown, and Bellagamba in the conferences and editorial meetings that led to the creation of this volume. Finally, we thank everyone who participated in the Toronto conference, including our team of student volunteers, along with the legion of African colleagues, oral historians, archivists, scholars, and ritual specialists who enabled our contributors' access to the sources included in this volume.

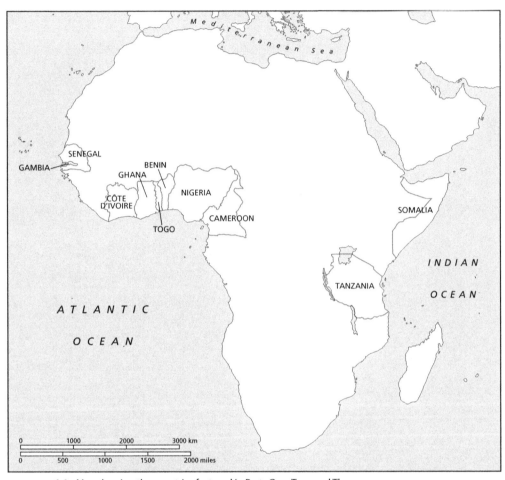

1.1. Map showing the countries featured in Parts One, Two, and Three.
Source: Based on a map published by *Africa Today*. Revised Edition (1990).

PART ONE

REMEMBERING SLAVERY AND THE SLAVE TRADE

1 INTRODUCTION: Oral Traditions, Historical Tales, and Interviews

Oral data on African slavery are a rich source of information, especially when one is trying to enrich historical interpretations with studies about the lives of real people. For a variety of reasons, however, such source materials are difficult to access and interpret, a problem that should never be underestimated.

Post-abolition African societies have confronted the distasteful legacy of slave-dealing and slaveholding mostly by obliterating it from all levels of public discussion. Many local communities also share an understanding that emphasizes the notion that digging into the past is a potentially conflict-laden exercise. Memories of enslavement and life in slavery can disrupt contemporary social alignments by reopening the wounds of past violence and suffering. In the course of the twentieth century, and even today, this has made both individuals and groups extremely selective about what they deem worthy of narration.

Forgetting, however, is a more complicated task than commonly assumed, even when oblivion is systematically organized. Memories that one section of a society considers dangerous another opts to preserve covertly. Things unspoken in public can be narrated in confidential settings, thus circumventing cultural and social censorship. Such narrative strategies apply not only to personal recollections, but also to the mnemonic reserves out of which oral traditions (which historians of Africa have depicted as often lacking direct reference to slavery and the slave trade) are built. It all depends on the ways historical knowledge is produced, shared, and transmitted in the social and cultural context under scrutiny and on the researcher's ability (and patience) to tackle the nuances of this multi-layered process.

The problem of interpretation comes next. It goes without saying that oral data that directly or indirectly refer to slavery, the slave trade, and enslaved individuals can help develop a robust and grounded knowledge of African slavery from an African point of view. But like more conventional historical sources, these data should not be taken at face value. The narrative structure of this kind of materials is deeply culturally embedded. The performer and the audience share a common reservoir of meanings and representation, which might sound confusing to outsiders. Proper historical and ethnographic contextualization is crucial to a full understanding of the messages oral data carry.

The chapters in this part of the volume present three different kinds of oral sources. The first are oral traditions from Ghana and the River Gambia. Following the classic definition developed by historians of Africa, oral traditions are information about the past transmitted across generations by word of mouth. The message usually refers to a historical period antecedent to the lifetime of the narrator, although some historians prefer a broader definition that includes personal and social reminiscences. The second category of sources consists of historical tales from Cameroon, Benin, and Togo. These differ from oral traditions not because of the mode of transmission, but because the content blurs the boundary between facts and fiction in the very eyes of the narrators and the audience. The third group presents a set of interviews from Southern Tanzania, Kano (northern Nigeria), and Senegal, and provides insight into the ways in which the research encounter shapes the production of historical knowledge.

ORAL TRADITIONS

In strict terms, the expression "oral tradition" denotes both the content of what is transmitted and the process of its transmission. This means that researchers have to pay attention to what is narrated and to the practices and contexts through which knowledge about the past is handed down through the generations, whether done deliberately or not.

In former times, the production and reproduction of oral traditions depended almost exclusively on the interests of the narrators and their audiences in talking about and listening to parts of their past. Oral traditions that stopped being performed simply disappeared. Transmission patterns, however, changed with the arrival of professional historians from the 1950s onward, and with the massive spread of Islamic and Western literacy in the second part of the twentieth century.

Today, the boundary between oral and written texts has become fuzzier. Researchers, for instance, can access oral data collected, transcribed, and edited by their predecessors (like the Asante and Gonja sources introduced by Sandra E. Greene in Chapter 2). The challenge, as Greene explains, is to clear up why certain sets of memories (in this specific case associated with the lives of eighteenth-century enslaved individuals) have been kept alive until the time they were recorded. Their political use to sustain legitimacy claims is one of the possible reasons. In Chapter 3, Alice Bellagamba presents an oral narrative about slavery produced in 2000 by Bakoyo Suso, a renowned twentieth-century Gambian griot and oral historian. By quoting examples from the nineteenth-century history of the River Gambia, Bakoyo offers a sensitive reflection on slavery and the slave trade, which is deeply rooted in local history, and addresses issues of moral, social, and political concern to contemporary Gambian society. What kind of social world sustained slavery and the slave trade? Is that past really gone forever?

HISTORICAL TALES

Messages from past generations are not always remembered and transmitted to others because of their historical content. At times, their moral script is more important. This does not prevent their use as historical source to uncover the social and intellectual history of the symbols, ideologies, and discourses on human beings and their sociality, which developed along with slavery and the slave trade and underpinned the daily lives of both slaves and masters. The two Cameroonian accounts introduced by E. S. D. Fomin in Chapter 5 comment on masters' disloyalty toward their slaves by taking a cue from the vicissitudes of two individuals whose memory, for tragic reasons, has been preserved across generations. The first account deals with a slave owner and sounds like a warning to all power-holders who abuse their subordinates. The second depicts the intrinsic vulnerability of the slave's condition by describing the dramatic death of a court slave. Alessandra Brivio's materials (Chapter 4), on the other hand, fade into myth, and their historical content is hardly detectable. Nonetheless, they testify to the moral debate spurred by enslavement and the slave trade in the coastal societies of West Africa, which supplied slaves to the Atlantic markets. By evoking the crude images of cowry shells growing on slaves' rotting corpses, these tales question the legitimacy of wealth accumulated through the systematic exploitation of human beings.

INTERVIEWS

Probably nothing highlights more the fact that oral data are not simply picked up from informants – as implied by the verb "to collect" to describe this kind of process – than the dynamic of interviewing, where data collection is deeply influenced by all those involved in the interviews. Researchers must become familiar with the etiquette of the society they study. They have to learn how to formulate questions in ways that sound neither offensive nor intrusive. If they deal with slavery, they need to be even more tactful. Most of the time, they are not alone, but accompanied by interpreters and other kinds of mediators. At times, recollections surface almost spontaneously in the midst of discussions on other topics. In other instances, people refuse to provide any answers at all to questions. In Chapter 6, Martin A. Klein reminds us of the importance of taking into consideration not only the content of the interview, but also the behavior of the people involved and the events that unfold between them. Mohammed Bashir Salau, in Chapter 8, emphasizes how dominant scholarly research interests in the 1970s molded the questions about slavery posed to Kano informants. Interviewers encouraged informants to focus on certain parts of the past, and in so doing, they ignored other elements (for instance, the part gender played in the organization of the Kano slave system). In Chapter 7, Felicitas Becker sensitively explores the field of social memories and personal recollections surrounding a slavery plantation in Southern Tanzania. As she notes, remembrances about slavery are interwoven with other recollections, and an analysis of the ways informants narrate their stories is as important as what is said in the course of the interview.

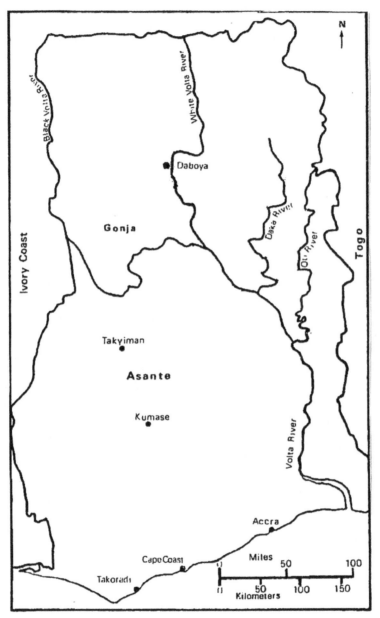

2.1. Map showing the location of Asante, Takyiman, and Gonja.

Source: Based on a map in Glenna Case, Wasipe under the Ngbanya (unpublished PhD dissertation, Northwestern University, 1979), xi.

2 Oral Traditions about Individuals Enslaved in Asante

SANDRA E. GREENE

The state of Asante was founded in the late seventeenth century in what is now central southern Ghana. In the approximately 200 years it existed as an independent polity, It developed a massive bureaucratic apparatus to manage affairs of state. It deployed sophisticated diplomatic means to negotiate with friends and enemies alike. It developed and managed a series of roads that linked Asante's economy to both the Atlantic coast and the savannah zone to its north. But it was also a state that did not hesitate to use military force. Between 1701 and 1774, Asante conquered all those polities and peoples located within a radius of approximately 100–250 miles, whose independence was deemed a hindrance to its political and economic interests. In its first imperial foray in 1701, for example, it conquered the polity of Denkyera. This was then followed by thirty-seven years of periodic but frequent warfare, as Asante extended its imperial control in all directions. By 1774, their military successes had expanded the boundaries of the Asante state to include much of what is now the modern state of Ghana. The warfare continued, however. For another 122 years, between 1774 and 1896 (when Britain conquered it), Asante continued to deploy its military largely to suppress the many rebellions organized by the conquered.[1]

One of the consequences of this military activity was the production of prisoners of war. Throughout the eighteenth century, many were conveyed to the coast where they were sold and transported to the Americas. Others were marketed to meet the local demand for domestic slaves. Still others were allocated to Asante military commanders in recognition of their leadership roles in battle. Most often the prisoners retained in Asante were used by their masters as agricultural laborers in underpopulated regions of the state, as a potential pool of funerary sacrificial victims, and as possible sources of additional income from the ransoms paid by the families of the enslaved. Not all prisoners were sold or distributed as booty to subordinates, however. The Asante king kept many for the state. Included in this

---

[1] For two excellent maps, which position Asante and its trade routes within the region, see T. C. McCaskie, *State and Society in Pre-colonial Asante* (Cambridge, 1995), 32, 77. On a discussion of Asante's imperial expansion and the development of a road network to control its conquered territories and the trade that was carried on these roads, see Ivor G. Wilks, *Asante in the Nineteenth Century: The structure and evolution of a political order* (Cambridge, 1975), 1–64. On the use of the military by the Asante, see D. J. E. Maier, "Military Acquisition of Slaves in Asante," in David Henige and T. C. McCaskie (eds.), *West African Economic and Social History: Studies in Memory of Marian Johnson* (Madison, 1990), 119–132.

group were royal family members from conquered territories and a number of Muslims, many of whom were deemed valuable because of their literacy. Information about such individuals is limited, however. We know they were captured. We also know how they were integrated into the state bureaucracy as valued assets.[2] But many questions remain. Some individuals were well remembered in the home districts from which they came. Others have been almost completely forgotten. The memories that do exist can vary considerably. In one place an individual is recalled as a major figure in their community; in another location, that same person is remembered only because they became so prominent in Asante. Why is this the case? This chapter addresses this question by focusing on the oral traditions associated with two individuals, Gyamana Nana and Kramo Tia, captured (or invited to take up residence in Kumase, the Asante capital) by a conquering Asante state in the eighteenth century. Both were retained (along with their descendants) as members of the Asante bureaucracy that served the Asantehene in Kumase. Whereas the next pages of this introduction explain why Gyamana Nana and Kramo Tia were remembered differently in different locations, the oral traditions themselves raise a number of other questions about slavery and the public discussion of this institution in West Africa.

GYAMANA NANA OF TAKYIMAN

In 1722–23, the state of Asante invaded the polity of Takyiman (also once spelled Techiman, situated to the northwest of Asante) and captured a member of the royal family, Gyamana Nana (also remembered as Nana Dwamenawa).[3] Even though she was taken to the Asante capital of Kumase as a prisoner of war and enslaved there until her death, memories of her remain. Oral traditions recited in both Kumase and Takyiman more than two hundred years after her capture still recall her existence and her suffering. One of the Kumase traditions is typical:

> When the Asante defeated Takyiman, they took as prisoner to Kumase a woman known as Gyamana Nana. She was a very wealthy woman. She was so rich, in fact, that a new cloth was woven for her every day, which she put on when she bathed. But when she was brought as a prisoner to Kumase she was made to sweep the rooms in the palace, and she learned what it was like to be poor. She was further humiliated by being asked to draw water: the vessel given her was a sieve.
>
> While she was in the palace, Gyamana Nana saw her own granddaughter there. Gyamana Nana was troubled. She approached the Asantehene and said that she did not mind how she herself was treated, but that she wanted her granddaughter to be cared for. So the Asantehene gave the girl to Bantamahene[4] so that he would look after her. It was her

---

[2] For the most comprehensive discussion of the production and use of slaves in Asante, see Maier, "Military Acquisition." On Muslim captives and non-captives in the Asante administration, see David Owusu-Ansah, "Power and Prestige? Muslims in 19th Century Asante," in Enid Schildkrout (ed.), *The Golden Stool: Studies of the Asante Center and Periphery* (New York, 1987), 80–92.

[3] Gyamana Nana is variously described as the Queenmother of Takyiman or a sister of the Queenmother. See Eva L. R. Meyerowitz, *Akan Traditions of Origin* (London, 1952) 43–44; Nana Kwame Nyame, "General Techiman History," in D. M. Warren and K. O. Brempong (eds.), *Techiman Traditional State Stool and Town Histories, Part I* (Legon, 1971), 20.

[4] The Bantamahene, a senior official in the Asante government, had his political base in Bantama, in the nineteenth century a village north of central Kumase. The community also held the distinction of being the location of the royal mausoleum.

descendants who became the Abanasehene.... The Abanasehene is responsible for the Asantehene's clothes.[5]

This memory of Nana Gyamana, like other oral traditions, has served a variety of purposes. It commemorates her capture as an historical fact, for she was indeed captured by Asante in 1772–73. But this particular account also animates these bare bones with anecdotes that despite their implausibility make the incident both memorable and useful for reinforcing a particular political perspective. Gyamana's experience of having to collect water in a sieve, for example, is a description not easily forgotten. At the same time, as a memory retained by her Asante descendants, it represents the affront they have opted not to forget even as they themselves continue to live in and remain affiliated with the Asantehene's bureaucracy. Other traditions retained in Takyiman itself, which focus largely on Takyiman's defeat, serve other purposes. They recall a once independent polity that as a consequence of its conquest was forced to provide Asante with soldiers throughout much of the late eighteenth century. These individuals were used as shock troops, taking the brunt of enemy fire and suffering far greater casualties than the members of the Asante military itself, even as their royal captives are remembered as having brought a more "civilized" culture to the Asante.[6] By remembering Takyiman's defeat and Gyamana's capture, Takyiman's leaders were able to use these memories to justify to their people more than one hundred years later their decision to rebel against Asante rule in 1896. The tradition probably served the same purpose when Takyiman unsuccessfully resisted in 1935 British colonial efforts to reintegrate it into the Asante Confederation, and it likely played no small part in the Takyiman-led effort by several states to secede from the Asante Confederation in 1951.[7]

Different reasons account for the tradition's survival in Asante. In 1973, Dr. Alex Kyerematen – a respected historian of Asante art and a descendant of Gyamana Nana – indicated that while the Asantehenes, Nana Prempeh II (1931–1970) and Nana Opoku Ware II (1970–1999) were well aware of this history, "it [was] not talked about in Kumase," in keeping with Asante law prohibiting the disclosure of someone's origins. Yet the memory of the enslavement of Dr. Kyerematen's ancestor was still very important for Asante. The existence of her descendants as servants of the Asantehene was a physical reminder of the historic power of the Asante to extend its influence over a now independent polity. Although they would not speak publicly about the origins of his ancestor, they remembered nevertheless. At the same time, the descendants of Gyamana Nana resident in Kumase had their own reasons for remembering. Her place in their family memories reinforced their own identities as citizens of a polity that they recalled as once larger, more wealthy, and independent of the state that would later enslave their ancestress. It was also served as the very basis for the periodic invitations they received to visit their ancestral home.

---

[5] Ivor Wilks, Conversations about the Past, Mainly from Ghana, 1956–1996, Vol. 4, 1968, July 10–1999, April 13: FN 96: Interview with Alex Kyerematen.

[6] On the Asante use of troops from conquered states as frontline troops, see Emmanuel Terray, "Contribution à une étude de l'armée asante," *Cahiers D'Études Africaines*, XVI: 61–62 (1976), 312–318. Takyiman appears to have been treated at times as a tributary state, and at other times as an inner province in which they participated in the Asante government. On Asante organization of its various provinces and Takyimans status, see Kwame Arhin, "The Structure of Greater Asante," *Journal of African History*, 8: 1 (1976), 65–85; and Wilks, *Asante*, passim.

[7] See William Tordoff, "The Brong-Ahafo Region," *Economic Bulletin of Ghana*, 3: 5 (1959), 2–18.

KRAMO TIA OF GONJA

Reasons for remembering in one place can constitute the very rationale for forgetting in another locale. Such is the case with the polity of Gonja. Present in both Kumase and Gonja oral traditions is the name of one 'Uthman Kamagatay, also known as Usmanu Kamara or Kramo Tia (the "little Muslim"). In the Asante capital of Kumase he is remembered quite clearly as a captive obtained during an 1844 Asante campaign against Gonja:

> [There was a] very powerful Kramo or Moslim who was gifted in the Koran and worked miracles.... This Moslem was captured red-handed and sent to Kumasi. He was known as Kramo Tia. When Kramo Tia arrived in Kumase, he became a permanent Moslem consultant of the Asantehene. He was captured with his two wives, namely Wurukye and Awuro Kyaah.[8]

Memories of Kamagatay are decidedly different in the Gonja town of Daboya and among Kamagatay's relatives in Kumase, however. There, he too is remembered in terms of his travels to Kumase, but not as a war captive who was enslaved at the court of the Asantehene, but rather as a guest of the Asante king. According to the Gonja traditions, Kramo Tia was invited to Kumase because of his learning; he then opted to remain of his own free will. The differences between these two traditions are a result of how two different communities have chosen to remember the past. For Asante, remembering Kamagatay as a prisoner reinforced its identity as a conquering power that had the ability to commandeer and benefit from the services of those over whom it exercised authority. For the Gonja, their emphasis on the voluntary nature of Kramo Tia's service worked to reinforce its image as a respected polity whose citizens had knowledge that was often sought without the threat of violence by neighbors both near and far. Denying Kamagatay's capture also served to de-emphasize the humiliation the Gonja polity experienced when it was indeed violently subordinated to the power of the Asante state.[9] In both cases, history was selectively appropriated to reinforce a valued image of the historical self within the larger region. Will we ever know whether or not Kramo Tia was enslaved or instead opted on his own to reside in Kumase? Perhaps not, but the oral traditions about him (as well as those about Gyamana Nana of Takyiman) can tell us a great deal about the past and the politics of memory.

QUESTIONS TO CONSIDER

On the traditions about Gyamana Nana and Kramo Tia

1. Both Gyamana Nana and Kramo Tia found themselves resident in Asante. The descendants of both these individuals – and in the case of Kramo Tia, he himself – came to hold central positions within the administration of the very state

---

[8] Cited in Glenna Case, Wasipe under the Ngbanya: Polity, Economy and Society in Northern Ghana (unpublished PhD dissertation, Northwestern University, 1979), 231.

[9] That the Gonja preferred to limit the ignominy of their 1844 defeat is evident in how they have also chosen to recall the war. Great emphasis in the oral traditions is placed on their resistance and the fact that they inflicted serious casualties on the Asante military leadership when they sought to make arrests in Daboya. Far less emphasis is placed on Asante operations thereafter (which were ultimately successful). See Case, Wasipe, 231–234 and J. A. Braimah, *The Ashanti and the Gonja at War* (Accra, 1970), 11–32. On the history of Asante-Gonja relations as it involved Kramo Tia, see Wilks, *Asante*, 275–279; and Bruce M. Haight, "*Pontonporon* and *Koko*: Asante-Gonja Relations to 1874," in Enid Schildkraut (ed.), *The Golden Stool: Studies of the Asante Center and Periphery* (New York, 1987), 60–72.

that had enslaved them. Why would slaves and strangers have been given such opportunity? Why would slaves and strangers be interested in participating in the very administrations that had removed them or their ancestors from their natal homes or conquered their home communities?

2. The traditions about Gyamana Nana and Kramo Tia refer to the Asante laws that prevent public discussion of one's origins. Why would such a law have been enacted?

On the traditions about Gyamana Nana

3. Included in the documents are traditions that describe her as either the Queenmother of the state, as the sister of the Queenmother, or simply as a wealthy woman. What might be the significance of these different descriptors?

4. Oral traditions often contain fanciful elements designed to make an incident so memorable that it can withstand the memory-eroding effects of time. What fanciful elements can you identify in the Takyiman traditions? What purposes do they serve beyond making the story memorable?

On the traditions about Kramo Tia

5. Of the conflicting explanations about the circumstances that brought Kramo Tia to Kumase, which do you find more plausible?

6. How does the fact that Kramo Tia and his descendants both acquired a number of slaves and at times were given as debt slaves to others impact your understanding of how slave systems operated in West Africa?

TERMINOLOGY

hajj: the pilgrimage to Mecca, a journey that all devout Muslims are encouraged to perform

-hemaa: the Asante term for the most senior woman political leader of the named location – for example, Daboyahemaa

-hene: the Asante term for the royal political leader of the named location – for example, Asantehene, Daboyahene, and the like

Imam: Muslim prayer leader

Limam: Gonja term for the head of the Muslim community

-wura: the Gonja term for a royal political leader whose full title included the name of the community over which he had authority – for example, Gbuipewura (royal head of Gbuipe), Daboyawura (royal head of Daboya)

ORAL TRADITIONS ABOUT GYAMANA NANA OF TAKYIMAN

1. Asante traditions maintained by Gyamana Nana's descendants

DR. ALEX KYEREMATEN: Interviewed by Prof. Ivor Wilks and Dr. Phyllis Ferguson, September 12, 1973, Kings College, Cambridge, England.[10]

---

[10] This interview can be found in the Ivor Wilks, *Conversations about the Past*.

CONTEXT: Dr. Kyerematen, a distinguished anthropologist and author of a number of studies on Asante royal regalia, agreed to answer questions about his own background in an interview that took place in Britain. Excerpted here are those portions in which he discussed his ancestors. The individuals mentioned included those ancestors who connected him to the royal families of Asante and Takyiman. His maternal grandfather, Kwame Boaten, was Kyidomhene in Asante (a military title, but in reality a position that involved overseeing the management of a number of towns and villages under the authority of that office).[11] This relative also participated in the 1895 Asante embassy to London, when Asante was seeking to negotiate directly with the British crown at a time when its independence was threatened by European colonial expansionism. Others mentioned included his maternal great grandfather, Akyeampong Tia, brother of the Asantehene Nana Kwaku Dua Panin and his ancestor, the Asante captive, Gyamana Nana of Takyiman.

My mother was the daughter of Kyidomhene Boaten, the one who was a member of the embassy to London. Kyidomhene Boaten's father was Akyeampong Tia. He was the brother of Nana Kwaku Dua Panin [the Asante king, Asantehene], and for that reason, the Asantehene always calls me grandson.

I am a member of the Abanase. The Abanasehene is responsible for the Asantehene's clothes.

I work closely with the new Asantehene [Nana Opoku Ware II]. Among other things, I am a member of the committee for building his new palace.

My ancestors were from Takyiman. Even now I am invited to go there on various occasions. But this is not talked about in Kumase. Neither [Asantehene] Nana Prempeh II [1931–1970] or [his successor] Nana Opoku Ware II [1970–1999] will refer to it, though they know about it. When the Asante defeated Takyiman, they took as prisoner to Kumase a woman known as Gyamana Nana. She was a very wealthy woman. She was so rich, in fact, that a new cloth was woven for her every day, which she put on when she bathed. But when she was brought as prisoner to Kumase she was made to sweep the rooms in the palace, and she learned what it was like to be poor. She was further humiliated by being asked to draw water: the vessel given her was a sieve. While she was in the palace, Gyamana Nana saw her own granddaughter there. Gyamana Nana was troubled. She approached the Asantehene and said that she did not mind how she herself was treated, but that she wanted her granddaughter to be cared for. So the Asantehene gave the girl to the Bantamahene so that he would look after her. It was her descendant who became the Abanasahene. Osei Bonsu built a new palace of stone, and created the position of Abanasahene

2. Takyiman tradition I

NANA KWAME NYAME: Interviewed by D. M. Warren and K. O. Brempong, August 16–17 and October 9, 1970, Takyiman.[12]

CONTEXT: According to D. M. Warren, and K. O Brempong, their interviews with Nana Kwame Nyame were initiated as part of a larger effort to record the histories of the chiefs

---

[11] Ivor Wilks, *Asante*, 475.
[12] Warren and Brempong, *Techiman* (Legon, 1971).

and towns that made up the Takyiman (in their report spelled Techiman) Traditional State. Initially they brought together the elders of a town or those associated with a particular stool (the symbol of political office) to relate these histories. This method, however, proved rather unwieldy. Trying to bring everyone together at a single time was difficult. Disagreements among the elders could derail the entire session. Accordingly, as noted by Warren and Brimpong, they abandoned this approach "and allowed only one narrator to present a history. If another elder disagreed with the first narration, he was then asked to present his version."

The account by Nana Kwame Nyame presented here is perhaps one of the most detailed and extensive accounts in their collection. While it might differ in one detail or another from other versions about the Takyiman past, the Asante's capture of Takyiman's queenmother, named in his account Dwamenawa rather than Gyamana Nana, is consistent with most other accounts recorded at the time.

It is believed that the Techiman[13] people came from a hole in the ground at a place called Amowi. They were very great in number and therefore they decided to build villages for themselves .... The people decided to build a capital which was called Maaso. Maaso was the abode of the Omanhene. The various families always came together to pay homage to the Omanhene at Maaso. Years elapsed and the Techiman people lived peacefully. Everything progressed, especially farming and hunting. The Bonohene [the ruler of the Bono state of which Takyiman was a part] stayed at Maaso for a long period until the First Techiman-Asante War. This war is dated from the reign of Asantehene Opoku Ware [c. 1720–50]. The war was a very grand one; they fought for seven good days without rest. Techiman fought so well that she nearly conquered Asante.

On the seventh day [of the war], the Asante decided to retreat because they had run short of gunpowder. Nana Bafo Pim, the Nkoranzahene [i.e., the leader of a group of refugees from Asante who had been allowed to settle on Techiman land] went to trick Nana Kese Bashyia, the Benkumhene [the commander of the left wing of the Bono-Takyiman army] … for some gunpowder. Bafo told him that he was going to help the Bono beat the Asante. Basahyia was at first reluctant to part with any gunpowder because he could not go back to Maaso to collect more. All the same, he gave half of his gunpowder to Bafo and Bafo's trick worked effectively … [for] Bafo fought for the wrong person. He gave the gunpowder to the Asante. Bafo's next trick [also] worked perfectly. He asked Kese Bashyia to put his guns in water, telling him how straight they would shoot the following morning if they were washed. Bafo also said that he himself had put all of his guns in water to wash them as he wanted to clean them for the next day. One of the Bono soldiers disputed this and told Kese Basahyia that it was a trick because he had tried it once, but the gun would not shoot. The soldier was rebuked and immediately beheaded for challenging the chief. The man accepted his death philosophically, but warned them about the future and told them that they would regret their decision. Benkumhene Kese Basahyia then put all his guns in water in the hope that they would be more effective against the Asante the next morning. At this time the war was being fought fiercely … Bafo informed the Asante of the trick that he had played. He told them to be courageous the next morning, as the Benkumhene had been deceived and would have to retreat. The fighting was now very fierce in … Techiman

---

[13] This is a different spelling for Takyiman.

Town.... The war continued the next morning. One section of the Asante infantry began to invade from the Benkumhene's side. They knew he was now handicapped and could not retaliate. The main reason for this particular attack was the capture of the Bonohene at Maaso .... The Asante were able to capture the Bono Queenmother, Nana Dwamenawa .... A messenger was sent to inform them.... [After] this calamity ... Techiman retired and the Asante won the war.

Techiman became a vassal state of Asante. She paid taxes to the Asantehene and her men were conscripted into the Asante army in time of war. Opoku Ware [the Asantehene] rewarded Bafo with the greater part of Techiman's land as his trick had worked perfectly and had resulted in the Asante victory. While Techiman remained a vassal state to Asante, Bafo and his people enjoyed the fruits of Techiman's land.

3. Takyiman tradition II

NANA KOFI BIANTWO: Interviewed by Eva L. A. Meyerowitz in 1945.[14]

CONTEXT: Nana Kofi Biantwo was the Krontihene (an administrative position within the royal court of Takyiman, which is part of the Bono state) at the time of the interview. He presented this tradition in an interview attended by two other royal officials: Nana Yao Doako, Ankobeahene, and Nana Kwasi Tabiri, Akwamuhene, as well as by an elder, Nana Kwame Nyama.

Note that the spelling of names here again is slightly different from the spelling found in the previous documents. Nevertheless, they refer to the same places and people. Baafo = Bafo; -hemmaa = -hemaa; Kumasi = Kumase; Mansu = Maaso.

One morning ... when consulting [his] god's oracle ... the High Priest of [the god] Tano in Takyiman ... got the "intelligence" that a most beautiful woman with evil designs on the kingdom was on her way to Mansu [also known as Maaso, capital of the Bono state of which Takyiman was a part]. He immediately sent a message to the King, warning him of this beautiful, light-coloured and charming stranger, and stated that if she succeeded in sleeping with him a battle would result which would be very serious for the Bono Kingdom. If, however, she could be taken prisoner and the insteps of her feet cut deeply, no harm would come to the state. When the message arrived in Mansu, [the king's son] Boyemprissi made fun of the oracle and said that Bono was so powerful no nation on earth could conquer it. A short while later the High-Priest of Tano sent another warning to the King, begging him to be [e]specially careful on a certain day, for by this time the High-Priest had learned the day on which the woman would arrive. He again advised the King to get hold of her straight away and to make the cuts in her feet.

The day came and the beautiful woman ... sat in the marketplace, where she was duly discovered by court servants of the Bonohene, whose job it was to bring any pretty woman they saw to the Palace. When they arrived, the councillors, remembering the warning of the High-Priest of Tano, wanted to seize her and make the cuts in her feet, but the King, at once enamoured, said that he could not bear to see so beautiful a woman hurt or disfigured. The councillors were angry, but when Boyemprissi sided with his father, the latter was strengthened in his resolve to have his own way. He seduced her the same night. Next morning the

---

[14] Eva L. A. Meyerowitz, *Akan Traditions*, 39–44.

strange woman had disappeared and when this news spread, gloom prevailed in the city; they all thought that she had taken the spirit of Bono with her and that the oracle's prophesy would come true. When the High-Priest of Tano received the news he told the King that Bono was now faced with war and that the Kingdom would fall in forty days …

Two days after the High Priest of Tano's last message, Baafo Pim [the leader of a group of refugees from Asante who had been allowed to settle on Takyiman land], had gone to Kumasi ostensibly to convey … gold dust [as a present from the Bonohene] to the Asantehene Opoku Ware. [In reality, Baafo Pim had used the money to provoke war between Asante and Bono to avenge an insult he had suffered from the Bono king's son.] [When Baafo] returned to Mansu, he told the Bonohene that the Asantehene was highly pleased with his present and that he would come to thank him in person and cement the growing friendship. In addition Baafo told him that he (Baafo) wished to perform the funeral rites for his late uncle.… As these final rites were long overdue, Baafo suggested they take place during the visit of [the] Asante …

It is always the custom at a funeral to fire shots into the air, and when during the conversation the guns were mentioned, Baafo remarked that it would be wise to bury the guns in the river for awhile, so that they should look clean and fresh on the day of the ceremony. Since the Bono knew little about firearms, having had no major war for a century … [they] allowed [themselves] to be persuaded.

As the day approached on which the Asantehene and his entourage were expected at Mansu, the Bonohene prepared to receive his royal guest as magnificently as possible. The day came, and just as [he] was putting on his state robes a messenger arrived from the High-Priest of Tano with the prophecy that there would be a battle that day, for the visitors…would come with an army.… A few hours later … shots were heard … and there was no doubt that a battle had begun.

What happened was this.… The Takyiman soldiers threw themselves between the enemy and [their] threatened city and for seven days fought a desperate battle. They hoped for reinforcements from Mansu, but none came.

At Mansu the confusion was terrible. When it was realized that the High-Priest's prophecy was coming true, everybody was paralysed with shock.… Then everybody prepared to [flee]. The chiefs would not fight; they were angry with the King for having ignored their advice… and one after the other they left with their people …

The Queenmother Dwamara Akenten hid … a few miles north of Mansu, from where she secretly ruled the remnants of her people for another two years; then she died. Her sister [Gyamana Nana], the heir apparent, who had hidden near Boyem with some of the princes and princesses, was betrayed and taken into captivity to Kumasi where she gave herself out as the Bonohemmaa.

It is not known what happened to her … but apparently they were quite well treated at first

Kumasi was indeed a poor place at that time compared with Bono-Mansu. In spite of the victorious battles and the great loot taken … Kumasi remained a provincial backwater and its people, including the court, lacked all refinement. According to the information [provided by] the present Asantehene – and his view is widely held in the country – … the Queeenmother's heir apparent [i.e., Gyamana Nana, and the other royal captives from Takyiman] … showed the Asante how things should be done. Their weavers wove fine cloth, their goldsmiths taught the Asante how to decorate the state emblems with gold, and how to make gold jewellery for the Queenmother and the royal women. Their musicians showed them how to play on new musical instruments and introduced new songs and dances. The Chief who was once in charge of the great market at Mansu organized the market of Kumasi for trade, and introduced the standard gold weights from Bono. As court etiquette was practically non-existent, [Gyamana Nana] for a while supervised the teaching of the princes and princesses [of Asante].

When [Gyamana Nana], later, however was made to sweep the most stinking parts of the Kumasi market, she died soon after.

ORAL TRADITIONS ABOUT KRAMO TIA OF GONJA

1. Asante traditions[15]

NSUMANKWA STOOL HISTORY OF ASANTE: Collected by J. Agyeman-Duah as part of the Institute of African Studies Stool Histories Project.

CONTEXT: The Nsumankwaafo, or the corps of royal physicians, had the responsibility for maintaining the health of the Asantehene. Their head, the Nsumankwaahene, as noted by David Owusu-Ansah, "search[ed] for the best medicine or charm to protect the Asantehene. He thus consult[ed] the *Adunsifo* (herbalists) and *Abosomfo* (priests possessed by a deity) … [as well as] prominent priests outside Asante if he [was] convinced that their services [would] be of benefit to the king." As leader of the Muslim religious community in Asante, Kramo Tia served the Asantehene under the Nsumankwaahene. If he sought an audience with the king, the request was sent through the Nsumankwaahene. And if the King wished to summon Kramo Tia, it was done through the Nsumankwaahene. It is for this reason that the Nsumankwaa Stool Histories have something to say about Kramo Tia and the history of his relationship with Asante.[16]

It is … said that he [a Gonja ruler] had a very powerful Kramo or Moslem, who was gifted in the Koran and worked miracles for him. This Moslem was captured red-handed and sent to Kumasi. He was known as Kramo Tia. When Kramo Tia arrived in Kumasi he became a permanent Moslem consultant of the Asantehene. He was captured with his two wives, namely Wurukye and Awuro Kyaah.

THE ANANTA STOOL HISTORY OF ASANTE: Collected by J. Agyeman-Duah as part of the Institute of African Studies Stool Histories Project.

CONTEXT: The Ananta Stool, according to Akosua Perbi was a "service stool," an administrative office created by Asantehene Opoku Ware (1720–50) for his servant Ofosu, "in recognition of the spirit of initiative and valour displayed when he repulsed an attack by … the chief of Assin." Ofosu's troops were "made a part of the king's personal guard." Their head, the Anantahene, was made responsible for the king's physical safety when he was engaged in a particular religious ritual. He also had authority over the Nsumankwaa, the

---

[15] The stool histories excerpted here were collected by J. Agyeman-Duah and are now housed at the Manhyia Archives in Kumase, Ghana. These excerpts come from Glenna Case, Wasipe, 231–232.

[16] The quote comes from David Owusus-Ansah, *Islamic Talismanic Tradition in Nineteenth Century Asante* (Lewiston, 1991), 4; for more information on the position of Muslims in Asante, see also David Owusu-Ansah, "Power or Prestige?", 80–92.

royal physicians, the latter of whom, in turn, were responsible for the Muslim community in Kumase. It was because of their authority over the Nsumankwaa and the Islamic religious community in Kumase that the Ananta stool history retains information about Kramo Tia.[17]

[It was the Asante military leader, Asamoa Nkwanta] who went to Daboya and captured Kramo Tia during the reign of Nana Agyeman I (Kwaku Dua I), the least pugnacious king.

2. Gonja Traditions[18]

WASIPEWURA MAHAMA SAFO II: Interview by Glenna Case with Mathilda M. Soale, February 14, 1976, Wasipewura's Palace, Daboya.

CONTEXT: Mahama Safo, age fifty at the time of this interview, became the political leader of the Daboya division of the Gonja state in 1954 at the age of thirty-eight. This February 14 conversation with Glenna Case was the third of some twenty-four exchanges she had with him over the course of nine months. In this particular interview, he had become much more comfortable sharing what information he knew about the history of his polity, but like many other Gonjas he also found it difficult to acknowledge the undeniable historical reality of Gonja's subordinate status under Asante during much of the eighteenth and nineteenth centuries. In this interview and in subsequent ones, he emphasized the status of Daboya as the supplier of imams to neighboring polities.

Usmanu Kamara [the Daboya name for Uthman Kamagatay or Kramo Tia] was not stolen! In the olden days the Kumasi people had their Limams from Daboya.... The Asante went to the Gbuipewura to ask him for a Limam. Then the Guipewura also sent a message to ... tell the Wasipewura he should give a Limam to him to give to the Asante ... then a Limam [was] sent to the Guipewura to be sent to the Asante.

IMAMU AL-HAJI HAMADU B. ZAKARIA, LIMAM OF DABOYA: Interview by Glenna Case with Ahmed A. Mahama, June 6, 1976, Limampe Ward of Daboya.

CONTEXT: In this thirteenth of twenty-one interviews with Glenna Case, Zakaria emphasized, as had the Wasipewura, Mahama Safo II, the existence of a relationship between equals as it pertained to Gonja-Asante relations. Equally important to Zakaria was the fact that Daboya was the source of so many of the imams who served in other polities in the region.

I have no knowledge of Daboya being under the Asante, but the relationship that existed between them was because of the salt from Daboya and the kola nuts from Asante. Asante brought Kola to this place for the exchange of salt. Also if they needed *mallams* they came to Daboya. Were it not for the *mallams* of Daboya all of the surrounding area would have no *mallams*.

[17] Akosua Perbi, "Mobility in Pre-colonial Asante from a Historical Perspective," *Research Review*, NS 7: 1–2 (1991), 72–86.
[18] Case, Wasipe.

3. Traditions maintained by Kramo Tia's Descendants

AL-HAJJ SUMAILA B. MUMUMI, ASANTE-NKRAMO IMAM, AND MALAM IMORU B. BUKARI, other elders of the skin (symbol of office): Interview by Ivor Wilks, August 3, 1965, Kumase.[19]

CONTEXT: This interview, conducted by Ivor Wilks and J. Agyeman-Duah, took place in Kumase and was organized with the *imam* of the Asante Muslim community. Although quite a few individuals were present, Wilks indicates that "Malam Imoru was the principle speaker." The purpose of the interview was to obtain information about the Asante Muslim community.

Kramo Tia came to Kumase at the time of Nana Kwaku Dua I [1834–1867]. He was from the house of the Daboya Limam. He was the Limam of Daboya. His true name was Uthman, and he used the *nasab* Kamaghatay.… The reason why Kramo Tia came to Kumase is this. The Chief of Daboya (Daboyahene) made himself a gold calabash. The Asantehene considered this improper, and sent three chiefs to the Chief of Daboya, namely Asamoa Nkwanta, Domfe Kyewa, and Apeagyei. They were ordered to bring the golden calabash to Kumase. Kramo Tia was then the Imam of Daboya. The wife of Kramo Tia was named Wurikye. She was the queenmother of Daboya (Daboyahemaa) and the sister of the chief of Daboya. The chief of Daboya was arrested and taken to Kumase. His sister Wurikye went with him. So Kramo Tia decided that he would also go to Kumase to accompany his wife. The Asantehene questioned the Chief of Daboya about Kramo Tia, and the chief of Daboya explained that Kramo Tia was a very powerful *mallam*. This was accepted, and Kramo Tia was asked to stay in Kumase.

AL-HAJJ SULAYMAN: Interviewed by Thomas James Lewin, July 10, 1970, Kumase.[20]

CONTEXT: Al-Hajj Sulayman, who was between eighty and ninety years of age at the time of this interview, had met with Thomas Lewin three previous times to discuss various aspects of the history of Asante. In this fourth interview, Al-Hajj Sulayman discussed his own family background. He had four wives and had made the *hajj* in 1949. He had studied with a number of Islamic teachers in Kumase, but had to end his educational training prematurely because of financial difficulties. Thereafter he pursued tailoring as his profession. In this interview, he drew on the family knowledge he had acquired as a grandson of Kramo Tia. Mentioned as well were the discursive norms that governed discussions in Asante about slave origins and his own experience as a debt pawn.

My grandfather's name was Osumana, nicknamed Kramotia. Kramotia was born in Buipe … in Gonja. He was brought to Kumase from Daboya by the Asantehene. Kramotia was a special *malam* for the Daboya chief before he was brought to Kumase …

Kramotia had the office of leader of the Muslim community in Asante. Abu Bakr [Kramotia's son and my father] succeeded Kramotia … Abu Bakr prayed for the Asantehene. This was his work.… Every Friday he prayed for the Asantehene. Abu Bakr took over from his father, Kramotia … I saw Kramotia when he was a very old man.… Every Friday Kramotia was carried to the Asantehene's palace on my and others' shoulders. Kramotia was then too old to walk …

---

[19] Wilks, Conversations about the Past.

[20] Thomas James Lewin, The Structure of Political Conflict in Asante, 1875–1900. Volume II – Asante Field Texts (unpublished PhD dissertation, Northwestern University, 1974), 65–75.

[Like his father, Kramo Tia], Abu Bakr also received slaves from the yearly tribute given to the Asantehene. Every year, one thousand slaves [men and women] were given to the Asantehene. Abu Bakr received five from the one thousand. The Asantehene's representative was stationed at Salaga [a major slave market in the polity of Gonja to the north of Asante]. He made sure that the Asantehene got one thousand slaves yearly [as tribute]. This happened during the time of Kwaku Dua I [1834–1867].

The area from the present army barracks [in Kumase] to Kwadaso had nine … huts for farming.… Seven or eight people stayed in one such [hut]. All the people there were Abu Bakr's slaves. Abu Bakr took them over from Kramotia, who had them first. The slaves paid in yams, eggs, fowls, goats, plantains, and other farm goods. Kramotia did not get [this] land from the Asantehene. He had money and developed the land. He put his slaves to work on this land. Anybody with money could stay anywhere in Kumase. Only slaves lived in these nine [farm huts]. Around forty people lived there in all. The slaves were taken from different tribes. Mossi men married Dagomba women, Dagartis married Mossis, etc.… Abu Bakr gave the women that were brought to the men slaves without wives. A child of two slaves was Abu Bakr's. Abu Bakr's first two wives were from Buna. They were not slaves. His other four wives were slaves. They lived in the nine [farm huts]. Any man with money could buy slaves in Salaga. Slaves were bought with kola nuts in Salaga. The slave cost more in Kumase than in Salaga. A man examined the feet to find if a slave was healthy: thin feet and ankles meant he was healthy; round feet and ankles meant he was not healthy. A slave cost 15 shillings, 18 shillings, one British pound. The cost depended on whether the slave was strong …

In the old days, it was hard to find out a person's place of origin. It was disrespectful to ask old people about their origins. It is not right to talk about origins in Asante.… The last four wives of Abu Bakr were brought to Asante as slaves … but once married they became Asantes. My mother was a slave. I myself was sold for eight pounds during the Yaa Asantewaa War [1896]. [My father], Abu Bakr [had been] caught by the British during the Yaa Asantewaa War. One hundred pounds was paid by some elderly persons in Kumase and some Asante chiefs to free him. I myself was sold for eight pounds. Others were sold for the rest of the one hundred pounds. My own brothers took me to a wealthy Asante to get the money to free Abu Bakr from prison. I served beyond Kwadso. I farmed and carried foodstuffs to Kumase. Food only sold here for three or four pence. At times the food had to be left behind because people did not buy it. For seven years I served at Ohwinase. A woman, Akosua Owusuwaa, bought me. She is now dead. Her son, named Kwaku Dua, is still alive. He is a Muslim. His Muslim name is Seidu. At the end of the seven years, I was freed when my elder brothers got the eight pounds.

SUGGESTED ADDITIONAL READINGS

ON SLAVERY IN ASANTE

Austin, Gareth. *Labour, Land and Capital in Ghana: From Slavery to Free Labour in Asante, 1807–1956.* Rochester: Rochester University Press, 2005. See in particular, chapters 6–10.

Mier, D. J. E. "Military Acquisition of Slaves in Asante," in *West African Economic and Social History: Studies in Memory of Marion Johnson.* Edited by David Henige and T. C. McCaskie (1990), 119–133.

Perbi, Akosua. "Mobility in Pre-colonial Asante: From a Historical Perspective," *Research Review, NS,* 7, 1&2 (1991), 72–86.

Poku, K. "Traditional Roles and People of Slave Origin in Modern Ashanti – A Few Impressions," *Ghana Journal of Sociology*, 5 (1969), 34–38.

Rattray, R. S. *Ashanti Law and Constitution*. New York: Negro Universities Press, 1911/1969. See in particular chapter V.

ON TAKYIMAN HISTORY AND TAKYIMAN/ASANTE RELATIONS

Tordoff, William. "The Brong-Ahafo Region," *Economic Bulletin of Ghana*, 33, 5 (1959), 2–18.

Wilks, Ivor G. *Asante in the Nineteenth Century: The Structure and Evolution of a Political Order*. Cambridge: Cambridge University Press, 1975. Passim.

ON GONJA HISTORY AND MUSLIMS IN ASANTE

Bravmann, René and Silverman, Raymond A. "Painted Incantations: The Closeness of Allah and Kings in 19th Century Asante," in *The Golden Stool: Studies of the Asante Center and Periphery*. Edited by Enid Schildkrout (1987), 93–108.

Haight, Bruce M. "*Pontonporon and Koko:* Asante –Gonja Relations to 1874," in *The Golden Stool: Studies of the Asante Center and Periphery*. Edited by Enid Schildkrout (1987), 60–72.

Owusu-Ansah, David. "Power or Prestige? Muslims in 19th Century Kumase," in *The Golden Stool: Studies of the Asante Center and Periphery*. Edited by Enid Schildkrout (1987), 80–92.

Wilks, Ivor, Levtzion, Nehemia, and Haight, Bruce M. *Chronicles from Gonja: A Tradition of West African Muslim Historiography*. Cambridge: Cambridge University Press, 1986. See especially chapter one: "The Rise of Gonja: An Historical Preamble."

"The Little Things that Would Please Your Heart…"

Enslavement and Slavery in the Narrative of Al Haji Bakoyo Suso (The Gambia)

ALICE BELLAGAMBA

Bakoyo Suso is a *jaloo* (the Mandinka term commonly translated as bard or griot).[1] In other words, he belongs to one of three main social categories that Mandinka culture recognizes as part of its historical legacy: freeborn, professional endogamous groups (bards and praise-singers, also known as griots – sing. *jaloo*, plur. *jali*; blacksmiths – sing. *numoo*, plur. *numoolo*; leatherworkers – sing. *karangkewoo*, plur. *karangkewoolu*) and descendants of slaves.[2] In the past, each category had its internal articulations. Freeborn could be part of the ruling class or commoners devoted to trade, farming, cattle-rearing, and Islamic studies. The *jali* specialized as oral historians, musicians, and praise-singers but also as hunter-bards, singers, and drummers for the youth and the elders. Their ability to enchant their audience with the deeds of past heroes stands as a living symbol of the way Africans preserved their historical memory through oral performances.[3]

In 2000, while carrying out fieldwork on memories of slavery and the slave trade along the River Gambia, I invited Bakoyo, whose historical ability I long knew, to talk about these topics. At first, he showed surprise, slavery not being something easily discussed in the Gambia. People and scholars used to approach him to inquire about the great leaders of the precolonial past or to know where their ancestors hailed from and how they became part of the Gambia River elite of warriors, chiefs, notables, and religious scholars. After a while, however, Bakoyo agreed. In 1996, the government of the Gambia established the Roots Homecoming Festival, a development aimed at attracting African-American tourists through the celebration of the connections between the river and the Americas created by

---

[1] "Griot" is a French-derived term for the ancient hereditary occupational class of the *jali*. T. Hale, *Griots and Griottes* (Ohio, 1998).

[2] In Mandinka, the slave is *jongo* (plural *jongolu*). Today, such term is not frequently used to talk of descendants of slaves, whose origins are often hidden under the more generic etiquette of *korewo* (member of the family but also herd of cattle) or *nyamaloo*. The last term refers to members of professional endogamous groups, which might be of free origins, like Bakoyo, or descendants of slaves originally given to the *nyamaloo* as compensation. The inclusion in this category of all descendants of slaves is a matter of courtesy, which amounts to the overlapping of some of the *nyamaloo*'s ceremonial tasks (like slaughtering animals) with those of descendants of slaves.

[3] Ethnographic and historical literature illustrates the *jali*'s ability to cope with the requests of new national and international markets, which since the 1960s and 1970s have profoundly transformed the context of their artistic production.

Bakoyo Suso, recorded by Alice Bellagamba and Bakary Sidibe, Dippakunda, The Gambia, May 2, 2000. Transcription and translation of Isatou Conteh.

the transatlantic slave trade.[4] Like other *jali*, Bakoyo felt marginalized. In spite of his reputation as oral historian, no government official ever contacted him, nor was he invited to contribute to the initiative. My request offered him a chance to display the density and depth of his knowledge in front of an audience of friends and acquaintants, which on that day followed his performance.

Unlike the other elders I met over the years, he did not talk in general and normative terms. Instead, he took specific historical episodes from his repertory of oral traditions on the nineteenth-century history of the River Gambia and used this reservoir of representations and meanings to illustrate details of enslavement, the slave trade, and life in slavery.

This chapter presents an extract from the resulting narrative. As it often happens with oral traditions, the text requires a lot of background knowledge to be understood. Bakoyo uses a language full of idiomatic expressions, names, and historical references – which today are unfamiliar to the majority of young Gambians (but not to men and women of his generation) – to touch on issues of contemporary moral and social significance. Is it fair to enslave other human beings? Could the slave descendant ever make others forget his or her origins? Without losing sight of the original narrative order, I divided the text into paragraphs preceded by a short comment, which helps further contextualize their historical content. Footnotes identify the major localities and historical characters, and help put Bakoyo's account into a dialogue with colonial records and Senegambian historical literature.

SOME BIOGRAPHICAL INFORMATION

Bakoyo was born in Eastern Gambia in the 1930s. By then, the Gambia was a British colony and protectorate.[5] The legal status of slavery had been formally abolished in 1930, after two ordinances (enacted respectively in 1894 and 1906) closed the traffic in slaves and opened opportunities for the emancipation of bonded men and women.[6] At the time of Bakoyo's birth, relationships between former masters and their ex-slaves were rapidly

---

[4] A. Bellagamba, "Back to the Land of Roots. African American Tourism and the Cultural Heritage of the River Gambia," *Cahiers d'Études Africaines*, Special Issue: "Creating Tourism Out of Culture," XLIX (1–2): 193–194 (2009), 453–476.

[5] British presence along the River Gambia dates back to the sixteenth century and to the involvement of British traders in the Atlantic slave trade. In 1816, Great Britain consolidated its political influence by founding Bathurst, a military and mercantile settlement at the mouth of the river meant to be a base for patrolling the coast against the traffic in slaves, which the British Parliament had outlawed in 1807. After independence (1965), Bathurst became Banjul, the capital of the Gambia. In 1823, the government established the settlement of McCarthy Island, which lies about 300 kilometers inland from the coast. In the next decades, Bathurst and MacCarthy Island hosted thousands of liberated Africans (locally known as Aku) displaced from Sierra Leone to the Gambia. The colony of the Gambia, which included Bathurst and the immediately adjacent mainland, came officially into being in 1888. By the end of 1892, the administrator of the colony began the creation of a protectorate, which was completed in 1901 when British rule was extended to Eastern Gambia. M. Gray, *A History of The Gambia* (London, 1966); B. Barry, *Senegambia and the Atlantic Slave Trade* (Cambridge, 1998).

[6] For a comparative analysis of the process of emancipation in French West Africa and the Gambia see M. Klein, *Slavery and Colonial Rule in French West Africa* (Cambridge, 1998); P. Weil, "Slavery, Groundnuts, and European Capitalism in the Wuli Kingdom of Senegambia, 1820-1930," *Research in Economic Anthropology*, 6 (1984), 77–119; A. Bellagamba, "Slavery and Emancipation in the Colonial Archives: British Officials, Slave Owners, and Slaves in the Protectorate of the Gambia (1890-1936)," *Canadian Journal of African Studies*, 39:1 (2005), 5–41.

changing. Former slaves sought recognition and rights; former masters insisted on rank and social discrimination. Groundnut commercial cultivation was the backbone of the rural economy.[7]

Bakoyo's family engaged in farming and trade while also offering their services as bards to the rural elite. Chiefs, traders, and cattle-owners retained the resources to promote the *jali* as artists and oral historians. Listening to a *jaloo*, who sang the epic of precolonial warriors and rulers and publicly praised the deeds of the contemporary elite, was a common and greatly appreciated form of entertainment. Such performances enhanced reputations and social identities. Bakoyo was socialized in this kind of environment. He saw his mother praising the big traders and their wives while former slaves danced for their masters. He attended the public performances of the most famous artists of the time, men like Jali Fode, who during and after World War II toured the major settlements along the River Gambia and sang about events taking place in other parts of the world. "Hitler said: I will take afternoon tea in London" was one of Demba Camara's songs, another famous performer of the time.

Bakoyo was also associated with Bamba Suso, who was one of the first *jali* to be recorded by the newly established national Radio Gambia in the early 1960s. Bamba's historical repertory included the epic of Sunjata Keita and the oral traditions of the major precolonial polities along the River.[8] Because of this background, Bakoyo has become a well-respected oral historian. Before independence, he migrated to the outskirts of the capital city of Banjul, where he performed for the emerging national political elite, businessmen, and high-ranking civil servants. As a young man, he sang and played the kora (the harp-lute used to accompany Mandinka *jali* oral performances). His compound was a long-important meeting point for Mandinka intellectuals and professionals, who visited Bakoyo to participate in lively political and historical discussions. Youth attended as well. The fact that he knows so much about slavery is in itself indicative of the enduring significance of the past associated with slavery and the slave trade in the contemporary Gambia. Like most of the *jali*, he did not expose the social origins of groups and individuals historically associated with him and his family. When I asked about the slave entourage of Alpha Molo Baldeh and Mussa Molo Baldeh of Fuladu, two of the war leaders of the second part of the nineteenth century with whom Bakoyo's family is connected,[9] he replied by quoting a famous statement of Jali Fode: "I have something in my head which is too big for my mouth" – in other words, I know more than what I am going to disclose (see Narrative 6). I assume this elegant mixture of revelation and silence is precisely what kept the audience

---

[7] K. Swindell and A. Jeng, *Migrants, Credit and Climate: The Gambian Groundnut Trade, 1834–1934* (Leiden and Boston, 2006).

[8] Mande oral traditions celebrate Sunjata Keita as the founder of the Mali Empire in the thirteenth century. Some of Bamba Suso's recordings were published. See G. Innes *Sunjata: Three Mandinka Versions* (London, 1974) and B. Suso and B. Kanute, *Sunjata* (London, 2000).

[9] Fuladu was one of the major polities of late-nineteenth-century Senegambia. Its influence stretched from the middle and upper Gambia down to Guinea Bissau. Alpha Molo Baldeh established the kingdom and ruled from about 1865 to 1881. The son Mussa Moloh took the leadership of Fuladu in the early 1890s and maintained it until colonization. See C. Quinn, "A Nineteenth Century Fulbe State," *Journal of African History*, 12:3 (1971), 427–440. An ancestor of the Suso *jali* associated himself to Alpha Moloh, when he had yet to become a successful military leader. G. Innes, *Kaabu and Fuladu: Historical Narratives of the Gambian Mandinka* (London, 1976). A consistent collection of oral traditions on Fuladu, recorded during the 1970s and early 1980s, is available in the archives of the Research and Documentation Division, National Council for Arts and Culture, Banjul, The Gambia.

fascinated and attentive while Bakoyo performed his narrative. The past is a battleground, and everybody admired his ability to cast light on some of the saddest turns of the river history without underrating the humanity and suffering of the men and women involved.

WHERE IS THE SLAVES' VOICE?

When Bakoyo ended his narrative, some of his friends and acquaintances prompted a discussion by reminding him that his family also owned slaves. Everybody knew that in the past, patrons compensated their *jali* with slaves. This happened also to Bakoyo's ancestors.

In the masters' eyes, slaves were dependants, people unable to take care of themselves and quick to exploit the situations out of which they could gain some material rewards. Is it therefore possible to retrieve the voice of the enslaved from Bakoyo's account? Is not his narrative but another expression of the masters' ideology that silenced the slaves?

I believe it is not. Slaves' voices whisper through the recollections of this former master. Bakoyo unveiled the role of rulers and merchants in the slave trade (Narrative 1). Slaves' subordination is explained by quoting examples from daily life (Narrative 4). The text details how their subjection to masters was reversed in the ritual space of public ceremonies. For one day, slaves took the stage and could publicly mock those masters who did not act generously. The slaves sang and begged so as to make the master ashamed (Narrative 4). There is agency in this picture as much as the recognition of interdependence between masters and slaves. Slaves' initiatives emerge through Bakoyo's description of their efforts to work once a week on their personal fields in order to improve their conditions and strive for the little things "that would please your heart" and make life bearable. The crucial role they played in the reproduction of their masters' social world is illustrated by the care they took in supervising their masters' children during the circumcision ceremony (Narrative 4). Their own children, instead, belonged to the master of the mother, and could be disposed of at his/her will. Bakoyo stressed that this lack of control of their offspring was one of the major deprivations slaves experienced. In the midst of a society that considered large families a major attribute of freeborn elderly men and women's identity, slaves often aged alone. After a life spent taking care of others, their time to be cared for never materialized.

The story of Momadou Fatima Jawla, who was the son of a slave woman and also a renowned military leader of the late nineteenth century, is touching (Narrative 7; Narrative 8). Momadou was never integrated into the Jawla family at the same rank as his freeborn brothers and sisters. He fought and brought the booty to his elder brother time and again but in the end he had to realize that the brother never truly respected him.[10] Even after the official abolition of slavery in 1930, remarks Bakoyo (Narrative 9), slaves obtained full recognition in the eyes of their former masters only by accepting the redemption rules that masters themselves established. The account closes with a few remarks about the resilience of the social stigma associated with slave origins in contemporary Gambia.

---

[10] B. Sidibé, *A Brief History of Kaabu and Fuladu (1300–1930). A Narrative Based on Some Oral Traditions of the Senegambia (West Africa)* (Torino, 2004), 87 and ff.

QUESTIONS TO CONSIDER

1. What does Bakoyo's narrative tell us about the continuation of the traffic in slaves out of the British settlement of Bathurst in the course of the nineteenth century?
2. How were people enslaved and who were the major actors at play?
3. How did the slave Mamadi Manyang acquire a social position?
4. What role did the slaves play in the ceremonial lives of their masters?
5. Can you figure out why Bakoyo wants to underline by quoting the proverb: "slavery, only a bad slave disowns it"?
6. What does the story of Momadou Fatima Jawla teach us about slaves who dared to rebel against their masters?
7. What is Bakoyo's opinion on slavery?
8. What is the relevance of Bakoyo's account for the history of slavery along the River Gambia, and for the general understanding of slavery as an institution?

1. "Let me first explain how this land was …"

Bakoyo's starting point is the mid-nineteenth century, as shown by some of the historical figures he mentions, like Mansa Demba Koro, who ruled the North Bank state of Niumi in the 1850s.[11] Raids, war, and the combined interests in slaves by external (the white man) and internal (big merchants, warlords, and religious scholars) forces made life perilous. This epoch of chaos and social disruption bequeathed contemporary Gambian society and culture with the shared idea that power always entails abuse and violence. The term "soninké," which recurs in the narrative, identifies the pagan ruling elite of the River Gambia. "Marabout" stands for the Islamic reformers and leaders, who successfully struggled to achieve political supremacy in this historical period. Military confrontations between the "soninké" and the "marabout" fed the internal traffic in slaves for several decades. This traffic, in turn, existed in response to the hunger for labor spurred by the expansion of commercial groundnut cultivation in the Senegambia region after the 1830s.[12] There is not enough evidence to state whether the events mentioned really took place although Bakoyo's narrative evokes the major phases in the history of the traffic in slaves, and of its abolition along the river Gambia.

The first person mentioned in the story is Findy, whom Bakoyo describes as a white slave dealer. He was probably a representative of the mulatto or African population of Bathurst whose lifestyle mimicked that of the Europeans.[13] At the time, British legislation outlawing the traffic in slaves was effective only within the restricted boundaries of British jurisdiction: in Bathurst, the immediately adjacent mainland (known as the Ceded Mile on

---

[11] D. Wright, *The World and Very Small Place in Africa* (Armonk, NY, 2004), reconstructs the precolonial and colonial history of the kingdom of Niumi, which was located at the mouth of the River Gambia.

[12] M. Klein, "Social and Economic Factors in the Muslim Revolution in Senegambia," *Journal of African History*, 8:3 (1972), 419–441; C. Quinn, *Mandinko Kingdoms of the Senegambia* (Madison, 1972).

[13] Bakoyo's Findy could be the son of Col. Alexander Findlay (the first Lieutenant-Governor of the Gambia, who was also called Alexander), or the colonial engineer James Finden who had a compound in Jeshwang in the 1850s (see J. M. Gray, *A History*, 391) and became the head of the Gambian militia in the 1860s. Another possibility is the trader of Ibo descent and leader of the liberated Africans' community in Bathurst, Harry Finden. A. Hughes and D. Perfect, *A Political History of The Gambia (1816–1994)* (Rochester, 2006), 62–63. I am grateful to David Perfect for his help in clarifying this point.

the north bank and British Kombo on the south one), and MacCarthy Island. Immediately outside these enclaves, the slave trade was endemic, and British documents clearly describe the involvement of the Bathurst mercantile community and its African associates.[14]

After Findy, the slave Mamadi Manyang is introduced. His story speaks of the movement of people between the Upper River Gambia and the Atlantic coast in the course of the second half of the nineteenth century. The master, whose surname was Ceesay, probably belonged to one of the trading families whose commercial connections linked the River Gambia to contemporary Eastern Senegal, Mali, and Guinea.

I will narrate what I heard from our elders and what I can remember of it.[15] Slaves left from the River Gambia for the white man's land. What I will try to tell is the history of how this happened. I will report what I heard. This is what I will narrate. Let me first explain how this land was, before the advent of slave trade. Then I will talk about slavery.

At that time the black race was pagan. Pagans loved tobacco very much.[16] Tobacco formed part of our tradition, it was a worthwhile thing because it could get you a wife; whatever you desired you could obtain it if you had some tobacco.[17] Today, the land I am talking of is the Gambia but yesterday it was not the Gambia. They used to say the ruler of Wuli, the ruler of Niani, the ruler of Badibu, the ruler of Kiang, the ruler of Kombo, the ruler of Niumi.[18] Each ruler had his area. They knew about each other but they governed independently. In the beginning, the white men did not come to rule over us. They came to trade and learn about these places. There were indigenous rulers. Prosperous traders were prominent as well. They engaged in farming. Farming allowed them to acquire wealth.

Rulers were freeborn and enslaved people. If you are more powerful than someone else, you can attack him or her forcefully and take him or her away. Some rulers would get up in the morning, and would go to raid other human beings, who in turn tried to hide. They would see children whom they knew were immature; they would capture them and take them away. If there were traders around, they would leave such children with the traders. The traders would say: "these are our slaves!" As they grew up, the majority would become hard working farmers. Farming was a prosperous activity; the merchants reinvested their wealth in cattle and gold ornaments. They captured slaves in this manner. We had slavery even before the coming of the white men.

I was told about a white man called Findy, who lived in Kombo. He came to meet the ruler of Niumi, who was called Mansa Demba Koro.[19] Findy said to Mansa Demba Koro: "I want to buy slaves. I need your assistance in getting a place to keep them before sending them away." Mansa Demba replied: "Fine." Findy looked at all the places around Essau in proximity

---

[14] C. Quinn, "Mandinko," 139.

[15] This is the formulaic expression Mandinka *jali* and elderly people in general use to introduce their historical narratives.

[16] The Mandinka term for pagan is *soninke*, which comes from the verb "so-ni." This means "pouring libations." P. Nugent, "Cyclical History in the Gambia/Casamance Borderlands: Refuge, Settlement and Islam from c. 1880 to the Present," *Journal of African History*, 48 (2007), 221–243. Popular memory recalls the *soninke* with a mix of fear and admiration. Fear depends on their unpredictable style of rule, which in the nineteenth century relied on raids and war. Soninke rulers, however, are admired for a number of qualities which Mandinka culture for long kept in high regard: cunning and secretiveness, bravery and loyalty.

[17] American tobacco was one of the major imported items of trade during the nineteenth century.

[18] The major precolonial centralized polities of the Gambia River. See Quinn, *Mandinko*, 29 and ff.

[19] This is Demba Adama Sonko, who was in power in 1833. See R. W. Macklin, "Queens and Kings of Niumi," *Man* (1935), 67–68.

of the sea but they were not apt.[20] Findy feared that the ship could not anchor there. He returned to Mansa Demba and asked to be introduced to Mansa Suling Jatta at Busumbala, so that Mansa Suling could assist him.[21] Suling invited him to survey the area that is today known as Jeshwang.

In Mandinka, Jeshwang means "jong suu," the home of the slaves. A Jola[22] woman lived in Jeshwang but she came later. She was called Joosuwaq, but the locality is not named after her. Findy came and settled there. He was buying slaves from Niumi, Fogni, Kombo, and many other places. He built a big enclosure. He bought slaves and put them there. He would load them on the ship and carry them to the white man's land. I do not know the place where they went.

This continued for long. By then, this land produced a very sweet honey. But the white men brought sugar. Findy would supply his slaves with sugar and biscuits so that they would forget where they came from. In such a way, he would keep them quiet. He also gave them tobacco to smoke and sent tobacco as a gift for those who provided him slaves. At times, he would get slaves for free. Findy acted in such a way. But there was a ruler in the land of the white man called Queen Victoria. As she came to power, she said that slavery had to be abolished. Findy received a message via sea. He had many slaves with him on the ship. They brought the slaves back to Jeshwang. Those who knew where they came from left but those who did not know where they came from remained.[23]

In Bathurst, there was an Aku man called Forster.[24] Findy realised that the slaves in Jeshwang had become useless. He decided to leave but he left the place into the custody of the Forster family. The Forster family put a man who had come from the East to live there.[25] He was called Mamadi Maniyang.

Mamadi Maniyang had come to the Kombo with his master Maniyang Ceesay. Mamadi became a very big wrestler. Forster loved wrestling. Thus, he took Mamadi and adopted him.[26]

---

[20] Essau is a locality in Niumi, on the northern bank of the river, which was related to the Sonko, one of Niumi ruling families. C. Quinn, "Niumi: A Nineteenth Century Mandinko Kingdom," *Africa*, 38:4 (1968), 443–455.

[21] In 1840, Mansa Suling Jatta signed an agreement with the British of Bathurst for a cession of a part of his territory, which became part of British Kombo. J. M. Gray, *A History*, 367. This shows that the events narrated presumably took place in the 1830s or 1840s, at a time in which Bathurst had already been established as a military base to fight the slave trade along the river.

[22] The Jola (or Diola) are one of the ethnic groups of Southern Senegambia. C. Quinn, "Mandinko," 25 and ff.

[23] This probably involved significant incorporation of slaves into Findy's entourage, which must have used them for agricultural production. Such a practice, which was common at the height of the Atlantic slave trade, intensified with the expansion of groundnut cultivation for commercial purposes from the 1830s until the beginning of the twentieth century. See K. Swindell and A. Jeng, *Migrants*, 37.

[24] Samuel John Forster (c. 1830s–1906) was a prominent member of the liberated African (Aku) community of Bathurst. He traded in rice and by 1875 was one of the wealthiest men in Bathurst and played an important role in the political life of the colony of The Gambia. A. Hughes and D. Perfect, *A Political*, 67–68.

[25] Mamadi Manyang was a Tillibunka, which in Mandinka means "somebody from the East." In colonial correspondence, this local word indicated immigrants from the Upper Niger Valley and Eastern Senegal, which for centuries also had been the main centers of enslavement for the Senegal and Gambia rivers. In the course of the nineteenth century, the expansion of groundnut cultivation along the River Gambia attracted a steady flux of seasonal laborers and settlers, but until the end of the century, the category of Tillibunka, included also displaced persons and groups of people, fleeing the wars of Al Haji Umar Tall and of Almami Samori Toureh, as well as the slaves who were the by-products of their military campaign. P. Curtin, *Economic Change in Precolonial Africa. Senegambia in the Age of the Slave Trade* (Madison, 1975), 177 and ff.

[26] This section of Bakoyo's narrative reminds the audience that Aku personalities, who had achieved predominant positions in trade as well as in the public life of MacCarthy and Bathurst, often protected individuals

Mamadi worked as a fisherman at Denton Bridge.[27] At that time when he got very good fish he would give it to the Forster. They brought him to settle in Findy's enclosure with the few slaves who were still there. Eventually he became renowned as the owner of Jeshwang. This is what I heard from the elders. Now, I will talk about the traders.

2. "Farli Kora bought so many slaves …"

From his maternal side, Bakoyo is associated with the Kora of Tambassansang, a family of traders who in early colonial times held the district chieftaincy of Fuladu East in the Upper River Gambia. Bakoyo explains the relationships between the Kora family and other prominent families of the area. According to him, the engagement of the Kora with the traffic in slaves continued up to the 1910s, well after the ordinance of 1906, which banned the slave trade in the whole Protectorate of the Gambia. Currently, Tambassansang, the home-town of the Kora, is one of the villages where slave descendants still agree to be recognized as such. This sections mentions the nineteenth-century religious scholar Simoto Kemo Sanuwo and also talks about Jula Jekere Bayo (to whose memory is attached a very famous kora tune), an extremely wealthy and powerful trader of the Upper River Gambia who stands as an icon of the historical connections between trade, wealth, and slavery. With regard to the slaves themselves, Bakoyo introduces Mansa Nyima, who contradicted his master Jula Jekere and, though being correct, was immediately chained as if he were mad. In Mandinka, "Mansa nyima" means "the good ruler." This is a reference not to the qualities of the slave himself but to Jula Jekere. Freeborn children used to be named after renowned personalities so as to be inspired by their glorious deeds. By contrast, slaves' names either recalled important events in their masters' life or praised their master's glory. This detail shows how the social subjectivity of slaves was always constructed in the shadows of their owners. The slaves lived for their masters in whose names the *jaloo* would recollect their achievements as energetic farmers, respectable trading partners or brave warriors.

Farli Kora bought so many slaves at Tambassansang that he could not recognize them.[28] When his slaves needed something, they would capture each other and go to Farli: "trader, buy this guy, this is a very good slave, he is a very good slave, he is a hard working person." Farli used to buy the "new" slave.

Farli's senior brother was Tanda Mamadu Kora. Tanda and Farli had the same mother and father. There were three women: Mansara Fadia, Sakala Fadia, Sohna Fadia. Mansara Fadia begot the ruler of Wuli who was called Yaka Sari Wali.[29] Sakala Fadia begot the marabout

---

like Mamadi, who belonged to marginal groups in society and were in the process of building a new life for themselves.

[27] The Denton Bridge was built in colonial time to connect Bathurst, which lay on an island, to the mainland. The locality is historically associated with fishing and the salt trade.

[28] This is how *jali* commonly praised the merchants of the late nineteenth century. At the time, prestige and wealth were represented by the number of people that formed the entourage of a powerful man, slaves included. In colonial times, the image of the big man surrounded by hundreds of slaves lost ground and was substituted by references to positions in the colonial administration, generosity toward the poor, and ability in agriculture and trade.

[29] Wuli is one of the most ancient and powerful kingdoms of the Upper River Gambia. Mansa Nkoi Wali or Yaka Sari became the sovereign of Wuli in 1827 and immediately signed an agreement with the British administrator of Bathurst so as to curb down the traffic in slaves. Oral traditions recollect his engagement with the expansion of groundnut farming in Wuli. W. Galloway, *A History of Wuli from the Thirteenth to the Nineteenth Century* (Unpublished PhD thesis, University of Indiana, 1975), 92.

Simmoto Kemo.[30] Sohna Fadia begot Farli Kora and Tanda Mamadu. The Kora lived in Tanda.[31] The slaves they obtained were their father's slaves. War came. At first, the slaves declared they would not escape but when they realized that it was becoming serious they took the youngest of the Kora and carried them on their shoulders. They ran from Tanda up to the place of Simoto Kemo in Wuli. Simoto was their elder, as their mothers were sisters. They lived with Simoto for some time.

Jula Jekere Bayo was a big trader, he was so rich that he did not know the extent of his wealth. He had a *jaloo* called Suu Saba Ansumana. One day he said to the *jaloo*: "go and if you see a son of a trader who hasn't got anything, come and tell me! I like to patronize poor people." The *jaloo* traveled till he reached the place of Simoto Kemo and found Tanda Mamudu Kora there. Tanda was plating rope out of grass. They chatted for a while. Then the *jaloo* asked whether Tanda was married. The man replied he was not. Suu Saba returned to Jula Jekere: "I have seen the son of a trader, he has nothing in his hands as I found him wearing torn trousers and plating rope out of grass. He is not married." Jula Jekere said he would give a wife to Tanda Mamadu. It was evening, and Jula Jekere was sitting with his children in the courtyard. "I have a wish. I want to give one of my children to Tanda Mamadu Kora at Simoto Kemo's place. Which of you would accept? Which would agree?"

His daughter Jamana got up and said: "Father, I am ready!" Jula Jekere was happy. He called the people and "tied" the marriage.[32] Then, the *jaloo* and the people escorted the woman to the husband. Twenty-five slaves accompanied Jamana. As she arrived, she found an incredible situation but she kept quiet. People were dancing to celebrate the happiness of Simmoto Kemo on that day. The slaves were naked and while dancing they were climbing one on top of the other like goats, male and female goats.[33] The talibe of Simoto Kemo protested.[34] Simoto replied that the same was happening at Jula Jekere's house. Let the slaves

---

[30] Simmoto Kemo Sanuwo was a religious personality of the late nineteenth century remembered in the oral traditions of the Upper River Gambia for his piety and relationships with the contemporary trading and ruling elite. The founding of Tambassansang, the hometown of the Kora, is said to be linked to one of his prophecies, which identified the locality as a favorable site for the family.

[31] Tanda was a prosperous commercial area in the Gambia River valley, located between Niokolokoba and the Nerico River. It is mentioned in travelers' accounts of the seventeenth, eighteenth, and nineteenth centuries as a territory of towns and markets linking the Gambia to the Upper Niger Valley. In the nineteenth century, Tanda trade declined and the area depopulated. In addition to Mandinka and Soninke, who were involved in trade, the region was inhabited by Koniagi groups, which constituted a slave reserve for the warring elite of the Upper River Gambia. In colonial times, Koniagi and other Tanda people began to migrate to the Gambia during the rainy season in search of agricultural labor. They used to live on the margins of local communities and were integrated in the lowest ranks of the social ladder, being considered pagans and foreigners.

[32] Marriage is a long process in Mandinka communities, which involves different steps and several actors. Bakoyo is referring to that part of the ceremony that today takes place at the mosque, where the marriage is formalized by sharing the kola nuts the bridegroom has provided for lineage elders and other notables. The next phase, which is also described in the narrative and takes place even years later, sees the bride transferred to her husband's home. The interesting point is that Jula Jekere did not ask any bride-wealth from Tanda Mamadu Kora and gave him not only a wife with prestigious family connections, but also a consistent number of slaves who possibly helped Tanda Mamadu clear the bush and establish himself as a farmer and trader.

[33] This is a reference to the fact that slaves and slave descendants could behave in ways that scandalized the freeborn. Obscene dances were part of their cultural repertoire and strategically used to obtain gifts and other concessions from their masters. S. Camara, *Gens de la parole* (Paris, 1992), 68.

[34] "Talibe" means student. Simoto's entourage included hundreds of youth that followed his Islamic teaching and worked on his farms. In such a way, they substantially contributed to his economic and social prosperity.

dance. But, at night Jamana set her hut on fire. The hut had a thatched roof and only one door. Jamana burned together with her bridal ornaments.[35]

That was a disgrace. People cried but Suu Saba, Jula Jekere's *jaloo* stopped them. He said: "Jula Jekere, he is a man who never says two words. He is a *sora* who does not eat *karaa*.[36] He does not eat animals with two tongues. He said he would give his daughter to Tanda Mamadu. Jamana died together with her bridal gowns. Please, wait!"

Suu Saba rode his horse and returned to Jula Jekere's place. To explain the tragic event to Jula Jekere, he praised him by using the name of his slaves who were Mansa Nyima, Sabou Nyima, Barakaa, and Duwaa Jabbia.[37] He began by saying: "God gave you all these! Your slaves are here! Your blessing is visible in these human beings!"

Mansa Nyima, the slave, had seen the *jaloo* coming. He had just said to Jula Jekere: "I am seeing someone from a distance. He looks like your *jaloo*." Jula Jekere replied: "I hope you are not crazy. I sent the *jaloo* with my daughter to Simoto Kemo's place just the day before yesterday. Now you are saying that he is coming. You are not well." The slaves of Jula Jekere had just returned from cutting a certain tree in the bush. People said that Mansa Nyima had gone mad because of the influence of that tree. They chained him. But soon it became evident that the man was right. The *jaloo* arrived and explained everything to Jula Jekere. Jula Jekere called his children and asked them who would replace Jamana. Mamanding said she would as Jamana and her had suckled the same breast milk.[38]

Whatever happens tomorrow, when this story is narrated, the courage of Mamanding will be also narrated. Jula Jekere added other twenty-five slaves to the dowry. Thus, Tanda got fifty slaves. Tanda and Mamanding remained at Simoto's place until Simoto died. Mamanding begot Tanda a boy called Mamadi Kora. The song "Ala le a ke," that still today is sang by the *jali*, was composed in honor of Mamadi Kora. He was the last trader to deal with slaves. He used to go to the East and buy slaves.[39] He spent three years without coming back. As he returned, he found that his junior Kemonding Kora had become chief. By then, when you came back from a very long journey, you would arrive at night. You would meet the family

[35] Bakoyo does not explain whether the behavior of the slaves shocked Jamana or whether she was not truly convinced to marry Tanda Mamadu. The story does not also clarify whether the fire resulted from an accident or arson. In any case, it carries with it an implicit message that stigmatizes the behavior of the slaves. They exaggerated, and such exaggeration corresponds to the Mandinka stereotype of the slave as a wild and savage human being without self-control. Social disruption resulted from their frenetic dances. Simmoto Kemo – who was responsible for them – should have disciplined them but he preferred to respect the custom, which allowed slaves to exhibit themselves freely during public ceremonies.

[36] The *karaa* is a big lizard, with a split tongue. It is the totem of the Bayo family. The praise song for Jula Jekere Bayo – "he is a *sora* who does not eat *karaa*" – depicts him as an honest man who kept his word. Both qualities were essential to build up confidence and trust in his commercial partners.

[37] Respectively, Mansa Nyma is "the good ruler," Sabou Nyima is "the good reason," Baraka is "blessing," and Duwaa Jabbia is "prayer answered." The names of these slaves symbolized the prestige and prosperity of Jula Jekere. As for the surnames, slaves either took the surname of their masters or retained their original ones. In the first case, slave ancestry became almost a family secret in the course of the twentieth century. In the second one, surnames are a historical source that reveals an original act of enslavement.

[38] This means that two girls considered each other strongly linked because they were breast-fed by the same woman.

[39] Bakoyo now shifts to the events related to Mamadi Kora and his struggle to obtain the chieftaincy of Fuladu East, after the death of Farli Kora, which occurred early in the 1910s. Mamadi competed with Kemonding until Mamadi was exiled from the district and the chieftaincy given to a different family. The *jali* commemorated the event by creating a Kora tune, "A la la ke," which means "God wanted it." In other words, the loss of the chieftaincy was not a result of Mamadi's misbehavior, but was part of the destiny of the family.

members whom you trust. They would inform you of what happened in your absence. They would narrate many things to you. At daybreak, people would come to greet you. By then you would have known a lot. Mamadi did like this. He learned that Kemonding had got the chieftaincy. Mamadi wanted the office. This led to a crisis that resulted in the lost of the chieftaincy for the Kora.[40]

3. "Slaves were brought to the River Gambia from various places …"

Bakoyo now comments on the interdependency of rulers and traders in the slave trade. He explains where most of the River Gambia slaves hailed from, and describes both the ruthlessness of the rulers toward their subjects and the trading families' pride in having large slave entourages.

Slaves were brought to the River Gambia from various places. People got them from Bundu, Dantilaa, from Tanda. They got them from the place that today is called Tillibou, the east. Niani is there, Bundu is there.[41] All these places are there. They got their slaves form all these different places. They got slaves from war and trade […].

Rulers caused the majority of wars. The ruler would reason in this way. First, he would let you free to manage your affairs until you are about to become powerful. Then, one day he would get up and assemble his men to come and attack you. On that day, all your strength would be destroyed. He would capture your people and enslave them.

This was a common practice among the rulers to prevent their subjects from becoming powerful enough to challenge their sovereignty. Then, as I already explained, there were those who stole children. These were not rulers. Traders used to buy those children, as owning a lot of slaves was a matter of pride for the trading families.

Rulers also asked the assistance of religious scholars and diviners when they were about to buy slaves. The divination advised them that a specific person, if bought, would bring luck and make their family entourages long prosperous. This is how things went. Rulers jumped ruthlessly on people and caused enslavement. But wealth also mattered. I was once adviced not to wish for wealth, as wealth entails wickedness and greed, and greed is what cursed *Iblis Shaytan*. Traders were happy when rulers attacked and captured people. Even today, if you look carefully at the way in which business operates, you would realize that when something is scarce and difficult to get, businessmen raise the price. So, also in the days of the slave trade, the trader was the one who gained more as he was more aware than the ruler. When a ruler sits on his throne, if you cajole him with sweet words, he would be generous toward you by giving out things, which value one hundred, for seventy.

4. "The slaves worked from upland to swamps …"

Certain categories of slaves, namely those who gained the confidence of their masters or who were born in their masters' families, played important ritual roles. During circumcision

---

[40] Bakoyo closes his recollection here, as he does not wish to reveal unpleasant details about the history of the Kora family. Colonial sources registered the case of Kemonding and Mamadi, which was one of the most famous chieftaincy conflicts of the early twentieth century.

[41] The regions Bakoyo mentions are all located in Eastern Senegal and were the major supplier of slaves for the River Gambia in the late eighteenth and nineteenth centuries. Curtin, *Senegambia*, 177 and ff.

ceremonies, boys were segregated in the bush for almost three months. Blacksmiths per-formed the surgery. The slaves taught the children how to bear thirst and hunger, how to sleep on the soil, how to talk to elders and conversely keep quiet when the elders talked. All this was designed to transform boys into respected members of their society. The train-ing included explanations on how to court a woman and behave as a proper husband. Slave children were circumcised together with freeborn ones, but the latter enjoyed spe-cial privileges. The slaves in the family would assist the freeborn children and report their progress to the mothers, who waited in the village. Beside creating solidarity across the social hierarchy, circumcisions prepared freeborn and slave children for different future positions in society.

First and foremost, they used the slaves to work, they gained a lot from the work of the slaves. Powerful and wealthy people bought many slaves. When the rains came – by then the rains lasted long and were heavy – the slaves worked from upland to swamps, they worked extremely hard during the rains.

Now, if you had slaves – and I had slaves – imagine that my slave wishes to have your slaves' child for marriage. You had power over that; whatever you say would happen. This is how the slaves married. If you have a slave woman with you, we would discuss until we agree and without saying a word to her. Only the two of us would talk. The agreement would be some money and a female goat. That is what I would pay and then we would tie the mar-riage. When you go, you would say to your slave woman: "your husband will be Bakoyo's so and so slave." When I return home, I would say to my male slave: "your wife is Mamadi's so and so slave woman." This is how they were married. My male slave, if he married your slave woman, their children belonged to you. They would be with you and work for you. If I had a female slave, and one of your male slaves took her, all her children would come and work for me. This is how slaves married in those days.

When the masters had a joyful occasion or a ceremony, for example a wedding, chris-tening, circumcision, the slaves did the cooking and the fetching of firewood and whatever errand ensured the success of the ceremony. At the time of circumcision, the slaves used to go with their masters' children to the bush for a period of about three months. They would stay with the children, train and assist them. They would inform the mothers of what the chil-dren dreamt. On the day of the "coming out," they would carry the children on their shoulders till they reached home. Whatever people gave to the children – wrappers, money, gold – belonged to the slaves. They owned it all. Because of this, there is a saying in the Mandinka language: "slavery, only a bad slave disowns it." On the day of the "coming out," the slaves were popular; benefits and glory belonged to them.

It is because of this that some slaves accepted their condition. For the rest, they worked for themselves only on Thursdays, the rest of the week they worked for their masters. They did not earn much out of that; in fact, if you count the Thursdays from the beginning to the end of the rainy season, you would soon finish them. They might be nine or ten; these ten Thursdays, one of them might find you sick. What they got was not much. Maybe, they had a wife and a child. The master took care of all their basic needs. But the little things that would please your hearth, those little things were provided by the Thursday you worked by your-self.[42] The slaves were not so interested in this kind of little benefit. What they really prayed

---

[42] Bakoyo refers to a little bit of tobacco, honey, spirit, wild fruits, and other little items.

earnestly for was for their masters to organize a joyful ceremony, as in that case, they would really enjoy themselves.

5. "Mussa was with Saloum Jobarteh for three years ..."

Masters traded their slaves in ways that escaped a narrow definition of selling. The Mandinka word, which is today used to talk about the traffic in slaves, is *sango*. This simultaneously refers to the act of buying, of selling, and more generally of transacting. The possibility of being traded or of witnessing the transaction that involved one's own children and grandchildren – spoke to the core of the slaves' social vulnerability. Bakoyo already illustrated the use of slaves as bride-wealth. Marrying a freeborn woman meant a gift of at least three or four slaves to her family. Other slaves would accompany her to the new house. Slaves were donated to religious scholars as compensation for their services.

It is worth remembering that spiritual work – divination, prayers, and the provision of ritual paraphernalia – sustained the symbolic apparatus of power and social prestige of warlords, big merchants, and religious scholars. Finally, pawns were more often slaves than freeborn. In strict terms, they were not slaves but persons given to secure a loan and who were supposed to return to their family when the debt was paid. Bakoyo takes a cue from the oral traditions associated with Mussa Moloh Baldeh's youth to show that that this form of subjection could be but a phase in the life cycle, as even powerful military leaders like Mussa experienced it.

In Kaur, there was a prosperous trader named Saloum Jebate.[43] He had many slaves and bought slaves until no one knew how many slaves he owned. When the white people came to Kaur, they would greet him and present him with a gift. Local people would say: "Saloum Jebate has become so powerful that even the white men pay taxes to him." Saloum Jebate was very rich. Mussa Moloh's father, who was called Alpha Moloh, ran out of gunpowder. He asked who among his children or younger people would agree to be taken to the trader as a guarantee so that he could get gunpowder. They were all quiet. Mussa was a young man. He said to his father: "I agree." Alpha Moloh asked: "Sure?" Mussa replied: "Yes."

Alpha Moloh walked from N'Dorna until he reached Saloum Jebate's place.[44] He left Mussa as a guarantee and Musa remained with Saloum Jebate for three years. When Alpha Moloh was eventually ready to retrieve Mussa, rains had already started. Mussa was working in Saloum's fields. Thirty people were behind him. He was their leader, and they were sowing seeds into the holes after him. These thirty people could not keep his rhythm. He was very ambitious and worked extremely fast. Whatever he engaged in, he would try to do something which people recognized as exceptional. Alpha Moloh arrived and said to Saloum: "Trader, I have come for my child. Now Allah has provided for me. Here, it is what you asked." Saloum replied: "What I really want is your child. I will give you two slave boys and cancel this debt but leave Mussa with me." Alpha Moloh laughed: "This is not the son of my elder

---

[43] Kaur is an ancient trading post on the northern bank of the River Gambia, whose foundation dates back the heydays of the Atlantic traffic in slaves. J. M. Gray, *A History*, 353 quotes the Bathurst trader Salim Jobarteh, who hailed from Bathurst and was based in Tendaba, on the southern bank of the river, around 1834. Tendaba is opposite to Kaur. Probably he is the same trader, and this would point to early relationships between native merchants and Bathurst settlers.

[44] N'dorna was Alpha Moloh's village in the Upper Casamance near the contemporary town of Kolda.

brother nor he is the son of my younger brother. This is my own son. A son, who did so many things for the man he was pawned to, will surely be able to substitute for the father when he is absent. I beg you to allow me to go with Mussa."[45]

Saloum knew that Alpha said the truth. Mussa Moloh was also given as a guarantee to Masirey at Jarra Sukuta and to Bulung Kono Bukasi at Jarra Soma. He was taken to all these places as a guarantee on behalf of his father. At the time, people would place their sons and daughter as a guarantee to survive periods of hunger. In exchange, they would get food supplies, which they returned at the time of the harvest, after the rains. But if they could not honor their debt, the child would stay with the creditor as a slave. Some children did not wish to be ransomed as the place in which they had been pawned was far better than their original homes.

6. "I have something in my head, which is too big for my mouth ..."

Respecting the loyalty that linked his forebears to Alpha and Mussa Molo Baldeh of Fuladu, Bakoyo is reluctant to talk about the slave-dealing activities of these two military leaders. Today the descendants of Mussa's slaves consider themselves (and are considered) as part of his extended family. This is the meaning of the expression: "I am from Mussa kunda," where the suffix *kunda* (literally, compound or dwelling place) indicates the web of relationships originated by Mussa's entourage. Not all the slaveholding families of the River Gambia pursued the same assimilation policy, however. The freeborn families of Fuladu accused Alpha Moloh's branch of the Baldeh family of being slaves. This slander should be understood to be an expression of discontent on the part of other freeborn families with both Alpha and Mussa. In their effort to limit Mussa's influence in the Upper Gambia and Casamance, both French and British colonial officials espoused the thesis that the Baldeh were usurpers, lacking historical legitimacy because of their slave origins.

Mussa 's character was complicated. He attacked people and went to places to fight, he and Fode Kaba fought most of the wars of their time.[46] Although it is really ridiculous not to talk about this (because it is history and has been recorded), if you mention these things, you can bring problems. Jali Fode[47] said: "I have something in my head, which is too big for my mouth!" This is what really worries me, otherwise I would narrate the little I know about certain areas which Mussa attacked and were he captured many slaves.[48] What I can say is that Mussa's home was made into a desirable place when you go and reach there. After some time, the people he captured would say: "I am from Mussa Kunda." They would not say: "I am a slave, or a *jaloo*, a black smith, or any other person." This is what they become, people of Mussakunda. The Baldeh would not address you as a slave because they were known to be slaves as well.

[45] Alpha Moloh's words clearly show that "son" was a classificatory term that included a wide range of relationships; Mussa, however, was his own son, and Alpha wanted him back. By quoting such an example Bakayo tries to explain how quickly pawns integrated into the families of the creditor up to the point of preferring them to their original home.

[46] That is, Fode Kaba Dumbuyaa, Islamic reformer and war leader of the second half of the nineteenth century. See Bellagamba, Chapter 31 in this volume, for major details on his slaving activities and his enmity with Mussa Molo Baldeh.

[47] Griots like Bakoyo often quote famous sentences from their predecessors when they want to stress a particular point. I already mentioned Jali Fode in the introduction.

[48] One of these famous places was, for instance, Bijini, a big Muslim village of Guinea Bissau, whose inhabitants refused allegiance to Mussa Moloh Baldeh. Another one was Jali in the Kiang area on the southern bank of the River Gambia. See B. Sidibé, *Kaabu*, 81 and ff.

7. "The day Musa betrayed Momadou Fatima …"

Bakoyo now turns to Momadou Fatima Jawla's vicissitudes. Momadou Fatima is one of the minor characters in the religious conflicts, which in the second half of the nineteenth century interested the northern bank of the River Gambia. He was associated with the Islamic reformer Mamadu Lamine Darame, whom the French saw as one of their major obstacles to the pacification of Eastern Senegal. Mussa Moloh Baldeh assisted them in sweeping away Darame.[49] Momadou Fatima, being an ally of Darame, was also on their blacklist. Mussa was asked to organize his assassination.

Bakoyo narrates what purportedly happened on that specific day. Mussa knew Momadou resented being of slave ancestry. He therefore explained to Momadou the personal interpretation he had developed of the contrast between ascribed and achieved status: to be called a slave and be really treated as a slave are two different things. Betrayal hid behind these sweet words. When the conversation ended, Mussa's men killed Momadou Fatima Jawla and troops were sent to destroy his home village and enslave his wives and children. The second part of the text provides details on the slave origins of Momadou Fatima himself.

The day Mussa betrayed Momadou Fatima, he talked to him nicely about slavery. Momadou Fatima was staying at Misira. Mussa sent him a message to come, but Momadou refused. Somebody from Mussa's entourage said he would be able to bring him. Mussa sent the man who found Momadou Fatima sitting at his place and said to him: "Hee, elder Momadou, haven't you heard that Mussa the warlord came and sent a message for you? You did not answer, I think you are afraid to go." Momadou Fatima replied "tie my horse!" Momadou found Mussa and other people in Nawu. Mussa got up to welcome him and asked him to sit. They chatted, and Mussa told him: "You should bear in mind that I called for you to discuss as now the war ended, and we do not see each other very often. What you are, everybody knows that." Mussa said to the people assembled there: "You are seeing a lion.[50] This is Momadou Fatima. You underrate him in the house, but if you meet him in the bush you would know who he is, he can overcome me completely. But Momadou, you, also, please forebear now, old age has come, please forebear because no one cannot prevent people from what they say. What they would tell you, you would not like it; up to the time you would die, you would always be hearing such words. Go there, and you would hear them saying that Momadou Fatima is a bastard. In your place, as well, they say: 'Haa, Mussa Moloh is not a free Fulah, but a slave.'" "Haa!" Mussa continued, "I am not a free Fula, I am a slave, but I am also your ruler although I cannot prevent you from calling me a slave. Let us bear it, Momadou!" Mussa kept repeating that kind of words to Momadou Fatima to put his mind to rest until evening. He later bid farewell from him. At this point, the betrayal took place. Momadou lost everything on that occasion: his life, the slaves that he had captured and become part of his family, his wives and children. When they really treat you as a slave, it is a great sufferance.

---

[49] See M. A. Gomez, *Pragmatism in the Age of the Jihad. The Precolonial State of Bundu* (Cambridge, 1992).

[50] Famous warriors of the past are often praised by the *jali* as the equivalents of the wildest and most dangerous animals of the time, namely lions and crocodiles. The lion is also associated to Sunjata Keita, the founder of the Mali empire. For the Mandinka *jali* of the Senegambia, the epic of Sunjata offered a model to narrate the histories of nineteenth-century military leaders like Alpha Moloh, Mussa Moloh, and Momadou Fatima himself. Innes, *Sunjata*; Suso and Kanute, *Sunjata*.

Momadou's mother, Fatumaa Sanneh,[51] was a *furubaa* slave. This meant that she belonged to the entire Jawla family. When Ha Fode Jawla[52] became interested in her, his senior brother said to him: "You should know that she is a *furubaa* slave.[53] She is now your mistress but in the case she gets pregnant and delivers, if the baby is a girl and you call her Kumba, for the family she will be Sira, if he is a boy and you call him Malamin, for the family he will be Mamadu."[54] Ha Fode's senior brother was ready to insist on this point [meaning: to stop the love affair between Ha Fode and this slave woman], but the pregnancy became manifested and the woman delivered a boy. War came and Ha Fode died without marrying Fatumaa Sammeh.[55] Momadou Fatima was therefore a slave as his mother before him.

8. "If a slave wants to become a free man . . ."

With the establishment of the British Protectorate, slaves obtained the opportunity to free themselves. Some did so by showing deference and loyalty to their former masters. Others simply severed the link with their masters' families. It is evident from the narrative that, like that of other master descendants, Bakoyo's sympathy was with the category of slaves who humbly asked for their freedom. Momadou Fatima enters the picture again, being the only case Bakoyo knows of a slave that rebelled against his condition in precolonial times.

In this area of West Africa, from Mali up to the Gambia, all the slaves were in one condition; a slave was never freeborn. Hardship was for him, and whatever he did, he was always a slave.

Abolition began with the white men. Since colonial times, if a slave wants to become a free man, he works for his master until the master is very happy. He explains what he wishes to the master in a respectful manner by going to one of the master's closest friends and asking him to intercede for his/her freedom. The friend chats with the master till the latter is convinced and agrees. You know that a slave is bought for 66 dalasis.[56] The slave will bring that amount of

---

[51] Sanneh is a Mandinka surname associated with the ruling class of Kaabu, one of the major polities of precolonial Southern Senegambia. Kaabu center was situated in contemporary Guinea-Bissau and its political influence reached the River Gambia. By the mid-nineteenth century, when the wars leading to the establishment of Fuladu began, Kaabu had almost disintegrated. It major settlements along the River Gambia had been destroyed by Fula raiders, while their populace had been either enslaved or scattered throughout the region. Many slaves of the second part of the nineteenth century bear Kaabu surnames, and there is a joking relationships between Fuladu Fula (mostly the Baldeh and other related Fula families) and Kaabu Mandinka, which plays around slave-master relationships. By addressing each as the slave of the other, the joke states the difficulty of ascertaining who dominated whom in the course of history.

[52] Ha Fode Jawla was one of the *marabout* military leaders of the mid-nineteenth century. He was killed in 1863. J. M. Gray, *A History*, 424.

[53] This detail provides an insight on how the control of slaves was distributed within the large domestic entourages of the time. Farming land was divided between family collective fields (*furubaa*) and individual ones. Similarly, slaves were owned either by the family at large and kept under the control of the family head for the benefit of the whole group, or by individuals who disposed of them according to their needs. For instance, the slaves that freeborn women brought along at the time of marriage remained attached to them and did not belong to the families of the husband.

[54] This is to illustrate that the children of a *furubaa* slave belonged to the family. The family could change the names the father had chosen for them.

[55] Marrying a woman of slave origins was a common practice among the freeborn of the time. This produced inequalities and different entitlements within the same family entourage of brothers and sisters, which at the death of the father would split into major and minor lineages.

[56] The customary price that elderly men like Bakoyo recollect for the freeing of slaves. The fact that they talk about dalasi, which is the currency of independent Gambia, is evidently an anachronism. Versions are also at variance. On other occasions, Bakoyo himself talked about 6 times 66; some others give the following interpretation: whatever the slave brings to pay for his freedom must be produced by 66; 66 pieces of cloth, 66 kola nuts, and so forth. This made redemption extremely expensive.

money, buy cola nuts and go to the master. They will pray for each other and then the master will say: "Today, this man is free. We have given him his neck. What we are, he also is."[57] There are cases, however, in which the slaves simply rebel and say: "Since slavery has been abolished, I am no one's slave today. Let no one call me slave again." Then, the master has a problem.

Before the coming of the white man, there was no great chance of rebellion. The only case I know is that of Momadou Fatima. Momadou was not a ruler but he was a very big warrior. During one of his battles, one day Momadou captured the son of Bokar Sada.[58] The boy was called Abdou Sey. Momadou put him on a horse, tied him, and brought him up to Kunting, where the Jawla family was.[59] He came and entrusted him to his senior brother, Nfali Soora. Momadou explained: "This is the son of a chief, what you eat, give him to eat, where you spend the night, let him also spend the night there, let no one lose patience with him, let no one insult him, let no one beat him, just be careful that he does not escape."

Nfali Soora agreed. Momadou had received a gift from God. People who knew him also feared him. Bokar Sada was afraid to go and meet him in order to ransom his son. He thus made a plan and went straight to Nfali Soora pleading to get his son back. Nfali Soora pitied him and gave him the boy. About three weeks later, Momadou Fatima asked for Abdou Sey. People informed him of what happened. Momadou therefore said to his elder brother: "I entrusted this boy to you, and you sent him away without even a message to me. You know, I go to war, whatever I get, I bring it here for the benefit of the family. I will stop this habit. I am no longer behind you, whatever I get will be mine." The dispute between Momadou Fatima and his family began like this. Momadou then settled in Misira. The slaves he got remained with him. They were farming and [doing] many other things. He did not send anyone to Kunting again. Momadou Fatima was a slave but also a warrior.

9. "People have realized that slavery is not correct..."

Slavery continues to be a disputed issue in the Gambia. Bakoyo gives examples of enduring discrimination against slave descendants and closes the narrative by stating his personal opinion. Addressing other people as slave descendants is a vestige of the past, morally and socially out of place in the contemporary context.

The discrimination against slave descendants is still alive.

Among the Serrahule and the Jahanka, slavery is practiced.[60] The majority of the Jahanka are marabouts. People who owned slaves took them to the marabout saying: "Please, pray for

---

[57] The ceremony included also a ritual bath, which was meant to remove from the person the impurity caused by enslavement (see also Paolo Gaibazzi, Chapter 46 in this volume). *Foroo*, which translates as "free" and *jongo*, which became historically associated with the word "slave," are used in the Mandinka language also to distinguish pure from impure gold or silver.

[58] The ransom of Bokar Sada's son is a renowned episode in the oral traditions of the Gambia river. Educated by the French, Bokar Sada was the ruler of Bundu, a state located north of the Gambia river, between the 1850s and his death in 1885. In 1866, he led a major invasion through Wuli that reached MacCarthy Island and forced the British to send troops to the island thereby abandoning their policy of nonintervention in native conflicts. He then allied with Alpha Moloh and the Almami of Futa Jallon, Alpha Ibrahima Jallow. For a number of years, he made almost annual raids to the Gambia. A. Hughes and D. Perfect, *A Political*, 202.

[59] At the time, Momadou Fatima controlled the region of Sandu and still recognized the leadership of the Jawla of Kunting, which was the center of the Jawla influence on the northern bank of the River Gambia not far from the British settlement of MacCarthy Island.

[60] The Serrahuli and the Jahanka are two of the ethnic minorities of the Senegambia region. For the Serrahuli, see Paolo Gaibazzi (Chapter 46 in this volume); Jahanka, like Simoto Kemo Sanuwo, were Muslim clerics and traders whose villages were widely scattered throughout the hinterland of the Senegambia. They

me!" As for Simoto Kemo, you would see someone, he would be taking ten slaves and give them to him. Even Mussa Moloh gave five slaves to Sheku Mafujii[61] at one go, and he did such kind of things in so many places.

In the village of Gambisara the graveyard[s] for slaves and freeborn are not the same. Even in Baddibu.[62] In Gambisara the slaves and the freeborn have different graves. I saw this the last time I was there.

Now, think of it: yesterday, your forebears had slaves but your forebears were pagan; the slaves were pagan too. The descendants of those slaves are in your hands up to today but how can you insist saying: "I have a slave or I own a slave"? People have realized that slavery is not correct. Where is the descendant of the ancient trader, who today stands to state "this man is my slave"? The traders of the old days, who are now dead, were known for buying slaves. Their descendants are here but they keep quiet…. They recognize they had slaves but to point to someone as their slave, they cannot do that today.

SUGGESTED ADDITIONAL READINGS

1. ON *JALI* AS ORAL HISTORIANS AND MUSICIANS

Hoffmann, Barbara. *Griots at war: Conflict, Conciliation and Caste in Mande*. Ohio: Indiana University Press, 2011.

Jansen, Jan. *The Griot's Craft: An Essay on Oral Tradition and Diplomacy*, Volume 8: Forschungen zur Sprachen and Kulturen Afrikas. Hamburg and Piscataway, NJ: Transaction Publishers, 2001.

Janson, Marloes. *The Best Hand Is the Hand That Always Gives: Griottes and Their Profession in Eastern Gambia*. Leiden: Research School CNWS, 2002.

Jawara, Mamadou. *L'empire du verbe et l'éloquence du silence*. Köln: R. Koeppe, 2003.

Schultz, Dorothea. *Perpetuating the Politics of Praise*. Köln: R. Koeppe, 2001.

2. ON ORAL SOURCES AND THE MEMORY OF SLAVERY

Clark, Andrew. "The Challenges of Cross-Cultural Oral History: Collecting and Presenting Pulaar Traditions on Slavery from Bundu, Senegambia (West Africa)," *Oral History Review*, 20:1 (1992), 1–23.

Greene, Sandra. "Whispers and Silences: Explorations in Africa Oral History," *Africa Today*, 50:2 (2003), 40–53.

Klein, Martin. "Studying the History of Those Who Would Rather Forget: Oral History and the Experience of Slavery," *History in Africa*, 16 (1989), 209–217.

Searing, James. *"God Alone Is King": Islam and Emancipation in Senegal*. Oxford: James Currey, 2002.

---

traced their origins back to Dia, a town in Mali, which had the reputation of being a very important religious center. P. Curtin, *Senegambia*, 67; L. Sanneh, *The Crown and the Turban: Muslims and West African Pluralism* (Boulder, CO, 1996) discusses the place of slaves in Jahanka society.

[61] Cheikh Mahfoudz, a Mauritanian Islamic scholar who spent the last decades of the nineteenth century traveling and preaching through Senegal, Mali, Guinea Conakry, and Guinea Bissau. Nugent, "Cyclical," 233.

[62] Gambisara is a populous Serrahule town of the Upper River Gambia. Baddibu is a region on the northern bank of the River Gambia, where the social stigma of slave ancestry is felt to this day.

4 Tales of Cowries, Money, and Slaves

ALESSANDRA BRIVIO

The trade in shell money – cowries – started in the fourteenth century and ended by the 1880s.[1] The shells arrived from the Indian and Pacific oceans and were traded all over the world. West Africa, where the mollusk that produces the shell did not breed, was the ultimate destination for many of the shells. They were brought by European slave traders as capital to buy slaves. Since their arrival on African coasts, they have come to symbolize the introduction of money and market expansion during the era of the Atlantic slave trade, but they also embody images of death. They represent "an alternative to the concept of market rationality and its encompassing discourse of modernization,"[2] while also offering a critique of Africa's entrance into the global capitalist economy. The first important cowry shipment probably arrived in Benin (Nigeria) from the Indian Ocean in 1515. It was in the course of the sixteenth century that the political elite of Benin appears to have monetized cowries. It was in the eighteenth century, however, one of the most intense periods of the slave trade, that traders imported more than ten billion shells.[3]

Along what was once known as the Slave Coast, a common myth (with many different versions) narrates a tale about slavery and money, wellness, death, and violence. The myth focuses on cowry shells, imagined as little vampires that reproduce themselves on the skin of humans, sucking their blood. Today, as in the past, these tales seek to describe the violent and troubling memories of the slave trade. Using images of witches, vampires, and cannibals, they reflect on the socially and morally problematic nature of money in general, and on how the capture and binding of slaves, in itself a process of disempowerment, transform human beings into alienable commodities.

---

[1] Cowries' shells are part of the family of seashells called *cypraea*. Two species were used: the *cypraea moneta* and the *cypraea annulus*. They arrived from the Indian and Pacific oceans. Probably the first important cowrie load arrived in Benin (Nigeria) from the Indian Ocean in 1515. It seems that, during the sixteenth century, the political elite of Benin was one of the first to monetize cowries. During the eighteenth century, the more intense period of slave trade, it is reckoned that traders imported tens of billions of shells. A. Ogundiran, "Of Small Things Remembered: Beads, Cowries, and Cultural Translations of the Atlantic Experience in Yorubaland," *The International Journal of African Historical Studies*, 35, 2/3 (2002), 427–457.

[2] R. Austen, "The Moral Economy of Witchcraft: An Essay in Comparative History," in J. Comaroff and J. Comaroff (eds.), *Modernity and Its Malcontents: Ritual and Power in Postcolonial Africa* (Chicago and London, 1993), 89.

[3] Ogundiran, "Of Small," 427–457.

This chapter presents three versions of the widely distributed myths about cowries.[4] The first was collected by Gregor Elwert (1989)[5] in Ayizo region in Benin; the second by Louis Adotevi (2001)[6] in southern Togo. The last is the version Kokou Atchinou narrated to me in Lomè (Togo) in 2007. Although the tales seem to repeat the same plot, the storytellers actually offer different views about the slave trade and how one should understand masters and slaves given the political and historical contexts described. The first tale represents the voices of the Ayizo, a people who fought to escape enslavement. Even though they themselves had never been enslaved by the Abomey king, and were therefore probably not descendants of slaves, they nevertheless remembered the history of their political and social subaltern position with regard to Dahomey and the state's role in profiting from the introduction of cowrie-money during the era of the Atlantic slave trade.

The second tale expresses the traders' point of view. The Guin-Mina people were able to enrich themselves from slave trade both selling humans beings and profiting of the "natural" growing of cowries on the bodies of drowned slaves. The third tale evokes the ancestors' mythical times. The tale expresses the voices of the masters' descendants who remember their grandfathers' past. They were hunters who, thanks to their professional skill and to the encounters with coastal people, were able to gain money and, as a consequence, forced to invest them buying an increasing number of slaves.

In all the different tales the relation between cowries and human bodies points out the idea of a zero-sum moral economy: the enrichment could just be accomplished to the detriment of vital energy of others humans. Nevertheless, the strong and cruel metaphor of the introduction of money in local economy entailed by the slave trade, and the implicit moral condemnation, do not prevent cowries to incorporate different and contrasting meanings. They are little vampires able to kill human beings and at the same time, as evoked by their name, "white-corn-money" – they feed people as maize does. Furthermore, as cited in the second narrative, cowries could be offered to divinities. They are, in fact, loaded with mystical powers and incorporate symbolical values of fertility and abundance. Their ambiguity could also help understand the thinking and the talk about the slave trade of Tchamba people. While evoking the implication of their families in the slave trade and its evident violence, they regret the past times when cowries were abundant, wellness was assured, and the "grandfathers" were great hunters and warriors. For Tchamba people, cowries remain objects of desire even if they are aware of the heavy price paid in the past to obtain them.

---

[4] Isikei shows the wide spread of these stories in Africa, which were probably independently invented or carried along the trade routes. She reports different versions of the myth recorded in Nigeria. According to Isichei, the first tale recorded was in 1907, in Central Nigeria, and was not related to slave trade. In 1978, in the Benue valley in Central Nigeria, the myth was linked with enslavement and the Hausa trading network. She found the same tale narrate, even if different in detail, by the novelist Soni Labu Tansi and related to the Zaire River. E. Isichei, *Voices of the Poor in Africa: Moral Economy and the Popular Imagination* (Rochester, NY, 2002), 66–69. In his historical novel, *The Viceroy of Ouidah* (1980), Bruce Chatwin has located the legend in the New Word: "*Mama Benz asked what cowrie really was. "Cowrie is a snail," he said. It lives in a river called Mississippi. In the old days, the Americans would throw a slave in the river, the cowries would feed on the body, and then they'd haul it up and that's how they got money to buy more slaves.*"

[5] G. Elwert, *An Intricate Oral Culture: On History, Humour and Social Control among the Ayizo (Benin)* (Berlin, 1989).

[6] L. Adotevi, "Contribution à l'etude de l'esclavage en pays Guin (mina) à l'epoque precoloniale (XVVIIe-XIXe seicle)," in Gayibor (ed.), *Le tricentenaire d'Aneho et du pays guin* (Lomé, 2001), 117–136.

QUESTIONS TO CONSIDER

1. What do you think about the ambiguity of the meanings associated with cowries? Do you agree or disagree with this idea?
2. How can you explain the present position of the Tchamba people in terms of facing the memory of the slave trade?
3. What do these tales suggest about the African agency in the slave trade?
4. What were the consequences of the slave trade in the political setting of the region?
5. In your opinion, what are the implications of the Kokou Atchinou association between slave trading and hunting?
6. What do these tales tell us about the present-day memory of the slave trade in West Africa?

1. An Ayizo Tale by Klikpo Cece

(translated from Ayizo into English by Gergor Elwert).[7]

The Ayizo live on the Allada plateau in Benin. They are the southern neighbors of the Fon-speaking people, whose capital, Abomey, stood at the political center of the Dahomey state. Starting from the eighteenth century, they suffered from the expansionist politics of the Fon people, who sought to control the slave routes to the coast.[8] The Ayzo people were sold as slaves or forced to serve in the king's slave-raiding army. Those Ayzo who escaped capture settled into less accessible forest regions such as Attotinga, Houéto, Hèvié, and Akassato, but they remained tributaries and potential slaves for the Abomey king. Cece's tale reflects their subaltern position: it denounces the violent politics of war and assimilation perpetrated by the Abomey kings and condemns their involvement in the slave trade and their role in introducing money into the local economy. Abomey's violent and cruel actions are directly linked to the absolute quest for wealth through the slave trade. The capital was supported by a complex system of taxation and tribute payments. The king imposed travel tolls and taxes on market's sales, on agricultural production, on inheritance, on money incomes, and on all adult men. During Annual Customs,[9] African traders brought to the king's palace at Abomey gifts in cowries according to the king's requests. Moreover, tributes were paid by all the states dominated by Dahomey. Prominent persons offered foodstuffs for the maintenance of the palace population, and people from lower social levels supplied young men for the army and young women for the palace organization.[10] Women drawn from the Fon population and war captives, who lived in the palace, were available to

---

[7] Elwert's translation was of the Ayizo text that had already been published in 1979.

[8] The Ayzo were centered in Allada and occupied the plains between the Kufo and Wo rivers. Theirs influence reached to the south the Lake Nokoue and the towns of Abomey-Calavi and Gbessou. Allada was defeated by the Fon king Agaja in 1724 and then heavily colonized by the Fon. The conquest of Allada and then of Ouidah brought Dahomey in direct contact with the coast and the European trade. E. Bay, *Wives of the Leopard: Gender, Politics and Culture in the Kingdom of Dahomey* (Richmond, 1998), 57–58.

[9] The Annual Customs was a ceremony celebrated to honor the royal ancestors. The aim was to legitimize the dynasty, assuring the support of the deceased kings for the ruling king. Annual Customs spoke both to the ancestors and to Dahomeans. They emphasized the supremacy of the royal line through lavish human and animal sacrifices and preventing other lineages from performing their annual ceremonies for ancestors before the king's Annual Customs.

[10] Bay, *Wives*, 122.

lower-ranking men as wives after they paid bride-wealth (that would have otherwise gone to the women's fathers or male elderly relatives) to the king.[11]

Money became the mean to obtain power and the cause of exploitation. The tale explains how the introduction of money into the local economy transformed human beings into objects, which were then vampirized by the new exchange value. The king's practice of capturing, immobilizing, and locking up the prisoners in order to feed and enlarge their bodies heightened the violence and exploitative nature of such political power.

The fattening of the people in Cece's tale references the practice of fattening brides before they were released to the public, usually as the wives of rich people. It was a widespread custom, according to Goddman,[12] "specially in some areas of Ashanti and Fanti territory [in Ghana] and in Nigeria, the bride-to-be is sent away to a 'Fatting House,' where her female relatives-in-law keep her in close confinement for several months during which she is overfed in an endeavour to bring her to that state of obesity which … is regarded as a sign of extreme beauty and fitness for marriage." Talbot wrote of similar practices in south-east Nigeria: "Among the Efiks and those Ibibios rich enough to bear the expense, free-born girls of good family go twice, and sometimes even thrice, into the Fatting house before the full marriage ceremony is performed."[13] According to some local folktales, fattening house did more than prepare a bride for marriage. Sometimes girls ran the risk of being "eaten."[14] A southern Nigerian folktale, for example, describes a king's daughter who was sold to a "spirit man." She "was put in the fatting house by the spirit man, and was given food; but a skull, who was in the house, told her not to eat, as they were fatting her up, not for marriage, but so that they could eat her. She therefore gave all the food, which was brought to her to the skull, and lived instead on chalk."[15] Finally she escaped.

It is possible that Klikpo Cece was inspired by this practice, even if the "fattening house" was not a Dahomey or Ayizo institution. It existed in neighboring countries and was probably known even if it never became a local practice. By referencing this marital custom, Cece underlined the important presence of female domestic slaves in local societies, while emphasizing the brutality of the slave trade in which the enslaved men and women were "fed like pigs in order to became big" to feed their captors. The message conveyed by Cece's tale is clear: the Dahomey king transported slaves from the interior to the coast (Ayizo lived close to the main road connecting Abomey to Ouidah) and then transported cowries from the coast to the interior. His wealth was linked with this trade, and his treatment of those he captured was absolutely contrary to the norms of Ayizo society.

In the beginning of the world we had the forge and we forged things, we had weaving-looms and we wove our clothes, we had oracle huts where we consulted the oracle, and we had boats from which we caught fish. We had no guns. We had no money (*akwá*). If you went to the market you took beans in order to barter them for sweet potatoes. You exchanged something specific for something else. You exchange something specific for something else, till

---

[11] Bay, *Wives*, 149.

[12] L. Goodman, "Obstetrics in a Primitive African Community," *American Journal of Public Health*, 41 (1951), 56–64.

[13] A. Talbot, *Woman's Mysteries of a Primitive People* (London and New York, 1915).

[14] In this tale, "eat" might mean that the spirits eat the "soul" of the girl, compelling her to become part of its mystical order.

[15] E. Dayrell, *Folk Stories from Southern Nigeria* (London, 1910), 98.

the time that the king brought the money. What did the king do in order to bring the money? He caught people and broke their legs and their arms. [Then] he built a hut in a banana plantation and put the people in it, he gave her [them] the banana and [they] ate it until [they] became big and fat. The king killed the person and he gave orders to his workers, and they put strings and pulled and put the corpses in the water of cowries-shells (*akwá*). When the cowrie-shells are numerous around the corpse and start to eat the corpse, they pulled him out and they pick the cowries-shells and put them in hot water [to kill them]. That is how one did till the time that money came to exist. This money was called money-grain-white (*akwé-kún-wéé*). The French came to break the country before they came to bring the metal money to this place. The second money of the French is called "billet" (paper money)."[16]

2. A Guin-Mina Tale

(recorded by Louis Adotevi, translated by Alessandra Brivio)

This second version of the cowry tale was collected in the Guin-Mina-speaking region of Togo. The Guin-Mina had been involved in slave trade since the eighteenth century. Their economic successes allowed the Guin-Mina to extend their political and economic rule from the Mono River (the present-day border between Togo and Benin) along the coast to Keta (in present-day Ghana). Agbodrafo (called Porto Seguro by the Portuguese) was one of the coastal ports to which people captured in the area were sent for sale as slaves to European traders' station on the littoral. Most, however, were first taken to the town of Dekpo (located on the northern side of the Togo Lake opposite Agbodrafo, which was situated on southern side of the lake on the Atlantic coast). Agbodrafo traders would travel to Dekpo to purchase them for export to the Americas.

Adotevi wants to give us a rational explanation for the cowries' presence on the corpses. The relevant point in this short narration is, however, once again, that money was obtained using humans as bait. Money grew on human skin; the market economy needed commodified bodies to develop. Emphasized as well, however, is a different notion. Cowries as noted in the first tale are called white-corn-money. Maize is one of the most widespread and appreciated cereals in the region. This suggests that cowries do not have a purely negative connotation but rather are imbued with ambiguous meaning: on the one hand, they kill humans, or perhaps more accurately they reproduce on the bodies of killed human beings. On the other hand, they also feed humans beings and can be used as ritual offerings.

In Dekpo, slaves did not willingly agree to embark in order to reach the south bank; to avoid the risk of sinking the boat during the passage, the more riotous slaves were simply thrown [overboard] and drowned in the water. After some days, according to Dekpo people, on the slaves' corpses began growing cowries. They plunged into the waters to gather the cowries on the bottom of the lake. Due to their harvest from dead bodies, they were also able to gain … from the slaves' corpses. Is it normal to find a profitable enterprise as this one was? … As far as the real cowries' origin, today we prefer to believe they were just shells, or may be money thrown by people from Agbodrafo, as a sacrifice to the lake's divinity, in compensation for the drowning crimes and for polluting the lake with corpses.[17]

---

[16] Elwert, *An Intricate*, 23.

[17] "À Dekpo les esclaves n'acceptaient pas volontiers l'embarquement pour la rive sud; et au cours de la traversée, ceux qui se montraient trop agités au risque de faire chavirer l'embarcation étaient purement

3. A Tchamba Tale by Kokou Atchnou

(translated by Alessandra Brivio)

I collected the third version of the cowries tale in Lomé, from Kokou Atchinou, the leader of GAMAT (Groupment des Adorateurs de Maman Tchamba). GAMAT is an association that helps families involved in the *vodun* religious order called Tchamba. *Vodun* Tchamba is currently considered the *vodun* of *ameflefle*, the *vodun* of the "bought people." Presently GAMAT consists of at least seventy associates and is involved in the organization of periodic ceremonies (*kpeta*) and other religious practices for Tchamba. The association also engages in a number of economic activities by marketing their cultural practices to tourists from the African diaspora.

Unlike the previous two tales that focus on remembering the horrors of the slave trade, Tchamba tales recall the business of the slave trade from the slave-traders' point of view. The leaders of Tchamba claim to be the descendants of traders, even if they acknowledge the existence of an enslaved person (usually a woman who had married into her master's family) as a family ancestor. They describe the origins of their worship by noting that "*once our grandfathers bought people,*" and so they are now forced to adore Mami Tchamba. They openly accept their ancestors' positions as active agents in the slave trade, and they engage in particular religious practices as a means to negotiate internal conflicts that can arise between the different components of their families.[18]

Kokou Atchinou offered this version of the cowries tale to answer the questions: Why slavery? Why were our parents involved in that particular business? The tale describes the passage from a barter economy to a market one. It also expresses the point of view of the Guin-Mina people – descendants of slave masters – who have never really felt it necessary to repent for the past actions of their ancestors. Tchamba religious practices are not organized to serve as collective contrition, but rather consist of rituals that reenact and evoke memories of the heroic actions of their ancestors. The worshippers' purpose is to propitiate the *vodun* in order to ensure well-being and the acquisition of richness. To achieve this, it is necessary to consider and assess all visible and invisible aspects of one's past and present life. Therefore the masters' descendants have had to confront their past and to assume responsibility for its ambiguous legacy.

In our grandfathers' times, money did not exist; people used to go to the market to exchange foods, maize, red oil, and yam. This system entailed some problems because people who had nothing to exchange could not go to the market and then they could not obtain what they were looking for. This is the reason why our grandfathers thought about employing cowries.

---

et simplement noyés dans le lac. Les gens de Dekpo racontent que sur leurs corps, quelques jours après, poussaient des cauris qu'ils allaient ramasser au fond du lac! Ainsi pouvait-on gagner de l'argent deux fois sur le dos de son cadavre. Est-il courant de trouver une entreprise aussi profitable ? ... Pour ce qui est de la provenance des cauris, nous préférons croire qu'il s'agit plutôt de lots de ce coquillage – monnaie jetés aux points de noyade par le gens d'Agbodrafo, en sacrifice expiatoire à la divinité du lac, à la fois pour le crime de la noyade et la souillure au lac infligée par les cadavres" (Adotevi, "Contribution," 132).

[18] For a more complete discussion on the *vodun* Tchamba, see: J. Rosenthal, *Possession, Ecstasy & Law in Ewe Voodoo* (Charlottesville, 1998); T. Wendl, "The Tchamba Cult among the Mina in Togo," in H. Behrend and U. Luig (eds.), *Spirit Possession: Modernity and Power in Africa* (Madison, 1999), 111–123; A. Brivio "'Nos grands-pères achetaient des esclaves ...' Le culte de Mami Tchamba au Togo et au Bénin," *Gradhiva*, 8 (2008), 64–79.

Where was it possible to find them? Never on the beach. It was necessary to enter the sea and reach its bottom. How was it possible to rich the deep sea? Hunters used to travel in the forest. To scare everybody, they began to hunt human beings. Helped by fishermen on the coast, the hunters brought the captives by boats into the middle of the sea. They bound the slaves' hands and feet. They attached big stones around their neck and they let them drop into the water. After some hours, the hunters recovered the bodies, which were completely covered by cowries. They took off all the cowries and then, after moving a bit further away, they threw the bodies into the water again. They went on in this way until the body was decomposed.

This was the way slavery got started. When the fishermen came back to the coast, they had money to buy more slaves. Others arrived from America to buy the slaves, but this occurred later. This was the origins of slavery. As a consequence, people started having a lot of money but, at the time, there were no banks where one could put the money. Since there was nothing to buy, no televisions, no cars, no houses, and no lands ... they were compelled to buy more slaves. Slaves were the only available commodity and the richer you were, the more you had slaves. It was as if today you were rich and you had a lot of money in the bank.[19]

SUGGESTED ADDITIONAL READINGS

Austen, Ralph. "The Slave Trade as History and Memory: Confrontations of Slaving Voyage Documents and Communal Traditions," *William and Mary Quarterly*, 58 (2001), 229-244.

Burton, Richard. *A Mission to Gelele, King of Dahome*. London: Tinsley Brothers, vol. I e II, 1864.

de Medeiros, François (ed.). *Peuples du golfe du Bénin (Aja-Ewé)*. Paris: Karthala, 1984.

Ferguson, James. *Expectations of Modernity: Myths and Meanings of Urban Life on the Zambian Copperbelt*. Berkeley: University of California Press, 1999.

Frank, Barbara. "Permitted and Prohibited Wealth: Commodity-Possessing Spirits, Economic Morals, and the Goddess Mami Wata," *Ethnology*, 34, 4(1995), 331–346.

Gayibor, Nicoué. *Histoire des togolais des origines a 1884*. Lomé: Presses de l'UB, 1996.

Herskovits, Melville. *Dahomey, an Ancient West African Kingdom*. Evanston: Northwestem University Press, 1938.

Koffi, Kodjo. "Note sur le thème de l'esclavage dans la politique togolaise actuelle," *Journal des Africanistes*, 70 (2000), 233-237.

Law, Robin. *The Slave Coast of West Africa 1550-1750*. Oxford: Clarendon Press, 1991.

Le Hérissé, Auguste. *L'Ancien Royaume du Dahomey. Moeurs, religion, histoire*. Paris: Émile Larose, 1911.

Lovejoy, Paul. *Transformations in Slavery*. Cambridge: Cambridge University Press, 2000.

Mignon, Alain. *La terre et le pouvoir chez les Guin du sud-est Togo*. Paris: Publications de la Sorbonne, 1985.

Taussig, Michel. *The Devil and Commodity Fetishism in South America*. Chapel Hill: University of North Carolina Press, 1980.

Watchel, Nathan. *Dieux et vampires: retour à Chipaya*. Paris: Seuil, 1992.

---

[19] Interview with Atchinou Kokou, Lome, January 2, 2007.

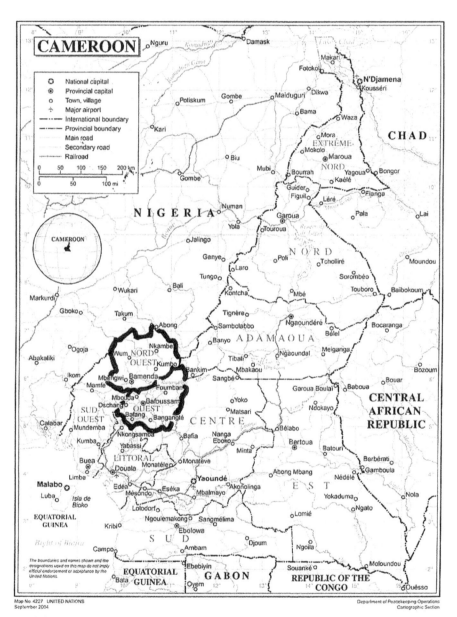

5.1. Map of Cameroon showing featured provinces.
Source: United Nations Map No. 4227.

5 Oral Accounts of Slave-Master Relations from Cameroon Noncentralized and Centralized Polities (1750–1950)

E. S. D. FOMIN

The Cameroon coast occupies a big portion of the Bight of Biafra. Between the fifteenth and the mid-nineteenth centuries, this was one of the major regions of Atlantic slave exports. New Calabar, Bonny, Old Calabar, Bimbia, Cameroon, and Gabon were key slave exit ports whereas coastal commercial networks extended as far as the old Adamawa Emirate in the north.[1] Slave caravans followed tortuous footpaths and rivers that connected the hinterland to the coast and crossed several ethnic polities and local communities.[2]

Many Africans participated in different ways in this shameful history, which in contemporary Cameroon is still rarely discussed. Some were raiders and traders, others slave owners, and the rest enslaved persons. The majority of Cameroonians involved in the trade were enslaved individuals who were either sold across the Atlantic, the Saharan desert to a limited extent, or locally enslaved. Slave-dealing engendered a high degree of violence and many ethnic conflicts, which have not yet been thoroughly explored. The trade continued well after the Atlantic slave trade networks were closed down in the first half of the nineteenth century,[3] and internal slave-dealing lasted well into the twentieth century. For decentralized polities, it was an important source of labor supply. For centralized ones, it had become a very reliable way of increasing families and political units.

As this chapter shows, oral accounts can provide useful details on slave-master relationships and life in slavery in both the noncentralized and centralized polities. Unlike the centralized polities, communities located in the coastal region and forest interior of Cameroon were generally not only decentralized but also homogenous in kinship and citizenship. They created small village communities through hiving-off as their living units became bigger. The new settlements remained linked together and to the home village by kinship and marriage bonds.

The Banyang people of the Manyu division in the southwest region of Cameroon are a classic decentralized people. Although sharing a common culture and language known

---

[1] David Richardson, "Slave exports from West and West-Central Africa, 1700–1810: New Estimates of Volume and Distribution," *Journal of African History*, 30 (1989), 17; M.Z. Njeuma, *Fulani Hegemony in Yola (Old Adamawa) 1809–1902* (Yaounde, 1978), 74.

[2] See the map at the end of the chapter.

[3] E.S.D. Fomin, "Female Slavery in Nweh Country (1850–1970)," *West African Journal of Archaeology, Special Edition on Archaeology and Slavery in Africa and the Diaspora*, 26:2 (1996), 140–154.

as *kenyang*, they created a multitude of small independent villages that seem not to have practiced any form of servitude before the advent of the trans-Atlantic slave trade. Elected leaders and leaders of traditional associations governed the Banyang villages.[4] Their social and political structures encouraged social equality, but the dependence of citizenship and belonging to kinship affiliations precluded the full incorporation of slaves, whom historical narratives always depict as outsiders, their length of slavery notwithstanding. Banyang slaves (*besem*; sing.*nsem*) were kept in settlements called *kesem*,[5] which were separated from those of their freeborn masters. Master-slave relationships appeared to have been potentially conflict-prone, and although masters did not appear as having ever treated their slaves harshly, nonetheless they kept them on the margin of their corporate life while slaves in their turn strove to achieve full integration.[6]

The first part of this chapter is a narrative I recorded from Ebeagwa village, in Upper Banyang, in 1981 and again in 1997. It is the story of the conflict between a slave master known as Ashunken and his slaves.[7] The second part focuses instead on Essoh-Attah, which is one of the centralized polities situated in the Cameroon Grassfields, an area in the hinterland of the country. Here, the traditional political organization consisted of a supreme hereditary ruler, variously called in different areas (*fon*, *fua*, *fou*, etc.), and many vassal chiefs. Rulers exploited the slave trade to build large harems and to recruit loyal state and palace functionaries. Slaves were given land and the latitude to accumulate wealth for themselves and their masters as if they were freeborn dependents. They were rapidly assimilated into the complicated system of ranks and titles, which characterized local hierarchies of power, performed important social and political tasks, like organizing court secret clubs and sacred associations.[8] Their integration into the corporate life of the polity was simple and largely attained through marriage. Masters married their female slaves. The offspring of such marriages were free and were assimilated among the freeborn dependants of the same entourage.

While Banyang narratives focus on master-slave economic and social interactions that often portray the hostility of slaves to social discrimination and abuse, those from the Grassfields show slaves (especially royal ones) as holding important political offices. The protagonist of the second story is Mbonghagesoh, who was a royal slave buried alive to mark the boundary between Essoh-Attah and Lebang, two neighboring kingdoms. Mbonghagesoh is portrayed as a hero whose unwilling sacrifice consolidated the kingdom, but the story also carries a hidden moral that warns slaves about the true intentions of their masters. Monarchs, in particular, should never be fully trusted, for no matter how much

---

[4] Edwin Ardener, *The Coastal Bantu of the Cameroons* (London, 1956). Though Douala today refers to some of their political units as kingdoms, all the coastal people of Cameroon were decentralized in their political organization previous to the trans-Atlantic commercial transactions.

[5] E.S.D. Fomin and V.J. Ngoh, *Slave Settlements in the Banyang country 1800–1950* (Limbe, 1998), 1–4; 42–46.

[6] See, for instance, E.S.D. Fomin, *A Comparative Study of Societal Influences on Indigenous Slavery in Two types of Societies in Africa* (New York, 2002), passim; U. M. Röschenthaler, "Translocal Cultures: Slave Trade and Cultural Transfer in the Cross River Region," *Social Anthropology*, 14:1 (2006), 71–91.

[7] The research I did in 1981 culminated in a doctoral thesis on "Slavery in Cameroon: Case Studies in Slavery in Selected Centralised and Non-Centralised Polities," unpublished PhD dissertation, Department of History, University of Yaoundé, 1985. In 1997, I went back to the Banyang country with some colleagues and students, on a grant from the Norwegian National Committee for Research and Education (NUFU), to update information on Banyang slave settlements.

[8] Often a trusted male slave took care of the sacred groves where the shrines of the state and palace gods resided. Slaves also preserved the instruments of the tuneful royal dance, *lefem*, reserved for members. Lefem took place in the sacred grove and was an occasion to display social hierarchies.

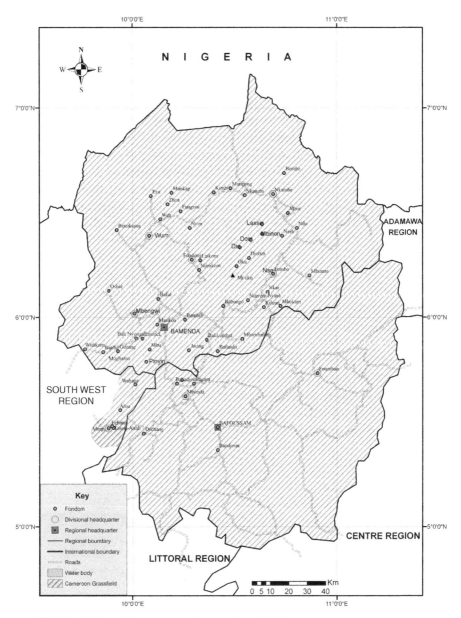

5.2. Map of featured Cameroon provinces and provincial towns.

confidence and personal affection they might display toward their slaves, if the need arose they would always privilege the interest of the state.

THE ACCOUNT OF ASHUNKEN AND HIS SLAVES

Banyang slaves could own property and had rights that they fiercely defended against the attacks of unscrupulous masters.[9] Their sense of corporate unity was high, and in colonial times they sought recourse in courts when they were mistreated by their masters. Because they were excluded from most of the freeborn corporate and ritual institutions, they created rival ones to consolidate their unity and capacity of collective action. Masters' dependence on slaves for the exploitation of the oil palm produce, which became a key economic crop in the eighteenth and nineteenth centuries, gave them a wonderful bargaining power. As freeborn Banyang never climbed the tall palms themselves, the slaves got a fair share of the proceeds, which they sold or exchanged for other commodities just like their masters did, in the same market. Banyang masters also feared the mystical power of their slaves, such as witchcraft, which they considered prevalent among slaves. This deterred them from exploiting male slaves callously and female slaves sexually as it happened in many other slaveholding societies. Elsewhere in Cameroon, indigenous traditional monarchs and princes of the Adamawa region, for instance, made it a point of honor to have the first night (*jus primaenoctis*) with every newlywed wife of their slaves and subordinates, including the Fulani immigrants.[10] This did not happen in Banyang country, where slavery was a fairly benign institution. Conflicts between slaves and masters stemmed more from the freedom Banyang slaves enjoyed than from mistreatment on the side of masters. Even today, slave descendants do not wish to quit the Banyang country, where they own lots of property.[11] Unlike their ancestors, they are striving for full integration in their masters' society.

QUESTIONS TO CONSIDER

1. How would you use the oral account to reconstruct a picture of slavery and slaves' living conditions in Banyang country?
2. How would you describe the role witchcraft played in Banyang slavery? Take a cue from Askunkem's vicissitudes.

THE ORAL ACCOUNT PROPER

Ashunkem was a wealthy slave owner. He was one the great slave owners of Ebeagwa town[12] in upper Banyang country. His slaves lived in the Ebeagwa slave settlement.[13] He had many

[9] I was told Ashunken'sstory by Nelson Egbemba and his account was corroborated by David Egbemba; although not having personally witnessed the incident, both were interested in the oral history of Banyang slavery as handed down across generations. They all hailed from Tali, a prominent village in upper Banyang.

[10] Njeuma, *Fulani Hegemony*, 12.

[11] Fomin and Ngoh, *Slave Settlements*, 37–47.

[12] The Banyang live in small villages and the inhabitants of each village build their houses close together. They adopted the same pattern for their slave settlements.

[13] This incident is also reported in Fomin, *Slavery in Cameroon* (1985), 198–208. He shows that slave settlements in Banyang country were owned collectively by members of a freeborn town, but wealthy individuals with many slaves created and maintained their own settlements.

male slaves, some of whom were married and had children. Ashunkem slaves, like those of most Banyang masters, were largely employed in the production of palm oil which they sold at Ebuensuk market. Slaves carried the oil in calabashes to this market. Like other Banyang he would sell his oil while his slaves also sold their own shares.

The Ebuensuk market was a major border market between the peoples of upper Banyang and those of the Cameroon Grassfields. Most Banyang masters also got slaves from this market.[14] The most important commodity that the Banyang could offer the Grassfields dealers in exchange for slaves and other goods was palm oil. It was because of this that Ashunkem and other Banyang slave owners valued palm oil a lot. The production of it in Banyang country was the job of the slaves because the climbing and harvesting of the palm fruits from which oil is extracted is risky. But Ashunkem slaves always bore the risk because he gave them a commensurate share of what they produced. In fact like other Banyang slave masters, he initially was fair to his slaves in sharing the wealth that they made.

For some unfortunate reasons Ashunkem got into a bitter acrimony with his slaves, as a group, over the sharing of palm oil proceeds. Indeed, it is one of the serious feuds between masters and slaves known in Banyang country. He appeared to have cheated them a number of times in sharing the palm oil which they produced from his estate. The slaves protested, but Ashunkem was unbending. They refused to produce oil and he meted out severe sanctions on them, threatening to deprive them of farmlands and other economic resources. He punished many of their ringleaders. It is alleged that their revenge took a mystical form as they caused the pretty daughter of their master, Ma-agbor, to suffer a paralysis from waist to toes on both legs. At this juncture Ashunkem opted for reconciliation rather than tougher sanctions. Ma-agbor's condition was never reversed. She is a well-known character in Upper Banyang cultural tales. She is known as the paralyzed daughter of Ashunkem, the owner of many slaves in the town of Ebeagwa. This mystical vengeance was the only way Ashunkem's slaves could punish him and go away without taking direct serious consequences. Ma-agbor was a wonderful singer and was sought after here and there to animate occasions. When she sang, every lover of good singing was on his/her feet. And as she could not walk on her own she had to be hired and carried around Banyang villages to animate both funerals and festivals. Ma-Agbor's very high ability in singing as well as the physical disability contributed to her renown and popularity.[15]

THE STORY OF THE SLAVE WHO WAS BURIED ALIVE IN A BOUNDARY PEACE PACT

I recorded the story of Mbonghagesoh from an interview with TeihBezanchong who in 1981 was the most authoritative palace historian of Essoh-Attah *fondom*,[16] where

---

[14] This infamous market is also cited in Fomin and Ngoh, *Slave Settlements*, 40–41. The front cover image of the same book shows the market as it exists today, but has nothing to do with slave trade.

[15] I interviewed Nelson Egbemba at Nguti where he was serving as a primary school teacher, on September 12, 1981. He hailed from Tali, one of the main slave market towns in Banyang country. Egbemba'sgreat-grandfather was a slave owner and he saw some of his grandfather's liberated slaves when he grew up. When Martin Bela, one of my assistants, interviewed David Egbemba at Tali on September 10, 1981, his information corroborated this account of the conflict between Ashunkem and his slaves and the misfortune of his daughter that is purported to have resulted from it.

[16] A *fondom* is one of the appellations for a traditional state in the Cameroon Grassfields. Essoh-Attah is one of such states, although administratively it is located in the Southeast region of Cameroon considered generally as being in the forest zone. It is believed to have been created around 1600 by Mankem who led

Mbonghagesoh served as a royal slave. Teih was older than seventy years when I interviewed him in 1981 but was not the oldest notable in the *fondom*. His prominence in palace
service stemmed from the fact that he was somehow literate. In addition to his proficiency
in oral narration, he kept some written records of colonial tax collection. He hailed from a
freeborn lineage in Essoh-Attah.

Like many Cameroon Grassfields polities, Essoh-Attah was deeply involved in the
enslavement of people from other areas in the sub-region.[17] The supreme ruler, his subordinate chiefs, and notables acquired slaves to increase their families and groups and used them
in a variety of economic, social, and political tasks. Slaves were crucial in the administration
of the palaces of the paramount ruler and of the chiefs under him. They performed such tasks
as tribute collection, caring for palace property including shrines, cultural musical instruments, and masks for secret and sacred associations, and running errands for their masters.

It was while serving in Essoh-Attah palace at Ateng-Attah that the ill-fated
Mbonghagesoh became the sacrificial lamb in a boundary peace pact between the
Essoh-Attah and Lebang polities. This happened around the second half of the nineteenth
century when Tanjoanji and Asonganyi were paramount rulers of Essoh-Attah and Lebang
polities, respectively. They decided to end the long-standing boundary dispute between
their two states by demarcating the boundary ritually so as to make it permanent. The two
rulers were still alive when the German colonialists subjugated Nweh country (Bangwa)
including their polities in the 1890s.[18] Both resisted the German colonialists but were
defeated and sent into punitive exile. It is said that they accepted exile to avoid the systematic destruction of their states.[19] Peace returned to Nweh country but under the brutal rule
of the German colonialists.

Though relatively recent, Mbonghagesoh's saga has become a classic tale of enslavement and slavery told and retold, interpreted and reinterpreted in this area of the Cameroon
Grassfields, and it shows how close and trusting slaves could be to their lords. Monarchs,
on their side, often betrayed and sacrificed their slaves to safeguard state interests. When
I interviewed a number of persons on what would have happened if there was no slave in
the palace to sacrifice on the occasion, they replied that such a possibility was rare, but if
such were the case, even a person of royal blood could be sacrificed. Even if slaves were
rapidly integrated into the social and political structures in the sub-region, their use in rituals as TeihBezanchong illustrated, showed their relative vulnerability. Human blood was
crucial in the preparation of protective charms for warfare, and slaves were often sacrificed
to obtain it. One would imagine that the plight of slaves was dangerously irksome in the
sub-region, but in reality it was not. From the many studies that have been done on slavery in Cameroon in general and this area in particular,[20] the general agreement is that the

---

his band of Bamilike people to this area. I reconstructed the date of foundation from the genealogy of the
fondom in E.S.D. Fomin, *Handbook on Essoh-Attah Chiefdom* (Bamenda, 1994), 23.

[17] Robert Brain, *Bangwa Kinship and Marriage* (Cambridge, 1972), passim; Fomin, "Female Slavery in Nweh
Country," 140–154.

[18] The Bangwa (*Beghnweh*) are a subgroup of the Bamileke ethnic entity of the Cameroon Eastern Grassfields.
See also Robert Brain, "The Bangwa (Western Bamileke) Marriage Wards," *Africa*, 39:1 (1969), 11–23.

[19] E.M. Chilver, "The Bangwa and the Germans: A Tail Piece," *Journal of the Historical Society of Nigeria*, 4:1
(1956), 155–160.

[20] The collection by BongfenChem-Langhee (ed.), on slavery and slave-dealing in Cameroon in the nineteenth and early twentieth centuries, in *Paideuma*, 41, 1995, is quite elaborate and comprehensive on
slavery in Cameroon.

treatment of slaves by masters was rather benign. In fact, the supreme rulers who wielded the authority to sacrifice slaves were few and used the authority often to protect them instead. Slaves and the weak free individuals were never frivolously maltreated. Masters, for instance, were never buried with their slaves as it happened elsewhere in Africa's other strong and centralized monarchies. Any appreciation of Cameroon Grassfields slave systems as harsh or benign is relative to the perceivers' knowledge of how the institution was organized. It is worth remarking that royal slaves belonged to the side of the rulers and not of the ruled. The creation of the heterogeneous centralized polities in the area involved conquest and subjugation of weaker autonomous chieftains, usurpation of more collaborative ones, and boundary pacts with other strong state builders, often involving slave taking and enslavement.[21]

The immediate conclusion from Mbonghagessoh's story is that he was the most expendable of Tanjoanji peoples, free and slave alike. From the story that follows, his ordeal was neither a punishment nor the result of any physical defects. His master appeared to have chosen him perhaps because he was the best-suited victim, and the various accounts of the tale depict him as a hero.

QUESTIONS TO CONSIDER

1. How would you use the details given in the story to reconstruct Mbonghagessoh's biography?
2. What does this story say about the trustful relationship between slaves and masters?

TEIHBEZANCHONG'S VERSION OF THE STORY OF MBONGHAGESOH

Mbonghagesoh was a first-generation slave of Ateng-Attah palace.[22] He came from a far Bamileke *fondom*. I do not know his exact place of origin but he could speak a distant Bamilike dialect, very different from *nweh* that Essoh-Attah and other *nweh*-speakers in this area spoke. He was sold to Tanjoanji, the *fon* of Essoh-Attah around the time when he succeeded Achemandeng as the supreme ruler of Essoh-Attah.[23] Mbongagesoh was one of the youngest slaves of Tanjoanji, a very handsome boy, strong, intelligent, and lovely looking. He was probably just a victim of circumstances, because there were many other slaves in Ateng-Attah palace at the time. No person can say for certain why he was chosen for this ritual peace pact.

I do not know his original name. His lord gave him the new name Mbonghagesoh, which is the short form of *Mbonghagessoh a tebehg*, which means there is no good Essoh-Attah person.[24] This name was an indictment of the people of his *fondom* rather than a curse placed on the young man. And the name had nothing to do perhaps with the circumstances that led to his being sacrificed for the state.[25]

---

[21] Interview with FuachehFualefeh, Nchu village, Essoh-Attah, March 19, 1981.

[22] This is the indigenous appellation of Essoh-Attah palace precinct.

[23] Fomin, *A Hand Book*, 23. According to the genealogy of the *fondom*, this took place around 1860.

[24] It would be recalled that most names among the Essoh-Attah and other Bamileke peoples have deep historical or philosophical meanings. The renaming of acquired persons did not involve any rituals as it happens instead in the case of freeborn named at birth.

[25] In the Cameroon Grassfields, masters usually gave new names to their slaves. Most of the names were the same as those of freeborn individuals.

The boundary conflict between Essoh-Attah and Lebang had lasted for long, but when Tanjoanji noticed the growing power of the young Asonganyi, the new ruler of the neighboring *fondom* of Lebang, he was eager to arrange on a permanent basis the boundary between their fondoms. And the way to make it so was to ritualize it. The most memorial ritual would no doubt be the one that involved human life.

Mbonghagessoh was among the few but important Essoh-Attah people who happily went to the ritual spot with their *fon*. All participants at that settlement knew that some solemn ritual would be performed to end the boundary conflict and mark the boundary in a lasting manner that day, but the victim of the ritual seemed to have been known only to Tanjoanji alone. At the site, precisely at Ahreankeng, a hole was dug in the ground. As the digging went on, Tanjoanji asked Mbonghagessoh to go in and measure it. He did so many times unsuspectingly. The last time the hole was deep enough to be his grave. Tanjoanji ordered that Mbonghagessoh be buried in it alive, and it was so done.

It took Mbonghagessoh and many who were there by surprise. He cried and cursed Essoh-Attah as he died. The people took the curse seriously. They have made many rituals of atonement (traditional and Christian) to reconcile with him and with God his creator for the act. The people of Essoh-Attah honor him today as a fallen war hero, and Ahreankeng is considered in the *fondom* as a pilgrimage site. *Fon* Asonganyi also buried on the same spot a gun and other royal ritual paraphernalia to eternalize the boundary.

And so like the biblical Isaac, Mbonghagessoh prepared the sacrifice in which he himself was the victim. But unlike Isaac, he was unlucky that the Lord God did not provide an alternative for the sacrifice. The people of Essoh-Attah regret the act of their ruler, especially the fact that the slave was buried alive, but Tanjoanj showed his love for Essoh-Attah more glaringly when he resisted the German colonialists to the extent of dying in exile.

SUGGESTED ADDITIONAL READINGS

Chem-Langhëë Bongfen (ed.). Slavery and Slave-Dealing in Cameroon in the Nineteenth and the Early Twentieth Centuries. Special issue of the journal *PAIDEUMA*, 1995.

Fomin, E.S.D. *A Comparative Study of Societal Influences on Indigenous Slavery in Two Types of Societies 1600–1950*. New York: Edwin Mellen Press, 2002.

Fomin, E.S.D. and Ngoh, V. J. *Slave Settlements in the Banyang Country 1800–1950*. Limbe: University of Buea Publications, 1998.

Klein, M. "The Slave Trade and Decentralized Societies," *Journal of African History*, 42 (2001), 49–65.

6.1. Map of Senegal.

6   "He Who Is without Family Will Be the Subject of Many Exactions"

A Case from Senegal

MARTIN A. KLEIN

When interviewing, unexpected incidents can occur that reveal something about the dynamics of slavery. This case involves a relationship between two men, one a former slave, the other a former master. It took place in Kaymor, a Wolof-speaking Senegalese area just north of the Gambia. The man of slave descent, Al Haj Biraan Ture, was 103 years old when I interviewed him in Sam, a hamlet he had created. He was a little weak, but still intellectually alert and coherent. He was one of the most impressive people I met during my research. In 1923, he moved out of the village in which he lived and cleared a piece of land. I could figure out the date because his fifty-four-year-old son said he was two years old when his father moved to Sam. This was a period when many slaves were establishing control over their own pieces of land, which I explore later in the chapter. Gradually Ture moved other members of his family out to his land, which became a prosperous hamlet, attached for tax purposes to the larger village, but in many ways autonomous. In 1975, when I interviewed him, he had about fifty people, divided into four households, living in his hamlet.

Ture and his family had long since ceased to work for anyone else, although they probably made a small payment called *assaka* to their "master." The *assaka* was originally a Koranic obligation to give to the poor, but somehow got converted into a payment slaves and former slaves made to their former masters. They may also have cooked for weddings, naming ceremonies, and other ritual occasions. At such affairs, they had the right to beg or request gifts. I do not know if Ture or other members of his family did so. Some ex-slaves refused deference, even though begging and gifts may have made a significant contribution to their income. Members of *jaambuur*, freeborn families, often insisted that they gave their "slaves" much more than they received from them. It was long after this interview that I began to take this claim seriously and to see the importance of begging as a means for those begging to affirm the nobility and generosity of the *jaambur* and by so doing reproduce the social hierarchy between those who give and those who take. Whether or not Ture engaged in this kind of activity, he seems to have been one of the more prosperous peasants in his group of villages.

The region of Kaymor was a major producer of peanuts. Senegal was one of the world's largest peanut producers, and during Ture's lifetime, peanuts were the country's largest source of income. The desire of both the French and their major chiefs to remove all restraints on peanut production meant that it was fairly easy for slaves to get their own land. Land was available in the areas between villages and thus, increasingly in the 1920s, many slaves were able to get land and thus establish their autonomy. They could establish their rights to land by clearing new fields, accumulate wealth, and even hold office in the most important rural institution, the agricultural cooperatives, which Senegal created to stimulate agricultural production. In spite of this, they were still seen as slaves and referred to as such, although usually not to their face. It was considered bad form to confront a slave or a person of slave descent with his status. Of the people of slave descent I interviewed, BiraanTure was the only one to openly speak of himself as a slave. There were a number of institutional practices that maintained social boundaries, the most important of which were probably the code of honor and the control exercised by the descendants of the free-born over Muslim institutions.[1] This meant a "slave" could not be an imam, nor could he make the pilgrimage to Mecca without being freed under traditional law.

I have included sections of the interviews with BiraanTure and with a descendant of his masters, Abdu Siise. Both of them bore the title Al Haj, which means that both had enough income to make the pilgrimage. This was not surprising for Siise, who was a chief, but it says a lot about Ture. Jacques Faye, a sociologist working in the same area, explained to me that Ture had sold seven cows to pay for the trip to Mecca. It was common through-out the region for slaves to seek the kind of religious education that had been denied to them as slaves. They often also took on the obligations of the Muslim faith that they were not able to follow as slaves. Only the more successful, however, could make the pilgrim-age. The two interviews I have excerpted indicate a significantly different attitude toward slavery by former slave and former master. The interesting thing is the contradiction within Siise's response. He explained at one point that a slave could save his money and buy his freedom, in which case he became a *jaambuur*, a free man. Ture, however, did not become a *jaambuur* because he had not been properly deferential. When he told me this, Siise was quite agitated. Once again, I asked Faye what was going on. The going rate for manumis-sions was 18,000 CFA francs, then worth about US$70. Ture had apparently walked into Siise's (his master's) home, plunked 70,000 francs on the table, and announced that he was going to Mecca. When I heard Ture tell his story, I looked at the wizened and frail man in front of me in a very different way. The situation was striking because it was clear that Ture resented any obligation to his master, and yet, although he was legally free in the eyes of both the French colonial state and its Senegalese successor, he felt that he had to make the payment and free himself under traditional law. On the other hand, what was striking about Siise was that even though he no longer received any significant economic benefit from the relationship, it was still important to him that the descendants of slaves remain properly deferential.

Both Ture and Siise were prosperous, but in other cases, both slave and master were poor, or the slave had, through hard work, become more prosperous than his former mas-ter. As Ture remarks in the text that follows, "hunger is democratic." Most African peasants were vulnerable. Prosperity was fragile and could easily be destroyed. One result was that both former slave and former master were often reluctant to break a link that could be use-ful if in need.

---

[1]   On codes of honor, see J. Iliffe, *Honour in African History* (Cambridge, 2005); M. Klein, "The Concept of Honour and the Persistence of Servitude in the Western Soudan," *Cahiersd'ÉtudesAfricaines*, 45 (2005), 831–852.

QUESTIONS TO CONSIDER

1. How does Ture's conception of traditional slavery differ from Siise's?
2. Can you imagine why BiraanTure would feel he had to pay for manumission before making the pilgrimage to Mecca?
3. What explains the attitude of Siise to Ture and vice versa?
4. How did Ture and Siise respectively explain the establishment of Sam? Do you see a conflict situation here?

INTERVIEW WITH AL HAJ BIRAAN[2]

BiraanTure: The slave was property, like the goats, who could be gotten rid of by sale whenever one wished. The *toubab* (white man) destroyed that order of things. The *jaam* had to work every day, at the discretion of his master, like his animals. In some cases, the adult slave could be autonomous and have a personal field. In this case, the *xumus*[3] and the *assaka* were given to the owner. There was no work limited to slaves except weaving. The *jaam* wove cotton cultivated by his *jaambur* without receiving any part of the product.

Q: How was the slave married?

BiraanTure: Those who depended entirely on the master were married by him, at his expense. Someone who was autonomous furnished money to his *jaambur*, who looked for a wife for him. The latter could have several wives if he was wealthy enough.[4] The slave could buy his freedom. He could also be sold.

Q: Were there slave flights?

BiraanTure: The slave who remembered his origin could flee. He could be pursued to his natal village, but they were careful to get away.

Q: Who inherited the *jaam*?

BiraanTure: Slaves were inherited like property and followed the same procedures. All of the slave's property was left to his master.

Q: What happened when the Europeans arrived?

BiraanTure: The *jaam* remained a *jaam*, although no longer alienable. Few knew their origins. Almost everyone remained where they were. Those who remained in the master's house continued to have the same life until maturity. At this time, a *jaam* could create his own household.[5]

...

---

[2] I have merged extracts from two interviews I carried out with Biraan Ture on different occasions.

[3] The *xumus* was a percentage of crops paid to the master by those slave families that were allowed to farm for themselves. After the formal end of slavery, most freed slaves worked for themselves in small family units. On the different ways slave labor in precolonial society was organized, see C. Meillassoux, *The Anthropology of Slavery: The Womb of Iron and Gold*. Translated from the French (Chicago, 1991), 116–121.

[4] Other informants confirmed that slaves could have more than one wife. It is doubtful that many did.

[5] In French West Africa, about a third of the slaves left the places of their servitude. Others gradually reduced their obligations and tried to establish their autonomy. With time, many drifted away. See M. Klein, *Slavery and Colonial Rule in French West Africa* (Cambridge, 1998).

Q: Was there much migration with colonisation?

BiraanTure: Yes, but most of it was individual. The *jaam* were not in hurry to break away from the *jaambuur* and found their own villages.

Q: Did they recruit here for the First World War?

BiraanTure: I do not know, but many young people were enrolled by family heads. Obviously, *jaam* without family were the first to go.

Q: Who suffered most during the First World War?

BiraanTure: By that time, the *jaam* had his own autonomous household. Hunger is democratic.

Q: What was the difference between the Bur [traditional ruler] and the *chef de canton* (French colonial chiefs)?

BiraanTure: The Burs made war. The *chefs de canton* did whatever they wished because the peasant never sees the white man. They could have access only through the intermediary of the chief.[6]

Q: Did the *jaam* have problem getting land?

BiraanTure: It is only recently that land has been scarce.

Q: To whom did the *jaam* give the *assaka*?

BiraanTure: To the *jaambur*. It is an old custom. In exchange, the master provided a hoe at the beginning of the rainy season. He could also give gifts. Everyone did not respect that.

Q: What was the position of the jaam in ceremonies?

BiraanTure: *Jaambur* presided over marriages, prayers, etc.

Q: How did the slaves see the white men?

BiraanTure: The *toubabs* [whites] prohibited the slave trade and dependence, but slavery persisted.

Q: When did you find Sam again?

BiraanTure: Between the two wars. I found one man in place. He left several months afterwards. This village was extinct, dead. I am the one who uprooted the bush that had taken hold. I was alone with my family.[7] One other person came a year afterwards. At present, there are four households at Sam, inhabited by brothers, nephews and grandsons who descend from the original migrants.

Q: Who inherits the slaves of the household head?

---

[6]   During the colonial period, the peasants' contact with the colonial state was generally through the chief. Few peasants had any contact with the administrator. As long as chiefs did the bidding of the administrators, they had great power and could be very exploitative.

[7]   In the Kaymore region, where Ture and Siise lived, there was until the 1970s a significant amount of free land between the villages.

BiraanTure: The slave bought or taken in war is inherited by the son. The slave born in the house remains at the disposition of the elder of the matrilineage, to whom he now pays the *assaka*.

Q: Is the slave prisoner more maltreated?

BiraanTure: He who is without family can be the subject of many exactions.

AL HAJ ABDU SIISE, CHIEF OF VILLAGE OF SONKORANG

I discovered only by accident that Abdu Siise was the master of BiraanTure. Like Ture, he was a well-off peasant, thanks in part to his position and his military service in the French army in Vietnam. I have selected only the relevant parts of this interview.

Abdu Siise: The slave worked for his proprietor in exchange for lodging and food. As a young man (fifteen to twenty years old), he had his own field, which he cultivated just like the *surga* (other male dependants).[8] The revenue from these fields provided clothing, casual expenses, and marriage expenses. For the unmarried slave, the proprietor owed both tools and seeds. Once married, the slave had to take all of that, and also to pay the *assaka*. The fields worked by the *jaam* have become the possessions of the slaves.

Q: Is there a difference between the acquired slave and the slave born in the house?

Abdu Siise: None. The proprietor dealt with them as he wished.

Q: Could the slave purchase his freedom?

Abdu Siise: He would save the revenues from his fields and confide it to his proprietor. Having paid the sum fixed by the proprietor, he became free and a *jaambur*. He had all the rights of a *jaambur*. And rich slaves could even possess other slaves. Once married, he only owed the *assaka*.

Q: What happened with colonization?

Abdu Siise: Everyone remained where they were, but the *jaam* worked henceforth for themselves. The trade disappeared. Our slaves did not leave. They stayed.

Q: Did slaves from other villages take refuge here?

Abdu Siise: No. None.

Q: Can a well-off *jaam* become chief of a village?

Abdu Siise: Not if there is a *jaambur* in the place.

Q: What are your ties with Samb?

Abdu Siise: Ali Kura Yasin left Sonkorang to inhabit Samb with his slaves. On his death, BiraanTure, his slave, was his successor. Ali left the village because of a lack of land.

---

[8] In the Kaymor region, many peasants also had migrant farmers from eastern Senegal and Mali working with them during the growing season. See P. David, *Les Navetanes* (Dakar, 1980); K. Swindell and A. Jeng, *Migrants, Credit and Climate: The Gambian Groundnut Trade, 1934–1934* (Leiden, 2006).

Q: It seems that BiraanTure bought his freedom before going to Mecca?

Abdu Siise: I heard that said, but he did not become a *jaambur*. He did not respect custom because he gave his master what he wished instead of demanding what he should pay. He pays the *assaka* regularly to the elder of his *jaamburs*.

SUGGESTED ADDITIONAL READINGS

Klein, A. Martin. "Servitude among the Wolof and Sereer of Senegambia," In *Slavery in Africa: Historical and Anthropological Perspectives*, eds. Kopytoff, Igor and Miers, Suzanne, 335–363. Madison: University of Wisconsin Press, 1977.

Slavery and Colonial Rule in French West Africa. Cambridge: Cambridge University Press, 1998.

Venema, L. Bernhard. *The Wolof of Saloum: Social Structure and Rural Development in Senegal*. Wageningen: PUDOC, 1978.

7 Common Themes, Individual Voices

Memories of Slavery around a Former Slave Plantation in Mingoyo, Tanzania

FELICITAS BECKER

Today's Mingoyo is an agricultural village just off the main road to Lindi, capital of the eponymous region in southeastern Tanzania. It is a fairly typical village of the coastal belt, where mainly small-scale cultivators produce food for themselves, as well as cash crops such as sesame.[1] A hundred years ago, however, it was the site of a major slave plantation owned by the al-Barwani, a family of Zanzibari-Omani slave traders, and their grandson still owns a large coconut grove in the village.[2]

The six extracts from interviews presented in this chapter (all collected from Mingoyo residents in the 2000s) offer different, sometimes conflicting, memories of this plantation and of its significance after the end of slavery. They show that the present-day coexistence of the descendants of both slaves and owners in the villages results from a series of renegotiations of the hierarchical relationships of the slave-trading era. To the mind of contemporary Mingoyans, the largest step toward equality between former masters and former slaves was neither the disintegration of slave regimes early in the twentieth century nor the official abolition of slavery in 1922, but the achievement of political independence in 1961 – that is, about two generations after the de facto emancipation of slaves.[3] A closer look at the history of slavery and its colonial aftermath in Mingoyo and its environs provides clues for understanding their view.

SLAVERY AND ABOLITION IN MINGOYO AND LINDI

Mingoyo is located in a region that, in the late nineteenth century, was characterized by poor access to surface water, a small, decentralized, and mobile population, and very simple agricultural methods (except on the slave plantations near the coast).[4] Beside Arab

---

[1] On present-day agriculture and economy in this region, see B. Kota and P. Seppaelae, *The Making of a Periphery: Economic Development and Cultural Encounters in Southern Tanzania* (Helsinki, 1998).

[2] Generally on the early colonial economy of this region, see N. Aas, *Koloniale Entwicklung im Bezirksamt Lindi (Deutsch-Ostafrika)* (Bayreuth, 1989); on the al-Barwani in Mingoyo, see Tanzania National Archive (TNA) G 9/46, 103 (Report on the "Mecca letter" affair, November 11, 1908).

[3] For the transition to independence in Tanzania, see J. Iliffe, *A Modern History of Tanganyika,* (Cambridge, 1979); for this region, see F. Becker, *Becoming Muslim in Mainland Tanzania, 1890–2000* (Oxford, 2008), chapter 7.

[4] Aas, "Koloniale Entwicklung"; A. Adams, *Im Dienste des Kreuzes* (St Ottilien, 1899), passim; P. Fuchs, "Die wirtschaftliche Erkundung einer Ostafrikanischen Suedbahn," *Beihefte zum Tropenpflanzer* 6 (1905), 241–247.

immigrants like the Barwani, at least five African ethnic groups were present: Swahili on the coast and Ngindo, Mwera, Yao, and Makua partly overlapping in different parts of the hinterland. The Yao and Makua populations were recent immigrants from further south. The disruptions caused by their arrival were compounded by frequent Ngoni warrior raids from the west.[5] Such raids were but one of several sources for slave exports from this coastal area, which were significant in spite of the thin population. Demand for slaves from East Africa persisted throughout the century, as some buyers from the Americas turned to East African supplies to make up for the increasing shortage of slaves from West Africa, slave markets in the Middle East stayed open until late in the century, and plantation owners on the Swahili coast itself needed to replenish their workforce. The town of Kilwa, in the north Lindi region, was East Africa's largest export harbor for slaves being transported to Zanzibar.[6] Many of these slaves originated beyond the borders of the region, in present-day Malawi or further west in Tanzania.[7] Nevertheless, the presence of several long-distance slave-trading routes leading toward Kilwa, Lindi, and a number of smaller destinations had far-reaching effects on social relations and political practice. In a sharp departure from established social hierarchies focused on local elders in small villages, it provided opportunities for militarized "big man" leaders, who typically both supplied captives for the slave trade and sheltered slave escapees from competitors' spheres of influence.[8] The uneasy coexistence of the decentralized elder-centered form of control over people and larger-scale, militarized big man rule is reflected in comments on elders and "chiefs" in the interviews I present in this chapter. On the coast, meanwhile, both long-established Swahili patricians and Omani immigrants took advantage of the booming slave supply to establish plantations.[9]

The disintegration of this complex political economy followed fairly swiftly upon the establishment of German colonial rule. Officially established in 1884, German authority was militarily asserted first in 1890 on the coast and then brought home to everyone with a brutal military campaign against the so-called Maji Maji uprising in 1905–07. By the time of the latter campaign, masters were already at the point of losing control of their slaves. The pervasive insecurity caused by warfare held up the process slightly, but by the end of German rule, in 1917, slavery was effectively dead. The official ordinance on abolition passed by the British in 1922, five years after they had taken over former German East Africa as a mandated territory, was largely symbolic.[10]

Masters' loss of control over slaves was not attributable to particularly aggressive anti-slavery measures by the German colonial regime. Rather, measures introduced by the German government in pursuit of self-interested goals turned out to have decisive consequences for slavery. The suppression of Ngoni military power ended Ngoni slave raids; more generally, the disarmament of indigenous military leaders made big man rule

---

[5] Iliffe, "Modern history," 54–57.

[6] On the slave trade through Zanzibar, see A. Sheriff, *Slaves, Spices and Ivory in Zanzibar: Integration of an East African Commercial Empire into the World Economy, 1770–1873* (Oxford, 1987).

[7] Iliffe, "Modern history," 40–51 and 168–192.

[8] Becker, "Becoming Muslim," chapter 1.

[9] On the tense social relations that resulted from the use of slaves on the Tanzanian coast, see J. Glassman, *Feasts and Riot: Revelry, Rebellion and Popular Consciousness on the Swahili Coast, 1856–8* (Oxford, 1995).

[10] For a detailed study of this process, see J. G. Deutsch, *Emancipation without Abolition in German East Africa* (Oxford, 2007). The following paragraphs follow his account.

unviable and flight from the plantations on the coast toward the interior more feasible for slaves. The suppression, albeit hesitant, of slave trading deprived owners of an important means for disciplining slaves. Even more important was the competition for labor between the established slave plantations and new wage-worker plantations started by German immigrants, which led to the development of a market in paid labor. Mzee Juma's interview clearly states this point.

Slaves, attentive to the power balances between themselves and their masters, took advantage of these changes to weaken or sever ties with owners. Some remained near or in former slave settlements while reasserting control over their labor; others moved small distances away to new independent villages; some left. But slaves' reestablishment of control over their sites of residence and work did not amount to full equality with people who had never been slaves, least of all with former owners.[11]

This was one of the partly intended, partly accidental consequences of British colonial policy after 1917. Motivated by expediency as well as racism, British officials near the coast cultivated Swahili patricians and Arab immigrants as intermediaries between themselves and the African population, and hence protected their status. In Mingoyo, they gave the highest political office open to nonwhites to a son of the plantation-owning Barwanis, Halfan bin Nassor.[12] His unpopularity and fiery temper led to his demotion, but Halfan and his peers continued to express their disdain for ex-slaves quite clearly, as Rajabu Feruzi Ismaili explains in his recollections later in the chapter. Economically, too, ex-masters retained advantages: they had better-established claims to land and could afford to hire labor. Ex-slaves often depended on marginal plots and the work of their own hands. The region as a whole lacked high-value peasant cash crops and efficient transport. It remained economically stagnant throughout the colonial period (and, in fact, beyond).[13]

In the 1950s, however, the independence campaign under Julius Nyerere gave ex-slaves and their descendants a powerful new language in which to claim equality. Although Tanzania was declared socialist only in 1967, "all people are equal" (*watu wote sawa*) was a central claim of Nyerere's since the 1950s.[14] His focus on progress and the future implicitly dismissed status claims based on ancestry or past greatness, and portrayed slavery as part of a benighted past to be overcome. Moreover, the independent government quickly moved to disempower those chiefs who had profited from British endorsement, including a Yao dynasty with a slave-trading past and influence in Lindi region. Rajabu Feruzi provides details on this point. The haughty Halfan bin Nassor was publicly humiliated. Nevertheless, memories of slave origin continued to be passed on in whispers (see, for instance, Esha Issa Baharia's recollections later in the chapter), and they retained the capacity to offend. As a result, Mingoyans (like people elsewhere in the region) today readily acknowledge that slavery was widespread, but avoid naming names of slave descendants.

---

[11] On the stark hierarchies and contested relations between masters and slaves in the late nineteenth-century, see Glassman, *Feasts and Riot*.

[12] For the explicitly racist rationale of this choice, see TNA 12800 vol. 2, 187–191 (Memorandum on a meeting with Provincial Commissioner Kitching by the Chief Secretary, Dar es Salaam, March 3, 1937); for Halfan bin Nassor's time in office, see interviews with Mohammed Halfan bin Nassor, Mingoyo, August 17, 2000; with Juma Sudi bin Juma, Mingoyo, August 12, 2000.

[13] Koda and Seppaelae, *Periphery*, passim.

[14] On Nyerere's campaign, see Iliffe, *Modern History*, 507–566; Becker, *Becoming Muslim*, chapter 7.

THE INTERVIEWS: DISCURSIVE STRATAGEMS, RECORDING AND EDITING

The accounts that follow stem from a research project into the colonial history of this part of Tanzania. They were collected with official permission and with the help of my Tanzanian research assistant, Zuhura Mohamed, from as wide a cross-section of Mingoyo's inhabitants as I was able to contact through local officials and word of mouth. Assuming that local information may have material consequences if fed into the technocratic machinery of the state, informants were keen to put their version of history on record. Questions were kept very open. Slavery was but one of many topics discussed.

The interviews display a way of speaking about the past that is different from both professional historians' and written sources of the period. The allegiances of the speakers are different from those of literate contemporary observers, and the interviews clearly display the influence of speakers' social positions on their views. Compare, for instance, the apologetic notes struck in the two interviews with descendants of slave owners (Mohamed Barwani and Sharifu Shehani) to the more graphic and damning descriptions by respondents without such antecedents. The interview extracts have been selected to represent a variety of stances toward the end of slavery: from the descendant of owners deploring the loss of social order (Sharifu Shehani) to the patriarch of plebeian origins recalling slave owners' disregard for gender hierarchies (Mzee Juma).

Other discursive stratagems at work here are less clearly partisan and instead point to the efforts of people with little formal education to find frames of reference for interpreting their history, in ways that avoid exacerbating social divisions. Thus the informants use a great number of social categories with little hesitation, which to the observer may cry out for qualification (as when Mzee Sefu characterizes the helplessness of slaves by saying they lived "like women"); African, Arab, European; Makonde and other ethnic names; chief (*mwenye*), patrician (*muungwana*), master, slave, slave wife (*sulia*); man, woman. Close up, these terms often serve to draw a line between "them" and "us", while placing the blame for slavery with "them" (most often Arabs, but also indigenous power brokers, especially in Bibi Esha's case).

There are further critical references, indicting among others the profit motive (said to have driven Africans to collude in the slave trade), European land hunger in the colonial period, and colonial racism and authoritarianism. The interviews leave little doubt that life was a struggle against many oppressive forces – not only for former slaves, but throughout the colonial period and also for the people telling their stories today. To decipher these subtexts, however, to notice implied criticism or apologies and notes of pessimism or hope, requires careful reading and attention to context.

The narratives that follow are the product of an editing process of several stages. I have removed questions and encouraging verbal cues to transform conversations into narratives, and replaced pronouns with proper nouns where necessary for clarity (e.g., written "the slaves" for "they" when "they" referred to slaves mentioned in a preceding question). I have also removed repetitions and off-topic references. For ease of reading, these excisions and substitutions are not marked, except for major omissions. As the original Swahili is idiomatically quite different from English usage, I have translated fairly freely (e.g., using "hire workers" where the Swahili reads "put people in the fields"). For ease of reading, I have in some places rendered the gender-neutral Swahili pronoun as "he," but this should not be read to exclude women. What the texts have lost in individuality they have, I hope, gained in comprehensibility.

QUESTIONS TO CONSIDER

1. In what way do interviewees appear to address the present as well as the past? What values, aims, and allegiances do they express that affect their view on the past?

2. What different social identities – Arab, African, Makonde, German, British, free-born, owner, slave, woman or man – are mentioned, and how are they characterized? How do these characterizations address the challenge of living with the memory of slavery?

3. How are slaves' lives described? What indignities and hardships are mentioned? How are slaves said to have interacted with their owners?

4. What, according to the informants, were the interests, rights, and motivations of slave owners? How important was control over slaves' labor to them?

5. How did the lives of slave women and slave men differ, and how did they intersect? What do these differences imply for gender relations after the end of slavery?

6. How did slaves' lives change after the end of slavery? What continuities and what transitions took place in the aftermath, and how do they affect the present?

1. Bibi Esha Issa Baharia

Bibi Esha was a single woman of about seventy, surviving as a cultivator.[15] She described herself as a Mingoyo native, and the relatively central location of her home and plots suggested that her entitlements were relatively secure. Bibi Esha knew a lot about ancient ritual, and as she was the first female informant introduced to me, her fellow villagers clearly considered her knowledgeable. Visibly frail, she conducted most of the interview from a *kitanda* bedstead (with a hand-plaited rope criss-crossing the bed frame in place of a mattress), having recently come back from planting. In keeping with the impression that her social position was relatively secure but not privileged, her account of slavery is less palpably partisan than the others presented here. It focuses on slave recruitment on one hand and the later integration of former Arab masters into village society on the other. Nevertheless, Bibi Esha was very cautious commenting on those aspects of slavery that most affected women and thus were closest to home, especially slave women bearing masters' children.

Bibi Esha blamed the development of slavery on the collusion of Arab immigrants with African rulers she calls *mamwenye*.[16] *Mamwenye* were among the types of chief who were

---

[15] "Bibi" for women and "Mzee" for men are polite forms of address in Swahili, which I will use to refer to the narrators on the assumption that this is how they would like to be referred to.

[16] *Mwenye* (plural *mamwenye*) is a political term corresponding only very roughly to the English notion of the "chief," derived from the Swahili root "-enye" that roughly means "in possession of something." They were leaders with ritual, judicial, and sometimes military functions chosen from among privileged lineages. In the parlance of this region, the word covered a multitude of political positions: the powerful Yao rulers who dominated the slave trade from southern Lake Malawi were referred to as *mwenye*, but so were fairly weak, small-scale rulers within the region. Sometimes, the term referred simply to urban patricians with quasi-aristocratic aspirations; this appears to be the way Esha uses it here. By contrast, elders are clearly local, village- or family-based notables who existed also among those ethnic groups in the region that did not recognize *mwenye*.

disempowered by the state after independence, and as Esha distinguishes them explicitly from the still-valid social category of "elders," she effectively places the blame for slavery safely in the past.

In the German era, slavery was part of the social order; the English abolished it.[17] The masters simply owned them. In the old days there were those mamwenye, in the towns, they would come here, presenting themselves as elders, so that people might come to the mwenye. And the mwenye might follow those people, abduct and sell them. He would obtain people easily as this was his home, and he was the ruler. The Arabs would take the people and leave with them. [...] There was a king here who took people and brought them to the Arabs, and their headquarters was at Mikindani,[18] and that building is still there where the slaves were bundled up to be taken away.[19] Those Arabs came here for business. Then they saw that this town is beautiful, so they stayed, while still buying people. The Arabs started buying people since before we begin to know their history.

Bibi Esha's account of what happened to Arab slave owners after emancipation is fairly typical: for those who married local people, their descendants became part of family networks; their separate status was reduced to the economic advantage of landownership. When discussing the Barwani's family history, she shows how divisive ex-owners' attempts to maintain superior social status could be.

After the slavery regime broke down, some Arabs were still living here, and now those slaves remained as if their children, though before they had been their slaves. When they were slaves, they cultivated, planted coconut, did housework. They planted sugarcane, custard apple and mandarin trees and date trees, but the ground here was not suitable [for the trees], they did not produce fruit. They did grow coconut and sugarcane successfully; we found this sugarcane still in place at our birth, after the end of slavery.[20] [...] The former owners' children took over the fields the slaves had worked, for those elders did not go away again, they procreated right here with those slaves, they chose some of the slaves to be as if their wives and had children with them, and now those children have inherited the valley.[21]

---

[17] Informants often spoke of the time preceding German colonial rule as the era of the Arabs, with reference to the influence that Arab-dominated Zanzibar and Arab immigrants then exerted on the mainland.

[18] Mikindani is a long-established coastal town south of Lindi and southeast of Mingoyo, off the Makonde plateau. In the nineteenth century, it served as an export harbor for both slaves and slave-produced goods from its environs.

[19] The "king" referred to here is most likely the immigrant Yao big man Machemba, who established a strong military position on the Makonde Plateau south of Mingoyo in the 1870s. He combined slave trading with the recruitment of followers from among plantation slaves and took tribute from caravans heading for Lindi or Mikindani. He was strong enough to defy German officials for a full decade after the military imposition of colonial rule in 1890. The putative slave market at Mikindani, however, is a building that dates to the German period but, built in the Orientalizing style favored by German administrators, is often attributed to Arab influence.

[20] The failed experiments with fruit trees are plausible, as the Barwani would have had little information on how best to use the land. Sugarcane and rice were typical plantation crops. According to Mohamed Barwani, small-scale sugar mills were run in Mingoyo under British control, in the 1940s. This would have been part of the "war effort" to reduce demand for imported goods.

[21] See the introduction and Mohamed Barwani's story later in the chapter for the ambiguous but nevertheless privileged status of the part-African descendants of major slave owners. Mohamed Barwani, however, is atypical in having managed to hang on to most of his landholdings. Most families formerly prominent because of slave ownership have lost their wealth, including the land.

[…] Our elders were not involved in slavery.[22] The Arabs were involved with slavery; they were rich because they owned us. […] Now after slavery ended, the English remained, the Arabs didn't have a voice anymore. Some of them went back home to Maskat,[23] and those others who stayed here just lived like our relatives, they had children right here and married here. Those of old, the "pure" Arabs from Maskat, are all dead, and the ones who remain were born here. They are mostly the grandchildren. Even if you go to Mikindani, you will only find a handful of real Arabs.

Some of the former slaves came from far away like Songea or Tunduru.[24] […] Some had grown old and did not know any more where they were from; they died right here. These days, their children remain, and they don't know these matters, and even if you tell someone, your history was like this, it is dangerous. […] Well, it is as if you tell them something that is over, and those were bad things. Whether someone's ancestors were slaves or owned slaves is a big secret. […] We have one child of Mzee Halfan, the pure Arab, living here, but even he these days would not say so and does not want to present himself as an Arab.[25] Mohamed Halfan is the one who remains and in other places there are others. We now call them *machotara* (half-castes), because they are black on their mothers' side, but they have straight hair. Mohamed Halfan, though, has not retained this trait; he just is a bit lighter in colour; that is all.

2. Mohamed Halfan Nassor bin Hamisi Barwani

Mzee Mohamed is the person that Esha Baharia mentioned in her last paragraph as the descendant of the owner of the valley. He openly acknowledged this ancestry, as well as the important role of his family, the al-Barwani, in slave trading not only from this region, but also from Western Tanzania to Zanzibar. Mohamed Barwani lived relatively comfortably off the large coconut grove into which the former plantation has been transformed. He also had a pension, having spent most of his working life away from Mingoyo as a policeman. This decision to pursue a profession that both took him away from Mingoyo and signalled his support for the postcolonial order was very politic, as his father had been extremely unpopular because of his involvement in the colonial administration and insistence on a status above that of Africans. Mohamed was a knowledgeable yet cautious informant. For instance, he was careful to portray his ancestors' actions as rational by the standards of a

---

[22] Bibi Esha is here making a point occasionally found in interviews with members of those ethnic groups, specifically Mwera and Ngindo, that defined themselves partly by their rejection of the institution of *mwenye*. They tended to liken living under a *mwenye* to living in slavery, and blamed the *mwenye* for selling their subjects. The abolition of chiefly privileges early on the postcolonial period makes it easier to express disdain for the institution in Tanzania than in many other African countries.

[23] Bibi Esha correctly identifies Maskat as one of the Southern Arabian harbor towns that Arab immigrants to East Africa set out from. There is, however, no concrete evidence that Arabs from the Lindi/Mingoyo area had particularly strong ties to this town.

[24] Songea and Tunduru are inland districts west of Lindi. In present-day Tanzania, Tunduru is often identified as the home place of people of Yao ethnicity. In fact, many enslaved Yao in the nineteenth century came from further south, but it is true that Yao chiefs and their subjects were deeply involved in slave dealing. Songea district contained the frontier of Ngoni settlement, and Ngoni raiding produced many slaves.

[25] Bibi Esha is referring to Halfan bin Nassor, the son of Mingoyo's biggest slave owners and father of the next informant, Mohamed Halfan. As his Arab ancestry was the reason why the British imposed Halfan as an intermediary ruler on Mingoyo in the 1930s, it is plausible that he made a big thing of his status as a "genuine" Arab. In fact, his mother was African.

7.1. Photo of Mzee Barwani. He claimed to be standing on the site of a former residence of one of his slave-owning ancestors.

different era. He also described their presence in Mingoyo as legitimate, in a way apt to forestall present-day challenges to his ownership of land in the village.

My name is Mohamedi Halfan Nassor bin Hamisi Barwani. I was born in the village of Mingoyo, on 7 January 1940. I had two grandfathers, Mohamed bin Halfan bin Nassor Barwani was the elder and his younger brother was Nassor bin Halfan bin Nassor bin Barwani.[26] They came to this village of Mingoyo in the 1870s and settled in the area called Lipanda, which is part of Mingoyo. [...]

They came to live here in the pursuit of the slave trade, in keeping with the times, and they had followed this pursuit since the 1830s, coming from Kigoma. [...] But the family as a whole came from Zanzibar in the 1820s. They had already been a long time in Zanzibar. My father was born here, but his mother was from Kigoma. She was Manyema.[27] [...] Normally,

[26] In Swahili, all brothers of one's father or grandfather are also referred to as fathers. He is talking about his grandfather and grand-uncle.

[27] The Manyema are an ethnic group from what is now Eastern Congo. Imported into Tanzania in large numbers during the heyday of the slave trade, they have retained a separate identity.

Arabs when traveling were not accompanied by women, but if they liked a woman, they went to the family and asked to marry her; these wives were called *sulia*. [...] They handed over a certain amount of money and they were given the woman. They could not marry a slave; that is not permitted by law. Therefore they went to the parents of this woman or girl, they put up a certain amount of money or a money equivalent, and then they were given the woman. My grandmother was called Latifa Binti Mbaraka.[28]

[...]

They found just forest here [in Mingoyo]. There were no people. [...] But they saw that there is a river here, so that water would be available, and they saw that they could obtain other necessary goods, so they decided to stay here. [...] At this time, you understand, this ground was very wet, and then there was no way of making the work easy, so they employed the slaves then available to do the necessary work. [...] They cut the trees, felled them, and then dug channels to let the water run off into the river. [...] My grandfathers were strangers here, and as you understand, strangers cannot just go anyplace. The people who they met here I have rather forgotten, but there were people present, only they didn't have the system of "chiefs" here. They were just people of small, small tribes, living together.[29] Therefore it was easy to meet them and to explain, we have come here to pursue a certain activity, so they built a relationship with them.

3. Sefu Selemani Makoreka

Mzee Sefu's account contrasts with Mzee Mohamed's efforts to present the use of slaves as a rational choice for its times. He described himself as a cultivator and appeared fairly typical of the poorer among this group in Mingoyo. His emphasis on Africans' difficulties in competing for land with ex-masters and European plantations suggests that he struggled in his own pursuits as an agricultural producer and perceived himself to be on the disadvantaged side of Mingoyo's social divides. In many Mingoyans' mind there is continuity between the precolonial, the colonial, and the postcolonial period: despite the decline of slavery, some Mingoyans still saw themselves on the losing end of their interaction with the immigrants among them. Concomitantly, Mzee Sefu emphasizes slaves' victimhood and masters' ruthlessness almost to the point of grotesque.

The Arabs followed this valley in order to plant coconut palm; wherever you find coconut palm, the Arabs have passed through for the sake of wealth, in order to plant coconut, rice, dates and sugar cane. [...] If the Arabs had known that on the hills too, goods of this kind are available, we Wamakonde would not have been allowed to live here; we would have been chased off.[30] [...] But they only followed the valley, by the time they realized that the hills can

---

[28] Mohamed Barwani is careful to assert that his grandmother was not actually a slave and likens the transaction whereby a *sulia* was acquired to bridewealth negotiations among African families. His account of what a *sulia* was is based on a narrow reading of Islamic law and not supported by other accounts (such as Mzee Juma's that follows) that are much more adamant about the fact that *sulia* were bought.

[29] He used a Swahili-ized version of the English term "chief" rather than *mwenye*. The observation on the absence of chiefs in the coastal hinterland tallies with both European precolonial and African accounts, while reinforcing the claim that there was no ruler over the valley where Mohamed's ancestors settled.

[30] See also Bibi Esha's assertion that the Arabs "were rich because they owned us." Generally informants were very attuned to the economic benefits of slave ownership.

provide wealth, their influence had ended. His fellow colonizer had beaten him at the *bao* game.[31] [...]

In the following paragraph, the description of slaves' living quarters as lacking any semblance of privacy emphasizes the slaves' subjection; in fact, this was only one of several possible arrangements, most of which were more like ordinary huts. The more demeaning circumstances, like the one described here, were characteristic of the most intensively worked plantations and most often used for recently arrived slaves. As slaves reacquired a semblance of identity, they sought to renegotiate living arrangements to approximate proper family dwellings.

Certainly the Arabs used slaves. In the era of the Arabs, people were really worked hard. The slaves lived together in one place. If there are many, well, the owner will build perhaps two buildings to house the slaves exclusively. [...] As you know, if you keep goats, you put them together in one pen, and in our past, when the Arabs made people slaves, they put them together in one pen, men and women together. [...] Swahili people had maybe one slave at a time. [...The slaves] were made to work; they were put into agriculture; the owner himself stays in the city, you slaves "off you go to the fields, you're going to cultivate." [...] The names [of the former Swahili slave owners] I can't remember.[32]

Mzee Sefu was particularly adamant in dismissing the possibility of slave resistance, in contrast with the evidence of slaves' increasing bargaining power in the late nineteenth century that historians have uncovered.[33] While he ends up sounding rather dismissive of his forebears, the main impetus is to emphasize and hence condemn the evils of the past, which he explicitly contrasts with the present.

To confront the masters – how would the slaves have done that? A slave has no fight in him. To confront the master – oh no, that was impossible. Slaves were in a state where they had no power to give orders. There was only one person to give orders, namely the master; slaves were just being kept like chickens. [...] The only one to own arms was the master. Those slaves have no arms at all, they just live sitting down (*wamekaa*), like women. [...] They were as if dumb, they were people without reason, and a person without reason cannot run away, where would they go? Where you come from you don't know [...] Today, if you abduct somebody they will have the wits to do something about it. In the past, people were loafers, they covered themselves with blankets and thought that way they could not be seen.[34] [...]

Mzee Sefu was also very explicit concerning the exploitation of domestic slaves:

The slaves worked a lot, were they not slaves? And is it not inevitable that slaves work? The person who makes him work is the master. You have to cultivate, to bathe the master [...] If he

---

[31] Mzee Sefu here likened the competition between successive colonial powers to a popular board game, *bao*, where two players try to appropriate each others' counters. Literally, he said "his fellow had already outnumbered his *kete*," meaning the seeds used as counters in the *bao* board game.

[32] This amnesia is certainly strategic. Mzee Sefu's description – owners living in town, slaves out in the fields – summarizes slavery in the era of plantations; see Glassman, *Feasts and riot*.

[33] Deutsch, *Emancipation*.

[34] The term "loafer" probably achieved currency in Swahili around the time of independence, when it was used to describe anybody who supposedly failed to make the requisite effort to advance the country, such as underemployed city dwellers. It means something like "lazy, hapless person; fool." The reference to blankets probably refers to stories about the kind of magic with which people in the past tried to protect themselves from slave raids.

saw you husking rice in a mortar, he would say no, for fear that the rice would break, instead "it is this slave's work to peel the rice by hand" until you have enough to make a meal.[35] A slave would not put the raw rice for the master into a mortar for husking, for fear of ruining the master's food. […] If the master goes for a bath, he will have water poured on him, and moreover the one doing the pouring will be a woman, while the one being bathed is a man. And the bed is right nearby: that is the origin of many of the half-castes you see here. […]

Slavery ended when the English arrived. The English were stronger than the slaves' masters; the masters had nothing to say against them. […] But the fields were the property of the masters and the masters retained them; the slaves had nothing. The masters still reaped crops, but not as before, because now their own slaves had been let go and they had to hire workers. […] The local people could get plots, but only with difficulty, as European-run plantations took up many hectares. For us individual cultivators the available land was just small plots, as you see it is until today. The fields had been taken by the Europeans for sisal planting, as for Europeans sisal was wealth. […] The workers for these sisal fields came from the mainland: from Tunduru, Songea, and the Wamavia from Mozambique.[36]

4. Rajabu Feruzi Ismaili

Instead of the brutality of slavery in the "era of the Arabs," Mzee Rajabu focused on the brutality of the status differences derived from slavery that characterized colonial Mingoyo. He gave a detailed account of his educational career, which was stunted by the shortage of access to state education (as opposed to mission schools, which Muslims often mistrusted). This sense of missed opportunity in his own life perhaps also informed his sensibility toward the many expressions of status difference in the post-slavery era. Moreover, Mzee Rajabu's parents came from Tunduru, where the British had instituted a more hierarchical form of indirect rule than in Lindi, and apparently were displaced to Mingoyo by the orders of a Tunduru chief. Consequently, Mzee Rajabu also transmits a strong sense of how much independence, which implied the abolition of Europeans', Arabs', and chiefs' claims to superiority, meant to people like him.

I am from Tunduru. I came here as a very small child, about 1939–40. My parents were Wayao, who came here to cultivate cotton. This was during a time of monarchic rule; the stronger would eat the weaker.[37] People were abducted, that is how this elder obtained slaves, and they came here to cultivate. They were taken to Ruo.[38] The first thing to say about our history

---

[35] The story of slaves being used to peel rice grains by hand, in a tedious process that could cause painful damage to the nails, was widely told in Mingoyo, though more often in informal conversation than in interviews. It is also a typical instantiation of owners disregarding established gender divisions of labor: using the mortar is a women's task, but apparently men were not secure from having to peel rice by hand.

[36] Sisal plantations were indeed an important part of the colonial economy in the coastal region, and their workforce in Lindi and Mingoyo came predominantly from outside the district. People from Songea and Tunduru migrated to the plantations to obtain cash with which to pay their taxes; the Wamavia were a Makonde-speaking group from Mozambique who migrated to Lindi region during the colonial period.

[37] Mzee Rajabu is referring to the system of "paramount chiefs" instituted by the British administration (following German precedents) among the Yao population in Tunduru. Justified with reference to the powerful slave-trading Yao *mwenye* of the nineteenth century, it contrasted with British reliance on small-scale "village headmen" in the areas closer to the coast.

[38] As Mzee Rajabu also hinted elsewhere in the interview that his parents had been quite wealthy, grown-up people in Tunduru before they were sent to Ruo; it appears that their displacement took place in the colonial period rather than the era of slave trading. This chimes with the recollections of some other informants

is to give thanks that I can talk to you like this, *memsahib*.[39] In the past, we could not speak to a white person, if you saw one you ran indoors. We thank Mwalimu Nyerere for having saved us from this state, so that I can now sit with you, and you greet me.[40] [...]

When the Arabs came here, to this town, they came saying "I am looking for slaves." Well, I might – at that time, a matter of history[41] – I might take a nephew of mine, my brother in law sees it but he does not dare do anything; I take him and sell him to the Arab. Every person would be paid for according to their specifics, their "grade."[42] Somebody might cost three rupees. [...]

Slavery was wiped out after Mwalimu J K Nyerere came into power.[43] Although the English had prohibited it, a claim to respect had remained with the owners. If an Arab was arrested, he could not be tried in primary court. [...] He would be taken to the district court, saying "I'm an Arab, I can't sit together with an African," and the provincial commissioner himself would be talking to the accused.

Slavery very much existed in Tunduru, and I will give you the history of slavery there: there was one person who was *mwenye*, chief, that is to say like Queen Elizabeth. If he died, well, they would take a young girl, like a grandchild of mine; they would obtain seven of them, and also seven boys, and they would be thrown into the grave, alive – but not in the era of the English, this is an era I was only told about, as history. They are put into the grave, then they take soil and begin to fill in the grave with these living people inside. Now if they sneeze they will say, take him or her out of there, the king has refused to go with him/her. So it goes on, until by bad luck two or three or five have remained, they haven't sneezed, so they are buried together with the king. If you ask, they will tell you that the women go to serve the king, and the men go to do his bidding.[44] [...]

When we obtained self-government in 1961, the hierarchies based on slavery died altogether, and they are not talked about any more either. Now I talk about these things with hesitation, for if you mention a person and say "this one was my slave," and it becomes known, you will be in jail, if not for twenty years then for fifteen. For now they say, all humans are equal, there is nobody who is more or less than another; rather, all people deserve one thing: respect.[45] If there are people who used to be slaves you cannot say so. [...] You do not

---

who said that the Yao "chiefs" recognized by the British used their privileged position to press others into migrant labor.

[39] Mzee Rajabu's use of this address, which perhaps was used for white or South Asian women in the colonial period, is unusual, but shows his familiarity with the interactions between Africans and employers from immigrant groups in late-colonial Mingoyo.

[40] "We" here evidently means as much as "Africans."

[41] This is one of several occasions when Mzee Rajabu used the English term "history" to place a claim safely in the past; an indirect acknowledgment that it would be divisive if applied to the present.

[42] The sale of nephews was reported by many informants on and off the coast. Among these matrilineal people, maternal uncles had strong claims over their sisters' offspring, while the position of fathers in the family was relatively weak.

[43] In this sentence, it is clear that slavery in fact refers not to the precolonial labor regime, but to the status differences of the colonial period.

[44] With this story, Mzee Rajabu is likening the Yao *mwenye* of the nineteenth century to the kings in a number of African societies – especially slave-trading ones – at whose funeral humans, normally slaves, were sacrificed. The written record is silent on the funerals of Yao rulers; given Mzee Rajabu's limited education, it cannot be assumed that he obtained this story from a written source and applied it to Yao circumstances. It is therefore not impossible that it is true, but it could only refer to events well before the establishment of colonial rule.

[45] "All humans are equal," *watu wote sawa*, was one of the most evocative catchphrases of the campaign for political independence and is still widely quoted.

have proof. You merely have been told by your father: do not look at this person like this, do not look at this person like that, he used to be our slave, that one. [...]

In Tunduru, slaves used to be available in the market, like if you go to buy fish. Somebody would examine the slave's body and his health and his weight, thinking "if I buy him, is he going to do my work well?" [...] The understanding necessary to run away exists now; in the past, a slave would not escape. They used certain cultural practices to make sure he does not go back, and the slave would forget his home and not know where he came from.[46] They would feed him something to confuse his understanding, so that he would not know where his home was. [...] The Arabs punished their slaves severely, without hesitation. [...] People like Halfan bin Nassor Barwani had high status then.[47] Our state was miserable; as I told you, in the past you and I would not have talked as we are doing. Halfan bin Nassor still continued to appropriate the labour of others, as I told you. [...] I stand by this claim.

In the following paragraphs, Mzee Rajabu expands on the racial and social hierarchies of the colonial period, with examples of the everyday humiliations that they implied for people like himself. He again emphasizes that independence, rather than abolition, was the crucial step toward the recognition of Africans' rights and citizenship.

If you, as a human, encounter another person who is stronger than you, inevitably you will fear that person. If he gives you to understand that he wants you to carry something for him, you will do so; if not, you'd be punished. That is how things were done; I have seen it with my own eyes. I have also seen that somebody had died in their own house, and the socially "stronger" person came and put a chair in front of the door, like this, and said "this burial will not leave the house today, it will wait until tomorrow." And that is how it was indeed done. You have come to look for history, I am telling you the truth, there was nobody who would have dared say "this is my sister or my maternal uncle, she/he has died and I'll bury her/him today," nobody.[48] [...]

And I tell you – I won't tell you the name or any such thing – there was one person who on occasion would go to another and tell him, you, *babu*, get up and go to my house, get up and wash my dishes, don't sit here in public before the people, eating.[49] The one who did this was an Arab, though I won't tell you which one.

After leaving school in fifth grade, I had not yet had any job, so I took one digging clay for three months, and how much did I earn? Twenty-five Shillings for three months, and you didn't even know how many Shillings you were supposed to receive per hour or day. [...] With these twenty-five shillings, I went to the shop of a certain South-Asian merchant, Ahmad Katchi. I went and bought a vest, in those days they sold woollen vests for eighty Shilling[50]; a

---

[46] What I have translated as "cultural practices" was *mila*, a word often translated as "custom." In the parlance of coastal towns, it often stands for the Swahili version of Islamic practice. Among villagers, the term tends to be used more loosely to denote any kind of "indigenous" practice. Mzee Rajabu appears to have the use of "medicine" (potions) in mind.

[47] This is again the Halfan bin Nassor mentioned by Bibi Esha, Mzee Mohamed's father.

[48] A speedy burial is considered mandatory among Muslims, and generally preparing a decent funeral is an essential mark of respect and solidarity among kin. To interfere with this was therefore a significant incursion into the affairs of a kin group.

[49] *Babu*, literally "grandfather," is a somewhat familiar way of addressing an older man. Rajabu is highlighting the speaker's lack of respect for the addressee.

[50] "Eighty shilling" must be a mistake as Rajabu had only earned twenty-five shilling altogether. He may mean eighty cent or, more realistically, eight shilling.

shirt of *bfata* cloth cost two shillings,[51] and I bought it, and there were trousers, khaki trousers called "Stapuli" with decorated edges, and I bought them for two shillings. It was 1944.

Well, I was arrested with my twenty-five shillings, because I had them, and I didn't have the stature to own twenty-five shilling, so the police took them away. […] I was held at the police station until the Indian came who had employed me as a laborer for three months, and told them "this man has worked for me; he has been digging clay and carrying it to my home in a canister." Then I was released. […] So let us pray to God that he puts Mwalimu Nyerere into a good place, I tell you. Even the *waungwana* were like the Arabs.[52] They would not eat in the same place as a slave.[53] They would say *mkazi na mkaziwe*, meaning "slave with his fellow slave and *muungwana* with his fellow muungwana."

5. Sharifu Shehan Zaina

Sharifu Shehani, past eighty years old in 2000, insisted on the address *sharifu*, a term of respect accorded to descendants of the prophet Muhammad. *Sharifu* continue to claim high status on the northern Swahili coast, but here at its southern end, the opinion is widespread that they have "lost" the particular blessing attendant on their ancestry. Nevertheless, Sharifu Shehani, living in the center of Lindi town among the trappings of former wealth, was an unapologetic elitist; his attitude chimes with Rajabu Feruzi's recollections of *waungwana* arrogance. The respect he was given at religious functions indicated that he retained high status, but he was also rumored to practice witchcraft and to have killed at least one member of his family with it. He was critical of my work and only spoke to me out of a desire to set the record straight.

What were ex-slaves going to do after the end of slavery? They were just slaves, they scattered; every one ran whichever way he wanted and that was the end of it, and it was mostly the British who made this possible – that the *waungwana* were no longer valued by their slaves. […] Some stayed and they have had offspring too, they are around, they know their origins themselves […] but today the *waungwana* have no more responsibility for them. […]

Slavery is slavery and slave descent still exists, only that now it is not mentioned. But slavery is slavery because it is written in the book of Islam, the Quran […] if you go to [the island of] Mafia [north of Kilwa], they take pride in saying I'm the slave of so-and-so son of so-and-so, they are proud of it to this day […] I went to Mafia in 1961 and was given a slave to show me around, his name was Maalimu Twalifu. Every time we reached somewhere where we had to walk through water, he would say, "Sir, wear my shoes" [so that Shehan Zaina's own would stay dry].

---

[51] I have not been able to identify the term "bfata." Mostly likely it would be a bowdlerized brand name for a new, synthetic kind of fabric.

[52] Characteristically, Sharifu Shehani appears to use the term *waungwana* in the particularly restrictive sense of "slave owner, master."

[53] *Waungwana* (singular *muungwana*) is a Swahili-language social category often translated as "free-born," meaning non-slave, fully entitled or even patrician citizen of the coastal towns. In the late precolonial period, contestation of who could claim to be *muungwana* was fierce as plebeians struggled to be included. In the interwar period, it appears that even villagers, especially Muslim converts, claimed to be *waungwana*, and today the term *kiungwana*, "in the manner of a *muungwana*," may be heard to denote simply "polite, cultivated." Nevertheless, respondents evidently recall the more specific meaning of the term in the past.

7.2. Photo of Mzee Juma with his youngest grandchild.

6. Mzee Juma Sudi bin Juma

Mzee Juma, in his late seventies in 2000, was an antipode to Sharifu Shehani: a man of obscure ancestry who had achieved a position of respect over a lifetime of working and networking in Mingoyo. A former recruiter for the independence campaign of the 1950s and a minor leader in a Sufi brotherhood that introduced Mingoyans to this form of Islamic ritual, he lived in the same neighborhood as Mzee Mohamed Barwani and met him on an equal footing. His detailed account of slaves' ways of exploiting early-colonial legislation chimes with the interests of people of humble background working to establish their autonomy.

As it was explained to me, at the beginning the Arabs came to this country, and brought the trade in slaves. Now, when this way of making money became known,[54] the people

---

[54] Like Bibi Esha and Mzee Sefu, Mzee Juma emphasizes the economic motivations of slave traders and owners.

living here went to their own neighbors in some regions, to make war against them, to grab the children and take them to a place where they could sell them. […] So now we sold one another, the Yao invade Ngoni territory; the Ngoni invade Nyasa territory; well, a great disorder developed this way, because of the desire for money. People went as far as selling their own children. […]

While this upheaval was going on, the Germans arrived. They declared that no person can own another in the way of slavery, "you are now all the slaves of the German government."[55] Now everyone was told, if they wanted to redeem themselves, go to the *boma*.[56] So I go to the *boma*, I find the DC there, "I'm the slave of such-and-such; I have come to redeem myself.[57] What is my price?" – "Sixty rupees; perhaps forty." Well, the government receives the money and calls the current owner: "Take your money, and this person, we give him a certificate today to say he is not your slave anymore." So it was that people went and redeemed themselves.[58] […]

A slave might also say "this master is very oppressive." This was the case especially for those owned by poor people, because a poor master would make his slave work hard day after day. So the slave goes to someone else and says: "Give me money so I can redeem myself from this master, so I may be your slave." He goes and sells himself to a new owner, so as to get out of his current position. […] When the English arrived, they abolished slavery completely. Whether you had money or not, there was no permission for one person to own another. And thus the country progressed.

The following discussion of the phenomenon of *sulia*, meanwhile, shows Mzee Juma's partisanship as a plebeian man struggling to achieve the role of a patriarchal elder. What he depicts most vividly is the fact that a *sulia*, albeit merely a young woman, could in principle achieve a status above that of an older man. Written sources suggest that few *sulia* in fact were so fortunate; in practice their status was often indistinguishable from concubinage.[59] But for ambitious men in post-slavery Mingoyo, establishing control over women within the family was an important step toward their aims.

Sulia were a phenomenon that occurred in connection with slavery. For the Arabs did not bring women. Now, a man needs to live with a woman. If he marries seven or eight slaves, there may be a beautiful youth among them, who he marries after she has grown – having bought her as a small child. After she has grown up, she is desirable; well, he takes her and makes her his lady. That is a *sulia*. It is not as if he goes anywhere to ask for her hand. No, he chooses one from among his property to make her his lady.[60] A light-skinned woman maybe,

[55] Mzee Juma's claim that the Germans treated everybody as a slave chimes with many memories of the particular brutality of former officials, while also capturing the leveling effect of German rule on indigenous hierarchies.

[56] *Boma* was the term commonly used since German times for the buildings housing the offices of white officials. Literally it means fortress.

[57] DC stands for District Commissioner, the colonial government's "men on the ground" in British taxonomy. The acronym is still used occasionally even to refer to the officials of the current government. The German term "Bezirksamtmann," which is intended here, has not survived in Swahili.

[58] Mzee Juma is describing the system of *Freibriefe*, "letters of freedom," which was an important element of German attempts to develop an anti-slavery policy without actually prohibiting slavery.

[59] Katrin Bromber, "Mjakazi, Mpambe, Mjoli, Suria: Female Slaves in Swahili Sources." In G. Campbell, S. Miers and J.C. Miller, *Women and Slavery, Volume One: Africa the Indian Ocean World and the Medieval North Atlantic* (Athens, OH, 2007), 111–28.

[60] Note the contrast with Mzee Mohamed's description of the proceedings for marrying a *sulia* earlier in the chapter.

if he wants to have children. [...] If she has children, this *sulia* is freed, she is not a slave any more. All the Arabs who are left now were born this way. [...]

It was impossible that someone should be made *sulia* and then run away. Here is her home. She is the lady of the home; she can slap the slaves who are beneath her; hasn't she advanced to a higher status? A master's lady is respected; water is drawn for her; her clothes are washed. She slaps people, she doesn't have to work at the mortar. She can call me, an old man like me: "You, Mzee Ramadhani, why didn't you bring firewood yesterday?" Slap, slap. I just stand there quietly. Where would she go, she is eating the dates the Arabs eat, she wears fine clothing from Muscat. She would run away again?! And it was the case that one Arab, or anyone, even an African, might have up to ten, fifteen women.

Mzee Juma's vivid account of the domestic face of slavery illustrates respondents' tendency to understand the past in terms relevant to their present lives. Pre-eminence in the gendered hierarchies of the household is still part of the making of a village elder. Meanwhile his fairly uncomplicated relations with Mzee Barwani indicate that both plebeian people like him and the descendants of owners have managed to "live down" much of the heritage of slavery in Mingoyo.

SUGGESTED ADDITIONAL READINGS

Alpers, Edward. *Ivory and Slaves in East Central Africa: Changing Patterns of Trade to the Later Nineteenth Century.* London: Heinemann, 1975.

Cooper, Frederick. *Plantation Slavery on the East Coast of Africa.* New Haven, CT: Yale University Press, 1977.

From Slaves to Squatters. New Haven, CT: Yale University Press, 1980.

Glassman, Jonathon. *War of words, War of Stones: Racial Thought and Violence in Colonial Zanzibar.* Bloomington: Indiana University Press, 2011.

Pouwels, Randall. *Horn and Crescent: Cultural Change and Traditional Islam on the Swahili Coast, 800–1900.* Cambridge: Cambridge University Press, 1987.

8 Slavery in Kano Emirate of Sokoto Caliphate as Recounted

Testimonies of Isyaku and Idrisu

MOHAMMED BASHIR SALAU

Kano is a major commercial, industrial, and agricultural center in Northern Nigeria. Historically, Kano's dominance in this region has been tied to its central functions in the precolonial trans-Saharan trade between West Africa and societies in North Africa and elsewhere. In the nineteenth century, jihad forces led by members of the Fulani ethnic group conquered Kano and integrated it into the Sokoto Caliphate,[1] then the largest Islamic empire in West Africa. With the jihad, the slave population in Kano expanded rapidly and this was largely because an increasing number of non-Muslims from the Ningi and other regions[2] were enslaved through slave raids, kidnapping, and the demand for tribute. In addition to non-Muslims, Muslim political rivals were also sometimes enslaved in Kano, especially during moments of major internal political conflicts such as the *basasa* (civil war of 1893-94).[3] By the end of the nineteenth century, at least half of the population in the Kano region consisted of slaves.[4] At this time, slaves were used in various capacities including in aristocratic households, merchant firms, craft production, agriculture, and the military.

This chapter presents the transcripts of two interviews dealing with slavery in Kano. Yusufu Yunusa recorded the interviews in Kano in 1975 as part of the Economic History Project initiated by Jan Hogendorn and Paul E. Lovejoy in that year. The intention of the project "was to improve on earlier interview techniques for the collection of historical material and to promote the collection of economic data for archival deposit and public use by other scholars."[5] To achieve this, Hogendorn and Lovejoy sent research assistants to the field with tape recorders to document interviews.

[1] For a history of the Sokoto Caliphate, see M. Last, *The Sokoto Caliphate* (London, 1967).

[2] For more details on the raids on the Ningi region, see A. Patton, Jr., "An Islamic Frontier Polity: The Ningi Mountains of Northern Nigeria, 1846–1902," in I. Kopytoff (ed.), *The African Frontier* (Bloomington, IN, 1987), 193–213, and M. G. Smith, *Government in Kano 1350-1950* (Boulder, CO, 1977), 274–277.

[3] Situated between present-day Kano and Bauchi, the Ningi region was then mainly inhabited by stateless people who spoke a variety of Chadic and Plateau languages. For example, on the enslavement of Muslims, see Smith, "Government," 233–235.

[4] The estimates of the Kano's population after 1807 largely derive from the accounts of contemporaneous European explorers, such as H. Barth, *Travels and Discoveries in North and Central Africa Being a Journal of an Exhibition Undertaken under the Auspices of H. B. M.'s Government in the Years 1849–1855* (London, 1965), 143–144, and so must be treated with caution.

[5] J. Hogendorn and P. E. Lovejoy, "Oral Data Collection and the Economic History of the Central Savanna," *Savanna* 7:1 (1978), 72.

Yunusa interviewed about thirty individuals, mostly male elders. All of them were interviewed in Hausa. Unlike other oral data collected during the project, which yielded information on commerce, agricultural production, craft specialization (dyeing, leather work, women's crafts), labor mobilization, family histories, salt mining, and the 1913–14 drought,[6] the oral data Yunusa recorded deals primarily with slavery.[7]

At the time, Yunusa was a student at Ahmadu Bello University. Following the conclusion of his field research in Kano, Yunusa wrote his B.A. research essay on slavery in Kano emirate. He later taught history, worked in educational administration and wrote a number of books in Hausa. Here, we are presenting abridged versions of his interviews with Malam Isyaku, an ex-slave who was ninety years old when interviewed; and Malam Idrisu, a descendant of a nineteenth-century Kano title holder, who was seventy-seven years old when interviewed.

When Yunusa interviewed Idrisu, the latter was working as a messenger although he was the grandson of a powerful royal slave official. Idrisu apparently did not do as well as his father. Unlike Idrisu, Isyaku was a privileged slave, who worked as an overseer on a royal estate, a position he took over from his father. Although Isyaku inherited his position, junior slaves were generally promoted on two main bases: the quality of their relationship with a patron (both senior slaves and the emir) and merit. As an overseer, Isyaku was responsible for the day-to-day operation of the royal estate at Dorayi. His testimony is of interest because it represents the voice of a royal slave official, and because it also represents a rural perspective on slavery.

Yunusa interviewed Idrisu and Isyaku at a time when scholarly debate on slavery and the slave trade had shifted from a focus on the consequences of the Atlantic slave trade on Africa[8] to a debate on the nature of slavery in the continent. This new debate was provoked by the publication of two major collections.[9] Although both collections agree on certain issues such as on the question of a slave's status as an outsider, they also disagreed on several other points. Suzanne Miers and Igor Kopytoff argue that slavery was an institution of marginality in Africa, and that western concepts of slavery cannot be used to analyze this "peculiar institution." For Miers and Kopytoff, in Africa, slavery involved rights in person and it primarily served the social function of integrating acquired persons into kin groups. Claude Meillasoux, on the other hand, sees slavery as an antithesis to kinship. In his view, slavery was a relationship of production and slaves were chattel.[10]

Considering the controversy sparked by these works, it is not surprising that Yunusa asked his informants questions related to slave treatment, slave assimilation, enslavement, slave use in household as well as in production, slave punishment, and slave resistance. It is also not surprising that other questions, such as many of those related to women and on the illegal slave trade during the early colonial era in Kano and other parts of Northern

---

[6] For more details on the Economic History Project, see Hogendorn and Lovejoy, "Oral Data Collection," 71–74.

[7] The Yunusa oral data collection has been deposited with the Northern History Research Scheme at Ahmadu Bello University in Zaria and at the Tubman Institute of York University in Toronto.

[8] This earlier debate was sparked by Walter Rodney. See W. Rodney, *A History of Upper Guinea Coast 1545–1800* (Oxford, 1970).

[9] I. Kopytoff and S. Miers (eds.), *Slavery in Africa: Historical and Anthropological Perspectives* (Madison, WI, 1977), and C. Meillassoux (translated by Alide Dasnois), *The Anthropology of Slavery : The Womb of Iron and Gold* (Chicago, 1991).

[10] Kopytoff and Miers, *Slavery*; Meillassoux, *The Anthropology*.

Nigeria,[11] that engaged the subsequent attention of scholars were largely ignored in the Yunusa interviews. Although the questions Yunusa asked Idrisu and Isyaku are limited, the answers provided by the informants tell us a lot about the nature of slavery in Kano.

The testimonies suggest that the emir of Kano and other rich slave owners were not primarily interested in integrating slaves into their kin groups. Based in the city, the emir and other rich slave owners consigned many of their slaves to rural estates where production was often based on gang labor and management of productive activities was partly based on the use of slave officials.

The interviews also indicate that the master-slave relationship in Kano was not always cordial. Not all slaves were hardworking. Many disregarded their masters' instructions or even escaped. For these and other reasons, slave masters sometimes punished their slaves. The sources inform us that punishment sometimes involved flogging, denial of food, imprisonment, and disposal of slaves.

Idrisu and Isyaku also suggest that there were avenues for the slave's advancement in Kano. In particular, the testimonies indicate that while many slaves could rise to important positions in the household and in society through hard work, bravery, and sexual union with male masters, others could buy their freedom.

Finally, the testimonies point to various ways in which Islam influenced the character of slavery in Kano. For instance, they indicate that enslaved prisoners brought into Kano were generally treated in accordance with Islamic theory. Although some were publicly executed at the various gates leading to the city, those enslaved were distributed according to the Hausa system of *humusi* (division of war booty) whereby the emir took one-fifth and the officers who took part in the campaigns shared the rest in adherence to Islamic law.

Overall, the two testimonies can be used to corroborate each other, even though they are not altogether similar.[12] However, based on their strengths and limitations, which are similar to those of other materials that form part of the Yunusa collection, the pictures Idrisu and Isyaku present us must be used together with other sources to corroborate or refute the pictures Idrisu and Isyaku present to us.[13]

QUESTIONS TO CONSIDER

1. What were the slaves' daily lives like in the royal estates?
2. What are the similarities and differences between the two interviews.
3. What do the two texts say about women in slavery?
4. What role did ritual and beliefs play in the sustenance of the Kano slave system?
5. What was the impact of the abolition of slavery on the Kano slave population?
6. Why did many slaves not care about abolition?

---

[11] For subsequent works on slavery dealing with such new problems, see, for instance, C. N. Ubah, "Suppression of the Slave Trade in the Nigerian Emirates," *Journal of African History* 32:3 (1991), 447–470, and C. C. Robertson and M. A. Klein (eds.), *Women and Slavery in Africa* (Portsmouth, NH, 1997).

[12] The personal histories of both informants are, for instance, completely different.

[13] I discuss the strengths and weaknesses of these accounts in "Voices of Those Who Testified on Slavery in Kano Emirate," in A. L. Araujo, M. P. Candido, and P. E. Lovejoy (eds.), *Crossing Memories: Slavery and African Diaspora* (Trenton, NJ, 2011), 129–145.

1. Isyaku

My name is Isyaku. My age is eighty and ten. My occupation is farming.

I work in the Emir's estate. My father was brought to Kano from Maradi.[14] He migrated here and gave birth to thirty-one children, including myself. I am the youngest and currently the only child alive. My father was captured during war, during the reign of Alu.[15]

Q: How many slaves were here when the royal estate was established?

A: We were about seventy in number. We cultivated the Emir's estate. All these locust bean trees you see form part of the royal estate.

Q: Oh, is that why this settlement is called Dorayi?[16]

A: Yes. This area is the original heartland of Dorayi. Slaves, including those captured in war, were settled here in Dorayi. Damagaram[17] captured people and killed them. Later, however, war captives were brought here and enslaved. You know that in those days war captives were usually killed.

Q: How were they killed?

A: About sixty slaves were sometimes brought to Jakara, and killed.[18] Their heads were cut off.

Q: Why do they take them to the gates?

A: Yes, war captives were usually brought there. Some who God favored were set free to go back to their towns while others who remained and were enslaved could be made the Dan Rimi[19] of Kano, or become very rich during their lifetime.

Q: Well, about those killed? Why were the victims not simply enslaved?

A: Where will they be enslaved? Slaves were numerous, mister, slaves were numerous.

Q: What types of food crops were planted here?

A: Here we planted groundnuts and cassava. Harvests principally belonged to the Emir. Groundnuts millet and guinea corn also primarily belonged to the emir. When I was the slave overseer, I used to tie hundreds of corn bundles. Other slaves and I did that. But when the Europeans came,[20] they started sending prisoners to this place to assist with farming, and this still takes place today.

Q: Now when the farm produce was harvested, what was done with such harvest?

A: It was given to horses.

---

[14] A major town in present-day Republic of Niger.
[15] Aliyu came to power in 1894–95 after the Kano civil war.
[16] Dorayi is also a Hausa term for locust bean.
[17] A Muslim state established in the nineteenth century in what is now southeastern Niger.
[18] The Jakara River is the major river that flows through the city of Kano.
[19] A senior slave official at the emir's palace in Kano who dealt with Kano's relations with other states.
[20] The British conquered Kano in 1903. They ruled it up to 1960.

Q: Don't they take part of the harvested crops to Kano?

A: No, no. The practice of sending harvests to Kano stopped long ago.

Q: Okay, how was the crop harvest conveyed to Kano in the past?

A: On the head. Donkeys and very poor people conveyed the harvest to Kano.

Q: Well I understand that royal estates were mostly managed by Salama,[21] or Shamaki,[22] or Dan Rimi or Turakin Soro.[23]

A: The Shamaki managed all the slaves here and those at the royal estate in Nasarawa were also under the Shamaki. And he managed the royal estate in Gogel.

Q: How did you go out for work before the arrival of the Europeans? How did slaves get ready for work?

A: All the slaves, including women, armed themselves with hoes and reported at the estate. In the morning? They finish after noon. They close after prayers,[24] then everyone goes home until the next day.

Q: You were once the overseer here? Did the overseer usually arrive at the royal estate earlier than other slaves?

A: Yes, he usually arrived earlier. The overseer assigned each gang a task. Everyone then proceeded to work. Men and women all worked together. Usually when slaves were many, both young men and women were asked to work at the estate.

Q: Were women assigned different tasks from those assigned to men?

A: Yes, men were assigned different tasks.

Q: What were the origins of those enslaved here? You mentioned, in your own case, that you are of Maradi background.

A: Yes, we were brought from there. Yes, while some were from Ningi and Adamawa.[25]

Q: Were they Fulani?[26]

A: Yes.

Q: Were the enslaved people from Maradi Hausa-speakers?

A: They spoke Hausa. Yes, some were Muslims. Some were non-Muslims. Some were uncircumcised. They had beards that reached to this point, but were uncircumcised.

---

[21] A slave official at the emir's palace who was responsible for the supervision of palace armory and palace eunuchs. He also served as the commander and instructor of the slave musketeers.

[22] The most important slave official in the emir's palace. He was in charge of the royal household.

[23] A slave official who served as the go-between for Dan Rimi and the emir.

[24] The Muslim Zuhr prayer typically ends around 2:30 PM.

[25] Located in the northeastern region of modern-day Nigeria.

[26] An ethnic group of people spread over many parts of west, central, and east Africa. Elements of this group spearheaded the holy war, jihad, which took place in Hausaland, including in Kano, between 1804 and 1808.

Q: What could excuse a slave from work?

A: If he is sick. If he was well, he had to work at the estate.

Q: Were slaves given plots to farm on their own account?

A: Yes.

Q: But did the small farm plot meet the food need of a slave?

A: It did. You know by then productivity was relatively high. This Emir's estate, you won't believe it produced about hundred or three hundred bundles of grain crops. Whatever the slave harvested at his assigned farm plot was his. They grew groundnuts or grains, and other crops. Yes, each slave cultivated his own plot, by God.

Q: Were slaves given gifts by the Emir?

A: Yes. He gave gifts like robes in the dry season. Yes, officials like me were given black-and-white-colored robes with trousers and with embroidery. Some were given more gifts than others.

Q: Were the gifts given to slaves awarded based on completed work?

A: Yes. That is how it was done. Overseers were given such gifts to distribute to those working under them.

Q: What about the *cucanawa*?[27] The slave's children, how were they treated? Were they also assigned gifts?

A: Yes.

Q: What is the duty of a slave overseer?

A: He farmed. He also ensured that other people worked properly in the estate.

Q: Did the slave overseer have slaves of his own?

A: No, only those asked to work under him by the master. Such slaves were his boys.

Q: What do they do for him?

A: Farming on the royal estate.

Q: As such, they didn't do anything else for him. They were simply under his control?

A: Those slaves were placed under the overseer.

Q: Could a slave own a slave?

A: A slave to own a slave?

Q: What kind of reward did overseers receive from the Emir?

A: They were given robes. They were given more gifts than other slaves.

---

[27] A second-generation slave is a *bacucane*. The plural is *cucanawa*.

Q: Were they given gifts on Sallah[28] days?

A: Yes, they were.

Q: Which days were assigned as rest days for slaves employed at the royal estates?

A: Only Fridays,[29] they do not work on that day.

Q: Were slaves engaged in other activities apart from farming?

A: By God, apart from farming, slaves largely did nothing. Their primary responsibility was farming.

Q: What I mean is this, when slaves were not doing the Emir's work, didn't they do other things so as to get some money, cowries?

A: I know that my father was weaving *mangala*[30] for sale. Everyone did something similar. Some made beds. We don't produce mats in this area.

Q: Weren't they involved in commerce?

A: They weren't. By God no. Except that some took cornstalks from here to the city to sell.

Q: Did slaves leave this place for the city to work?

A: No. By then royal slaves were employed mainly in agriculture.

Q: What if a slave just wanted to get some pocket money to spend?

A: Oh, by then an Emir's slave was relatively better off, though he worked continuously.

Q: Did a slave work during Sallah day?

A: When it is Sallah day all a slave was expected to do was to go to the master's house to eat in the morning and then leave.

Q: Was slaves' escape common in this area?

A: In the past, yes, slave escape was common.

Q: Were they ever pursued and recaptured?

A: Who will waste time running after a slave? Now will they go to Ningi to catch someone? A lot of them ran, by God. They ran away.

Q: Were slaves employed here granted freedom through self-purchase? If so, was such freedom granted by the Emir or by the Shamaki?

A: Through the Shamaki. He had powers and could even sell a slave.

Q: But if he sold a slave, was he expected to inform the Emir?

A: Yes, he was expected to do that.

---

[28] Muslim festivals.

[29] Muslims slave owners believed that Fridays should be devoted to congregational prayers and to other devotional acts. This partly explains why they made Fridays rest days for their slaves.

[30] A donkey's bag, rectangular in shape, meant for carrying manure.

Q: For what reasons would he sell a slave?

A: Because he has them under him. The Shamaki mainly sold lazy and troublesome slaves.

Q: But the Shamaki did not expel a slave from the estate?

A: No. It was better to sell a slave.

Q: But what I am getting at is did slaves buy their freedom?

A: Yes. Formerly a slave with the means could ask his master for freedom.

Q: But I mean those slaves employed at the royal estate.

A: The royal slaves? That was not possible with the royal slaves.

Q: They couldn't take money to the Emir and ask for their freedom?

A: No.

Q: They, therefore, remained here forever.

A: They remained here forever, and that is all.

Q: Well in the past, what sign indicated that a slave was up for sale? How could such a slave be identified?

A: They were tied with chains and some were taken to Isyaku, the slave dealer.

Q: In the city?

A: Yes, such slaves were then taken there. Usually, they were asked to sit down in an organized manner. If a slave was too stubborn, however, he was promptly taken to the market and sold. The master was then given the money to buy another slave.

Q: Which place was assigned for slave marketing in Kano?

A: In the past? By the market. Yes, Kurmi market.[31] Yes, that was where slaves were lined up. About a hundred slaves were usually lined up for disposal. Men and women.

Q: Were they given any sign on their bodies to indicate that they were meant for disposal?

A: Yes, that was done. Ashes were usually rubbed on the faces. Announcement was also made, for instance, that this was a stubborn slave of so and so.

Q: I heard you mention Isyaku. Now, apart from Isyaku, which slave dealer do you remember?

A: Isyaku. Right from my early years Isyaku was the major slave dealer in Kano.

Q: Okay, apart from him, wasn't there anyone else?

A: No, except Musa, his junior brother. Any slave sold in the market was through them.

---

[31] Kurmi Market is one of the oldest and largest local markets in Africa. It used to serve as an international market where North African and some European goods were exchanged for domestic goods through trans-Saharan trade.

Q: For how much was a slave sold?

A: He was sold for two hundred thousand cowries. Deals were struck at the market. After bargaining, the money was taken for payment. After a deal had been struck at the market, a buyer then proceeded home to bring money for payment. Such amount was usually tied in grass mat bags. Female slaves were sometimes stubborn. Some of them could tell a potential buyer that they disliked him, and this made reaching agreements difficult.

Q: Why were slaves given facial marks?

A: Well you know that when the Europeans came, by then Rabeh[32] from the east used to enslave many. Such slaves were tied up and an iron instrument placed in the fire to tattoo the slaves. That was how Rabeh used to give marks to slaves.

Q: But I noticed that royal slaves have three marks on the lower part of their face.

A: Yes, that practice persists. Those from both Dan Rimi's and Shamaki's lines have such marks. Any slave you see now, even if a child, in the palace without these facial marks is not a *cucane*.[33]

Q: But, why is the mark given to them?

A: There was once a Shamaki named Barka. He introduced the practice of giving marks to slaves.

Q: Was it aimed at differentiating between the Emir's children and the *cucanawa*?

A: Yes, certainly.

Q: What is the meaning of *murgu*?

A: *Murgu*?[34] Payment made daily by a slave to his master in lieu of service. Cowries were used for payment.

Q: Who were the rich people in Kano with plantations?

A: Here in Kano? I remember Musa Dan-Maraya. He lived in the city, but his estate was here in Dorayi. We observed that Musa Dan-Maraya had about a hundred slaves in his estate. He was a merchant. He used to trade to Gwanja.[35] Those with plenty of slaves were many, but most of them did not have as many slaves as he did. After him, then Kundila.

Q: That means he had more slaves than Kundila?

A: No, he did not have more slaves than Kundila. Kundila was exceptional. Kundila was a merchant.

---

[32] A Sudanese who was formerly an associate of an Egyptian slave trader known as Zubayr Pasha, and who attacked and conquered Borno, in what is now northeastern Nigeria, with his army in 1893. Following his 1893 military success, Rabeh ruled the Borno region briefly until the French defeated him at the turn of the twentieth century.

[33] A second-generation slave. See discussion later in the chapter.

[34] The definition of *murgu* offered later in the chapter by Isyaku differs from the colonial understanding of the term. To most British colonial administrators in Northern Nigeria, *murgu* refers to payments slaves made to purchase their freedom.

[35] Gonja or Gwanja was a state north of the Asante Empire.

Q: What did he sell?

A: Kolanuts. They go to Gwanja to bring kolanuts with about a hundred donkeys. There was no one in Kano with Kundila's wealth. Kundila was very rich and had estates by each of the city gates. When you see him, you see an ordinary person on his horse. But then you are told he is Kundila. He himself did not know precisely how many slaves he had. Hence he usually asked his slaves questions like: how many are you in that estate of mine? Are you up to a hundred slaves there? In some cases slaves informed him that "Master we are more than that." You don't ask of the number of slaves in Kundila's house. Slaves were from everywhere. Some were Barawa, some Adamawa. They were all there. There was no ethnic group that was not there. That is Kundila. He bought all his slaves.

Q: That makes two; was there any other rich slave owner?

A: Except for Danda. Danda had started acquiring slaves. He was a butcher. If it is a hundred slaves, he had such. Do you wish to be informed about people like Daku? A person with thirty slaves, are you interested in knowing about him?

Q: Apart from the city, were there slave markets in the villages?

A: Actually there was a slave market everywhere. Slaves were advertised and sold even in villages.

Q: How do slaves marry in Dorayi?

A: Co-slaves, male and female, fall in love. And that is all.

Q: But did slave children from such union belong to the woman's master?

A: Yes. Certainly, they become his *cucanawa*.

Q: Could a master seize the *cucanawa*?

A: He could take them and lock them indoors.

Q: Could such locked-up children become their master's concubines?

A: Yes.

Q: Did they give birth to children?

A: Certainly, they had children. Where young female slaves were numerous, about fifty or thirty, or twenty, or five of them could be given as gifts, specifically as concubines, to any of the Emir's children who was getting married.

Q: Could a slave marry a free woman?

A: Yes, when a slave saved enough money he could marry a free woman.

Q: Were such children the Emir's slaves?

A: No.

Q: Even though their father was a royal slave, they were not the Emir's slave?

A: Yes. Since he married a free woman.

Q: What is the difference between a slave employed at home and a slave employed at a plantation?

A: A house slave belongs to the master. He is like a son of the master. If such a slave was female, she could have a child by the master.

Q: Do female slaves cover their faces like married women?

A: No, they don't. Even if today you go to the palace and see a lady with wrappers covering up to the breast but not the face, then she is a slave.[36]

Q: Was this because a female slave was not married?

A: Yes.

Q: Will she, therefore, cover her face once she gets married?

A: She will.

Q: Did female slaves in the palace take care of their own children?

A: Yes. Many female slaves looked after their own children, but some gave Uwar Soro[37] the responsibility of taking care of their children. In that case, if the child was female she remained with this guardian until she starts menstruating.

Q: Could a slave buy a slave?

A: Certainly. He will work for him. Any assigned work. He could work until he was able to free himself.

Q: As the master of the slave who bought his own slave, do I have authority over the slave of my slave?

A: You do mainly because the slave who bought a slave is your slave. Whatever task you assign your slave, his own slave could do for you.

Q: If my slave buys a slave, the Hausas have a saying: The head and the load are all under the jurisdiction of the neck. Then it implies that my slave's slave is my slave?

A: Yes.

Q: Then what really is the benefit of buying a slave to my slave?

A: The point is that the practice existed, and we witnessed a lot of it. Aybu bought a female slave who gave birth to a son. The son then became a man before he was freed.

Q: What is the meaning of *mudabbar*?

A: *Mudabbar* is a written promise given to a slave that at the death of his master he shall receive freedom.

---

[36] Covering the face by women in Kano generally has religious significance. However, not all women use veils today even at the Kano palace, and this is partly because the mode of dressing of any given female also symbolizes her ancestry (whether slave or free).

[37] Head of female palace slaves.

Q: Let us go back to the issue of slave dealers. When slaves are taken by their owners to a slave dealer, could they work for the dealer before he sells them?

A: Yes. It was allowed. Remember, the slave dealer was responsible for feeding the slave about to be sold.

Q: Wasn't the master of the slave responsible for sending money and food?

A: No. No matter the number of days the slave remained with dealer.

Q: Okay, were slaves sold on credit in the past?

A: No. Only if the slave is lazy, then he could be sold on credit.

Q: What were the reasons for selling a slave?

A: Stubbornness or laziness of a slave or lack of peaceful coexistence between master and slave. Now don't you know that a slave could be beyond the master's control, and this usually encouraged the disposal of the slave for another one?

Q: Could a *bacucane* be sold?

A: Yes, they were sold.

Q: But some say that if a master sells *bacucane*, such a slave owner will become bankrupt or be afflicted by poverty.

A: There is no doubt about that.

Q: Was there anybody who went bankrupt because he sold his *bacucane*?

A: Yes, don't you see them here. Now if this is a Fulani man. With time you are told your slave is a Fulani man. Why will he be sold? Selling this one is poverty.

Q: Was it economic pressures that forces people to do that?

A: Yes, some were sold forever. Yes, we witnessed many cases here.

Q: Could a slave owner pawn his slave?

A: Yes, this was common. When a slave master is in dire need, and his slave is valued at about two hundred pounds, he could ask someone to advance him some money in exchange for his slave, and that he will collect back his slave if he pays back the loan. This was done.

Q: Do commoners give facial marks to their slaves?

A: Yes, some gave their slaves *yan baka*.[38] Some gave theirs *bille*.[39] They were given marks because some may attempt to escape.

Q: Were charms really used to prevent slave escape?

A: Yes, of course. When charmed, the slave will go out and will not be able to determine any escape path.

---

[38] Facial marks by the sides of the mouth.
[39] Diagonal facial marks.

Q: Were royal slaves also charmed?[40]

A: Yes.

Q: Did slave overseers here have assistants?

A: My father had no assistant. He was the leader here in Dorayi. He established the Dorayi estate. My father was the one who established this estate, and I worked here for about twenty one years before I took over the position of overseer from him.

Q: Where in Kano were stubborn slaves taken to for punishment?

A: They were taken to the house of Ma'ajin Watari.[41] Such slaves were usually beaten until they defecate. His master beat the slave until he repents. The slave was tied and severely punished. Slaves were punished so that they will give up bad habits.

Q: But, who gave them permission to punish slaves at that location? Was it the Emir?

A: Yes, the Emir authorized that.

Q: Punishments usually lasted how many days?

A: Some may spend up to a year at that house.

Q: Do private slave owners pay for punishment services received?

A: They usually offered rewards for such services, mister. Whenever such slave owners had a soft spot for a stubborn slave they brought the slave to Ma'ajin Watari's house for punishment.

Q: A slave was sometimes punished because his owner liked him?

A: Yes. Because the master did not want to sell slave.

Q: What is the difference between *rinji* and *gandu*?[42]

A: A slave owner who had a *rinji* usually had numerous slaves. He knew the character of some, but not all of them. *Gandu* means plantation. *Rinji*? That refers to slaves.

Q: Did *rinji* refer to slave's quarters?

A: Yes, it refers to slave's quarters. That is it.

Q: A *rinji* was usually located within a *gandu*, right?

A: Yes, that is so. The situation has changed. In the past, no free person lived in the midst of royal slaves here. Now anyone can move here.

Q: How was war organized in the past?

A: The Emir would go to Damagaram and capture people. He captured the people of Damagaram and brought them here. Some of them might eventually prosper. One brought here as a child might grow up to be a nice man who everyone admires.

---

[40] In this context, charmed means bewitched. In other words, it means using spells or magical powers to control another person's mind and action.

[41] A slave prison situated less than a kilometer northeast of the emir's palace at Kano city.

[42] Both of these terms also refer to plantation.

Q: Were slaves used in the army during wars?

A: Are you asking if slaves were taken to the war front? In those days slaves were at the war front in the battle against the Yanyam,[43] pagans who, in those days, lived to the south.

Q: But my question is that were slave soldiers used in the war front?

A: Of course, slaves were used in the war front.

A: They were required to carry loads. Food. Even mortar.

Q: Mortar for pounding?

A: Women were also engaged at the war front. Yes, female slaves. They also carried items like mats for war purposes.

Q: Apart from carrying loads, did slaves fight?

A: No. By God they didn't.

Q: Weren't donkeys used for carrying loads?

A: Palace based mules and camels were usually taken to the war front. They carried cereal powder, grain crops, and other items. They were meant for feeding the army.

Q: Who did the cooking?

A: Women. Female slaves.

Q: How did the Europeans conquer Kano?

A: Europeans? Early one morning, we were sitting outside when we noticed the whole town was becoming hazy.

Q: Was it dust?

A: Yes. I wondered what was happening. Then I heard that it was the Europeans. They were on horses, although the horses were not many.

Q: Did they break the city gate?

A: Yes, they broke all the frames. Some blacks were involved. Those soldiers were from there around the river side.[44]

Q: Did the Europeans stop slavery?

A: Oh! They were responsible for stopping slavery.

Q: Was the selling of slaves stopped?

A: Everything was stopped. Everything related to slavery.

Q: But, what was the reaction of the people to all this change?

A: People adapted.

---

[43] This appears to refer to the region south of Zaria.

[44] The Royal West African Frontier Force established by Lord Lugard, who became the British high commissioner of the protectorate of Northern Nigeria in 1900, consisted of local recruits drawn from the region south of River Niger or from southern Nigeria. Here, Isyaku refers to such locally recruited colonial soldiers.

Q: Everyone continued with his activities?

A: Yes, and the Europeans were less concerned. But any offender caught was punished. That was the reason why the Europeans eventually stayed in Kano.

Q: Did the Europeans enter the palace?

A: Yes, they entered the palace. They raped any concubine of the Emir they encountered until the situation became pretty bad. That was when their commander said he would not tolerate that.

Q: The Europeans or their black soldiers, who were those that committed these atrocities?

A: The whites.

Q: Were their black soldiers involved?

A: Yes, they were.

Q: I heard that the Europeans gave out papers to the slaves proclaiming them free. Is it true?[45]

A: Yes, it happened.

Q: Now, did you get that paper?

A: No. How could we get it? We belonged to the Emir.

Q: But I heard that every slave, including those of the Emir, was given such papers.

A: Yes. Some who collected the document even returned to stay. They stayed as slaves.

Q: Between the royal slave and a commoner's slave, who suffers more?

A: Well, a commoner's slave experienced more hardship. The commoner's slave was monitored more closely by the owner than the royal slave.

Q: Were slaves not punished at the royal estate?

A: Rebellious slaves were usually caught and punished.

Q: Were there rebellious slaves among those owned by private holders?

A: Yes.

Q: Were such slaves usually targets of punishment everywhere?

A: Yes.

Q: But in terms of workload at the royal estate, do the emir's slaves here work more than those employed in private estates?

A: Yes, they do.

---

[45] It is difficult to establish the precise date that colonial administrators started issuing freedom papers to slaves in Kano. However, we know that such documents were issued after the 1903 British conquest of Kano.

Q: Did slaves engaged at the royal estate suffer more than those at the palace or those employed by the peasants?

A: Yes, they did.

Q: Did a slave eat before going to work?

A: Yes, he did. Food was also taken to him be it *tuwo*, *kunu*,[46] or anything that was cooked. Usually such meals were served in clay bowls.

Q: Was it the Emir who distributed food or what?

A: Yes. Will you deny your slave food?

Q: I thought that it was prepared from the slave's house?

A: No, it was supplied from his master's house.

Q: Was provided food usually adequate for the slaves?

A: Yes.

Q: Which food was eaten most?

A: Beans. It is a king among foods.

Q: Beans only, or was it cooked with rice?

A: No. Who knew of rice then?

Q: How are these slave leaders chosen? Was it hereditary?

A: Some inherited their title.

Q: But do children of concubines rule in Kano?

A: Well, there are examples of that. Such children could inherit wealth and other things from their father.

Q: But do they consider a slave's character in appointing a leader?

A: Yes. Usually they consider someone with good character, probably inherited from his father.

Q: How many female slaves were in the Emir's palace at the peak of slavery?

A: The female slaves, including those who cooked, were many.

Q: Is it s hard to know their precise number?

A: It is hard.

Q: Where were eunuchs obtained from?

A: Mostly from the east.[47]

---

[46] *Tuwo* is food made from grain flour, while *kunu* is a drink made out of the same material.

[47] Kano obtained eunuchs from areas like Damagaram. According to R. A. Dunbar's work entitled "Slavery and the Evolution of Nineteenth Century Damagaram (Zinder, Niger)" in Kopytoff and Miers, *Slavery*,

Q: Could a female slave buy a slave, either male or female?

A: She could.

Q: What sort of work could she ask the slave to do for her?

A: Any assigned work.

Q: What sort of work do the female slaves do in the palace?

A: Grinding, pounding. That was their work. And cooking food. And sweeping.

Q: Could any of the female slaves be called to spend the day with the Emir if he wishes?

A: Yes, they were his slaves. Abdullahi even had a hundred concubines.

Q: Well, a majority of the slaves brought here were not Muslims. Were they taught Muslim prayers here?

A: They were taught here.

Q: Were they taught how to read the Qur'an and other subjects?

A: They were taught all.

2. Malam Idrisu

My name is Idrisu. I am seventy-seven years old. My great-grandfather was the Galadima of Kano during the reign of Sulaiman. Currently, I am a messenger. I don't have any link with any other town since the time of Sulaimanu, the Emir of Kano Sulaimanu who was succeeded by Dabo.[48]

Q: Where were the slaves sold in Kano obtained?

A: They were usually from Ningi, Zaria, and Gwari lands. Apart from these, some were captured during the war with Damagaram. Those caught were enslaved. We didn't kill them except when a person was tough and uncooperative. He was then killed. But when a town was conquered, all those captured became slaves. Both old and young ones among them were war booty. They were then enslaved.

Q: Were the people of Damagaram Muslims or pagans?

A: They were Muslims. The war thus was Muslims versus Muslims. Damagaram and Kano were both Muslims.

Q: Were they enslaved?

A: Of course. Only those who deserved death were killed at the war front.

163, castration was illegal under Islamic law, so Damagaram bought eunuchs from non-Muslim societies, especially from Christian and Jewish merchant groups. Unfortunately, the validity of this claim has yet to be established, bearing in mind that the study of the eunuch phenomenon is generally far from rich.

[48] Dabo (1819–1846) actually succeeded Suleiman (1807–1819).

Q: Who were those deserving of death?

A: When, for instance, you bring out your weapon and I also do the same but I feel you will hurt me then I will be the first to kill you.

Q: What was done with war captives?

A: When they arrived at Kano, the Emir could enslave some, while others were sent to Sokoto as tribute. Many were tied and taken to Sokoto and that is why there were lots of slaves in Sokoto. They included those taken as tribute from Kano and everywhere that a flag-bearer of Shehu[49] was based. Such slaves were usually taken to Sokoto as tribute during the dry season.

Q: Were slaves the only item taken to Sokoto, or were other items also forwarded as tribute?

A: I am only aware of slaves.

Q: How were those brought to Kano sold?

A: In Kurmi market there is a place called Yan Bayi where slaves meant for disposal were lined up. Usually they had ash rubbed on their body and were also chained. Anyone who wanted to buy a slave would go there and make an offer. After an agreement has been reached, the slave was then untied for the buyer to take home. A slave could be sold at twenty or sixty *zambar*.[50] In fact, their prices were not the same, and it was even possible to get one for a hundred *zambars*.

Q: Did buyers carry money to the market or did they pay at home after the bargain?

A: Buyers went to the market with money. The bargain for any slave took place in the market around where such slave was seated. When an agreement was reached, the buyer paid. The ropes are then untied from the slave's neck before he was handed over to the buyer to take home. Such a buyer could ask the slave, "Do you like me?" If the slave says, "I don't like you," then the buyer could seek another slave. Surely, he usually wouldn't buy someone who does not like him. He therefore looks for another slave who gives a positive response to his question to buy. There has to be an agreement, the slave had to state that "I like you." Would anyone buy a slave who does not like him?

Q: Was the slave usually informed about the type of work which he was expected to do for his new master?

A: No. No. When a slave was purchased, he did any task assigned to him. If he was unable to do an assigned task, then his master taught him. For instance, a farmer might buy a slave who claims he does not know how to harrow. Such a master could then ask the slave to hit a spot directly under his foot with a hoe. The slave would usually then avoid striking his own foot by hitting the ground with the hoe and widening both legs. The master would

---

[49] Shehu refers to Uthman dan Fodio who led the Sokoto jihad in the first decade of the nineteenth century, while a flag-bearer refers to his military commander.

[50] *Zambar* refers to a thousand cowries. In this case, twenty or sixty *zambar* means twenty thousand or sixty thousand cowries.

inform the slave that his action confirms that he was capable of farm work. Yes, a slave was taught in this manner. When he comes to a place and says that he did not know how to do the assigned task, then a master could give him a test to find out.

Q: Was there any mark given to slaves meant for sale?

A: Was it possible to take a slave to the market for sale without rubbing him with ashes? It was only after the slaves body was rubbed with ashes that he was then tied down. His body will be all ashes. It shows that he is a slave. With a rope and ashes, that becomes obvious.

Q: What part of the slave's body was usually tied? The neck, leg, or hand?

A: Their necks were usually tied. But in the market, they were tied to each other and lined up. Both hands were tied to prevent escape. They were tied in this manner.

Q: Were female slaves also covered with ashes as the men?

A: A female slave was usually rubbed with ashes, when she got home then she was cleaned.

Q: Do you know the names of any slave dealer in Kano?

A: There was one called Dikko. We even once bought a female slave from him, but I cannot recall her name.

Q: Here in Kano, apart from Jakara, where else were slaves sold?

A: That was the only slave market, to the west of the market. Where else do you expect? But I wouldn't know if you mean in another town. Here, that was the slave market at *yan bayi*.[51] There was nowhere else where slaves were taken to for sale.

Q: Well, was it possible to steal slaves?

A: Of course. If a person is stolen, he could be rubbed with ashes and sold. For example, a child walking around could be captured, disguised, and rubbed with ashes for sale.

Q: Were there people who opposed slavery in the past?

A: Everyone disliked being a slave, but anyone who had the means usually purchased a slave because he also disliked doing things, especially tedious tasks, by himself.

Q: Was there any place here in Kano where errant or stubborn slaves were taken to for punishment?

A: There is no such place. Most people discipline their own slaves.

Q: What kind of discipline was given, if one wanted to do so?

A: Something like refusing him enough food when you see he likes eating. Then hunger alone is a form of punishment. When a slave likes to eat, and at the same time he was rebellious, then a master could deny him food, or you give him what will not suffice him. On his own, the slave will come back begging for work to do.

Q: But won't the slave decide to run away?

---

[51] Literally *yan bayi* means slave offspring.

A: No. People in the past did not handle slaves in that manner. Slaves were usually charmed as soon as they were bought. Hence, when a slave tried to escape, he goes westward, he sees that he has nowhere to go. If he goes south, he cannot go anywhere. So also northward, Allah will make his intellect to be of no use and as such he will not be able to go anywhere.

Q: Could someone buy as many slaves as he desired from the slave market?

A: One could buy as many as he could afford.

Q: Why is it that the Emir's slaves have three marks on their faces?

A: So as to distinguish them from other people's slaves.

Q: So these were given mainly to children of the royal slaves?

A: Yes, they were given to children of the royal slaves. Anyone born was given these marks right from birth, except if exempted.

Q: But can't the commoners give facial marks to their slaves just like the royal slaves?

A: They don't do that. Who have you seen doing that? They don't do that.

Q: Don't war captives have facial marks prior to their capture or prior to their introduction to the palace as slaves?

A: There were many people, both males and females, enslaved through capture. The Emir usually paired a male and female slave together for procreation. Just as sheep give birth, these slaves multiply in number. Marks were then usually made on the newly born children so that when they grow up they identify with this place.

Q: Does this apply to the royal slaves or to other slaves?

A: To the palace slaves.

Q: When someone wants to buy a slave, can the slave refuse and say "don't buy me?"

A: When someone wants to purchase a slave, he had to first draw the slave's attention to this fact. Specifically, a buyer shows interest by telling the slave dealer that "I want to buy this slave." The slave dealer will direct the potential buyer to the slave, and potential buyer will ask the slave "Do you like me?" If the answer is negative then the buyer will pass the slave and look for another.

Q: Can slaves purchase slaves?

A: What prevents a slave from having a slave? Didn't the Emir's slaves have slaves? The important slaves of the Emir also had slaves, but they were all also slaves. Both a slave and his slaves were all slaves, they were all the same.

Q: Was there any difference between how a town slave and a slave captured through warfare were sold?

A: No difference. Any slave owner who wanted to sell his slave simply took that slave to the market for disposal. It does not make a difference whether or not the slave owner was acquainted with the slave.

Q: At that time, were there many slave dealers?

A: There were not many. They traded from their houses.

Q: What is the meaning of *murgu*?

A: *Murgu*? Masters with many slaves sometime asked each of their slaves to pay them money in lieu of working personally, but not in shillings. Each slave was sometimes expected to bring cowries ranging from five to ten. Each slave submitted the amount daily to master in the evening.

Q: What sort of work did slaves do to earn money for such payment?

A: They did any work possible. They could either work for another person for a stipend, or cut grass or firewood for sale.

Q: What is the meaning of *bacucane*?

A: Someone born into slavery by slave parents. In the past, when a slave master was not in good mood, he could sell his *bacucane*.

Q: Was it possible for a slave to prevent his master from selling him?

A: If that was possible, that means no one can sell a slave if a slave was against the act. But that was not possible since it was the master who decided what to do with the slave. The slave is the master's property. Is it possible for a sheep to prevent its owner from selling it?

Q: What is the meaning of *dimajo*?[52]

A: That is the meaning, "he is our slave" or someone born into slavery by slave parents.

Q: What duties did slaves employed in the house perform?

A: Whatever job or work the master assigned was what they did. It was not possible for a slave to say that he will only do such and such work, since he belonged to the master. A slave did whatever the master wanted. The Emir's slaves worked tirelessly. Some were taken to the estates while some were given horses and houses, especially if they were trusted. Wasn't that the case? Some slaves were also involved in warfare. If such a person proved his bravery in the wilderness then he was made an important personality in the palace.

Q: That means that once you buy a slave, he does any type of duty for you, right?

A: He does. Commerce, farming, any type of work. Either he works in your house or you send him on an errand, anything. Haven't you heard of a Gwari who bought a slave and was sitting close to a calabash? Despite her closeness to that object, she still insisted that the slave must get up from where she was and bring the calabash, and in the process the calabash got broken. You see that was the end of her services.

Q: Was it possible for a slave to carry out business transactions on behalf of his master, and travel from one town to another in the process?

---

[52] *Dimajo* refers to someone born into slavery by slave parents.

A: It was possible, if he was trusted. Trusted slaves were treated like family members, hence they could go anywhere on behalf of the master.

Q: Who were the rich slaveholders who had plantations in Kano?

A: There was one Madaki Dan Bello who was the grandfather of the late Sarkin Dawaki.[53] He had a large number of slaves who searched for firewood every morning. They would all go westward and each person would return with a tied heap of firewood. They would do the same thing the next day, and they would stockpile a great heap of firewood which they used.

Q: But this person you mentioned is among the aristocrats.

A: Of course he was an aristocrat, but he was not exercising power here. Madaki Dan Bello was the son of the Emir of Dutse,[54] Dallau. The grand child was the one who brought him to stay, and he was not acting as the ruler. He stayed at San Kurmi and got educated. The ruler of San Kurmi commissioned him to make native cloths with stripes whenever an Arab died, and also to share inheritance. He refused to take up a royal position and even his son Sarkin Dawaki Na ta'alla accepted a position only after his death.

Q: Can you tell me something about Kundila? I heard that he also had slaves.

A: He had many slaves.

Q: What about Sharubutu?

A: Sharubutu is of the relatively recent past, and we were together with him. Sharubutu the father of Mallam Na Alhaji, I presume. He was wealthy and had slaves. He also had many children because of the large number of concubines he had. In fact his children were numerous to the extent that he did not know some of his children. As you are aware, the legal wives a Muslim can have is four. Well he did not know the number of his concubines. As such a child of his would come to the house, and he, Sharubutu, will ask: "Whose child is this?" He will be then be informed that "This child belongs to this house, he is from that lady."

Q: Who suffers more between a slave employed at home and a slave employed at a plantation?

A: A slave employed at an estate suffered more because he tilled the land. In fact, a slave could be transferred from the house to the estate as a form of punishment, especially when a master was not satisfied with the services he provided at home.

Q: But who normally owns an estate?

A: When a slave owner had many slaves, he could then acquire a large parcel of land and erect a big compound on the estate. All the male slaves together with their wives and children were then kept there. They farm for the master. Even if they don't farm for the master, they were still his slaves and the estate was his. All his slaves stay there.

---

[53] Chief or Ruler of Dawaki.
[54] Dutse was another Hausa state subject to the Sultan of Sokoto.

Q: Are you suggesting that rulers and wealthy individuals were those who had plantations?

A: They were. Apart from those here in Kano, there are royal estates in all the towns that you know of nearby. To the best of my knowledge, the largest was the Nasarawa estate, which has now been turned to a housing estate. In the past, the Emir usually had gunshots fired for seven days at the beginning of the rainy season. Then planting of grain crops would commence. The slaves and all those employed at the palace would take part in the planting on a daily basis for seven days after the first gunshot was fired. As you know, in the past no one planted until the royal guns have been shot, and the Emir goes out to the Nasarawa estate for planting. Thereafter, everyone could cultivate his own land. Everyone would then go and plant. Once the guns were shot and the Emir plants, then everyone knows that the rainy season had started.

Q: Was it normal to transfer slaves from one estate to another?

A: A person might be taken from the estate and brought to the palace if he was lucky. Isn't it luck for one to be brought and made part and parcel of the royalty? That is luck. If one was not lucky, would he get this? To be brought from the estate into royal household?

Q: Could a slave make use of his personal wealth to ensure his transfer to the city?

A: What I mean is that a slave could be singled out for his wisdom, and as such transferred to the palace.

Q: How were estates established and managed?

A: Once anyone acquired land, he could build houses there and acquired slaves to work there. The owner of the land runs the estate.

Q: Do slaves surrender all of the harvest to their master?

A: They do that because everything technically belonged to the master. Slaves usually gathered everything before the overseer informed the master about the harvest.

Q: Who managed an estate?

A: A slave like others. But one who has been found competent to control the slaves.

Q: What time do the slaves go out for work?

A: Once it is daybreak. That is when they go to work.

Q: What time of the day do they close altogether?

A: It depends on the instruction of the overseer. Would they close in the afternoon or work until nightfall? It all depended on the overseer since they are under his control.

Q: When the slave was asked to make payment in lieu of personal work, did he still do any other slave work for his master?

A: Making the payment was his only responsibility for the day. When it was daybreak, the slave was free to do whatever he could. In the evening, he was expected to make the day's payment of a fixed amount to the master.

Q: Just like paying tax?

A: Certainly. Whatever has been fixed for him, he brings every evening. That is *murgu*. Favor is from God. Sometimes he may not earn anything hence he will be left alone. If he didn't earn anything today, tomorrow he might.

Q: Will he be obliged to pay in the future what he couldn't pay previously?

A: He will have to pay later when he earns significantly, and especially if the master did not forgive the debt.

Q: What is the meaning of *humusi*?

A: This relates to war. For instance, after an expedition, everyone was expected to submit whatever they obtained as war booty, be it slaves, horses, or whatever. Following this, the Emir usually took his share from the material submitted by each individual while the rest was given back to the owner.

Q: Well, what is the meaning of *mudabar*?

A: *Mudabar*? A master may write a paper and give it to his slave indicating that "Whenever I die, show this piece of paper. When I die you become free. But as long as I am alive you are a slave." As such *Mudabar* was a written will given to a slave by his master indicating that once the master died the slave was freed.

Q: What was the slave's view or idea on slavery?

A: Slavery was never happily embraced. People were usually forced into bondage. Slaves disliked slavery. Does anyone like slavery?

Q: Certainly not. Well, did the slaves have the belief that if they were not slaves in this world, they will be in the hereafter?

A: They embraced that belief. Whether it is true or not, that was what people believed.

Q: Non-native slaves captured in war were brought to Kano and sold. Can we say that all slaves in Kano today were non-natives?

A: Some were non-natives from Damagaram while some were stolen. In the past, no matter your status, you could be stolen and sold into slavery. As such, a person captured in war was different, while a person stolen and sold into slavery was also different. However, the captured one had more prestige. The second one was caught without war while walking or traveling just like that. Will this one be equal with a person captured together with other people after the defeat of their town?

Q: The Emir of Zaria used to send them here to Kano for sale?

A: He used to send them here and everywhere.

Q: They were brought to Kano and sold?

A: Yes. Then the colonialists had conquered Kano. But the Emir of Zazzau persisted in selling slaves until the colonialists stopped him. Had it not been that slaves were sold during the early days of colonialism, I would not have known where they sold slaves, and how they sold slaves in Kano. During the early colonial period here, slaves were sold in the market.

Q: That is about seventy-two years now. Was it done secretly?

A: Openly, until the Europeans stopped it.

Q: That is true. But for example, did the Europeans seal up the market and stop people from selling?

A: Did the Europeans have to seal up the market? At that time if they ordered that something should not be done, was there anyone who would do it?

Q: When the Europeans abolished slavery, how did the slaves react?

A: Some were happy while some were angry and questioned the rationale behind it. The Europeans gave papers to many symbolizing their freedom, and that nobody should be called a slave. [They] gathered all slaves including the royal ones and gave them their paper of freedom. Yet after collecting the paper some of the slaves said: "What a useless statement, what business do we have with them." All the royal slaves were given such paper. Including their descendents. They were all given freedom papers by the colonialists.

Q: Is it possible for me to see such a paper?

A: This is impossible because no one around still has it.

Q: But the non-native slaves, didn't they go back to their towns?

A: Where will they go? Will a person go back into hardship? Isn't here, where they were slaves, better than their towns?

Q: The slaves' towns?

A: Yes. A person who was in a bad place and brought to the city where he ate what was good; he had no clothing before until he came here. Would you then say that such a person should go back to his town? Those who went back were those who knew that they would be better off if they went back. Coupled with the fact that they know their way back. But would a contented slave go back to his town? That is a joke.

SUGGESTED ADDITIONAL READINGS

Hamza, Ibrahim. "Slavery and Plantation Society at Dorayi in Kano Emirate," in *Slavery on the Frontiers of Islam.* Edited by P. E. Lovejoy. Princeton, NJ: Markus Wiener, 2004, 125–148.

Hill, Polly. "From Slavery to Freedom: The Case of Farm Slavery in Nigerian Hausaland," *Comparative Studies in Society and History* 18, 3 (1976): 395–426.

Population, Prosperity and Poverty: Rural Kano, 1900–1970. Cambridge: Cambridge University Press, 1977.

Hogendorn, J. S. and Lovejoy, Paul E. *Slow Death for Slavery: The Course of Abolition in Northern Nigeria, 1897–1936.* Cambridge: Cambridge University Press, 1993.

Nast, Heidi J. *Concubines and Power: Five Hundred Years in a Northern Nigerian Palace.* Minneapolis/London: University of Minnesota Press, 2005.

"Islam, Gender, and Slavery in West Africa circa 1500: A Spatial Archaeology of the Kano Palace, Northern Nigeria," *Annals of the Association of American Geographers* 86, 1 (1996): 44–77.

Philips, John Edward. "Slavery in Two Ribats in Kano and Sokoto," in *Slavery on the Frontiers of Islam*. Edited by P. E. Lovejoy. Princeton, NJ: Markus Wiener, 2004, 111–124.

Salau, Mohammed Bashir. "Ribats and the Development of Plantations in the Sokoto Caliphate: A Case Study of Fanisau," *Africa Economic History* 34 (2006): 23–43.

Stilwell, Sean. "'Amana' and 'Asiri': Royal Slave Culture and the Colonial Regime in Kano, 1903–1926," *Slavery and Abolition* 19, 2 (1998): 167–188.

"Culture, Kinship and Power: The Evolution of Royal Slavery in Nineteenth-Century Kano," *African Economic History* 27 (1999): 177–215.

Paradoxes of Power: The Kano "Mamluks" and Male Royal Slavery in the Sokoto Caliphate, 1804–1903. Portsmouth, NH: Heinemann, 2004.

"Power, Honour and Shame: The Ideology of Royal Slavery in the Sokoto Caliphate," *Africa* 70, 3 (2000): 394–421.

"The Power of Knowledge and the Knowledge of Power: Kinship, Community and Royal Slavery in Kano, 1807–1903," in *Elite Slavery in the Middle East and Africa: A Comparative Study*. Edited by Toru Miura and John Edward Philips. London: Kegan Paul, 2000, 117–158.

Stilwell, Sean, Hamza, Ibrahim, and Lovejoy, Paul. "The Oral History of Royal Slavery in Sokoto Caliphate: An Overview with Sallama Dako," *History in Africa* 28 (2001): 273–291.

PART TWO

THE VERBAL ARTS AND EVERYDAY OBJECTS

9

INTRODUCTION: Songs, Prayers, Proverbs, and Material Culture

Songs, prayers, proverbs, and the material cultures of Africa constitute an often over-looked source of information about slavery and the slave trade in Africa. More often than not, these repositories of information are considered to be of interest only to those who study present-day Africa. Closer scrutiny indicates, however, that they can also reveal a great deal about the past. Songs, prayers, proverbs, and material cultural practices often encapsulate – like few other sources – the very thoughts and memories of both the enslaved and the enslavers. The examples presented in the following chapters come from a variety of places: southern Somalia, eastern and western Nigeria, northwest Côte d'Ivoire, and southern Togo. In their range, they reveal the variety of ways different African peoples have remembered slavery and the slave trade. In their memorializing of the past, these sources also speak of a legacy that continues to live into the present.

SONGS AND PRAYERS

Songs about slavery and the slave trade are sung today in communities throughout Africa, even though both slavery and the slave trade were officially abolished more than a century ago. Their ongoing performance can be attributed to a number of factors, among them the power of the lyrics and the mesmerizing music that accompanies them, as well as their usefulness in recalling historical events and educating the youth about the past. They also serve to reinforce social identities and religious beliefs in ways that continue to be relevant for the present. Still they can be difficult to interpret. At times, the lyrics themselves are often cryptic, obscure in meaning. Lyrics about a lion attacking a community can be understood to be about such an event, or it can be interpreted as a reference to slave raiders descending upon a village. Which is correct? Only by knowing something about the history of the community where such a song is sung can one determine its possible meanings. Other songs (and prayers), however, can be more transparent. Some speak quite explicitly about slave raiders and the desire to wreak vengeance upon the attackers. Expressions of fear, anger, and defiance are clearly articulated along with the sorrow felt about the loss of family and friends. Together the song lyrics and prayers presented here by Francesca Declich, Jeanne Maddox Toungara, and E. S. D. Fomin reveal critical forms of memory found in many African communities, which can tell us a great deal about slavery, the slave trade, and the quest for freedom.

PROVERBS

Proverbs, like many songs, can defy easy analysis. They too are often obscure in meaning and can be subject to multiple interpretations. Those explored here by Olatunji Ojo, however, speak quite explicitly about slavery. They refer to the enslaved according to their condition. More importantly they focus not so much on the historical memories of former slaves as on the perspectives of their masters and society in general. They frequently admonish slaves to accept their status. They warn of the consequences of disobedience. They enshrine the social values that once underpinned the hierarchical relationship that existed between master and slave. That such values continue to influence contemporary social relations indicates the potential for proverbs to offer a window onto the past as well as the present.

MATERIAL CULTURE

If the study of proverbs, prayers, and songs is uncommon for understanding the history of slavery and the slave trade in Africa, an analysis of material culture is even more unusual. Artifacts made of perishable materials (wood, cloth, or clay) from the era of the slave trade have often not survived into present times. And when less perishable commodities do withstand the elements (iron shackles, for example), their individual stories are frequently lost. More revealing are those material objects that continue to be used today. Dana Rush describes how southern Togolese use particular material objects (cowries –also known as shell money – and murals, for example) to remember and commemorate the past. Images of what would otherwise look like ordinary bracelets and paintings to the uninformed eye obtain new meanings that allow us to understand how material cultures in Africa are used today to remember the slave past.

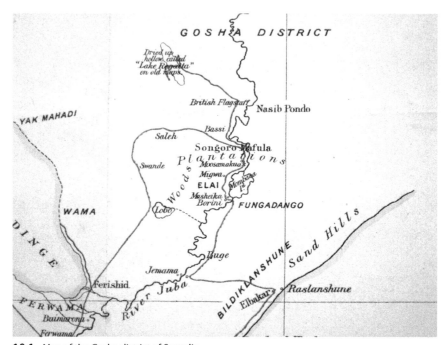

10.1. Map of the Gosha district of Somalia.

Source: C. H. Craufurd, map accompanying Geographical Report to the Marquess of Salisbury (13 July 1896) (ASMAI) Pos. 62/2.

Singing Songs and Performing Dances with Embedded Historical Meanings in Somalia

FRANCESCA DECLICH

In Southern Somalia, in the immediate hinterland of the Juba River, there exist several villages settled from the 1840s by descendants of slaves who had escaped from slavery.[1] These people claim their ancestors came from disparate areas in East Africa and were brought to Somalia as slaves. The earliest leaders referred to themselves as being Yao, Makua, Machinga, Massaninga, Mchenya, Makale, Mwera, Ngindo, Nyasa, Nyka, Nyamwesi, and Zigula. The Yao-speakers and their subgroups (among which the Machinga, Massaninga, Mchenya, Makale, and Mwera) came from areas broadly covering present-day northern Mozambique, southeastern Malawi, and southern Tanzania; Nyasa was the name of a region in present-day northern western Mozambique that borders Malawi and Zambia; in Tanganyika, this name was often used to refer to slaves coming from the south. The name "Nyka" is used in reference to different people from the hinterland (bush areas) of the Kenyan coast; the Nyamwesi is one of the ethnic groups of Tanzania, and Zigula is one of the major linguistic group in present-day Tanzania. The area where these escaped slaves gathered after emancipating themselves from slavery is called Gosha, meaning "the forest." In Gosha villages, the performance of ritual dances is a very important marker of identity, but they are also imbued with miracle-producing powers. For instance, secret celebrations held among elders in conjunction with the dances are believed either to treat people for infertility, to produce rain during a drought, or to prevent people from been killed on the battlefield. Knowledge of the wondrous aspects of ritual dances called *mviko* is inherited mostly through matrilineal ties, with each attached to one or another form of dance.[2] Through initiation, dancers are also introduced to the higher and/or hidden meanings of

[1] F. Declich, "'Gendered Narratives' among Zigula and Shanbara: Two Hundred Years along the Juba River," *History in Africa*, 22 (1995), 93–122; F. Declich, *I Bantu della Somalia. Etnogenesi e rituali 'mviko' nella Somalia Meridionale* (Milano, 2002); Cassanelli, "Bantu Former Slave Communities (Somali)," in I. Kopytoff (ed.), *The African Frontier: the Reproduction of Traditional African Societies* (Bloomington & Indianapolis, 1987); V. L. Grottanelli, "I Bantu del Giuba nelle tradizioni del Watzegua," in *Geographica Helvetica*, 8 (1953), 249–260; K. Menkhaus, "Rural Transformation and the Roots of Underdevelopment in Somalia's Lower Jubba Valley" (unpublished PhD thesis, University of South Carolina, 1989); O. Kersten, *Baron Claus von der Decken's Reisen in Ost-Afrika in den Johren 1862 bis 1865* (Leipzig, 1871).

[2] By matrilineal inheritance in this context I mean that the knowledge of the dance and its secrets are transmitted by the mother's relatives to the sons and daughter of such woman. Thereafter, the male children of

The research for this paper was made possible by financial support of the Italian National Research Council. I am grateful to Martin Klein and Sandra Greene for very valuable advice on the final version of this paper.

the dances, which often relate to the history of flight from slavery. Many such dances imply initiation into adulthood (right at the beginning of adolescence), which often coincides with initiation into the dance society. A period of segregation is established for a group of initiates; during that phase, among other teachings, they hear narratives of the escape from slavery and learn how people used to defend themselves from re-enslavement. The dances used to be performed on specific occasions, both to attract fortune and to celebrate special events. They were also done when people wanted to solicit forecasts of the future through divination and believed that it was important to please the ancestors through these dances as part of the process of divination. The performance of such dances could also be prompted by somebody's dream, whereby an ancestor could appear in a dream asking for the performance of such and such a dance.

In this chapter, I describe two of the dances: *massewé*, a dance performed by the descendants of the Yao of Malawi and northern Mozambique; and *mseve*, performed in villages of the Zigula speakers of Tanzania.

QUESTIONS TO CONSIDER

1. Was the *massewé* dance described in this article simply a leisure activity, or did it play further roles? Can you explain which ones?
2. How many audiences can you trace in the performance and songs of the *massewé* dance? How do the meanings of the song reach the audience?
3. Which historical meanings are embedded in the *mseve* dance and how were they conveyed?

MASSEWÈ AND THE YAO CHIEF MACHINGA

The *massewé mviko* dance is said to have been brought to the Gosha area by Nassib Bundo.[3] Today, only men dance the *massewé*. They wear skirts made of straw, decorated with *mbuji* (harness-bells) made of bamboo. The chests of the dancers are bare, and black lines and spots are traced on their breasts, shoulders, and faces. The words of the songs that accompany the dance are in the Yao language. Dance initiates taught not only the literal meanings of the songs texts, but also the relationship between drum rhythms and the meanings of the songs' words. In the past, the drum rhythms recalled the words of the songs sung by Nassib Bundo's warriors. They also conveyed messages on how to behave in battle. According to oral accounts, people in the old days used to bring a lion into the middle of the dancers and the dancers were to avoid the lion's attack by following the drum's advice. It is unclear whether or not this was a real lion or simply a mask representing a lion. But when masks representing animals have appeared in the villages, people tended to point at them as if they were actual wild animals to be feared. One informant insisted that he had

---

a family will not transmit this cultural inheritance to their children, unlike their sisters who are the repositories of the tradition. They will, instead, convey such traditions to the children of their sisters. When a *mviko* dance performance is requested, only the descendants from the mother's side are compelled to participate.

[3] Nassib Bundo died in an Italian prison in 1906 after leading a resistance against the Italians. Around 1891, he was allied with the Somali Tunni of Brava town and protected Brava from attacks of a number of Somali clans by controlling Gosha as a buffer zone. He is reported to have sent emissaries to estates in the hinterland of Brava to convince slaves to escape to the freed slave villages of Gosha.

NASIB BUNDA, CAPO DI GOSCIA.

10.2. Photo of Nassib Bundo, c.1903.
Source: Ugo Ferrandi, *Lugh: Emporio commerciale sul Giuba* (Roma: Società Geografica Italiana).

seen in this dance real lions that had been drugged. The lion's presence was also a meta-phor for one's enemies. The dancers were to learn through the song's words how to behave in front of their enemies. Performances involving lions at initiations among Yao, according to a Mozambican Yao linguist from Lichinga, typically convey advice to the youth to dis-trust humans more than wild animals. Wild animals can be managed but humans may turn back against you at any time.[4]

The rhythms of this specific song could order a group of dancers to take their machetes and be ready to attack the enemy or to be ready to proceed in a queue so as to move in an orderly fashion to another location. In addition to defense purposes, *massewé* was also performed as a *mviko* dance, a ceremonial dance that could produce miraculous events.

Chingangana chakulenje	We must play the drums well
Masimba gaga nkenei	The lion has arrived inside
Walanganani chepanga	You must be separated from one another
Walanganani ma samba	Separated from the lion
Kaulenji wandu	People must stand one by one [in a queue]

By 1986, only initiated people knew the meanings of the words of the *massewé* songs. People complained that some of the best dancers had died and that young ones were not yet ready to replace them. Moreover, they believed that if too many attendees did not believe in the miraculous implications of the *massewé* dance, it could lose its magical pow-ers. This sentiment should be understood as an expressed form of powerlessness. Many in the Gosha area had expected to be freed from the stigma of slave descent after Somalia's independence and with the socialist revolution of 1969. Yet this had not happened. Instead, especially in the 1980s, the years that preceded the Somali civil war that began

---

[4] I thank the young Yao linguist, Cubilas Messope, for this insight given during a conversation held in 2011.

in 1990, Gosha people felt that their subjection to the despotic Somali government was a new slavery.[5] Young people from the area were kidnapped and sent by force with the army to the north. Some parents completely lost contact with their children. Often the news of their death was not even conveyed to their families. Gone were the golden days in which the villages of the slave descendants, then headed by Nassib Bundo, had defended themselves from Somali slave owners and even protected the population in nearby Brava from Somali raids.[6] When the *massewé* dance was performed in the village of Mareerey in 1987, the dancers were so emotionally moved, one even cried while dancing. Villagers pointed out that one dancer had been brought to tears after remembering some dancers who had recently died. The dance was then stopped by some Somali soldiers to avoid an outbreak of violence. The memory of the old victory over Somali slavers symbolically reenacted by the *massewé* dance and the present condition of submission to the despotic government of Syaad Barre, as well as the visible arrogance of his policemen, together had created an emotional context that could indeed have led to a brawl.

This particular song refers to historical events. The text of the song recalls memories among the people who listen and/or sing them when there is a performance. This remembering is encouraged by the intertwining of the song text with the learning of the dances and rhythms within the context of initiation rituals. Its continued performance fosters knowledge among the youth about historical events that are important to their own identities.

THE *MSEVE* AND THE FLIGHT FROM SLAVERY OF THE ZIGULA

Another dance performed by the Zigula subgroup in Gosha is the *mseve*. It celebrates their escape from slavery. There are a number of different stories about their enslavement and escape,[7] but the main narrative goes as follows. The Zigula had been promised jobs along the Somali coast and only on their arrival did they find out that they had been enslaved. They immediately began to devise ways to escape. To organize their flight from Tumba (metaphoric name of the place where they were enslaved), they started going to the bush where they prepared and hid bows and arrows. They also cast spells, performed special protective dances, and began singing in their native tongue to inform their people that they were preparing to flee. The leader was the prophetess Wanankhucha, who was accompanied according to different versions either by Mze Migwa and/or by the warrior Majendero. On their journey to freedom, the Zigula arrived in the Gol area – the forest on the Juba River. At some point the warrior Majendero was killed by the Boon, the hunters in the area. Thereafter Wanankhucha performed a sacrificial celebration, killing a wild fowl. The land began to tremble, and she forecast that the Zigula had arrived in the right place to settle. They then resolved to stay. Some Zigula wanted to go further to reach their country of origin, but they were stopped by the outbreak of an epidemic. Their stay in Gosha was not easy. They had to fence their villages to defend themselves from attack. They also fought a number of wars (recalled sometimes as the seven wars) to defend themselves from the surrounding people and to acquire land.[8]

[5] F. Declich, "Can Boundaries Not Border on One Another?' in M. Hohne and D. Feyissa (eds.), *Divided They Stand: The Affordances of State Borders in the Horn of Africa* (London, 2010), 170.
[6] U. Ferrandi, "Diario: viaggio nelle regioni del Giuba," in *L'Esploratore Commerciale*, vii, V (1892), 140.
[7] F. Declich, "'Gendered Narratives' among Zigula"; F. Declich, *I Bantu della Somalia*, 231.
[8] The number seven, however, is a sort of stereotypical perfect number in local narrations, and one can see from the many stories that, in reality, more than seven wars were fought by the Zigula.

According to the Zigula elders, the *mseve* was performed in preparation for battles against the ex-masters who wanted to re-enslave them. The words of the song were designed to encourage the warriors before they went into battle. The entire *mseve* addresses the preparation for battle and involves a number of spells, called *mphande*, which were to protect the warriors during the conflict. Today *mphande* can be found in the *mbuji*, the bells that dancers wear on their ankles. In the past, warriors are said to have worn these in battles because enemies were bewitched upon seeing them. The first documentary reference to *mseve* appeared in the 1934 Handeni District Book.[9] According to this record, a Zigula man from Kisimayo, Abdallah bin Simba, spoke of the *mseve* as a dance the Somali Zigula performed to prepare themselves for their flight from slave villages in the hinterland of the Benaadir coast. This suggests that the *mseve* was perhaps one of the most important dances of the Zigula. In 1988, however, during my fieldwork, the *mseve* was not performed as often as other dances, but was staged when it was deemed necessary to invoke the ancestors so they could help address the problems that troubled the entire community: serious disputes, quarrels with the government, droughts, or illnesses.

Many *mseve* songs recall the Zigula's escape from captivity (metaphorically named Tumba). Tumba, however, not only indicates a geographical area often associated with coconut trees and the coast, but also means captivity in general.

Mnazi ugua Tumba	The coconut tree of Tumba has fallen down
Chirangiro ugua oh mame	It has fallen where we were, oh mother
Nazagavirapo kuamdame	Let us leave the things in Mdame
Mphongesi nkhondo chuia[10]	We are safe, we come back from the war

The oral sources that speak of the route followed by the Zigula during their journey from the hinterland mention Mdame, the first site where the Zigula settled after escaping from slavery. The song starts with a metaphor: "The coconut tree of Tumba has fallen down." This means that the slaves escaped from Tumba, which had plenty of coconut trees. The war had started, but the people were now safe in Mdame where they could settle peacefully.

A number of songs of the *mseve* also celebrate the fact of having acquired freedom. The contents of the following song speak of a desire for Zigula independence while they were captives. It also expresses a scornful attitude toward their masters. "Closing the door," in addition to being the metaphor of having left slavery, may also refer symbolically to a geographical location at the entrance of the Gosha area. One toponym along the Juba River, up north from the town of Jamaame (later called Margherita by the Italians) in three old maps dating to the turn of the twentieth century, was called *fungalango*,[11] *fungatango*, or *fungadango*,[12] meaning "close the door," and was considered the door of Gosha.[13]

---

[9] District Books were records of events compiled by the administrative officers in the districts of Tanganyika. Such books reported data and news considered relevant in a specific year. Among news concerning the district, the Handeni District Book of 1934 reports a Somali Zigula, Abdallah Bin Simba, who visited the Handeni district in the 1930s, having travelled from the Gosha area of Somalia to Handeni, a district capital of Tanganyika, seeking the origins of his ancestors.

[10] F. Declich, Fieldnotes, 1988, p/sto: 121.

[11] Enrico Perducchi, Map as of December 30, 1901, "Dal rilievo fatto a bordo della pirobarca inglese 'Geraldine' 20 settembre – 7 ottobre 1901," Historical Archive of the Ministry of Italian Africa (ASMAI) Pos. 68/1.

[12] C. H. Craufurd, Map Accompanying Geographical Report to the Marquess of Salisbury, July 13, 1896, (ASMAI), Pos. 68/1.

[13] C. H. Craufurd, to the Marquess of Salisbury, Mombasa, July 13, 1896, 5, (ASMAI), Pos. 68/1.

Fundi kuaheri	Fundi (master), goodbye
kamakutuma kusokera, djero	I am tired of receiving orders, today
nakugamba kuaheri, funga mnango	I am telling you goodbye, close the door

The last song speaks of the man Muia, who was working as a slave, looking after cattle. He decided to escape because of the nostalgia he had for the time when he was free. The song also indicates that a number of Zigula people were employed as cattle herders. People who lived in the towns and villages in Somalia used to give their cattle to be herded by others who lived in a better environment for the animals. As reported by Cerulli,[14] nomadic people often entrusted the pasturing of their cattle to individuals who had become their clients by being captured in raids. The song tells us that the Zigula may have become clients of nomadic people or that they may have been given the task of pasturing animals by people who were settled in the towns and villages. Oral records suggest that this song was sung often when the Zigula came together after escaping from slavery. It fostered feelings of mutual satisfaction for having achieved the freedom they very much regretted having once lost.

Muia Muia	Muia Muia
Kalekerezi ngombe	Leaving the cows
Akaira lungole	Because you regretted much the freedom

CONCLUSION

Embedded in the songs of the descendants of slaves are memories of historical events and information about the socioeconomic conditions and status of the slaves. Analysis of the songs, however, is dependent on also having an understanding of the cultural and historical contexts of their production and performance. The more we know, the more we can unearth the hidden meanings in the songs. I have discussed in this essay those songs that seem related to slavery.[15] The very existence of group dances performed in languages from far-away countries is evidence of the many areas from which the slaves who escaped to Gosha originally came. *Mseve* is a dance used by the Zigula to aid their flight from slavery. The lyrics are directly related to this flight. *Massewé*, by contrast, is a war dance and also an initiation ceremony. Dances called *massewé* exist in Mozambique, in Malawi, and in Tanzania, although further comparative studies are needed. In Somalia, *massewé* songs with embedded historical meanings are played together with other chants that are designed to teach the young. The very fact that the *massewé* songs are loaded with historical meanings shows how important dances were as a form for training and communication, as well as for the reproduction of memories in this area.

SUGGESTED ADDITIONAL READINGS

Abdallah, Y. *The Yaos Chiikala cha Wayao*, arranged, edited, and translated by Meridith Sanderson. London: Cass, 1973.

---

[14] E. Cerulli, *Somalia. Storia della Somalia, l'Islam in Somalia, il libro degli Zengi*, vol. 1 (Roma: 1957), 67.

[15] The fieldwork was carried out in 1985–1986, 1987, and 1988 in the Gosha area, first in the village of Mareerey and later in the one of Mugambo, both on the Juba River. Of course, during that period many other locations and villages were visited.

Alpers, Edward. "Trade, State, and Society among the Yao in Nineteenth Century," *The Journal of African History* 10, 3 (1969): 405–420.

ARPAC. *As dinastias dos Matakas*. Maputo: ARPAC, 2004.

Beidelman, T.O. *The Matrilineal People of Eastern Tanzania (Zaramo, Luguru, Kaguru, Ngulu, etc.)*. London: International African Institute, 1967.

Declich, Francesca. "'Gendered Narratives', History, and Identity: Two Centuries along the Juba River among the Zigula and Shanbara," *History in Africa* 22 (1995): 93–122.

"Dynamics of Intermingling Gender and Slavery in Somalia at the Turn of the Twentieth Century," *Northeast African Studies* 10, 3 (2003): 45–69.

Fair, Laura. *Pastimes and Politics: Culture, Community, and Identity in Post-Abolition Urban Zanzibar, 1890–1945*. Athens: Ohio University Press, 2001.

Ferrandi, Ugo. *Lugh. Emporio Commerciale sul Giuba*. Roma: Società Geografica Italiana, 1903.

Freeman-Grenville, G. S. P. *The East African Coast: Select Documents from the First to the Earlier Nineteenth Century*. London: Rex Collings, 1975.

Kratz, Corinne. *Affecting Performances*. Washington, DC: Smithsonian Museum Institution, 1994.

Pender-Cudlip P. "Oral Traditions and Anthropological Analysis: Some Contemporary Myths," *Azania* 7 (1972): 3–24.

Ranger, Terence O. *Dance and Society in Eastern Africa, 1890–1970: The Beni Ngoma*. Oxford: Clarendon Press, 1975.

Shaw, Rosalind. *Memories of the Slave Trade: Ritual and the Historical Imagination in Sierra Leone*. Chicago and London: University of Chicago Press, 2002.

Stroebel, Margaret. *Muslim Women in Mombasa, Kenya, 1890–1973*. London and New Haven, CT: Yale University Press, 1975.

Vansina, Jan. *Oral Tradition as History*. London: James Currey, 1985.

Williams, Drid. *Anthropology and the Dance. Ten Lectures*. Urbana and Chicago: University of Illinois Press, 2004.

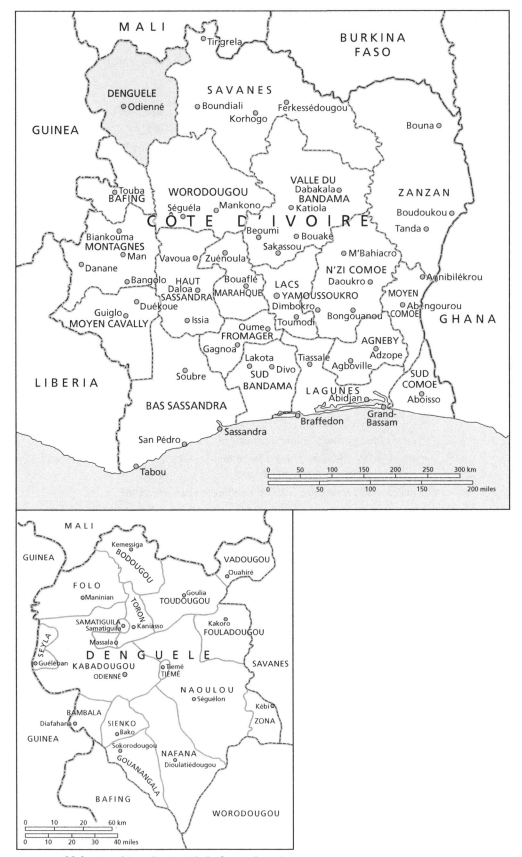

11.1. Map of Cote d'Ivoire with the featured province.

Source: http://www.nationslonline.org/oneworld/map/cote-divoire-admin.

Song Lyrics as Pathways to Historical Interpretation in Northwestern Côte d'Ivoire

The Case of Kabasarana

JEANNE MADDOX TOUNGARA

This chapter examines the use of song lyrics as a supplement to oral traditions often used in the reconstruction of African history.[1] Oral traditions form an important element in the corpus of resources used to infuse the historical record with the multi-layered voices of complex societies. Consequently, they may serve to empower those who otherwise might be perceived as peoples "without history."[2] Sometimes, written sources may be so scarce that the historian must rely on oral narratives to provide the dominant storyline as well as alternative interpretation of times past. In fact, written sources on northwestern Côte d'Ivoire before the French occupation in 1898 (following the conquest of the West African empire of Samori Toure) are somewhat scarce, limited to a brief references in military reports and a few missives from the wandering nineteenth-century explorer, René Caillié.[3] The Mande-speaking peoples of the western Sudan are known for their bards, aka *griots*, whose principle task is to broadcast "state" versions of history that portray their kings in a positive light.[4] Yet, these highly visible and skilled professionals are not the only sources of oral narratives. The historian must seek to balance the *griots*' versions of history with input from other members of society whose versions may carry a different perspective.

While searching for information on the founding of Kabasarana (ca. 1848), I discovered song lyrics that led to new insights into the highly stratified nineteenth-century Malinke society, making it possible to explore relations that might escape the "state" narratives broadcast by bards. After all, the bards were customarily dependents of the ruling lineage and handsomely rewarded for their ability to shape the historical record in favor of

---

[1] The songs presented here were included in a paper given at a conference on "Finding the African Voice: Narratives of Slavery and Enslavement" in Bellagio, Italy, in 2007. I am grateful to the organizers for providing an opportunity to examine this perspective and for their commentary on this work, particularly Alice Bellagamba.

[2] Eric Wolf, *Europe and the People without History* (Berkeley and Los Angeles, 1982).

[3] Louis Binger, *Du Niger au Golfe de Guinée par le pays de Kong et le Mossi (1887–1889)*, 2 vols. (Paris, 1892); René Caillié, Journal d'un v*oyage `a Tombouctou et a Jenné*, 2 vols. (Paris, 1830).

[4] The term "Mande" is a linguistic classification used interchangeably with "Manding" to include peoples whose ancestry emerged within a broad swath of territory from Senegambia eastward to the Volta River and from the western Sahel southward to the forest fringe. They are divided into several subgroups whose histories and geographical dispersions have resulted in distinct identities. The peoples of Kabarasana in northwestern Côte d'Ivoire refer to themselves as Maninka, Malinke, and so on – descendants of Manden, the heartland of old Mali and speakers of Mande.

their patrons. The song lyrics that originated among subordinate groups sometimes defied representations of ruling-class largesse. They allowed the researcher, as an outsider, to become more familiar with the "worldview" of the Malinke. Jan Vansina noted the challenge for outsiders seeking to understand worldviews, noting:

> Worldview is a representation of ultimate reality in all its aspects visible and invisible. It includes views about the creation of the world, about the kinds of beings that are in it and their taxonomies, on its layout, and on its functioning.... Everyone knows them and the main principles are not often talked about, precisely for this reason. It will therefore be difficult for the outsiders to discover the impact of worldviews on messages because knowledge of them is supposedly known. The first question is to know how an outsider can discover a worldview.[5]

The oral traditions and song lyrics that I collected among the Malinke peoples in several districts of northwestern Côte d'Ivoire in the 1980s and 1990s shed light on relations between masters and subordinate classes in Kabasarana from its formation, circa 1848 to the liberation of captives during the first decade of the twentieth century. The lyrics were rich with revelations about the negotiated terrain of power and authority between rulers and the vanquished. Passed along from generation to generation, the lyrics provided a pathway to understanding the Malinke worldview of social stratification, power, and subordination.

BACKGROUND

I pieced together the master narrative or principle storyline about Kabasarana from interviews with clan heads, village chiefs, and bards (*jeliw*) throughout the fifteen provinces that made up the original state. The interviews were usually carried out in the presence of family members, friends, and neighbors who benefited from the opportunity to hear the history again and bore witness to the veracity of the testimony. Basically, the formation of Kabasarana had followed prescribed patterns of migration, settlement, conflict, and reintegration familiar to most members of the Manding communities of the western savannas. Kabasarana (named after the founder's mother – Saran Kaba) was founded by Vakaba Toure, a member of a Muslim patrilineage based in Dia (Mali) renowned for its role in the expansion of Islam. Vakaba Toure replicated political and socioeconomic relationships based on a deep understanding of both Islamic and Manding ideologies of statehood and social relations.[6] He extended Toure Muslim hegemony over a region of the Manding frontier largely populated by non-Muslims – both Senufo and unconverted Mande peoples. The formation of Kabasarana was a continuation of Muslim Manding political dominance moving south from the Sahel in search of trading activities and opportunities to study or expand *dar-al-islam* – the land of peace, or Muslim-occupied territory. After Vakaba's death, weaknesses emerged in the articulation of elite functions and led to internal dissension. Toure rule was continuously challenged by emerging leaders who tried to regain control of their provinces. To avoid total destruction, the Toure rulers (descendants of Vakaba) yielded to Samori's invitation to join his conquest of territories eastward, away

---

[5] Jan Vansina, *Oral Tradition as History* (Madison, 1985), p. 133.
[6] Igor Kopytoff, *The African Frontier: The Reproduction of Traditional African Societies* (Bloomington, 1987). The introduction explains how the proliferation of political and cultural practices carried from the homeland through migration results in continuities with frontier societies.

from the path of French occupation. Kabasarana was absorbed in its entirety as an ally (ca. 1881); the warrior elite and enslaved cavalry (*sofaw*)[7] fought with the Samorian forces as they advanced toward the Gold Coast. The Samorian empire had the same ideological foundations and philosophical underpinnings as Kabasarana because they shared a common ethnic origin, patronymic affiliation, and commercial interests. It was dismantled by the French colonial occupation after the Samori's 1898 capture and exile. The French reduced Kabasarana's territorial reach (more than fifteen provinces) to a simple administrative canton (Kabadugu) composed of the villages surrounding the capital Odienne, and restored the leadership of the provinces (*kafuw*) that Vakaba and his armies had defeated to descendants of their founding families. These provinces became separate administrative cantons of the colony of Côte d'Ivoire.

Many of the political alliances Vakaba Toure established were predetermined based on notions of patronymic affiliation, occupational status, and class that spread southward from the Manding heartland along with the people who migrated to seek their fortunes in new territories where they could establish hegemony as firstcomers. The song lyrics collected from descendants of those persons who participated in the formation and defense of the state reveal a highly negotiated terrain that engaged a great deal of interdependence among the castes and classes of people involved. Malinke kin groups were organized by lineages based on patronymic affiliation. Status was determined by class (slave – *Jon* or freeborn – *horon*), religion (Muslim clerics), and identity as members of endogamous occupational castes (*nyamakalaw*), composed of ironworkers (*numuw*), leatherworkers (*garankew*), and praise singers or bards (*jeliw* and *fune*). The wars of conquest severely affected the territorial integrity of their original settlements as thousands of people (both Malinke and Senufo) were displaced by war and enslaved. Several large clans of freeborn farmers were enslaved on their own lands and inhabitants of caste villages of ironworkers or leatherworkers were forced to serve under caste groups loyal to the Toure.[8]

The emergence of the state reflected Toure prowess in dominating people and resources. In the formation of Kabasarana, Vakaba Toure conquered several disparate communities situated in an intermediary zone between major poles of production (salt from the Sahara, kola from the forest zone, and cattle raised in the grasslands of the savannas). Toure warlords amassed hordes of captives from conquered provinces and dispatched them to designated "crown" villages where they farmed to provide food for the Toure and their dependents, warriors, and other slaves. From these resources, the Toure redistributed wealth, rewarded allies, and exercised their influence over the region. After the formation of the state, Vakaba and his descendants forged a regional economy from a variety of preexisting and recognized forms of exploitation, such as tribute, slavery, and long-distance trade. The Toure dynasty exacted tribute from sedentary farmers in the form of agricultural surplus, delegated imams to collect prescribed Islamic offerings, and enlisted lieutenants to levy taxes on commerce. They benefited from the activities of professional Muslim traders, the *julaw*, who supplied firearms, slaves, and prestige items for the defense and

---

[7] In the Mande language, *sofa* is literally the father or master (*fa*) of the horse (*so*). Slave armies played a significant role in state formation in the western Sahel. Many captured warriors were made to fight as mounted cavalry on behalf of their new masters.

[8] Women of the ironworker caste engaged in pottery-making. Leatherworkers also serve as bards. The *funew* devote themselves strictly to Islamic performances, such as chanting of verses from the Koran.

support of the ruling class.[9] Toure rulers established a network of markets and redirected trade routes to ensure the prosperity of religious and commercial elites. Markets thrived and Muslim clerics lived from production of slaves the Toure made available to them. The song lyrics composed during this period assist in articulating the dynamics of hegemony and subordination. The songs reveal the voices of the vanquished and provide vital clues for understanding social relations between masters and slaves.

As I began collecting oral narratives of family and state histories, I discovered that an intricate web of social relations existed within the established narratives. The lyrics helped by shedding light on Mande endogenous knowledge, values, and ideologies and revealing aspects of the norms and mores undergirding the society. Interestingly, the search for song lyrics provided an opportunity for more women to participate in the storytelling, because the informants' female ancestors had composed and performed several songs in the past, both formally and informally, as entertainment, on ceremonial occasions, as accompaniment at work, and on the battlefields to encourage warriors toward victory. Each category of performers had its own repertoire of songs acceptable for its rank and social standing. The three examples that follow are from a bard, a slave warrior, and a slave born in captivity.

QUESTIONS TO CONSIDER

1. What can we learn about hegemony and subordination from the song lyrics?
2. Can song lyrics help fill in the history with the voices of the vanquished?
3. Do the lyrics explain social relations and sensitivities between the classes?
4. Could the lyrics influence the behavior of masters toward slaves, and vice versa?
5. Would you describe Mande social relations as fixed or fluid? Why?
6. What is the role of song lyrics in releasing tensions in social hierarchies?

1. Big Millet

Nabounou Diabate (May 1992), a female bard (*jeli*) of about sixty years of age from a clan affiliated with the Toure, performed a song about millet as a food given to slaves, which reflected the social hierarchy. Mande rulers were highly concerned about public oral recitations that would eventually communicate their legacies to their progeny, and the Toure were no exception. Vakaba Toure's designated praise singers, the Diabate clan, established a viable and lasting legacy for him and his lineage. The Diabate are members of the Toure *kabila*, a neighborhood of family relations and affiliated clans. They arrived with Vakaba as the ruler's official bards and assisted him and his descendants in their wars of conquest. Women of this Diabate clan are attached to Toure women on ceremonial occasions and also defend the interests of the Toure rulers' legacy. They helped dynastic rulers carefully preserve the perceived notions of superiority, obligation, and subordination between themselves and their subjects. The *jeliw*, *griots*, or bards entrusted with the safekeeping of hegemonic traditions through wisely crafted public demonstrations, songs, and recitations were essential players in this process. The very existence of *jeliw* illustrates the importance of song lyrics and speech in Manding communities. This clan was dedicated

---

[9]   Person, in *Samori une révolution dyula (Nimes, 1968–75)*, suggests that the long-distance traders played a central role in transforming the geopolitical configuration of the western Sahel from non-Muslim to Muslim domination.

to music, merrymaking, and public discourse. Nabounou Diabate learned this song from her grandmother.

The *sofaw* were captives who fought on behalf of the *horonw* – the freeborn farmers and other noncaste groups – the class from which rulers emerged. The slave warriors lived apart from the freeborn in their own camps known as crown villages. Several provinces (*kafuw*) were nearly wiped out by the Toure wars of expansion. One of the largest districts, the Nafana had boasted 177 villages that by the time of French colonialism had been reduced to 15 villages. At Noolo, the Kone warlords conquered peoples in surrounding areas (mostly Senufo, but not their own people) and forced them to drink *dege*, a millet drink that conquered communities were forced to consume. The lyrics confirm the practice used to humiliate captives. They establish the legitimacy of rulers and illustrate disdain masters held for their captives even though they were called upon to defend the state.

> *Big millet, big millet, big millet*
> *Millet is not a food for horonw*
> *Go give it to the sofaw*
> *Millet is not a food for horonw*

2. Slave Warriors' Bravado

Ahmadou Doumbia (January 1992), an elder of the blacksmith caste, offered the song lyrics that follow in response to my inquiry about the wars of Kabasarana. According to Doumbia, the vanquished were enslaved and their territories (*jamanaw*) subjected to pillage. The expansion of slaveholding was essential to the functioning of the ruling class and its clients, the freeborn militiamen. This freeborn warrior class relied on the slave warriors to reproduce themselves through warfare – the incorporation of new captives into the ranks of *sofaw*. Slave warriors strived not only to survive their battles and Toure domination after the destruction of their villages; however, in some instances they found opportunities to improve their ranking within slavery. Although masters held authority over the life or death of a captive (a captive could be executed or sold at any time), they understood that their success or failure during warfare rested with the prowess of their fighting forces, including the captives.

These song lyrics, reflecting the interdependence between the enslaved and the master, the ruler and the ruled, were originally performed by the renowned *sofa*, Sogona-Koma (aka Tchekoma), and his flute-playing companions, likely *komo* association initiates, the secret society of blacksmiths. Once again, evidence of interdependence between slave and free becomes apparent when African voices are allowed to tell their own story. This highly venerated *sofa* was "invulnerable," meaning that neither knives nor bullets could pierce his flesh. Women fabricated many of the protective objects and ointments that warriors applied to make their bodies impenetrable to bullets or knives. In addition, Sogona-Koma wore a special comb underneath a braided crown of hair. This coif identifies him as a *soma*, a sorcerer of the blacksmith clan who exercised extreme powers and rose to greatness, as indicated in the lyrics that follow, because his memory has been preserved.[10] Such

---

[10] Patrick McNaughton, *Mande Blacksmiths: Knowledge, Power and Art in West Africa*. (Bloomington, 1993), p. 49. "The [*komo*] cult gives smiths great political clout, because it is extremely influential spiritually, and political leaders cannot be successful without spiritual alliances"; p. 130.

men were stoned to death in the battlefield because they could not be killed by any other means. Sogona-Koma was also burned and his ashes were used to make healing ointments in order to extend the benefits of his supernatural powers. The lyrics to his song reveal a daring attitude toward the Toure rulers who could have benefited more if Sogona-Koma had lived and continued in his role as a valiant warrior and collaborator than if they had executed him for his bravado. It appears that conquest and enslavement did not reduce all captives to the same element.

> *If the warrior is attacked*
> *Isn't Vakaba likely to be attacked as well?*
>
> *The warrior stands between Vakaba*
> *And the war!*
>
> ---------------------------------------
>
> *Tchekoma says we go hand-in-hand*
> *If someone like him is not there,*
> *The freeborn becomes a slave!*
>
> *Sogona-Koma says we go hand-in-hand.*
> *The day he is no longer,*
> *The freeborn becomes a slave.*

3. Pity, Fear, and Revenge

Maaba Doumbia (January 1992), a woman in her mid-fifties, told of her *woloso* status and revealed some very important issues about this category of captive born to an enslaved mother in the custody of a master. This slave evokes pity because she has no home to remember. These types of slaves, specifically the *wolosow*, composed and performed a genre of music that reflected their status in society and their relationship with their masters. They supposedly knew no shame and benefited from the largesse of the master on ceremonial occasions. Warfare resulted in poverty, displacement, and isolation on occasion causing some individuals to relinquish their independent status voluntarily in return for the security of enslavement by a benevolent master. Maaba Doumbia's father, who descended from a blacksmith clan, was impoverished during the colonial period and voluntarily submitted himself as a slave to the Toure. He then acted out behaviors in keeping with his diminished status (e.g., he swore to never eat from the same dish as a *horon* again).

Maaba followed the traditions set in motion by her father and thus continued to perform *wolosow* dances and exercised the privileges (and pain) of her status below the *horonw*. If the *woloso* did not get her way with the master, she insulted or cursed the master by exposing her buttocks or genitals in public. Masters moved quickly to satisfy when the *wolosow* were nearby, giving money or gifts to move them out of the way. Maaba's song about a gazelle (*sinzin*) and its power (*nyama*) illustrates Manding sensitivities to the weak, including the lowest class, and the injustices heaped upon them. This small, graceful animal is a symbol for the weak and the infirm. Yet, its inner strength (often malevolent power) can overcome the most adept hunter, leaving him sickened or dead if he is not well prepared (metaphysically) to kill the gazelle. The song reveals the capacity of the weak and most compromised individuals – usually captives and orphans – to overcome rulers and masters through highly charged symbolic acts that could ruin or kill a miserly, selfish *horon*. The song calls out the names of several well-known rulers and commemorates their demise. Maaba delegates occult power and the capacity for revenge to her mother, father, and Fakoli who is the ancestral clan patriarch for all blacksmiths.[11]

> *"Sinzin Nyama"*
>
> *I say, that sinzin power, the power is in it.*
> *Oh mother!*
> *Oh, mother, is the power in you?*
> *I say, good mother, is the power in you?*
> *Big-headed Fakoli, is the power in you?*
> *Eh! My father, the power is in you.*
> *Big-headed Fakoli, is the power in you?*
> *Kenife-Moktar, the power got him.*
> *Zacharia, the power got him.*
> *Malonden-Sori, the power got him.*
> *Siran-Siridi Toure, the power got him.*
> *Kemissaden Karanmogo, the power got him.*
> *The sinzin power, I say, sinzin power,*
> *The power!*
> *The sinzin power, I say, the sinzin power*
> *The power!*

A second song about merrymaking indicates Maaba's acceptance of her birthright as a member of the blacksmith clan. Her clan in particular was charged with managing occult powers, sorcery, and excision ceremonies. She did not practice pottery-making. Notice the sense of fulfillment and pride in carrying out the prescribed roles both as a service to the community and in respect for one's ancestry.

> *"Nyangan Nyangan"*
>
> *We, the laughing stock, are the village clowns!*
> *I say, we are the clowns!*
> *We clowns bring out the merrymaking in the village.*
> *Village clowns are here,*
> *Fakoli (blacksmiths) are the town clowns!*
> *Giant Fakoli is the village clown.*
> *Eh! Merrymaking in the village,*
> *Fakoli brings out the merrymaking!*

The songs of Kabasarana reveal aspects of the tensions between the freeborn, the enslaved, and the caste members of society. Each had scripted roles that were reinforced by the song lyrics created, performed, heard and repeated, throughout time.

---

[11] Fakoli is credited with the bringing mystical powers to Manden. He is prominent in the Sunjata epic as an important general and confidant who plays an essential role in the preservation of Manden and the authority of *horonw* (freeborn) over endogamous castes and slaves. His supposed dwarf-like body and big head make him the laughingstock at social gatherings. David Conrad, "Oral Traditions and Perceptions of History," in Emmanuel Akyeampong, *Themes in West Africa's History* (Athens, 2006), pp. 87–91.

SUGGESTED ADDITIONAL READINGS

HISTORY OF NORTHWESTERN IVORY COAST

Person, Yves. "States and Peoples of Senegambia and Upper Guinea," in J. F. Ade Ajayi, ed., *General History of Africa - 19th c. - 1880s, Vol. VI.* New York: UNESCO, 1989, 636–661.

HIERARCHY IN THE MANDE WORLD

Conrad, David. *Sunjata: A West Africa Epic of the Mande People.* Indianapolis, IN: Hackett Publishing Company, 2004.

Conrad, David and Barbara Frank, eds. *Status and Identity in West Africa: Nyamakalaw of Mande.* Bloomington: Indiana University Press, 1995.

McNaughton, Patrick. *Mande Blacksmiths: Knowledge, Power and Art in West Africa.* Bloomington: Indiana University Press, 1993.

Mande Music and Performance:

Charry, Eric. *Mande Music: Traditional and Modern Music of the Maninka and Mandinka of Western Africa.* Chicago: University of Chicago Press, 2000.

Hale, Thomas A. *Griots and Griottes: Masters of Words and Music.* Bloomington: Indiana University Press, 1998.

Hoffman, Barbara G. *Griots at War: Conflict, Conciliation and Caste in Mande.* Bloomington: Indiana University Press, 2000.

White, Luise, Stephan Miescher, and David William Cohen, eds. *African Words, African Voices: Critical Practices in Oral History.* Bloomington: Indiana University Press, 2001.

12 Slave Voices from the Cameroon Grassfields

Prayers, Dirges, and a Nuptial Chant

E. S. D. FOMIN

In the centralized polities of the Cameroon Grassfields,[1] captives on the way to enslavement usually prayed to their gods for forgiveness against crimes that might have caused their ordeal. The ones already enslaved in different communities in the area also acted as dirge composers and singers for the funerary ceremonies, which lasted up to three or four days, respectively for women and men. Dirge singing was not, however, a prerogative of slaves but of talented individuals in spite of their gender and origins. The traces of such poetic and musical performances are still alive in personal and social memory, providing access to the experiences and feelings of long-gone men and women in bondage.

From my extensive research in this area,[2] I have learned that asking about slaves' activities in the past is one of the strategies that help such recollections emerge. If questioned appropriately, people often end up recalling what the slaves did and said or sung while performing those tasks. For example, there is a song among the Babungo people that female slaves are alleged to have composed and sang while cooking for the workers of the Babungo ancient iron industry. In this song, they express their disgust and resentment for the insatiable appetite of the foundry workers, who were mainly male slaves:

> *Foundry laborers eat too much,*
> *They never eat to the full,*
> *No matter the amount of food you give them.*[3]

Although the song does not display any explicit reference to slavery, it provides good information about the organization of the industry that, if read in the context of the history of

---

[1] The Cameroon Grassfields are located in the western quadrant of Cameroon. The appellation connotes the savannah vegetation of the subregion. It also has common cultural features of which the creation of centralized polities was one. A centralized polity is a traditional political unit with a well-defined territorial area, supreme hereditary authority called *fon* (plur. *afon*), and its variants. Such political units were created from conquest and annexation of weaker chieftains and the usurpation of the authority of collaborative ones. Many such powerful polities were in existence in this area during the slave trade era.

[2] This area is one of the case studies I investigated for my doctoral thesis in 1981 and have since gone back to from time to time to collect information for other publications and conference papers.

[3] NjobehNgufor, "Babungo in the Grassfields Trade 1840–1960" (unpublished dissertation, E.N.S. Yaounde, University of Yaounde 1, 2007), 48. As Njobeh's and many other works on the ancientiron industry in Ndop plain in the western Grassfields show, the industry employed many laborers who were often the immediate family members, relations, and slaves of the industry owners.

the subregion, reminds one of the long-standing slaving[4] activities in the area. And the fact that women were employed to cook collectively for the male laborers is an indication that they were not free workers.

The first section of this chapter presents a selection of five prayers that captive Yamba[5] people are alleged to have recited when they were in the hands of slave drivers, who marched them from the Cameroon Grassfields to distant intermediary markets and finally to the European trading posts on the coast. The second part contains two dirges and a nuptial chant that were sung by a male and a female slave probably in the 1940s in two different villages of the chiefdom of Essoh-Attah.[6] At the time, first-generation slaves could still be found in many societies in the Cameroon interior. The man, who had been sold into slavery when he was a child sometime in the 1920s, was called AbenNzembong.[7] The woman's name was Nkeng Tanya and she was a first-generation slave as well.

I recorded the two dirges and the chant in interviews with Stephen Forcha and Stephen Tanya, who had witnessed the dirge performances during their childhood. It is worth remarking that such performances continue to be staged frequently even nowadays in different areas of the Cameroon Grassfields. All death ceremonies are marked by dirge performances. The dirges of this chapter clearly demonstrate great abilities in oratory, rhetoric, and philosophy on the part of their singers and evoke the plight of displacement and solitude of the enslaved who find himself/herself kinless in the masters' society. According to my informants, the performances were solemn and tear provoking.

PRAYERS AND SONGS OF ENSLAVED YAMBA PEOPLE

Background: I found these four prayers and the song in the unpublished collection of Florence Ndifor while collecting information for this chapter. She was a graduate social researcher working in the Ministry of Higher Education in Yaounde when I met her. She had collected extensive oral accounts of the Yamba. The Yamba live in the Nwa subdivision in the Northwest Region of Cameroon. Florence Ndifor kindly authorized me to use the information in my own writing.

The prayers address different problems, as they emerge from the texts themselves. The first calls for the assistance of the Yamba god (Nwi), as Yamba people considered enslavement a curse for some wrongdoing by the enslaved. The second requests the protection of three other divinities in the Yamba pantheon for those whom the enslaved left behind, while the third prayer calls for evil to rain upon slave-dealers. The fourth prayer, in contrast,

---

[4]   The Bali, who were notorious slave-dealers, supplied the Douala and Bimbia coasts with many slaves from the nineteenth right into the first half of the twentieth century. *Source*: Cameroon National Archives, Buea, British Assessment Reports on Bali clan 1925, file cb (1937), 1.

[5]   The Yamba people are one of principal ethnic entities in Donga and Mantung Division of the Northwest Region of Cameroon. Like many other weaker groups in that area, the Yamba were frequently raided by Fulani from Adamwa, who took many captives and sold them as slaves.

[6]   Essoh-Attahchiefdom (*fondom*) is one of the centralized polities in the Bangwa region of the Eastern Grassfields. It is in Lebialem division of the Southwest Region of Cameroon. As shown in E.S.D. Fomin, *Handbook on Essoh-Attah Chiefdom* (Bamenda: Patron Publishers, 1994), 23 The chiefdom was founded around 1600.

[7]   Cameroon came under German colonial rule in 1884. The German colonialists were ousted from Cameroon and replaced by the British and French during World War I. All three colonial powers tried in varying degrees to stop slave-dealing in the territory of Cameroon but did not succeed until the late 1930s.

asks for the mercy of Nwi. This specific type of prayer usually took the form of praises, like those reserved for Yamba supreme ruler. The last text is a war song that captured, and enslaved Yamba individuals are alleged to have recited or sung to encourage themselves to resist their captors through rebellion and escape at the least given opportunity.

QUESTIONS TO CONSIDER

1. How did the Yamba perceive capture, enslavement, and sale of an individual?
2. What were some of the traumas of the Yamba captives?
3. What was their attitude toward slave drivers?
4. What to the captives was the way out of their plight?

1. The prayers

"Nwi, you are most high,
Nwi, you are most mighty
You are the greatest god,
You are the most powerful god.
We entreat you to listen to our plea.

We no longer live in peace,
Fear has overwhelmed our children,
Fear has overwhelmed our wives,
They lose us, their dear ones day by day,
Who are taken to the land of no return.

We know we must have annoyed you,
Nwi forgive our trespasses,
Protect our people from these raiders,
Send your bees to sting them,
Send your snakes to bite them,
So they will know you are our greatest god."

"Nwantap, Chimbi, Soh,
Bring harmony among those we have left behind,
Let them live as one person,
Nwantap, you are the owner of calabashes,
Chimbi, you are the owner of bowls,
And Soh you are the owner of farms.

Oh Nwantap,Chimbi,Soh,[8]
Let our absence make our children grow even stronger,
Let our absence give our wives greater courage,
Let our absence make our king stronger,
Let our absence make our people more united,

---

[8] These are some of the names of Yamba deities.

Let them not fall into this same plight.
Bring this our Supplications to the Almighty Nwi."

"Oh Nwi, You ordained that,
When the dyer prepares the dye, her hands first get stained,
When a cam wood dealer prepares it, her hands first get colored,
Nwing that invites the rain first gets it on his own land,
Who ever put us in the hands of these devils?
Whether they are *afon*
Let same evil beset them and their accomplices,
Let them also be captured, tied and driven away
Let the same cords be used to tie them."

"Have mercy on us our lords,
The husband of all maidens,
The lion of the forest,
The light of the season,
The pasture of all herds of cattle,
Stop beating us lords, we are tired.

You who speak once and things happen twice,
You who cause the mountains to tremble,
You whose name goes beyond the setting of the sun,
You who cough and rocks break,
Stop beating us lords we are hungry lords.

You who cough and women urinate on their dresses
You who cough and men breathe faster
You who cough and lions starve in their dens
You who laugh and children cry
Have mercy on us."

2. A song of enslaved Yamba

"When we sit silent,
Are we men?
When we sit motionless
Are we women?
When we succumbed so easily
Are we children?
The more you push a calabash into the water the more it floats
Take Courage, take action men
Our friends who escaped into the forest are many
Though their injuries are countless, they survived
These slavers took us like foxes pick up strayed chickens
Let us make them bow to us or we die

Let them know that we are men
Let them know we are heroes born to end this evil."

DIRGES AND NUPTIAL RECITATIONS

Informant: Stephen Forcha,

Stephen Forcha, the informant on the performance of AbenNzembong, was born in Essoh-Attah chiefdom around 1930. He knew AbenNzembong as a popular dirge singer in Nchenmbin village as he grew up. I interviewed him at Buea in 1985, when he was a civil servant of the Cameroon state, working with the then Ministry of Finance. In 2006, when I met him again to update this information, he had retired and had become chief of Abwet village in the same chiefdom. It should be noted that Abwet and Nchenmbin of Fuankengacheh are neighboring villages in Essoh-Attah.

According to Stephen Forcha, AbenNzembong, was a first-generation male slave of Fuankengacheh of Nchenmbin village in Essoh-Attah chiefdom in Lebialem division of the Southwest Region of Cameroon. He appeared to have been enslaved as a boy around the 1920s. The informant knew him by the 1940s when he had been emancipated[9] and given land on his former master's estate. He had a wife, who was also a first-generation slave of the same master. They had children and their descendants are well-known members of the same village. He had a farm of palms and other economic trees. He was constantly disturbed by trespassers on his farm and he could be very violent toward them. And quite often he cursed them as thieves who should be plagued by elephantiasis of the scrotum.

But his voice is better heard in the dirges that he sang regularly at funerals than curses he placed on his trespassers. The informant claims that AbenNzembong was a good dirge singer, indeed a good mourner who brought tears to the eyes of all mourners when he sang his dirges. Dirges are still very popular in this part of Cameroon (Nweh country).

Both male and female persons of free and servile origins sing them even today. But not many are as gifted as AbenNzembong. Good singers like him are admired and remembered for a long time.

From the text, one would think that AbenNzembong should be a happy person, but the sentiments his dirges evoke are quite different. They speak of loneliness and solitude following the tradition of dirge singing, which often recalls only traumatic events in the lives of their singers and of the people they loved. In fact, their purpose is to induce mourners to weep.

It would be misleading to conclude from what he expresses here that he was not happy in his host society. He appeared to have found pleasure in dirge singing probably because of the latitude that dirges provide singers to express themselves. They often say what they think and feel about people and the society without getting into problems with others. Critiquing society was common in dirge singing even by freeborn singers.

---

[9] The people of the Cameroon Grassfields did not emancipate their slaves. The slaves were rather absorbed into the free society through different social and political processes: deconstruction of their identity, marriage, assigned functions, and acquisition of nobility ranks. Formal legal emancipation was a European colonial administrative measure, which became effective in this area only around the 1930s.

QUESTIONS TO CONSIDER

1. What is the main regret of AbenNzembong as expressed in this dirge?
2. Had AbenNzembong any friends in his host society?
3. How can one tell from this dirge that the society was not an egalitarian one?

1. AbenNzembong'sdirge performance

The chorus is:-*wou-ouhwouah, wou-ouhwouah*
"I, Nzembong, is the one singing – -chorus,
I am singing for whom to hear me? – -chorus,
I without a 'back'! – -chorus
I am weeping for whom to comfort me? – -chorus
I without a father! – -chorus
I am weeping for whom to comfort me? – -chorus
I without a mother! – – chorus
I am weeping for whom to comfort me? – -chorus
I without a brother-chorus

All good friends have gone and left me – -chorus
To whom shall I go for help? – -chorus
Who shall weep when I die? – -chorus
Who shall bury me? – -chorus
Oh death, why not take me now? – -chorus
Why don't you leave the mighty? – -chorus
Please death, take but us the helpless." – -chorus

THE VOICE OF NKENG TANYA

Informant: Stephen Tanya

Stephen Tanya is another informant who gave me an eyewitness account about Nkeng Tanya's dirge performance, one of the female slaves of his grandfather. Stephen Tanya was born in Nzanchen in Essoh-Attah in the early 1950s. Before he was born, Nkeng Tanya had long been bought and integrated into their family. His father Tanya Akutie was the successor of the slave owner and inherited Nkeng Tanya among other widows. The informant, Stephen Tanya, was interviewed on January 12, 2000, at Buea where he was working as a civil servant of the Ministry of Urban Affairs, a member of the delegation of the Southwest Region of Cameroon.

Nkeng Tanya was one of the many slave wives of Mbe Tanya. She is said to have been bought from slave-dealers when she was still a very pretty young woman. According to the informant, she was very friendly, a good animator, and a wonderful dirge singer. But the informant did not know where she came from. The dialect she spoke is said to belong the Bamileke language, which is one of the main indigenous languages of the Cameroon Grassfields. Thus, she must have come from one of the Bamileke Grassfields chiefdoms in the Cameroon Grassfields. In addition to the dirges, which she sang, she also prepared brides for their weddings and entertained at nuptial ceremonies. Unfortunately she had no children of her own. The nuptial song presented here let surface the voice of a childless slave widow and tells a lot of her expectations and disappointment in her host society.

QUESTIONS TO CONSIDER

1. What was Nkeng Tanya's greatest regret?
2. Why did Nkeng Tanya not know her society of origin?
3. How can we tell from the dirge that Nkeng Tanya was deeply religious?
4. Who does Nkeng Tanya blame for her plight of childlessness?

1. Nkeng Tanya's dirge performance

The chorus is this: - *Yea eyea yea eyea*
"I Nkeng Tanya am the one crying – -chorus
Crying for the people so dear to others – – chorus
The people so dear to this country – -chorus
The people with children and relations – -chorus
Who will cry for me when my own turn comes? – -chorus

Where can I have come from? – -chorus
Is there any one still in that country? – -chorus
Who can go tell them my saga? – -chorus
The saga of my great misfortune – -chorus
My misfortune in this blessed country – -chorus
Where lucky women bear but twins – -chorus

Tell them that it was a cursed history for me – -chorus
That I shall return to the creator as I came – – chorus
I must weep for myself and for them – – chorus
For them who are long gone to the creator – -chorus
For no one is there to do so after me – -chorus

My own parents of that unknown land – -chorus
I know I will never see them again – -chorus
I may not even recognize them if I see – -chorus
Perhaps I shall do so in the eternity – – chorus
That will be wonderful for us both – -chorus

And you our good husband Mbe Tanya – -chorus
Did you journey well to the creator? – -chorus
I want to thank you for the good marriage – -chorus
That those you gave me to care for me well – – chorus
I want to inform you that I did not desert your Compound – -chorus
But soon I shall do so to meet you in eternity – -chorus/

NKENG TANYA'S NUPTIAL CHANT

Nkeng Tanya was also a wonderful and extremely versatile singer at nuptial ceremonies. She was very good at preparing brides for their wedding. According to my informant, when a "fattened" teenage[10] bride had to be taken to the husband at the end of the period of

---

[10] According to my informant, a female teenager here was usually confined and fed well for several weeks to give her the size that made her a good wife and future mother.

confinement, she was well cleansed and polished with camwood, adorned with beads, and presented publicly at the weekly market square. The most difficult aspect of the preparation was spraying her, using the mouth, with harsh camwood paste. The task was not reserved for slave women but was indeed a prerogative of experts like Nkeng Tanya.

The preparation had two main components that were the actual spraying and the chanting of praises and wishes for the new bride. This custom is no longer practiced in the area. Like in the case of dirges, each verse of the nuptial chant had a chorus that the audience sang along with the singer.

QUESTIONS ON THE CHANT TO CONSIDER

1. How can one tell the extent to which Nkeng Tanya was integrated into her host society from this chant?
2. What was the greatest wish that she had for the bride?
3. What did she ask the bride? Why did she wish having many namesakes?

1. Nkeng Tanya's nuptial chant

Chorus: Abap meh ndemêh (so be it god)
"You pretty young bride – -chorus,
Sharp and straight as Mbelebong[11] – -chorus,
Bright and beautiful as the moon – -chorus,
Kind and generous as god – -chorus,
Meek and innocent as a lamb – -chorus,
This is a great day for you – -chorus.
You are a most beautiful wife – -chorus,
And MbeTankeng[12] must be proud of you – -chorus,
He is a great and vigorous man – -chorus,
He will make you happy to night – -chorus,
And you will bear him twins – -chorus,
Many more twins and single children will follow – -chorus.

You will deliver yours and mine – -chorus,
Never has any bride failed me – -chorus,
You too cannot fail me – -chorus,
And do not forget to name Nkeng Tanya – -chorus,
I need many namesakes in this land – -chorus,
So that Nkeng Tanya is not forgotten – -chorus.

SUGGESTED ADDITIONAL READINGS

Brain Robert. *Bangwa Kinship and Marriage*. Cambridge: Cambridge University Press, 1972.

---

[11] This is a type of plant of the bulrush family that grows in this area. It is very straight and smooth, thus the local saying "as straight as *mbelebong*."
[12] MbeTankeng is used here to represent any of the bridegrooms whom she named in her chants.

12.1. At the funeral of Chief Forcha Ankanju, Essoh-Attah.
Source: The album of Chief Fuatabong-Leke, son-in-law of the decease.

12.2. At the funeral of Chief Forcha Ankanju, Essoh-Attah.
Source: The album of Chief Fuatabong-Leke, son-in-law of the decease.

Chem-Langhëë Bongfen, ed. "Slavery and Slave-Dealing in Cameroon in the Nineteenth and the Early Twentieth Centuries," *PAIDEUMA*, 1995.

Chem-Langhëë Bongfen and Verkijika G. Fanso. *Royal Succession in the African Kingdom of Nso': A Study in Oral Historiography.* New York: Edwin Mellen Press, 2008.

Chilver E.M. "Nineteenth-Century Trade in the BamendaGrassfields, Southern Cameroon," *Afrika und Ubersee* XLV, 4 (1961), 233–258.

Fomin, E.S.D. "Female Slavery in Nweh Country, 1850–1970," *West African Journal of Archaeology, Special Edition on Slavery* 26, 2 (1996), 140–154.

A Comparative Study of Societal Influences on Indigenous Slavery in Two Types of Societies 1600–1950. New York: Edwin Mellen Press, 2002.

Fomin, E.S.D. and Ndobegang M.M. "Slavery Artifacts and European Colonialism: The Cameroon Grassfieldsfrom 1600–1950," *Journal of the European Legacy* 11, 6 (2006), 633–646.

Warnier J.P. "The History of the Peopling of the Western Cameroon and the Genesis of Its Landscapes," in *Nso' and Its Neighbors: Readings in Social History.* Edited by B. Chem-Langhee and V.G. Fanso. Amherst, MA: Amherst College, 1996, 41–75.

MAP OF YORUBA ETHNIC GROUPS, c.1820

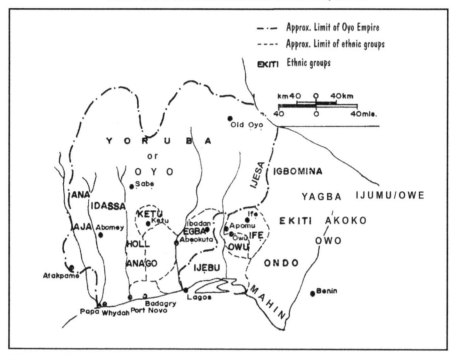

13.1. Map of Yoruba ethnic groups.

13 Silent Testimonies, Public Memory

Slavery in Yoruba Proverbs

OLATUNJI OJO

Oral traditions constitute an important source of historical information in nonliterate societies. This is true for the study of slavery in Yorubaland because of the late development of writing and the general paucity of source materials. However, scarcity of data does not imply the absence of slavery. Historical data are scattered in various oral traditional forms: *oriki* (praise poems), *ese ifa* (ifa rhymes), *iwi/esa* (mascot's poems), *alo* (riddles and folktales), *ekun iyawo* (bridal songs), *ijala/iremojo* (hunters' poems), *eewo* (taboo), *ofo/ayajo* (spells), and *owe* (proverbs), among others. While there are similarities in the structure and content of these traditions, they differ based on whether they are composed as songs, prose, verses, and phrases; aimed at juveniles or adults; and depict joy or sadness. There are also differences based on the age and gender of performers and the mode of performance.[1]

In the course of my research on the links between warfare and slavery in eighteenth- and nineteenth-century Yorubaland, I noticed how frequently my informants used proverbs in their narratives. They buried proverbs either within a long narrative or inside other oral forms to explain, illustrate, or summarize their views. Proverbs serve as metaphorical statements useful in putting things in historical and literary contexts, and they give deeper meaning to other experiences. At times, my informants clarified a proverb with another. In answering a question on the ineligibility of a family for a chieftaincy post, the plaintiff invoked a proverb: *Igbagun ni igbagun* (Everything has a place). When asked to explain the meaning, he replied: *Ki eru mo ara re leru ki iwofa mo ara re ni iwofa* (The slave should know s/he is a slave and the pawn should know s/he is a pawn).[2] In other words, the proverbs stated that slaves should accept their status as slaves and strangers and not pretend to be free persons. According to the plaintiff, the respondent was unqualified to be chief because he descended from a slave. Descent from slaves emblematizes weakness, otherness, and deprivation.

---

[1] B. Awe, "Some Ibadan Place Names, A Source of Historical Evidence," *African Notes* 6:2 (1970–71), 85–93; B. Awe, "Praise Poems as Historical Data, the Example of the Yoruba Oríkì," *Africa* 44 (1974), 331–49; W. Abimbola (ed.), *Yoruba Oral Tradition, Poetry in Music, Dance and Drama* (Ile-Ife, 1975); O. Adewoye, "Proverbs as Vehicle of Juristic Thought Among the Yorùbá," *Obafemi Awolowo University Law Journal* 3–4 (1987), 1–17; and K. Barber, "Documenting Social and Ideological Change Through Yoruba Oriki, A Stylistic Analysis," *Journal of Historical Society of Nigeria (JHSN)* 10:4 (1981), 39–52.

[2] Interview with Samuel Ojo, age seventy-six, Omu-Ekiti, August 5 and 6, 1999, July 31, 2001, and June 20, 2009.

This chapter focuses on proverbs and has three goals. First, it seeks to validate proverbs as a source of data on slavery. Second, it considers how slavery is memorialized across generations. Third, given that slave proverbs remain popular several decades after the legal abolition of slavery, the chapter establishes the continued salience of slave origins and uses this to modify certain received ideas about the institution. It pays attention to popular attitudes about slavery and slaves. The essay is divided into three parts. It begins with an overview of proverbs as a form of oral tradition and the mode of data collection used and its consequent complications. Part two provides an overview of slave-related conflicts in Yorubaland, and part three examines some slave proverbs and their (possible) origins, use, and meaning.

THE YORUBA PEOPLE

The Yoruba are a West African people who number some forty million today and live in western Nigeria. They are internationally known for their beautiful plastic arts, including the elaborate wood sculptures often associated with their kingdoms, and for their impact on the diasporic religions in the New World. Today millions of people in the United States, the Caribbean, and Latin America worship Yoruba gods and practice religions variously called *Santeria, Candomble,* and *Shango* or *Orisa.*[3]

Until the late nineteenth century, the Yoruba, contrary to widely held view, did not constitute a single ethnic group or had a common name. Rather, they belonged to multiple ethnicities namely in the west (Anago, Ketu, Egbado, Sabe, and Idaisa), east (Ijesa, Igbomina, Ekiti, Owo, Ondo, Akoko, Bunu, Owe, Oworo, Yagba, Ijumu and Ikale), north (Oyo), and the south (Ijebu, Owu, Egba, and Awori), some not more than a city-state. The name Yoruba was of Hausa origin, referring to Oyo, the biggest and most northern Yoruba state. After 1840, the name was applied to people sharing the same language and culture with Oyo. Each Yoruba ethnic group or state was governed by an *oba* (king) who ruled with elaborate bureaucracies representing lineage heads, military forces, and powerful occupational groups. Each *oba* ruled a capital town and subordinate towns, villages, markets, and farmlands. These city-states were also sites of elaborate crafts and professional production – weaving, dying, leatherwork, sculpture, and so forth. A vibrant network of markets linked them one to another and to the trans-Saharan and later coastal Atlantic trades.[4]

Despite their ethnic diversity, the Yoruba people have common myths of origin, which relate the founding of the world. One of the myths states that in the beginning the earth was

---

[3] J. Houlk, *Spirits, Blood, and Drums, The Orisha Religion of Trinidad* (Philadelphia, 1995); S. Palmié, "Against Syncretism, Africanizing and Cubanizing Discourses in North American Òrìsà-Worship" in R. Fardon (ed.), *Counterworks, Managing Diverse Knowledge* (London, 1995), 73–104; P. C. Johnson, *Secrets, Gossip, and Gods, The Transformation of Brazilian Candomble* (Oxford, 2001); D. H. Brown, *Santeria Enthroned, Art, Ritual, and Innovation in an Afro-Cuban Religion* (Chicago, 2003); C. Ayorinde, *Afro-Cuban Religiosity, Revolution, and National Identity* (Gainesville, FL, 2004); J. L. Matory, *Black Atlantic Religion, Tradition, Transnationalism, and Matriarchy in the Afro-Brazilian Candomblé* (Princeton, NJ, 2005); D. Trotman, "Reflections on the Children of Shango: An Essay on a History of Orisa Worship in Trinidad," *Slavery and Abolition* 28:2 (2007), 211–234; and L. N. Pares, "The Nagoization Process in Bahian Candomble" in T. Falola and M. D. Childs (eds.), *The Yoruba Diaspora in the Atlantic World* (Indianapolis, 2004), 185–208.

[4] W. Bascom, *The Yoruba of South Western Nigeria* (New York, 1969); R. Law, "Ethnicity and the Slave Trade, 'Lucumi' and 'Nago' as Ethnonyms in West Africa," *History in Africa (HA)* 24 (1997), 205–219; and J. D. Y. Peel, "The Cultural Work of Yoruba Ethnogenesis" in E. McDonald and M. Chapman (eds.), *History and Ethnicity* (London, 1989), 198–215.

covered with water, and God sent Obatala and sixteen mortals, carrying a bowl of sand, to create land and establish a settlement at Ile-Ife. Another tradition attributed the origin of the Yoruba to immigrants from the Middle East fleeing to Ile-Ife in the aftermath of a religious uprising in Mecca. Later in the history of Ile-Ife, a new leader emerged in Oduduwa, whose descendants founded other Yoruba states. Henceforth, Ile-Ife has been the spiritual capital of the Yoruba people and – though never having the military power of Oyo, one of the successor states – had a considerable moral authority over the people of the region.[5]

Until the late eighteenth century, the Yoruba people lived in relative peace with the neighboring kingdom of Edo dominating Eastern Yorubaland, while Ijebu controlled the coastal district and the bulk of areas in the north and west including Egba, Egbado, Anago, Igbomina, and Ijesa subjugated to an empire called Oyo. The fact that Oyo empire, which existed between the sixteenth and eighteenth centuries, embraced a number of non-Oyo Yoruba districts marked a major attempt at forming Yorubaland into a single ethnicity and polity. The empire was founded in the early-seventeenth century and expanded into the most powerful Yoruba state, renowned for its cavalry of horses supplied through their northern trade routes.[6] Within some decades, Oyo had become one of the largest and most powerful states in the Guinea forest zone of West Africa, and their power and authority ensured peace and security within and beyond its boundaries.

The whole empire imploded, however, in the 1780s for a number of reasons still being debated by scholars. For our interest in slavery, the importance of this collapse is twofold. First is one interpretation of the series of crises that led to the collapse of Oyo. According to this explanation, a rebellion of Muslim slaves held by the Oyo occurred in their capital city, also known as Oyo, and in a military headquarters at Ilorin, southeast of the capital. This deepened a constitutional crisis between several government officials and so weakened Oyo that it could no longer ensure security within its territory and maintain the delicate alliance of neighboring states.[7] Violence within Oyo spread to other Yoruba districts and from this point thousands of Yoruba-speakers began to appear in the various slave ports on the West African coast and Yoruba slaves poured into the New World. The collapse of Oyo led to eight decades of warfare that severely devastated Yorubaland. On the other hand, the wars produced several new states that experimented with new terms of unity, political structures, and social organization. Two such states were Ibadan and Ijaye, which emerged out of war camps during the turmoil and became warrior states in which kinship and religious power held no currency for political power. Ibadan and Ijaye came into prominence after 1830. Both cities began originally as small Egba towns located at the intersection of Yoruba forest and savannah belt. Following the fall of Oyo in the 1820s, refugees and warlords from the old Oyo empire seized Ijaye and Ibadan and transformed both into Oyo enclaves welcoming adventurers from all over Yorubaland. Authorities in the two cities took on the task of rebuilding the old Oyo empire by positioning their respective towns as the center of a future empire. With their armies constantly at war, Ibadan and Ijaye became

---

[5] S. A. Crowther, *A Grammar and Vocabulary of the Yoruba Language* (London, 1852), i–iv; R. Law, "The Heritage of Oduduwa, Traditional History and Political Propaganda among the Yoruba," *Journal of African History* 14 (1973), 207–222; and R. Smith, *Kingdoms of the Yoruba* (3rd edn., Madison, WI, 1988), 3–28.

[6] R. Law, *The Oyo Empire c. 1600–c. 1836, A West African Imperialism in the Era of the Atlantic Slave Trade* (Oxford, 1977); and Smith, *Kingdoms of the Yoruba*, 29–41.

[7] For details, see S. Johnson, *The History of the Yorubas from the Earliest to the Beginning of the British Protectorate* (Lagos, 1976 [1921]), 161–273; and Law, *Oyo Empire*, 245–302.

terrors to their neighbors, seizing huge tracts of territory and establishing, especially at Ibadan, a new sociopolitical framework based on merit and devoid of hereditary rights.[8] Proverbs treat the legacies of this war and the impact of slavery and slave trading on the Yoruba communities that were thrown into chaos for most of the nineteenth century. We discuss this in more detail later in the chapter.

SLAVE PROVERBS AS ORAL HISTORY

Owe (proverb) is a Yoruba oral literal and figurative tradition whose full meaning is subject to translation and unpacking. Consisting mostly of simple sentences and couplets, and rich in metaphors, *owe* conveys feelings and sentiments that are impolitic to express in literal terms or require deeper contexts for more complete understanding. When a proverb appears as a couplet, the object is to describe or establish an antithesis between two consecutive lines, in which a noun answers to a noun and verb to verb. Proverbs provide images of a particular worldviews. Isaac Delano says, "Proverbs are self evident truths which have the gist of what one wants to say in a brief and unmistakable form," while Isidore Okpewho describe them as "piece[s] of folk wisdom expressed with terseness and charm."[9] Like other oral traditions, proverbs are in the public domain and belong to the realm of folklore or popular memory. They are available for teaching or to remind the public about the past. Hence, William Bascom notes that folklore validates culture and justifies its rituals and institutions to those who perform and observe them. They also serve as a means of applying social pressure and exercising social control.[10] In other words, proverbs teach behavioral lessons, ancient wisdom and traditions, good neighborliness, and provide short summaries for long stories. Proverbs also justify certain ideologies by stipulating boundaries of social behavior.

The value placed on proverbs as words of "wisdom" and educational tools also extends to those, usually elders, who are skilled in their use. They are revered in the community for their ability "to get to the heart of a matter" by using appropriate proverbs. In conversations between people of different ages, it is considered appropriate to illuminate discussions with proverbs and to defer to elders. The symbolism lies in the fact that proverbs, like elders, manifest ancient wisdom. Because proverbs are mutable and adaptable to time and context, it is vital for a verbal artist to use them at the right time and context. There is the term *asipa owe* or wrong proverb-making, and anyone able to detect *asipa owe* and come up with a counter-proverb is also deserving of respect in the community. In referring to social relationships, proverbs about slaves encourage masters to be fair to their slaves, yet they also require slaves to be obedient and accept their status. Thus, slave proverbs provide a window on the world of slavery and illustrate and justify social disparities.

---

[8] B. Awe, "The Rise of Ibadan as a Yoruba Power 1851–1893" (unpublished DPhil thesis, Oxford University, 1964); G. O. Oguntomisin, "New Forms of Political Organisation in Yorubaland in the Mid-Nineteenth Century, A Comparative Study of Kurunmi's Ijaye and Kosoko's Epe" (unpublished PhD thesis, University of Ibadan, 1979); and Smith, *Kingdoms of the Yoruba*, 125–140.

[9] Delano, *Owe L'Esin Oro, Yoruba Proverbs – Their Meaning and Usage* (Ibadan, 1966); Okpewho, *African Oral Literature, Backgrounds, Character, and Continuity* (Indianapolis, 1992); and O. Olatunji, *Features of Yoruba Oral Poetry* (Ibadan, 1984).

[10] Bascom, "Four Functions of Folklore," *Journal of American Folklore* 67, 266 (1954), 333–349.

THE COLLECTION PROCESS

The proverbs used in this essay come from published texts and archival sources as well as interviews. Between 1843 and 1897, authors such as Samuel Ajayi Crowther, Thomas Bowen, and Alfred Ellis collected, translated, and sometimes annotated collections of Yoruba proverbs including some addressing the issue of slavery.[11] In addition to being a valuable archival source, these materials present an eyewitness account of historical events and real-life perceptions. This is especially the case in Crowther's collection because he was one of a group of educated Yoruba writers who had either experienced slavery or descended from slaves.[12] Since these nineteenth-century publications, other collections of Yoruba proverbs have been written, the most notable being the many works of Oyekan Owomoyela. He published most recently, in 2005, a collection of some 5,207 proverbs drawn from interviews and published works.[13]

I was interested in collecting data on those areas of Yorubaland about which little had been collected. To research these largely neglected areas I interviewed people in the Ibadan, Ekiti, Ondo, and Ikale districts from 1998 and 2009. My informants may be divided into three age categories: seventy years and older, forty to seventy years, and fifteen to thirty-nine years. I asked them to speak about the nineteenth-century Yoruba wars, slavery and its impact, and attitudes and contemporary stereotypes of slavery. Informants in the first group, whose memories were near-contemporary to the era of slavery, proved more likely to use proverbs as figures of speech. They did so to illustrate or summarize stories and draw parallels between related events. These elders were ready to speak on general issues and proverbs, but less willing to provide data on their personal lives. With the second group, most of the informants were teachers, farmers, traders, and professionals. They also gave me access to local historians and custodians of local culture. Because the individuals in this last group were mostly educated, their views of slavery were often influenced by readings and scholarly lectures on the Atlantic slave trade. Even though adults used more proverbs in their conversations, children have not been excluded from this tradition. Informants in the youngest group told me that they learned proverbs by listening to conversations, radio and television programs, and local music. Additionally, formal training in proverbs takes place in schools where students are tested on the proper use of appropriate

[11] Crowther, *Grammar and Vocabulary*; T. J. Bowen, *Adventures and Missionary Labours in Several Countries in the Interior of Africa from 1849 to 1856* (London, 1968 [1857]), 288–293; T. J. Bowen, *Grammar and Dictionary of the Yoruba Language* (New York, 1858), 56–69; and A. B. Ellis, *The Yoruba-Speaking Peoples of the Slave Coast of West Africa* (London, 1894), 134–157.

[12] Crowther, originally Ajayi, was born in the Oyo town of Osogun around 1806. In 1821, he was captured by slave-raiders who swept up Osogun in the early phase of the decades-long Yoruba wars. He was destined for the New World on a Portuguese slave ship when it was intercepted by a British warship, and was taken to Sierra Leone where he was liberated and baptized with the name Samuel Crowther. Crowther attended the Fourah Bay College in Freetown, ordained a priest of the Church Missionary Society in 1846, and became the first Black Anglican Bishop in 1864. He died in 1891. See J. Page, *Samuel Crowther, The Slave Boy who became Bishop of the Niger* (London, 1888); and J. F. Ajayi, *A Patriot to the Core, Bishop Ajayi Crowther* (Ibadan, 2002).

[13] J. O. Ajibola, *Owe Yoruba* (London, 1947); D. Ladipo, *Egbokanla le ogoorun owe Yoruba* (Ibadan, 1955); C. O. Fasanya, *Akojo awon Owe Yoruba* (Ilesa, 1962); A. Bamigbose, "The Form of Yoruba Proverbs," *ODU* 4:2 (1968), 74–86; S. O. Bada, *Owe Yoruba ati Isedale Won* (Ibadan, 1979); K. Akinlade, *Owe Pelu Itumo (A-GB)* (Lagos, 1987); Y. K. Yusuf, "A Speech Act Study of English and Yoruba Proverbs about Women" (unpublished PhD thesis, University of Lagos, 1996); and O. Owomoyela, *Yoruba Proverbs* (Lincoln, NE, 2005).

proverbs in Yoruba as proof of competence in indigenous knowledge and the art of public presentation.

The interviews were not without challenges. Many of the interviews reflected the political alliances that were made during the nineteenth-century Yoruba wars, which continue to influence how individuals identify themselves and others. The interviews were conducted in Yoruba and English depending on the informant's choice. Because slavery is a very sensitive topic, not all informants agreed to speak on tape. Some questioned my interest in slavery and wanted to know if the research was linked to chieftaincy and land contests involving my family. To persuade many informants that this was solely a scholarly project, I had to meet them multiple times and repeatedly explain my interest in slavery and the rationale for the research. Nonetheless, some informants remained unconvinced and either rejected an interview, refused permission to record their testimony, or requested anonymity. In deference to their concerns, I have refrained from using their names. As an "insider" – I am a scholar from these very communities in Yorubaland – who knows "too much" about certain "places," "people," and "things," my task was difficult. The study reveals my several identities. In Ekiti, I was X from lineage A or Y from town Z. At Ibadan, my identity ranged from the "Ekiti man" to the "University boy" and "one of the people we [Ibadan] used to capture." In some other places, I was the "man from America." In all, however, I discovered that few of the thousands of proverbs studied addressed slavery. It is unclear whether this has always been the case or whether they are disappearing because of the legal abolition of slavery.

Before analyzing the proverbs themselves, it is important to discuss the Yorubaness of these slave proverbs. As we have seen from the earlier discussion, a pan-Yoruba ethnicity did not emerge until the nineteenth century, and some would argue it did not develop until the early decades of the twentieth century.[14] Each Yoruba district, in fact, has a unique history and dialect, all of which are blended into local folklore to make them unique to the locality. To this extent, some proverbs popular in one part of Yorubaland might be unknown in other places, such as Ekiti proverbs attacking Oyo and Ijebu proverbs condemning Ibadan. For instance, one Ijebu proverb recorded around 1890 says, '*Afi Ijebu afi Oyinbo, dede aye dede eru ni won* (Besides the Ijebu and Whites every other person are slaves).[15] Proverbs are founded on local wisdom and realities, so it was no surprise that they express a changing provincial orientation. As living traditions, each proverb has its origin in one Yoruba town or district after which it spread through published texts, via oral traditions, and later by radio and television programs, newspapers, audiotapes, CDs, films, and schools. In the process of diffusion, proverbs were adapted to suit local needs.

SLAVERY IN YORUBA HISTORY

Slavery has a long history in Yorubaland. Most writers agree that it played an important role in Yoruba state formation and administration. Slaves functioned as administrators in the Oyo kingdom and were a powerful force in supervising provincial chiefs. Additionally, slave soldiers were important in the creation of such ancient kingdoms as Oyo, Ijebu, Ile-Ife, Ondo, and Ijesa, some dating back to the tenth century. Leaders in each of these states

---

[14] Law, "Heritage of Oduduwa" and Peel, "The Cultural Work of Yoruba Ethnogenesis."

[15] Johnson, *History*, 610.

employed slaves as bodyguards, soldiers, consuls, advisers, and toll collectors. Without slaves, it seems the processes of state consolidation in the region would have been different and probably less effective.[16] This indigenous slave system later grew as the Yoruba began to participate in the Atlantic slave trade.

Until the mid-eighteenth century, it has been argued that slaves sold by the Yoruba came largely from among their non-Yoruba neighbors especially the Hausa, Nupe, and Borgu in the north and Dahomey in the west. Some historians have argued that the sourcing of slaves from non-Yoruba-speaking areas (and the concomitant practice of not enslaving fellow Yoruba) was attributable to cultural similarities and a sense of pan-Yoruba identity.[17] But as we have noted, pan-Yoruba ethnic consciousness was born in the nineteenth century and was a product of the slave trade. So, if modern Yoruba identity was a recent invention, it could not have obviated the enslavement of people with no prior collective identity. This theory is buttressed by the fact that attacks were carried out by one Yoruba-speaking group against another. There are numerous accounts of Oyo invasions of Ijesa, Ekiti, and Igbomina in the east and Anago, Egba, Sabe, and Egbado in the west between 1600 and 1800.[18] We can assume that in these wars, Yoruba-speakers were enslaving other Yoruba-speakers.

Although commercially profitable, slave trading was detrimental to the Yoruba. Ethnic wars legitimized the enslavement of the enemy or ethnic others, resulting in wars and slave raids spreading to places hitherto untouched by violence. Slavery heightened internal sociopolitical and economic divisions and forced politicians and traders to compete for power and authority. For Yorubaland, the crisis was aggravated by the eighteenth-century religious reform movements that spread from the Futa Jallon Mountains in the hinterland of the Upper Guinea coast throughout the West African Sahel. The Fulani jihads were a movement that used Islam as its core moral and political authority. For the Yoruba, the key political impact was the establishment of the Hausa-Fulani Sokoto caliphate in the early nineteenth century, which put a theocratic state right on the border of Yorubaland, just at the time when the unifying power of Oyo began to decline. The result was the incorporation of the northern Yoruba polity, Ilorin, into the Islamic Sokoto Empire in 1823. Hausa slaves (Gambari) had been employed for centuries in Ilorin and played an important role in this revolutionary conversion.[19] In 1804, following the outbreak of the Sokoto jihad in the Hausa area of modern Northern Nigeria, Oyo lost its major source of slaves. If this were not bad enough, in 1817, forces loyal to Sokoto Empire/Caliphate attacked the Oyo capital,

[16] Johnson, *History*, 57–69; B. Awe, "The Ajele System, A Study of Ibadan Imperialism in the Nineteenth Century," *JHSN* 3 (1964), 47–60; and E. A. Oroge, "The Institution of Slavery in Yorubaland with Particular Reference to the Nineteenth Century" (unpublished PhD thesis, University of Birmingham, 1971), 15–99.

[17] See Ajayi, "West African States at the Beginning of the Nineteenth Century" in Ajayi and I. Espie (eds.), *A Thousand Years of West African History* (Ibadan, 1967), 255; and Oroge, "Institution of Slavery," 115–116, 144; Robin Horton, "Ancient Ife, A Reassessment," *JHSN* 9, 4 (1979), 69–150; B. Adediran, "Yoruba Ethnic Groups or a Yoruba Ethnic Group? A Review of the Problem of Ethnic Identification," *Africa: Revista do Centro do Estudos Africanos de USP* 7 (1984), 57–70; and Akinjogbin (ed.), *The Cradle of a Race, Ife from the Beginning to 1980* (Port Harcourt, 1992), xi–xvi.

[18] See P. Morton-Williams, "The Oyo Yoruba and the Atlantic Slave Trade, 1670–1830," *JHSN* 3 (1964), 25–45; and Law, "Ethnicity and the Slave Trade."

[19] J. A. Atanda, "The Fulani Jihad and the Collapse of the Old Oyo Empire" in T. Falola (ed.), *Yoruba Historiography* (Madison, WI, 1991), 105–121; and Lovejoy, "The Clapperton-Bello Exchange, the Sokoto Jihad and the Trans-Atlantic Slave Trade, 1804–1837" in C. Wise (ed.), *The Desert Shore, Literatures of the African Sahel* (Boulder, CO, 2000), 201–227.

seized the Oyo army garrison at Ilorin, and began a piecemeal conquest of Yorubaland. The immediate response from Oyo was to sell slaves sympathetic to Sokoto, but this did not abate the spread of violence. Individual Oyo chiefs and traders depended on slaves for their sustenance while the state relied on Central Sudanese slaves and horses for its army. The search for alternative sources of slaves and new systems of military reorganization exposed decades, if not centuries, of internal dissension and pent-up anger that exploded into a destructive wave of violence. This warfare and subsequent slave raids had a far-reaching impact on the Yoruba. It exposed ethnic and political diversity and hostilities that have proven resilient in modern times.

By 1830, many parts of Yorubaland were in total ruins. The kingdoms of Owu, Oyo, and Egba had been destroyed and retained little or nothing of their old glory. Refugees, slaves, and bandits massed in the forest region to the south of Oyo and created new cities like Ibadan, Ijaye, Abeokuta, and Ago Oja (new Oyo) while expanding existing ones like Osogbo, Lagos, Ijebu, Ogbomoso, Ilorin, and Ilesa. Many thousands of Yoruba-speaking slaves were sold into the Atlantic trade and left their cultural imprint on the Atlantic world. Because these events coincided with the era of British abolition and intensified surveillance of slaving on the coast, few slaves captured after 1850 entered the Atlantic trade. Rather, slaves not sold into the foreign trade worked in the new legitimate trade in agricultural and manufactured products within West Africa.[20] Thus, ironically, abolition tragically led to an increase in local slavery. A large number worked as farmers, porters, canoe men, guards, and domestics and became wives and concubines. In the palaces, for instance, a group of slaves worked as eunuchs, serving the monarchs, their wives, and their children. Female slaves were employed as nurses, traders, and mostly as concubines. The children of female slaves born to their freeborn husbands and lovers were termed *eru ibile* (house-born slaves). Another group of slaves fought in the army. The confidential household guards of military chiefs, called *omo ogun*, were originally selected from among slaves.

To date, the volatile conflicts of the nineteenth century continue to prevent Yoruba unity of the various groups causing lingering suspicions about one another among the different Yoruba communities. Many Ekiti families do not encourage their children to marry anyone from "Oyo," Egba, or Ijebu. All these antagonisms dated to the era of slavery when one region preyed on another, such as when Oyo soldiers captured Ekiti people and sold them to the Ijebu/Egba.[21] The suspicion is reinforced by occupational choices and wealth

---

[20] S. Johnson, *History*, 178–283, 403–445; J. F. A. Ajayi and R. S. Smith, *Yoruba Warfare in the Nineteenth Century* (London, 1964); A. Akinjogbin (ed.), *War and Peace in Yorubaland 1793–1893* (Ibadan, 1998); Oroge, "Institution of Slavery"; Falola, *The Political Economy of a Pre-Colonial African State, Ibadan, 1830–1900* (Ile-Ife, 1984); K. Mann, *Slavery and the Birth of an African City, Lagos, 1760–1900* (Indianapolis, 2007); C. Sorensen-Gilmour, "Badagry 1784–1863, The Political and Commercial History of a Pre-Colonial Lagoonside Community in South West Nigeria" (unpublished PhD thesis, University of Stirling, 1995); Francine Shields, "Palm Oil and Power, Women in an Era of Economic and Social Transition in Nineteenth Century Yorubaland (South-Western Nigeria)" (unpublished PhD thesis, University of Stirling, 1997); Olatunji Ojo, "Warfare, Slavery and the Transformation of Eastern Yorubaland c.1820–1900" (unpublished PhD thesis, York University, Toronto, 2004); and Ann O'hear, "Ilorin as a Slaving and Slave-Trading Emirate" in P. E. Lovejoy (ed.), *Slavery on the Frontiers of Islam* (Princeton, NJ, 2004), 55–68.

[21] On the demographic impact of Yoruba wars, see Nigeria National Archives Ibadan (NAI) CSO 26/29834, H. F. Marshall, Intelligence Report on Ara District of Ekiti Div. (1932); NAI CSO 26/29800, N. A. C. Weir, Intelligence Report on Itaji District of Ekiti Div. (1934); Ondo State Chieftaincy Review Commission, 1978, Day 75; interviews with Madam Wuraola Ogundeyi, age eighty-two, and Lawrence Adeyemi, age seventy-six, Omu, June 29, 2001; G. I. Olomola, "Demographic Effects of the Nineteenth Century Yoruba

disparities between coastal and inland Yoruba. The Ijebu/Egba on the coast profited more from the European trade than the Ekiti located in the hinterland, who then blamed the former for its socioeconomic deprivations. In an era of misery, it is not unusual for the Yoruba to associate commercial wealth with witchcraft (*ajẹ*).[22] Proverbs capture these events. The following section discuses Yoruba representations of slavery in proverbs. These include concepts of legal and illegal enslavement; depictions and stereotypes of slaves and modes of enslavement; links between slavery and ethnicity; slavery and religion; contrasts between slaves, freeborn, and pawns; treatment of slaves; and local concepts of slave abolitionism.

QUESTIONS TO CONSIDER

1. In what ways do slave proverbs content, use, or reluctance of use tell us about the way the institution as being understood today? What do we learn from the content of slave proverbs about the institution of slavery in Yorubaland?
2. What are the special burdens that confront a local researcher when interviewing communities about Yoruba slavery?
3. What are the relative strengths and weaknesses of Yoruba slave proverbs as historical sources?
4. How "Yoruba" are Yoruba slave proverbs?
5. How does social change impact the use of proverbs as historical data?
6. What other innovative methods could be used to study slavery if people are generally uninterested in discussing the topic?
7. How do we preserve Yoruba oral traditions and ensure those who possess them do not die with their wisdom/knowledge of slavery?
8. What slave proverbs exist in your own society.
9. Why were slaves used to perform such important political offices during the precolonial period?

CONTENT ANALYSIS OF SOME YORUBA SLAVE PROVERBS

1. Yoruba, Hausa, Slavery and Ethnicity

A ni ki Gambari ta okiti, o ni ile le, se ataye la ni o ta ni, tabi ataku.

We ask the Gambari to somersault and he complains of landing on a hard surface, no one wants him to survive.[23]

Gambari pa Fulani ko lejo ninu.

A Hausa kills a Fulani there is no case to answer, who cares (or there should be no trial) when a Hausa kills a Fulani.[24]

Wars" in *War and Peace*, 371–379; and G. Oguntomisin and T. Falola, "Refugees in Nineteenth Century Yorubaland" in *War and Peace*, 381–398.

[22] See R. Baum, *Shrines of the Slave Trade, Diola Religion and Society in Precolonial Senegambia* (New York, 1999), 108–129; and R. Shaw, *Memories of the Slave Trade, Ritual and the Historical Imagination in Sierra Leone* (Chicago, 2002).

[23] Interview with Adeola Eniola, Kosofe Street, Obalende Lagos, July 3, 2001.

[24] Owomoyela, *Yoruba Proverbs*, 315.

Ethnicity features prominently in Yoruba slave proverbs. The Yoruba recruited Hausa (Gambari) slaves during the eighteenth and nineteenth centuries, and this had an impact on the Hausa-Yoruba relations. In particular, the incorporation of Ilorin, a Yoruba town into the Sokoto caliphate in 1823, from where Sokoto sent soldiers against the Yoruba, produced entrenched anti-Hausa feelings that are felt even now and expressed in these proverbs.[25] The idea that no one cares about a Hausa or a Fulani captures the role of slavery in the Sokoto-Yoruba relations and is used to describe relationships with and within a community.

2. Slavery, Work, and Patrimony

Omo eni i ba jo ni a ba yo; omo ti Gambari ba bi okun ni yoo ran

If a child resembles the parents one would rejoice; the Hausa child will inherit the trade of rope-making.[26]

This proverb addresses ideas of kinship, community, and inheritance. Apart from categorizing slaves and slavers based on their ethnicity, proverbs also link slavery and ethnicity with particular skills. Samuel Johnson describes the use of Gambari (Central Sudanese) slaves as horsemen, pastoralists, and rope-makers in nineteenth-century Yorubaland. These skills are instanced in proverbs linking Hausa slaves to rope-making.[27]

3. Slavery and Freedom, Slaves and Freeborn

A kii pe e leru ka pe e lóbí

If it is a slave it cannot be a child.[28]

Eru kii se omo igi, eru ku iya ko gbo omo ku ariwo ta, eru se omo ni ile iya re ri

A slave is not a senseless block of wood. When a slave dies, his/her mother hears nothing of it. But when a (freeborn) child dies, there is lamentation though the slave was once a child in his mother's house.[29]

There is a popular view that African slavery was benign and distinct from slavery in the Americas.[30] The view gained ground in the eighteenth century as slavers on both sides of the Atlantic debated the merits and demerits of British abolitionism. On the European side, abolitionists, humanitarians as well as traders attacked slavery in Africa, especially the element of human sacrifice, to argue that the Atlantic slave trade saved slaves from ritual killers and cannibals.[31] In Africa, on the other hand, the theory was that slavery was

---

[25] Johnson, *History*, 288. On Ilorin, see I. Mustain, "A Political History of Ilorin in the Nineteenth Century" (unpublished MPhil thesis, University of Ibadan, 1978) and O'Hear, "Ilorin as a Slaving and Slave-Trading Emirate."

[26] Owomoyela, *Yoruba Proverbs*, 435–436.

[27] Johnson, *History*, 123, 193 and Law, *Oyo Empire*, 183–199.

[28] Owomoyela, *Yoruba Proverbs*, 401.

[29] Crowther, *Grammar and Vocabulary*, 98; Bowen, *Grammar*, 63 and Owomoyela, *Yoruba Proverbs*, 367, 389, 430.

[30] S. Miers and I. Kopytoff (eds.), *Slavery in Africa, Historical and Anthropological Perspectives* (Madison, WI, 1977); and J. Inikori (ed.), *Forced Migration, The Impact of the Export Slave Trade on African Societies* (London, 1982).

[31] W. Snelgrave, *New Account of Some Parts of Guinea and the Slave-Trade* (London, 1971 [1734]), 5–24.

a familial institution in which slaveholders and slaves had a patron/client relationship. Abolition, they argued, would destroy the family and lead to socioeconomic chaos. Oroge, for instance, argues that evidence of the benevolence of Yoruba indigenous slavery is illustrated in the discourse of slavery. Slaves were called *omo* (child) rather than the negative term *eru* (slave).[32] The import here, from Emmanuel Oroge's standpoint, is that slavery was a familial institution in which slavers and their slaves had a parent/child connection. But slavery in Yorubaland was much more complex than this. It is true that the Yoruba, regardless of a person's social origin, espoused varying forms of dependency, but compared to similar ties between parents and children, slaves occupied the lowest cadre of the "family." In particular, Oroge ignores the fact that slaves were required to publically indicate their status through "alien" symbols like particular scarification, distinct haircuts, and unusual names. The *ilari* (royal slaves) of Oyo were identified by their partially shaved heads. Other slaves wore bead necklaces (Ekiti: *kele*) identifying their social status. Thus, when a slave was redeemed, the best proof of freedom was to remove the necklace.[33] William Marsh and James Johnson, both ex-slaves, explained that slaves were not *omo* (child), but *omo odo* (servant).[34] Therefore, to call slaves *omo* was to imply a state of permanent minority and not to identify them as free children (freeborn) with ancestral rights. This proverb attests to inferiority of slaves and the better treatment given to the freeborn and how slavery negated freedom. The inference is that one must be clear about one's attitude toward a thing or person (ambivalence causes trouble).

4. Exploitation of Slaves

Gidigidi ko mo ola, ka sise bi eru ko da nnkan.

Scurrying around does not ensure prosperity; working like slaves yields no benefit.[35]

This proverb equates arduous work with slavery. As property and aliens, slaves took on tasks not obliged of the freeborn. The proverb urges people not to work themselves to death.[36]

5. Accommodation and Elite Slaves

Imado i ba se bi elede a ba ilu je; bi eru ba j'oba, ilu o ni ku enikeni.

A wild boar in the place of a pig would ravage the town; a slave made king would spare nobody.[37]

Ika iba la, a ba ilu je; eru iba j'oba, eeyan iba kukan.

[32] Oroge, "Institution of Slavery," 135–142.

[33] C. H. Gollmer, *Charles Andrew Gollmer, His Life and Missionary Labours in West Africa* (London, 1889), 215.

[34] Church Missionary Society Archives (CMS) CA2/067, W. Marsh, journal, April 17, 1850 and J. Johnson, CMS CA2/056, Annual Report for 1879.

[35] Interviews with Abraham Folorunso, Omu-Ekiti, July 4, 2001; Abiola Ajibola, Idikan Ibadan, June 22, 2001; and Pa James Okunoye, Ikole-Ekiti, June 10, 2001.

[36] Interview with Olusola Adejare, Ado Ekiti, August 3, 1998.

[37] Crowther, *Grammar and Vocabulary*, 24; Ellis, *Yoruba-Speaking Peoples*, 239; Delano, *Owe Yoruba*, 78; Owomoyela, *Yoruba Proverbs*, 575; and interviews with Bello Akinyeye and Yusuf Saka, Ayeye Ibadan, July 12, 2001.

Were the wicked to prosper, they would ruin the town; were a slave to be made king, no one would be left in the town.[38]

These proverbs teach that trusting matters to the hands of an unfit person guarantees disaster. They assume that slaves were unfit to serve in political office. Each warns that to put the affairs of a community in the hands of a wicked or unreliable people is to destroy the community. We have noted links between Yoruba state formation and slave labor and the treatment of elite slaves. The rise of Ibadan to the status of a "republic of warriors" hinged on the effort of its leaders (warlords), ably assisted by their slave soldiers, to create the biggest and most egalitarian state in nineteenth-century Yorubaland.[39] In fact, in the volatile days of military rule, characterized by coup d'états and factional conflicts, slaves were the cannon fodder, law enforcers and soldiers on whom the power of Ibadan chiefs rested. Yoruba chiefs, afraid of losing power, maintained power through elite slaves.

At Ibadan, the power of elite slaves became more noticeable in the 1860s as powerful slaves were sent to the provinces as consuls. Not later than 1870 some chiefs demanded policies reducing the power of elite slaves. According to Johnson, Baale (the head chief) Orowusi advised his chiefs to end both the appointment of slaves to sensitive positions and the choice of slave wives as favorite wives. His view was that, as strangers, slaves could not have the interest of Ibadan at heart and could become fifth columnists, while slave wives could poison their spouses. Very few, if any, senior chiefs heeded the plea, however, and continued to use elite slaves. Yet the proverb remains in circulation, warning of the danger of allowing power to slip into the hands of slaves.

6. Slave Control

Eni ti o ni eru lo ni eru.

The slave owner owns the slave's property.[40]

This proverb means no matter the wealth of the slave, he or she is still property. In a Yoruba primer, the author, Joseph F. Odunjo, narrates the story of a slave belonging to a rich man who loved him dearly. On his deathbed, the owner instructed that his only son should inherit not more than a piece of his property while the bulk should go to the favorite slave. The son was sad that the father left almost everything to a slave, but the happy slave hired a drummer to sing his praises in anticipation of imminent freedom and wealth. Many people in the community were also saddened by the deceased's decision. Unsure of what to pick as inheritance, the son consulted every wise man in the town each of whom identified different items as the most valuable property. Hours before the properties were to be shared, the son went to a poor old man for advice. The man counseled him to choose the favorite slave, whose own inheritance would transfer automatically to the new master. At a public forum attended by many, the boy touched the favorite slave as his item of choice. There was a loud "Alleluia" while sorrow and sadness descended on the slave.[41]

---

[38] Owomoyela, *Yoruba Proverbs*, 487.

[39] Johnson, *History*, 281–608; Awe, "Rise of Ibadan"; and Falola, *Political Economy*.

[40] Interview with Ibidun Akinlade, Odojomu Street, Ondo, June 24, 2001; and Owomoyela, *Yoruba Proverbs*, 442.

[41] Odunjo, *Alawiye Apa Kefa* (Lagos, 1972).

7. Age and Slavery

Ati kekere se eru ko mo iyi ote

S/he who has been a slave from childhood knows not the value of rebellion (slave wars/raids).[42]

OR

Atikekere se eru ko mo iyi omoluwabi

One who has been a slave from childhood does not appreciate being a freeborn.[43]

These figurative expressions on human vulnerability indicate how strangers to freedom do not appreciate it. They suggest that people born into slavery (*eru ibile*) and to some extent people captured during childhood possessed very little memories of the initial days of slavery – the period of seasoning.[44] In particular, the former lacked memories associated with the processes of enslavement such as separation from relatives, death of close family members, loss of property, hunger, and the tortuous process of seasoning. To this extent, resistance was more likely to be staged by adult and first-generation slaves than children and creoles. Three informants, Chief Akin Ajibade, Julius Afolayan, and Mathew Babalola, all of Omu-Ekiti, believed this proverb had its origin in differential attitudes to slavery held by first- and later-generation slaves.[45] Similar to the tension between African-born and Creole slaves in the Americas, the latter in Yorubaland also had more privileges than their slave parents, including laws banning their sale. They also shared with the freeborn common language/dialect, body marks, and knowledge of local custom that they could pass off as free.

8. Slavery and Rituals

A kì í fi ọmọ Ọrẹ bọ Ọrẹ.

We do not sacrifice the children of *Ọrẹ* (an Ife *Orisa*) to appease *Ọrẹ*.[46]

Eru kii d'ere, iwofa kii d'Otomporo.

Slaves cannot wear masks and pawns are banned from parading as Otomporo masquerade.[47]

These proverbs, also comment on the distinctions between slaves and freeborn and deal with acceptable codes of conduct in the society. *Ore* and *Otomporo* are two of the numerous Yoruba *Orisa* or gods associated with human sacrifice. Because of their lowly status, slaves dominated the list of victims killed during religious and funeral rites and, as strangers, they could not learn the secrets of specific religious rites. The first proverb has an Ile-Ife origin where *Ore* was one of the most senior *Orisa* and the second from Ikirun closely

---

[42] Interview with Samuel Ojo, Omu Ekiti, July 24, 27, and 29, 2009.

[43] Owomoyela, *Yoruba Proverbs*, 363.

[44] Seasoning was a process relating to the "breaking" of slaves. The practice conditioned the newly enslaved to their new status such as learning new tasks, languages, and culture, among others.

[45] Interviews with Akin Ajibade, Julius Afolayan, and Mathew Babalola, Omu-Ekiti, July 30, 1999.

[46] Cf. A. O. Oguntuyi, *History of Ekiti, From the Beginning to 1939* (Ibadan, 1979), 37.

[47] Interview with Adeniyi Adebayo, Ikirun, August 5, 2001.

associated with *Otomporo* masquerade.[48] At Ile-Ife and Kabba, the idea that only strangers (slaves) could be offered in sacrifice but not allowed to join the priesthood underlies many decades of communal conflicts between slave descendants and those of the freeborn.[49] According to Oyo and Ife traditions, between the 1780s and the 1940s, the Ife preyed on Oyo refugees and brought Ijesa slaves into the town. With reference to the 1880s, Johnson noted how Ife people often recruited sacrificial victims from Ijesa area even though both fought as allies against the Oyo during the second half of the nineteenth century.[50]

9. Slavery and Pawnship

Rira la eru yiya la ya iwofa.

We buy slaves and hire pawns.[51]

Asotele ko je ki a pe iwofa ni eru.

A firm contract keeps the pawn from being called a slave.[52]

These proverbs discuss the differences between pawns and slaves. *Iwofa* (pawning) involved the pledging of individuals to a lender to work in lieu of interest payments in money.[53] The pawn was the debtor's representative or the debtor himself. Child pawns lived with the creditor and worked for him until the debt was redeemed. Most adult pawns lived in their own homes, working some days for themselves and others for the creditor. Pawnship is a contract in which the liquidation of a debt leads to the release of a pawn from bondage. Slavery was different. A slave was purchased or caught in war, and it was for the slaveholder to decide whether to release the slave or not even when the latter had the means to redeem him- or herself. Pawns received better treatment than slaves on the expectation of future redemption and because pawns and creditors generally came from the same community. Nonetheless, an unpaid debt or the transfer of a pawn far away from their kin could and often did result in enslavement. According to an Egba chief in 1876, "the interest upon … money … lent, added to the original sum, [and] may in due time lead to the [pawn] being sold as a slave."[54]

CONCLUSION

From the preceding discussion, it is clear that proverbs contribute to the study of slavery. Yoruba slave proverbs in particular enhance our understanding of Yoruba history. They

---

[48] *Otomporo* is a Yoruba masquerade feared for brutality in whipping the audience. It is closely associated with *Ogun*, the Yoruba god of metals.

[49] S. Omoniyi, "Inter-clan Rivalry in Oweland" (unpublished BA essay, University of Ibadan, 1979); and P. Akanmidu, "The Socio-Economic Impact of Caste System in Oweland, 1834–2000" (unpublished BA essay, University of Ilorin, 2004).

[50] CMS CA2/049, David Hinderer, journal, August–September 1858; and Johnson, *History*, 21.

[51] Interview with Samuel Ojo, Omu-Ekiti, March 17, 2009.

[52] NAI CMS (Y) 2/2/3, D. Williams to J. Maser, November 24, 1879.

[53] On *iwofa*, see CMS CA2/031/78, Crowther to T. Hutchinson, September 10, 1856; Johnson, *History*, 126–130; Lovejoy and Falola (eds.), *Pawnship, Slavery and Colonialism in Africa* (Trenton, 2003), 137–163, 325–408; Peel, *Religious Encounter and the Making of the Yoruba* (Indianapolis, 2001), 59–63; Shields, "Palm Oil and Power," 106–108, 123–134; and Ojo, "Warfare, Slavery and Transformation," 234–250.

[54] E. Roper, "What I Saw in Africa, Part II," *Church Missionary Gleaner (CMG)* 3, 27 (1876), 34–36.

contain substantial data on public perceptions of freedom, slavery, and related institutions of bondage. They also allow us to see the complexity of Yoruba identities and aspects of Yoruba worldviews on slavery group relations, political concerns, economic relations, religious beliefs, systems of dependency, and social change. These are rich materials that enhance our understanding of a topic for which written sources are inadequate. Finally, unlike many long narratives, slave proverbs are less susceptible to change. Every proverb recorded by Crowther in 1843 is known today in the same form, whereas each of his longer narratives has since been modified and altered.[55]

SUGGESTED ADDITIONAL READINGS

Adeeko, Adeleke. *Proverbs, Textuality, and Nativism in African Literature.* Gainsville: University Press of Florida, 1998.

Akintoye, S. Adebanji. *A History of the Yoruba People.* Dakar: Amalion Publishing, 2010.

Awe, Bolanle. "Praise Poems as Historical Data: The Example of the Yoruba Oríkì," *Africa* 44, 4 (1974), 331–349.

Bailey, Anne C. *African Voices of the Atlantic Slave Trade: Beyond the Silence and the Shame.* Boston: Beacon Press, 2005.

Bowen, Thomas J. *Grammar and Dictionary of the Yoruba Language.* New York: Smithsonian Institution, 1858. See pp. 56–69.

Crowther, Samuel A. *A Grammar and Vocabulary of the Yoruba Language.* London: Seeleys, 1852.

Greene, Sandra E. *West African Narratives of Slavery.* Indianapolis: Indiana University Press, 2011.

Klein, Martin. "Studying the History of Those Who Would Rather Forget: Oral History and the Experience of Slavery," *History in Africa* 16 (1989), 209–217.

Lawal, Babatunde. "Some Aspects of Yoruba Aesthetics," *British Journal of Aesthetics* 14, 3 (1974), 239–249.

Lovejoy, Paul E. and Toyin Falola, eds. *Pawnship, Slavery and Colonialism in Africa.* Trenton, NJ: Africa World Press, 2003.

Okpewho, Isidore. *African Oral Literature: Backgrounds, Character, and Continuity.* Indianapolis: Indiana University Press, 1992.

Olatunji, Olatunde. *Features of Yoruba Oral Poetry.* Ibadan: University Press, 1984.

Owomoyela, Oyekan. *Yoruba Proverbs.* Lincoln: University of Nebraska Press, 2005.

---

[55] Crowther, *Grammar and Vocabulary.*

14 In Remembrance of Slavery

Tchamba Vodun (Bénin and Togo)

DANA RUSH

Tchamba me so gbenye me nya senao
Tchamba me so gbenye bu.

> I come from Tchamba, no one understands my language.
> I come from Tchamba, my language is lost.

Mia mamawo kpo hotsui wo fle agbeto kodi.
Amekle nya ne noanyi na ye looo. Elava kplom yi afiadi.
Bada bada nenoanyi nam looo.

> Our grandparents were rich, and they bought people.
> I am proud of who I am, though it risks bringing me troubles.
> May bad luck stay far away from me.

> > Tchamba Vodun songs, collected in Vogan, Togo, February 8, 1999.

Vodun, or Vod*ou* as it is known in the Caribbean and the Americas, is the predominant religious system of southern Bénin and Togo. It is organized around a single divine creator and hundreds of spirits who govern the forces of nature and society. As an orientation to the world, however, it is much more all-encompassing, permeating virtually all aspects of life. Its existence in Haiti is a testament to the strength of Vodun/Vodou in the face of the transatlantic slave trade. West African Vodun in Bénin and Togo also attests to the impact of slavery.

Domestic enslavement is the source of a Vodun complex known as Tchamba. This spirit grouping has been critical in the maintenance and proliferation of histories and memories of domestic slavery, sustained to the present by the progeny of domestic slaves and their owners. Tchamba Vodun has also been influential in bringing to the fore contemporary debates regarding the owning and selling of slaves and slave ancestry. Such discus-

This essay set the foundation for the in-depth study undertaken during 2010–2011, which I am currently expanding into a book and documentary. Although I learned of Tchamba in the late 1990s, a major impetus for pursuing this research further was my participation in the international conference "Tales of Slavery: Narratives of Slavery, the Slave Trade and Enslavement in Africa" (University of Toronto, May 20–23, 2009). I thank Martin Klein, conference organizer and Professor Emeritus at University of Toronto, for the opportunity to present this preliminary work. I extend my appreciation to conference participants for good feedback. I also thank the Fulbright Africa Regional Research Program and the Council for International Exchange of Scholars for supporting my fieldwork on this topic in Bénin and Togo during 2010–2011.

sions help Beninese and Togolese people address the multiple roles their ancestors played in transatlantic and domestic slavery, as either the sellers or the enslaved.

I begin this essay with some general information about transatlantic and domestic slavery in this region. I then introduce an example of domestic slavery via a landmark piece of African francophone literature. Next, I demonstrate how the visual within Vodun marks people and spaces as dedicated to the remembrance of slavery. I focus on Tchamba Vodun shrines and temple paintings as primary documents, emphasizing the main iconographic symbology. I then introduce a new Tchamba spirit with contemporary meanings derived from the growing cognizance of the transatlantic slave trade. I follow with two field stories addressing present-day complications revolving around histories of domestic slavery. Throughout this writing, I demonstrate that Tchamba Vodun spirits reify reversal: the once-enslaved are now divinities.

BRIEF BACKGROUND

"When our forefathers bought a slave, this was just as if they put money into a bank account. If you buy yourself a slave and [s]he produces children, they will belong to you; they will till your fields and build houses for you." Bonifatur Foli[1]

Between the fifteenth and nineteenth centuries, an estimated 11–12 million slaves were purchased in Africa by European traders, 80 percent of whom left the African continent between 1700 and 1850.[2] The town of Ouidah, Bénin (formerly Dahomey) was a major embarkation point for slaves from the 1670s through the 1860s, accounting for more than one million people.[3] In the 1690s, the slave trade through Ouidah reached a volume of about ten thousand slaves per year, and in the years 1700–1713, the exportation number reached approximately fifteen thousand slaves annually, which may have accounted for up to half of all slaves leaving the continent.[4]

The section of the western African coast between the Volta and Lagos rivers was not only a major source of slaves for the Atlantic slave trade, but was also an area where domestic slavery was commonplace. Although there is uncertainty regarding the date that domestic slavery began, Le Hérissé notes that in the nineteenth century it was more common for Dahomeans to purchase slaves for domestic use from the interior northern regions of contemporary Bénin and Togo than to receive slaves as gifts from the king.[5] Those from the king were likely obtained in warfare, and many were bound for the Atlantic trade, while Dahomean citizens who financed their own purchase were engaging in a system different than that of the transatlantic trade.

Thus, the overseas trade amplified the already established tradition of domestic enslavement. By the 1670s, the English, French, and Danish had built forts in Ouidah to facilitate their roles in the slave trade, and in 1721, the Portuguese built a fort. The staff of the European forts was overwhelmingly African, although most of these slaves were not local in origin. A large number of domestic slaves came from about 300 miles north of the

[1] Dietrich Westermann, *Worterbuch der Ewe-Sprache* (Berlin, 1905).
[2] Paul E. Lovejoy, "The Volume of the Atlantic Slave Trade: A Synthesis," *The Journal of African History* 23, 4 (1982), 473–501.
[3] Robin Law, *Ouidah: The Social History of a West African Slaving "Port" 1727–1892*, (Athens, 2004), 1–2.
[4] Law, *Ouidah*, 2004. Lovejoy, Paul E. *Transformations in Slavery* (Cambridge, 1983).
[5] Le Herissé, A. *L'ancien royaume du Dahomey: Moeurs, religion, histoire* (Paris, 1911), 52–53.

coast. Tchamba and Kabre peoples, from northern central Togo, seem to have been the most sought after as domestic slaves in the south.[6]

In 1723, Ouidah's French fort reported a purchase of "[T]Chamba" slaves, in reference to this northern ethnicity.[7] Today, Tchamba is not just a region of Togo and the name of the main city and ethnic group therein. Along the coast, Tchamba is also a particularly strong Vodun complex honoring domestic slaves, addressed later in the chapter. But first, here is an example of domestic slavery from a local piece of African francophone literature.

FÉLIX COUCHORO'S *L'ESCLAVE*

In 1929, Ouidah-born author Félix Couchoro published his first novel, *L'Esclave* (The Slave), which to this day stands as an important contribution to African francophone literature. Couchoro's *L'Esclave* is a passionate story of an inheritance dispute between a domestic slave, Mawulawoé, and his brother, Komlangan. Couchoro's character of the "slave," the relationships between the "slave" and the members of the family who bought him, and the social and economic milieu in which the story unfolds present a contextual backdrop for Tchamba veneration, referring directly to a domestic slave's presumed origins, ethnicity, and ancestry.

A key passage from, *L'Esclave* follows:

> Komlangan's father purchased eight-year-old Mawulawoé from far, far away in the northern region of Okou-Okou. The slave's adorable face pleased his master so that he could not bring himself to disfigure it with the scarification of slaves. He named him Mawulawoé, which means "God will provide." Nothing distinguished him from Komlangan with whom he grew up. They shared their games and worked together as brothers.... The boys grew into men and took wives.... At his deathbed, the father blessed his two sons preaching to them his mutual affection. They closed his eyes for him.[8]

This point in the novel sets into motion the brothers' fight over their inheritance. Komlangan, the birth son, claims that Mawulawoé, the "slave," has no rights to their father's estate. Thus Mawulawoé's revenge begins and instigates multiple events that elicit love, jealousy, hate, and ambition, which ultimately lead to several murders. The theme of Couchoro's *L'Esclave* is current, and the ramifications of domestic enslavement play out in contemporary Tchamba veneration.

When Couchoro mentions that Komlangan's father purchased an eight-year-old child from "far, far away in the northern region of Okou-Okou," he is referring to the more widespread name for the Nyantroukou ethnic group in northern Togo.[9] A large number of the domestic slaves brought to the south came from the same region as Mawulawoé, 300 miles north of the Atlantic Ocean. It is estimated that as many as three million people were brought to the coast, but much like Mawulawoé, not all of them were destined for

---

[6] Tobias Wendl, "Slavery, Spirit Possession & Ritual Consciousness: The Tchamba Cult Among the Mina of Togo" in Heike Behrend and Ute Luig (eds.), *Spirit Possession: Modernity & Power in Africa* (Madison, 1999), 111–123.

[7] In Law, *Ouidah*, 39.

[8] Félix Couchoro, *L'Esclave* (Paris, 1929), 81, my translation.

[9] The Nyantroukou, along the Dassa, Holli, Ifé, Itcha, Mahi, and Oyo, are listed by Cornevin in a subsection entitled "Yoruba-speaking groups," although he mentions that both the Holli and the Nyantroukou are "marginal" in the Yoruba collective. Robert Cornevin, *Histoire du Dahomey* (Paris, 1962), 44, 202–205.

the Atlantic trade.[10] Neighbors of the Nyantroukou peoples are Bassar, Moba, Taberma, Tchamba, and Kabre. It is the latter two, however, that seem to have been the most sought after as domestic slaves.[11]

In the Mina language of coastal Togo, "-to" at the end of a word refers to a person "of" or "from" the first part of the word. Accordingly, the terms *kabreto* and *tchambato* were used to designate enslaved Kabre and Tchamba peoples in the south.[12] In association with domestic slavery, however, only the name Tchamba survives to the present. In the section that follows I analyze Tchamba material culture.[13]

QUESTIONS TO CONSIDER

1. Why is Tchamba, originally a Vodun spirit venerated by the progeny of former slave owners, now revered by the descendants of the formerly enslaved?
2. In the contemporary world, why is it challenging to determine who is the descendant of a slave and who is the descendant of a slave owner?
3. Why is domestic slavery a difficult topic to address? Think about guilt, shame, and pride from both perspectives.
4. Whose "voices" are represented in the Tchamba songs at the beginning of the essay?

TCHAMBAGAN: READING THE VISUAL

Within Tchamba Vodun, the visual marks people and spaces dedicated to the remembrance of slavery. The most important attribute of Tchamba veneration is a tricolored metal bracelet. A person wearing this type of bracelet can be recognized as being affiliated with Tchamba and associated with domestic slavery as either a descendant of slaves or slave owners (Figure 14.1). Within Vodun practice, however, the same tricolored metal bracelet may represent an entirely different spirit, completely removed from Tchamba veneration. Because of this, context and associated symbols are of critical importance in reading Tchamba iconography.

---

[10] Charles Piot, "Of Slaves and the Gift: Kabre Sale of Kin during the Era of the Slave Trade," *Journal of African History*, 37 1 (1996) 31–49.

[11] Wendl, "Slavery," 114.

[12] Wendl, "Slavery," 114. Perhaps the term *kabreto* has lost its currency in association with domestic slavery because of the thirty-eight-year regime of late Togolese dictator Eyadema. Because Eyadema was Kabre, a southerner (Mina or Ewe) could have been detained, or worse, by Eyadema's military if heard speaking badly about Kabre peoples. At present, *kabreto* means someone of Kabre ethnicity and has nothing to do with slavery.

[13] Tchamba has been the subject of four short studies: Judy Rosenthal, *Possession, Ecstasy, and Law in Ewe Voodoo* (Charlottesville and London, 1990). Rush, Dana, "Eternal Potential: Chromolithographs in Vodunland," *African Arts* 33, 4 (1999), 60–75, 94–96. Wendl, "Slavery"; Alessandra Brivio, "Nos grands-pères achetaient des esclaves: Le culte de Mami Tchamba au Togo et au Bénin," *Gradhiva au musée quai Branly* 8 (2008), 65–79. According to Wendl, it is "the descendants of former slave masters who are afflicted by the spirits of their former slaves" (111). Judy Rosenthal's study, focusing on Ewe Vodun in Togo, addresses Tchamba in terms of its "quasi-historical and . . . imaginary geography and genealogy of the slave trade with its attendant mixings of populations and lineages in marriage, procreation, and production of the sacred" (23). She attends to this topic in the chapter entitled "Romance of the North," in her book *Possession, Ecstasy, and Law in Ewe Voodoo*. In her recent article, "Nos grands-pères achetaient des esclaves: Le culte de Mami Tchamba au Togo et au Bénin," Alessandra Brivio analyzes how slave spirits evoke a mythical heroic past of both slave traders and slaves themselves, in terms of the ambivalence of current memories of slavery.

14.1. Tchambagan bracelets for purchase at a Vogan market.
Source: Dana Rush, December 1999, Vogan, Togo.

This tricolored metal bracelet, called *tchambagan*, has a metonymic relationship to the shackles and irons used in the transport of slaves from the north to the south. *Ga(n)* is the Fon, Mina, and Ewe word for metal itself, or something that is metal. Thus *tchambagan* translates as the "metal of Tchamba."[14] According to collected histories,[15] slave owners presented their slaves with such a bracelet to mark them as enslaved people. Upon the death of a slave, the family who owned him/her removed the bracelet (or, in some versions, an anklet or a ring) and added it to a shrine dedicated to the family's former slaves in gratitude for their lifetimes of service.

The bracelet's three colors of metal (black, white, and red) are sometimes said to represent three different northern spirits. Black, represented by iron, is called *boublou* (stranger), and is known to be a turbulent, aggressive, excitable spirit who is associated with iron, thunder, and fire. White, represented by silver, is called *anohi* (a presumed Hausa spirit, sometimes called "Hausa," other times called *adonko*), and is known as a source of calm spirituality, associated with the rainbow. Red, represented by copper or bronze, is called *yendi* (a contemporary town in northeastern Ghana) and is known for its powers of healing and its association with the earth. These three spirits are likely a contemporary mixture of southern Vodun – Heviosso (thunder), Dan Aida Wedo (rainbow serpent), and Sakpata (the earth, healing, and disease), for example – with romanticized northern spiritual identities. Of course, these "northern spirits" do not really exist in the north. Wendl's

[14] Many of the words I translate may not have exact origins in the ethnic groups to whom I refer. Because Tchamba crosses southern ethnic borders, some words associated with the Tchamba might originate in Mina, Ewe, or Fon, but are used in all three languages. I am not addressing tonal differentiations.

[15] These histories were collected mainly along coastal Togo and into southeastern Ghana in a series of interviews during December 1998 through March 1999. The interviews collected in Bénin were usually with people originally from Togo, but who had moved because of political unrest.

interpretation of the southern representation of "northern spirits" is that they are "projective transfigurations, by which Mina [Fon, Ewe] have articulated their own experience with the otherness of the people from the north in symbolic and ritual terms."[16]

Wendl explains that if a person learns, possibly through a divination, that s/he has a Tchamba spirit, s/he must begin to honor the spirit by purchasing two *tchambagan* as the initial component of a shrine. Similarly, I was often told that when a person learns of her/his Tchamba spiritual obligations, s/he is obliged to purchase a new *tchambagan*, add it to a generations-old shrine piled with old *tchambagan*, and then choose a replacement from among the accumulation of bracelets and rings to wear as a pronouncement of his/her newly affirmed Tchamba affiliation. Sometimes, I was told, a farmer will find a *tchambagan* while cultivating the field, digging a well, or constructing the foundation of a house. Such a find would be read as a sign that the family who owns the land used to own slaves. A family meeting would be called, divination would be carried out, and the family would begin to venerate Tchamba in gratitude for the service of the now deceased slaves. Depending on the divination, a family might be obliged to host a large Tchamba celebration as an apology for years of neglect and as a harbinger of future commitment to devotion. In most cases, after acquiring a *tchambagan* and learning of an obligation to a northern spirit, a Tchamba novice would also purchase a *tchambazikpe*, or wooden stool, to welcome the Tchamba spirit and to provide it with a seat. The stool also is a direct reference to the role of the domestic slave to carry her/his master's stool. Cowry shells are also important to a Tchamba shrine, in that they were the currency used to purchase slaves. Wendl stresses that "iron bracelets, wooden stools, and cowry shells are the focus of every Tchamba shrine, representing the slave as a chained person, a stool carrier, and a person who had been bought."[17]

The same symbols help identify Tchamba in mural paintings, which evoke histories, memories, and stories about domestic slavery. These murals articulate slave status and foreign (northern) origins through their painted details. Metal bracelets, northern scarification markings, clothing, accoutrements, stools, cowry shells, Islamic paraphernalia, "northern" food and drink, as well as Tchamba himself, sometimes accompanied by a female (his mother or wife known as Mama Tchamba), are painted on Vodun temple murals.

Ghanaian artist Joseph Ahiator has painted a handful of Tchamba temple murals throughout Bénin, Togo, and Ghana. His earliest Tchamba painting (Figure 14.2), which he dates to the 1970s, shows Tchamba's mother on the left with a bowl of kola nuts, some of which she is giving to her son before he journeys. Kola nuts are a key symbol commonly associated with northern Muslims, used culturally as well as medicinally to suppress hunger, thirst, and fatigue. Both mother and son have northern-looking scarification markings on their faces. Between them Joseph painted an Islamic watering kettle and a *tchambazikpe*, or stool, upon which are *tchambagan*, the tricolored bracelets which Tchamba also wears on both wrists. His hat is decorated with abstracted cowry shells.

Vertical facial scarification markings are pervasive markers of a northern identity and play an integral role in contemporary Tchamba veneration. Along the same lines as the refusal of Mamulawoé's father to have his "son" scarified in *L'Esclave*, coastal people

---

[16] Wendl, "Slavery," 116.
[17] Wendl, "Slavery," 116.

14.2. Maman Tchamba and Tchamba temple mural painted by Kossivi Joseph Ahiator.
Source: Dana Rush, April 1996, near Lomé, Togo.

in general disapprove of northern facial scarification markings. A Mina proverb demonstrates the extent to which enslaved people did not want to draw attention to their facial markings and, in turn, their enslaved status: *Adonko mekploa fetridetsi o*, which translates as "A slave does not draw strings while eating okra soup."[18] The proverb is a direct reference to mucilaginous texture of cooked okra (*fetridetsi*), which, when lifted from bowl to mouth, produces long, thin, gummy vertical strings, similar to northern facial scarification markings. In the contemporary spiritual context, when a person is seized by a Tchamba spirit, s/he or a nearby initiate will draw temporary kaolin markings on her/his face or the face of the person in trance mimicking northern scarification. Some adepts are said to go as far as to have real markings permanently incised on their cheeks, but I have never seen this. Alternatively, adepts may use charcoal to color their faces a dark black to represent a very distant, unknowable place – specifically the north. The scarification markings are clearly "northern looking," but in reality, they are often an amalgamation of various northern ethnic markings (Bariba, Logba, Dendi, Nyantroukou) combined to communicate the idea of a generalized northern ethnic identity.

In a painting from the late 1990s, Joseph paints much of the same iconography, making Tchamba easily identifiable: tricolored bracelets, a stool upon which the bracelets are placed (corner of stool can be seen on bottom left of image), a cowry-shell-covered hat, and northern-looking scarification markings (Figure 14.3). Joseph added Tchamba's wife and drummer to another temple mural located in Togo. The threesome is en route to the "north" (Figure 14.4). Tchamba's wife carries his stool on her head, and is dressed and adorned in a "northern" style. The only explanation Joseph provided concerning her draped cloth, the nose ring, and the six hooped earrings (three in each ear) is that she is

[18] Westermann, *Worterbuch*, 122.

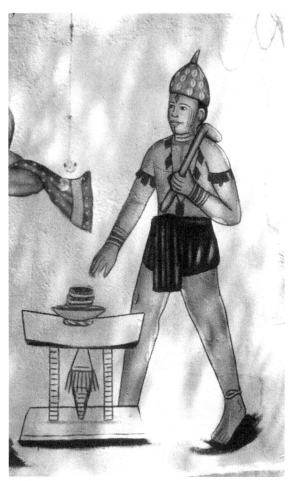

14.3. Tchamba temple mural painted by Kossivi Joseph Ahiator.
Source: Dana Rush, December 1999, near Lomé, Togo.

"northern."[19] To Joseph, "northern" represents a vast conceptual realm offering a rich reservoir of symbolism. Two Mama Tchamba mural paintings in Aneho, Togo also show similar iconography. In Figure 14.5, Mama Tchamba functions as guardian for her family's wealth, represented in the bowl overflowing with gold. She is adorned with a cowry-shell-covered hat and gold jewelry, also attesting to the wealth of the family who could afford to own her. Once again, facial scarification markings refer to her "northern" identity and slave status.

A Tchamba shrine might be near such a mural painting (Figure 14.6), but more often than not, the shrine is kept out of sight to be viewed only for offerings only on certain sacred days of the week. There are many types of offerings given to Tchamba, but the ubiquitous favorites are *tchoukoutou*, a highly fermented northern Togolese millet-based drink; *tchapkalo*, an unfermented sugar-sweetened northern Togolese millet-based drink; and kola

---

[19] Adornment in the south does not traditionally include nose rings or multiple ear piercings. Thus, identifying this type of adornment as "northern" likely reflects the fact that it is *not* southern. Much like "northern" scarification, "northern" adornment is an amalgamation of multiple types of northern ethnic body ornamentation.

14.4. Tchamba with his wife temple mural painted by Kossivi Joseph Ahiator.
Source: Dana Rush, November 1999, near Lomé, Togo.

nuts. Other offerings made to Tchamba and/or associated slave spirits are combinations of the following: gin; *sodabi*, a locally distilled palm wine; and *liha*, a corn drink that must be prepared by a postmenopausal woman. Other common offerings are rice, beans, yam, and manioc prepared together; corn, millet, or cassava products, as well as black chicken, black pigeon, and male goat. Sometimes there is a container of *karité* butter because on occasion, based on divination, a *tchambagan* must be anointed with this butter. When I was fortunate to have access to old Tchamba shrines, photography was generally forbidden.

Tchamba is decidedly an old Vodun spirit based on domestic African enslavement. However, there is a new Tchamba spirit with contemporary meanings derived from the growing cognizance of the transatlantic slave trade. Tchamba appears to be increasingly associated with Mami Wata, the female water spirit. This association is twofold in explanation. Some Mami Wata adepts who venerate Tchamba hold that they have ancestors who were sold in the transatlantic trade. Those who claim this often say that other people worshipping Tchamba (usually other Mami Wata adepts) do not always have the spirit in their families. Others relate the possession of Tchamba to the prestige associated with a family who at one

14.5. Maman Tchamba temple mural with a bowl of gold.
Source: Dana Rush, April 1996, Aneho, Togo.

time could afford owning slaves. Mami Wata is known to bring wealth, and thus if one has Mami Wata as a familial guiding spirit, one should have had enough money to have bought slaves. Tchamba is thus often regarded as a modern-day sign of old money.

TRACING TCHAMBA ROOTS

Today it is not uncommon for stories to circulate regarding which families owned slaves and whether their slaves married into their families. Some of the descendants of slaves are just recently learning of their slave ancestry. Most of these accounts follow a general format.

The story usually begins with a group of young men, usually Catholic, walking around town. They pass a compound in which a Vodun celebration is taking place. One young man in the group stops walking and starts shuffling his feet to the *brekete* drumming rhythm, which is known to be from the north. He is then seized by a Tchamba spirit and starts speaking an unrecognizable language, also said to be from the north. The language is often

14.6. Maman Tchamba temple mural with bowl of kola nuts…
Source: Dana Rush, January 2000, Aneho, Togo.

referred to as "Hausa," as a generic term for "northern." Some claim that Tchamba always sends an angel to translate the incomprehensible messages from the ancestral north, whereas others maintain that the person in trance is truly speaking a northern language based on her/his northern ancestry manifesting itself via the will of Tchamba. Whether this is a form of xenoglossy (knowledge of a language one has never learned), glossolalia (speaking a language one does not know), or articulated mumbling is irrelevant. What matters is that Tchamba is connecting to and communicating with those who hold his spirit. While shuffling his feet, the young man in a trance might stop for a moment to draw scarification markings on his face from earth retrieved from under his feet.

Following this spirit encounter, the chosen person meets with a diviner who often endorses Tchamba veneration. Some people learning of their slave ancestry travel to the north in search of their roots and long-lost families. In Lomé, Togo, the name Dogbe-Tome was mentioned to me several times in relationship to a story – still in circulation – of a woman who had learned of her slave ancestry and journeyed north to find her roots. The following is based on a summary of my interview with Cécile Akpaglo, in Lomé, Togo:

> In the early 1800s, the father of a very wealthy Ewe family sent a slave buyer to the area in and around Upper Volta (contemporary Burkina Faso) to purchase a strong, male slave. The slave was known by his surname Tomi. He served the Ewe family well, and grew up. Through his hard work and honesty, he became a well-respected man. He married into the Dogbe family and had children ... time passed.... In the 1950s, a young girl from the wealthy Catholic Dogbe family in Lomé, woke up one morning in trance. She took her school chalk and drew northern scarification patterns on her face and starting speaking in an incomprehensible language. Her father was worried so he took his daughter to a very well-respected diviner for a consultation. The diviner asked questions and consulted with the Fa oracle. He also recalled that there had always been talk in the local community of a male Dogbe ancestor being of Burkinabe origins. The diviner advised the girl to go to Burkina Faso to find her family. She traveled with her father to Ouagadougou. They learned that everyone in the family was dead except for a very old man. They went to meet with the old man who remembered his own grandfather telling him of slavery and tearing up when he recalled the sale of one of his own brothers to an Ewe family in the south. The old man's surname was Tomi. From that point on the family adopted the name Dogbe-Tomi, and began Tchamba veneration. The girl grew up, and when she died in the 1990s, the family had already gone back to Catholicism.[20]

This search for family origins has haunting similarities to heritage tourism, also known as "roots tourism," in which people of African descent in the Americas travel to former slave port cities such as Cape Coast, Ghana, and Gorée Island, Senegal, in search of their roots. The idea of "return" and the deep longing for origins and homeland transcend time and space and have relevance in both Africa and the United States.

I have only one case history in which I was able to meet the daughter and granddaughter of a "bought person" (*amepleple* in Mina and Ewe) named Tonyewogbe. I conducted a series of interviews in 1999 with these women in the town of Adidogome, Togo. The last surviving child of the "bought person," Adono Zowaye, was a frail, though vibrant, centenarian at the time. Her youngest daughter, Notuefe Zowaye (b. 1952), had just begun the process of Tchamba initiation upon the advice of a diviner. The following is a summary of their story:

> In the late nineteenth century, there was a wealthy farmer named Kofi Zowaye. He had no wives nor children. Because of his wealth and his desire to leave it to a beloved child, he purchased a baby girl from the north, whom he named Tonyewogbe. He raised the girl as if she were his real daughter, and kept her purchase a secret so that his daughter would not feel "different" from other family members, even though rumors of her "bought person" status circulated. Tonyewogbe married into the family and had three children, the youngest of whom was named Adono Zowaye. Tonyewogbe died when she was quite young, but Adono remembered that her mother had scars on her light-skinned face and stomach like nothing she had ever seen in the south. Adono stated that she thought her mother might have been Peul because of her light skin, her facial features, and her scarifications. While acknowledging that her own skin is quite dark, Adono pointed to her very straight nose and high cheekbones claiming that she had features like her mother. Adono later

---

[20] Interview with Cécile Akpaglo, Lomé, Togo, February 9, 1999. Although I tried, I was unable to meet with any members of the Dogbe-Tomi family. I was told that many of them had moved to Europe and only came back to Lomé periodically.

14.7. Adono Zowaye with her youngest daughter Notuefe Zowayè in front of the beginning stages of a Tchamba shrine.
Source: Dana Rush, January 2000, Adidogome, Togo.

learned that her mother's scarification were likely those of Kabre peoples in the north.... Tonyewogbe was raised not knowing that she was a "bought person" until issues of inheritance cropped up. Her father wanted his daughter to inherit his estate, but once he died, his brothers refused to allow her to acquire the land and wealth of her father. Tonyewogbe never received much of what her father bequeathed to her, and inheritance problems continue to trouble her daughter, Adono, and her granddaughter, Notuefe, to the present.

Because of these ongoing problems, Notuefe had begun Tchamba initiation in 1999, but she was still gathering funds to continue the long and somewhat costly process. The discussions we had were emotional. At one point, Adono began crying because of the ongoing divisive effect the inheritance issues play in her family in general and with her daughter Notuefe in particular. However, since Notuefe began Tchamba initiation, things have been improving in her life. When she prays, she claims that it is like her grandmother is with her; it makes her feel happy and brings her good luck. Her Tchamba shrine was quite modest, with only a *tchambazikpe* painted white and *tchambagan* (Figure 14.7). Notuefe avoided Tchamba initiation for years, even though she knew through her dreams that Tchamba was calling her. Because she now understands her great-grandmother's northern "bought person" status, she has become very proud of her mother's history and her own ancestry.[21]

Couchoro's *L'Esclave* – with all of its drama and pain – is a "living story" in which the characters may change but the human downfalls of jealousy and greed continue to the present, as presented in the preceding account. Complications based on "bought people" and inheritance have become even more nefarious in that stories currently circulate of brothers and sisters who have been reported to isolate and identify a sibling born of the same parents as a "bought person," only to deny that sibling her/his inheritance.

[21] Interview with Adono and Notuefe Zowaye, Adidogome, Togo, February 1999.

CONCLUDING THOUGHTS

The open-endedness of Vodun has been critical in the maintenance and proliferation of histories of domestic slavery from the perspectives of families whose ancestors owned domestic slaves, were domestic slaves, and/or were sold in the transatlantic slave trade. Vodun is able to produce spirits to address the changing needs of contemporary society. As more discussions surrounding slavery take place, Vodun spirits with new personae will materialize to help answer newly emerging questions. Accordingly, the centuries-strong and fervently reimagined memories of slavery are alive and growing.

SUGGESTED ADDITIONAL READINGS

Cornevin, Robert. *Histoire du Dahomey.* Paris: Editions Berger-Levrault, 1962.

Law, Robin. *Ouidah: The Social History of a West African Slaving "Port" 1727–1892.* Athens: Ohio University Press, 2004.

Lovejoy, Paul E. "The Volume of the Atlantic Slave Trade: A Synthesis," *The Journal of African History* 23, 4 (1982), 473–501.

Piot, Charles. "Of Slaves and the Gift: Kabre Sale of Kin during the Era of the Slave Trade," *The Journal of African History* 37, 1 (1996) 31–49.

Rosenthal, Judy. *Possession, Ecstasy, and Law in Ewe Voodoo.* Charlottesville and London: University Press of Virginia, 1998.

Rush, Dana. "Eternal Potential: Chromolithographs in Vodunland," *African Arts* 33, 4 (1999), 60–75, 94–96.

Wendl, Tobias. "Slavery, Spirit Possession & Ritual Consciousness: The Tchamba Cult among the Mina of Togo," in *Spirit Possession: Modernity & Power in Africa.* Edited by Heike Behrend, and Ute Luig (Madison: The University of Wisconsin Press, 1999), 111–123.

PART THREE

DOCUMENTING OUR OWN HISTORIES AND CULTURAL PRACTICES

15 INTRODUCTION: Written Accounts by African Authors

Slavery and the heritage of slavery have been important in many African societies. It has been so important that many Africans have tried to suppress memories about them. There are, however, many others who have passed on stories and others who have written them down. There are also Africans who openly defended what they saw as their right to enslave others. This section gathers together three very diverse documents in which Africans tell us what they thought about the institution of slavery. The first comes from Cameroon. Ahmadou Sehou, a scholar from that country, has found documents associated with Lamido Iyawa Adamou, a powerful chief who defended slavery and maintained control over slaves in his chiefdom until his death in 1966. In Chapter 16, Sehou discusses a letter the *lamido* wrote, a list of punishments to which slaves were subject, and a manumission certificate. A letter from a French administrator suggests that Iyawa Adamou's success was rooted in the limited authority of the colonial state and its dependence on men like the *lamido*. The second document comes from Ute Röschenthaler, who did research in an area that was on the major trade route to the coast in Cameroon and southeastern Nigeria. Her research assistant, who was interested in local history, collected and synthesized information gathered from elders. The result, presented in Chapter 17, is an account that gives a picture both of how a participating society saw the organization of the slave trade and how the slaves fit into and influenced the community. The third document comes from Ghana, known as the Gold Coast during British rule. Bayo Holsey in Chapter 18 gives us an excerpt of a text written by a local Gold Coast political leader. Instead of passing in silence the memories of the trade, the author – a lawyer and politician named E. J. P. Brown – celebrates the role of Birempon Kwadwo, who traded with the Europeans. According to the tale Brown tells, Birempon Kwado outsmarted the Europeans and kept many of the slaves he bought, saving them from a worse fate.

These documents, along with others presented in this book, indicate the diverse ways Africans related to slavery and the slave trade. Some traded. Some were traded. Some profited. Many suffered. They also suggest that memory takes many forms. People sometimes choose what they want to remember, but often memories are rooted in the subconscious and can impose themselves on those who would rather forget.

16 Some Facets of Slavery in the *Lamidats* of Adamawa in North Cameroon in the Nineteenth and Twentieth Centuries

AHMADOU SEHOU

In Cameroon, a country of Central Africa which stretched from Lake Chad to the Gulf of Guinea, slavery had a triple dimension. In the coastal fringe, it was oriented to the export trade to the Americas; in its northern part, it was oriented to the trans-Saharan trade; and everywhere, there was a local dimension influenced by the other two, which existed before and after official abolition. We are concerned with Fombina, an area found in the southeast corner of the Sokoto Caliphate founded by Usman dan Fodio after 1804. The Emirate of Adamawa with its capital at Yola was created by one of his lieutenants, Modibbo Adama. Seeking to spread Islam and eliminate paganism, the heads of several Fulbe clans used military means to stake out fiefs for themselves and to capture and reduce local populations to slavery. Differences of religion and economic interests were crucial in the subjection and exploitation of native people by an Islamic aristocracy. Five large *lamidats*[1] were established on the Adamawa plateau under the authority of *lamibé* (sing. *lamido*, which means chief or king), with power passed by hereditary succession.[2] The German (1902–15) and French (1916–60) colonial conquests of this area, where the *lamibé* considered themselves masters and owners of their subjects, with control over life and death, revealed the contradictions between the moral principles of the colonizers and the need to consider local realities.

Slavery and the slave trade had the particularity of increasing in Adamawa at the very moment when abolition was spreading in other parts of the world. The trade was well integrated into trans-Saharan networks, which extended to Adamawa, and was staffed largely by Hausa traders from Nigeria. For the *lamibé* it was an important source of wealth through taxes they took, the supplies in exotic goods it permitted, and the possibilities of selling the local slaves. For colonial administrators, slaves represented the bulk of the laborers provided to them by the *lamibé* (for the construction of buildings and roads, porterage, transport of European personnel, etc.) and they were in charge of making available most of the foodstuffs needed for individuals in administrative posts.

The German and French colonizers tried to stop the trade and efforts to capture new slaves, but those already enslaved were ignored. For the colonial officials, slavery was part

---

[1] The Lamidats were Muslim polities created in the Northern Cameroon in the beginning of the nineteenth century by a jihad led by Ousman dan Fodio from his home base in Northern Nigeria. Each *lamidat* was commanded by a Muslim chief called a *lamido*.

[2] They are Kontcha (1823), Tignère (1828), Tibati (1829), Ngaoundéré (1830), and Banyo (1862).

of local customs that they accepted for practical reasons. The colonial rulers did not want to abolish slavery for fear of seeing the social structure crumble and provoking anarchy. Until 1948, the French colonial authority was not interested in doing anything to end slavery. It avoided addressing this crucial issue. The situation changed when the United Nations was created and Cameroon was put under trusteeship. UN missions of inspection pushed the French colonial administration to make confidential inquiries into the situation of the slaves.[3] Between 1953 and 1955, five reports were made on "the situation of slaves in the *lamidat* of Banyo and what measures to take to ameliorate it."[4] Those reports made by local colonial administrators were intended to inform their hierarchy about the true situation of slaves in the region before it came to be known by the visiting missions of the UN.

But neither in Banyo nor in the other *lamidats* of Adamawa was any radical measure taken to liberate the slaves until 1960, when Cameroon became independent. Since then, the question has hardly been posed in public, and until today, the descendants of slaves continue to consider themselves property of the masters of their parents. It is why even today, some slaves request certificates of emancipation from their masters; without that formal emancipation, their testimony cannot be accepted in a customary court, they cannot marry free women, and they cannot make the pilgrimage to Mecca no matter how much money they have.[5] The following documents localize the region concerned and present some facets of slavery as it developed in nineteenth- and twentieth-century Adamawa.

DOCUMENT 1. LETTER FROM THE *LAMIDO* TO THE CHIEF OF THE REGION OF ADAMAWA OPPOSING THE PROGRESSIVE ELIMINATION OF SLAVERY

This letter was written on May 7, 1955, by Iyawa Adamou and addressed to the Chief of the Region of Adamawa, M. Noutarie, who was visiting Banyo. The context of the visit was an attempt to change French policy on slavery, which was maintained in the region up to this point. To carry out the desired changes, the Chief of the Subdivision had to convince the *lamido* and the leading men to progressively free their slaves. The two methods proposed threatened the power and the revenues of the *lamido* and his dignitaries because they took away an important part of their inheritance in slaves and in products. Through the village chiefs, they exercised their authority, using it to take concubines, extort agricultural products, and extract labor for different tasks. To preserve their privileges, they strongly opposed the transformation of the system. The French colonial administration approached this question of personal statute and social relations with caution. It avoided taking any administrative or legal decision to simply abolish slavery.

---

[3] After World War I, as a former German colony, Cameroon became a League of Nations mandate territory, divided in two parts, administered by France and Great Britain. In 1948, it became a UN trust territory.

[4] See Ahmadou Séhou, "*Lamido* Iyawa Adamou de Banyo (Nord-Cameroun): chef traditionnel, parlementaire et esclavagiste (1902–1906)" (unpublished paper delivered at the Conference on Tales of Slavery: Narratives of Slavery, the Slave Trade and Enslavement in Africa, University of Toronto, May 2009); Ahmadou Séhou, "Nègres au pays des Noirs: statuts, representations et situation des esclaves dans les *lamidats* de l'Adamaoua (Nord-Cameroun), XIXe-XXe siècles" (unpublished paper delivered at the Colloquium on Constructions historiques de la notion de "race" et hierarchies socials en Afrique septentrionale et occidentale musulmanes, Dakar, Sénégal, December 2008).

[5] After World War I, as a former German colony, Cameroon became a League of Nations mandate territory, divided into two parts administered by France and Great Britain. In 1948, it became a UN Trust Territory.

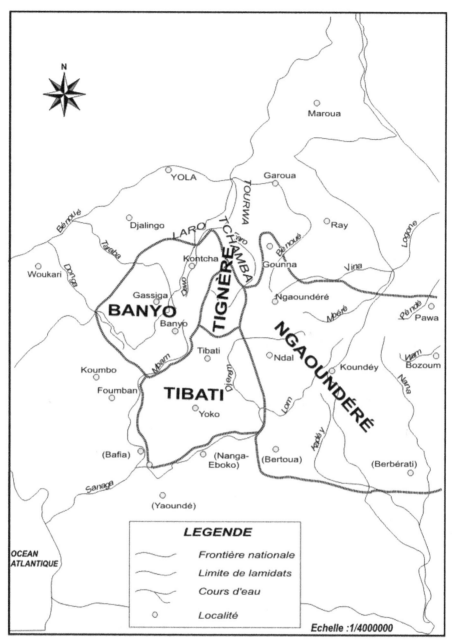

16.1. The *lamidats* of the Adamawa Plateau in the nineteenth century: Ngaoundéré, Tignère, Banyo, and Tibati.

Source: Eldridge Mohammadou, *Les Royaumes Foulbe du Plateau de l'Adamaoua au XIXe siècle*. (Tokyo: ILCAA, 1978), p. 433.

QUESTIONS TO CONSIDER

1. What is the word used to designate slaves in this correspondence and why?
2. What were the two ways proposed for the suppression of slavery in the *lamidat* of Banyo?
3. Why were the *lamido* and his dignitaries opposed to ending slavery?

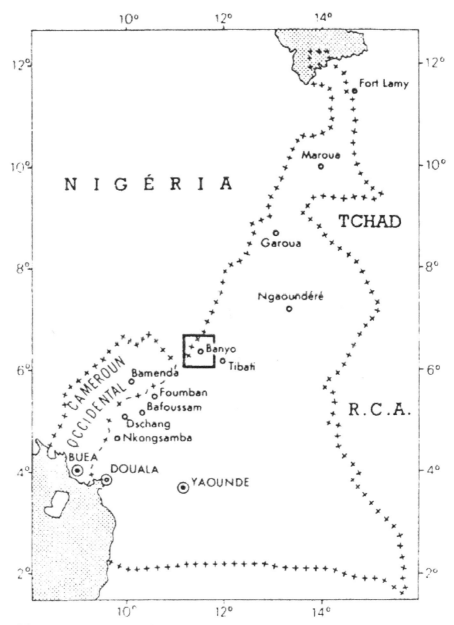

16.2. Location of the *lamidat* of Banyo in Cameroon.

4. How do you interpret the following statement of the Lamido: "We do not refuse to free the servants, but we do so only when they make a demand based on ill treatment by their new masters. Mr. Administrator in Chief, I have the will to execute your orders, but in this case, excuse me, I cannot take responsibility"?

5. How do you understand the following sentence: "I regret that it is a new Chief of Subdivision, just arrived, who finds himself confronted with difficulties and will not know how to understand the region"?

Banyo, 7 May 1955

Iyawa Adamou
Lamido of Banyo,

To: Administrator in Chief of the Region of Adamawa

[This letter deals with a series of questions, the first of which was the freeing of slaves after the death of their Master.]

… As far as the freeing of servants[6] after the death of their Master, last December already … following instructions that you gave me, there was a long discussion between the leading men and the chief of the subdivision, who agreed to write you on this subject. All of our criticisms were noted and sent to you. I regret that I do not have a copy at hand, but as you know our grievances, we plead with you to study this affair with good will. You are the only father and boss in our region. We wish to suggest to you that studies as important as this should be made in the capital of the region and not in a little post like Banyo and that a single rule should be applied throughout the region. With the obligation to which you have entrusted to me to apply the law when a case of succession comes before me, I have submitted the question to the local dignitaries, who have requested that the consideration of their views be given to the Chief of the subdivision. We do not refuse to free the servants, but we do so only when they make a demand based on ill treatment by their new masters. Mr. Administrator in Chief, I have the will to execute your orders, but in this case, excuse me, I cannot take responsibility.

[The next paragraph of the letter deals with the *lamido*'s opposition to reforms in the selection of village chiefs, which would have reduced the *lamido*'s control over the villages.]

I regret that it is a new Chief of Subdivision, just arrived; who finds himself confronted with difficulties and will not know how to understand the region….

Iyawa Adamou

DOCUMENT 2. CONFIDENTIAL LETTER FROM THE CHIEF OF THE ADAMAWA REGION TO THE CHIEF OF THE SUBDIVISION OF BANYO FORBIDDING HIM FROM PROCLAIMING THE LIBERATION OF SLAVES

This confidential correspondence is addressed to the Chief of Banyo Subdivision by his superior, the Chief of the Region of Adamawa. As a result of a meeting with Iyawa Adamou, Regional Chief Noutarie asks Sablayrolles to leave the *lamido*'s hands free in the application of political reforms in the *lamidat*, particularly in the course to be followed in the liberation of the slaves. Clearly, he is disavowing his collaborator, proclaiming the maintenance of the authority of the *lamido* in that issue, and forbidding any announcement of the liberation of the slaves in Banyo by the local colonial administrator. This letter shows that the threats made by the *lamido* were taken seriously and that henceforth, slavery could continue in the *lamidat*.

---

[6] The French word used here is *serviteur*, but this is clearly code for slave, as indicated by the local context.

QUESTIONS TO CONSIDER

1. Is the *lamido* the best person to undertake the liberation of the slaves? Why?
2. What explains the attitude of the Regional Chief? Why does he forbid the proclamation of the liberation of the slaves?
3. Can the Chief of Subdivision and the *lamido* collaborate after this in the harmonious fashion recommended by the Regional Chief?

14 June 1955

The Chief of Adamawa Region,
to the Chief of Subdivision of Banyo

As a result of a meeting I had recently with the Lamido of Banyo, I would like to put out, hereafter, what should be your line of conduct, in the immediate future, in the application of political and social reforms which have recently been decided.

In spite of the risks which this tactic presents, I ask you to have confidence in the Lamido, whose authority should be maintained at any cost. For the moment, it is up to him and him alone, to inform the population of new dispositions. His intention is to talk to the dignitaries and heads of households to indicate to them, with all the desirable tact, that in the future it will no longer be possible to get rid of servants as they would wish or to use violence or coercion in dealing with them. (Noutarie's underlining)

By contrast, it is not desirable, for the moment, to proclaim to one and all the "liberation" of servants, nor to send away – unless they ask it expressly – those who are at present in the service of the Lamido and the dignitaries of Banyo, their residence from now on being the place where they were counted during the census, with no possibility of change without the agreement of the Subdivision.

[The rest of the letter deals with administrative organization.]

Noutarie

DOCUMENT 3. SANCTIONS APPLICABLE TO SLAVES IN ADAMAWA
IN THE NINETEENTH AND TWENTIETH CENTURIES

This table presents the different penalties and sanction to which the slaves of the *lamidats* of Adamawa were subject. It is based on colonial archives[7] and on discussions in the field with persons knowledgeable about the practice of slavery in different parts of Adamawa. The list of faults and misdemeanors and of sanctions and penalties is far from being exhaustive. It provides an indication of the condition of slaves in this region at least up to the middle of the twentieth century. As elsewhere, the situation of slaves was far from being

---

[7] For the colonizers, the inquiries made and the reports written contributed to a better understanding of slavery as it was practiced locally, the better to take expected decisions (which never came). These reports were usually confidential because it was difficult for administrators to justify the survival of such a practice in an area under their authority. A reading of these reports makes clear the embarrassment of the situation in which they found themselves, the cruelty of practices they observed in the field, and a fear that it could be known internationally. This explains the nervousness they felt every time a UN mission was scheduled to visit the region. There were five UN mission visits before independence in order to verify the respect of the terms of the trusteeship by French and British administrators of the territory.

Faults and misdemeanors	Sanctions or penalties	Judicial authority charged with application	Observations
Defects and incorrigible vices	Sale, exchange, removal	Master	
Acts detrimental to master or his family	Punishment according to gravity of act until slave mends ways	Master	
Acts detrimental to other persons	Punishment according to gravity of act until slave mends ways	Master	Master is responsible for damages done
Theft within master's family	50 lashes	Master	Conditional on object being found
Repeated theft	Whipping and irons	Master	Length of punishment according to master
Wrongs or insults to master	Whipping and irons	Master	Number of lashes and length fixed by master
Repeated wrongs or insults	Sale	Master	Sanctions can be extreme because honor is involved
Sexual relations with master's concubine	50 lashes for the slave and 100 for the concubine; torture	Master	Sanctions can be extreme because honor is involved
Sexual relations with master's free wife	50 lashes for the slave; torture; wife is stoned to death	Master	Sanctions can be extreme because honor is involved
Sexual relations with master's sister, married or divorced	50 lashes for the slave; torture; woman is stoned to death	Master	Penalty determined by master
Murder of another slave of master	Death or 100 lashes and irons, sale, 12 months imprisonment	Master and Lamido	Master must report punishment to Lamido (public security concern)
Flight (when captured)	Lashes, deprivation of food, forced labor, irons, sale	Master	
Repeated flight	Prolonged period in irons, cutting kneecap or Achilles tendon	Master	

16.3. Table of penalties and sanctions used against slaves in Adamawa in the nineteenth and twentieth centuries.

Sources: Archives Nationales de Yaoundé, 1AC 1744/2 Rapport annuel sur les Foulbés et leurs esclaves 1921, pp 6–7. Also miscellaneous interviews.

uniform. It depended largely on the master and on the tasks the slave was expected to carry out. Despite the disparity in number or scale, it is clear that the range of sanctions is so varied that it has nothing to envy in cruelty and refinement to what was applied to slaves in plantations throughout the Americas.

QUESTIONS TO CONSIDER

1. What are the most grievous errors for slaves?
2. Why are slaves, free persons, and concubines punished differently for the same act?
3. How is the irresponsibility of the slave expressed in the application of sanctions?
4. How do these penalties compare to those inflicted on slaves on the American continent?

DOCUMENT 4. CERTIFICATE OF MANUMISSION

This certificate of manumission was issued on August 12, 2006 by the *lamido* of Banyo, Hamagado Yaya. While doing field research, I was received by the *lamido* in his office at the palace. After I asked how the emancipation of slaves took place and if there were documents attesting to it, he called one of his slaves who was waiting in the doorway. This slave was waiting for the *lamido* to give him a written document certifying his manumission. After the document was signed in my presence, I asked if I could film it and use it in my work. This request was granted by the *lamido* and by the person he had just freed. The witnesses were all princes eligible for the throne. This was a supplementary guarantee for the person freed. To the best of my knowledge, Banyo is the only *lamidat* of Adamawa where the *lamido* is still allowed to deliver or to refuse certificates of manumission. Others free slaves discreetly or verbally in the presence of several witnesses. This is an indirect way of recognizing that slavery still exists in this Muslim and strongly Arabized society a half-century after independence.

QUESTIONS TO CONSIDER

1. What is the utility of such a document in contemporary society?
2. Why is the document written in Arabic?
3. Can it have any value under modern republican law?
4. Can modern law abolish slavery in a Muslim society?

Translation:

Hereafter,

In the name of Allah, the Just and merciful; Peace and the blessings of his Messenger Mohammed and his companions.

By this written testimony,

I, the lamido of Banyo, Al Hadj Mohammad Gabdo Yahya,

free Sadou the son of Hama Djabbo;

In the presence of the following witnesses:

- Yerima Oubandoma,
- Al hadji Djika Saïdou the son of Yerima Hamoua Abdourahman Yahya,
- Yerima Baba Aboubakar son of Yerima Babbada Hama'adama.

Dated: 8 December 2006 17/7/1427 after the Hegira
Sealed and Signed: Lamidat of Banyo Adamawa Cameroon

Lamido Hamagabdo Yaya

CONCLUSION

Through oral sources collected in the field, archival documents, and the correspondence of colonial administrators in Adamawa, we have shown the positions taken by a Muslim traditional chief among the Fulbe, on the practice of slavery in his *lamidat*, and French efforts to end it. The confidential character of the struggle between partisans and adversaries of slavery, symbolized by *lamido* Iyawa Adamou and Sablayrolles, involved the fate of tens of thousands of persons. The victory of the status quo delayed for several decades the end of slavery, born on particular circumstances in Adamawa. The interplay of interests and the complacency of the colonial masters led to the denial of rights and distanced Adamawa from the goals of a certain universal humanitarian ideal that justified colonial enterprise. Banyo was one of the vastest subdivisions of Adamawa, which also included for some time neighboring *lamidats* of Kontcha, Tignère, and Tibati. The survival of slavery there consequently had an influence on other parts of Adamawa. The history of slavery is definitely very complex and made up of particular cases, making any generalization hasty or improper. While the colonial powers seem to have abolished slavery elsewhere and freed slaves, in Adamawa, the colonial officials allied themselves to the masters to perpetuate the slaves' exploitation.

SUGGESTED ADDITIONAL READINGS

Bah, Thierno Mouctar. "Les armées peul de l'Adamawa au 19ᵉ siècle." In *Etudes africaines offertes à Henri Brunschwig, XXVIII*. Edited by J. Vansina et al. (Paris: Editions de l'EHESS, 1982), 57–71.

"Le facteur peul et les relations inter-ethniques dans l'Adamaoua au XIXᵉ siècle." In *Peuples et cultures de l'Adamaoua (Cameroun): Actes du colloque de Ngaoundéré du 14 au 16 Janvier 1992* (Paris: ORSTOM/Ngaoundéré-Anthropos, 1993), 61–86.

"Slave-Raiding and Defensive Systems South of Lake Chad from the Sixteenth to the Nineteenth Century." In *Fighting the Slave Trade: West African Strategies*. Edited by Sylviane A. Diouf (Oxford: James Currey, 2001), 15–30.

Burnham, Philip. "Raiders and Traders in Adamawa: Slavery as a Regional system," *Paideuma. Mitteilungen zurKulturkunde*, 41 (1995), 153–176.

Büttner, Thea. "On the Social-Economic Structure of Adamawa in the 19th Century. Slavery or Serfdom?" In *African Studies*. Edited by W. Markov (Leipzig: Karl Marx University Press, 1967), 43–61.

Cordell, Denis D. "Warlords and Enslavement: A Sample of Slave Raiders from Eastern Ubangi-Shari, 1870–1920." In *Africans in Bondage: Studies in Slavery and the Slave Trade, Essays in Honor of Philip D. Curtin on the Occasion of the Twenty-Fifth Anniversary of African Studies at the University of Wisconsin*. Edited by Paul Lovejoy (Madison: University of Wisconsin Press, African Studies Program, 1986), 334–365.

Eckert, Andreas. "Slavery in Colonial Cameroon, 1880s to 1930s," *Slavery & Abolition*, 19, 2 (1998), 133–148.

Eldridge, Mohammadou. *Les Royaumes Foulbé du plateau de l'Adamaoua au XIXe siècle: Tibati, Tignère, Banyo, Ngaoundéré*, Tokyo: ILCAA, 1978.

Hurault, Jean. "Les noms attribués aux non-libres dans le lamidat de Banyo," *Journal des africanistes*, 64, 1 (1994), 91–107.

Njeuma, M. Z. *Fulani Hegemony in Yola (Old Adamawa), 1809–1902*. Yaounde: CEPER, 1978.

Saïbou Issa, "Paroles d'esclaves au Nord-Cameroun," *Cahiers d'Etudes africaines*, 45, 179–180 (2005), 853–878.

VerEecke, Catherine. "The Slave Experience in Adamawa: Past and Present Perspectives from Yola (Nigeria)," *Cahiers d'Etudes Africaines*, 34, 133–135 (1994), 23–53.

17 Etchu Richard Ayuk's Manuscript on the Slave Trade and Social Segregation in the Ejaghamland

UTE RÖSCHENTHALER

Great Britain abolished the slave trade at the African Atlantic coast more than 200 years ago. The European colonial powers suppressed the interior slave trade in Africa more than 100 years ago. Still, the Ejagham people, located today in Cameroon and Nigeria, maintain clear knowledge of who is the descendant of a freeborn and who is the descendant of a slave. The first document presented here is by Etchu Richard Ayuk, a young Ejagham man who explains what the elders in his home village told him about the slave trade. His description reminded me of a paragraph I had read in the travelogue of the German explorer Eugen Zintgraff. This paragraph follows Etchu's document for comparative purposes. The third document consists of two *nsibiri* signs related to the slave trade, which were collected by the British colonial officer Percy Amaury Talbot in the area in the first decade of the twentieth century. *Nsibiri* is a graphic sign system and a mime language used by members of secret societies.

Etchu Richard Ayuk was born in 1966 in the village of Inokun, which is one of the Ejagham villages in the immediate hinterland of Calabar and Rio del Rey. He has worked with me as a research assistant since 1998 when I traveled to the Ejagham villages to record the histories of their settlement, cults, and associations. At the time, Etchu also worked for the rural radio station Voice of Manyu in Kembong. He worked there as a technician but also hosted a program on culture for which he himself collected oral materials and music from the Ejagham villages. Etchu was very interested in researching and documenting the culture of his people. He had no education in the humanities, but had studied electronic engineering at Calabar. He then focused on media technology. He had a good command of the English language, and so I encouraged him to continuously document interesting events and stories from the various villages while I was at home in Germany. The first document presented here is one of the accounts he wrote in English and sent to me. In this document, he discusses the slave trade with two elders from his home village. They still

This chapter is based on field research in southwest Cameroon and southeast Nigeria. Between 1987 and 1988, research was supported by the *Nachwuchsförderung des Landes Berlin* and the German Academic Exchange Service, between 1998 and 2001 by the German Research Council in cooperation with the Goethe University, Frankfurt, and in 2008 by the Cluster of Excellence "The Formation of Normative Orders" at the Goethe University Frankfurt, Germany. I am also particularly grateful to the many informants in Cameroon and Nigeria who patiently took the time to discuss their culture with me.

17.1. Richard Etchu Ayuk (second from left) at his initiation ritual into the Ekpe society in Inokun, 2008.
Source: Photo by Ute Röschenthaler.

remembered slave trade based on what they saw with their own eyes or heard from those elders who had been slave-traders themselves. Etchu's documentation of these memories is unusual. In contrast to Nigeria, where almost every village group has its own local historian, trained or self-made, and who has produced the group's history,[1] the people of Cameroon have hardly begun to document their history for the public. Historical knowledge is still a privileged and valuable resource largely held by elders and chiefs.

SLAVERY, THE SLAVE TRADE, AND SLAVES' CULT ASSOCIATIONS

Etchu's home village, Inokun, belongs to the Ekwe Ejagham, which is one of the three Ejagham subgroups in Cameroon.[2] The Ejagham people live in a sparsely populated and hilly rain forest crisscrossed by many rivers and streams. It is part of the Cross River area that today is divided by the international boundary between Cameroon and Nigeria. This area extends from the Atlantic Ocean at Calabar, in Nigeria, far into the hinterland of Cameroon. The Southwest Region ends at the foot of the mountains of the Cameroon Grassfields where the Northwest Region begins. Most of the slaves came from there. This is a fertile and densely populated highland with many larger and smaller kingdoms and chiefdoms. The northern part of the Grassfields was linked to the trans-Sahara trade networks.

---

[1] For more on this topic, see A. Harneit-Sievers (ed.), *A Place in the World: New Local Historiographies from Africa and South-Asia* (Leiden, 2002).

[2] There are about sixty-five Ejagham villages in Cameroon. They make up the Eyumojock Subdivision, which is part of the Manyu Division in the Southwest Region. About eighty more Ejagham villages are situated in the Cross River State of Nigeria. In precolonial times, these villages regarded themselves as autonomous political units.

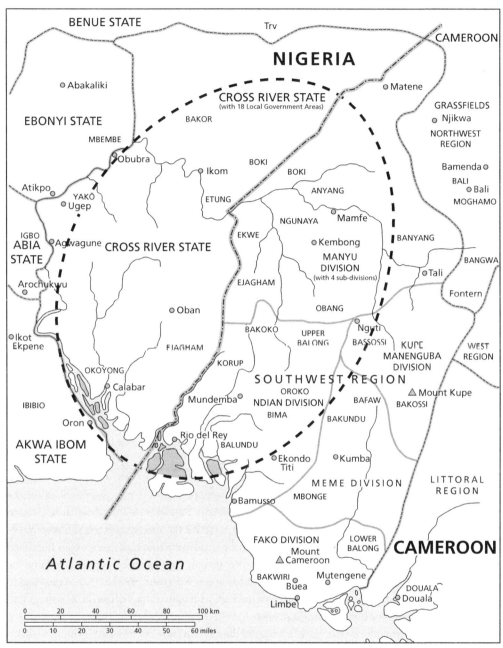

17.2. Map of the Cross River region.

The slave trade in the Cross River area began at Rio del Rey. It was the first place where in the early sixteenth century European traders anchored their ships. They contacted the local people and indicated that they wished to trade with them. European traders began to exchange cloth, Venetian beads, brass and copper rods, cowries, and bottles of rum and wine they had taken along as trade goods for African ivory, beads, ebony, and other forest products – at first – and then also for slaves. The African traders at the coast understood

17.3. Village with square compounds, on the Cross River, 1912.
Source: Photograph from Percy Amaury Talbot, *In the Shadow of the Bush* (London: W. Heinemann, 1912), opposite p. 336.

that they could act as middlemen with the hinterland villages (and developed a trade system that gradually extended into the hinterland as far as the Cameroon Grassfields to the northeast. In the late seventeenth century, European traders discovered that west of Rio del Rey on the Cross River was a more convenient place to trade, which they called Calabar. Calabar then gradually took over the trade from Rio del Rey until it had become the most influential trade center in the region in the nineteenth century. When the European demand for slaves grew, slaves were brought in ever-greater numbers from the Grassfields to the coast at Calabar.[3]

Most of what we know about the slave trade from this region has been written by European traders, missionaries, and colonial officers, all of whom were located on the coast. We know little from firsthand accounts about the organization of the slave trade in the hinterland, even from a present-day perspective. Etchu's document provides some insights in this direction. He starts his text by explaining that individuals who had been convicted of witchcraft or another crime were usually sold as slaves. He then explains the organisation of the slave trade, the tasks those slaves who were not sold to the coast had to carry out, and the rituals or associations through which memories of the social segregation of slaves and free born are still kept alive.

Etchu mentions Okongo as a "cultural dance." This is more precisely a men's association into which the firstborn sons of the freeborn families in a village are initiated. It is one of the older associations or secret societies. Secrecy surrounded many of their activities, including their sign language and some of the knowledge of how they functioned, even

---

[3]   See E. Ardener, "Documentary and Linguistic Evidence for the Rise of the Trading Polities between Rio del Rey and Cameroons, 1500–1650," in I. M. Lewis (ed.), *History and Social Anthropology* (London, 1968), 81–126; A. J. H. Latham, *Old Calabar 1600–1891: The Impact of the International Economy upon a Traditional Society* (Oxford, 1973); S. Behrendt and E. Graham, "African Merchants, Notables and the Slave Trade at Old Calabar, 1720: Evidence from the National Archives of Scotland," *History in Africa*, 30 (2003): 37–61.

17.4. Funeral dance at which slaves used to be sacrificed. Note the warriors 1908 with Dane guns and the big community slit gong.
Source: Photograph from Alfred Mansfeld, Urwald-Dokumente: Vier Jahre unter den Crossflussnegern Kamerune (Berlin: D. Reimer, 1908), 201.

though their members were known to the public. Their secret sign language involved the use of words, but it was mostly mimed or written on the ground and immediately erased afterward. The visible form of this sign language was developed by specialized women as a decorative art. They painted it on their faces, on house walls, and decorated calabashes with it. Talbot and other colonial officers collected these *nsibiri* signs with meanings. Some of these, which the women shared with Talbot, relate to the slave trade. The first sign shows a husband and a wife with many children and many servants who are slaves. This means that they are wealthy. The other two signs depict a convicted criminal to be sold as a slave and the local currency, consisting of brass rods, which was used to buy slaves but could also be worn as decoration.[4]

The villagers emphasized that one of the purposes of Okongo was to unite the free-born families in the village. It thereby also operated an association that in the past had the means to control the slave trade, although this was always surrounded by much secrecy and the exact details are difficult to ascertain. Of course, Etchu would not disclose anything he was bound to keep as a secret. This also helps explain why little is known about the slave trade in the hinterland. The Ejagham, as the other ethnic groups of the region, have many other men's and women's associations and cult agencies. The cult agencies are used to detect theft, witchcraft, and other transgressions of law concerning the invisible domain. The associations facilitate trade, act as courts, collect debts, perform at festivities,

---

[4] Many of the older men's associations of the Ejagham were initially organized to recognize hunters and warriors who had been successful in killing enemies and dangerous animals. They owned and danced the skin-covered masks for which the Ejagham are well known in the Western world. Their faces can sometimes have painted *nsibiri* signs. These masks are usually known under the ethnic name Ekoi, which is the Efik word for the hinterland groups with whom they traded.

and serve as social meeting places for members, but many also perform some of their activities in secret.

Not all slaves coming from the Grassfields through the Ejagham country were sold immediately to the coast. Some remained with the Ejagham, not in the main village but in separate settlements. Some slaves arrived with the knowledge of associations and cult agencies and disclosed this to their new masters in exchange for favorable treatment. So, some of the older associations and cult agencies were originally in the possession of the slaves. Okongo is the institution that still maintains the social difference between the descendants of slaves and the descendants of the freeborn villagers. The slaves, however, kept their own Okongo in which the freeborn did not participate, just as the freeborn excluded the slaves. Even when there were relationships between slave women and freeborn men,[5] their children were strictly excluded from becoming members in the more important secret associations, namely in the Okongo of the freeborn. They were also not allowed to hold responsible positions in the village. The descendants of the freeborn keep strict records as to who was of slave descent and could participate in Okongo.

SLAVERY'S ENDURING LEGACY

Many villages had large slave settlements. When the first explorer – the German Eugen Zintgraff – traveled through the forest as far inland as the Grassfields in the late nineteenth century, he still encountered these slave settlements. In his travelogue he wonders why the slaves never made any attempt to escape. As was typical for early explorers, Zintgraff portrayed the more centralized people from the Grassfields in more positive terms, depicting them as intelligent, strong, and disciplined, qualities the more decentralized forest people lacked, in his opinion. Most interesting is that many people in the forest areas also saw the Grassfields people in a similar way. Zintgraff's observations are echoed in Etchu's document when he talks about the slave villages and how the freeborn perceived the personalities of the slaves, even though Etchu has not read Zintgraff. Nevertheless, they were regarded as slaves, and people assured me that the slaves could not have escaped because they were under the authority of their master who was like a father to them and also cared for their well-being.

Obviously European or Western ideas about the slaves' status were different from the actual situation in Africa. When Cameroon became a German colony after the Berlin Africa conference in 1884, the Germans decided that one of their first tasks should be to end the slave trade and free the slaves. One of the early colonial officers was the German Theodor Seitz who later became one of the governors of the German colony of Kamerun. He reached Cameroon for the first time around 1895, and his task was to fight slavery. He quickly became disappointed when he failed to encounter what he understood to be slavery. He even regretted that he was unable to locate any slave markets among the Douala (an ethnic group that controlled another slave port to the southeast of Rio del Rey), or any slave caravans or slaves who were carrying out forced labor. Slavery was almost invisible. Because the German government did not recognize slavery as an institution, even cases of runaway slaves were not handled by the courts. According to Seitz, however, this was not

---

[5]   B. Chem-Langhëë, "The Banyang Slave System: Social Differentiation and Citizenship, *Annales de la faculté des Lettres et Sciences Humaines (Université Yaoundé) Série sciences humaines*, 1:1 (1985): 163–182; D. Fomin and J. Ngoh, *Slave Settlements in the Banyang Country 1800–1950* (Limbe, 1998).

the problem. Rather on the contrary, some slaves refused to leave their masters despite their masters' wishes. He recalled that once a Douala chief came to him and begged him to legally free the slave he owned because the slave only bothered and insulted him. The slave who had accompanied him argued that he refused be to freed, and that his master tried to get rid of him simply because he hated him, but he, as a slave, had nowhere to go and insisted on remaining his master's slave.[6]

When the German colonial officers at the beginning of the twentieth century reached the Ejagham country, they officially freed the slaves not only on the coast but also in the hinterland. To their surprise, most of the slaves did not want to return to their home countries as free people. They preferred to remain where they were. The slaves had to work for their masters, harvesting palm nuts and producing oil, but they were also free to work for themselves. To eradicate all visible signs of slavery, the colonial officers forced the slaves to settle with the freeborn in the main villages, which made both the Ejagham and the slaves feel they lived uncomfortably close to one another. Still, this did not end the slave trade, which continued occasionally until at least about the 1920s, despite the colonial presence. For the colonial officers, this was a completely different form of slavery from that on the plantations in the Americas with which they were familiar.

In 2001, Inokun was a growing village of about forty compounds. Most of the remaining slave descendants had left Inokun and the other smaller villages and moved to larger towns and cities where their descent is of less relevance. Bigger villages such as Kembong still have an entire quarter in which the descendants of slaves live, called Obiola, which means "palm tree," referring to the slaves' task of harvesting the palm nuts for the production of red oil. In these villages, conflicts occasionally arise about who is allowed to participate in the men's associations and who is not. Officially, slave descent no longer matters, but in daily village life it is still felt. So, descendants of former slaves have occasionally tried to sue the freeborn villagers in court for discriminating against them. They have not succeeded, however, because the court treats these cases as a traditional matter to be judged according to customary law.

One reason for the maintenance of social differences between freeborn and descendants of slaves is that the post of the village chief, confirmed by the state authorities, is one of the most respected posts in the Ejagham country and beyond. Another reason is the fear of people in the Southwest Region that those from the Grassfields could outnumber the villagers and take their land, as has occasionally happened. The problem is particularly pertinent further south near Mount Cameroon, where large plantation enterprises were created during German colonial times, and on which many workers from the Grassfields are employed. These fears have recently been politically instrumentalized by the government that convinced the majority of the Southwest Region to vote for the ruling party and not for the opposition, which – by coincidence – has many members in the Grassfields.[7]

---

[6]   This information is taken from an article by Theodor Seitz, "Eingeborenenrecht im alten Kamerun" (native law in the ancient Kamerun), which appeared in the anthology *Die deutschen Kolonien in Wort und Bild* (The German colonies in word and images) edited by H. Zache (Berlin/Leipzig, 2004, reprint of 1926), 270.

[7]   For more details on the consequences of migration and plantation work, see E. Ardener, S. Ardener, and W. A. Warmington, *Plantation and Village in the Cameroons* (London, 1960); E. Chilver and U. Röschenthaler, *Cameroon's Tycoon: Max Esser's Expedition and Its Consequences* (Oxford, 2001); F. Nyamnjoh and M. Rowlands, "Elite Associations and the Politics of Belonging in Cameroon," *Africa*, 68:3 (1998): 320–337.

17.5. Slave climbing palm tree, 1908.
Source: Photograph from Alfred Mansfeld. *Urwald-Dokumente: Vier Jahre unter den Crossflussnegern Kameruns* (Berlin: D. Reimer, 1908), 98.

The way Etchu and his elders talk about the slave trade shows that they perceive the slave trade as having had a beneficial impact on their village and the country. Yet, Etchu carefully selects his words to avoid being accused of any direct form of discrimination. The history was not shared freely with the youth. The details of a village's history were only incidentally discussed – for example, when a conflict about land or other resources arose with other villages. The elders felt that this history should not be generally known because they could then adapt and use it as an argument to win court cases. Etchu had some basic knowledge because he grew up in the area. For the details, however, he had to ask the elders. For different reasons, the descendants of slaves did not wish to talk about this part of their past. They preferred not to be reminded of it and preferred to assume a normal Ejagham identity.

QUESTIONS TO CONSIDER

1. In which way does Etchu's account of slavery differ from those of the explorers and colonial officers?
2. What was the attitude of the Ejagham people toward their slaves (as related to work, treatment, relationships)?

3. Where did the slaves in the Cross River area come from? Which individuals had become victims?
4. How was the slave trade organized and who were the organizers?
5. Why did the slaves not resist being sold?
6. Why did the slaves not escape or rise against their masters?

SLAVE TRADE AMONG THE EJAGHAM PEOPLE OF CAMEROON, BY ETCHU RICHARD AYUK

The slave trade in the Ejagham area occupies a pivotal position in the development of the Atlantic trade in slaves in the nineteenth century. The Ejagham of Cameroon and Nigeria find themselves in a transitional position vis-à-vis where the slaves were being brought and where they were to be sold. The North West Region of Cameroon was the main source from where the slaves came from before being taken to the coastal regions of Isangele and Calabar in Cameroon and Nigeria for onward transportation to the overseas countries.

But who was involved in this particular activity, and why and how? As the story goes, stubborn children of both sexes, as well as men and women who were accused of practicing a lot of negative witchcraft, were prime victims of slave trade. They were then sold to traders by their own parents or relatives. These influential chiefs and rich men who came from the villages to the southwest used either precolonial currencies or material wealth acceptable at the time to buy these slaves. They were the benefactors of the slave trade. At that time also, other precious items were used as a medium of exchange in the process of buying and selling of slaves. These included durable clothes, nice-looking empty bottles of whisky, and cowries.[8]

As narrated to me by Eking Bassey, the oldest person in my village of origin, Inokun, in Eyumojock Subdivision of Manyu Division in the Southwest Region of Cameroon, who is presently more than ninety years of age, the transaction was in the following mode. As soon as a slave-trader arrived in a village with a contingent of slaves from the northwest direction, he went straight to the chief of that village, who would in turn ask his town crier to announce throughout the entire village that "some business commodities had arrived in the village," and whoever was interested could get in touch with the trader through the chief. Individual villagers, beginning with the chief himself, then bargained with the slave-trader and bought their slaves depending on each person's financial might. If all the slaves were bought in that village, the slave-trader ended his journey there, but if not all of them were bought, then he had to continue to the next village. If, however, the slave-trader came in contact with another slave-trader in one of the villages, then the next trader would buy the remaining slaves from his counterpart and continue with the process, which ended right at the coast of Calabar in Nigeria for onward transportation to the overseas countries. The slaves were simply deceived by their owners before leaving their respective places, which is why the slaves never showed any resistance wherever they were going around the villages and beyond. Putting them in chains was common only along the coastal areas.[9]

---

[8] Beside cowries, brass, and copper manillas, rods and spirals served as a medium of exchange and standard of value precolonially in the region, and were an efficient and well-working currency.

[9] In the northern Grassfields region, slaves were occasionally caught by raids, but most slaves came from within their own society. In the previous paragraph, Etchu talked of people who were stubborn, had negative witchcraft, or had committed a crime and were then sold as slaves. This was so in the Grassfields and in the forest region. The Ejagham sold locally enslaved people as quickly and as far away as possible. They

Not all of the slaves were sold to the coast. Some of them remained with their new masters who forced them to embark on a particular activity that was risky and hitherto unknown to the indigenes of the village, such as the children of their masters. For instance, they introduced to their masters the climbing of tall palm trees in order to tap palm wine and to harvest the palm nuts without cutting the tree. This particular activity the slaves carried out deep inside the forest where their masters merely supervised them from time to time.[10] Back at home, the slaves were allocated pieces of land that were situated at the outskirts of the village to build their houses and settle.[11] The production of the palm oil and palm wine was the only activity their masters would expect them to carry out. Otherwise slaves could form their own households, produce food crops, and become self-sufficient. They did not depend on their masters for everyday subsistence. Neither were they obliged to produce food surpluses for their masters.[12] When their population eventually increased, their settlement area was given a name in the Ejagham language, the meaning of which either referred directly to their daily activity, to their status, or was simply called "Etek Asung," meaning the "village of slaves." Each village named the slaves' quarter using their own terminology in the Ejagham language. It was considered an abomination for someone coming from an indigenous family to marry a slave. Masters would take slave women as concubines, but the offspring of these unions would not be acknowledged by the father as descendants.

The Ejagham describe their former slaves and their descendants as being proud and boastful, always successful and prosperous in their endeavors, and generally being both beautiful and handsome people.[13]

Perhaps the most interesting paradox about the day-to-day activities of the slaves is their cultural dance. This was later revealed to me by my second interviewee, Asong Ojong-Asick Mathias, from my home village. He is a grandson to Nta-Asick Ntui-Etem, the founder of Inokun village who got married to seven wives with whom he had several dozen children, and he also owned many slaves. It was from his story told to him by his late father about the Ejagham slave trade that I picked out two important facts about who used to be but no longer is referred to as slave.

According to Pa Asong Ojong-Asick Mathias, the most secretive cultural dance among the Ejagham performed during the funeral celebration of elderly respected men is called Okongo by the Ekwe Ejagham of Eyumojock Subdivision. The slaves introduced it to their masters, or better, their masters appropriated it from the slaves, yet they [the slaves] are

did not, however, sell all the slaves from the Grassfields, at least not in the late nineteenth and early twentieth centuries when the trade still continued. Very old people could still remember how people were sold, or knew about it from their fathers.

[10] To harvest the nuts, they had to climb the prickly palm trees, cut the heavy fruits, and let them drop. This was dangerous work, and after returning from the tree one was completely covered in dust. They climbed high trees with ropes attached around the palm trunk, their waist, and feet. The palm nuts were used for the production of palm oil. The slaves climbed the palm trees and tapped palm wine from the trunk at the tree top. The Ejagham never climbed palm trees but made palm wine by tapping the tree after felling it.

[11] Slaves had their own houses, farms, and families and moved freely from their village to the forest to carry out their work.

[12] Most Ejagham villages produced only as much food crops as was necessary to survive. Some Ejagham villages, however, are situated in more fertile areas where it is worthwhile to undertake more farming. Here, I was told, the slaves were also forced to do farm work for the villagers.

[13] It is interesting that the Ejagham themselves talk with admiration about their slaves. This is similar to remarks of Eugen Zintgraff who thought that slaves in a Bafaw village east of Ejagham were physically and spiritually superior (see the paragraph by Zintgraff later in the chapter).

the ones who are prohibited from taking part during the performance of the dance. As an initiate of this particular traditional dance, I can confirm that this was so when I recall the secret told me by my "grand masters" at the concluding segment of the performance of the Okongo dance during the funeral celebration of our former chief, Obhasi Asong Asick. This happened more than a decade and a half ago in this same village of Inokun where I maintain the position of one of the great-grandsons of Nta Asick Ntui Etem, its founder. My second interviewee also revealed to me another salient point: It is about the famous slave owner Asong Asick, who at that time had inherited his father's throne as the next chief of Inokun. He was invited to a meeting of chiefs by the then Senior Divisional Officer of Manyu in Mamfe. Prior to the meeting, the protocol officer announced that everybody must stand up as the Divisional Officer made his way into the meeting hall. Then Chief Asong Asick, who was quite aware that the Divisional Officer hailed from the Northwest Region of Cameroon being the main source of slaves, defied the order on the grounds that he has "several of such people like the Divisional officer working for him as slaves." How on earth, therefore, he continued, can he honor by standing some other person coming from the same area as his slaves.[14] This was the simple explanation that he gave when asked why he did not stand up. So there was no reaction from within or from any quarter afterward. This confirms that people from the Northwest are even today tainted with the reputation of slaves.

This discriminatory attitude shown toward those considered or known to be descendants of slaves today is a common phenomenon among the peoples of the entire Manyu Division. It is manifested in situations such as marriage relationships, participation in certain traditional rituals and dances, as well as the choice of who can sit on a chieftaincy stool no matter your position in the society.[15] The accompanying effect of this social ill among us, the Manyu people, is devastating and perhaps a hindrance to our development effort.[16]

EUGEN ZINTGRAFF

The following paragraph by Eugen Zintgraff complements the text by Etchu Richard Ayuk. Before Eugen Zintgraff reached the Cameroon Grassfields for the first time in the 1880s, he passed the Bafaw villages to the southeast of the Ejagham. He spent a night in the Bafaw village of Ikiliwindi, and when he left with his carriers, he wondered about the slave villages. My translation from Zintgraff, Nordkamerun (Berlin, 1895), pp. 80–82.

The next morning, on March 7, 1888, the chief took my hand and accompanied me to the end of the village. Then he returned and we continued. After half an hour on foot, we reached an extensive slave village. These were the people who had arrived in great numbers the day before to witness my visit in the main village. These slave villages are generally called Batáng,

---

[14] It did not matter for the Ejagham whether the Divisional Officer was actually of slave descent or whether he just came from the Northwest Region where formerly the slaves came from. The mere fact that he came from the same region was enough for the chief to indulge in this form of protest.

[15] Maintaining this difference is of utmost importance to most people to this day. Freeborn daughters still do not marry descendants of slaves. They cannot obtain the upper positions in the *Ekpe* association, another very important men's society, and they cannot become the village chief.

[16] Many of the descendants of the former slaves are today in important positions in the administration and the education sector. At the beginning of colonial times, they were the first who went to mission and government schools, because the freeborn villagers did not wish to send their children there and meet the risk of them being punished by white people. Compare this to Zintgraff's remark later in the chapter about the powers of the slaves from the Grassfields.

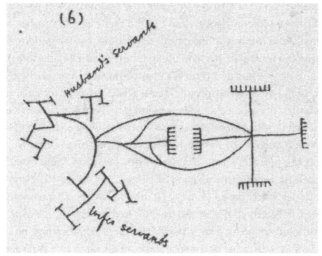

17.6. Image of a Nsibiri sign, 1912.
Source: Percy Amaury Talbot, *In the Shadow of the Bush* (London: W. Heinemann, 1912).

and among the Duala they are called Ninga, obviously a mock name of the English "nigger," a contemptuous name for the negro.

The slave villages are a remarkable institution. As the name indicates and as I have alluded to in the previous chapter, in these villages live the slaves who belong to the free people in the main village. They live under their own chiefs who are also slaves. No slave may spend the night in the village of the freeborn people. This is a rule, partly to maintain the necessary respect, and partly because of fear, since these people who were brought from the interior of the country are superior to their masters not only in numbers but also as to their physical and spiritual powers. Slavery as a social institution has recently been treated quite extensively, so it will suffice here to remark that explorers should not consider the slaves as a negligible factor.[17]

I have never fully understood why these people who come from regions of a more or less uniform language and custom do not unite and, as the spiritually and physically stronger race, abandon their masters to found independent communities.[18] Possibly, even certainly, this will happen when, without the hindrance by trade spheres between the coast and the hinterland, their freeborn compatriots will be able to move to the coast. We will encounter certain signs of such future transformations as we continue our story.

Be it as it may, the many slaves who stood in the doors of their houses watched mutely and almost without answering our greetings how we passed. Did they foresee that the White man was about to go to these regions from where their despotic rulers had banned them, and that one day they would hear again their mother tongue from their own tribal people

---

[17] With this, Zintgraff addresses the German government, which was about to take over the country as its colony.

[18] Zintgraff mentions here the physical and spiritual powers to which Etchu had earlier referred to when saying the slaves were successful, prosperous, proud, and boastful. My Ejagham informants always insisted that the slaves could never have overtaken the free villagers because the slaves were under the authority of their masters who, with the help of their ancestors, had the power over the land; also, people from the neighboring villages would come to help defend them.

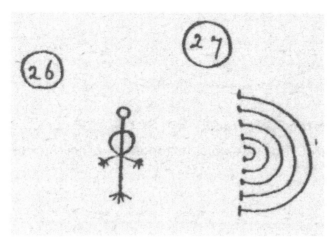

17.7. Image of another Nsibiri sign, 1912.
Source: Percy Amaury Talbot, *In the Shadow of the Bush* (London: W. Heinemann, 1912), 448–449.

who would travel to the coast as free companions of the White man?[19]

After the slave villages, came extensive farms of plantains, corn, cocoyam and beans …

NSIBIRI SIGNS (FROM PERCY AMAURY TALBOT "IN THE SHADOW OF THE BUSH" (1912: 448–449)

According to Talbot, this sign denotes "ardent love between husband and wife. They have many servants."

According to Talbot, the left sign shows a "slave with hands tied together." The right sign "denoting plenty of money."

SUGGESTED ADDITIONAL READINGS

Chem-Langhëë, Bongfen and E.S.D. Fomin. "Slavery and Slave Trade among the Banyang in the Nineteenth and Early Twentieth Centuries," *Paideuma*, 41 (1995): 191–206.

Klein, Martin. "The Slave Trade and Decentralized Societies," *Journal of African History*, 42 (2001): 49–65.

Röschenthaler, Ute. "Translocal Cultures. The Slave Trade and Cultural Transfer in the Cross River Region," *Social Anthropology*, 14, 1 (2006): 71–91.

Purchasing Culture. The Dissemination of Associations in the Cross River Region of Cameroon and Nigeria. Trenton, NJ: Africa World Press, 2011.

Warnier, Jean-Pierre. "Slave-Trading without Slave-Raiding in Cameroon," *Paideuma*, 41 (1995): 251–272.

---

[19] Zintgraff obviously understood that the slaves were rarely caught in raids but mainly sold by the "despotic rulers" of chiefdoms and kingdoms who longed to obtain European commodities in exchange for them.

Writing about the Slave Trade

Early-Twentieth-Century Colonial Textbooks and Their Authors

BAYO HOLSEY

In 1929, the British colonial government published and distributed in the Gold Coast (what is now Ghana) a volume entitled *Gold Coast and Asianti Reader, Book II*, by E. J. P. Brown. Its purpose: to serve as a history textbook for the colony's schools. School textbooks, like Brown's *Reader*, if carefully analyzed, can tell us a great deal about how scholars thought about the past, what issues they deemed important for inclusion, and what topics they thought better to omit. They also permit us to see how scholarly approaches affect what ordinary people learn about the past. Analyses of textbooks that were written during the early part of the twentieth century for use in the colonies can, in fact, reveal a great deal about the ways in which both European officials and African educators sought to use history in the context of colonialism. The slave trade is a particularly interesting topic for review. While early textbooks in the Gold Coast generally treated the slave trade only briefly and did not provide any remarkable details about it, Brown's book was an important exception.

Born in 1872, Brown was a lawyer, author, and politician in Cape Coast, a town located on the Atlantic coast of the Gold Coast Colony. He was a member of the Board of Governors of Mfantsipim School, a boys' secondary school in Cape Coast, where he also served as an instructor.[1] He wrote several textbooks for use in Gold Coast primary and secondary schools.

In the preface to *Gold Coast and Asianti Reader*, Brown lamented the dearth of school textbooks devoted to local history. In response to this situation, several educators had already begun to publish texts in the period following World War I. *A History of the Akan Peoples of the Gold Coast*, written by the Englishman W. T. Balmer (also a teacher at Mfantsipim School) in 1925, was popular with secondary school teachers.[2] But many Africans also began to write their own textbooks during this period. In addition to Brown's reader, there were J. B. Anaman's *Simple Stories from Gold Coast History*, J. B. Danquah's *Akim Abuaka Handbook*, and J. W. de Graft Johnson's *Historical Geography of the Gold Coast*.[3] This generation of African educators was interested in creating a history in which

---

[1] I. Ephson, *Gallery of Gold Coast Celebrities: 1632–1958* (Accra, Ghana, 1969), 190.
[2] D. Kimble, *A Political History of Ghana: The Rise of Gold Coast Nationalism, 1850–1928* (Oxford, 1963), 526.
[3] Kimble, *Political History*, 527–528.

their students could take pride. Indeed, David Kimble, author of the study, *A Political History of Ghana: The Rise of Gold Coast Nationalism, 1850–1928*, argues that the awakening of national consciousness was part of the reason for the growing interest in local history during this period.[4] He quotes J. W. de Graft's brother who, in a report to the educationists' committee, stated that "any people who disregard their customs and ignore their past history will soon cease to be a people."[5]

The overall goal of Brown's text was certainly in line with a nationalist agenda, particularly in its focus on African agency. One portion of the text recounted the early history of Elmina. Here, Brown told the story of the now famous meeting between the Portuguese captain Don Diego d'Azambuja and chief Kwamena Ansa in 1482 during which d'Azambuja requested permission to build a fort (which later became Elmina Castle). Brown described Ansa in glowing terms as "the most enlightened monarch of his day."[6] He explained that Ansa foresaw European domination of the region and therefore initially refused d'Azambuja's request. Brown notes that although Ansa eventually conceded, the Portuguese and later the Dutch were required to pay rental fees to the local rulers for the use of their land. In this way, Brown presented Ansa not as a helpless victim, but rather as a savvy politician.

Brown's focus on African agency is even more pronounced in a later section of the book, which was composed primarily of biographies of prominent African figures. One of the chapters in this section is entitled "Birempon Kwadwo (A Tale of the Slave Trade)." After announcing his intent to focus on the slave trade in the subtitle, he went on to explain that Birempon Kwadwo was a prominent member of the elite coastal African trading community during the slave trade. He was born in the 1700s and became one of the chief traders in Cape Coast. He was also a relative of Philip Quaque, who was the first African chaplain of the Church of England. Known by the British as Cudjoe Caboceer,[7] Birempon Kwadwo was often entrusted by them with large sums of money with which to buy slaves. Kwadwo would purchase the slaves; however, he would often retain some of them as his domestic servants. When the British asked him for the slaves, he told them that some of the slaves had died and he then showed them graves that had been recently filled and claimed that they were the graves of these slaves. Kwadwo peopled four villages with the people he acquired in this fashion. The British continued to hold Kwadwo in the highest regard, which attests to their ignorance with regard to his ruse, and in 1774, they presented him with two silver goblets with an inscription that read, "A present from the committee of the company of Merchants Trading to Africa to Cudjoe, Caboceer for his faithful service and adherence to the subjects of his most sacred Majesty King George III."[8]

In his *Gold Coast and Asianti Reader*, Brown presented Kwadwo as something of a hero. He opined that "by this trick, which was really a blessing in disguise, he saved many of his countrymen from miserable bondage and death in far-off lands."[9] We can glean from this statement that for Brown, the story of Birempon Kwadwo was useful because

---

[4] Kimble, *Political History*, 523.

[5] Kimble, *Political History*, 527.

[6] E. Brown, *Gold Coast and Asianti Reader* (London, 1929), 18.

[7] *Caboceer* is a corruption of the Portuguese term *caboceiro* or captain.

[8] Brown, *Gold Coast*, 125; see also B. Holsey, *Routes of Remembrance: Refashioning the Slave Trade in Ghana* (Chicago, 2008), 31.

[9] Brown, *Gold Coast*, 124.

it allowed him to tell a story about the slave trade in which a local individual, who might have otherwise been cast as a heartless slave dealer, was rather reinterpreted as the savior of slaves bound for export. Despite the fact that these individuals appear to have become Kwadwo's slaves, it remained noteworthy for Brown that he had saved them from the Atlantic trade.

Brown insisted that this particular African slave-trader, Birempon Kwadwo (and by extension others who were also in the business of selling human beings), did not operate in perfect collusion with Europeans, but rather worked to subvert their interests. In this way, Brown attempted to reform the image of the African slave-trader that was being developed at the time by early-twentieth-century British historians. These historians focused on the willing participation of Africans in the slave trade while insisting that it was a despicable trade. W. T. Balmer, for instance, author of a 1925 text about the Akan peoples of the Gold Coast, used the example of Osei Tutu, the seventeenth-century founder of the Asante state, to discuss African participation in the trade. He noted that "in those day men had not learnt that it was wrong to trade in human beings." He then went on to state that Tutu's "ancestors had made slaves of the poorer and weaker people, both of his own country and of others" and that "he [Osei Tutu] saw nothing wrong with it."[10] To Osei Tutu, according to Balmer, trading with the Europeans "simply meant more trade and more wealth."[11] This picture of African immorality set the stage for his later celebration of British colonialism. Balmer wrote that "the British at last put forth their strength and acting as a nation, imposed their power upon the hinterland as well as upon the coast, so bringing about a condition of things in which the whole Gold Coast might dwell together in peace and learn the lessons of civilization and history."[12]

By providing an example in which African participation was actually a subversion of the Atlantic slave trade, Brown attempted to demonstrate the strong moral fiber of at least some Africans during the slave trade. By using history to challenge the negative image of African slave-traders, Brown also sought to raise his own cultural capital and that of his contemporary coastal Africans – a politically astute move in the context of the increasing disenfranchisement of his class of educated Africans in the Gold Coast under British colonialism. By the 1920s then, at least some local African historians had begun to paint a more ambivalent picture of the involvement of local slave-traders in the Atlantic slave trade. Furthermore, by challenging the image of the one-dimensional immoral African slave-trader, they constructed a positive national identity. In this light, the story can be read as an early precursor of contemporary attempts to redefine the meanings of the slave trade within African history.

Significantly, the story of Birempon Kwadwo was included in later published works by a number of local West African historians including Isaac Ephson's *Gallery of Gold Coast Celebrities, 1632–1958*, published in 1969, and J. Erskine Graham's *Cape Coast in History*, published in 1994. European historians, however, did not relate the story. While many reference Cudjoe Caboceer as an important slave-trader, the story of his ruse was not mentioned in their texts, relying as they did on European records, not on the works of local historians.

---

[10] W. Balmer, *A History of the Akan Peoples of the Gold Coast* (New York, 1969), 57.

[11] Balmer, *A History*, 57.

[12] Balmer, *A History*, 73–74.

QUESTIONS TO CONSIDER

1. What do you think were the motivations behind Birempon Kwadwo's decision to hide slaves from the European slave traders?

2. What does this story tell us about the relationship between domestic slavery in West Africa and the Atlantic slave trade?

3. What effect did Birempon Kwadwo's actions have on the social composition of the region's population? What broader conclusions might you draw about the effects of the slave trade on the social composition of the population of West Africa?

4. What does this story suggest about the power of European slave traders in their dealings with African traders?

5. Does this story change the way in which you think about the variety of forms of African agency in the Atlantic slave trade?

6. How does an understanding of Brown's identity as a politician as well as a historian, and an understanding of the context in which Brown wrote his discussion of Birempon Kwadwo's story, influence how you read this excerpt from his textbook?

Gold Coast and Asianti Reader

E. J. P. Brown

London: Crown Agents for the Colonies, 1929.

An Extract

34. BIREMPON KWADWO[13]

(A Tale of the Slave Trade.)

1. Birempon Kwadwo was the son of an Ekumfi-Adansi man and Akuwa, a very handsome woman, who was the sister of another Ekumfi-Adansi man sojourning at Efutu, who had gained wealth and influence there. Akuwa being dissatisfied with the treatment of her husband at Ekumfi, aforementioned, went up to Efutu to seek financial assistance from her brother to go and pay off her husband, and divorce him. Egyir Panyin, king of Efutu and Cape Coast, was present at a large public meeting of chiefs and other people at Efutu, when he saw Akuwa carrying a baby at her back. Egyir at once paid the money wanted. She went back to Ekumfi-Adansi, paid off her husband, and divorced him. She had three children by the divorced husband. On returning to Efutu, she was wedded to the Omanhin. The child she was carrying at her back when the Omanhin saw her was Kwadwo Mensa – that is, the third child – afterwards Kwadwo Edyir, or Birempon Kwadwo. He was the son of the Kwonna or Ebiradsi Clan. Egyir Panyin had a son by Akuwa, named Egyir, who afterwards became King as Egyir Enu (Aggrey II).

2. Kwadwo Mensa was carefully brought up by his stepfather, King Egyir Panyin. He grew up to be an industrious and well-to-do man, gained great power and influence, and was made a Caboceer of Cape Coast. To Europeans he was generally known as Caboceer Cudjoe (Kwadwo) or Cudjoe. It is related of him that he picked up a few of the languages

---

[13] He flourished during the slave trade, and was born about the end of the seventeenth century, or at the early part of the eighteenth century. He died on the March 24, 1779.

of the white slave traders to the Coast of Guinea, and was, for that reason, taken into their confidence. They left him with large sums of money to buy slaves for them.

3. He accordingly bought a large number of slaves, but secreted a good many of them far away in the bush. When the white man returned to load their vessels with their human cargo, Birempon Kwadwo, as he was then called, owing to his immense wealth in those days, showed them graves recently filled as those of slaves who had died since he replenished his last stock of human goods. They believed him and accepted the survivors. This went on for a long time, until he was able to people about three or more villages with these poor slaves, who, in course of time, became his domestics.

4. By this trick, which was really a blessing in disguise, he saved many of his countrymen from miserable bondage and death in far-off lands. The villages he founded with these slaves are now known as Kakumdu, Mpeansem and Siwdu, afterwards known as "Parson's Croom." The inhabitants of these villages are now known as Werempidom, and are the rural section of the Ntsin Asafu (No. 3 Company) of Cape Coast. Latterly the Werempidom founded another village in perpetuation of their acknowledgements to Ohin Kwasi 'Tu for many kindnesses received, which they named "Abura," after the Abura Division of which the said Ohin Kwasi 'Tu was the paramount Ruler.

5. In modern times Siwdu became the seat to the fetish-craft of Cape Coast, under the sway of the well-known priestess Komfu Araba of Asorful. The inhabitants largely fished in the Fosu lagoon, which is near the village, and manufactured salt on its banks during the dry season. They also produced plentiful food crops and grew cocoanuts, etc. Kakumdu and the other two villages produced sugar-cane, besides corn, cassava, yam, tiger-nuts, ground-nuts and fruits; raised cattle and poultry, and manufactured palm-wine, which they sold in large quantities to the inhabitants of Cape Coast and adjacent towns. In the nineteenth century lodges were made near some of these villages by the elite of the educated classes in Cape Coast, which became fashionable rural resorts.

6. During the Seven Years' War between England and France, Birempon Kwadwo became purveyor to the garrison at the Castle. In recognition of his many public services two silver goblets were presented to him by the Committee of the Company of Merchants trading to Africa, bearing the following inscription: -

    "A present from the Committee of the Company of Merchants trading to Africa, to Cudjoe, Caboceer, for his faithful service and adherence to the subjects of his Most Sacred Majestry King George III. Anno Domini 1774.)

7. His fame, which spread far and wide, gave birth to the well-known byword "Birempon Kwadwo n'enyim kamn' onyimpa bo-e"[14] (The tribal incision on Birempon Kwadwo's face was made by man), meaning that no person, how great soever he or she may be, is above censure, which Shakespeare, in *Measure for Measure*, has made Vincentio (Duke of Vienna) well describe in a soliloquy, after his meeting with Lucio in the guise of a Friar, as follows:-

    "No might nor greatness in mortality
    Can censure 'scape; back-wounding calumny
    The whitest virtue strikes. What King so strong
    Can tie the gall up in the slanderous tongue?"

---

[14] This saying is claimed by some to refer to Nana Kwadwo – that is, Egyir Panyin – King of Cape Coast, and not to Birempon Kwadwo.

It will be noted that the Mfantsi-Akan people bear distinctive tribal marks on the face and sometimes on the nape, incised in early childhood.

8. He died on the 24th March 1779, and was the father of the celebrated Reverend Philip Quaque who, for upwards of fifty years, was Chaplain to the Merchant Government of the Gold Coast.

SUGGESTED ADDITIONAL READINGS

Adjaye, Joseph K. "Perspectives on Fifty Years of Ghanaian Historiography," *History in Africa*, 35 (2008): 1–24.

Farias, P. F. M. and Karin Barber. *Self-Assertion and Brokerage: Early Cultural Nationalism in West Africa*. Birmingham: Centre of West African Studies, University of Birmingham, 1990.

Jenkins, Raymond G. Gold Coast Historians and their Pursuit of Gold Coast Pasts, 1882–1917. PhD dissertation, University of Birmingham, 1985.

Kimble, David. *A Political History of Ghana: The Rise of Gold Coast Nationalism, 1850-1928*. Oxford: Clarendon Press, 1963.

Korang, Kwaku L. *Writing Ghana, Imagining Africa: Nation and African Modernity*. Rochester, NY: University of Rochester Press, 2003.

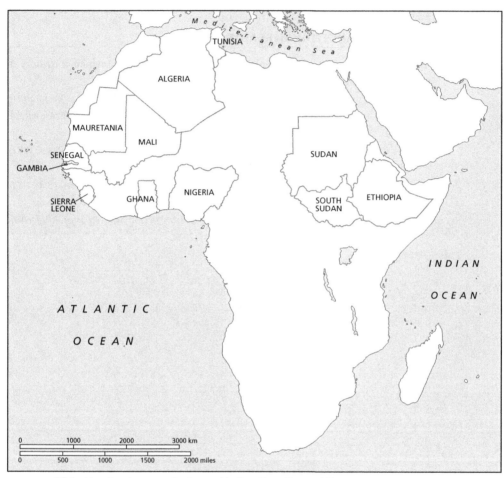

19.1. Map showing countries featured in Parts Four, Five, and Six.
Source: Based on a map published by *Africa Today*. 1990. Revised Edition.

PART FOUR

SLAVERY OBSERVED: EUROPEAN TRAVELERS' ACCOUNTS

19 INTRODUCTION: Accounts by European Travelers

Pre-twentieth-century Europeans have long reported on their experiences in Africa. As travelers, traders, and colonial officials, they were moving around the continent from as far back as the late fifteenth century. Diaries, official reports, and published accounts abound with information on what specific individuals saw, heard, and experienced while in Africa. Because slavery was ubiquitous, it is mentioned in many of these accounts, often as simply a fact of life, whether reported prior to or after the European abolition of the slave trade in Africa in early nineteenth century. The abolition certainly brought change, as the export in human beings to the Americas and North Africa gradually came to a halt, but indigenous slavery – the buying and selling of men, women, and children – continued in Africa through at least the end of the nineteenth century. Thus, while European travelers' accounts of slavery are not uncommon, rarely have they been examined as a means of unearthing the voices of the enslaved. The task is difficult. Written by Europeans, it is their voices that predominate in these records. Still, glimpses of life in slavery from the perspective of the enslaved can sometimes be found, if only in reports of their actions: silent sullenness, their refusal to speak to strangers about their past lives, their efforts to make life better for themselves and others in difficult circumstances. The reports included here span several centuries and geographical locations. They range from the seventeenth-century Gold Coast (Pierluigi Valsecchi in Chapter 23), when indigenous slavery was of greater importance politically and economically than the trans-Atlantic slave trade, to the mid-late nineteenth century in Tunisia (Ismael M. Montana, Chapter 22), the Sahara (Benjamin Claude Brower, Chapter 20), and Egypt (George Michael La Rue, Chapter 21), a time by which the slave trade had already been abolished but indigenous slavery continued to thrive. The influence of the writers' perspectives, shaped by their own personalities and social positions, the prevailing values of the time, and the politics of the day, is clear, but so too are the possibilities of using these sources for understanding slavery as experienced by the enslaved.

20 The Story of Saaba

Slavery and Colonialism in the Algerian Sahara

BENJAMIN CLAUDE BROWER

The following chapter tells the story of a young Fula-speaking woman known as Saaba (Sa'aba) who was sold as a slave in the Algerian Sahara in 1877. It comes from a French explorer named Victor Largeau (1842–96), who first bought Saaba to serve as his cook during an extended summer sojourn in the French-controlled oasis of Ouargla. Situated in the north-central Sahara, between the Niger River (roughly 2,000 km to the south) and the Mediterranean Sea (800 km to the north), Ouargla had once been a major hub of commerce between sub-Saharan Africa and the Mediterranean world. When the French started their occupation of Algeria in 1830, they soon realized the strategic importance of the Saharan oases, and by 1871 they had defeated a local rebellion and occupied Ouargla as part of a larger plan to extend their rule across the desert into West Africa.

Largeau, who knew Arabic but not Fula, interviewed Saaba through an interpreter, a Fulbe woman, who came to the Algerian Sahara as a slave herself. Many people had arrived in the Sahara as slaves as a result of the endemic wars that plagued the middle Niger River region in the second half of the nineteenth century. Unleashed by the expansion of Umar Tal (ca. 1797–1864), who led a jihad against his neighbors, the violence and insecurity continued well after his death, producing conditions in which the slave trade flourished: war produced prisoners and these prisoners represented profits as slaves. Thus even as the Atlantic demand for African slaves had come to an end, the wars produced a flourishing trade in slaves sold in sub-Saharan Africa or sent to markets into the Sahara and northward into the Muslim Mediterranean.

A text like this presents a challenge to the historian. Its origins and authorship make it inherently problematic, yet it represents a tantalizing opportunity to pull from oblivion a life so sadly typical of thousands of others. Most of all it is exceedingly short: a few paragraphs of a larger life. It consists of both direct quotations of Saaba, presumably as Largeau transcribed them in his notes, and a first-person narrative told by the explorer recounting events surrounding the interview, such as Saaba's sale and her first days in his service. Saaba speaks to us through two intermediaries (the translator and Largeau), and her voice undergoes four changes in language (from Fula to Arabic, Arabic to French, and, now, French to English). Thus her words come to us in indistinct form. Moreover, Saaba has little to say herself. She is taciturn when describing her homeland and family, capture, and dangerous journey into Saharan slavery. There is hardly the stuff in this austere narrative to inspire the historian seeking to write a rich, detailed history of Saharan slavery. Nothing of her subjective experiences, feelings, and emotions come through for the historian, and she was in no position to comment on the larger political and social forces that shaped her life. After she concludes her interview with a pessimistic assessment of her circumstances, the archive falls silent. The only other extant documentation of her life is a photograph (taken by Largeau) and an offhand passage in an unpublished French military report discussing the passing of her caravan.[1]

This lack of sources is not an accident. Such a deficit is linked to the fact that Saaba's enslavement was illegal on several counts, and because she was at the bottom of slave system that tried to stifle the voices of slaves in order to hide its very existence. Concealing slavery was important at this time when, on one hand, colonial leaders had publically pledged themselves to abolishing slavery in Africa (France did so for Algeria and other colonies in 1848), and on the other, when slave-traders sold captives from Saaba's homeland, the middle Niger River region (modern-day Mali), despite the fact that they were freeborn Muslims like she. Such sales represented a clear and egregious violation of Muslim law that regulated slavery in most of northwest Africa prior to colonialism. Thus, Saaba was one of many who received neither the emancipation promised by colonial rule nor the full protection and rights of the precolonial legal system. A witness and victim of criminal activities on both sides of the colonial situation, Saaba was destined to oblivion. Thus her case is typical of so many enslaved people who, their voices largely silenced in their own times, remain silent as the historian tries to reconstruct this past.

In other words, we can say that it is not the passage of time that is at the root of the problem of sources, but the fact that Saaba and others like her were expunged from the historical record in the very process of its creation. Thus a call emanates from this silence, a call for further research that might uncover overlooked sources, and, even more urgently, a call to think in methodological and theoretical terms about how we might approach slavery's archive and understand how its erasures and repressions are part of the historical process itself. In the end, what this document teaches us about slavery is *precious*, in the double sense of this word: something of great value and something to be treated carefully.

QUESTIONS TO CONSIDER

1. This document raises as many questions as it answers. Identify three that you think are in need of further explanation and research.
2. How did Saaba fall between the gaps of colonial laws abolishing slavery and the protections of Islamic law?
3. How reliable do you feel Largeau is as an observer? At what points in his account does he establish himself as credible or problematic?

Victor Largeau, *Le Pays de Rirha–Ouargla–Voyage à Rhadamès* (Paris: Hachette, 1879), 223–229.

[Three original footnotes, relating to transcriptions, place names, and ethnographic definitions, have been deleted. The text has been repunctuated for sense, and the spelling of place names has been adapted.]
Sunday, 8 July 1877

[1] B. Brower, *A Desert Named Peace: The Violence of France's Empire in the Algerian Sahara 1844-1902* (Columbia, 2009), 188.

Today at four o'clock I went to the slave market accompanied by several Arab notables and my servant Bouzid …

For quite a while Bouzid had complained about having to cook in the [summer] heat … I sympathized with his suffering and I looked for an old local woman who would be willing to come and serve as my cordon bleu. The first who came to me was of such uncleanliness that my stomach turned in disgust. I paid her for her troubles and asked her to return home. A second presented herself who seemed to be relatively clean. The first day all went well, [but] the next day she said that the neighborhood women heckled her because she cooked in the home of a *Nasrani* (Christian), [and] she could no longer serve me.

Thus I was in a big predicament when the Arabs came to see me. One of them told me that he wanted to buy a Negress and couldn't do it because he didn't have enough money: the [slave] merchants, who wanted to leave quickly, would not extend him credit until the date harvest [later in the fall].

I proposed to this Arab that I would pay the price of the Negress, on the condition that she stayed in my service until the day of my departure from Ouargla; he would then reimburse me and she would become his property. My proposition accepted, we left straight away for the slave market, which was held in the Beni Sisin quarter [of the oasis], in a large, old home that the [French] demolishers had not touched [when they occupied Ouargla]: indeed it belonged to a shaykh who emigrated to Biskra during the insurrection, and who, for this act, was considered as a friend of the French.[2]

[…]

In the courtyard of this old house, a dozen young black girls, clothed in blue cotton robes, stood or crouched against the walls, their eyes lowered and full of tears. In the corner a group of fifteen children swarmed about, several of whom were not quite five years old. Squatting in the middle, a few Arabs chatted with the marabout slave trader

The regularity of the features of these young Negresses struck me. Several even had, on their face and in their bearing, a distinction that is not typical of the Negroes of the Soudan [i.e., the region at the Sahara's southern edge]; several of them had almost thin lips, and their skin was hardly darker than that of the Saharan Negroes.[3]

The marabout came to greet me, [and] I quietly explained the purpose of my visit. He wanted to immediately undress the Negresses, [but] I strongly refused: "As a doctor," I told him, "I will easily see, though a simple examination of the mouth, legs and the chest, if they are healthy or not."

After a fifteen-minute inspection, my choice settled on a young girl of about 16 years of age (the eldest was not quite 18). She had a nice figure and a distinguished look that attracted my attention and her tears moved me to pity. Her name was Saaba. I left to the

---

[2] Ouargla had been at the center of several movements resisting the French. In 1851, a man named Muhammad ben Abdallah rallied the people of Ouargla in a famous rebellion. The troubles mentioned here occurred in 1871, when a new leader, Bou Choucha, led another round of armed resistance. The Beni Sisin of Ouargla pledged their support and paid dearly for it when a French punitive expedition put down the revolt and destroyed their homes and confiscated their property in retaliation.

[3] Largeau, like many French, found the Fulbe physically attractive. Living across the West African savanna from Senegal to Lake Chad, the Fulbe were originally pastoralists, but by the nineteenth century, many had settled. They tended to be slender and light-skinned.

Arab for whom I made this deal, having approved my choice, the task of negotiating the price. After long and loud negotiations, the deal was concluded at the price of 650 francs, a sum that would be paid in only three days, unless, during this period, we found any redhibitory defect in the bought person.

According to Muslim traditions and laws the redhibitory cases that entail the annulation of the sale are a slave's pregnancy, even if this state is not seen until after the payment, a penchant for theft or anger, secret illnesses, and, something funny, the defect, if you can call it that, of snoring at night.

It is explicitly forbidden to sell Muslims. But the person who was idolatrous at the time they were reduced to servitude and who then converts to become Mohammedan is not emancipated for this act, if their master would like to keep them. No one can force an unbelieving slave to embrace Islam; but it is the duty of the master to instill morals in young slaves.

When it came time to leave the market, poor Saaba began to sob violently, [but] pulling herself together, she bid farewell to her companions and followed me with a firm step.

I took her home, still surrounded by my escort of Arabs, who did not leave me until sunset.

As the dinner hour approached, Saaba, on her own initiative, stirred up the fire and attended to the cooking of the food. Bouzid was overjoyed by the idea of finally being free of a chore that had become unbearable. Saaba washed her hands before eating, something I had never seen done by any of the local Negresses, and she ate with a good appetite.

The poor girl did not understand Arabic, yet she pronounced the sacramental words "bismillah" (in the name of God) before eating, and after eating I clearly heard her say "alhamdulillah" (praise God). Was she a Muslim? To find the answer, I began reciting the profession of faith, "la illah illa Allah…," and I made a sign for her to continue. She took up the words very distinctly, although with a strong foreign accent, "la illah illa Allah, sidna Muhammad rasul Allah [sic]," or "There is no other god but God and our lord Mohammed is the prophet of God!"

I raised my eyes to Bouzid, who himself looked to me with surprise: "Since when do the Arabs sell Muslims?" I asked him.

"Maybe she learned that on the route."

The next morning, I gave Saaba two long white gandouras, a scarf as a belt and two turbans; I gestured to her to make a dress of blue cottonade, a color especially liked by the Negros of the Soudan, and I finished by buying her some sandals. Before dressing, she gestured that she wanted to wash. My improvised bathtub, situated under the stairs and hidden by curtains, was soon filled, and a half-hour later Saaba showed herself very well dressed.

A young local Negro, whom I had hired to shop for me in town or in the kasbah, offered to go find a woman [he knew] who spoke Saaba's language, a woman who, having come very young to the region as a slave, had since been freed and married by her master to one of his servants.

I sent him off forthright, and in an hour he came back accompanied by a tall and beautiful Negress; I saw on first sight that this woman belonged to the same race as my slave, to the Fulani race, as I rightly suspected. Here is what Saaba told me through the intermediary of the Negress.

"I am Fulani [Fulbe], born on the banks of the *Mayo Balleo* [the central reach of the Niger River] in a village situated between Yamina [Niamina?] and Ségou. All the Fulani are nobles and Muslims, but they do not speak the language of the Arabs.

"The brother of my father was a leader of the country. My father was himself a powerful man among the Fulani, and the Bambara people feared him greatly because of his strength.

"My country is very fertile, there is a lot of water and large trees, and the people are not poor like here.

"One day we were at war with the Arabs, although I do not remember why. The Arabs arrived in great numbers at a time when the Fulani didn't expect them. They killed all the men and all the boys. I saw my father fall in a battle against ten of the whites. Although my father was very strong, the Arabs killed him with their guns.

"After all the men and young people were dead, the Arabs rounded up the young girls and those young children who could walk and placed us in their midst to take us along with them.

"My mother followed me for a long time, wailing and crying, but all of a sudden I did not hear her anymore. I think the Arabs killed her.

"We followed the *Mayo Balleo* passing by Ségou, Djenné, Hamdallahi, Dioouarou (Joouarou) [sic], and we arrived at Timbuktu. Up to there we saw pretty country and lacked nothing.

"They wanted to sell us at Timbuktu, but they were not allowed because we are Muslims. Then we crossed horrible deserts on foot, where there was neither water nor vegetation. Many of us died on the journey. We ended up putting all the little ones on the camels, otherwise they would have all died.

"We arrived at In Salah, where they sold us. Then we were brought here, traveling only at night because of the heat.

"This country is ugly and those who live here are poor and wretched. The Arabs told us that farther on there are the French, who eat blacks."

Such was the story of Saaba.

CONCLUSION

"Such was the story of Saaba": With these words Largeau ends Saaba's testimony. When the French explorer left Ouargla, he does not tell us if he turned Saaba over to the unnamed man who served as his proxy in the slave market or if he took her with him as he continued his travels. Like most of the slaves who came to Algeria, Saaba probably stayed in the Sahara, becoming part the slave community that represented roughly 10–15 percent of the total population in the Algerian oases. Or she might have been smuggled into the home of an Algerian master living in a northern city. Here she would serve as a domestic servant or concubine, hidden from the 1848 abolition law as a wife or otherwise absorbed into the household in a way that obscured her true status as a slave.

The somber note on which she concludes her story in Ouargla – among the ruined, facing the barbarians – is worth considering. Certainly, Saaba's future looks bleak. Her family had been destroyed, and all that this family represented, such as economic and physical security, as well as a claim to her labor, sexuality, and children, was lost to her. A slave's life in a poor oasis like Ouargla was a precarious one. At the same time, it might not mean utter annihilation. Like other slaves, Saaba might have been able to reconstitute a community among her peers in Ouargla (or where ever she eventually settled) and partake of social support such community might offer. Moreover, although few had respected the law in her case, she might hope that her master would one day. If her owner was a man, Muslim law afforded her certain legal rights if she conceived a child with him and thus became *umm walad* (mother of a child), a status by which the law forbade her resale and proscribed her manumission upon the master's death. If her master was a pious person, she or he might follow Islam's repeated encouragements that masters liberate their slaves. Likewise, the French colonial authority might one day choose to enforce the abolition law in the oases and emancipate Saaba – a distinct possibility inasmuch as she would have been in her mid-forties in the first decade of the twentieth century, when the French made a concerted effort to end slavery in the Algerian Sahara.

SUGGESTED ADDITIONAL READINGS

Brower, Benjamin Claude. *A Desert Named Peace: The Violence of France's Empire in the Algerian Sahara 1844–1902*. New York: Columbia University Press, 2009.

Cordell, Dennis D. "No Liberty, Not Much Equality, and Very Little Fraternity: The Mirage of Manumission in the Algerian Sahara in the Second Half of the Nineteenth Century," in *Slavery and Colonial Rule in Africa*. Edited by Suzanne Miers and Martin Klein (London: Frank Cass, 1999), 38–56.

Ennaji, Mohammed. *Serving the Master: Slavery and Society in Nineteenth-Century Morocco*, trans. Seth Graebner. New York: St. Martin's Press, 1999.

Goldenberg, David M. *The Curse of Ham: Race and Slavery in Early Judaism, Christianity, and Islam*. Princeton, NJ: Princeton University Press, 2003.

Hunwick, John, and Eve Trout Powell. *The African Diaspora in the Mediterranean Lands of Islam*. Princeton, NJ: Markus Wiener, 2002.

Jennings, Lawrence C. *French Anti-Slavery: The Movement for the Abolition of Slavery in France, 1802–1848*. Cambridge: Cambridge University Press, 2000.

Klein, Martin A. *Slavery and Colonial Rule in French West Africa*. Cambridge: Cambridge University Press, 1998.

Lethielleux, Jean. *Ouargla, cité saharienne: des origines au début du XXe siècle*. Paris: Geuthner, 1983.

Lovejoy, Paul E. and Jan S. Hogendorn. *Slow Death for Slavery: The Course of Abolition in Northern Nigeria, 1897–1936*. Cambridge: Cambridge University Press, 1993.

Wright, John. *The Trans-Saharan Slave Trade*. New York: Routledge, 2007.

21 Zenneb and Saint-André's Cruise Up the Nile to Dongola

An Enslaved Woman from Dar Fur (Sudan) and Her Self-Presentation

GEORGE MICHAEL LA RUE

Zenneb was an enslaved woman from Dar Fur who became the female companion of M. Saint-André, a French pharmacist serving in the Egyptian army. Through an unusual set of circumstances, some of her words and actions have been preserved. Zenneb and Saint-André were observed from December 1833 to February 1834 by the young Saint-Simonian traveler, Edmond Combes, who shared their cruise from Cairo to Dongola where Saint-André was posted.[1] There were several other reports about one or both of them by Reboul (another Saint-Simonian) in 1834 and early 1835, and by an anonymous European (tentatively identified as Amadée D. Ryme) in 1838.[2] Combes provided the most detailed information on Zenneb, but together these sources reveal some of her views, her range of self-presentation, and the complexity and evolution of her position as a slave companion of a European male in Muslim Egypt in the 1830s.

Slavery was a very old institution in Egypt and the Sudan. The trans-Saharan trade from Dar Fur, Sinnar, and the Lake Chad region had been going on for centuries. From medieval times, merchants brought many trade items including gold, ivory, ostrich feathers, and slaves to Egypt by caravan. The slaves were captured in local wars, kidnapped from their families, or captured in slave raids launched by the sultans of Dar Fur and Sinnar or by nomadic groups, and then sold to trans-Saharan merchants. In Egypt, the black slaves were used for a wide variety of work, including porters, nursemaids, shop assistants, artisans, domestic servants, concubines, and soldiers. In 1820, the Egyptian government invaded the Sudan and occupied it until 1882. This transformed the means by which slaves were acquired and distributed. During the conquest of the Sudan, many Sudanese were enslaved, and for several decades thereafter, the Egyptian army in the Sudan engaged in annual slave raids. The Egyptian army recruited many of the male slaves as soldiers for the *nizam al-jadid*, the new European-style army that Egypt's modernizing leader, Muhammad Ali, created with the help of European military advisors. The female slaves

---

[1] E. Combes, *Voyage en Egypte, en Nubie, dans les deserts de Bayouda, des Bischarys, et sur les côtes de la mer Rouge*, 2 vols. (Paris, 1846). In Combes's text, her name is spelled both Zenneb and Zennab. This is likely to be his personal transliteration of the classical Arabic, Zaynab.

[2] P. Santi and R. Hill, "A Saint-Simonian in Kordofan: Reboul's Journal of an Expedition to Collect Live Animals, 1834–1835" in their *The Europeans in the Sudan, 1834–1878* (Oxford, 1980), 35–51, and R. Hill, *On the Frontiers of Islam: Two Manuscripts Concerning the Sudan under Turco-Egyptian Rule, 1822–1845* (Oxford, 1970), xiv.

were often sold to merchants who transported them to Egypt for sale. Muhammad Ali also recruited a new wave of European doctors and other medical staff to treat his soldiers, train Egyptian doctors and midwives, and improve the health of the Egyptian nation. Although most of the enslaved Sudanese ended up serving Egyptians, some of them were purchased by Europeans living in Egypt, and sometimes working for the Egyptian government.

In the nineteenth century, enslaved Sudanese interacted with European medical personnel in Egypt. Muhammad Ali, the viceroy of Egypt, recruited European doctors as medical officers in his army, as physicians in his court, and quarantine monitors in his lazarettos. Beginning in 1827, he established an Egyptian medical school headed by a French surgeon, Clot-Bey. A further influx of French and other European medical personnel staffed the medical school (which included midwifery), provided support for new hospitals and smallpox vaccination programs in Egypt, and staffed hospitals and army posts in the Sudan.[3] These European doctors, pharmacists, and professional midwives often described Sudanese slaves they treated, encountered, or owned, and their accounts can be used to investigate slavery in nineteenth-century Egypt and the Sudan.[4] These particular texts were found by looking for accounts by and about European medical personnel in Egypt.

THE NARRATOR

Working with this material presents its share of challenges. Edmond Combes, the primary narrator of the text presented here, is best known for his subsequent two-year mission to Ethiopia with Maurice Tamisier beginning in January 1835. In 1838, the two published their well-known account of their travels, *Voyages en Abyssinie, dans le pays de Choa et d'Ifar, précédé d'une excursion dans l'Arabie heureuse (1835–1837)*.[5] Only after Combes had achieved a certain degree of fame as an explorer of Ethiopia, worked unsuccessfully on behalf of the French Compagnie Nanto-Bordelaise to open up trade with Abyssinia, and then negotiated for the purchase of the port of Edd on the Red Sea, did he publish (in 1846) the account of his earlier voyage with passages about Zenneb and Saint-André in 1833 and 1834. After his travels in Ethiopia, Combes kept company with Anna, a 'Galla' (Oromo) woman, who was described as his widow at his death in 1848.[6]

Combes indirectly mentions that he had kept a journal of this first voyage, but he must have done so because he gives dates throughout his *Voyage en Egypte*. The noted British historian of the Sudan, Richard L. Hill, described this book as "a purple-tinted account of his journey," implying that it included material that was both gossipy and sexually

---

[3] For a description of Muhammad Ali's efforts to build up the Egyptian medical service, see LaVerne Kuhnke, *Lives at Risk: Public Health in Nineteenth-Century Egypt* (Berkeley, 1990). For a general introduction to slavery in modern Egypt, see G. Baer, "Slavery in Nineteenth Century Egypt," *Journal of African History*, 8, 3 (1967): 417–441.

[4] For examples of my previous use of these sources, see G. M. La Rue, "African Slave Women in Egypt, from ca. 1820 to the Plague Epidemic of 1834–1835" in G. Campbell, S. Miers, and J. C. Miller (eds.), *Women and Slavery: Volume One – Africa and the Western Indian Ocean Islands* (Athens, OH, 2007), 168–189; and G. M. La Rue, "The Fatal Sorbet: An Account of Slavery, Jealousy, Pregnancy and Murder in a Harem in Alexandria, Egypt, ca. 1850," unpublished paper presented at an International Conference on *Sex, Power and Slavery: The Dynamics of Carnal Relations under Enslavement* at McGill University, Montreal, 2007.

[5] E. Combes and M. Tamisier, *Voyages en Abyssinie, dans le pays de Choa et d'Ifar, precede d'une excursion dans l'Arabie heureuse (1835–1837)*, 4 vols. (Paris, 1838).

[6] C. J. Jaenen, "The Combes-Tamisier Mission to Ethiopia, 1835–1837: Saint-Simonian precursors of Colonialism," *French Colonial History*, 3 (2003): 153–154.

salacious.[7] But Combes' work seems complementary to the two fascinating and detailed accounts that Hill later translated and annotated in *On the Frontiers of Islam*, describing the lives and circumstances of Europeans living in the Sudan, including their interactions with Sudanese slaves. Those accounts Hill admires as being "refreshingly free of cant" – that is, very straightforward and unbiased – and together they provide context and further details on Saint-André and Zenneb.[8] This text by Combes is both detailed and potentially controversial because it goes beyond descriptions of the Sudan, Egypt, and slavery, to describe the feelings of a particular slave woman from Dar Fur and the gritty details of her life with a French master in the Egyptian Sudan. The challenge is to discern Zenneb's actions, words, feelings, and situation through the text created by Combes, a young, French Saint-Simonian man who is in Egypt for the first time, and to understand the meaning of her later actions in forming a closer relationship with Saint-André's Nubian servant, Musa, as reported by another source.

The narrator, Combes, was just twenty-one when he began his voyage up the Nile, and he states that his youthful curiosity was strong but he knew little Arabic:

> I was still a child (I was twenty-one years old) but a curious child, eager to see and to know: I did not know then at what price one buys the satisfaction of such desires.... I had yet to learn the Arabic language, as necessary for a voyager in the Muslim lands as French is today in Europe. By the time I had finished this trip, I had attained my double goals – my strengths were developed and I spoke Arabic passably well.[9]

This tone of an accomplished man looking back at his naïve and tentative beginnings obscures his cultural and linguistic preparations for this journey, and also suggests that he may have had conflicting views of what he witnessed – that he was torn between his first innocent understanding of what he saw and his later, perhaps more cynical and experienced, views as a well-traveled man when he was actually writing the book in 1846.

Despite his youth, Combes was not as naïve and linguistically challenged as his self-description might suggest. In both his books, Combes downplays or neglects to mention how he (and Tamisier) came to Egypt as part of the Saint-Simonian movement.

The Saint-Simonians were a very interesting group of idealists who believed in a form of socialism that sought to raise the status of workers and women. By 1832, their leader, Prosper Enfantin, had been arrested by the French government, which inspired his followers to look to the Orient as a potential new site for their activities. They formed a group called the *Compagnons de la Femme* to seek out a female leader in the East, and divided themselves into three bands. The first Saint-Simonian delegation is the best known and was led by Emile Barrault to Constantinople as part of the *Compagnons de la Femme*, and eventually ended up in Egypt in 1833. That group had prepared themselves by beginning to learn Arabic and reading about Muslim culture.[10] This was part of a broader plan by Père

---

[7] For Hill's dismissive comment, see Richard L. Hill, *A Biographical Dictionary of the Sudan* (London, 1967), 102–103, entry on Edmond Combes.

[8] Hill, *On the Frontiers*, xxvi.

[9] Combes, *Voyage en Egypte*, 1: xi–xii.

[10] For a quick introduction to the Saint-Simonians, see Jaenen, "The Combes-Tamisier Mission," 144–145. For more details, see P. Regnier, *Les Saint-Simoniens en Egypte, 1833–1851* (Cairo, 1989). See also I. Urbain, *Voyage d'Orient suivi de Poemes de Ménilmontant et d'Egypte*. Ed. P. Regnier (Paris, 1993), 47–202; P. Regnier, "Thomas-Ismayl Urbain, Métis, Saint-Simonien et Musulman: Crise de personnalité et crise de Civilisation (Egypte, 1835)" in Jean Calude Vatin (ed.), *La Fuite en Egypte: Supplément aux voyages*

Enfantin (the Saint-Simonian leader) to leave France, and the other Saint-Simonian members of the *Compagnons de la Femme*, including Combes, came to Egypt more directly and were similarly preparing themselves for their new experiences.

When he arrived in Egypt, Combes had very little money, so he was quite pleased to be able to accompany the French pharmacist, M. Saint-André, to his new post at a military camp in Dongola in the northern Sudan. The pharmacist traveled up the Nile at the expense of the Egyptian government and offered Combes a free ride and food for the journey.

THE VOYAGE

On December 13, 1833, Saint-André left Cairo by boat, accompanied by Edmond Combes, the young traveler who is the principal source of information on the relationship between the pharmacist and Zenneb. In 1833, Combes described Saint-André as 'a man of mature age, with an excellent heart' who treated Combes with every consideration during their voyage together from Cairo to Dongola. He also thought him a timid soul who feared that the Nile boat would capsize. The older man frequently ordered the crew to take in the sails and tie up the boat to the shore if the wind was blowing vigorously, and he rarely permitted them to sail at night, and stayed awake if they did.

Saint-André was not a newcomer to the Middle East or Egypt. After serving in the French army and leaving France at the end of the Napoleonic wars, he had spent more than twenty years in the Levant without ever managing to learn Arabic. Egyptian troops had been sent to Greece in 1825 (under the command of Ibrahim-Pasha, the son-in-law of Muhammad Ali), to fight against the Greeks on behalf of the Ottoman Empire. The Egyptian contingent included both the newly enslaved black troops captured during the Egyptian invasion of the Sudan and various European medical personnel serving in the Egyptian army.[11] In 1828, Mangeart, a French traveler in Greece, met a group of the European medical men including six Frenchmen, two Piedmontese, and three Italians. They had all been engaged for four years' service, were well paid and granted not only suitable food but fine clothes. Their contracts stipulated that they would not be forced to convert to Islam and that they would receive termination pay and a return fare to France. "Each one of them had only one [slave] woman with the exception of Monsieur Saint-André of Lyon, who had three of them."[12] One wonders why Saint-André required three slave women. He was

européens en Orient (Cairo, 1989), 299–316; M. Levallois, "Ismayl Urbain: Elements pour une biographie" in M. Morsy (ed.), *Les Saint- Simoniens et l'Orient vers la Modernite* (Paris, 1989), 53–82. Specifically on their preparation for life in the Orient, see Regnier, "Thomas-Ismayl Urbain," 304–305; and Urbain, "Voyage d'Orient," 134–140, 148–154, 162–167.

[11] For a standard introduction to the formation of the new Egyptian army, the *nizam al-jadid*, see K. Fahmy, *All the Pasha's Men: Mehmed 'Ali, His Army, and the Making of Modern Egypt* (Cambridge and New York, 1997), 86–93. For a description of the use of Sudanese slaves in the Egyptian military, see R. Hill and P. Hogg, *A Black Corps d'Elite: An Egyptian Sudanese Conscript Battalion with the French Army in Mexico, 1863–1867, and Its Survivors in Subsequent African History* (East Lansing, 1995). For specific information on the units serving in Greece, see R. L. Hill, *Egypt in the Sudan, 1820–1881* (London, 1959), 18; R. R. Madden, *Egypt and Mohammed Ali: Illustrative of the Condition of His Slaves and Subjects* (2nd edition, London, 1841), 67; G. E.J. Durand-Viel, *Les Campagnes Navales de Mohammed Aly et d'Ibrahim* (Paris, 1937) 1: 456; G. Douin, *Une Mission Militaire Française Aupres de Mohamed Aly: Correspondance des Generaux Belliard et Boyer* (Cairo, 1923), xvii–xviii.

[12] J.-S. Mangeart, *Souvenirs de la Morée recueillis pendant le séjour des Français dans le Pélopenèse* (Paris, 1830), 29. All translations are mine unless otherwise noted. Saint André was nicknamed "Dragoon" after his unit during the Napoleonic wars.

nicknamed Dragoon, as he had apparently served in a French cavalry unit. He had been briefly in the Greek army but quit and switched sides to join the Egyptian army because of broken promises and mistreatment. One of the other French medical men had fathered a child by a very pretty Negro woman and intended to have his child naturalized as a French citizen when he returned home. She occupied herself with her child and lavished attention on her man as well. Mangeart "especially noted in her a great deal of orderliness, cleanliness and economy" and was impressed with her during his short stay, but Saint-André had a longer period to observe her.[13] Saint-André's three slave women are not described, but they could have been Greeks, as many in the Egyptian forces there bought Greek women as slaves.[14] Little is known of Saint-André's activities between 1828 and 1833, but it appears that he remained in the service of the Egyptian army. Not long after his return to Egypt from Greece, he purchased Zenneb. Although their relationship became more complex, Saint-André's enthusiasm for female slave companionship, and the example of his colleague's African slave wife in Greece, may have shaped his initial intentions for his relationship with Zenneb.

In addition to Saint-André and the boat's crew, the voyagers up the Nile included an unnamed Spanish "renegade" who was to be a nurse in Dongola. The Spaniard tried hard to convince Combes that he had converted to Islam out of conviction, but Combes noted cynically that the Spaniard favored Islam because men were permitted to take four wives. The Spaniard's first wife (who had produced two sons for him) began the voyage in Cairo, and the Spaniard married for the second and third times between Cairo and Dongola, to the alarm of his first wife. Despite this enthusiastic adhesion to Islam, he had not renounced the consumption of wine. The Spaniard served as Saint-André's interpreter on the voyage, and would help interpret in Dongola.

Saint-André also had two male servants, one a fellah (Egyptian peasant) from the Cairo area and the other a Nubian, named Musa (Moussa in the French original). According to Combes, they were eager to serve because they knew that domestics in the employ of Europeans, particularly those working for the Egyptian government, could escape military conscription. The Nubian was literate and quite religiously conservative, and often entertained the crew and the voyagers with long recitations. There was one more voyager on their Nile-boat: Zenneb, Saint-André's female slave companion.

Zenneb had both a history and a considerable physical presence. She had been captured during the invasion of the Sudan. She was reportedly from a princely family from Dar Fur, the major sub-Saharan sultanate to the west of Kordofan. The invading Egyptian forces did not reach Dar Fur itself in this time period, so she was probably captured in Kordofan, then a province of Dar Fur. From Combes's account one cannot tell whether she was part of a noble family sent out from Dar Fur to rule over Kordofan or one of the noble families of Kordofan. But her proud demeanor and interactions with Saint-André, her command of Arabic, and her adherence to Islam support her claim of being from a princely family rather than a commoner. After capture, she had been brought to Egypt where she was put

---

[13] *Ibid.*

[14] Col. Sèves, commonly known as Soliman-Bey, had trained the new black and Egyptian troops of the *nizam al-jadid* in Upper Egypt. He arrived in Greece with Arsana, a black slave woman, and bought three Greek women, one of whom became his new favorite, and Arsana, after making a scene over her displacement, was sent away. C. Deval, *Deux années a Constantinople et en Morée, 1825–1826, ou Esquisses historiques sur Mahmoud: les janissaires, les nouvelles troupes, Ibrahim-Pacha, Solyman-Bey, etc.* (Paris, 1828), 210–211.

on sale in a slave market, probably in Cairo, and purchased there by Saint André in about 1828.[15] Little was told of her history from the moment of capture until the French pharmacist bought her, although as was typical for slaves brought from the Sudan, she had several masters in the interval.[16] It was quite common for Europeans living in Egypt to buy slaves. Several other European medical officers purchased African slave women and then formed very stable unions and had children with them.[17]

In his first impression of Zenneb, Combes followed a common circumlocution in describing physically attractive Negro slave women by referring to Venus, the Roman goddess of love. Venus de Milo, the famous statue now in the Louvre, was often invoked to suggest the physical attributes of the women in question. But here Combes goes farther and refers to the Hottentot Venus, whose body had been described in clinical detail by the famous French doctor, Georges Cuvier.[18] Literate French men and women of that time would have immediately been able to conjure up an exaggerated mental image, based on Combes's brief description of Zenneb.

Aware of earlier descriptions of Nile voyages, Combes did not provide a complete running commentary on the sights and sounds of the journey, but did give some historical background on Muhammad Ali and his modernization efforts, on his admirers and his critics. The Egyptian crew sailed, and as necessary hauled, the boat while consuming a very basic diet featuring raw onions, salted cheese, and Nile water. Near Beni Suef, Saint-André purchased a sheep and gave three-quarters of it to the crew as encouragement.[19] Combes also discoursed on the proselytizing zeal of Muslims, but felt that there was still a distinction in their minds between those who were born Muslim and new converts, with "the latter ordinarily considered less than the others."[20] When it came to slaves:

> The first concern of a believer is to learn what [the slave's] religion is, and to impose on him his own, which is a meritorious act in the eyes of God. The jallabas [trans-Saharan merchants] for their part are the most intolerant and despotic missionaries on earth: difficult conversions are accomplished with blows of the whip. Fortunately, the timid and credulous slaves do not generally put up much resistance for they have enough martyrship already as slaves. The Muslims do not raise any doubts about the good faith of the African neophytes and they are right, but they are less certain about the Europeans converted to their faith.[21]

---

[15] For comparative information on this generation of enslaved Sudanese women, see La Rue, "African Slave Women in Egypt."

[16] See J. McCarthy, *Selim Aga: A Slave's Odyssey* (Edinburgh, 2006), 21. The original narrative by Selim Aga is available in electronic form: Selim Aga, *Incidents Connected with the Life of Selim Aga, A Native of Central Africa*. http://docsouth.unc.edu/neh/aga/aga.html (accessed January 22, 2006). See also G. M. La Rue, "'My Ninth Master was a European': Enslaved Blacks in European Households in Egypt, 1798–1848" in K. Cuno and T. Walz (eds.), *Race and Slavery in the Middle East: Histories of Trans-Saharan Africans in Nineteenth-Century Egypt, Sudan and the Ottoman Mediterranean* (Cairo and New York, 2010), 99–124.

[17] See the marriages of Dr. Dussap and his wife Halima, Dr. Del Signore and his wife Catherine, and Dr. Alfred Peney and his wife. The broader phenomenon of Europeans owning slaves in Egypt is discussed in La Rue, "My Ninth Master."

[18] George Cuvier died in 1832, which may have led to renewed discussion of his work on the Hottentot Venus. See Georges Cuvier, "Extrait d'observations faites sur le cadavre d'une femme connue à Paris et à Londres sous le nom de Vénus Hottentotte," *Mémoires du museée nationale d'histoire naturelle* III (Paris, 1817), 259–274.

[19] Combes, *Voyage en Egypte*, 1: 132.

[20] *Ibid.*, 1: 126.

[21] *Ibid.*, 1: 132.

Here one can detect the views of the older Combes who had picked up the prevailing skeptical attitudes of the French toward Muslims in Africa by the time he was writing his account for publication in 1846.

One early incident of their trip revealed something about Zenneb's empathy for others and her interactions with Saint André. As the Nile-boat moved slowly up the river, they spotted a young woman on the bank with an infant in her arms. Exhausted, she hailed the passing boat, and the crew stopped to offer assistance. She clambered on board the boat without a word and collapsed on the deck. Zenneb and the Spaniard's wife moved quickly to help her. She lived in Beni Suef, but her husband had been absent for six months. Pregnant and increasingly aware that her delivery date was approaching, she had hoped to go upriver to Minieh to her parents' house to get her mother's assistance, but had started to deliver en route, gave birth to her baby, and had hailed their boat half an hour later. All aboard did everything they could to care for her.

This led to a conversation between Zenneb and Musa the Nubian servant who criticized her as too tolerant of the Europeans, which he believed showed that her faith was weak. After further discussion with Zenneb, Musa concluded that Saint-André would make a good Muslim, and the conversation turned to the fine clothes that Zenneb wore and the luxurious goods the Europeans imported into Egypt. For Musa, these were only signs of a pact between the Europeans and Satan, who had shared his secrets for a price.[22]

Zenneb's end of the conversation showed several things about her. Not only did she retain her humanity and empathy for others; she recognized Saint-André as a benign person, not only in his compassion for the new mother they rescued, but in his kind treatment of Zenneb herself, compared to earlier Muslim masters she had encountered who had beaten and injured her. While she appreciated his kindness and the quality of the clothing he provided her, she still regretted her kinless condition, as an enslaved person removed from all her original familial and social context.

Perhaps because of his Saint-Simonian background, the young Combes is working on the question of race himself, and this makes him a close observer of the Sudan and a curious interlocutor who often pursues issues of race and hierarchy with Zenneb. One interesting feature of the book is that there is a bit of tension between the young Combes's idealistic views as seen in his eyewitness reporting of what he experienced in 1833–34 and the digressions that seemingly reflect Combes' views as he was writing the book after extensive acculturation through travel in the Horn of Africa, associating with both local people and the range of Europeans in the area. In one of his digressions, the experienced Combes reveals he considered whites superior to blacks:

> While there exist notable differences between the various black races and even greater differences between the negro with thin legs and wooly head, and the Nubian, the Abyssinian, the Galla, and most of the tribes of Africa's East coast, one can boldly affirm that the black populations in general are inferior in nature in comparison to white populations.[23]

Perhaps remembering his youthful idealism, Combes is a bit uneasy with this and talks about aptitudes of specific peoples and individuals: he counters the notion of the brotherhood of men with the notion that some are elder brothers and others are younger brothers and extends this analogy to peoples.

[22] *Ibid.*, 1: 139–140.
[23] *Ibid.*, 1: 244.

Reconstructing the views that Saint-André and Zenneb held on race is a challenge. Saint-André's views on race were not expressed explicitly, but he certainly showed no qualms about owning slaves, and he may well have acculturated to a combination of the local attitudes toward slaves and the pragmatic view of other long-term European residents of the Sudan who lived with slave women.[24] For Zenneb's views on race there are several general clues in Combes's account, specific statements that he attributes to her, and revealing situations. Combes cites a folk story that he first learned from a slave woman from the Dar Fur region. He does not attribute this to Zenneb, but she may have heard a version of this either at home or after her enslavement. Perhaps Combes found this story charmingly naïve and gratifying, as it reinforced his sense of racial superiority and symbolically showed that whites had advanced by washing away their primitive origins. One can also question whether it reflected the folklore of the Sudan or was offered by others to enslaved Sudanese as a justification of racial differences and hierarchies.[25]

No doubt based on his later experiences, Combes wrote several discursive passages on race, using the well-known racial hierarchy of Muslim harems in Egypt and the extension of those preferences to Abyssinnia and Dar Fur as proof that black Sudanese accepted that hierarchy.[26] The crew of his Nile-boat consisted mainly of Nubians and Egyptians, but included one sailor who claimed Arab descent and felt superior because of it, despite the fact that his skin color was as dark as his fellow sailors.[27] Combes reported that the Nubians accepted this racial hierarchy without question, but denied that this specific sailor was white, which led to endless discussions.

It was in this context that Combes decided to press Zenneb on her racial views and asked her whether she would rather be black or white. Her response speaks volumes about Zenneb's understanding of the position of the "other" in European, Egyptian, and Sudanese societies.

LOCAL INTERACTIONS

Not long after these discussions, Zenneb, moved by empathy for a young Nubian woman, played the role of intermediary for her as she sought help from the pharmacist Saint-André. The Nile-boat had been tied up at Tééffah, a village on the Nile's left bank, south of Aswan. As the travelers were about to re-embark, Zenneb approached Saint-André to ask him to help the young Nubian woman who had been married for six months. Because she had not yet conceived, her husband was threatening to divorce her as infertile. The Nubian thought that she had been cursed, and Zenneb asked Saint-André to break the spell. Saint-André, taking the rational, medical approach, explained that it was too early to despair after only six months, and that she might soon be complaining of being too fecund! The Nubian woman left dissatisfied, and Zenneb turned her back on the pharmacist, obviously displeased with his refusal to honor her request.[28] Zenneb had tested her position as client to

---

[24] Hill, *On the Frontiers*, xxiv–xxvii.

[25] Another similar story involving the washing of hands and feet in a river, collected from a Muslim pilgrim in Asyut, portrays whites and blacks as created by God and Satan, respectively; M. T. Renouard de Bussierre, *Lettres sur l'Orient écrites pendant les années 1827 et 1828* (Paris, 1829), 2: 71.

[26] Combes, *Voyage en Egypte*, 1: 247–253.

[27] *Ibid.*, 1: 274–275.

[28] *Ibid.*, 1: 278–279.

Saint-André, her patron, to ask his help to benefit the Nubian woman. His refusal to act was embarrassing and humiliating to her as it put her status in question.[29]

Beyond her status as a dependent of Saint-André, Zenneb's position in the broader upper Egyptian society was demonstrated by an incident that occurred when the Nile-boat tied up at the village of Dekkeh, south of Dendour. First there was a discussion between Combes and Zenneb as she looked in a mirror while preparing to go ashore. Again, Combes captures Zenneb's growing self-awareness, her sense of multiple standards of beauty, and her ability to reframe differences not only as they related to different social contexts, but also in light of a larger divine plan. But ashore, not everyone was as tolerant of her position.

Generally in Egypt and the Sudan there were implicit sumptuary standards. Everyone dressed in a manner that reflected their standing in the society. The royal families of Egypt, Dar Fur, and Sennar dressed in expensive finery, wealthy merchants dressed well, and peasants dressed simply. The clothing of slaves reflected the rank of their masters, with the slave women of royal harems dressed in finery and the ordinary slaves of poor households dressed in rags and barefoot. Zenneb stepped ashore into a rich mix of standards by which she would be evaluated. She was judged by racial type, by sumptuary display, by her comportment and speech, and of course by her presumed religious beliefs.

Zenneb was an unusual "other" in Dekkeh. At first she attracted a crowd because she was an obviously black woman from Dar Fur dressed in elegant Egyptian clothes. There is no detailed description of her appearance on that occasion, so it is impossible to say for certain whether she was dressed *à la Turque* or *à l'Européenne* (in the Turkish or European styles), though the former seems more likely. The local people admired her gold bracelets and fine silken clothes, and combined with her height and ample figure, she must have been quite an unusual sight for them.

Her two French companions left her on her own: Saint-André settled in for a nap under a palm-tree, and the young Combes set off to see the local ruins. When he returned, Combes found her again at the center of a crowd. But this time, a devout Muslim was haranguing her for turning away from Islam to associate with Christian foreigners, and for being tempted by the luxurious clothing she had so proudly worn. Zenneb at first defended her master, but was soon quite rattled at this unexpected turn of events. The crowd had turned against her, and Combes found her in tears. He used a whip and his "superior" European status to rescue Zenneb. Saint-André had slept through the whole incident, but now wanted to complain to the local *shaykh* about this treatment. Instead, they chose to sail on.

Zenneb's safest course of action might have been to take refuge in her status as the slave/client of the European pharmacist who was in turn protected by the power of the Egyptian viceroy Muhammad Ali. But she remained open to other options.

INTO THE SUDAN

As they neared Wadi Halfa and the second cataract, the travelers followed the common practice of leaving behind their Nile-boat, to travel overland. To renew their provisions,

---

[29] For a discussion of master-slave interactions as patron-client relationships, see E. Toledano, *As If Silent and Absent: Bonds of Enslavement in the Islamic Middle East* (New Haven, CT, and London, 2007), 23–34.

Saint-André applied at the government depot and got new supplies. The young Combes was excited to travel by land, but Saint-André – older, diminished in vigor, and less impatient – would have preferred traveling further by boat if possible. His status enabled him to apply to the local *kachef* in Wadi-Halfa for the necessary camels. Zenneb, who already traveled northward along this route in a slave caravan under the eye of the *jallabs*, appreciated the opportunity to cross it again, this time as a "'princess' as the pharmacist put it when in his better moods."[30]

They joined a small caravan about to depart for the south and soon settled into the routines of desert travel. These were made more challenging because it was Ramadan, the holy month when Muslims fast from sunrise to sunset. Just before they reached the watering spot of Sakiet-al-'Abd about halfway through the land leg of their journey, it was the last day of Ramadan. One of their fellow travelers had made an extra effort to obtain a goat for the feast marking the end of fasting, and they also sent someone up a hill to look out for the new crescent moon, the first sign of the new month. Soon they were feasting, and celebrating and including the Europeans in the festivities.

Zenneb was revisiting familiar ground, and was once again in the Sudan. Her appearance was less the polished, well-groomed female slave companion of the European, and more a fellow traveler in the caravan, a Muslim Sudanese woman celebrating the end of Ramadan with a traditional dance. This scene astonished Combes, but was familiar to the others, and very comfortable for Zenneb who could reclaim a part of her pre-enslavement identity.

Soon enough they reached Dongola. M. Drouart, a doctor and an old friend of Saint-André, stationed there with the Eighth Regiment of the Egyptian Army, had heard of their imminent arrival and sent one of his servants to announce that he would come out to meet them. They arrived in his company on February 17, 1834, at Dongola-al-Ordi after thirteen days of travel in the desert. Combes described Drouart's living arrangements, but the young traveler only stayed in Dongola until April 6, 1834.[31] While there, he says nothing more about Zenneb. Dr. Drouart had a comfortable house in Dongola, and lived in the "oriental style" with slaves, and kept his favorite female slave, an Abyssinian woman in Drouart's case, out of sight.[32] Perhaps Saint-André imitated this pattern, and Zenneb and Combes were no longer in contact.

OTHER SIGHTINGS

Other sources provide some glimpses of Zenneb and/or Saint-André. On June 12, 1834, Reboul arrived in Dongola with Georges Thibaut, a French traveler and collector of exotic animals, and met up with M. Drouart, a medical officer there, and Saint-André ("the Dragoon"). Thibaut and Reboul stayed with Saint-André in "his commodious house" until July 1, 1834, when they left for Kordofan. Reboul also mentions that Reboul and Saint-André had shared a residence in Cairo, presumably while they were both working there.[33] They were to also stop in Dongola for six months (February 5 to August 3, 1835) on the return trip with six giraffes, and found Drouart and the Dragoon "as full of health as ever."[34]

---

[30] Combes, *Voyage en Egypte*, 1: 332–333.

[31] *Ibid.*, 2: 39.

[32] *Ibid.*, 2: 4.

[33] Santi and Hill, "Saint-Simonian in Kordofan," 35, 45.

[34] *Ibid.*, 50.

By 1837, Drouart is no longer mentioned, having been replaced by a Dr. Iken. The Eighth Regiment has become substantially Sudanese, through the replacement of Egyptian soldiers with Sudanese captured in slave raids.[35] Puckler-Muskau, who visited Dongola, never mentions Saint-André by name but he does mention an apothecary there "who used to be a French captain of the Dragoons" and told some stories of his time in the French Army.[36] Dr. Iken's immediate predecessor had been a Dr. Germain, and the apothecary calmly recounted how he had been present when Germain had been poisoned by a slave woman he had married:

> The poison had been prepared from the juice of the noxious shrub, which is everywhere at hand, and it was so potent, that in a few moments vomiting and convulsions ensued, and the unhappy victim expired the same night, retaining the use of his faculties to the very last. He pardoned the negress, though she manifested little contrition for what she had done and only made an awkward attempt to deny it. However she thought proper, as M. Germain with great magnanimity had hindered her from being arrested, to collect everything of value that she could lay her hands on, and to abscond before daybreak.[37]

Saint-André's comments are not recorded, but this poisoning of his close colleague must have made him reevaluate his own situation.

Other Europeans present in the Sudan also make note of Saint-André's coming and goings. He was mentioned by A. D. R. as arriving in Kurusku on December 19, 1837: "Saint-André, formerly a captain of the Dragons Napoléon and now pharmacist to the 8th Regiment, has arrived."[38] He was reportedly in Wad Madani (a town and military post on the Blue Nile) on September 6, 1838, and again on October 18 of that year. This suggests that he may have shifted his home base from Dongola to Wad Madani where the Eighth Regiment had relocated as part of the general preparation for war in Abyssinia.[39] By December 12, 1838, the pharmacist was thinking of leaving that town as well:

> Gassier and Saint-André had each bought a house and had afterwards exchanged houses but without notifying the qadi. Saint-André now wants to sell his house, but the qadi refuses to recognize Gassier's title, which is quite absurd of him.[40]

Gassier was the principal medical officer of the Eighth Regiment, the successor to Drouart, Germain, and Iken, Saint-André's earlier colleagues in Dongola.[41] Another European doctor, Sulayman-Effendi (known as Dr. de Pasquali before his conversion to Islam), accompanied him to Khartoum, leaving Wad Madani on December 24, 1838.

Several new pieces of information emerge here: Zenneb had a daughter by Saint-André, and Zenneb and Musa, his longtime Nubian servant, appear to have conspired against him to take control of his possessions. Zenneb and Musa had been living together in spite of her long association with Saint-André, and his advanced age. He was in poor

---

[35] Hill, *On the Frontiers*, xxi.

[36] Puckler-Muskau, *Egypt under Mehemet Ali* (London, 1845), 1: 163, 168–169.

[37] *Ibid.*, 1: 170; Dr. Germain is also mentioned in E. Cadalvène and J. de Breuvery, *L'Égypte et la Turquie de 1829 à 1836* (Paris, 1836), 2: 141–142.

[38] Hill, *On the Frontiers*, 129.

[39] *Ibid.*, 125, 169, 173.

[40] *Ibid.*, 176.

[41] *Ibid.*, xiv.

health and retreated to Egypt for medical leave. Two days later on December 26, 1838, the rumor was confirmed. Zenneb abandoned Saint-André completely to take up with Musa, and she had made the decision to conform to the Nubian marriage customs to please her new man. She had an operation that was ordinarily performed on girls before the age of twelve, to prevent "illicit sexual intercourse."[42] Of course in a small town like Wad Madani, everyone knew that she had undergone the operation.

NEW DEVELOPMENTS?

Quite obviously something had happened in the relationship between Saint-André and Zenneb in the time period from 1834 to the end of 1838. At this point there is no direct evidence of what occurred. One of them could easily have violated the other's trust. Saint-André was not a saint, for he was the only one among his group in Morea to have three female slaves, and in Dongola there was a sexual undercurrent among his visitors' reports that he is "very healthy." He was undoubtedly aware of Zenneb's physical attractions at the time he bought her. Perhaps he took other lovers and acquired syphilis or some other sexually transmitted disease, but there are no details on the health issues that led him to leave the Sudan.

Zenneb also knew that she was physically attractive, and Saint-André's job as a pharmacist to the Eighth Regiment put her in close proximity to many Egyptian and Sudanese soldiers in Dongola and the other military outposts where he was stationed. It is likely that she attracted the soldiers' attention and may have found a lover there. The reference to Saint-André abandoning his "putative daughter" (presumably Zenneb's child) leaves open the possibility that she took a European or some other lighter-skinned lover at some point. Perhaps Saint-André had lost some of his youthful vigor, or perhaps she had retaliated for his sexual wanderings.

It is interesting that Zenneb moved to marry Musa. Was he merely a convenient option as Saint-André was leaving? She could have found another man to take her in, but the fact that she was willing to voluntarily undergo circumcision as an adult woman to please him suggests that Musa was not her easiest option. She must have selected him for his familiarity to her through long association, for his piety, or possibly because he was the father of her child.

Zenneb's new partnership with Musa in taking control of Saint-André's possessions suggests that both felt betrayed by the pharmacist for some violation of their trust. One story, told among various instances of the bad behavior of Europeans toward their slaves in the Sudan, may suggest a parallel case:

> A French pharmacist who lives in Dunqula got very angry one day with a slave of his (I call him 'slave' for thus they are treated by the Europeans who employ them, though our law does not recognize them as slaves) because this slave had gone to see some girl who was his lover. In his anger the Frenchman wrote a note to the doctor of the place asking him for the loan of his box of instruments in order to castrate his slave. The doctor sent to him telling him that he hoped the sight of them would cause him to change his mind and be more

---

[42] *Ibid.*, 25. There is a detailed description of the operation.

humane. The doctor did wrong in sending them for the Frenchman carried out the crime and was not punished.[43]

No dates are given, and the pharmacist involved was not named, though the document covers events from 1822 to 1841. There is no evidence that Saint-André, Zenneb, or Musa were involved in that incident, yet it is suggestive of the sort of event that might have outraged Zenneb and Musa.

CONCLUSION

Zenneb's words and actions reveal her views, her range of self-presentation, and the complexity of her position as the slave companion of a European in a Muslim society. She was adjusting to living in a world that was more racially varied than the one she was raised in. She remained appreciative of kind treatment, and open to the suffering of others, especially young women. She used the behavioral models of her culture to become an intermediary for those she sought to help.

She could defend Saint-André against Musa's accusations by praising his treatment of her, which she contrasted to that of her earlier Muslim masters who had insulted and beaten her. She did acknowledge that her enslavement still caused her pain because of the separation from her family. Her own views of racial differences are not known, but she may have heard the explanatory stories about the original universality of black skin and the mythical use of lake or river water to create white-skinned people. Contesting versions emphasized superficial differences or deeper similarities between races.

Aware of cultural differences in the perception of racial hierarchies and standards of beauty, she sought to present herself to her best advantage according to the culture of the places she was in. In Egypt, she had adopted the dress and habits of elegant Egyptian women. But in upper Egypt and the Sudan, some local people "read" her clothing as an indication that she had abandoned Islam for the lure of European material goods, and she was chastised for renouncing Islam. This reaction caught her off guard. Later, she embraced the opportunity to behave like a daughter of the Sudan. To celebrate the end of Ramadan, she joined her fellow travelers' party and chose to dance for them, doing a stunning imitation of a camel in motion.

After Combes left to continue his travels, there is less detailed information about Zenneb, and the conditions of her daily life in Dongola and later Wad Madani can only be suggested. The available information suggests that her attachment to Saint-André was severed and her trust in him ended, without providing clear reasons for these changes. She apparently had a child, perhaps by him. He became ill. Zenneb took up with Musa, the pharmacist's Berber servant, and eventually married him. Together they had been "robbing him blind." To please Musa, she had arranged to have an operation, a female circumcision, so that she could present herself as a virgin bride.

Although Saint-André mistreated her, it was Zenneb who made new domestic arrangements, made financial arrangements for her own support, picked a new partner, and remained in the Sudan. Saint-André, the Frenchman, had to leave the country for medical reasons, but Zenneb stayed. She was free of his control, and set about to make a new life in the Sudan for her child, her new man, and herself.

[43] *Ibid.*, 38.

QUESTIONS TO CONSIDER

1. One definition of slavery is as follows:

   Slavery is one form of exploitation. Its special characteristics included the idea that slaves were property; that they were outsiders who were alien by origin or who had been denied their heritage through judicial or other sanctions; that coercion could be used at will; that their labour power was at the complete disposal of their master; that they did not have the right to their own sexuality and by extension to their own reproductive capacities; and that the slave status was inherited unless provision was made to ameliorate that status.[44]

   Which of these aspects of slavery are most relevant in Zenneb's case? Which aspects of her status as a slave remain the same throughout the time period described here and which changed? What are the reasons for the changes and continuities?

2. Combes, Zenneb, and Saint-André are all living in a society that is not their own. How does each one of them cope with the challenges of assimilating to life along the Nile? What are their coping mechanisms? How do they change? Who changes the least and who changes the most? Which culture is Zenneb trying to fit into? How can you explain these differences?

3. Consider Combes's shifting perceptions of Zenneb as a person. What resources does she have to survive life as a slave?

4. How does Zenneb perceive her life as Saint-André's slave woman in 1833–34? Does she consider herself to be sexually exploited at that time? Was her life difficult in other ways?

5. From the text, is it possible to understand why Zenneb left Saint-André in 1838 to marry Musa? Why did she undergo an operation before marriage to him?

1. FROM EDMOND COMBES

A. First Impressions

Monsieur Saint-André also had with him a pretty negress[45] of whom he was quite proud: she was a young woman of considerable height, extraordinarily shapely and who could have made the Hottentot Venus jealous.[46] She said that she was from one of the princely families

---

[44] P. E. Lovejoy, *Transformations in Slavery: A History of Slavery in Africa* (2nd ed., Cambridge and New York, 2000), 1.

[45] The French word, "négresse," was commonly used by Combes to refer to black slave women he encountered in Egypt and the Sudan. The male form of the word, "nègre," was definitely pejorative in French at the time, but the female form was more ambiguous in connotation. The word "negress" is used here to try to give something of the flavor of Combes's language, and that of the other contemporary sources.

[46] Saartjie Baartman, the well-known woman from southern Africa, whose physical appearance had impressed the French to such a degree that after her death her body was preserved and put on display in Paris. Her body was described in clinical detail by the famous French doctor, Georges Cuvier, and she was cited in many subsequence studies and essays on race and related matters. Her caricature was also frequently published in newspapers and journals. For a useful review of Saartjie Baartman's history, see S. Qureishi, "'Displaying Sara Baartman, the 'Hottentot Venus'," *History of Science*, 42 (2004): 233–257. http://www.shpltd.co.uk/qureshi-baartman.pdf. For a recent monograph focusing on Saartjie Baartman, the Hottentot Venus, see R. Holmes, *African Queen: The Real Life of the Hottentot Venus* (New York, 2007). For the broader phenomenon which she represented, see T. Denean Sharpley-Whiting, *Black Venus: Sexualized Savages, Primal Fears, and Primitive Narratives in French* (Durham, NC, 1999).

of Darfour, and supported her pretensions with a show of grand airs. Made prisoner by the troops of the viceroy [Muhammad 'Ali], she was taken to Egypt where M. Saint-André had purchased her in the slave market. But for a long time their roles had been reversed, and the negress had absolute dominion over her master.[47]

B. Talking to Musa, Zenneb defends Saint-André as a good man

'You see,' said the negress, 'that the Christians are not so bad as you keep telling me; you weren't paying any attention to this poor woman who was about to die of fatigue, and it was they who had the charity to collect her.'

'In the eyes of the all-powerful the actions of the infidels are indifferent, only Muslims will find grace before him on Judgement Day …'

After a few exchanges in this vein, Zenneb responded

'I don't really understand all that fancy talk, but you will not stop me from thinking that my master is the best of men, and you will not persuade me that these Muslims that you revere are more cherished by God than my master who only does good. I have often changed masters, none of whom spared me insults and blows, yet all were fervent Muslims. Allah and the prophet finally had pity on me, and I became the wife rather than the slave of one of these Christians who you want to make me hate and mistrust. With him, I have never been unhappy, liberty has been given back to me, and I would have nothing to desire, if the memory of my family didn't return to me at times to make me sad.'[48]

C. Combes relates a Dar Fur folktale on the origins of race?

A naïve tradition preserved by a few African tribes proves that they did not have any choice in their color, and if the Creator would have consulted them before forming them, they would have been white like us. This tradition was told to me for the first time by a black slave woman from the region of Darfour. It is common knowledge that in blacks the soles of their feet and hollows of their hands are nearly white. One day I asked this black woman why that was so.

Long ago at the beginning of the world, there was only color in the world – all humans were black like me. But in one country then uninhabited there was a large lake whose marvelous waters could whiten skin. The populations which are now white like you were the first to arrive in this favored land, and plunging into the waves of this enchanted lake, changed colors. But each diver absorbed a bit of the precious water, and the lake was already nearly dried up when the populations who stayed black came to take their turn. Despairing of arriving so late, they threw themselves on the wet mud of the lake bottom, and that mud still had the ability to whiten the bottoms of their feet and hands.[49]

D. Combes asks Zenneb a question about Race:

I profited from the circumstance to ask the negress [Saint-André's slave woman] the following question: 'If you had the ability to choose your color, would you prefer to be white

---

[47] Combes, *Voyage en Egypte*, 127–128.
[48] *Ibid.*, 1: 139.
[49] *Ibid.*, 1: 246.

or black?' But with such good sense that it disconcerted me and momentarily shook my convictions, she answered, 'I would want to be white if I were born in the midst of whites, and I am satisfied to be black as I am undoubtedly destined to live among blacks,' and after a moment's reflection she added, 'but as I belong to a European master, I would prefer to be white....' A white who was asked the same question would not have hesitated over the choice, boldly and without hesitation, he would have declared that he preferred to be white, because he would have had the vague or rational belief in his innate superiority.[50]

E. Zenneb reflects on racial differences:

The negress of M. Saint-André who intended to go on shore, dressed herself in her best clothes. I said earlier in speaking of black races that it was false that for blacks perfection consisted of having big lips and a very crushed nose. The pharmacist's slave, glorious in her brilliant outfit, had remained for long time in front of a small mirror which unfortunately only allowed her a partial view of herself.[51] After having admired with a naïve satisfaction the richness of her attire, she looked at her face, and could not prevent herself from a revealingly wry expression. She pinched her lips, and pressed her nose with her fingers. 'Here's what spoils everything,' she said turning towards us and trying to smile to hide her discontent, 'no nose and too much lips. What do you do in your country,' she added to me, 'to have such long and soft hair?' One must agree that the world is very extraordinary.

'It is likely,' I told her 'that you would not have thought of that if you had always lived among blacks.'

'Maybe,' she said with a worried expression, 'but my countrymen know that whites exist, and they speak ill of them, no doubt out of jealousy and to console themselves for being black.'

The negress again ran her eyes over her pretty clothes and refound her gaiety, 'No matter what color – white or black – we are all the children of Adam, and the servants of God. Let's go ashore and stop talking about ourselves.'[52]

F. Zenneb goes ashore in Dekkeh: How the Nubians perceived her

M. Saint-André's slave wore the clothes of the great ladies of Cairo. As soon as the [Nubians] of Dekkeh saw her she became the center of a crowd of men and women whose surprise and admiration must have flattered her self-worth. With an envious curiosity the Nubian women examined the various elements of her outfit one by one, and were astonished that a black woman, who in their view occupied the lowest rank of the human hierarchy should have managed such a fate. One of them told her, 'You had a happy fate,' as her hands touching her silken clothing and gold bracelets, 'your master must be very rich or very loving.'

We left Zennab (that was the slave's name) alone to enjoy her triumph. M. Saint-André sat in the shade of a palm tree, while I went to visit the temple of Dekkeh....

[50] *Ibid.*, 1: 276.
[51] Mirrors were not common in the Sudan at the time, and the fact that Zenneb had one for her personal use in Egypt and the Sudan suggests that she was being provided with all the material objects that an Egyptian woman married to a government official would have had. This set her apart from not only the ordinary people of Dar Fur, but from the vast majority of peasant women in Egypt.
[52] *Ibid.*, 292–293.

When I returned to the slave woman, the scene had changed. A cruel disdain had replaced the admiration to which she had been subjected. Blacks in general are not fanatics, but like all weak natures, they let themselves be carried along by evil. Among the [Nubians] gathered into a mob around her was a <u>hajji</u> (pilgrim) who had brought back from Mecca those narrow ideas and the affected intolerance which distinguish the majority of Muslims.[53] According to him and his co-religionists, all blacks without exception belonged or should belong to Islam. A Christian owner of a black slave encroached on their rights and was in their eyes very guilty. Despite the fact that a slave was everywhere sacred property, the Muslims never neglected to incite those who had infidels as masters to flee. In many provinces under their domination, Christians are prohibited from buying slaves, and those who possess them are obligated to get rid of them. In no country do good Muslims ever see without displeasure a black slave pass into the hands of an infidel, and the seller and buyer have thus an equal share in their scorn.[54] The pilgrim in Dekkeh, like all those who have performed the pious journey to Mecca and Medina, and who live among the blacks enjoyed in his village an enormous consideration and a great influence. Jealous, no doubt to no longer be in this moment the exclusive object of the attention of his compatriots, he wanted to avenge himself for their indifference towards him by trying to trouble the innocent joy of Zennab. He started by insinuating to her that her cohabitation with a European was a crime in the eyes of men and of God and that she would be punished for it sooner or later. 'If you still have in your heart,' he added loudly to make himself heard by the onlookers, 'the feelings of a good Muslim woman, hasten to abandon your master, come into our houses, where you will find asylum and protection. We'll know how to shield you from the pursuit by the infidels, and you will be free like us. No doubt you will not find here the rich clothing and silk garments like those you are now wearing, but you will live in the midst of good Muslims, instead of being the slave of these Christian dogs.' These words were welcomed with a greater favor since the women had viewed the slave woman's clothes with envy. Grateful towards her master, she had thought it necessary to defend him, and the Nubian women, glad to humiliate her, showed no pity. Excited by the pilgrim, they shouted invectives at her and left her alone like a leper. Zennab[sic] stunned and saddened, had tears in her eyes. When I got close to her I heard the pilgrim, who had been the last to move away from her, say triumphantly, 'That's what happens when you choose infidels over believers.'

Seeing the slave's face, I didn't even take the time to understand what it was about, and throwing myself on the insolent pilgrim who had hastened his steps when he saw me, gave him a blow of the whip across his body. I told him, 'Here's what happens to a real believer who insults an infidel's woman.' I took a risk in striking a man that everyone in Dekkeh respected, but in the East an energetic act is rarely compromising, and there is even a high regard for anyone who thinks himself strong enough to obtain justice himself. In the view

[53] The *hajj* or pilgrimage to Mecca (in what is now Saudi Arabia) is one of the five pillars of Islam, and those who have performed this journey are called *hajji*. Combes adds his own interpretation that the effect of this religious experience was to make the newly returned pilgrims less tolerant of Muslims who associated with people of other religions, including European Christians.

[54] Combes was well aware that a number of European and Egyptian Christians owned slaves in Egypt, and that the legal right of non-Muslims to own slaves had varied from place to place within the Ottoman world, and had been granted and withdrawn in some places.

of the Nubians, I must be a powerful person, since I dared to attack a Muslim who had performed the pilgrimage, and the furious pilgrim although disconcerted, contented himself with throwing me a look full of hate and kept moving away while cursing....

M. Saint-André was asleep where I had left him. When Zenneb told him of the insult that she had just received, the pharmacist wanted to make a complaint to the local shaykh, but I let him know that he could be satisfied with my actions, and we thought of nothing more than continuing our voyage.[55]

G. Zenneb's Dance at the end of Ramadan[56]

To celebrate, they thought of organizing dances, and everyone, Turks and Nubians alike, set themselves with good grace to compose a dance. Of course, music was lacking, but someone dug out an old cracked tarabouka [drum], and the clapping of hands, singing and rhythmic shouts supplied the rest. Those gathered took turns performing warlike dances and grotesque pantomimes.

M. Saint-André's negress wanted to participate, and to give us a sample of the dances of her native land. I have already said that this slave woman was tall and sturdily built, and I was more than mildly astonished that I saw her join these festivities. She nonetheless delighted the assembly, and I must admit that I never saw a stranger, or more outlandish dance. The undulations of her body showed a fascinating flexibility, and she perfectly embodied the movements of a walking camel.[57]

2. SIGHTINGS OF SAINT-ANDRÉ AND ZENNEB IN 1838 FROM OTHER SOURCES

A. Saint-André leaves for Khartoum and Cairo

Dr. Sulayman Effendi [Dr. Pasquali][58] left this evening for Khartoum in company with Saint-André who has got leave to go to Cairo without having to hand in his resignation and at government expense on account of his health. Saint-André is abandoning his putative daughter and his black woman Zaynab [Zenneb] who, in collusion with his [Nubian] servant Musa, has robbed him of nearly everything. At least Saint-André has had his eyes opened, for the black woman was living with Musa and took no trouble to show her attachment to Saint-André in spite of the fact that she has been with him for ten years and that Saint-André was over 60.[59]

---

[55] *Ibid.*, 1: 293–298.

[56] Another one of the five pillars of Islam is the requirement that Muslims should fast – not eat and not drink at all – from sunrise to sunset during the month of Ramadan, one of the twelve lunar months of twenty-eight days in the Muslim calendar. Exceptions to this requirement are made for the very old and the very young, for pregnant women and soldiers, for the ill, and for travelers if fasting would be harmful to their health. After sunset, Muslims are naturally eager to eat a good meal, and after the last day of fasting they usually have a feast.

[57] *Ibid.*, 1: 359–360. In the northern Sudan, Kordofan, and Dar Fur, there is a long tradition of women imitating interesting movements, including those of animals as they dance. One famous dance was the pigeon dance.

[58] This Italian doctor was originally known as de Pasquali, but after his conversion to Islam was called Sulayman Effendi.

[59] Hill, *On the Frontiers*, 177–178.

B. Zenneb Marries Musa after her Operation

Saint-André's black woman has been married to Musa, his [Nubian] servant, with all possible nuptial ceremony. Some months before, she went to the doctor to undergo female circumcision in order to simulate the condition of a Nubian virgin.[60]

SUGGESTED ADDITIONAL READINGS

Austen, Ralph A. "The Mediterranean Islamic Slave Trade Out of Africa: A Tentative Census," in *The Human Commodity: Perspectives on the Trans-Saharan Slave Trade*. Edited by Elizabeth Savage. London and Portland: Routledge, 1992, 215–248.

Baer, Gabriel. "Slavery in Nineteenth Century Egypt," *Journal of African History*, 8, 3 (1967): 417–441.

Fahmy, Khalid. *All the Pasha's Men: Mehmed Ali, his army and the making of modern Egypt*. Cambridge: Cambridge University Press, 1997.

Hill, Richard. *Egypt in the Sudan, 1820–1881*. London: Oxford University Press, 1959.

Hunwick, John and Eve Trout Powell (eds.), *African Diaspora in the Mediterranean Lands of Islam*. Princeton, NJ: Markus Wiener, 2002.

Kuhnke, LaVerne. *Lives at Risk: Public Health in Nineteenth - Century Egypt*. Berkeley: University of California Press, 1990.

La Rue, George Michael. "African Slave Women in Egypt, from ca. 1820 to the Plague Epidemic of 1834–1835," in *Women and Slavery: Volume One – Africa and the Western Indian Ocean Islands*. Edited by Gwyn Campbell, Suzanne Miers, and Joseph C. Miller. Athens: Ohio University Press, 2007, 168–189.

Walz, Terence. *The Trade between Egypt and Bilad as-Sudan, 1700–1820*. Cairo: Institut Français d' Archéologie Orientale du Caire, 1978.

---

[60] *Ibid.*, 178. This operation involves removing the clitoris and sewing up the labia majora, leaving only a small opening for the passing of bodily fluids.

22 The Ordeals of Slaves' Flight in Tunisia

ISMAEL M. MONTANA

Most of our knowledge of enslaved Africans' experiences of slavery and enslavement has come through the Atlantic slave trade. In contrast, we know little about slaves' experiences within an ongoing system of slavery that sent more than eight million Africans to the Muslim world over twelve centuries. There are few accounts of slaves' voices. Some stories were recorded by European diplomats – for instance, the story of Khadeja. Initially bought in Cairo in the late 1850s by a Turkish slaver, she was illegally resold in Istanbul (Turkey) where the slave trade had been prohibited and the slave market closed down since 1847. Then, in 1860, Salem Agha of Monastir bought Khadeja and took her to Tunisia where slavery had been abolished in 1846. Resisting her illegal enslavements, Khadeja escaped three times to European sanctuaries and eventually procured her manumission through the British consulate. Although Khadeja could not read or write and, therefore, did not author an account of her ordeal, her "actions speak louder than words" and warrant attention to her inner voice and intentions. Not surprisingly, a large body of Tunisian state correspondence with European consuls, some of which is discussed in this chapter, reveal similar slaves' ordeals. These ordeals are a macrocosm of untold stories and experiences of enslaved Africans in the Muslim world. Although much of the literature on slavery during the modern period tends to focus on Africa and the Americas, millions of sub-Saharan Africans were enslaved in various lands of the Muslim world, including North Africa, which had been a regular destination of slave influx from several states in present-day West Africa. Scholars have pointed out that most slaves in the Muslim lands were employed in domestic chores. They lived unsegregated lives and were incorporated into their masters' households. As such, they had more intimate bonds with their masters. According to these scholars, enslaved Africans in Muslim societies endured more benign and humane experience than their counterparts in the Americas, whose experience was shaped largely by the brutality of the plantation complex. Further, they argue that, based on Islamic law, which governs slavery in the Muslin context, both the rights of the enslaved and that of their master were regulated, which often translated into a greater rate of manumission. But while Muslim slavery has been portrayed as "benign," when European abolitionists sought to ban the slave trade and slavery in the Muslim lands in the 1840s, enslaved Africans escaped in droves to European sanctuaries.

In these documents, the struggles of enslaved black Africans in the Muslim context are narrated. In each of these documents, the slaves at the center of European diplomats and

Tunisian state officials' correspondences did not leave us accounts of their own. Instead, European diplomats and merchants who witnessed their plight reported the account of their ordeals to us. We have this documentation because of the existence of a sizeable European community in Tunis. Nineteenth-century Tunisia was intensely cosmopolitan and prosperous in foreign trade. Several European states maintained consuls there. Beside the diplomatic corps, European merchant groups also lived in many parts of Tunisia. The saga of slave flights began in April 1841, when the Bey of Tunis launched an Anti-Slavery Program and promised Sir Thomas Reade, the British consul, that he would ban the African slave trade and abolish slavery throughout his country. As soon as the Bey's promise became public, slaves began to escape at alarming rates to European consulates and legations. But what really triggered the Bey's promise and why did the enslaved Africans flock to European consulates and legations? Following the examples of Great Britain and the United States in 1807–08, some European nations abolished the slave trade and by the late 1830s were outlawing slavery altogether. The trade across the Sahara and to the Muslim world was, however, alive and well. Ahmad Bey's decision to outlaw the slave trade and slavery was greeted by abolitionist societies in the Mediterranean, especially the British Foreign and Anti-Slavery Society in Malta, with jubilation. The Society hoped that the Bey's measures would set a good example for other Muslim countries still involved in the slave trade. Moreover, the Society lauded the Bey's measures and sent letters of approbation aimed at stirring the Tunisian ruler toward the total extinction of slavery.

Inevitably, both the Society and European diplomats' push for abolition and sympathy for runaway slaves encouraged fugitive slaves to target European institutions such as the British consulate. For example, in December 1845, James Richardson, Chairman of the British Anti-Slavery Society in Malta, who visited Tunis twice between 1841 and 1845, reported that during this period, the British consulate alone manumitted more than 1,000 slaves. Richardson's estimates suggest an average of 16.7 cases of slave flights per month at the consulate. During this trip, after which he wrote a report about the manumission of slaves at the British consulate, he witnessed a ceremony of freeing of five runaway slaves at the British consulate. Richardson informs us that slaves manumitted at the consulate were ill-treated slaves who were fleeing the cruelty of their masters. According to Richardson, the manumission of most of these slaves occurred only through the intercession of Ahmad Bey and with the consent of slaves' masters. Once freed, they were issued *atqas*[1] as evidence of their freedom. With these certificates, they could no longer be sold, inherited, or transferred to another owner. But the process of the manumission, according to Richardson, was "difficult," because not all slave masters consented to the British consulate manumitting their slaves. Even though the manumission of runaway slaves occurred only through the Bey's intercession, a number of runaway slaves' cases resulted in a dispute between the consulate and slave masters. As a case in point, Richardson reported a case of a certain runaway slave whose manumission caused an intense dispute between his master and the British consul. Because of the nature of this dispute, the consul was forced to keep the boy in his own house until he was freed as a result of the death of his elderly master. A similar case lingered for more than a year and was still pending when Richardson departed Tunis to Malta in December 1845.

---

[1] Certificates of manumission.

As you can see in Documents number 1 and 3, procuring one's freedom was not always easy. At times it came at a high cost. There were often severe consequences for those who failed. The case of the thirty slaves outlined in Document 2 also reveals that even slaves who resorted to religious sanctuaries such as the Muslim *zawiya* were not always guaranteed freedom or protection from abusive masters. The enslaved Africans in Tunis were fully aware of this risk but still seized the opportunity presented by European sympathy for their pursuit of freedom. Before you read these documents and answer the questions posed at the end of this chapter, you should first note the background to the slave flights and the political circumstances that enabled them to begin escaping en masse in pursuit of their freedom.

THE BACKGROUND

In April 1841, a Greek vessel *Brig. Miltiades*,[2] carrying fourteen black African slaves bound from Tunis to Constantinople,[3] was detained by Greek port authorities on the Island of Ionian for violating the laws banning the African slave trade. The detention of this vessel uncovered an illicit and little-known African slave trade across the Mediterranean. Investigations into this traffic, which had been ongoing since mid-1835, described it as occurring to an "incredible extent." The investigation implicated Joseph Gaspary, a French citizen. Gaspary was a consular agent of the British Consulate in La Goullette (Tunis port) and also a consular agent for several other European consuls at large in Tunis. A few days after the *Miltiades* affair became public, Sir Thomas Reade (the British Consular General) interviewed Ahmad Bey on the slave traffic. An abolitionist, Reade told the Bey that prohibiting this traffic would "be truly gratifying, not only to the British Government itself, but also to the British Nations generally."[4] Ahmad Bey promptly agreed and within a period of five years he abolished the slave traffic and slavery.

The context of this abolition should not be overlooked. During the turn of the nineteenth century, Tunis's political position in the western Mediterranean was weakened by political developments occurring in the region, in particular the rivalry between the Europeans and the Ottomans for control of the Mediterranean.[5] For example, in 1827, Tunisian warships fought alongside the Ottoman fleet and were destroyed at the Battle of Navarino. But Tunis was technically part of the Ottoman Empire. Thereafter, Tunis's fate in the Mediterranean, like that of the Ottoman Regencies of Algiers and Tripoli, became inextricably intertwined with the demise of the Ottoman Empire. Even before Navarino, France wanted to connect Egypt and the Ottoman North African Regencies of Algiers, Tunis, and Tripoli into a Mediterranean empire. In 1830, France used a dispute between the French consul and the Dey of Algiers about an alleged debt as a pretext for occupying Algiers. In the aftermath of the occupation, Tunis was caught between France's rivalry with Great Britain and, then, with the Ottoman Empire.

Since coming to power in 1705, the Husaynid Beys ruled the Regency. With recognition from the Ottoman Empire, they enjoyed a level of political autonomy amounting

---

[2] Spelled Miltiades in proper Greek.
[3] Istanbul.
[4] O. Kahl, "A Letter from Ahmad Bey of Tunis to Queen Victoria of England," *Journal of Semitic Studies*, 31, 2 (1986): 188.
[5] Kahl, "A Letter," 187–190.

to almost complete independence, allowing them to conduct diplomatic relations with European nations while maintaining their spiritual allegiance to the Ottoman Empire.[6] France's annexation of Algiers in 1830 and Constantine in 1837 threatened this status quo. In the Regency of Tripoli – once a semiautonomous state like Tunis – the Ottoman Empire had overthrown the local Karamanly rulers and imposed direct rule. When France occupied Constantine, the Ottomans sent a war fleet to Tunis, but France prevented the Ottoman fleet from landing. Tunis was embroiled in imperial battle for supremacy in the western Mediterranean between the Ottoman Empire and France.

Threatened by the two powers, the Tunisian Beys sought British support to maintain Tunis's status quo. Britain responded favorably, although its response was conditional. "So long as Tunis remained loyal to the Ottoman Porte," Lord Palmerston, the British Foreign Secretary, assured Ahmad Bey of Great Britain's full support. Needing Britain's support, the Bey complied with Reade's request that he outlaw the exportation of slaves from Tunis. He also liberated all of his own slaves and promised Reade that he would extirpate slavery throughout Tunisian territories.

This move marked a turning point on three counts. First, it encouraged European abolitionists, especially the British Foreign and Anti-Slavery Society's Maltese branch in the Mediterranean, to divert their efforts from Egypt, Tripoli, and Turkey to Tunisia. These abolitionists needed a success story from a Muslim state against slavery to convince hard-liners in the aforementioned states to ban the slave trade. Ahmad Bey's encouraging actions against slave traffic fulfilled this desire.

Second, encouraged by abolitionist propaganda, the enslaved increasingly began to escape to European institutions. Before this, however, slaves had recourse to the *ulama*, the Muslim clergy who traditionally act as the moral conscience of Muslim societies. According to Islamic law, the *ulama* had the legal right to free slaves, especially in cases where slaves were mistreated. Historically, the *zawiya* (a Sufi convent) had provided protection of slaves from abusive owners. Slaves who sought a refuge in a *zawiya* could not be forcibly removed from it.

Mention should also be made of a local mechanism. The institution of Bash Agha, known to have existed in Tunisia since the first decade of the nineteenth century, was established for the sole purpose of protecting runaway slaves. Accordingly, slaves faced with mistreatment could complain to the office of the Bash Agha. Designated as chief eunuchs and chief judges over the enslaved population, the Bash Aghas were derived mostly from the enslaved population themselves and had to speak the various languages of the slaves they represented. They played an intermediary role between the enslaved blacks and their owners. If a slave sought refuge with the Bash Agha, the owner could not repossess that slave without paying six piastres (an equivalent of US$6.00) to the Bash Agha's office, which mediated the disagreement between slave and master. Despite these traditional avenues available for the enslaved, after April 1841, they fled largely to European institutions. In response to this situation, Ahmad Bey launched his anti-slavery program. Only two months after the prohibition of the slave traffic, the *Malta Times* reported that during the first week of June, a black slave escaped to the British consulate seeking protection

---

[6] On the History of the Regency of Tunis, see M. Asma, *The Regency of Tunis and the Ottoman Porte, 1777–1814: Army and Government of a North-African Ottoman Eyalet at the end of the Eighteenth Century* (London, 2004).

22.1. Tunis: Souk el Birka – old slave market.
Source: Cie Alsacienne des Arts photomécaniques, Strasbourg.

from the cruelties of her master. Meeting with the Bey the following morning to intercede on the slave's behalf, Reade used the incident to induce the Bey to extend his measures against the Mediterranean slave traffic to the slave trade from the African interior and to fulfill his promise to end slavery in Tunisia. By August, the Bey promulgated the first of his preliminary measures to extirpate slavery in the Regency and informed slave dealers that the authorities should free any slave setting foot in Tunisian territories.

Then, on September 7, he abolished the public slave market in Tunis. To reinforce the previous measures prohibiting the slave trade from the African interior, the Bey again issued circulars to all the provincial governors in March 1842 that slaves who should find their way into Tunisian territories were to be considered "absolutely and bona fide free." By December 1845, the Bey extended the decree granting automatic freedom to slaves setting foot in Tunisia to slaves owned by foreigners. In January 1846, a month after the enforcement of the decree affecting foreign slave owners, the Bey completed his anti-slavery program and declared slavery illegal throughout Tunisia.

QUESTIONS TO CONSIDER

1. In what ways might slave flights be understood as a voice rather than simply escaping abusive masters?

2. Why did Khadeja and Mohamed Ali opt to run away to European consulates and legations and not to Muslim institutions such as religious sanctuaries, the Muslim *ulama* (clergyman), or the office of the Bash Agha?

3. Do the accounts of Khadeja and Mohamed Ali challenge the idea that Muslim slavery was benign?

4. How are the struggles and ordeals of Khadeja and Mohamed Ali in Document number 3 similar to or different from the slaves whose stories are narrated in Documents number 1 and 2?

THE SOURCES

Document #1. A case of an unnamed runaway slave who sought a protection of the British Consulate in Tunis in January 1846

Source: Archives Gouvernment Tunisienne (AGT)

This document, a selection from the Tunisian National Archives, illustrates the role of Thomas Reade (The British Consul General in Tunis) in protecting and securing liberty for slaves who sought a refuge at the British consulate. Reade served as the British Consul during the reign of Ahmad Bey and was the mastermind behind the Bey's anti-slavery program. He provided shelter to a number of runaway slaves and showed tremendous interest in seeing slavery abolished in Tunisia. Although the female in question did not author this account, it is not difficult to tell the ordeal that she went through to secure her freedom.

* * *

From Sir Thomas Reade to Ahmed Bey
23rd January 1846

We wish to bring to your attention that a female slave belonging to the honorable Sidi Mohammad Bey has fled from Hammam Lif[7] to the British Consulate General. In accordance with your recent orders respecting the mass emancipation of slaves, we have sent the slave with our own escort to the zawiya of Sidi Mehrez (one of the three zawiyas the Bey furnished with religious notaries to issue freedom certificates for manumitted slaves). Upon appearing at the zawiya, the slave was surprisingly abducted and taken forcibly to the residence of her owner, Sidi Mohammad Bey, even though she was being sent directly from the consulate.

Under this deplorable circumstances and inasmuch as the slave in question was let into the zawiya directly from the British consulate's premises in accordance with your esteemed instructions, we found her assault and abduction was unjustified. Furthermore, this act is not only oppression (*zulm*), but also as an encroachment on the British consulate's jurisdiction and a clear violation of its immunity. We therefore demand the return of the female slave concerned in this matter to the consulate premise.

Written on the 23rd January 1846

Document #2. Sir Thomas Reade to Aberdeen, (Enclosure: extract of a letter from Mr. Davis, a missionary to Sir Thomas Reade), March 31st, 1846.

Source: National Archives (NA), Kew F.O. 84 1846/648

This document, a selection from National Archives (NA), Kew on slavery in Tunisia, reported by Natalie Davis (a British missionary who was visiting the Tunisian interior), tells the story of the ordeal that the enslaved encountered at the hand of Tunisians who objected to Ahmad Bey's decree banning slavery in 1846. Among those who defied the

---

[7] A residential area located in north of Tunis.

abolition decree were the *marabouts*[8] at the *zawiya* where every slave appearing was to be issued a manumission certificate according to Ahmad Bey's orders banning slavery. Davis wrote reported a number of similar case to abolitionists newspapers in Malta informing them of the state of Tunisian violations of the decree of 1846 and calling on Sir Thomas Reade (the British Consul General) to urge the Tunisian government to punish those violating the decree.

* * *

Gafsa,[9] March 24th, 1846.

You will, I am sure, be very glad to hear to that the measures His Highness (Ahmad Bey) has adopted for the abolition of slavery are carried into effect even in the most distant parts of the Regency. The leader of the camp having been informed that a Marabout near Seriana[10] about thirty Blacks were in chains because they desired their liberty. He instantly dispatched a number of *bawabs* (military guards) to have them brought to the *mahalla* (a mobile military camp). They arrived this morning and the Bey instantly gave orders to have their *Atkas*[11] written and gave them their liberty.

I have made enquiries in other parts and I am convinced, it may now be safely declared, that slavery is abolished in the Regency of Tunis.

I inform you of this because I know it will give you pleasure.

Rev. N. Davis

Document #3. Edmund Calvert to Sir H. Bulwer, G.C.B, Monastir, (enclosure: reporting two cases of runaway slaves who have taken refuge with foreigners, February, 6th, 1863.

Source: National Archives (NA), Kew FO 84/1204

In the second half of the nineteenth century, Tunisia became attractive to European commerce and investment, with many Europeans residing in the richly agricultural towns of Sousse and Monastir in the Sahel region. Many European states whose citizens were trading in the Sahel region appointed consular representatives there. Two decades following the outlawing of the slave trade and slavery in Tunisia, rich Tunisian families, many of whom were trade partners with the Europeans, were violating the 1846 Abolition decree by importing fresh slaves from abroad. But constant slave flights to the European institutions and legations caused embarrassments and disputes between the wealthy Tunisians and their European trade partners and between them and European diplomats, as well. The following document illustrates such embarrassment and tension surrounding the slave flights in Monastir.

* * *

---

[8] An Islamic religious term in North and West Africa used to denote religious and spiritual teachers based mostly in *zawiyas*. Historically, the term *marabout* is derived from the Arabic term *ribat* or *murabit* (a garrison or one who is attached to it). The term is still used to refer to the Sufi religious scholars known for spiritual healing.

[9] A major in the south of Tunisia.

[10] A town in northeastern Tunisia.

[11] Certificates of manumission.

Monastir, February 6th, 1863

Sir,

I have the honor to report to your Excellency the following two cases, which have again occurred here, of runaway slaves placing themselves under the protection of foreigners.

The first is that of a Negro named Ali, 25 years of age, who took refuge at the Russian Consulate some weeks since. He was bought seven years ago by a certain Mustapha Bey of this place, who died the year before last. Although the poor man thus possessed a clear title to his liberty, according to the provisions of the Mohamedan law, he was, on the death of his master, transferred to the possession of Hadji Bey, the son of Mustapha Bey. The local authorities have nevertheless used every effort to obtain from the Russian Consul his restitution. Overtures to this effect were made at first, in the official form, but M. Hitroff having declined to give up the man until receiving instruction from his legation, the parties interested finally had recourse to a charge of theft, which was conveyed in an official note from Hadji Ali Pasha to the Russian Consul. Your Excellency will perhaps remember a similar pretext in the question of the two negresses claimed by Ahmed Pasha, and which was described by Mr. Consul Longworth in his dispatch from Monastir No. 2 of the January 1859, as already a "a stale practice in such cases".

The Pasha's note contained a demand for the delivery of the alleged thief to the local authorities, "together with the "stolen property." Mr. Hitroff again declined to act in the matter pending the receipt of instruction. He further took umbrage at the Pasha's demand for the restitution by him, the Consul of (alleged) stolen property. Although sufficient time had elapsed for the receipt of the expected instructions from Constantinople before Mr. Hitroff's departure hence, the question does not appear to have been yet settled between the Russian legation and the Porte. The Man, Ali, meanwhile remains at the Russian Consulate.

The second case I have to report is that of a negress named Khadeje, age 24 year and owned by one Mohmoud Bey of Monastir. The master for some reason decided [to part] with his slave sent Khadije to a *dellal*, an auctioneer of slaves. After remaining with this man's family for three weeks, in default of a purchaser, she took flight [sic] on the 25th January. She made her way, in the first place to the British Consulate. I happened to be away at the time, and the fugitive addressed herself to Gulfidan, the manumitted slave whose case was reported in my last dispatch of this series. By her advice, the poor woman went over to the Russian Consulate. M. Hitroff being already embarrassed with the case above related, did not encourage her application; and it seems she was advised by some person at the Russian Consulate to apply to the Austrian Vice Consul. She found her way by mistake to the house of Mr. Guz, a Swiss merchant under the protection of the French Vice Consulate, who willingly gave her shelter and with whom she has since remained. The case thus falls within my competency as Acting Vice Consul for France. Mahmoud Bey's endeavors for the recovery of his property were in the first instance limited to direct personal communication with Mr. Guz, with whom he has had several friendly interviews on the subject. As Mr. Guz, however, did not consider himself at liberty to comply with the Bey's request, an official application has been addressed to me through Hadji Ali Pasha. I have begged His Excellency to allow the matter to remain over pending a reference of it to Constantinople. I therefore now have the honor to solicit your Excellency's instructions with regard thereto, leaving it to your

Excellency to communicate with the French Ambassador on the subject, should you judge that course proper.

It is necessary to state to your Excellency that the requirements of the Musulman law with respect to manumission do not seem to have been fulfilled in the case of the woman Khadeja. She has changed hands twice, by regular purchase, since she was first bought by a certain Abdullah Pasha at Constantinople 12 years ago: and her longest term of service under any one master has not exceeded five years. She had served Mahmoud Bey three years.

In none of these cases of runaway slaves which I have lately had occasion to report does the ill-usage on the part of the owners appear to have been of a very aggravated nature. The leniency generally speaking of domestic slavery in Turkey is proved by the fact that these cases, occurring as they do from time to time, are by no means so numerous on the whole as might be expected. Still, however, there are exceptions to these leniency, and instances of illegal retention in slavery, such as those of Gulfidan and Ali, appear to be of not infrequent occurrence. Under any circumstances the occasional repletion of fugitive cases, such as those now reported, is a contingency to be looked for. Hadji Ali Pasha took occasion to observe to me in reference to the present instances, how desirable it was in his opinion that some fixed rule of action should be adopted with regard to these embarrassing questions; and the force of the remark is felt no less by the Consular body here than by the local authority.

I have Sir

[Signed] Edmund Calvert

SUGGESTED ADDITIONAL READINGS

Abun-Nasr, Jamil M. "The Beylicate in Seventeenth-Century Tunisia," *International Journal of Middle East Studies*, 6, 1 (1975): 70–93.

　A History of the Maghrib in the Islamic Period. Cambridge: Cambridge University Press, 1987.

Brown, L. Carl. *The Tunisia of Ahmad Bey, 1837–1855*. Princeton, NJ: Princeton University Press, 1974.

Brunschvig, R. "Abd," in *The Encyclopedia of Islam*. Leiden: Brill, 1960.

Ennaji, Mohammed. *Serving the Master: Slavery and Society in Nineteenth-Century Morocco*, 1st ed. New York: St. Martin's Press, 1999.

Kahl, Oliver, "A Letter from Ahmad Bey of Tunis to Queen Victoria of England," *Journal of Semitic Studies*, 31, 2 (1986): 187–194.

Larguèche, Abdelhamid. "The Abolition of Slavery in Tunisia: Towards a History of the Black Community," in *The Abolitions of Slavery: From L.F. Sonthonax to Victor Schoecher; 1793, 1794, 1848*. Edited by Marcel Dorigny (New York: Berghahn Book and UNESCO Publishing, 2003), 330–339.

Moalla, Asma. *The Regency of Tunis and the Ottoman Porte, 1777–1814: Army and Government of a North-African Ottoman Eyalet at the End of the Eighteenth Century*. London: Routledge Curzon, 2004.

Montana, Ismael M. "Bori Practice among Enslaved West Africans of Ottoman Tunis: Unbelief (Kufr) or Another Dimension of the African Diaspora?" *History of the Family*, 16 (2011): 152–159.

Toledano, Ehud R. *As If Silent and Absent: Bonds of Enslavement in the Islamic Middle East.* New Haven, CT: Yale University Press, 2007.

Slavery and Abolition in the Ottoman Middle East. Seattle: University of Washington Press, 1998.

Valensi, Lucette. "Esclaves chrétiens et esclaves noirs `a Tunis au XVIII siècle," *Annales Economies Sociétés Civilizations,* 6 (1967): 1267–1285.

Van Der Haven, Elisabeth. "The Abolition of Slavery in Tunisia (1846)," *Revue d'Histoire Maghrebine,* 27, 99–100 (2000): 349–464.

Wright, John, "Enforced Migration: The Black Slave Trade Across the Mediterranean," *The Maghreb Review,* 31, 1–2 (2006): 62–70.

23 African Slavery and the Slave Trade in the Manuscript of Jean Godot

PIERLUIGI VALSECCHI

For the past five centuries, slavery constituted the most striking aspect of personal dependency in Africa. It affected quite high percentages of the population and only came largely to an end in the early twentieth century. Studying the history of African slavery, however, is often quite challenging. Documentation can be scarce. That, however, has not always been the greatest problem. Written materials from the period are not lacking for at least some areas along the Atlantic coast, like the pre-nineteenth century Gold Coast (Ghana and Ivory Coast). In this particular case, researchers have actually had to work their way through a number of good sources, written in several different European languages that have remarkable chronological depth. Most were written by adventurers, merchants, officers, and missionaries. Some were long-term residents on the coast. In a limited number of cases they were native Africans or individuals of partial African ancestry. As a result, the knowledge they conveyed could vary greatly given their identities. Common to all the sources, however, is the fact that they were written for a public who was neither African nor resident in Africa. Instead their content was geared toward addressing a general European interest in travel accounts, or to meet the needs of more specialized readers of commercial and political reports, or court proceedings. All were written to describe aspects of the African world that might be perceived as peculiar and different. All also sought to "translate" these peculiarities into terms that could be understood by the public to which they were addressed. Emphasized was the gap between African and European/Christian standards, rules and accepted norms. Early-modern writers – whether European, African, or Euro-African – also shared a common perception of slavery and personal dependency. None felt the need to dwell on those aspects of African slavery that resembled Euro-American slavery. Accordingly, their texts, on the whole, contain very few details about those aspects of slavery and servile dependency the authors viewed as unremarkable.

Despite the limitations of the European-language sources, we know there existed a spectacular range of different individual conditions within the institution of slavery and bonded status in Africa. Some were poor wretched creatures who were totally

I thank S. E. Greene for commenting on the draft of this chapter, and Claude Hélène-Perrot for liberally providing me with copies of the Godot's original manuscript and the transcription of Jean-Claude Nardin, and much information on the subject.

disadvantaged, subject to all sorts of abuse. Others were of bonded or slave status who were powerful and influential individuals, operating at the top of the power pyramid in their communities, as king' servants, confidents or ministers, high military officers, and powerful traders. Some of these people might have been even wealthier than their masters. Every variation in personal status was also to be found between these two extremes. In other words, slavery and other forms of bondage[1] were extremely widespread at all social levels and within all social institutions.[2]

More challenging is the task of finding African slave voices within the early-modern European-language sources on African slavery. Such voices do exist in these texts. For even though the documents were consciously written from the perspective of an "outsider," and were never intended to convey an "insider" understanding of the Africa's social environment, the authors themselves were either deeply conversant with the African social and cultural environment they described or relied heavily on African informants and sources. Accordingly, "African voices" are definitely interspersed, albeit somewhat hidden, in the early European-language sources on African slavery. In many cases one can trace the often anonymously provided information to African informants. In a few cases the writer even gave the names of their informants as well as data on their social positions and roles. In the majority of cases, however, we can only guess at their identities. Nevertheless, the task of finding these "voices" is essential for writing history, for they allow us to hear how the African enslaved themselves understood their own societies and situations, even if their voices are enveloped in the words of a European author. For this reason alone, we have no choice but to use European-language sources as we seek to understand the institution of slavery in Africa.

THE MANUSCRIPT OF JEAN GODOT AND THE FRENCH AT ASSINI

The document presented in this chapter is an early-eighteenth-century French manuscript in two volumes (totalling 500 pages) listed in the Bibliothèque Nationale de France under the label *Voyages de Jean Godot tant a l'Amerique, Afrique, Asie, etc.*[3] The manuscript, long forgotten in a miscellanea collection, was brought to the attention of African studies scholars by Jean-Claude Nardin and Hermann Spirik, who realized its relevance not only for the history of the French presence in West Africa, but as an important source of information on African societies. Nardin transcribed the text, and then both Nardin and Spirik conducted historical research on Jean Godot and the circumstances that allowed Godot to document

---

[1] People pawning as a result of debtor insolvency and the use of hostages in the context of wars or political negotiations were very common. See T. Falola and P. E. Lovejoy (eds.), *Pawnship in Africa: Debt Bondage in Historical Perspective* (Boulder, CO, 1994)

[2] European-language writing about slavery changed in the course of the eighteenth century with the spread of the movement against slavery and the slave trade in Europe and America. At that time, critics of the slave trade focused mainly on its most cruel and inhuman traits to emphasize the necessity of radical reform or wholesale abolition. To counter this perspective, apologists for the slave trade tended to stress the gruesome aspects of African slavery so as to portray the acquisition of slaves by Westerners and transportation overseas as a form of liberation from uncontrolled barbarity. Clearly both arguments were widely used in contemporary written sources. Researchers need to be aware of this when critically assessing the phenomena of dependency in Africa, and especially the modalities of slavery and subjugation in Africa.

[3] J. Godot, *Voyages de Jean Godot tant a l'Amerique, Afrique, Asie, etc.*, 2 volumes, 1704 (unpublished manuscript, Bibliothèque Nationale de France, Ms N. Acq. Fr. n. 13380).

all he saw on his travels.[4] They never completed a comprehensive critical edition, however, and to this day, the manuscript remains unpublished.[5]

Jean Godot was a simple *particulier*, a sailor and workman for the French Compagnie de Guinée (Guinea Company). The main journey he described in his manuscript took place in the context of France's activity in the Gulf of Guinea and its efforts to establish permanent trading posts on the Gold Coast. Attempts to settle at Komenda and Takoradi began in 1685, but were unsuccessful because of fierce Dutch opposition.[6] A French expedition that sailed down the coast about two years later, between November 1687 and February 1688, visited Assini – spelled Eissinie by Godot – in the southeasternmost corner of present-day Republic of Côte d'Ivoire, where the French commander, J.-B. Ducasse, signed an agreement with the principal chief of the polity to establish a trading post.[7] Ducasse obtained two hostages, Aniaba – a boy of high social status – and Banga, whom the French government educated in France and then returned home at different times: Banga around 1695 and Aniaba in 1701.[8] The French presence in Assini was not continuous, however. In 1697, Louis XIV sent an expedition under the command of *chevalier* Damon[9] to renew the bond with the king of Assini. Damon left four Frenchmen to reside with the king and then returned on June 15, 1701, to construct the first French fort in the area, garrisoned with thirty men, including officers and a few Dominican friars as missionaries.[10] The history of the small settlement was short. The Dutch attacked it on November 13, 1702. Although the French successfully repulsed the assault and inflicted considerable losses on the attackers, they evacuated the fort in 1703, when relations between the French and the locals started to deteriorate.

The expedition in 1701, whose purpose was not only to construct a French fort at Assinie but also to convey Louis Aniaba home, returned him with all the honors due to the rank accorded him by the French court as a member and heir of a friendly royal family.[11]

---

[4] J.-C. Nardin and H. Spirik, "Un Nouveau Document pour l'Etude des Populations Lagunaires de la Côte d'Ivoire du Début du XVIIIe Siècle: Le Voyage du Jean Godot à Assinie (1701)," in *Proceedings, VIIIth Congress of Anthropological and Ethnological Sciences*, 1968, Tokyo and Kyoto, vol. 3 (Tokyo, 1970), 78–81.

[5] Gérard Chouin and myself are currently working on an edition of Godot's manuscript.

[6] In 1685, Louis XIV established the *Compagnie du Sénégal, de la Côte de Guinée et de l'Afrique*. For the events surrounding the French attempt to establish a presence on the Gold Coast, see P. Roussier (ed.), *L'établissement d'Issiny, 1687–1702* (Paris, 1935), v–xxxix; A. van Dantzig, *Les Hollandais sur la Côte de Guinéè a l'époque de l'essoir de l'Ashanti et du Dahomey: 1680–1740* (Paris, 1980), 56–66.

[7] J.-B. Ducasse, "Mémoire ou relation du sr Du Casse sur son voyage de Guynée avec 'La Tempeste' en 1687 et 1688 (1688)," in Roussier, *L'établissement*, 29.

[8] Aniaba became Louis XIV's godson, acquiring the Christian name Louis, and achieved a degree of fame in France. For information on Aniaba and Banga, see Roussier, *L'établissement* (particularly the introduction); Nardin and Spirik, "Un Nouveau Document"; R. M. Wiltgen, *Gold Coast Mission History: 1471–1880* (Techny, 1956), 78–88. For a fictional reconstruction, see Diabate, H. (avec la collaboration de G. Lambert), *Aniaba. Un Assinien à la cour de Louis XIV* (Paris/Dakar/Yaounde, 1975).

[9] Damon's name was also regularly spelled Damont and Damou; his Christian name is not known. A *chevalier* (knight) was a low-ranking nobleman.

[10] Damon also visited Komenda, continuing his journey to Angola and then to Martinique. In Assini, the principal chief, Akassini, granted Damon the right to set up forts and trading posts, promised future access to the gold mines of the interior, and guaranteed the supply of the materials needed to start building.? Damon, "Relation du voyage de Guynée fait en 1698 par le chevalier Damon (1698)," in Roussier, *L'établissement*, 76–78.

[11] Ducasse had introduced Aniaba to the court of Versailles as a son of the King of Assini and the "heir to the throne." This rigid interpretation of his status was later tempered when the French acquired greater knowledge of African customs in matters of succession and the rules of matrilineality that prevailed in Assini and the Gold Coast.

He was accompanied by a retinue that included the nephew of the duchess of Villart to serve as his First Gentleman of the Bedchamber;[12] a head butler, Mr. Du Mesnil; and other gentlemen and attendants. Jean Godot was a member of Aniaba's retinue.

Proximity to the black prince gave Godot an excellent vantage point for observing the dynamics of the complex relations that developed between Aniaba, his fellow countrymen (in particular the members of the local ruling group), and the French. Godot details the events that quickly widened the gap between Aniaba on the one hand and Damon and the missionaries on the other. It was after the final rupture in these relations that Aniaba publicly distanced himself from Christianity and reverted to the customs of his land. This development occurred at the same time Aniaba became involved in local politics, which further damaged his relations with Ducasse and the French, as well as with the local power-holders.[13] Godot's writings are by far the richest source we have at the moment on Aniaba's return to Africa and his role in Euro-African relations.

GODOT AS A SOURCE ON ASSINI COMPARED WITH OTHER CONTEMPORARY SOURCES

Godot's manuscript is particularly intriguing because it represents the very rare example of a text written by a person of a low social status and background. His literary skills were limited, his style unpretentious. As noted by Nardin and Spirik, his "is the precious testimony of a man whose condition is modest beyond doubt, who has apparently no ulterior motive, and is almost devoid of any prejudice: for sure a document of a very rare type."[14] All this accounts for the considerable interest in the book, which was consciously written as a "vision from below." The only other substantive source we have on Assini for this period was written by another member of the same expedition in which Godot took part – Father G. Loyer, a Dominican friar. His account, which documents his eleven-month stay in Assini, is one of the most sophisticated and comprehensive descriptions we have of early-eighteenth-century African coastal societies.[15] Understanding the Godot text in relations to that of Loyer offers a unique opportunity for the modern researcher to use

---

[12] A Gentleman of the Bedchamber was an officer in European royal or princely households. He was usually of noble extraction and his duty was to closely attend to the prince, waiting on him when he was dressing and dining, and guarding access to his apartments. Indeed he was often a crucial figure who controlled access to the prince by other courtiers, officers, and so on.

[13] Relations between Damon and Aniaba were already strained in France. However, they turned for the worse during the voyage from France and fell apart completely after the landing in Assini (Nardin and Spirik, "Un Nouveau Document"). The French commander perceived his former protégée as an obstacle to his plans, or perhaps even an adversary. Leaving aside any personal matters between Damon and Aniaba, this cooling of relations was clearly also related to contrasting aims in terms of local politics. After his arrival, Damon attempted to discredit Aniaba in the eyes of Akassini and the other chiefs. The young man was marginalized by the French, while Louis XIV's gifts intended for him as the "King of Assini" were given to Akassini. See also Roussier, *L'etablissement*, Introduction and infra;? Damon, "Relation très curieuse du voyage que M. le Chevalier Damon a fait aux Indes pour faire un établissement a Issigny (1702)" in P. Roussier, *L'établissement*, 91–107.

[14] Nardin and Spirik, "Un noveau document," 81.

[15] G. Loyer, G., "Relation du voyage du royaume d'Issiny, Cote d'or, Païs de Guinée en Afrique (1714)" in Roussier, *L'établissement*, 109–235. The 1701 Assini expedition left to posterity a mass of information and analyses unparalleled in many other parts of the West African coast. They are important for a variety of reasons. They not only document the Europeans presence, their interests and plans; they are works, really masterpieces of massive documentation, written by individuals who showed genuine interest in crucial aspects of African society, culture, and history.

critically the rich information they provided about the same place in the same period – not a common occurrence in African studies. More importantly for our purposes here, it helps us better understand how to read Godot. There can be no doubt, for example, that Loyer, the Dominican friar, was far more cultured and intellectually sophisticated than Godot. His work is an astonishingly accurate ethnography that provides a powerful portrait of the world of early-eighteenth-century Assini. It is a societal study, enhanced by a concern to report accurately the history of this community. Apart from his evident desire to satisfy his own intellectual curiosity, he sought primarily a means to access a world that was to be the object of his missionary work. Godot's motivations were clearly different. He could not rely on his meager education and erudition to record the history of Assini. He wanted only to chronicle and analyze the events he took part in or witnessed. The man he was ordered to serve, Aniaba, is a central character in his manuscript. Godot reported on his actions and behaviors during the journey from France to Assini and discussed Aniaba's progressive detachment from his European allies, a development Godot depicted as open treason, compounded by capricious and malicious ungratefulness, manifested by his abjuring the Catholic faith and slipping back into his former beliefs. Godot also documented with considerable insight Aniaba's political conflicts in Assini.[16] More broadly, he penned a fascinating description of what he saw and experienced of local society, institutions, customs, beliefs, and mentality during his three-months stay. It is an account no less comprehensive than Loyer's, but is less systematic effort to provide an overview of Assini than an attempt to describe and analyze his own experience of daily events.

Godot's frank and almost naive notes are particularly interesting for the historian of slavery. His descriptions of personal dependency in West African coastal communities during the period when the slave trade was increasing were largely based on personal observation and experience. But as indicated, he also often had access to the insights of another man by the name of Parisien (one of the four Frenchmen left by Damon in 1679 at Assini) who had been in the country for the past seven years. Parisien had traveled to Assini as one of two young servants (*valets*)[17] attached to a couple of heavily indebted gentlemen deployed to Assini under the protection of its king to await the establishment of a permanent trading post. Both gentlemen, however, died of fever not long after Damon left them in Assini. So their two servants (including Parisien) were cared for by the king, who fed and housed them in the best residence in his capital, Nsoko. Parisien adapted quite well to local life and acquired some degree of fluency in the local language. This made his role crucial to the 1701 expedition that brought Godot to Assini.[18] Godot wrote that Parisien "knew better than any other the way these people governed themselves" and was therefore an authority for the French in matters of local social and political institutions and beliefs.[19]

The only "African voice" that Godot mentioned by name as a source of information was Banga, Aniaba's companion who had returned earlier to his home country around 1695.[20]

[16] It is exactly this insight that sometimes leads the reader to question whether the reasons behind Godot's manuscript are not purely gratuitous and that some political motivation might have been relevant in pushing him to write his experience. However, there is no evidence for the time being to support any speculation in this sense.

[17] Parisien was from Paris. The other servant Frenchman besides Parisien was La Serre from Saint Malo.

[18] Godot, *Voyages*, 103–107, 165 [Nardin's transcription, 60–61], 84.

[19] Godot, *Voyages*, 262–263 [N, p. 122].

[20] Godot, *Voyages*, 312 [N, p. 147].

The perspectives Banga offered Godot might well be taken as a "slave voice." According to an authoritative source, when he was sent to France with Aniaba, Banga was a dependant (a "slave") of one of the main chiefs of Assini. His real name was Anouman, but on leaving the country he was given his master's name, Banga.[21]

Thus, not only was Godot, the writer, a sailor and workman, but his two main sources were also individuals of low status: the personal servant of a French gentleman (Parisien) and an African who started his career as a bonded member of the household of a local high officeholder (Banga). All this accounts for the considerable interest in the book that was consciously written as a "vision from below," which makes it even more attractive for the historian of dependency and slavery.

AFRICAN SLAVERY AND DEPENDENCY AS DESCRIBED BY GODOT

Throughout his manuscript, Godot uses the term "slavery" to describe the extensive and strong bonds of personal dependency that characterized the Assini social hierarchy. The bonds he described, however, included a very broad spectrum of social relations that were in reality markedly varied and which do not fall within the standard definition of a master-slave relationship.

According to the conventional definition in Roman law, a slave was an object (*res*), totally subject to the power of another person. This relationship was based on the right of ownership and not, for instance, on a condition of generic dependency within the family or other forms of subjugation, however binding they might be.[22] "A slave was property," writes Peter Garnsey. "The slave owner's rights over his slave-property were total, covering the person as well as the labour of the slave. The slave was kinless, stripped of his or her old social identity in the process of capture, sale and deracination, and denied the capacity to forge new bonds of kinship through marriage alliance. These are the three basic components of slavery."[23] Such a definition, derived from the ancient Roman world, fits perfectly with one of the more extreme forms of personal dependency found in the eighteenth-century Gold Coast. An *akyere* (*akɛlɛ* in the areas in question) was a foreign-born slave acquired through traumatic means that resulted in personal dispossession and depersonalization. Such individuals were most often captured in war, kidnapped, or sold abroad as judicial punishment. The *akyere* was mostly a chattel, totally at the mercy of his or her master. No matter how varied the actual condition of any individual *akyere* was – whether they experienced the greatest exploitation or were virtually integrated into the group that had acquired them – their status was marked by the stigma of perpetuity and irreversibility, at least in principle.[24]

---

[21] Tibierge, "Extrait du Journal du Sieur Tibierge principal commis de la Compagnie de Guinée sur le vaisseau 'Le Pont d'Or' au voyage en l'année 1692 (1692)" in Roussier, *L'établissement*, 67. Tibierge, a top officer of the Compagnie de Guinée, was in Assini in 1692. In his journal he gave important details about the country, the communities inhabiting it, and the relations between the ruling groups of various polities in the area, including information on the rulers of Assini and those of the neighboring Eotilé communities. Indeed he maintained that Aniaba himself was a prisoner or hostage from the Eotilé adopted by the rulers of Assini (*Ibid.*).

[22] I. Biezunska-Malowist, *La schiavitù nel mondo antico* (Neaples, 1991), 7–8.

[23] P. Garnsey, *Ideas of Slavery from Aristotle to Augustine* (Cambridge, 1996), 1.

[24] Cases of virtual "emancipation" of an *akyere* amounting to full integration into the social body are variously documented, though opinions differ about the possibility of a complete disappearance of the stigma attached to slave origins.

There were other forms of bonded status, however, that were extremely common during the period Godot lived in Assini. To any external observer, these forms would have appeared very similar to slavery, even though they were substantially different in terms of status and condition. Hostages, for example, could become fully enslaved or worse, but their situation was not irreversible. They could be ransomed by their relatives or elevated by their captors, once they proved their loyalty, to serve as a representative of their adopted community in their own home districts. Human pawns – usually persons handed to lenders as a pledge for a loan – might experience the same in treatment meted out to an average slave. Still, there was one fundamental difference: reversibility. The pawns' status was tied to the debt and ceased once the sum was repaid (although in many cases insolvency could lead to pawnship for life and even slide into slavery and sale). Moreover, pawns were accorded juridical guarantees denied slaves and hostages. Their status was definitely different. Temporary forms of enslavement issued by local courts as a sentence for various types of crimes, which Godot termed "slavery," were also quite different from slave status because of their reversibility. By using the term "slave" to describe these substantially different forms of personal dependency, Godot made no such distinctions among them at all. More importantly, it was his all-inclusive categorization that accounts for the stringent social hierarchy he observed in Assini.

The power and wealth of a big man (or woman) in Assini (whether he or she be an officeholder – a "noble" in Godot's words – or simply a rich person) was measured in terms of the number of dependants an individual could effectively muster. This entourage could consist of hundreds of people, including relations, offspring, clients, pawns, and real slaves. All these formed his estate and, in Godot's view, they were all his or her slaves. Godot provided lengthy descriptions of the retinues of big men that paraded through the town on public occasions, all of which he termed "a music band" to emphasize the role played by percussions, wind instruments, singing, and dancing in marking the pace of the marching entourage. A crucial component of these retinues was the women or wives who attended to the big men. Godot automatically included these women among the enslaved. Indeed, he extended the category of "slave" to include all women in terms of their relationships with their fathers, their husbands, and their male siblings. He portrayed women as a saleable property at the disposal of their male relations. Godot, in fact, made the mistake very common among Europeans who came from societies where dowry payments were the responsibility of the bride's family (usually the father or the brides's tutor). This cultural practice predisposed Europeans to see the African custom of bridewealth (compensation paid by the groom to the bride's parents or family) as an outright purchase of the woman. Godot's notion that there existed a close association between marriage and female slavery in Assini was not so much wrong as only partly correct. Many wives were certainly not their husbands' slaves, yet there were most definitely a large number of slave wives.

Some of Godot's most interesting remarks concern the slaves' own perceptions of their position in society and their relationship to their masters. Enslavement meant in its most extreme form that slaves could be killed in order to serve a deceased master in the afterlife. According to many sources, it was a big man's slave wives or concubines who were most subject to such a fate. Willem Bosman, a contemporary of Godot's and perhaps the most important source of information about the Gold Coast in the late seventeenth and early eighteenth centuries, specified that slave wives in particular could be commanded to follow their husband into his afterlife.[25] They could also simply be killed. Immolation (human sacrifice) in connection with death and funerals was not per se restricted to slaves, however. When a big man died, all his wives (free or slave) found themselves in a precarious position, and even free women could be pressured to join their husband in death by committing suicide or volunteering for execution.[26] Nevertheless, it was because of their marginal position in society that enslaved individuals, as well as condemned criminals and outsiders kidnapped for this purpose, were the favored victims, qua "cheaper" lives.[27] At different points in his manuscript, he writes of slaves so reconciled to their totally subordinate position that they happily accepted sacrificial death simply to follow their masters in death or to help them reinforce their powerful status in the hereafter. Godot remarked – definitely on the basis of hearsay – that it was common for slaves chosen as victims to compete for the acknowledged honor of being the first to be killed in sacrifices. It would be an exaggeration to read Godot's words as evidence that slaves (more often foreigners than not) fully accepted their purported position in society, no matter how low and disfavored their status was. It was not that simple. However, one can still read his remarks as hinting at how effective the hierarchical ideology may have worked by creating a consensus among some of the enslaved that they should feel privileged to have the opportunity to be killed so as to be part of their deceased master's entourage.

Godot also writes about the slave markets in Assini, where slaves were sold to Europeans in exchange for munitions.[28] This large-scale trade was a royal monopoly. The king and those controlling the relevant military forces had the right to capture large numbers of slaves, obtained largely through the taking of prisoners of war. But the king reserved for himself the right to engage in major slave transactions. He did so to retain his preeminence over his subordinate chiefs and big men. From the slave sales he obtained, in addition to arms and strategic materials, a variety of other Western goods, which he retailed to Africans.

Godot's book describes a society marked by pervasive hierarchy. Most individuals were subject to some form of stringent dependency; very many were members of the slave

---

[25] W. A. Bosman, *New and Accurate Description of the Coast of Guinea* (London, 1705), 199.

[26] Godot reiterates his point with reference to other parts of Africa. He writes, for instance, that in Congo a woman is her man's slave and may be sold at his pleasure. Godot, *Voyages*, 468h [N, pp. 217–218]. At Whydah, on the other hand, people used to go aboard merchant vessels "bringing along their wives in order to sell them. They can afterwards buy others, and sell them again if they are not satisfied with them. The king of Whydah sold two of his to M. Damon." Godot, *Voyages*, 317–318 [N, pp. 150–151].

[27] There were definitely a set of hierarchical principles that governed these killings. If the deceased was a high-status individual, possible sacrificial victims included bonded or "free" people who had an intimate relationship to the individual: wives, slave-wives, personal attendants, and often close advisors in the case of rulers and high-ranking officers. According to Godot, the king of Congo was accompanied into the grave by twelve young men and twelve young women from good families. All were buried alive in order to serve the king in the other world. Godot, *Voyages*, 469f–470 [N, pp. 218–219]. For someone of a lower rank, slaves might be killed to constitute his retinue in the afterlife. These were considered "cheaper lives" compared with the lives of relatives of higher-ranked individuals. Slaves might also be killed to "deliver messages" to the ancestor or as sacrifices to spiritual entities demanding valuable offerings.

[28] After leaving Assini, the French expedition called at Whydah, the main slave market on West coast of Africa in those days. Godot provides few details about the trading procedures, modalities of payment, or the presence of consuls of the European nations involved in the traffic. He also writes that slaves were clearly recognizable among the population by their half-shaved head. Maize, peas, and fava beans were the only food for slaves in Whydah. Godot, *Voyages*, 317–320 [N, pp. 150–152]. In Congo, slaves were fed with a type of red fava bean. Godot, *Voyages*, 465c [N, p. 216].

section of the community whose ranks were constantly renewed by war, judicial proceedings, and other means. Many were freeborn people, though freedom at birth often proved to be a volatile condition: at any point in a person's life, it was very easy for an individual to lose this free status and thus fall into a condition of dependency. It is not easy to assess the exact meaning of the word "freedom" when applied to the society of Assini – and West Africa in general – in the age when Godot was writing. What can be said with a degree of confidence is that individuals were free only if they were capable of guaranteeing their own person and their subordinates against the constant danger of running into debt, receiving a fine, being captured, or suffering similar ever-present misfortunes. In one word: "freedom" belonged more or less to the rich and the powerful.

QUESTIONS TO CONSIDER

1. How useful and what are the limits of European written sources for the history of slavery and dependency in precolonial West Africa?
2. What sort of "African voices," if any, can be detected in a source like Godot's manuscript?
3. How would you describe the various forms of bondage in eighteenth-century Assini? How do they compare with those in the West?
4. When Godot used the term "slave," where did he use it appropriately and where does it refer to other forms of bondage?
5. What did it mean for someone to be a slave in eighteenth-century Assini?
6. If slaves were chattels, who had the power to dispose of them?
7. It appears that Godot endorsed the idea that slaves accepted the chance to be victims in sacrifices at funerals, and perceived this as a peculiar form of social mobility. What do you think about this?
8. Consider the distinction between the status of a slave and his condition as a slave.

VOYAGES DE JEAN GODOT TANT A L'AMERIQUE, AFRIQUE, ASIE

A translation of selected passages on slavery at Assini By Pierluigi Valsecchi[29]

… When we [the French expedition] landed at Eissinie, the king[30] issued a warning to those living all along the coast not to steal anything from us, under threat that offenders will be enslaved for six years. This did not prevent them from steeling whatever they could from us. We complained with the king, who had them return what they took from us.[31]

---

[29] What follows is an approximate English translation of selected passages from the annotated transcription of Godot's text provided by Jean-Claude Nardin. These passages deal specifically with personal dependency and include data and remarks on slavery as a social phenomenon, the involvement of slaves as victims in rituals, slave trade, gender relations, and so forth in Assini. The information provided by Godot about these same topics in other parts of Africa are not dealt with directly, but occasionally referred to in the footnotes. These countries include Senegal, Whydah on the Slave Coast (present-day Republic of Benin), Congo, Angola, and the southern section of the Indian Ocean coast. I indicate where each passage can be found in both Nardin's transcription by preceding the page number with (N) for Nardin and (G) for Godot's original manuscript.

[30] The name of the king, or principal chief – local terms still in use for such an office are *belemgbunli*, or *blemgbin* – was Akassini. Godot uses the spelling Achasigni.

[31] N: 111; G: 235.

[Silver chandeliers were stolen from Damon's tent. Two thieves were identified by a prominent chief, Aymont, who wanted them decapitated in order to set an example. Asked by Damon, he dropped the death sentence. The culprits were severely tortured][32]... and later they are brought to Sauco[33] in order to be made slaves for six years. This is the way they make justice when the offender did not deserve death.[34]

When a man likes a woman, he asks her father for her and reaches an agreement on the amount he will give him[35] to get his daughter as a wife. Law allows a man as many women as he can feed. These women are the slaves of their men, who sell them when they like, and take others.[36] This is the reason why, when a man marries a woman, he pays an amount to her father, and when she has no father, the amount goes to her brothers in their capacity as their father's heirs,[37]... if the son-in-law dies within three full years of marriage, the father has the right to take back his daughter with the children she may have had from her late husband, by just paying back to his son-in-law's heirs the amount he received when he gave the girl to him in marriage. At this very moment the daughter becomes her father's slave for the second time, and the father can sell her again, if he likes, keep her with him or give her away in marriage again; but in this case he cannot get any more gold powder for her, as it happened when he married her the first time, rather he gives her away[38] in exchange for other slaves provided by his second son-in-law. In the event of the daughter being widowed a second time, her father has no power to take her back, and she is now declared free.[39]

... When someone becomes ill, they let him touch the fetish,[40] and a promise is made that if he recovers within twelve days, that is the normal term, one or more oxen will be sacrificed, or some slaves can be promised in honour of the fetish; if the ailing person recovers within twelve days, what has been promised must be sacrificed: if he dies within 12 days, the dead's relatives rejoice and say that the fetish needed him in the next world, that is why he died. If on the contrary he dies after 12 days, those who made the vow for the ill one are accused of lack of faith in the fetish.

When these people go to war, they vow before their departure to sacrifice one or more slaves to their fetish if their enterprise is successful; which they do very precisely, when the

---

[32] G: 241.

[33] The town of Nsoko was the capital of Assini, located on the island of Monobaha, in a Lagoon just a short distance from the seashore.

[34] N: 112; G: 238–241.

[35] G: 245.

[36] In Father G. Loyer's account no stress is put on the subject condition of wives to their husbands. The Dominican friar emphasizes the hierarchy between the first wife – who is "absolute master of all slaves" in her husband's house – and all further wives, who can be married by the man only with the approval of the first one (Loyer, "Relation," p. 176).

[37] Though the people of Assini were matrilineal in terms of succession to offices and wealth, the bond with the father was nevertheless extremely strong for many personal and social reasons. Adult children, males especially, were expected to reside in their father's house, work with him, help him in old age, worship the same spiritual entities, and take over his responsibilities after his death.

[38] G: 247.

[39] N: 114–115.

[40] Fetish, from the Portuguese *fetiço*, derives from the Latin *factitius*: made, artificial. The word was used by the Europeans in West Africa as a generic term to indicate all charms and cultic objects created or adopted in order to host some form of supernatural or magic power, be they statues ("idols"), stones, pots, or metal basins containing potions or any kind of objects. Per *extenso*, the word was used to describe the religious forms peculiar to West Africa. In the case mentioned by Godot, fetish indicates the material abode of any god (*bosonle*) or spirit that was the object of worship by the individual affected by illness.

result satisfies their request. None of his women dares to sleep with the man who made the vow before he has fulfilled it; and after he has performed the sacrifice, he goes, accompanied by all his women, to the sea or to the river, if it is nearer, and washes all over his body (his women wash as well). After that, he goes back home, where he is allowed communication with them.[41]

During the war he was waging when we reached Assini, Achasigny consulted his fetish about the fact that he had had no news from his general for the past month, and if he shall win over his enemies. This fetish promised Achasigny that his general will win the battle. Indeed he wins it; five days later, the news reaches Sauco, where the king fulfils the vow he made, by personally chopping off the heads of two of his women whom he sacrificed to the fetish. And the king's brother, named Hyamaque, also sacrificed three oxen, and the great lords one or more oxen.

Besides the frequent sacrifices that take place often in order to fulfil vows, the king performs another one each month in sacrificing a slave to his own fetish, while the great lords sacrifice one or more oxen.

One day, while I was in Sauco with M. Damont, I saw the king himself sacrificing to his fetish a slave, whose head he cut with his own hands, and with the blood spilling from this innocent victim, he reddened a jug in which his god was placed. After executing this sacrifice, he ran to the river to wash himself all over the body, and when he was back, he presented a white cloth with black stripes[42] to cover the dead body and bury it.

It is a great honour for the slaves to be sacrificed to the fetish, and has even been known for them to argue amongst themselves over who would be the first to be put to death.

It is also a great honour for them to be put to death in order to be put into their master's grave.[43]

These peoples do not wage war against each other in order to conquer towns, but rather to take slaves of both sexes,[44] and these are their riches.[45]

In this country adultery is punished with a fine or with slavery. When a man has communication with another man's woman and the fact can be proved, the man who had the affair is sentenced to pay a one benda[46] fine, which amounts to fifty *ecus* of our currency; and if this man has no means to pay the fine within three months from the day he is sentenced, he becomes for three years the slave of the man whose woman he had an affair with.

It happens that some women give up themselves to men with the design of later telling their own husbands, who, on the grounds of their wives' witnessing, collect the fine

---

[41] Loyer provides a description of the ritual of purification after a killing. See Loyer, "Relation," 207–208.

[42] All over this part of West Africa, a simple black-striped white cloth was the distinctive dress for slaves until the colonial abolition of slavery. Clothing their slaves was the prerogative of the masters. In providing a new piece of such cloth for the burial and transit to the afterlife of his slave, the king of Assini was asserting his fundamental right of property over the person whose blood he had just offered to his divinity.

[43] N: 118–119; G: 253, 254, 55, 256. Godot writes that in Angola, where slaves are sacrificed to spiritual power in private and public ritual circumstances similar to Assini, they are, however, not executed in order to serve dead people, due to belief that afterlife has no needs. Godot, *Voyages*, 472b–473c [N, pp. 220–221].

[44] In Senegal, Godot witnessed the return from war of the army of the *damel* (king) of Cayor with 2,000 slaves (men, women, and children), tied to each other in a chain. Godot, *Voyages*, 35–36 [N, pp. 28–29].

[45] N: 125. According to Father G. Loyer, the king and principal chiefs had control over slaves in the hundreds. The nephew of Akassini and successor appointed to the royal stool (spelled Emond, by Loyer, Aymont by Godot) had a following of 500–600 slaves. Loyer, "Relation," 208.

[46] The *benda* was a unit of mass used for gold dust on the Gold Coast, corresponding to two ounces.

imposed by the judges, which however does not amount to fifty *ecus*, because there is no sufficiently convincing evidence that this man had an affair with this woman. They are just sentenced to pay some bushels of millet or other similar things. But after that, the man who has seen the woman due to which she had him pay the fine can have her pass for a prostitute and enjoy her when he likes.

There is another particular rule when it comes to cuckolding the king: the fine is much higher when they are involved, and a man who is not a noble and has had an affaire with any of these women will be a slave throughout his life,[47] if he is caught; even when he is rich, it won't be enough for him to pay two and a half bendas, which amount to three hundred seventy five pounds of our currency.

The king has four hundred women and more, and he cannot satisfy them all, and the consequence is that they are left very much alone. However they are very discrete and do not say a word.[48]

…When someone dies, slaves are killed and buried with him. Gold powder, clothes and other things are also buried in order, they say, to service the dead in the next world, where they believe the body lives without ever dying [sentence erased in the text: and say it takes six weeks to go there]. It is only the most affectionate slaves who are killed, and often they even fight to be put to death as the first to go to the other world with their master.[49] They are killed according to the rank of the dead. If he is a chief, three are killed, who are buried with him in the same grave. Twenty-four oxen are also killed as a present to those who attend the funerals.[50]

Apart from the enormous trade in ivory these people have with the French and other nations, they engage in one that is even bigger. They sell slaves, or rather barter them against guns, bullets and other munitions.[51] There are public places where these unfortunates are displayed, and there are connoisseurs who visit them and see if they are of good complexion and fit for work [this phrase is added to the original text]. This trade is carried out by the king, who then retails the goods he derives from it to those who need them. For instance, when one inhabitant needs a knife or a gun or other things, he goes to the king, where he is sold anything he needs, even down to two pence of tobacco.

---

[47] Interestingly, death is not mentioned by Godot as a penalty for adultery with the king's wives, while capital punishment in this case is commonly referred to by many other contemporary and later sources. According to Bosman, death is generally mandatory in cases of adultery committed by a slave, with the addition of a fine imposed on his master. Bosman, *A New and Accurate Description*, 208.

[48] N: 128–129; G: 276, 277, 278.

[49] These sentences appear to be specific references to those categories of high-ranking attendants who were in a particularly intimate relation with a royal master. In central Akan areas, those categories included, among others, the *nkradwerefo* – literally the washers of the *kra*, the soul – who were the bath attendants of the king, directly connected with the rituals for preserving and strengthening his well-being and the intrinsic power of his body. They were recruited among his favorite slaves, but also personal friends of the king and were meant to be killed (or volunteer to be) at his death. See T. C. McCaskie, *State and Society in Pre-Colonial Asante* (Cambridge, 1995, p. 293).

[50] N: 136; G: 294, 295.

[51] Godot does not give any figure for the number of slaves traded in Assini. On the contrary, he reports a highly questionable figure provided by the interpreter for the French in Whydah, where the annual sale was supposed to amount to 75,000. Actually, the number in the manuscript was corrected by inserting a "4" in order to raise it to the totally unreliable figure of 475,000. Godot: 317; N: 150. One has to be suspicious of Godot's demographic estimates for towns and countries, and the size of armies. Sometimes his figures are clearly extravagant, as when he writes that the king of Assini can mobilize an army of 400,000 men. G: 270.

No one but the king is allowed to carry out the large deals, because the great lords would not buy their provisions from the king, if they could buy them from the Europeans, and this would affect his income.[52]

SUGGESTED ADDITIONAL READINGS

Bosman, W.A. *New and Accurate Description of the Coast of Guinea.* James Knapton, 1705. Reprinted: London; Frank Cass and Co., 1967.

Biezunska-Malowist, I. *La schiavitù nel mondo antico.* Napoli: Edizioni Scientifiche Italiane, 1991.

Damon, "Relation du voyage de Guynée fait en 1698 par le chevalier Damon," in *L'établissement d'Issiny, 1687-1702.* Edited by P. Rousier. Paris: Larose, 1934, 71-89.

Damon, "Relation très curieuse du voyage que M. le Chevalier Damon a fait aux Indes pour faire un établissement a Issigny," in *L'établissement d'Issiny, 1687-1702.* Edited by P. Roussier. Paris: Larose, 1935, 91-107.

Diabate, H. (avec la collaboration de G. Lambert). *Aniaba. Un Assinien à la cour de Louis XIV.* Paris: ABC; Dakar: NEA; Yaounde: CLE, 1975.

Ducasse, J.-B. "Mémoire ou relation du sr Du Casse sur son voyage de Guynée avec 'La Tempeste' en 1687 et 1688," in *L'établissement d'Issiny, 1687-1702.* Edited by P. Roussier (Paris: Larose, 1935), 1-47.

Falola, Toyin & Paul E. Lovejoy (eds.) *Pawnship in Africa: Debt Bondage in Historical Perspective.* Boulder, CO: Westview Press, 1994.

Garnsey, P. *Ideas of Slavery from Aristotle to Augustine.* Cambridge: Cambridge University Press, 1996.

Loyer, G. "Relation du voyage du royaume d'Issiny, Cote d'or, Païs de Guinée en Afrique [1714]," chez A. Seneuze et chez J.-R. Morel, in *L'établissement d'Issiny, 1687-1702.* Edited by P. Roussier (Paris: Larose, 1935), 109-235.

McCaskie, T. C. *State and Society in Pre-Colonial Asante.* Cambridge: Cambridge University Press, 1995.

Nardin, J.-C. et H. Spirik. "Un Nouveau Document pour l'Etude des Populations Lagunaires de la Côte d'Ivoire du Début du XVIIIe Siècle: Le Voyage du Jean Godot à Assinie (1701)," in *VIIIth Congress of Anthropological and Ethnological Sciences.* Vol. 3 (Tokyo: 1970), 78-81.

Tibierge,? "Extrait du Journal du Sieur Tibierge principal commis de la Compagnie de Guinée sur le vaisseau 'Le Pont d'Or' au voyage en l'annéee 1692," in *L'établissement d'Issiny, 1687-1702.* Edited by P. Roussier (Paris: Larose, 1935), 49-69.

---

[52] N: 145–146; G: 310.

PART FIVE

ADMINISTRATIVE RECORDS

The colonial state was a bureaucracy. It wrote things down and preserved written records. The colonial state is gone, but it has left behind masses of paper, which can be found in the capitals of former empires and in administrative centers all over Africa. They record both the minutiae of daily administrative life and the larger questions, both the ways Africa's colonial rulers saw the people they governed and how they responded to Africa's problems. These colonial rulers were limited in many ways. They rarely knew the languages of the people they governed, and thus depended on African intermediaries, clerks, interpreters, and chiefs. Fearing disruption, they were often obsessed with the maintenance of order and thus averse to development policies that might lead to conflict. Also, despite being pressed by European public opinion that was hostile to slavery, they often had little sympathy for the slaves. They tended to identify with the chiefs and other members of the elites, through whom they governed Africa. Finally, once they had banned the slave trade, ended slave raiding, and taken action against slavery itself, they were convinced that it was over, that they had ended slavery.

Neither slavery nor its heritage disappeared quickly. Working in colonial archives involves a lot of persistence, but it can be fruitful. Some of it is easy. There are files labeled "Slavery" in many archives. They often date to periods when the colonial administration was struggling over what to do about slavery. They also include reports that colonial governors asked the administrative officers to make. Some include African voices, albeit filtered through European eyes. There is also information about runaways who fled to European consulates or of slaves freed by navy ships that cruised the Atlantic and Indian oceans. They sometimes record the stories of the slaves they freed, though usually briefly. There were also situations in which a local administrator found himself faced with a crisis: for example, the refusal of slaves to continue working for their masters, massive slave departures, or the murder of slave women who returned to the sites of their enslavement to claim their children. We present two such cases here. One –by Pierluigi Valsecchi in Chapter 25 – involves an effort by a kidnapped man to avoid being shipped out into the Atlantic trade. The other is a case – discussed by Benjamin Acloque in Chapter 26 – in which colonial administrators investigated the murder of a slave accused of witchcraft. In all such situations, administrators had to talk to slaves and, even when unsympathetic, report their language and their grievances. Finally, there are grievances and petitions both from slaves and from those troubled by the loss of their labor as seen in the contributions by Hideaki Suzuki

(Chapter 27) and Marie Rodet (Chapter 28). Some wrote their own letters or depended on missionaries or relatives. Others depended on public letter-writers, who proliferated in many African cities and who translated the thoughts of the illiterate and helped them formulate their grievances. The range of issues addressed by colonial officials makes the use of these records indispensible for the study of slavery in Africa despite the frequent brevity of their accounts.

How Kwadwo Regained His Freedom and Put the Slave-Traders in Big Trouble

PIERLUIGI VALSECCHI

Most pre-twentieth-century European-language sources contain few, if any, voices of the enslaved. When they do, the stories contain an amazing amount of detail and can evoke tremendous empathy from the reader. Most often, however, their stories are told in the third person, making them fundamentally narratives "about" slaves rather than ones by the slaves themselves. The opportunity to read the story of a slave told by him- or herself is a rare occurrence indeed. The present chapter is concerned with one of these rare instances. It is a peculiar story. It took place on the western Gold Coast between late 1818 and early 1819. Kwadwo (spelled Cudjoe in the records) was a trader from Wassa, an important polity in the interior of the western Gold Coast. He was seized to serve as security for a debt contracted by one of his townsmen. His captor sold him in Axim, a trade port and the site of a Dutch fort, where he was purchased by an unnamed European slave-trader, apparently a Spaniard, who seemed to have operated in collusion with the Dutch commander at Axim. Their alleged intent: to force Kwadwo onto a ship so that he and a number of others could be transported illegally as slaves to America. Kwadwo, however, succeeded in escaping with two other companions. He then placed himself under British protection and appears to have regained his freedom. He later served as a witness against the Dutchman, a prominent officer on the Gold Coast, who was accused of engaging in the illegal sale of slaves. The officer was later removed from command.

Most interesting is the fact that Kwadwo was no ordinary peasant. He was a retainer of a prominent titleholder who employed him as a "messenger." In a word, he was a member, albeit a subordinate one, of the local political establishment.[1] Moreover, he was himself a

---

[1] This story of Kwadwo was reported in letters exchanged between British and Dutch officers stationed on the Gold Coast in 1819. They can be found in the National Archives of the United Kingdom (ex-Public Record Office, Kew Gardens), under the reference T 70/1605, T stands for records inherited from the archives of the Treasury. T 70 includes the records of the Company of Royal Adventurers of England Trading with Africa and successors, spanning from 1660 to 1833. Indeed, one of these documents provides a very happy surprise for those searching "the slave voice." It is a short annex to one of the letters, containing a written record of the oral examination of Kwadwo by the commander of the British Fort in Dixcove, John Fountaine, a seasoned resident on the Gold Coast and credibly acquainted with local languages. The questions posed by Fountaine are answered by Kwadwo in the presence of at least one European witness. The records do not specify whether the Wassa sword-bearer had any language in common with his interviewer and witness or not.

I thank S. E. Greene and M. Doortmont for commenting on the draft of this chapter.

trader. This alone makes Kwadwo's case very interesting. It was a time when most Europeans were forbidden from participating in the trans-Atlantic slave trade, but the related practice of Europeans owning slaves and controlling dependants (for instance, persons put in pawn for debts) was still legal and widely practiced. Kwadwo was not a passive, uninformed victim, however. He knew things and also knew how to deploy his knowledge in ways that served his own cause.

THE BACKGROUND

In 1807. Britain outlawed the slave trade.[2] It then pressured other countries to follow suit. The United States abolished the trade in 1808; Sweden did the same in 1813, as did the Netherlands in 1814. France took a gradual approach by agreeing in 1814 to reduce the size of its trade in slaves. It then completely outlawed the trade for its citizens in 1818. Portugal also took a gradual approach. It imposed successive limitations on its citizens' slave trade activities in 1810, 1815, and 1817; Spain did the same, imposing limited restrictions in 1814, but finally abolishing the trade in 1817.[3] These formal abolition acts, however, fell far short of actually ending the trade. After experiencing a serious decline in the 1810s, the trade actually revived in the 1820s, especially in the Bights of Benin and Biafra. To a lesser extent this trend was apparent on the Gold Coast too. After the 1807 abolition, slave exports from this region declined drastically, but illegal shipments continued nevertheless.[4] Indeed, after 1815, the region actually experienced a limited resurgence in the trade. European documents record the illegal export of more than 7,000 slaves between 1815 and 1821 from western and eastern ports on the Gold Coast, especially from Axim and Accra.[5] Although the numbers were relatively small in comparison with those from the end of the previous century, the problem was of concern to abolitionists.[6]

Especially important for understanding Kwadwo's case was the new framework that the British and Dutch governments put in place in May of 1818 to enhance the prosecution of the illegal slave trade. The two powers agreed to take action against the trade by establishing the right of each government to visit the other's ships suspected of slave trading.

---

[2] British law abolishing the trade did not go into effect until January 1, 1808.

[3] The ex-Spanish colonies in America suppressed it after getting their independence in the 1820s. The importation of slaves in Spanish Cuba was forbidden in 1821, though the ban was hardly observed. For details and dates, see P. E. Lovejoy, *Transformations in Slavery: A History of Slavery in Africa. Second Edition* (Cambridge, 2000), pp. 290–294.

[4] P. E. Lovejoy and D. Richardson, "The Initial 'Crisis of Adaptation': The Impact of British Abolition on the Atlantic Slave Trade in West Africa, 1808–1820," in R. Law (ed.), *From Slave Trade to "Legitimate Commerce": The Commercial Transition in Nineteenth Century West Africa* (Cambridge, 1995), 33–38.

[5] E. Reynolds, E. *Trade and Economic Change on the Gold Coast, 1807–1874* (London, 1974), 40–42. According to Reynolds, the known export of slaves from the Gold Coast from 1811–1820 (7,724 units) amounted to 1.95% of the total exported from Africa during the same period: 394,500 according to Curtin's calculation. See P.D. Curtin, *The Atlantic Slave Trade: A Census* (Madison, 1969), 234, 258.

[6] Shipments from the Gold Coast continued to take place periodically until at least 1839, in spite of British efforts at offshore naval patrolling. See David Eltis, *Economic Growth and the Ending of the Transatlantic Slave Trade* (New York, 1987), 168. Slaves were also occasionally smuggled to ports east of the Volta, where European influence was weak. This went on as late as 1842. See E. Reynolds, *Trade and Economic Change on the Gold Coast, 1807–1874* (London, 1974), 89. Vessels flying the Portuguese (and later Brazilian), Spanish, and U.S. flags and manned by crews from the United States, France, and elsewhere were the ones principally responsible for these illegal slave exports.

The treaty also established mixed courts in Sierra Leone and Surinam to deal with those breaking the ban.[7]

This determination to suppress the overseas export of human beings was not yet accompanied, however, by an equal effort to condemn slavery and to prosecute those involved in this local practice. Indeed, British and Dutch subjects who resided on the Gold Coast and worked in the two European nations' establishments were still allowed to buy slaves, to employ and exploit them, and to sell them provided they did not try to take them out of the region. Britain, in fact, did not formally forbid her citizens from holding slaves until 1833, when the government abolished the institution of slavery in Crown Colonies.[8] The British settlements on the Gold Coast did not constitute a Colony, however, and did not become part of one until 1874 when Britain created the Gold Coast Colony. And only in 1860 did the Dutch parliament abolish slavery in its own Dutch colonies.[9] These facts deeply influenced how both the Dutch and the British opted to handle Kwadwo's case.

THE MAIN CHARACTERS IN THE STORY

Kwadwo's story is crowded with the names of Europeans important in the history of the Gold Coast and West Africa. J. Hope Smith was the Governor in Chief of the Company of Merchants Trading to Africa (British)[10] from January 1817 to March 1822. He was based in Cape Coast Castle, the British headquarters on the Gold Coast. Frantz Christian Eberhard Oldenburg was his Dutch counterpart, and served as Governor of the Dutch possessions from May 1818 to his death in January 1820. He resided in Elmina Castle,[11] just a few miles west of Cape Coast Castle. The British commander Sir George Ralph Collier headed the West Africa Squadron, based in Freetown, which patrolled the coast to prevent illegal slave shipping. Sir Collier arrived in West Africa in late 1818 and retained command until 1821. He had the particularly difficult task of having only six ships to patrol 3,000 miles of coastline.[12] William Henry Blenkarne and John Fountaine also appear in the records. Both officers had long service records with the Company of Merchants.[13] They commanded the two

---

[7] These courts included Dutch and British judges. However, by the time the agreement was stipulated, no Dutch ship had been caught in illegal trafficking since the 1814 Dutch abolition. See P.C. Emmer, *The Dutch Slave Trade, 1500–1850* (New York/Oxford, 2006), 117–118; J.M. Postma, *The Dutch in the Atlantic Slave Trade, 1600–1815* (Cambridge, 1990), 290–291.

[8] 'Anno Tertio & Quarto, Guglielmi IV. Regis. Cap. LXXIII. An Act for the Abolition of Slavery throughout the British Colonies; for promoting the Industry of the manumitted Slaves; and for compensating the Persons hitherto entitled to the Services of such Slaves. [28 Aug 1833]', in *The Debates in Parliament – Session 1833 – on the Resolutions and Bill for the Abolition of Slavery in the British Colonies, with a Copy of the Act of Parliament* (London, 1834), 929–964.

[9] Its application of the ban on slavery was delayed, however, to 1863 in Suriname and the Dutch West Indies. Planters were to be accorded a "transition period" of ten years in order to achieve full emancipation. During this length of time, the ex-slaves were not yet completely free. See Emmer, *The Dutch*, 127–128.

[10] The Company of Merchants Trading to Africa (a.k.a. African Company of Merchants) was incorporated in 1750 as the successor of the Royal African Company (established in 1660). It was dissolved in 1821.

[11] Elmina castle was the first European establishment in the Gulf of Guinea, founded by the Portuguese in late fifteenth century. The Dutch seized it from the Portuguese in 1637.

[12] C. Lloyd, C., *The Navy and the Slave Trade: The Suppression of the African Slave Trade in the Nineteenth Century* (2nd ed., London, 1968), 64–70.

[13] J. Fountaine resigned from service in 1822, after the Company of Merchants was divested of the management of the establishments, which was taken over by the Crown until 1828. W.H. Blenkarne – a captain of the infantry, who entered the service of the African company of Merchants in 1804 – continued in service under the management by the Crown, and was later governor of Accra Fort and Member of Council. See

British forts to the windward of Cape Coast: Dixcove fort in the Ahanta district and Fort Appollonia located in Beyin, in the Nzema area, respectively. These forts were the two sole British bases in this section of the Gold Coast over which the Dutch also claimed jurisdiction.[14] J. H. Sels was the Dutch commander of Axim at the time the events involving Kwadwo took place. The captain of the Spanish brig accused of cruising the area in search of slaves in collusion with Mr. Sels is left unnamed.

Equally important were the Africans associated with Kwadwo's case. Kwadwo's lord and master, Attobra (Attabrah), was a powerful chief and the most prominent military leader (*safohene*) in Wassa.[15] Amihyia (Amanaheer Longcong) was another "big man" in the western Gold Coast. He was the uterine nephew of,[16] and appointed as successor to, the king of Appolonia (Nzema), Nyanzu Aka (who reigned from 1816 or 1818 to ca. 1832). Amihyia is mentioned in the story as the seller of a slave to Sels who was on a trade visit to Appolonia. In the event of Sels's absence, Kwadwo was brought to Axim by his captor and sold. Yet another prominent African was Kofi Amu, a chief from Axim and a man of economic consequence. According to Kwadwo, it was Amu and another resident of Axim, Badu Kwadwo[17] (Badow Cudjoe), a Castle slave[18] and bricklayer, who bought him on behalf of the Spanish slave trader who was ultimately supposed to take possession of him. Amu and Badu purchased Kwadwo from yet another African, Ano Benga (Anoe Bengar, also Bingar in one of the records), the man who had kidnapped him in the first place and then sold him as a slave. According to Kwadwo, Benga was from Busua (Bushwah), the principal Ahanta town where the Ahanta king had his residence. Kwadwo claimed that Benga kidnapped him to obtain compensation for a debt owed him by Kwadwo's townsman, Akasa (Accassa).

The most important character in this entire story, of course, is Kwadwo. As a servant (*ahenkwaa*), but more precisely a "sword-bearer" (*afenasoani*, pl. *afenasoafo*) of Attobra, he was permanently attached to his office-holding master, who employed him as a messenger. His daily proximity to power meant that Kwadwo and other sword-bearers could

J.J. Crooks, *Records Relating to the Gold Coast Settlements from 1750 to 1874* (2nd ed. Portland, 1973), 151–153. In the course of their career the two commanded different forts in succession, as the rule of frequent turnover among the few European resident officers was generally observed.

[14] The Ahanta district was under the nominal rule of the king of Busua (near Dixcove). On their part the Dutch claimed to hold a right of protection, and some form of jurisdiction over Busua and Ahanta, on the bases of an agreement they stipulated in 1656 with the local chiefs. The Dutch main settlement after Elmina stood in Axim, to the west of Ahanta. It was St. Anthony Castle, built by the Portuguese around 1552 and conquered by the Dutch in 1642.

[15] Attobra gained fame among the Europeans in 1809 when, under the leadership of his overlord Ntsiful, king of Wassa, he marshalled the Wassa army and joined an anti-Asante coalition of Fante forces that engaged in a number of failed attacks on pro-Asante Elmina and Accra.

[16] Uterine kin are those issued from the same womb (woman) and their descendants through a line of women: i. e. those sharing the same mother, or mother's mother, etc. Matrilineal kinship prevails in this part of West Africa and plays a crucial role in establishing property rights and in the transmission of office and wealth. All individuals belong in the first place to their mother's lineage (or family), and the successor of any individual is supposed to come from his or her maternal side. Amihyia shared the same maternal ascendants with the king of Appolonia: for instance, he might have been the son of one of his sisters from the same mother, or the son of his mother' sister's daughter, and so forth.

[17] Kwadwo was kept in Badu's house while waiting to be taken on board a slave ship.

[18] Badu Kwadwo was styled "Company's Slave" as all slave dependants attached to the Dutch establishments on the Gold Coast were still commonly known, though the Dutch West India Company had been dissolved in 1792 and all his territories and competencies, slaves included, taken over by the Dutch Royal government.

wield considerable influence in spite of their status as personal dependants.[19] Kwadwo was also a trader, working on his own behalf and possibly for his master as well. Sword-bearers and other servants often conducted their own and private business while also carrying out their state responsibilities because their official duties frequently required them to travel from place to place conveying orders and administrating dependencies, while also serving as supervisors, arbitrators, and collectors of tribute.[20]

KWADWO'S STORY

Kwadwo first came to the attention of the British Company of Merchants Commander J. Fountaine, in Dixcove, in January 1819 (*Record 1*). Kwadwo had come to town, where Fountaine recognized him as the one who had committed a trade crime, some time earlier. Kwadwo had tried to cheat one of the middlemen working for the British fort. He had entrusted this middleman with a sum of money in gold dust – a common currency in the region – that the middleman was to use to buy goods from a British vessel that was at anchor near the town. Kwadwo's gold dust was adulterated, however.[21] This crime came to light when the middleman went on board the ship. Immediately the middleman was accused of attempted fraud. In the meantime, Kwadwo – having discovered that his ruse had been detected – absconded from Dixcove before he was apprehended. His subsequent return to the scene of his crime was therefore seen by all as quite curious. The middleman brought Kwadwo before Fountaine to obtain satisfaction from him. On further enquiry, however, Fountaine realized that Kwadwo had had very good reasons for coming back and for giving himself up to the British commander even if this meant he would not be able to escape punishment for his crime. The Wassa sword-bearer had recently been the victim of circumstances that had nearly seen him being loaded onto a slave ship to be transported across the Atlantic. He came back to Dixcove to obtain British protection from those who would have transported him to the Americas.

According to Kwadwo, he had been kidnapped on his return from a trade journey to Appolonia, by a man from Busua, Ano Benga, who sought to hold him as a security for a debt contracted and left unpaid by one of his fellow citizens, Akasa. This practice was known as *panyarring*, from the Portuguese-derived *panyar*; it was employed by creditors to obtain satisfaction for neglected or ignored contractual obligations. As an established juridical institution, *panyarring* was based on the principle of corporate responsibility. The person (or persons) kidnapped – often the debtor himself – was taken as collateral by the creditor with the object of pressuring the debtor (or his or her family, village, town, or even the wider polity to which the debtor belonged) to repay the debt in order to obtain the release of the person kidnapped. Though in theory the condition of the *panyarred* was reversible upon the payment of the debt, in practice it could easily result in a long or even

---

[19] For the role of sword-bearers in Asante, see I. Wilks, *Asante in the Nineteenth Century: The Structure and Evolution of a Political Order* (Cambridge, 1975), 439–440, 447–448.

[20] In Asante, the horn-blowers (*asokwafo*) and drummers (*akyeremadefo*) provided the recruiting backbone for state traders. See Wilks, *Asante*, 455.

[21] Gold dust was the sole currency in Asante. On the Gold Coast it began to be scarce in the 1840s, which prompted the Europeans to import growing quantities of cowries, or shell money. See Wilks, *Asante*, 688–689. In different historical periods, cowries were used as currency in many parts of Africa and the Indian Ocean.

permanent loss of freedom. The *panyarred* could become the only "capital" the creditor was able to get back from the debtor's community. This, in turn, could – and often did – lead to abuse. During the days of the trans-Atlantic slave trade, *panyarring* became a shortcut for creditors to recover their capital. They did so by selling the *panyarred* overseas. In fact, this practice became one of the principle means by which many in Africa experienced a violent change in their status as they saw themselves transformed from free individuals in Africa to plantation slaves in the Americas. This is exactly what was about to happen to Kwadwo, at least according to his own evidence. His captor did not follow the expected procedure of informing Kwadwo's community of his capture. This would have given Kwadwo's community the opportunity to pay the debt owed by Kwadwo's countryman and thus obtain Kwadwo's release. Instead, Ano Benga hurried to sell Kwadwo outright at the slave market of Axim, where men, women, and children were in ready demand by whites who were trying to complete the cargo for a Spanish slave brig.

Kwadwo stated he was sold in exchange for Spanish goods, commodities with which he was quite familiar because he himself had sold a slave recently for the same sorts of merchandise. Ano Benga received these goods from two Axim men: Kofi Amu, a chief, and Badu Kwadwo, a slave associated with the Dutch fort. Kwadwo testified that these two were just middlemen for the real buyer, a Spaniard who was a guest of the commander of the Dutch fort at Axim, J. H. Sels. Sels was not in Axim, however, when the deal took place. He was on a trip to Appolonia, from which he returned a few days later with yet another slave for the Spaniard whom he had bought from Amihyia, one of the main chiefs of Appolonia and the appointed heir to the royal stool.

After his sale to Amu and Badu, Kwadwo was entrusted to Badu, who chained him to a log. Significantly he was not then consigned to the "slave hole" (i.e., the slave hold) located in the official Dutch seat of power in Axim, St. Anthony Castle. This was where most slaves had been kept while they waited to be loaded onto slave ships when the Dutch slave trade was still legal. Instead Badu kept Kwadwo with a number of other slaves in his own house in town. At the same time, the Spanish slavers stored on shore the goods they intended to use to purchase slaves in both the fort and in Badu Kwadwo's house. Once Sels returned from his slave-buying trip to Appolonia, he visited Kwadwo and his companions at Badu's house. In finding them in possession of a bayonet and some rope, he suspected them of preparing to commit suicide and reacted by flogging them. Only later did he accept Kwadwo and the other slaves' explanation that they had only used the rope and bayonet to supplement their diet by catching rats. Shortly thereafter, Kwadwo escaped with two of his fellow enslaved companions. Upon reaching the bush immediately outside Axim, he freed himself from the log, ran to Dixcove so as to avoid recapture, and then sought the assistance of the British. He succeeded.

The British Company of Merchant's commander in Dixcove, J. Fountaine, launched an investigation into the matter. He also asked his subordinate, William Henry Blenkarne, to gather information on Kwadwo's presence in Appolonia immediately before his kidnapping (*Record 2*). Although Blenkarne found no definitive evidence about the case in Appolonia, he was inclined to believe Wassa sword-bearer's account because of the information he had obtained about the Spanish brig. Many in the area were well aware of the presence of the ship and its crew and knew of their movements. Few also doubted that it was involved in the slave trade. Rumors even circulated that the loading of its human cargo was almost complete. When Blenkarne made a sudden visit to Axim, he again found no direct evidence of slave trading. He did observe, however, the arrival of the alleged Spanish trader (also identified in the records as possibly Portuguese or French)[22] at the fort. This prompted their Dutch host to have them quickly removed from sight before they could be introduced to him. Fountaine and Blenkarne were not the only British officers to take an interest in the case. Sir George Collier, commander of the West African anti-slave trade squadron of ships, observed the Spanish brig while cruising off the coast of Axim. His arrival caused several canoes that were approaching the ship to turn back immediately toward the shore (*Record 5*). On seeing this, he suspected the canoes were bringing human chattel to the slave ship. He wrote a letter to Sels requesting an explanation, but received no reply. Ultimately, Blenkarne failed to muster enough evidence to justify stopping the ship and detaining its crew, but he did inform the British governor, John Hope Smith, about the matter (*Record 2*). While Sels refused to respond to Collier's enquiry, he did write to Blenkarne (*Record 3, 2, 5*). He denied any involvement in the illegal slave trade or association with the Spanish brig. He also stressed instead that he was the lawful owner of a number of slaves. Kwadwo was one of these slaves. Sels then described Kwadwo as a malicious fellow whom he bought to employ on his plantation and that he had had to be put him in a log because of his unruly behavior. He went on to claim that Kwadwo was now simply trying to damage his reputation as he had done earlier when a few weeks before he had tried to run away with two of his other slaves. According to Sels, the three were involved in a wicked pact in which one of them would try to hang himself. He had moved Kwadwo and the others to Badu's house to avoid any such suicide attempt taking place within the walls of the Dutch castle. This was how he answered the accusation that he stored in town the human cargo intended for the Spanish brig. He then sought to have his legitimate property returned, and expressed his surprise that his British interlocutor would believe the word of a runaway black slave over that of his white master. This would not happen in his castle, he remarked.

Sels's explanation failed to free him of suspicion. As a result, Fountaine sent Kwadwo to be examined by the British governor at Cape Coast castle, J. Hope Smith, who in turn sent him to the F. C. E. Oldenburg, the governor of the Dutch establishments. The letter that Smith sent with Kwadwo requested a thorough enquiry into the matter, based on well-founded suspicions about the activities that were taking place in Axim, under the walls of the Dutch castle.

The British archival record ends at this point of the story. Sir George Collier, the commodore in charge of the anti-slavery squadron, did remark in a later document that the Dutch eventually took action against Sels. They removed him from his post.[23]

---

[22] Kwadwo maintained that the captain was a Spaniard. The Company of Merchants employee, John Fountaine, who questioned Kwadwo about his plight, speculated that the captain may have been either Spanish or Portuguese. On the other hand, Sels, the Dutch commander at Axim, maintained he was a Frenchman. It was most common for trade ships to be staffed with officers and crews whose nationalities where different from the flag the ship flied. In those years the definition of Spanish applied also to people from Spain's huge American dependencies, and Brazil was still a Portuguese land. Sailors from the United States were very common aboard slave ships. All these countries hosted substantial interests involved in slave dealings, while France still tolerated them to a large extent.

[23] West African Sketches. Compiled from the Reports of Sir G. R. Collier, Sir Charles McCarthy, and other Official Sources, *1824* (2nd ed., Legon, 1963), 221.

THE VOICE OF THE MASTER AND THE VOICE OF THE SLAVE

Kwadwo's case provides a rich set of materials to explore a range of issues: the circumstances faced by local government officials in their efforts to suppress the slave trade; the extent to which relations between different Europeans powers influenced their relations with one another in Africa; and the different ways Africans and African institutions interacted with Europeans and European institutions. Of concern here, however, is the question of the "voices" of the enslaved.

Kwadwo's enslaved voice has reached us thanks to J. Fountaine, who made a transcript (or at least a summary) of his testimony. Such documentation was quite uncommon at the time and can be explained as a product of British concerns about their political and diplomatic relations with the Dutch on the Gold Coast. The fact that these concerns produced a written record and that Kwadwo's words were probably filtered through a translator[24] require that the documents themselves be read with a degree of caution, considering that the issues they raised were extremely sensitive, and the wording of Kwadwo's testimony in particular was to add strength to a move to push the Dutch government to question the behavior of its representatives on the Coast. In spite of all political implications and undertones that might have influenced their formulation, the documents are revealing nevertheless.

Especially interesting is the way the language recorded in these materials illuminates notions about hierarchy and dependence. From Sels's letter alone, we see how Europeans viewed the institution of slavery and those whom they enslaved. Any person could be "lawfully" reduced to slavery; they could be bought and sold, disposed of in many different ways, as the complete property of another. This was what European law allowed. African law was no different. Kwadwo's responses to Fountaine's inquiries reveal he too believed in the legitimacy of buying and selling other human beings. He was himself a slave-trader. And although he had the misfortune of becoming a trade good himself, he never questioned the justness of slavery and the slave trade, or the legitimacy of the financial and commercial institutional practices which had made him a victim when he was kidnapped for someone else's debt. He knew perfectly well what was happening to him.

Equally significant is the fact that his knowledge about the logics of power and the various interests in the region allowed him to operate very effectively on his own behalf. When he successfully escaped from Badu's house, he consciously fled to the British. He did so well aware of the fact that his actions would place him at the center of an international incident on the Gold Coast. More importantly, he used his overall knowledge of European policies and practices to regain his freedom.

QUESTIONS TO CONSIDER

1. What were the costs and benefits of the practice of *panyarring* for all who were resident on the western Gold Coast?
2. The ban on the trans-Atlantic slave trade left unaffected the institution of slavery in western Africa. This created problems for those seeking to abolish the slave trade, as indicated in Kwadwo's case. But what other problems might have emerged as a

---

[24] There is no mention in the records of Kwadwo speaking English, which cannot, however, be excluded.

result? How might the ban on slave exports, the emergence of an illegal slave export trade, and the continued practice of slavery in western Africa have affected relations between the European establishments and local traders, as well as between the European establishments and the local African political elite?

3. Do you think the abolition of the slave trade had the power to change European and African perceptions of slavery in the nineteenth-century Gold Coast?

4. The analysis of Kwadwo's case presented here suggests that individual responses to enslavement could differ based on a person's social position. Was Kwadwo in a better position to gain his freedom than others? What difference did it make that he was a sword-bearer and a trader? Was one of his roles more important than the other?

NATIONAL ARCHIVES, UNITED KINGDOM
T 70/1605 DETACHED PAPERS 1819

Letters by J. Fountaine, W. H. Blenkarne, J. H. Sels, J. H. Smith and Questions put to a Warsaw Man Cudjoe, by Mr Fountaine with his Answers thereto
(Transcribed and annotated by Pierluigi Valsecchi)[25]

Record 1. J. Fountaine to Gov. J. H. Smith

J. H. Smith Esqr. Dixcove Fort
January 31st 1819

Sir

A circumstance has lately transpired with which I deem it is my duty to make you acquainted particularly as Sir George Collier made enquires on the subject when off this place.

Some time back, a Warsaw[26] Man, named Cudjoe, Sword bearer to the Caboceer[27] Attahbrah, gave to a Windward Man in my service 14 ack.[28] gold to purchase a few things from Captain Hatting of the Brig Mars, then at Anchor, in these roads, whose Gold taker[29] discovered it to be base Mettal, the Crew man declared he thought it was good, or never would have attempted to pass it. Captain Hatting fined him 14 ack. and permitted him to return on Shore, The Warsaw man had some knowledge of his being detected, and fled.

---

[25] What follows is a transcription from the handwritten copies of the original letters and documents that are to be found in T 70/1605. I apologize for all misunderstandings and mistakes I might have made in reading those copies.

[26] *Warsaw* is a very common spelling for Wassa in eighteenth–nineteenth-century European language documents.

[27] The word c*aboceer* (*cabocier* in Dutch), derived from the Portguese *caboceiro* (headman), was used generally by the English to indicate a range of African political and military officers. Later it was substituted by the term 'chief'.

[28] The *ackie* was the 16th part of 1 gold ounce (1 ounce = 16 ackies).

[29] Gold dust was very commonly adulterated or counterfeited. Local experts (*gold takers*) could be found in all trading ports whose services were employed by European merchants and trading ships to collect the gold from African trade counterparts, and assess and weigh it, in order to avoid being cheated. Because of their knowledge of European trade languages, the gold takers were often crucial in mediating trade disputes. See M. Huber, *Ghanaian Pidgin English in Its West African Context: A Socio-Historical and Structural Analysis* (Amsterdam and Philadelphia, 1999), 43, 46–47.

About 8 days ago Cudjoe again appeared in this town, he was instantly recognised by his friend the Crew man, who requested I would allow the Warsaw man, to be brought into the Fort, to which I consented, in a few minutes he was before me, and acknowledged his having given the base Mettal, for this offence, I intended punishing the fellow, and liberating him; the following affair to which I now request your attention; prevented my doing so, and induced me to send him to you.

It appears Cudjoe went some time back to Apollonia, and purchased of Mr. Blenkarne, oz 2 of Cloth, returning he was panyarred by a Native of Bushwah named Anoe Bengar, and carried to Axim Fort where he was purchased for oz 6^{30} of Spanish goods, in the possession of Mr. Sels, the assistant Governor, – the prisoner was with three others sent in town to a Co.[5] (?) Slave Bricklayer's house, named Badow Cudjoe, from where they effected their escape, then is now residing in the Fort of Axim, a Spaniard, or Portuguese with his Domestic, who arriving the few hours Mr. Blenkarne was there, were secreted in one of the Apartments; from enquires I have made, little doubt remains of Mr. Sels having landed goods to a considerable amount from a Spanish Brig, then at Anchor in the roads, when Sir George Collier was off Axim, and for which Vessel the Governor of that place I have every reason to think, is purchasing Slaves. I wrote Mr. Blenkarne on the above subject, and enclose you his answer, as he permitted me to make any use I pleased of it. I also wrote Mr. Sels, and send you his reply. – The Warsaw Man's evidence I have taken down, and enclose herewith, much light may be [therein?] thrown on this affair, if strictly investigated.

I am
Etc.etc. etc
(Sig.) Jn: (Jn) Fountaine

Record 2. W. H. Blenkarne to J. Fountaine

Dear Fountaine Apollonia Fort 22nd January 1819
Your express letter has this moment been handed me, and on questioning my Boys as to the truth of a Warsaw Man, named Cudjoe, having been here lately, and bought oz 2 of goods of me, it appears to them false, however the fellow may be right for I perceive here such timidity exhibited when the character, connexions, or person is called in question under the impression, that such information might alternately turn upon themselves.

The current report here is that the Spaniards are living in Axim Fort, and have been some time, also that the vessels cargo is now nearly ready, she runs into the Roads every 4 or 7 days, you may naturally inquire, as my stay was so short there I could not pry into particulars. – Sir George Collier was informed when off here, of the Spaniards being at Axim, and having landed the Cargo, when he wrote me stating the impropriety of detaining her, unless she was actually engaged in Slaving. – which now by the bye is clear enough. –

---

[30] The Dutch (as did other nations) made a distinction between "ounces merchandise" and "ounces gold." The ounce merchandise was based on an assortment of trade goods, presumably representing a fixed value (although in practice the actual value fluctuated). In this period the fixed value of the ounce of gold was 40 Dutch guilders, that of the ounce merchandise 36 Dutch guilders. For a discussion of prices for slaves in this period, see P. E. Lovejoy, and D. Richardson, "The Initial "Crisis of Adaptation": the impact of British abolition on the Atlantic Slave Trade in West Africa, 1808–1820," in R. Law, *From Slave Trade to "Legitimate Commerce"*, 33–7.

It must be obvious to every one 50 miles E. or W. of Axim what has been going on there, it is needless my entering into a detail of circumstances the more so as my information is entirely from Blacks report, the Man's evidence whom you send down, I should imagine would be quite sufficient to bring about an exposure of Mr. Sels conduct. He seems alarmed and has written me a long foolish Epistle on the subject of yours to him, I shall not notice it for surely he cannot be so weak, as to suppose for a moment I am totally ignorant of his transactions.

I am etc. etc. etc.
W. H. Blenkarne

Record 3. I. H. Sels to W. H. Blenkarne

Axim 23rd January 1819

Sir

I have received your letter before yesterday evening and was very astonishing on the containing.

The Slave who has taken refuge by you is one bayed by me to work at a plantation which two months ago I began to make, but being told by the men who sold him, that he was of a bad character, I put him in Irons in the Fort, until I could be assured of him, three weeks ago, one of the three would hang himself up, which was told by the other two, and I not liking that this should rise in the Fort, gave them to the care of a Co. Slave, named Badoe Cudjoe, but not for the reason of being afraid of the visit of Mr. Blenkarne but for the reason before mentioned.

What concerned there was a Spaniard or Portuguese in the Fort is not there, but a Frenchman with his domestic on which account I can give all eclairessment[31] that are required.

I never buyed a Slave for Spanish goods, but for very good English and Dutch goods and never buyed Slaves, or shall buy Slaves for a Vessel, you knowing as well as I that Slaves are not to be have had in the Country.

I shall always reclame[32] like I reclaim by these the Slave being now in your power, as a Slave being legitimately buyed by me, and who has run away – and I am very astonished that he has had the heart, to take refuge in an English Fort, there very light by the Governor would have believed a White Man, more than a Black but very happy for him, that like not to have been the case here.

What concerned the accusation that I have put a deal from the Cargo of a Vessel, in the house of a Co.s Slave, believe me that if I would do it, the Fort is great enough to hold instead of one Ship's cargo, ten of them, and [?] I am sorry of nothing than of the trouble that this business will give you, otherwise I should be very quiet,

I have the honor to be

Sir
Your most obedient Servant
(Signed) J. H. Sels

---

[31] Clarifications.
[32] Claim back.

Record 4. Questions put to a Warsaw Man Cudjoe, by Mr. Fountaine with his Answers thereto

Question. Who panyarred you?

Answer. Adoe Bengar, a Bushwah Man.

Question. On whose head did Adoe Bingar panyar you?

Answer. On the head of Accassa, one of my Townsmen.

Question. What did Adoe Bengar with you after he panyarred you?

Answer. Adoe Bengar, took me to Axim Fort and sold me.

Question. Who paid the assortment,[33] and what was the amount?

Answer. Two Men one named Coffee Amoe Caboceer of Axim Town, and the other a Co.s Slave Bricklayer, named Badoe Cudjoe, the Amount was Oz 6.

Question. Were the goods English or Dutch?

Answer. They were neither but Spanish goods.

Question. How do you know they were Spanish goods?

Answer. I am a trade Man, and know very well they were not such as Warsaw people usual buy from the English or Dutch, they were of the same description as a Spanish Factory,[34] kept some time ago at Adjuah,[35] paid for Slaves, and such an assortment, as I received for one.

Question. By whom were you examined when taken to Axim Fort, before the assortment was paid?

Answer. By the Spaniard he looked at my eyes and […?…] Members.

Question. Was Mr Sels the Governor of the Fort there present?

Answer. The Governor of Axim was gone for a few days to Elmina, and returned 5 days after I was bought.

Question. Did he see you after his return?

Answer. The Governor of Axim did see me.

Question. Did Mr Sels purchase any other Slaves while you were in irons at Axim?

Answer. Yes, he purchased one from the king of Apollonia's Nephew, Amanaheer Longcong[?]

Question. While you were in confinement, did you hear of a Spanish Vessel visiting Axim?

Answer. I did, it was the day after, Mr Blenkarne on his return, to Apollonia, and she went out to Sea again.

---

[33] The unit of account in slave dealings was an assortment of goods corresponding to the average price of a first choice adult male slave.

[34] An ad-hoc market.

[35] A town in Ahanta.

Question. Did you hear of there being much Spanish property at Axim?

Answer. I heard there was a great quantity landed from the Spaniard, part of which, I was told was taken into the Fort, and part in the Bricklayer, Badoe Cudjoe's house.

Question. Did you or any of your companions attempt to hang yourselves?

Answer. No, Mr Sels thought we meant to do so, from finding a Bayonet and String in the Slave hole, but we told him the former was to kill rats with, and the latter to catch them by the neck, and in proof of our assertion showed him two we had killed, In his passion, he flogged us, but afterwards dashed us half a Gallon of Liquor to drink.

Question. How did you get away from your confinement at Axim?

Answer. I watched an opportunity, when every person was asleep in Badoe Cudjoe's house, with two of my companions in same situation, as myself – then jumped into the Bush where we broke our Irons.

Witnessed this 30th day of January
in the year of our Lord, One thousand
eight hundred and nineteen
(Signed) Lewis Huthwaite

Record 5. J. H. Smith to F. C. E. Oldenburg

F. C. E. Oldenburg Esq.

Sir Cape Coast Castle 5th February 1819
When Sir George Collier, arrived here he stated to me his suspicions that a Spanish Vessel which he boarded off Axim had landed some Slaves at that place, having observed as he approached her several Canoes pulling hastily towards the Shore. He in consequence wrote to the Officer in Command of Axim Fort for information on the subject, and requested that he would forward his letter to Cape Coast Castle. No communication was however received from Mr Sels by the Commodore serving his stay here. Since Sir George Collier has left this, I have more than once, heard it reported that the Spaniard was Slaving at Axim, and I have now received the accompanying documents from Mr. Fountaine which fully confirms it.
Should any doubt exist in your mind of the truth of the circumstances which are therein set forth, I have no objection to send the Warsaw Man Cudjoe, to Elmina for your examination

I am, Sir
Your most obedient Servant
(Signed) J. H. Smith

SUGGESTED ADDITIONAL READINGS

Curtin, P. D. *The Atlantic Slave Trade: A Census*. Madison: University of Wisconsin Press, 1969.

Crooks, J. J. *Records Relating to the Gold Coast Settlements from 1750 to 1874*. London/Portland: Frank Cass and Co. Ltd., 1923/1973.

The Debates in Parliament – Session 1833 – on the Resolutions and Bill for the Abolition of Slavery in the British Colonies, with a Copy of the Act of Parliament. London: Maurice & Co., 1834.

Eltis, D. *Economic Growth and the Ending of the Transatlantic Slave Trade.* New York: Oxford University Press, 1987.

Emmer, P. C. *The Dutch Slave Trade, 1500–1850.* New York/Oxford: Berghahn Books, 2006.

Huber, M. *Ghanaian Pidgin English in Its West African Context: A Socio-historical and Structural Analysis.* Amsterdam/Philadelphia: John Benjamins Publishing Co., 1999.

Lloyd, C. *The Navy and the Slave Trade: The Suppression of the African Slave Trade in the Nineteenth Century.* London: Frank Cass and Co. Ltd, 1949/1968.

Lovejoy, P. E. *Transformations in Slavery. A History of Slavery in Africa.* Cambridge: Cambridge University Press, 1983.

Lovejoy, P. E. and D. Richardson. "The Initial 'Crisis of Adaptation': The Impact of British Abolition on the Atlantic Slave Trade in West Africa, 1808–1820," in *From Slave Trade to "Legitimate Commerce": The Commercial Transition in Nineteenth Century West Africa.* Edited by R. Law. Cambridge: Cambridge University Press, 1995, 32–56.

Postma, J. M. *The Dutch in the Atlantic Slave Trade, 1600–1815.* Cambridge: Cambridge University Press, 1990.

Reynolds, E. *Trade and Economic Change on the Gold Coast, 1807–1874.* London: Longman, 1974.

West African Sketches. Compiled from the Reports of Sir G. R. Collier, Sir Charles McCarthy and other Official Sources, 1824. Legon/London: Institute of African Studies, University of Ghana, Legon /Seeley and Son, 1824/1963.

Wilks, I. *Asante in the Nineteenth Century: The Structure and Evolution of a Political Order,* Cambridge: Cambridge University Press, 1975.

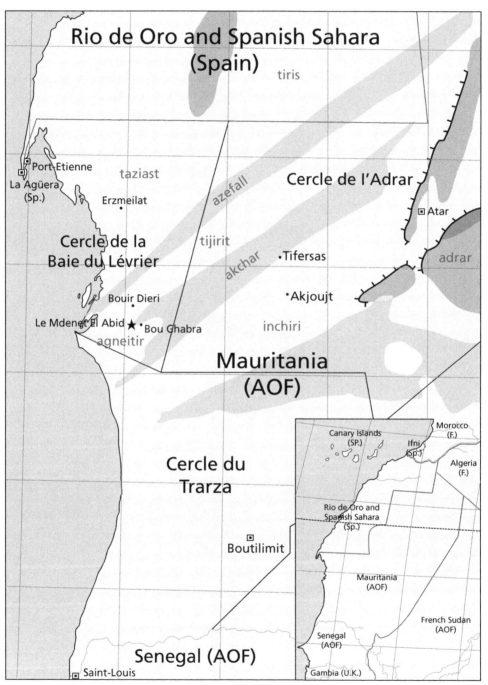

26.1. Map of Mauritania with featured administrative regions and locations.

26 Witchcraft and Slavery

Accusations of Remote Vampirism – The Colonial Administration of Mauritania Investigates the Execution of Three Slaves (1928–1929)

BENJAMIN ACLOQUE

In the course of my research in the archives of the Governor-General of French West Africa in Dakar in April 2007, I came across an enigmatic file on "the religious and social condition of Islam in Mauritania."[1] There I found thirty-one pages dealing with an affair involving important members of the tribal group that was the subject of my doctoral thesis.[2] The documents described an investigation conducted in 1928 and 1929 following the murder of three slaves accused of witchcraft in northwest Mauritania. As I had never heard of this episode, and because of the incoherence of the various elements contained in the file, I decided to wait for an upcoming trip to Mauritania to clarify matters.

In October 2008, I had the opportunity to travel through the area where the events took place.[3] I thus took advantage of the occasion to question various parties about what they knew of the episode. Despite a thorough search, the quite badly maintained and organized Mauritanian archives provided only a few complementary documents of secondary interest.[4] Interviews, conversely, turned out to be very fruitful. Many old people and a few younger ones shed new light on the remembered events and on beliefs about the "remote vampirism" of which the three slaves were accused. About the slaves themselves, documents and testimonies said very little. Even their names were uncertain.

Certainly speakers of Hassaniyya Arabic,[5] purchased from other Bizhan in southwest Mauritania where they are said to have already been accused of witchcraft, the three

---

[1]   Senegalese National Archives, Dakar (ANS) 9G86 (107). The archive documents reproduced later in the chapter are from this file.

[2]   Thesis in Social Anthropology and Ethnology, École des Hautes Études en Sciences Sociales, Paris, under the supervision of Pierre Bonte (CNRS, LAS, Collège de France), titled "Construction symbolique et sociale de la hiérarchie : noblesse, statut et état pour les Ahl Barikalla (Mauritanie)."

[3]   Research for the Pacoba program on the peopling of the Banc d'Arguin national Park and territorial dynamics partly published in B. Acloque, "Mémoire et enjeux territoriaux sur la côte mauritanienne : Le conflit d'Eyznaye et la convention de 1930 sur les puits et la pêche." in *Le littoral mauritanien à l'aube du XXIᵉ siècle: Peuplement, gouvernance de la nature, dynamiques sociales et culturelles.* Edited by S. Boulay and B. Lecoquierre (Paris: Karthala, 2011), 125–149.

[4]   Mauritanian National Archives, Nouakchott (ARIM) E1-75. This was correspondence between the governor of Mauritania and that of French West Africa, as well as with lower-level authorities. The most important documents were transmitted to the French West African governor. Access to the archives was particularly difficult, and I would like to acknowledge the kindness of Heybetna Ould Sidi Heyba, assistant director of the National Archives in Nouakchott.

[5]   A dialect of Arabic spoken by the Bizhan, an ethnic group characterized as Moorish in colonial writing. They inhabit Western Sahara and Mauritania and extend into neighboring countries.

slaves were owned by Cheikh Ould Abd El Aziz, a notable of the religious *qabila*[6] of the Ahel Barikallah.[7] They were two brothers (Hamadi and Souélim)[8] and a sister (Zénabou), apparently in the prime of life who, I was told, had been a great beauty. Suspected, among other things, of having bewitched Cheikh's son, Sid Ahmed, the three were reportedly put to death in early October 1928. Great caution should be exercised regarding the scattered and uncertain evidence regarding their case. Information collected at the time, if not distorted in memory, seems to have undergone reconstruction intended to orient colonial investigations. Besides, the administration was not really interested in learning more about the three slaves, or about their possible practices of witchcraft or their origins. Indeed, it showed more interest in the accused than in the victims. The probable extinction of this family at the time of the events made their perpetuation in memory through genealogy impossible. Here as elsewhere, subordinate groups are left in history's shadow. But their memory is inscribed in geography: a place name, le-Mdenet el-Abid (slave hill), is said to be the site of the execution and burial of two of these slaves, but also in this case, their identity is not certain.

REMOTE VAMPIRISM

As a first step, it is necessary to explain Bizhan beliefs about magic, particularly the remote vampirism that led to the death of the three slaves. Many varieties of magical practices are known in Mauritania: divination, relations with the *Jnunn*,[9] propitiatory rites, protective objects, and so forth. Not all of these are socially condemned. The major religious figures are also known for their supernatural powers, first among them *baraka*, in part inherited, in part acquired, which gives its holder blessing, protection, and fortune of divine origin that his disciples may hope to acquire through contact, perhaps indirect (an item of clothing, the dregs in a glass), or even through incantation (this is true of the Ahel Barikallah as a whole as descendants of the saint and miracle worker Ahmed Bezeid). Some families are known to possess a *sirr* (secret) that has been handed down, which gives access to various supernatural powers (this is true of the family of Abd El Aziz Ould sheikh Mohamd El Mami). Still others are *hajjabe* and have the ability to produce talismans (*hajab*) for specific magical actions. There is a distinction between *hajab ebyad* (white talisman) and *hajab ekhal* (black talisman), one of Islamic inspiration (notably through the use of verses from the Koran), unlike the other. Finally, there is what is considered witchcraft (*sihr*), although it is condemned by Muslim orthodoxy because it is maleficent.[10]

It is impossible to know what were the magical practices of the accused slaves, or even if there really were any. Both archives and recollections carry only the label of "witchcraft."

---

[6] I use *qabila* (pl. *qabail*) rather than the ambiguous "tribe." A *qabila* is a family group with a common ancestor from whom the group's name is usually taken.

[7] The largest religious *qabila* in the Sahel (the vast coastal region straddling Mauritania and Spanish Sahara).

[8] To facilitate understanding and in the absence of phonetic spelling, I have adopted the spelling most commonly used by colonial administrators.

[9] Known in the West from the tales of the Arabian Nights, genies (*jnunn* in Hassaniyya) make up a parallel world to the visible world. Their existence is attested by the Koran.

[10] The Koran explicitly condemns recourse to *sihr*. The word is ambiguous and can designate any magical practice. On magical customs and their judgment by Islam, see C. Hames (ed.), *Coran et talisman: Textes et pratiques magiques en milieu musulman* (Paris, 2007).

This may only be a matter of perspective, just as Haitian voodoo is a religion seen from the inside and witchcraft seen from the outside.[11] Whether the three slaves engaged in real magical practices – the cult of ancestors, for example – or were suspected "by nature" of following these occult practices is now impossible to determine. Their Muslim names tell us nothing – they were perhaps merely names given them by the purchaser with a view toward eradicating old attachments or practices. All we have are the accusations made by the group that killed them, because confessions under beating, torture, or the threat of being shot obviously have no value in themselves.[12]

The real confessions available have essentially to do with suspicions of bewitchment by supposed victims and by their social milieu.[13] Some attribute their designation to the recourse to divination, or the word of an unidentified visitor. All agree that they arrived preceded by their reputation as *sellal*. *Sell* is a process by which the *sellal* (pl. *sellale*) sucks the blood of his victim, the *meslul*, from a distance.[14] It is considered *sihr* (witchcraft), although the *sehhar* (sorcerer) and the *sellal* (extractor) are generally not the same individuals. The appearance of phenomena akin to *sell* was certainly enough to designate them as suspect.

The existence of *sell* is recognized by its effects. The sudden appearance of unexplained illnesses, particularly the loss of consciousness, leads to its diagnosis. According to testimonies I collected, food shortages, particularly the lack of meat, give rise to accusations of *sell*. Indeed, the *sellal* is said to suck the blood of his victims and "eat" their hearts for nourishment. He does it from a distance and invisibly, usually, it is believed, by looking – but it also can be done by talking to, or touching the victim or the victim's shadow. It is believed that the *sellal* can see his victim's heart and feed on it without the victim's knowledge. It is sometimes supposed that he has exchanged the heart with that of an animal. Most of the time, it is thought, the *sellal* acts consciously, but sometimes he is believed to be overwhelmed by this involuntary power, and attempts are made to eradicate it with a *hajab*.[15] A *hajab*, or consultation of a *hajjabe*, can also be used to establish the existence of *sell* or to unmask a *sellal*. It is also used as a preventive or a cure. Magical practices or objects

---

[11] See, for example, L. Hurbon, "Sorcellerie et pouvoir en Haïti," *Archives des sciences sociales des religions* 48:1 (1979), 43–52.

[12] Testimony at the time as well as present-day testimony, all acknowledging constraint, is very contradictory on the subject.

[13] Malicious gossip as the primary source on witchcraft is also true of Western Europe: "Unfortunately, we know less about what the sorcerers and witches themselves believed than what was believed about them. Possibly witches and sorcerers had more complicated emotions and systems of beliefs than those who believed in them. And this makes them more difficult to study." J. Caro Baroja, *The Witches and Their World*, trans. O. N. V. Glendinning (Chicago, 1964), 243. It therefore seems imprudent to conclude, following E. Ann McDougall, that *sell* may be "evidence of slave resistance against an oppressive master society." E. A. McDougall, "Slavery, Sorcery, and Colonial 'Reality' in Mauritania, c. 1910–60," in C. Youé and T. Stapleton (eds.), *Agency and Action in Colonial Africa: Essays for John E. Flint* (New York, 2001), 75. I would incline toward the contrary view, that it is a manifestation of the fear of the masters of an overthrow of the social order, which would occur if slaves began to control the fate of those who dominated them.

[14] The verb is *sell*, *isell* (tear off, remove, extract); in the south, more common is *mass*, *imass* (suck) for the same practice, and the person doing it is called *massa*.

[15] This does not make it possible to make an absolute distinction between witchcraft and sorcery, in Evans-Pritchard's terms, one unconscious and inherited, the other voluntary and acquired. E. E. Evans Pritchard, *Witchcraft, Oracles, and Magic among the Azande* (Oxford, 1937). In the case considered here, people seem to have believed rather in a possession or a gift. A piece of written testimony mentions that some slaves are "destined" for *sell* (letter of Ahmed Baba Ould Mohamed, presented later). In addition, Cheikh Ould Abd El Aziz is said to have attempted to eradicate the evil with a *hajab* (statement of Mohamed Ould Batta, Nouakchott, January 13, 2009, presented later).

imported from black Africa are reputed to be remedies for curing *meslul* or means of identifying a *sellal*. But usually, in the hope of curing the victim, an attempt is made to force the *sellal* to return the blood. Blows and torture are then customary, even if a threat may be enough. If the accused survives, an attempt is made to drive him off, and in the past, if he was a slave, he was sold. But a *sellal* may die before he has given back the blood, and it is sometimes said that he may be unable to return it. Accusations are sometimes made against blacksmiths and against Haratin,[16] but primarily against slaves. In the past, most recently acquired slaves were easily suspected because they both had the lowest status and were most foreign in the area.[17] Women seemed to be particularly targeted, although the accusation often was made against an entire family. Some regions and camps were reputed to be infested with *sellale*.

AN IMPORTED BELIEF?

Although Bizhan society harbors many magical practices and belief in witches' evil spells, several indications suggest that the specific belief in *sell* is imported.[18] One witness says that before this event, *sell* was unknown in the region (Ahmedou Ould Moni, later in the chapter). Nor does it appear to be a belief originating in the Maghreb. In his detailed research on magic in Morocco, Algeria, and Tunisia, Edmond Doutté does not mention any form of vampirism.[19] But the belief is found in black Africa, and among the Bizhan, black populations have the reputation of being powerful sorcerers.[20]

In the earliest known description of *sell*, Ahmed Lemin ech-Chingiti reports the prevalence of this type of witchcraft in the towns of the trab el-Bizhan in the nineteenth century, particularly in his town, Tidjikja.[21] The residents called on an exorcist from black Africa, probably from the Niger valley, to counter the practices of their Bambara slaves. He identified them by fumigation and proceeded to eradicate their power by causing vomiting. But because the practices continued, the suspects were massacred, which, according to the author, sharply reduced the number of cases. Always in the nineteenth century, there is a very interesting description of beliefs in forms of vampirism farther west, among the Wolof of Senegambia. The book describes "soul eaters" thirsting after blood and acting invisibly. What is particularly instructive is that the people convicted of being sorcerers were made slaves and "sold to the Moors of the desert."[22] But although *sell* appears to be part of beliefs

---

[16] The Haratin are a social group of dependents, reputedly of slave origin but free, traditionally employed in agriculture and small animal raising.

[17] There is a persistent rumor that blacksmiths are the descendants of Jews.

[18] This idea is developed by E. A. McDougall, "Slavery, Sorcery, and Colonial 'Reality' in Mauritania." However, she wrongly identifies witchcraft in general with the particular case of *sell*.

[19] E. Doutté, *Magie et religion dans l'Afrique du nord* (Algiers, 1909). He does mention the belief in witches flying on broomsticks, who suck blood, in Kheibar in Arabia, *Magie et religion*, 51.

[20] This belief is shared farther north: "Blacks are generally thought of throughout the Maghreb as particularly adept at witchcraft," *Magie et religion*, 34.

[21] A. L. Ech Chenguiti, *El Wasît*, trans. Mourad Teffahi (Saint-Louis du Sénégal, 1953). Ann McDougall's article includes a summary of this passage in English. The author speaks only of *sihr* (witchcraft) in his description, never of *sell* (vampirism from a distance) (Personal communication from Abdel Wedoud Ould Cheikh, April 2009). It is probable that his audience of eastern Arabs (the Arabic original was published in Cairo) would not have understood the second expression. Trab el-Bizhan means the land of the Bizhan, an expression designating the territory occupied by Hassaniya-speakers, roughly from Goulimime in southern Morocco to Timbuktu in Mali and Saint-Louis du Sénégal.

[22] Abbé P. D. Boilat, *Esquisses sénégalaises* (Paris, 1853), 315ff. Thanks to Alice Bellagamba for this reference.

existing further south, since the nineteenth century it has been adapted to the ways of life and beliefs of the Sahara.

A link has been made between vampirism and shortages of meat, an essential food source for nomadic herders. Some evidence suggests a connection between episodes of famine and accusations of *sell*. It turns out that food shortages brought many slave owners to sell off their slaves. Instead of recognizing the economic reasons for such sales, it was frequently believed that they were a way of getting rid of the cause of misfortune. Further, because a slave sale was a consequence of famine, people were inclined to believe the slave himself was the famine's cause. This derives from a vision of the world in which the search for a solution to a problem is reduced to the search for and neutralization of an agent, a person responsible.[23] In addition, as Ann McDougall has pointed out, *sell* shares with the everyday evil eye (*'ayn*) some common characteristics: action through the gaze and the motive of envy or jealousy. Slaves were not the only ones suspected of such practices. Blacksmiths, traditionally accused of witchcraft, were also held in suspicion, an adaptation of the belief to older patterns. More generally, changes in or the persistence of patterns of local political domination were largely interpreted in terms of magical practices, at least by religious groups who feared that *sell* might lead to a reversal of the existing social hierarchy.

Colonial administrators sometimes echoed these beliefs in *sell*, which seemed particularly prevalent in southern Adrar in the 1930s. In his 1936 "political report on the subdivision of Atar," Busquet devotes two pages to a "note on witchcraft,"[24] and observes that in southern Tungad, these cases of remote vampirism have overshadowed all other questions. *Hajjabe* had worked out remedial practices, but executions were frequent, with female slaves as the principal victims. Hesitating between repression and permissiveness, Busquet points out the dilemma faced by the colonial administration: "Here too, political and administrative considerations conflict. Should we pretend to adopt the beliefs of the Moors or repress all violence against these alleged witches and simply deny their existence?"[25]

Frequent in the past, *sell* is now in the process of disappearing.[26] These changes are probably connected to the end of the slave trade, which produced a scarcity of new slaves of unknown origin with unfamiliar customs. It may also be related to improvements in food and sanitary conditions and to the progress of education. The affair under consideration seems to have been the first that came to the attention of the administration.[27] Out of the large amount of information that has been gathered I have chosen to present three documents from the archives and excerpts from two interviews. Before, however, I will describe the course of events.

---

[23] See A. Zempleni, "La 'maladie' et ses 'causes'," *L'Ethnographie*, 96–97 (1985): 13–44.

[24] Busquet does not distinguish between *sell* and *sihr*. Many passages from this document have been translated into English by E. A. McDougall, "Slavery, Sorcery, and Colonial 'Reality.'"

[25] ARIM E1–8 (?) (the classification number is not fully legible). Political report on the subdivision of Atar, July 1936. On the language of administrators about slavery, see B. Acloque, "Embarras de l'administration coloniale: La question de l'esclavage au début du XXe siècle en Mauritanie," in M. Villasante-de Beauvais (ed.), *Groupes serviles au Sahara* (Paris, 2000), 97–119.

[26] One case of the execution of a Haratin for that reason was reported less than ten years ago.

[27] The cases of witchcraft in Adrar and Tagant known to the administration since 1900 and catalogued by Ann McDougall do not seem to clearly involve *sell* before 1934, with the possible exception of a case in 1922.

HOW THE EVENTS UNFOLDED

The correspondence between various administrative bodies shows that reports of what happened to the two slave brothers and their sister climbed the administrative ladder in the following way. In late October 1928, Mohamed Ould Ely, chief of the *qabila* of the Ouled El Lab designated by the French administration, informed the commander of the circle of Adrar[28] of a widespread rumor in northwestern Mauritania (Agneitir and Inchiri) concerning the execution by Cheikh Ould Abd El Aziz, an Ahel Barikallah notable, of three of his slaves accused of witchcraft. The location of the events was not yet clearly established, but it was at the junction of three territorial administrations:[29] the circles of Trarza, Adrar, and the Baie du Lévrier. Battalion commander Dufour, in charge of the administration of Adrar, entrusted the investigation to the neighboring administration of Trarza, in this case to the Nomad Group led by Lieutenant Génin. Génin went to the region where the events had occurred and conducted some discreet interrogations of witnesses. He reported the information he had gathered and his conclusions in a report dated November 19, 1928 (presented in full later in the chapter). On November 29, the commander of the circle of Adrar sent a telegram to the governor of Mauritania briefly setting out the facts. He informed him that the protagonists would soon be coming to see him and asked his superior which administrative body was authorized to pursue the investigation.

In his November 30, 1928 political report, Captain Bousquet, commander of the circle of the Baie du Lévrier, the territory where the events had occurred, mentions the affair.[30] On December 1, the governor of Mauritania radioed the circle of Adrar that the circle of the Baie du Lévrier had administrative authority. In January, various participants were brought before Captain Bousquet in Port-Étienne to present testimony. Two of them were interrogated, one as an accused (Cheikh Ould Abd El Aziz, whose report is reproduced later), the other as a witness (his nephew, Mohamed Abdallahi Ould Mohamed Ould Abd El Aziz), on January 29 and 30. Choteau, of the government of Mauritania, heard of this and expressed concern about the consideration owed to Cheikh Ould Abd El Aziz in a letter to his subordinate on February 2, 1929. His letter crossed one from Bousquet dated February 3 reporting the interrogations conducted at Port-Étienne, in which, he said in a February 8 letter, Cheikh Ould Abd El Aziz, "as well as those who accompanied him to Port-Étienne, were treated with all appropriate consideration."

Embarrassed by the number and status of the people involved, including the chief of the neighboring *qabila* of the Ouled Bou Sba,[31] Bousquet referred back to the governor of Mauritania before rendering any judgment. In addition to transcripts of interrogations, he attached to his letter various letters in support of Cheikh Ould Abd El Aziz (a translation of one, from Ahmed Baba Ould Mohamed Ould Abd El Aziz, Cheikh's nephew and official

---

[28] The circle was the lowest-level administrative region of the colony of Mauritania to which the listed *qabail* or groups were attached. The administrator in charge of a circle was usually called a commander, even if he was a civilian.

[29] At the time, the region of Inchiri was attached to the circle of Adrar. The post of Akjoujt was not made a circle until 1931.

[30] I have not been able to locate this document, which is mentioned in another letter.

[31] The Ouled Bou Sba are a large *qabila* of traders, who mostly came to Mauritania in the early nineteenth century, that imposed its presence by arms. For this reason it was in a state of conflict with almost all the *qabail* of the region.

head of the Ahel Habiballah, is presented later in the chapter). The governor of Mauritania, for his part, received tribal delegations favorable to the accused at Saint-Louis.[32]

Then, on February 18, the governor of Mauritania, who postdated the events to January 1929, brought the affair to the attention of the governor general's office for French West Africa (Afrique Occidentale Française or AOF) in Dakar. He sent most of the documents[33] and, setting out political reasons, asked for authority "to stop the pending judicial action." This was granted in a letter from Carde, of the Directorate of Political and Administrative Affairs, on March 13, 1929, which suggested that the only sanction against the murderers be a "particularly harsh warning." This decision was transmitted to the circle of the Baie du Lévrier in a letter dated March 25, 1929. As far as I know, there is no trace of the certainly oral reprimand.[34]

The event, which allegedly occurred in early October 1928,[35] was attested by the French administration in November. The AOF governor general was officially informed in February 1929, and in late March the case was closed. Six long months of investigations and debates were needed to finally dismiss what might have led to a troublesome trial.

SOME HISTORICAL BACKGROUND

To grasp the complexity and delicacy of the affair, it is necessary to have a sense of the context. By the late 1920s, France had been present in Mauritania for about thirty years. After a lengthy and conflict-ridden relationship between the colony of Sénégal and the various Bizhan *qabail* moving through the Sahara, it occupied Trarza in 1902, founded Port-Étienne in 1906,[36] and gained a foothold in Adrar after a large-scale military campaign. But it still had incomplete control over vast desert regions. Armed resistance to the colonial administration did not come to an end until 1934.

Tijirit, where the events took place, is a 400-mile-long corridor wedged between two ranges of dunes running from northeast to southwest, Azefall and Akchar. The region was traversed at long intervals by Nomadic Groups, military units mounted on camels, more intent on marking their presence felt than conducting effective policing. The camel-raising populations were administered by the three circles of Adrar (Atar), Trarza (Boutilimit), and the Baie du Lévrier (Port-Étienne). A military post then under the jurisdiction of Adrar, Akjoujt, although closer, was located 100 hard miles from the site of the murders. The Spanish border, on the other side of which another part of the nomadic population

---

[32] Although located in Sénégal, Saint-Louis remained the capital of Mauritania until the eve of independence.

[33] Even though they date the events to early October 1928. Was the January date just a mistake? In a preliminary draft, Carde was already writing "in the second half of January." I have found no satisfactory explanation for this difference in dates.

[34] Aside from the file from the Dakar archives (ANS 9G86 (107)), which contains the correspondence from the governor general, I consulted Mauritanian archives, in which I located some documents (ARIM E1–75) containing the correspondence of the governor of Mauritania, but the condition of the files suggests that documents might have been lost or mislaid. Other information may be in the local archives of Nouadhibou (formerly Port-Étienne) and Atar.

[35] According to the testimony of Mohamed Ould Batta later in the chapter, it is possible that the execution happened around August.

[36] Military control there was long limited to the peninsula of Cap Blanc. An edited book on this port city on the border with the former Spanish Sahara is now in preparation: *Nouadhibou: Fortunes et infortunes de la "capitale économique" mauritanienne* (provisional title), B. Acloque (ed.).

was officially located, although it crossed the border freely, was only 120 miles away.[37] On the Spanish side, the administration was confined to the fishing and trading centers of La Agüera and mainly Villa Cisneros.

The French occupation, which was chronically undermanned, relied on religious groups (Zwaya, Tolba, or Mrabtin, known as *marabouts* in the colonial archives) that had some interest in securing colonial protection against warrior groups called Hassan or 'Arab. The return for this support was respect for the customs of the Bizhan, the most important of which was Muslim law and property. Most disputes were therefore heard by the *qadi zawaya*, with the appeal courts and criminal courts presided by the circle commanders. In this framework, slavery could not be combated as such. Recognized by *shari'a*, and more importantly by the Koran, a slave, as in Roman law, had a status distinct from that of a free man. As a commodity, he was completely dependent on his master, whose consent was necessary even for him to choose a mate. His freedom of action was dependent on the degree of trust his master placed in him. The administration, it seems, had not tolerated any slave trading between its African possessions since the decree of December 12, 1905. But property transfers, notably through inheritance, were not blocked. Administrators also worried about harsh treatment, which was also denounced in *shari'a*.

The events took place in the territory of the Ahel Barikallah, a large *qabila* of Zwaya; the land through which they traveled, extending for more than 500 miles, overlapped the boundary between Mauritania and Spanish Sahara. Their aura had increased the number of their *tlamid* (students, disciples, sg. *telmidi*) and their wealth the number of their slaves. The category *tlamid* is very broad and includes free dependents who pay a variable tribute, as well as sometimes powerful warriors seeking supernatural protection. The administration had divided the Ahel Barikallah into six groups; the events had taken place in the territory of the Ahel Habiballah, near the coast. In the nineteenth century, the Ahel Habiballah had been led by the great figure sheikh Mohamd el-Mami, both a *wali* (saint) and an *'alim* (doctor of the law), whose legal controversies were known throughout the trab el-Bizhan. The leadership had remained in his family, passing through his son Abd El Aziz, his grandson Mohamed, to his great grandson Ahmed Baba, who had just taken over at the time of the events. His uncle Cheikh, the owner of the slaves, had, it appears, been removed from the succession because of his non-*zawiyya* mother, of the Ouled Tidrarin. In this context, the colonizers wondered about what sanctions to impose for the death of the three slaves.

The first issue was legal. The administrators were aware that the murder of the three slaves could be similar to the execution of a sentence, passed, of course, by a body normally considered unauthorized by the French because crimes came under the jurisdiction of the circle commander. Each administrator pointed it out in his way: the population would see this as a pronouncement of capital punishment after a legitimate trial from the point of view of Muslim law and tradition. Convicted of witchcraft, the accused were executed by the legitimate authority – their owner. Captain Bousquet confirmed this: "It is appropriate to take into account the fact that all of them believe themselves to be covered by Muslim law and that they acted exactly as their ancestors would have. I have consulted the Muslim code by 'Khallil,' who says in article 1958 that 'pursuit of the crime and application of the

---

[37] On this border and the way it was perceived over time, see B. Acloque, "L'idée de frontière en milieu nomade," in M. Villasante Cervello (ed.), *Colonisations et héritages actuels au Sahara et au Sahel* (Paris, 2007), II, 351–382.

penalty is the prerogative of the magistrate alone, and as an exception to the owner of the guilty party if he is of servile condition, unmarried, or married to a slave.' That is the case here." In any event, this fact led the administration to avoid a public trial where the contradiction between colonial and Muslim law might come to the fore, which would be politically harmful.

Next came the question of responsibility. The person directly responsible was identified by the administration as Cheikh Ould Abd El Aziz, seconded by his two sons, Mohamed Nami and Sid Ahmed. But the general opinion among the population was that he was not only a guilty party but also a victim. His son was the one who was chiefly affected by their witchcraft, but as the governor general of the AOF pointed out, taking account of property rights over slaves in Muslim law: "There is no doubt that in the eyes of the Moors, in this case the real civil harm was suffered entirely by the current owner of the victims, that is, by the principal co-perpetrator of the attack." Moreover, opinions converged in seeing the events less as individual acts than as the effect of collective fanaticism. More than on those directly responsible for the murder, the administrators emphasized the complicity of the entire camp, the Ahel Barikallah as a whole, and even the neighboring Ouled Bou Sba. The governor of Mauritania pointed out their lack of full authority over these *qabail* on both sides of the border: "In fact, the Ahel Barikallah of Port-Étienne, like the Ouled Bou Sba, are 'protected' rather than really 'administered' nomads." If there was fear of the military power of the Ouled Bou Sba and the "prickly" personality of Sidi M'Bareck, the leader of the Démouissat cited by name, with regard to the Ahel Barikallah, the worry was about the influence of the family of the Ahel Abd El Aziz. The governor wrote: "The personality of Cheikh Ould Abd El Aziz and the religious and political influence his family has acquired in the Sahel, an influence that from the beginning of the occupation to the present has always been put at our service, are worth considering in a region bordering on Rio De Oro in which our political action has not yet produced all the results we expect it to have."[38] He also expressed his worry to the governor of the AOF that repression that was too harsh would be "exploited against [them], if not by the authorities in the neighboring colony at least by dissidents and nomads of the Sahel who are hostile to us."

What sanctions would be appropriate given these political interests? All levels of the hierarchy agreed they should avoid any punishment that might be considered humiliating by Cheikh Ould Abd El Aziz. Following the advice of his subordinates, the governor of Mauritania suggested to the governor of the AOF a verbal reprimand of Cheikh accompanied by a collective fine. The Directorate of Political Affairs of the AOF, through Carde, acknowledged that "considering the serious reasons of a political order invoked, [it cannot but] share [his] way of thinking as to the necessity of there being no judicial consequences of the witchcraft affair." The fine was excluded, because the laws invoked did not apply in this case. Indemnification of the victims' relatives that had been spontaneously envisaged was excluded allegedly because there were none (although that was never established). This was a response to explicit political concerns that might be provoked by the public search for any relatives.

---

[38] In several documents, the importance given to the support of the Ahel Abd El Aziz is evident. The administration seemed to have blind faith in their reliability. But it is hard to know how real this support was. The manipulative skills of these clever politicians, as we shall see, cast doubt on their apparently unshakeable loyalty.

The authorities merely issued a respectful oral reprimand. We have no knowledge of the tenor of what was said to Cheikh. Was he told that he had narrowly escaped a death sentence? We have no way of knowing, but that is unlikely, especially because it was never mentioned in the documents. Based on the information they had gathered, the administrators had opted for a solution that was least likely to cause political trouble. Yet questions remain about the sincerity of the investigation. There is no space here to bring out the contradictions in the facts reported that an attentive reading reveals.[39] They are what induced me to question people who might have preserved memories of the events. At a distance of eighty years, despite failings of memory, the outline of the story takes on a different cast.

I was able to speak to a dozen people whose testimony points in the same direction. I offer two examples later in the chapter: one from the great grandson of Cheikh Ould Abd El Aziz and grandson of Sid Ahmed (the alleged victim of witchcraft), Mohamed Ould Batta, who told me the story known in his family; the other from Ahmedou Ould Moni, an old man in the region from a nearby *qabila*, the el-Graa, who knew various people involved in the story. According to various sources, Cheikh was in no way implicated in the murder of the three slaves. At the time of the events he was in Atar, nearly 400 miles from the scene.[40] It was his son, Mohamed Nami, who, believing his brother Sid Ahmed had been bewitched by the three slaves, tried to make them give back the blood and then executed them with his rifle.[41] Fearing prosecution by the administration, Mohamed Nami allegedly tried to leave French-controlled territory. Halted in his flight by relatives from a neighboring *qabila*, the el-Graa, he looked for another way out.[42] It was probably a delegation from the Ahel Habiballah, mentioned at the time of the events, that took charge of working out an account of the events that would have less harmful consequences.

The official version gathered by the administration was thus quite different from the facts remembered.[43] Despite their divergences on many details, understandable given the lapse of time, the general sense of the testimonies – particularly the sole responsibility of Mohamed Nami Ould Cheikh – seems highly probable. To save Mohamed Nami from the wrath of the colonial administration, it seems that a fictitious version of events was developed to which all witnesses, with a few slips, conformed. In his deposition, Cheikh voluntarily assumed responsibility for the death of the slaves, in place of his son. One might assume that it was a way, risky for himself, to mask the illegality of the execution from a Muslim perspective, because only a master can accept the execution of his slave because it is his possession that has been harmed. He may also have known that the administration would not dare punish him, whereas his son was more vulnerable.

What was the strategy used to mislead the colonial administration? On the basis of some indications,[44] I can formulate a few hypotheses. Information available to us in the archives was collected by three military officers: Battalion Chief Dufour in Atar, Lieutenant Génin in the region of Tijirit, and Captain Bousquet in Port-Étienne. The known sources of

---

[39] Some remarks on this issue are in the notes to the documents presented later.

[40] According to Mohamed Ould Batta (testimony later in the chapter), he was engaged in the *getna* (date harvest) in Adrar, which would place the events in or around August 1928.

[41] See the testimony of Mohamed Ould Batta later in the chapter.

[42] See the testimony of Ahmedou Ould Moni, Joffriyat (Agneitir), January 10, 2009, presented later in the chapter.

[43] The administration's investigation and the oral reprimand seem to have left no traces in memories.

[44] See particularly the testimony of Ahmedou Ould Moni later in the chapter.

information were: the voluntary testimony of Mohamed Ould Ely (chief of the Ould El Lab in Atar), information gathered in Tijirit by Lieutenant Génin (particularly from Mohamed Abdallahi Ould Mohamed Ould Abd El Aziz and from some unnamed Ouled Bou Sba, presented later), the interrogations of Cheikh Ould Abd El Aziz (presented later) and again of Mohamed Abdallah Ould Mohamed Ould Abd El Aziz conducted in Port-Étienne in late January 1929, the undated letters of support for the accused from Ahmed Baba Ould Mohamed Ould Abd El Aziz (nephew and nominal chief of the group to which the principal accused belonged),[45] from an assembly of important notables of Adrar (including the emir), and from Mohamed Ould Khalil (chief of a part of the powerful *qabila* of the Rgueibat). Finally the governor general of Mauritania received delegations of Rgueibat, Ouled Delim, and Ouled Bou Sba – that is, the preponderant *qabail* of the Sahel still partly in conflict with French authorities, as well as the emir of Trarza and sheikh Sidati of the Ahel sheikh Sidiyya (an influential religious *qabila* of Trarza close to the colonial administration), who had come to "intercede on behalf of Cheikh Ould Abd el Aziz and his accomplices."

In addition to the statements of all the Ahel Habiballah, it was also necessary to turn to testimony from figures outside the group in order to substantiate the official version of the facts. That is where relations established with their warrior *tlamid* turned out to be decisive. The Ahel Barikallah mobilized their networks of allies, dependents, and relatives. Mohamed Ould Ely, of the Ouled El Lab, informed the commander of the circle of Adrar, and the Ouled El Lab were the closest allies of the Ahel Barikallah. According to the testimony of Ahmedou Ould Moni,[46] Cheikh Ould Mouknass of the Ahel Laghzal informed the commander of the circle of Port-Étienne, where he represented the el-Graa, and he used his influence to delay the outcome. The Ahel Laghzal were *tlamid* very close to the Ahel Abd El Aziz. It also seems that a central role was played by his relatives from a family of the Ahel Boutrig (el-Graa) in preventing the flight of Mohamed Nami into Spanish territory, which certainly would have designated him as guilty in the eyes of the colonial administration. Finally, written testimony came first from Mohamed Ould el-Khalil of the Rgueibat, who was the personal *telmidi* of Cheikh Ould Abd El Aziz, but also from the emir of Adrar, whose family had long enjoyed the ritual protection of the Ahel Barikallah. In addition, the warrior *qabail* were on good terms with the Ahel Barikallah, who had no reason to fear harmful statements from them and could expect support from most of them. The same thing was true of the neighboring religious *qabail* (Ahel Elfagha Khattat, Ahel Hadj El Moctar, Ahel Mohamed Salem, Ida Ou Ali, and Smacide), who joined their support to that of the emir of Adrar.[47] Only the Ouled Bou Sba had tense relations with the Ahel Barikallah, and, rightly or wrongly,[48] the Ahel Barikallah tried to protect themselves by discrediting the testimony of the Ouled Bou Sba. This is why Mohamed Ould el-Khalil wrote in his letter that "the Ouled Bou Sba heightened the accusations because of their enmity against the Ahel Abd El Aziz." The Ahel Barikallah also implicated the Ouled Bou Sba in the affair (according to the statements of Mohamed Abdallahi Ould Mohamed Ould

---

[45] One of his letters sets out the jurisprudence concerning slaves' witchcraft (presented later), the other warns against "slanderers."

[46] See the testimony of Ahmedou Ould Moni later in the chapter.

[47] Who was then Sid Ahmed Ould Ahmed Ould Sid Ahmed Ould Aïda.

[48] We know nothing of the statements made at the time by the members of this *qabila*. A delegation nonetheless did come to support the Ahel Barikallah (probably because of internal divisions), according to the governor of Mauritania.

Abd El Aziz and of Cheikh, presented later in the chapter), although no current informer remembers their presence. Finally, the two Tendra mentioned as present during the events by Cheikh Ould Abd El Aziz (presented later) were his brothers-in-law, the maternal uncles of Sid Ahmed and Mohamed Nami. By neutralizing discordant voices, this was the way in which the Ahel Barikallah prompted the construction of an official version of the events for the colonial administration.[49]

QUESTIONS TO CONSIDER

1. What conclusions did Lieutenant Génin reach? What were his sources?
2. Why is the testimony of Cheikh Ould Abd El Aziz contained in the archives to be read with caution?
3. What does Ahmed Baba Ould Mohamed Ould Abd El Aziz try to bring out in his letter?
4. What can be said about what Cheikh and his son Mohamed Nami thought of the danger posed by the three slaves, according to the testimony of Mohamed Ould Batta?
5. How does Ahmedou Ould Moni bring to the fore the action of his *qabila* in defense of the interests of the Ahel Abd El Aziz?

TERMINOLOGY

Bizhan (sg. *Bizhani*) – Ethnic group called also Moors inhabiting the whole western Sahara. It designates particularly people of free ascendance.

Hajab – Talisman product by a *hajjabe*.

Haratin (sg. *Hartani*) – Statutory group of reputed slave origin but free, in a clientelist relationship with their master. It can also be a euphemism for slave ('*Abd*).

Hassan or '*Arab* – Noble statutory group of warlike honor.

Hassaniyya – Arabic dialect spoken by inhabitants between Goulimime (Morocco) to Saint-Louis (Senegal) and Timbuktu (Mali). It is the vernacular language in Mauritania and Western Sahara.

Qabila (pl. *qabail*) – Tribe in the sense of patrilinear family group, which refers to a common ancestor.

Sell – Specific sorcery made by a *sellal* (pl. *sellale*) who sucks from a distance the blood of a *meslul*, his victim.

Sihr – Witchcraft practiced by a *sehhar* (sorcerer).

Tlamid (sg. *Telmidi*) or students, disciples. For *Zwaya*, people following them, as well as free dependents who pay a variable tribute and warriors recognizing their supernatural power.

Zwaya, Tolba, or *Mrabtin* – Noble statutory group of religious values, more commonly known as *marabouts* in the colonial terminology.

---

[49] Doubt remains as to the administration's ignorance, particularly that of the governor of Mauritania, regarding the artificial construction of the Ahel Habiballah's defense. The embarrassment of the colonial authorities over the question of slavery suggests that they may have been showing accommodating stance. See Acloque, "Embarras de l'administration coloniale."

DOCUMENTS

1. Génin Report

Tifersas[50] November 19, 1928
Mauritania
Nomad Group[51] of Trarza
No. 639 A

Copy[52]

*Report of Lieutenant Génin, commander of the Nomad Group of Trarza;
Concerning murders committed in the camp of Cheikh Ould Abd El Aziz.*

Toward the end of October 1928 the rumor spread through the nomadic tribes in Agneitir and Inchiri[53] that Cheikh Ould Abd El Aziz, of the tribe of the Ahel Barikallah, had put to death three of his servants accused of practicing witchcraft. This information was conveyed by Mohamed Ould Ely, chief of the Ouled El Lab,[54] to the battalion chief commanding the Adrar circle,[55] who charged me with conducting an investigation.

I went to Agneitir and the Tijirit[56] to question, without prior warning, the witnesses to the events. In particular, I collected the statements from two Ouled Bou Sba notables[57] and from Mohamed Abdallahi Ould Mohamed Ould Abd El Aziz, nephew of Cheikh Ould Abd El Aziz.

From these statements and various information reaching the Nomad Group, the following conclusions can be drawn:

1. With respect to the facts themselves, no doubt should remain.[58] In early October in a camp located to the west of Bou Rabrah,[59] two servants of Cheikh Ould Abd El Aziz, named Hamadi and Souélim, and a female servant named Zénabou, accused of practicing

---

[50] For clarity, names of places and persons have been uniformly presented in the form most common in the colonial period. This is also the case for the notes. Tifersas is located north of Akjoujt, more than 100 miles northeast of the site of the events.

[51] Abbreviations have been replaced by complete words. Nomad Groups were mobile camel-mounted military units that marked the colonial presence in desert zones. Trarza is the region in southwestern Mauritania occupied by the French since 1902.

[52] In the document, which is typewritten unless otherwise indicated. This copy made in Port-Étienne (established in 1906 on the Nouadhibou Peninsula) was one of the seven documents initially sent to the central administration of Mauritania in Saint-Louis du Sénégal, transmitted to the governor general of French West Africa in Dakar.

[53] Agneitir is the coastal dune region near Cape Timiris, an extension of the dunes of Akchar. Inchiri is the rocky plain of the Akjoujt region in southeastern Akchar that in 1931 gave its name to a circle.

[54] The Ouled El Lab were a small warlike *qabila*, separated from their Ouled Delim cousins whom they led in the late nineteenth century and close allies of the Ahel Barikallah.

[55] The Adrar is the mountain range southeast of Sahel, the large northern coastal region of Trab el-Bizhan. It was made into a circle in 1909, following a difficult military conquest.

[56] The Tijirit is the long valley located between the lines of dunes of Azefall and Akchar, running 300 miles from northeast to southwest.

[57] The persons questioned from this *qabila* remain unknown.

[58] Génin's conclusions are the same as those reached by various administrators in their letters, despite blatant contradictions, particularly as to the unfolding of events, that came out in the depositions. See later in the chapter.

[59] Bou Ghabra on current maps, a well in the extreme southwest of Akchar.

witchcraft, were put to death.[60] Cheikh Ould Abd El Aziz beat Hamadi to death with a pestle; his elder son Mohamed Nami killed Souélim with a pistol, and his second son Sid Ahmed killed the female servant with a rifle shot. No one dreams of denying these facts; their notoriety is so great they cannot be questioned.

2. Cheikh Ould Abd El Aziz did not commit these murders entirely willingly.[61] Not that he was held back by a feeling of pity or respect for the laws, but because his avarice made him aware of the loss of wealth represented by the death of his servants. He resisted, hesitated, and acted only after having been urged on by his relatives, friends, and neighbors, and especially being threatened by the Ouled Bou Sba nomadic warriors in the region.[62]

3. All those who did not take part in the murder but nonetheless encouraged it have hastened to deny their responsibility by stating that they opposed the murder with all their strength, but they were not listened to. We can be sure that each of them will say "Cheikh Ould Abd El Aziz acted entirely alone. The servants are his and it's his business."[63]

4. The Ahel Barikallah are so afraid of reprisals from the Ouled Bou Sba that they prefer to bear alone the consequences of their actions and not to denounce the participation of the Ouled Bou Sba. Mohamed Abdallahi, who made the frankest statement, decided to speak only after having made protestations of his wish to harm no member of another tribe, to denounce no one, to not be the cause of friction between his tribe and the neighbors.[64] He does not like Cheikh Ould Abd El Aziz or his cousins, with whom he has often had disputes, and would be happy to affirm his influence on the tribe[65] of the Ahel Habiballah by taking charge of the settlement of this affair,[66] but although he conceded to me that the Ouled Bou Sba had driven the Ahel Habiballah to murder, he will probably not dare

---

[60] It is worth noting that the distinction between slaves according to sex adopts the local terminology that reserves *'abd* (slave) for a male slave and *khadem* (female servant) for a female slave. The identity of the slaves, their origin, and the possible practicing of witchcraft gave rise to no investigation by the administration. Slaves, even as victims of murder, were of little interest to administrators. In his letter 248 AP/d of March 13, 1929 (ANS 9G86 (107)), the director of political and administrative affairs of the AOF, however, wrote to the governor of Mauritania: "The victims were indeed 'born servants'; the transcript of one of the interrogations mentions that they had changed masters about thirty years ago; they had thus lost any contact with their natural relatives, whose domicile is unknown and who besides could not receive indemnification in these circumstances without provoking new political difficulties." If the change in masters thirty years earlier was indeed mentioned by the principal accused, it was not established (see later in the chapter). Moreover, nothing in the archive documents allows one to say that they were born slaves or that they had no existing family connections. As for the location of any possible relatives, nothing was done to establish it. Political questions undeniably trumped the exercise of justice.

[61] Phrase underlined in the margin.

[62] Phrase underlined in the margin. The pressure exerted by the Ouled Bou Sba, notoriously on bad terms with the Ahel Barikallah, was reiterated in all the colonial writings. And yet, a delegation of Ouled Bou Sba came to the administration to support the Ahel Barikallah (letter 8 BP from the lieutenant governor of Mauritania to the governor general of the AOF, February 18, 1929, ANS 9G86 (107)). Recent testimony attributes no role to them and does not even recall their presence (see later in the chapter).

[63] From the point of view of Islamic law, the master alone has the authority to inflict punishments of mutilation or death on his slaves. The emphasis witnesses apparently place on this point is worth noting.

[64] This was a frequent form of statement from the Ahel Barikallah as from most religious *qabila*, for whom reserve is the basis of diplomacy.

[65] Génin erroneously characterizes the Ahel Habiballah as a tribe. They were in fact one of the six groups of the Ahel Barikallah recognized by the French administration. It was the only one to be listed by the circle of the Baie du Lévrier (Port-Étienne).

[66] Among the Ahel Habiballah, the succession to the chieftainship of Mohamed Ould Abd El Aziz was still recent (1926). His brother Cheikh was allegedly excluded because the origin of his mother (Ouled Tidrarine) was not sufficiently noble in the eyes of the Ahel Barikallah and because of his judged-too-warlike conduct. His nephew Ahmed Baba Ould Mohamed Ould Abd El Aziz was quickly designated by the *djemaa* (assembly of notables), although his authority was never fully established, particularly over Cheikh.

repeat his deposition in contradiction to warriors who could bring their anger to bear on his tribe.

5. No one who witnessed the murder or heard about it has shown the slightest feeling of fright, regret, or pity. They all say they are convinced that the servants were witches, that they had caused the death of several people, that they had the power to steal the blood of their victims, and that for that reason they had to be done away with.[67] They invoke Muslim law, traditions and customs. No one has the feeling that a crime was committed. They only worry about the reactions of the French authority.

To sum up, we are in the presence of an act of collective fanaticism responsibility for which must be shared by all the notables in the region where it happened, whether marabouts or warriors.[68] But the principal instigators of the murder were the Ouled Bou Sba, in particular Sidi M'Bareck,[69] whose threats overcame the reluctance of the Ahel Habiballah.

Signed: Génin
Certified copy
At Port-Étienne, 30 January 1929,
Circle Commander
(Bousquet's signature)

2. Transcript of interrogation of Cheikh Ould Abd El Aziz

January 29, 1929[70]
Interrogation of Cheikh Ould Abd El Aziz[71]
January 29, at 9 AM[72]

---

[67] Administrative documents repeatedly use the term "witch" (*sorcier*), whereas vampirism, although identified with witchcraft, was clearly differentiated for the Bizhan.

[68] This sentence is underlined in the margin. The words "marabouts" and "warriors" adopt an indigenous distinction between the *Zwaya* noble groups, who do not bear arms and justify their position through religious authority, and the *'Arab*, who acquired their position by arms. The two groups, who have different codes of honor, consider intermarriages to be misalliances. Captain Bousquet in Port-Étienne and the lieutenant governor of Mauritania limited responsibility for the murders to the Ouled Bou Sba notables (warriors, at least as far as the colonial administration was concerned) and the Ahel Barikallah (*marabouts*).

[69] Sidi M'Bareck Ould Ahmed Baba, chief of the Démouissat, principal warrior group of the Ouled Bou Sba, was well enough known to the administration for it to be unnecessary to use his full name.

[70] Handwritten.

[71] Many typos and spelling and punctuation mistakes, made because of the direct transcription of the interrogation, have been corrected for greater clarity. Cheikh Ould Abd El Aziz was the principal person accused of the three murders. He was initially summoned to Atar like the others involved. But because it was established that the events took place in the territory of the circle of the Baie du Lévrier (Telegram no. 924A, Mauritania to Atar Circle, December 1, 1928, ARIM E1/75), he was heard in Port-Étienne by Captain Bousquet. Learning of his questioning, Governor Choteau of Mauritania wrote in a telegram (no. 403 P, February 2, 1929, ARIM E1/75) to his subordinate to "treat him with consideration and to urgently inform [him] of [his] opinion about [the] political repercussions [of] this affair and [the] solution that it would be appropriate [to] come to." In reply (no. 16 p, February 8, 1929, ARIM E1/75), Bousquet offers reassurances: Cheikh, "as well as those who accompanied him to Port-Étienne, have been treated with all the requisite consideration. All continued to enjoy complete freedom. In my opinion and for the reasons set out in my letter 14/P previously mentioned, this affair should be settled by making the Ahel Barikallah understand, without offending them, that in the future they will have to refrain from such acts."

[72] The next day at the same time, his nephew Mohammed Abdallahi Ould Mohamed Ould Abd El Aziz, who had already been heard by Génin, was questioned. I will point out the most important divergences

QUESTION: You are indicted[73] for having, in early October 1928, in the immediate vicinity of Bouir Dieri, in the region of Azefall,[74] in the circle of the Baie du Lévrier, killed by your own hand a person named Hamadi Ould Abd El Moyla[75] and contributed to the death of two other people: Souélim Ould Abd El Moyla, Hamadi's brother, and a woman named Zénabou, sister of the two others, all three in your service. What do you have to say in your defense?

ANSWER: Hamadi, Souélim, and Zénabou were my servants. I purchased them about thirty years ago[76] from Mohamed Delimine Ould Abdallahi of the Ideïkoub group (Ahel Barikallah).[77]

About six years ago, some witches in the service of the Ahel Mohamed Salem a marabout tribe of Adrar, were sentenced to death by the *djemaa*[78] of the Ahel Mohamed Salem for having practiced witchcraft.[79] Before they were killed, the convicts were questioned,[80] and confessed that the servants of Cheikh Ould Abd El Aziz, Hamadi, Souélim, and Zénabou had initiated them into these practices.

At that time, my father, the venerable marabout Abd El Aziz was still alive and asked me to kill my captives. I refused. My father said that since that was so I should leave the camp with my servants, which I did.[81]

between the two in the notes. On the other hand, his two sons, Sid Ahmed Ould Cheikh and Mohamed Nami Ould Cheikh, who were "deeply implicated, one [being] ill in his camp and the other in the north sent by the Ahel Barikallah to deal with a matter involving the return of camels," as Bousquet wrote (no. 14 P, February 3, 1929, ANS 9G86(107)), were not questioned.

[73] This is the only point at which there is a suggestion of a judicial proceeding against Cheikh Ould Abd El Aziz. The transmittal letter (no. 14 P, February 3, 1929, ANS 9G86 (107)) shows a reluctance to carry it out: "there was a preliminary investigation. Before continuing it, I thought I should explain the reasons for my reluctance to go any further."

[74] This well is more precisely located in southwestern Tijirit.

[75] The father's name of the slaves appears only three times in the whole documents: twice in this interrogation, once in the transmittal letter (no. 14 P, February 3, 1929, ANS 9G86(107)). The spelling is each time different: "Ould AB EL MOYLA," "OULD AB EL SOYLA," and "ould AB EL HOVLA." The appellation "Abd el . . ." is usual for Muslims. It means "slave of. . ." and it is followed by one of the ninety-nine names of God. It is not reserved for slaves. Cheikh father's name "Abd el Aziz," "slave of the Beloved," or of his nephew Mohamed "Abdallahi," "slave of God," are two examples. It might be "Abd el Moula," "slave of the Lord," which is why I use the closest spelling. In today's testimonies, neither name nor first names are known.

[76] Thirty years earlier, the French were not present in Mauritania. Repression of the slave trade, particularly enforced after the law of December 12, 1905, was thus not applicable if the transaction has taken place before that date. The statement may have taken that fact into account. That possibility is bolstered by the fact that they were in the prime of life in 1928 and, according to Mohamed Ould Batta (see later in the chapter), the fact that they had been tortured for witchcraft before their purchase. It is hard to imagine young children being tortured for that reason. Moreover, some remember that the events took place shortly after their arrival (Ahmedou Ould Moni, presented later).

[77] This is a mistake. The Ahel Barikallah had separated from the Ideïkoub in the seventeenth century. They were thus two independent, albeit related, *qabail*.

[78] A *djemaa* is an assembly of notables of varied composition that meets to make common decisions working toward a consensus.

[79] Mohamed Abdallahi Ould Mohamed Ould Abd El Aziz sets these events back "about ten years."

[80] The word is ambiguous. It may suggest the use of the torture technique called the question. It appears later on with the same ambiguity.

[81] Cheikh's father, Abd El Aziz Ould sheikh Mohamed El Mami, died at the very beginning of the twentieth century. There is certainly confusion here between him and Cheikh's brother, Mohamed Ould Abd El Aziz, chief of the Habiballah group, who died in 1926, which agrees with the statement of Mohammed Abdallahi Ould Mohamed Ould Abd El Aziz.

Afterward, everything was normal.[82]

About four months ago, I traveled to Atar; on my return to camp, my family told me: "While you were gone the servants Hamadi, Souélim, and Zénabou practiced witchcraft against the girl Aminetou Mint Cheikh, who was saved by the intervention of some Ouled Bou Sba who knew how to cure these ailments."

A few days later these same servants took the blood of my son Sid Ahmed. I was there and I could clearly see it. I am convinced of what I am saying. My second son Mohamed Nami had a gris-gris that he had gotten in Saint-Louis. He set the gris-gris beside the nose of his brother Sid Ahmed who, after breathing, said "it was Hamadi who took my heart."

I seized the servant Hamadi myself and told him to give back my son's heart. Hamadi answered: "I am not a witch and I haven't done anything."

I and my entourage, which includes many men of my tribe and of the Ouled Bou Sba, including Ahmed Salem Ould Abidine, Ahmed Baba Ould El Mami, El Hareitani Ould Sidi Béchir, hit Hamadi to make him confess. After he was beaten, Hamadi dragged himself to my son, placed his mouth on his heart, and my son immediately felt better. Hamadi was left alone.[83]

Two or three hours later, my son felt worse, and this time he accused Souélim.[84] Souélim was struck by me as well as by all those present.

The sister of Hamadi and Souélim was called, and when questioned she said that she and her two brothers had eaten the venerable marabout, my father Mohamed Abd El Aziz and his daughter Fatimatou and others.[85]

When my nephew, Chief Ahmed Baba, who was traveling further north, learned of these events, he sent me his father Mohamed Abdallahi[86] escorted by several others to kill the servants.

At the same time, Sidi Sinnie came to see me; he had been sent by Sidi M'Bareck, chief of the Ouled Bou Sba, who told me: "You have to kill your servants because they have eaten several Ouled Bou Sba." It was in the presence of five men of the Tendra marabout tribe named Mohamed El Mami Ould Moctar Lahi, his brother Sid Ahmed Ould Moctar Lahi,[87] I don't know the names of the three others, several Ouled Bou Sba, among whom I recognized Ahmed

82 According to Mohamed Abdallahi Ould Mohamed Ould Abd El Aziz, three or four years earlier, the three slaves "were again accused of stealing the blood of two Ouled Bou Sba of the family of the Ahel Sidi Béchir," then of causing the death of Mohamedun Ould Ahmed (Ahel Meki) and of Minita (Aminata or mint (daughter of)?) El Hajj Omar (Ahel Maouloud) of the Ahel Barikallah and of Toybani Ould Mohamed El Moctar of the Ideïkoub.

83 This account of events is confirmed by Mohamed Abdallahi Ould Mohamed Ould Abd El Aziz, who concluded: "Hamadi dragged himself to Sid Ahmed, who told us that Hamadi had given [him] back his blood, but no one saw the blood. Hamadi died a few moments later from the blows he had gotten from all of us."

84 According to Mohammed Abdallahi Ould Mohamed Ould Abd El Aziz, it was following another application of the *gris-gris* that Sid Ahmed accused Souélim.

85 The mistake here is obvious: Mohamed Ould Abd El Aziz was the brother of Cheikh Ould Abd El Aziz. He did have a daughter named Fatimatou. Their death was attributed to these three slaves by Mohamed Abdallahi Ould Mohamed Ould Abd El Aziz.

86 Another mistake: Mohamed Abdallahi Ould Mohamed Ould Abd El Aziz was the brother of Ahmed Baba Ould Mohamed Ould Abd El Aziz. Mohamed Abdallahi said he had been sent to his uncle to "tell him that he absolutely had to kill the three witches." He also said he arrived three days before Cheikh returned from his trip. According to him, Sid Ahmed complained that his blood had been taken. To the demand to give back the blood, Zénabou "answered that she had already given her part back, that Hamadi had not given his back." Hamadi had run away and only returned with Cheikh and Souélim three days later. The administration did not seem to have any doubts of the presence of both throughout the events. The delegation was probably sent after all of this in order to present a common version of events.

87 These were Cheikh's brothers-in-law, uncles of Mohamed Nami and Sid Ahmed.

Salem Ould Abidine, El Hareitani Ould Sidi Béchir, Ahmed Baba Ould El Mami,[88] and many Ahel Barikallah, among them the chief's brother named Mohamed Abdallahi Ould Abd El Aziz, Mohamed Sidamine, Ahmed Maraba, El Boukhari Ould Mohamed Mahmoud, Sidati Ould Ahmed Ha, Mohamed Labdor, Abd El Aziz Ould El Boukhari, El Boukhari Ould Sidi, and others, almost all the notables of our group,[89] that the three servants were killed.

The three servants were struck simultaneously by me and all the others until they died. We used sticks; the three servants were tied and lying on the ground. When they were dead, my sons Mohamed Nami and Sid Ahmed, the first with a pistol, the second with a 74 rifle, each fired one shot into the corpses of Hamadi and Souélim.[90]

Q: Were Hamadi and Souélim already dead when your two sons shot them?

A: Yes, that is certain. They had already been dead for two or three hours when my sons shot at the corpses of Hamadi and Souélim.[91]

Q: Don't you regret the act you committed and have been charged with that cost the life of three of your servants?

A: Yes, I regret the death of my three servants because that deprives me of a considerable source of income. But what they did deserved death. It is our law that our fathers taught us. We only obeyed their will and the will of God. We are not reprehensible.[92]

Q: Were you asked to kill your three servants?

A: Yes. My nephew, chief of the Ahel Barikallah[93] and Sidi M'Bareck, chief of the Ouled Bou Sba, particularly insisted, and in short all the Ahel Barikallah and Ouled Bou Sba notables demanded the death of my servants insistently. I was forced to surrender my servants to the vengeance of my brother,[94] chief Ahmed Baba, Sidi M'Bareck, chief of the Ouled Bou Sba, and all the notables.[95] I admit that I hit the servants myself, I was angry at them. But everyone who was there hit them as I did.

---

[88] These were the only three people outside the Habiballah whose presence was confirmed by the statements Mohamed Abdallahi Ould Mohamed Ould Abd El Aziz.

[89] These were probably the members of the delegation of Habiballah sent by the chief of the group Ahmed Baba mentioned earlier.

[90] The two versions diverge seriously. According to Mohamed Abdallahi Ould Mohamed Ould Abd El Aziz, the death of the slaves was not decided on; it was the result of beating them to make them confess. Hamadi first, then at nightfall "Souélim did not want to confess to being a witch: he died from the blows we all struck him with." When the others went out to pray, Mohamed Nami Ould Cheikh Ould Abd El Aziz fired a shot into the corpse of Souélim. It was not until two days later, after Sid Ahmed suffered a relapse, that the presentation of the *gris-gris* led him to designate Zénabou. "Like her brothers, she protested that she was not a witch; she was beaten until she was dead." Again taking advantage of a prayer, this time it was Sid Ahmed who fired "a pistol shot into the corpse of Zénabou." These differences were not picked up by the colonial administration.

[91] This assertion did not convince the administration. Sid Ahmed and Mohamed Nami were considered co-perpetrators of the murders to the same degree as Cheikh.

[92] This argument carried some weight. In his transmittal letter, Captain Bousquet wrote: "It is also appropriate to take into account the fact that they all believe they are covered by Muslim law and that they acted as their ancestors would have acted" (no. 14 P, February 3, 1929. ANS 9G86(107)).

[93] In reality chief of the Ahel Habiballah group of the Ahel Barikallah.

[94] Nephew.

[95] This accusation carried conviction in the administration. Captain Bousquet, for example, wrote that if the "original" guilty parties were Cheikh and his two sons, that this was "an act of collective fanaticism"; "the principal instigators were the Ouled Bou Sba, in particular Sidi M'Bareck, whose threats overcame the reluctance of the Ahel Barikallah" (no. 14 P, February 3, 1929, ANS 9G86(107)).

Port-Étienne January 26, 1929
Circle Commander (signature of Bousquet)[96]

3. Letter from Ahmed Baba Ould Mohamed Ould Abd El Aziz (Translation)[97]

In the name of God the merciful, may he grant his blessing to his generous prophet Mohamed.[98]

Greetings to the Honorable Governor Gaden.[99]

I inform you that the Most High decreed witchcraft[100] as the fate of some of our captives. We have deeply examined this question with the marabouts of the Ahel Mohamed Salem, Ahel Elfagha Khattat,[101] and other learned marabouts. We have found in our laws only their execution. We tried to bring them to you, but they refused.[102] We had them executed in accordance with the word of God (Great and Powerful) and that of his prophet (may God's blessing be upon him).[103]

A Moorish proverb says: "The Ahel Barikallah should not be wrongly suspected for the love they bear to captives."[104]

Previously, the French did not prevent us from inflicting, as we did, the punishments provided by the law.

We would like to leave us in the tradition of our father (may God pardon him).

Ahmed Baba, son of his sheikh, Mohamed Ould Abd El Aziz Ould sheikh Mohamd El Mami (may God pardon all of them).

(undated)[105]

4. Account of an interview in English of Mohamed Ould Batta, January 13, 2009, Nouakchott

My grandfather was Sid Ahmed Ould Cheikh Ould Abd El Aziz Ould sheikh Mohamed El Mami. He and Mohamed Nami had the same mother, Fatimetou Mint Moctar Lahi.

Cheikh Ould Abd El Aziz owned many things, many slaves and camels. He had his own camp even though his brother Mohamed was chief of the Habiballah. Mohamed

---

[96] Handwritten.

[97] Translation of one of the two letters written by Ahmed Baba Ould Mohamed Ould Abd El Aziz, chief of the Ahel Habiballah group of the Ahel Barikallah. Two other letters, one from a "*djemaa* of the residents of Adrar," the other from Mohamed Ould El Khalil of the Rgueibat, and all the originals in Arabic, are included in the file. They seem to have been provided by Cheikh Ould Abd El Aziz first to the commander of the Adrar circle, then to the commander of the circle of the Baie du Lévrier. They then went up the chain of the hierarchy and were finally translated in writing at the request of the AOF administration by Touradou Ben sheikh Kamara in February 1929. The entire document is handwritten.

[98] Customary introductory formula.

[99] Colonel Henri Gaden was governor of Mauritania from 1916 to 1926 (with the title "Commissaire du Gouvernement général de l'Afrique occidentale française" until 1920, and then "lieutenant gouverneur" when Mauritania became a separate colony). Alphonse Choteau held the office in 1928–29.

[100] The Arabic text reads "witchcraft (*sihr*) called *sell*."

[101] These *qabail* were small nomadic religious groups that had good relations with the Ahel Barikallah.

[102] Assertion not confirmed by any testimony.

[103] Idiomatic formulas that the translator chose to put in parentheses.

[104] Although the attachment of the Ahel Barikallah to their dependents and their reluctance to free them are still well known in Mauritania today, this "proverb" is unknown to me.

[105] The document was probably written in late 1928. The last letter of Ahmed Baba Ould Mohamed Ould Abd El Aziz was certainly later, because it only intended to warn against "slanderers."

Nami was the oldest of Cheikh's sons; he also had his own camp, whereas Sid Ahmed stayed with his father.

One day when Cheikh was in the south at the camp of a family of the Ideïkoub, cousins of the Ahel Barikallah, he saw them torture slaves accused of stealing people's blood. They might have killed them, but they couldn't or wouldn't, so they kept on torturing them. Then he bought the whole family for nothing, for two tent poles. He made a *hajab*[106] for them and it was said that he made them safe. Than he brought them back to Tiris.[107]

They stayed there for a long time without causing anyone any harm. But one day Sid Ahmed fell ill. Many people said they were the ones who had stolen his blood. Cheikh was then at the *getna*[108] in Adrar and Mohamed Nami was in charge of the camp.

Mohamed Nami had horses, guns, all that.[109] He took them and demanded that they give back the blood. They started to give back the blood and it was said that Sid Ahmed was feeling better and better. But seeing that, Mohamed Nami realized they were dangerous; he took them away and shot them.

The story we know in the family says that he was alone. Sid Ahmed also used rifles, but Mohamed Nami didn't need anyone. It is said that he took them not far from the tent and he shot them in the plain sight of everyone. People then said to him: "You shouldn't have killed them, they haven't given back all the blood. Sid Ahmed is better, but it's not over." But the fact is they were dead.

Sid Ahmed was better, but after two days, he fell ill again. Then his health improved and so on. Later there were problems to be solved with the slaves in Inchiri; Sid Ahmed went there and that's where he died. He is buried in Akjoujt. He must have been around thirty; that was around three or four years later....

When Cheikh came back from the *getna*, he criticized Mohamed Nami for killing his slaves: "How can you say they stole his blood when I made a *hajab* for them and they must have been safe? What happened is bad." I heard that Cheikh was angry at him because they were not his slaves and he thought they were safe. But he wasn't there.

5. Account of an Interview in Hassaniya of Ahmedou Ould Moni (El-Graa, Ahel Laghzal), January 10, 2009 in Joffriyat (Agneitir)[110]

I have been told that Mohamed Nami went south and brought back two slaves and a female servant[111] to the camp that is now called for that reason Le Mdenet El Abid.[112] Mohamed

---

[106] A *hajab* is a talisman of Islamic inspiration or not made by a specialist to obtain a particular magic effect. See introduction.

[107] Tiris is a vast plain with famous pastures in northern Azefall, mainly in the formerly Spanish zone.

[108] Date harvest that took place in July and August in regions with oases, the occasion for festive gatherings. The events, therefore, took place two or three months before the colonial administration thought they had.

[109] The custom among the *Zwaya* groups, including the Ahel Barikallah, was to be unarmed. Horses, as well as rifles, are warrior objects associated with the *'Arab* nobility.

[110] The translation (into French) was made by Farida Mint Habib and Ahmed Mouloud Ould Eida, in the presence of Hélène Artaud. My interlocutor said he got this information from his father and from Hamadi Ould Saguti, who will be mentioned later.

[111] This interlocutor is the only one who attributes ownership of the slaves to Mohamed Nami. He does not even mention his father, Cheikh.

[112] The hill of slaves.

Nami had a brother who was very dear to him, Sid Ahmed Ould Cheikh, who shortly after their arrival suddenly had nosebleeds that caused his death. It was said that he had been bewitched[113] by the slaves. They noticed that after the slaves came several residents of the camp fainted. That coincided with the visit of someone who was familiar with that kind of witchcraft, *sell*, because the residents didn't know about it at the time. The visitor told them that what was happening resembled the effect of *sell*, because after the slaves came the residents of the camp were devastated.

There was an El Graa (Ouled Mehlbel, Ouled Melhel) named Hamadi Ould Saguti who was also bewitched. Mohamed Nami threatened to kill the slaves with his gun to force them to cure him. Because of those threats they restored him to life.

I knew Hamadi Ould Saguti personally, and it is true that he was cured of *sell*. But he spent the rest of his life having a crisis every Friday during which he lost consciousness…

When he sensed the camp was in danger, with Hamadi Ould Saguti, Mohamed Nami took the two slaves and the female servant to Le Mdenet, and they shot them. The shots killed one slave and the servant, but one of the slaves ran away. They chased him and shot him to death under a tree, an *atil*. The graves of the slaves, whose location I know very well, are on Le Mdenet for one of the slaves and the servant, but the one who was shot under the *atil* is buried there. After this, Mohamed Nami decided to emigrate.[114] He took a *hartani*[115] and headed north. He joined an El Graa family named Ahel Boutrig, and then went on to Morocco for fear of the French.

In the family of the group of Ahel Mhemed of the El Graa that he joined were two men, Abd El Aziz Ould Boutrig and his brother Lemjed. At that time the camp was not far east of Erzmeilat.[116]

When Mohamed Nami told the two brothers he intended to emigrate to Morocco, they advised against it. The told him that if he did, they would follow him and abandon their territory. They were very attached to him and asked him to stay for a while to see what was possible.

One of the Ahel Boutrig went to Nouadhibou[117] to see Cheikh Ould Mouknass[118] who was then very valiant. Cheikh went to see the French and went to great pains to persuade the French not to put him on trial and not to bother him. Finally Cheikh secured Mohamed Nami's pardon. He then returned to his camp.

---

[113] The verb used (*sell*, *isell*) is translated as "extract." See introduction.

[114] The verb used (*hajer*, *ihajer*) refers to the Prophet's flight to Medina from the domination of the polytheists in Mecca, the origin of the Muslim calendar (Hegira). It is the word used in Mauritania to designate the flight from colonial domination to unoccupied territory. The Spanish did not travel through the territory granted by treaty until after 1934. See Acloque, "L'idée de frontière".

[115] *Hartani* (pl. *Haratin*) designates a freedman or an assimilated foreigner in a clientelist relationship with his master. He belongs to the category of the *tlamid*. It can also be a euphemism for slave.

[116] Located in the Taziast (north of Azefall), 45 miles north of the site of the events, Erzmeilat was 60 miles south of the border with Spanish territory. It was also on the road to Port-Étienne.

[117] The post of Port-Étienne was always known to the Bizhan by the name of the peninsula, Nouadhibou, now the name of the city.

[118] Cheikh Ould Mouknass of the Ahel Laghzal represented the El-Graa *qabila* before the colonial administration in Port-Étienne. He was very influential there. The Ahel Laghzal were *tlamid* (religious disciples) of the Ahel Abd El Aziz, the family of Mohamed Nami Ould Cheikh.

SUGGESTED ADDITIONAL READINGS

ON THE EVOLUTION OF SLAVERY IN MAURITANIA DURING THE COLONIAL PERIOD

Acloque, B. "Embarras de l'administration coloniale: La question de l'esclavage au début du XXe siècle en Mauritanie," in *Groupes serviles au Sahara: Approche comparative à partir du cas des arabophones de Mauritanie.* Edited by M. Villasante-De Beauvais (Paris: CNRS, 2000), 97-119.

Bonte, Pierre. "Esclaves ou cousins: Évolution du statut servile dans la société Mauritanienne," in *Terrains et engagements de Claude Meillassoux.* Edited by B. Schlemmer (Paris: Karthala, 1998), 157-182.

McDougall, E. A. "A Topsy-Turvy World: Slaves and Freed Slaves in the Mauritanian Adrar, 1910-1950," in *The End of Slavery in Africa.* Edited by S. Miers and R. Roberts (Madison: The University Press of Wisconsin, 1988), 362-390.

"Slavery, Sorcery, and Colonial 'Reality' in Mauritania, c. 1910-60," in *Agency and Action in Colonial Africa: Essays for John E. Flint.* Edited by C. Youé and T. Stapleton (New York: Palgrave, 2001), 69-82.

"Living the Legacy of Slavery: Between Discourse and Reality," *Cahiers d'Études Africaines,* XLV, 3-4 (2005): 957-986.

"'Si un homme travaille, il doit être libre...': Les serviteurs *hrâtîn* et le discours colonial sur le travail en Mauritanie," in *Colonisations et héritages actuels au Sahara et au Sahel: Problèmes conceptuels, état des lieux et nouvelles perspectives de recherche (XVIIIe-XXe siècles).* Edited by Villasante Cervello (Paris: L'Harmattan, 2007), I, 237-270.

Ould Cheikh, A. W. "L'évolution de l'esclavage dans la société maure," in *Nomades et commandants: Administration et sociétés nomades dans l'ancienne AOF.* Edited by E. Bernus, P. Boilley, J. Clauzel, and J.-L. Triaud (Paris: Karthala, 1993), 181-192.

Villasante-de Beauvais, M. (ed.) *Groupes serviles au Sahara: Approche comparative à partir du cas des arabophones de Mauritanie.* Paris: CNRS, 2000.

ON THE QUESTION OF WITCHCRAFT

Doutté, E. *Magie et religion dans l'Afrique du nord.* Algiers: Adolphe Jourdan, 1909.

Evans-Pritchard, E. E. *Witchcraft, Oracles, and Magic among the Azande.* Oxford: Clarendon Press, 1937.

Hamès, C. (ed.) *Coran et talismans: Textes et pratiques magiques en milieu musulman.* Paris: Karthala, 2007.

Zempleni, A. "La 'maladie' et ses 'causes,'" *L'Ethnographie,* 96-97 (1985), 13-44.

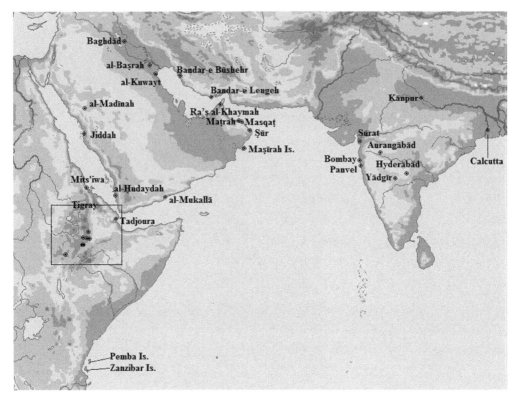

27.1. Map of the Indian Ocean region.

27 Tracing Their "Middle" Passages

Slave Accounts from the Nineteenth-Century Western Indian Ocean

HIDEAKI SUZUKI

In the last three decades, our understanding of the Indian Ocean slave trade has greatly expanded. Recent studies document that African slaves were moved quite extensively around the western Indian Ocean that included the East African coast, the Arabian Peninsula, and the Indian subcontinent.[1] We also know that East African exports did not end in 1873,[2] despite earlier claims and that in the Indian Ocean world, slaves had not only African origins.[3] Individuals from South Asia, Central Asia, and Middle East as well as from Africa were all bought and sold as slaves in the region. Yet many questions remain. We still have no definitive information about the number of men, women, and children who were circulated as commodities in the area. Estimates do exist, but they vary considerably. In 1971, C. S. Nicholls indicated that by the 1840s, 15,000 slaves were exported annually from the Swahili coast to the northward markets, whereas A. Sheriff estimated in 1987 that during the first half of the nineteenth century, about 3,000 slaves were exported from the Swahili coast to the north annually.[4] These estimations comprise an important part of the study of the slave trade. They offer a useful means for grasping the magnitude of the trade. They also allow us to compare the Indian Ocean slave trade with the slave trade in other regions. Too often, however, readers find numbers magically persuasive. Viewed as fair

---

[1] See, for example, S. de S. Jayasuriya and R. Pankhurst, "On the African Diaspora in the Indian Ocean Region," in Jayasuriya and Pankhurst (eds.), *The African Diaspora in the Indian Ocean* (Trenton and Asmara, 2003), 7–17.

[2] See, for example, M. S. Hopper, "The African Presence in Arabia: Slavery, the World Economy, and the African Diaspora in Eastern Arabia, 1840–1940" (unpublished PhD thesis, University of California, Los Angeles, 2006); B. A. Mirzai, "Slavery, the Abolition of the Slave Trade, and the Emancipation of Slaves in Iran (1828–1928)" (unpublished PhD thesis, York University, 2004).

[3] G. Campbell, "Slave Trades and the Indian Ocean World," in J. C. Hawley (ed.), *India in Africa, Africa in India: Indian Ocean Cosmopolitanisms* (Bloomington and Indianapolis, 2008), 21.

[4] C. S. Nicholls, *The Swahili Coast: Politics, Diplomacy and Trade on the East African Littoral, 1798–1856* (London, 1971), 205; A. Sheriff, *Slaves, Spices and Ivory in Zanzibar: Integration of an East African Commercial Empire into the World Economy, 1770–1873* (Oxford, 1987), 40. For other estimations, see R. A. Austen, "From the Atlantic to the Indian Ocean: European Abolition, the African Slave Trade, and Asian Economic Structures," in D. Eltis and J. Walvin (eds.), *The Abolition of the Atlantic Slave Trade* (Madison, 1981), 117–139; R. A. Austen, "The 19th Century Islamic Slave Trade from East Africa (Swahili and Red Sea Coasts): A Tentative Census," in W. G. Clarence-Smith (ed.), *The Economics of the Indian Ocean Slave Trade in the Nineteenth Century* (London, 1989), 22–30; E. B. Martin & T. C. I. Ryan, "A Quantitative Assessment of the Arab Slave Trade of East Africa, 1770–1896," *Kenya Historical Review*, 5 (1977): 71–91; T. M. Ricks, "Slaves and Slave Traders in the Persian Gulf, 18th and 19th Centuries: An Assessment," in Clarence-Smith (ed.), *The Economics*, 67.

and objective, statistics tend to mesmerize. Yet the numbers available on the Indian Ocean trade fail to capture the fact that the trade varied across time and space. Because of this, the quantitative approach needs to be supplemented with a qualitative approach, for the significance of the statistics can only be understood by also knowing something about the actual conditions that shaped the slave trade.

What qualitative materials have scholars consulted to obtain a better understanding of the Indian Ocean trade? Many studies have relied on observations found in contemporary travelogues and official reports that were specifically written to describe and investigate the actual conditions of the slave trade.[5] Each of these observations, however, documents only a segment of the trade. For an overview of the entire system, we would need many more such observations. These simply do not exist. More revealing are those accounts provided by (ex-)slaves and slave-dealers. Their narratives vividly illustrate how the trade was conducted and with what impact. They include ex-slave autobiographies and orally transmitted life histories, most often collected and published by Christian missionaries and modern scholars.[6] As sources, they provide us with quite interesting and useful material about slavery as experienced by individual men and women. They do have their own problems, however. Most were edited by Christian propagandists long after the formerly enslaved experienced the events they described in their narratives. In addition, whatever may have happened after their emancipation but before they narrated their life stories may have influenced their accounts. Memories can be faulty; the missionaries who recorded and edited their accounts had their own agendas. For these reasons one must read these life histories or autobiographical sources with a degree of circumspection.

There are, however, plenty of archival accounts of (ex-)slaves that were recorded by British officers. Many have yet to be fully utilized. Once British officers stationed at consulates and other (local) agencies in ports around the rim of the western Indian Ocean (i.e., Masqaṭ, Zanzibar, Bandar-e Būshehr) heard of a case of slave trading, they recorded the results of their investigations after conducting a series of interviews with the (ex-)slaves and sometimes with the owners and the dealers. They recorded these accounts not for the purposes of public or Christian propaganda, but rather to document the workings of the slave trade and to respond to the enquiries of higher officers in Bombay or London about how slaves were being treated. These documents are more reliable, having been written immediately at the time the British officers interviewed the ex-slaves. They also have greater objectivity. The documents on which we focus in this chapter consist of these accounts. Before discussing them, however, it is important to situate the testimonies in their appropriate historical context.

---

[5] See, for example, E. A. Alpers, "The Other Middle Passage: The African Slave Trade in the Indian Ocean," in E. Christopher, C. Pybus, and M. Rediker (eds.), *Many Middle Passages: Forced Migration and the Making of the Modern World* (Berkeley, Los Angeles, and London, 2007), 20–38; R. W. Beachey, *The Slave Trade of Eastern Africa* (London, 1976), 11–66; C. Lloyd, *The Navy and the Slave Trade: the Suppression of the African Slave Trade in the Nineteenth Century* (London, New York, and Toronto, 1949), 248–257; I. McCalman, "The East African Middle Passage: David Livingstone, the Zambesi Expedition, and Lake Nyassa, 1858–1866," in Christopher, Pybus and Rediker (eds.), *Many Middle Passages*, 39–51.

[6] For studies on slavery based on autobiographies and interviews with ex-slaves in East Africa, see S. Mirza & M. Strobel, *Three Swahili Women: Life Histories from Mombasa, Kenya* (Bloomington and Indianapolis, 1989); M. Strobel, "Women and Slavery on the East African Coast," in C. Tominaga (ed.), *Rethinking African History from Women's/ Gender Perspectives: Slavery, Colonial Experience, Nationalist Movement and After* (Osaka, 2004), 45–65; M. Wright, *Strategies of Slaves and Women: Life-Stories from East/Central Africa* (New York and London, 1993).

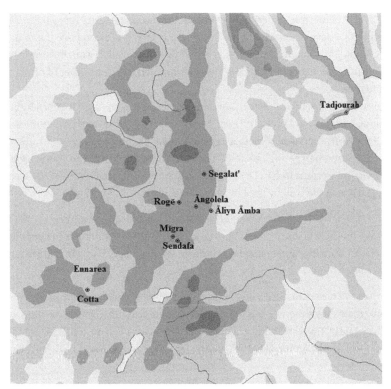

27.2. Map of the featured region in Ethiopia.

THE SLAVE TRADE IN THE NINETEENTH-CENTURY WESTERN INDIAN OCEAN

The western Indian Ocean is the vast maritime region located between the western coast of the Indian subcontinent and the East African coast. It also includes the Red Sea and the Gulf. Trading in slaves is known to have taken place in this region as late as when *Periplus Maris Erythraei* was written (c. 150 AD).[7] In this long history of slave trading in the western Indian Ocean, the nineteenth century stands out as especially important. It was in this period that the traffic in humans reached its heyday in terms of volume. Apart from pre-existing local needs for slaves as soldiers and domestic servants, and a demand for labor on plantations in the Mascarene Islands that had been in place since the eighteenth century, a demand that came from the Atlantic Ocean emerged as a result of the progress of anti-slave trade patrols on the Atlantic Ocean. Furthermore, the greatest local demand for an enslaved labor force developed after the 1820s with the emergence of the plantation economy along the East African coast, especially on the Islands of Zanzibar and Pemba. An expanding pearl industry in the Gulf, especially from the second half of the nineteenth century, also contributed to the demand.[8] These demands for labor, however, do not explain fully why trading in slaves reached its heyday in this century. Another aspect is found in

---

[7] The existence of slaves is found in much earlier records. Ur-Nammu tablets compiled in Mesopotamia in c. 2300 BC are the earliest known record of slaves not only in the western Indian Ocean but in the world. See J. Goody, "Slavery in Time and Space," in J. L. Watson (ed.), *Asian and African Systems of Slavery* (Berkeley and Los Angeles, 1980), 18.

[8] Hopper, *The African Presence.*

a note by E. A. Emerton, a merchant from Salem who visited Zanzibar on the East African coast in 1849: "slaves are owned here because it is fashionable to have them, not because it is profitable."[9] In fact, A. Hamerton, the first British consul in Zanzibar, observed that "a man's wealth and respectability … is always estimated by the number of African slaves he is said to possess."[10]

So, what sorts of people were traded in the nineteenth-century western Indian Ocean? In general, females were preferred over males, even though several case studies, especially about East African coastal societies, reveal a relatively balanced gender ratio among the enslaved. Rather than gender, it seems age was more significant. The young were preferred as slaves in the western Indian Ocean.[11] The reason for this is found in an 1842 report about the slave trade in the Gulf by the Persian Gulf resident A. B. Kemball:

> The slaves of either sex, whether Hubshee[12] or African, of an age exceeding twenty years, on their first sale, are of less comparative value, from their being at that mature age less tractable, and taking less kindly to the language, religion, and customs of their masters.[13]

The prices recorded in this same report substantiate this situation. According to this resident, males aged between ten and twenty were the most valued in the Gulf. Buyers paid 7–15 Maria Theresa Thaler (MTT)[14] for a boy age seven-to-ten; 15–30MTT for a boy age ten-to-twenty; and for over age twenty, the price was 17–20MTT.[15] Another observer,

---

[9] N. R. Bennett and G. E. Brooks, Jr. (eds.). *New England Merchants in Africa: A History through Documents 1802–1865* (Boston, 1965), 427.

[10] Zanzibar National Archives, Zanzibar, Tanzania (ZZBA) AA/12/29/43 [Hamerton to the secretary to Bombay government, 2 January 1842]. Emerton also found that there were slaves who owned other slaves; some even possessed several slaves (Bennett and Brooks, *New England Merchants*, 427).

[11] See, for example, G. Campbell, "Introduction: Slavery and Other Forms of Unfree Labour in the Indian Ocean World," in Campbell (ed.), *The Structure of Slavery in Indian Ocean Africa and Asia* (London and Portland, 2004), xxi; F. Morton, "Small Change: Children in the Nineteenth-Century East African Slave Trade," in G. Campbell, S. Miers, and J. C. Miller (eds.), *Children in Slavery through the Ages* (Athens, OH, 2009), 55; H. Suzuki, "Indo-yō Nishi Kaiiki Sekai to 'Kindai': Dorei Ryūtsū ni tazusawaru Hitobito wo cyuushin ni (The 19th century western Indian Ocean World and 'Modernity': a case study of people around the slave trade)" (unpublished PhD thesis, University of Tokyo, 2010), 202–204.

[12] This term is derived from an Arabic word "ḥabashī" and a Persian word "ḥabshī," which means "an Abyssinian (Ethiopean)" (H. Yule and A. C. Burnell, *Hobson-Jobson: A Glossary of Colloquial Anglo-Indian Words or Phrases and of Kindred Terms, Etymological, Historical, Geographical and Discursive* [new ed. edited by W. Crooke, London, 1986], 428 s.v. Hubsee). In the nineteenth century, "Siddy" or "Seedy" (various spellings exist) often was a counterpart to "Hubsee." It is derived from a Hindi word "sīdī" and an Arabic word "sayyid," which generally means "lord," "master," and "decedents of Prophet." Yule and Burnell explain that this term is "properly an honorific name given in Western India to African Mahommedans, of whom many held high positions in the service of the kings of the Deccan" (Yule and Burnell, *Hobson-Jobson*, 806 s.v. Seedy). In the context of the nineteenth-century western Indian Ocean, this term was widely applied to non-Ethiopian African population, particularly those from eastern Africa. For example, R. F. Burton noted that "Seedy boy" is an Anglo-Indian term for a Zanzibar man (R. F. Burton, *The Book of the Thousand Nights and a Night* [edited by L. C. Smithers, 12 vols. London, 1894], VI, 231). For both terms, see also Jayasuriya and Pankhurst, "On the African Diaspora," 8.

[13] A. B. Kemball, "Paper relative to the Measures adopted by the British Government, between the Years 1820 and 1844, for Effecting the Suppression of the Slave Trade in the Persian Gulf," in R. H. Thomas (ed.), *Arabian Gulf Intelligence* (Bombay, 1856), 649. The same content is found in *British Parliamentary Papers* (*BPP*), Slave Trade, XXIV, Class D, 26 [Kemball to Robertson, 8 July 1842].

[14] Maria Theresa Thaler is a silver coin that was widely circulated in the first half of the nineteenth century throughout the western Indian Ocean region.

[15] Kemball, "Paper relative to the Measures," 649.

M. Wilson, also stated that the most frequently purchased slaves ranged between ten and fourteen years of age regardless of sex, whereas slaves aged past thirty were rarely purchased.[16]

A similar preference for child slave was also found on the East African coast. As R. F. Burton noted, the slave owners most valued the *mzalia* (in Swahili; *muwallad* in Arabic) who were slaves who were born of slave parents. Owners treated them as if they were members of their own family, "because the master's comfort depends upon the man being contented."[17] These slaves shared the language and customs with the owner; some even conducted business on behalf of their owners.[18] Children just brought from the interior of the African continent were also prized, because it was possible for them to acquire more easily the language and the customs of their owners.[19] Not so highly prized were newly enslaved adults brought from the interior. They were regarded as being less obedient and "alter little by domestication."[20] These observations correspond as well with local Swahili views as found in several Swahili-language proverbs. Among the sayings compiled by W. E. Taylor, a Church Missionary Society missionary who worked in East Africa during the latter half of the nineteenth century, is the following: "*Mtumwa mwenyi busara ni Azawao* ('Born-here' is the sensible slave)."[21] Taylor explains: "An 'mzalia,' i.e. a slave of the first or second generation, gets accustomed to the ways of the coast; in contrast to the mshenzi, the bumpkin from the interior, that never quite loses his clumsiness."[22] If an owner had to sell a fully integrated first- or second-generation slave, he was thought to have engaged in disgraceful behavior.[23] In such cases, a slave owner was prepared to pay a premium for a newly enslaved person, especially if he or she was young. Their youth allowed them to acquire quickly the owner's language and culture, but if necessary the owner could also sell them with less shame.

BRITISH ANTI-SLAVE TRADE ACTIVITIES IN THE WESTERN INDIAN OCEAN

The 1820 General Treaty of Peace that the British concluded with all major sheikhs along the Arabian coast of the Gulf (except that of Masqaṭ and of Kuwayt) can be regarded as the starting point of British anti-slave trade activities in the western Indian Ocean.[24] Two years later, in 1822, Britain succeeded in concluding an anti-slave trade treaty with Sayyid

[16] *BPP*, Slave Trade, XXIV, Class D, 32 [Wilson to Government, 28 January 1831].

[17] R. Burton, *The Lake Regions of Central Africa: From Zanzibar to Lake Tanganyika* (2 vols., California, 2001), II, 310.

[18] *Ibidem*, 311; C. Velten, *Desturi za Wasuaheli na khabari za desturi za sheri'a za wasuaheli* (Göttingen, 1903), 257–258.

[19] Burton, *The Lake Regions*, II, 311. See also, Campbell, "Introduction," xxi; Morton, "Small Change," 55; Suzuki, "Indo-yō," 202–204.

[20] Burton, *The Lake Regions*, II, 311. See also C. New, *Life, Wanderings, and Labours in Eastern Africa: With an Account of the Equatorial Snow Mountain, Kilima Njaro and Remarks upon East African Slavery* (London, 1971), 56–57. Modern scholars follow their view about the contrast between a child slave and an adult slave.

[21] W. E. Taylor, *African Aphorisms; of Saws from Swahili-Land* (London, 1891), 78. See also *Ibidem*, 71.

[22] Taylor, *African Aphorisms*, 78. See also Glassman, *Feasts*, 85.

[23] F. J. Berg, *Mombasa under the Busaidi Sultanate: The City and Its Hinterlands in the Nineteenth Century* (unpublished PhD thesis, University of Wisconsin, 1971), 171; J. Glassman, *Feast and Riot: revelry, rebellion, and popular consciousness on the Swahili Coast, 1856–1888* (Portsmouth, 1995), 89.

[24] For the text of this treaty, see "Translation of the General Treaty with the Arab Tribes of the Persian Gulf," in C. U. Aitchison, *A Collection of Treaties, Engagements and Sanad: Relating to India and Neighbouring Countries* (13 vols. Calcutta, 1909), XIII, 172–176.

Year	Number of slaves liberated
1852	3
1853	63
1854	12
1855	0
1856	72
1857	26

27.3. Chart showing the number of slaves liberated by Britain (Indian Ocean), 1852 through June 1858.
Source: APAC IOR/R/15/1/171/30–33 [Report on the Slave Trade in the Persian Gulf extending from January 1, 1852 to June 30, 1858 compiled by H. Disbrowe].

Sa'īd, the ruler of Masqaṭ who eventually moved his headquarter to Zanzibar around 1830. By 1839, the British negotiated an agreement with the chiefs including Ra's al-Khaymah, Sharjah, and Masqaṭ to allow their cruisers to detain and search any vessel belonging to those chiefs and their subjects suspected of having on board individuals whom the crews may have kidnapped.[25] By 1848, Britain also concluded a series of treaties with most of the polities along the Gulf, banning the slave trade between Africa and Asia.[26] Despite these agreements, the British captured no slave vessels in the Gulf until 1842.[27] Even in the 1850s, the Indian Navy[28] – which played the major role in patrols in the western Indian Ocean – liberated only a small number of slaves as indicated in Figure 27.3. In fact, British anti-slave trade efforts in the western Indian Ocean remained ineffective up to the mid-1860s.[29]

Complex procedures after slave vessels were captured and the associated cost caused the Indian Navy to pursue the suppression lackadaisically.[30] The Indian Navy also had a shortage of vessels. In 1858, for example, the Navy had only 252 officers and 31 sea vessels to patrol the vast region from the South China coast to the East African coast.[31] Simultaneously, they were expected to engage in emergency military operations such as those in Burma and China.[32] Thus, though the Gulf was important for Britain as a commercial and communications route, the Indian Navy simply could not perform all its duties. After repeated requests for reinforcements,[33] officers working for the suppression of the slave trade managed to improve the Indian Navy's performance. Nonetheless, a shortage of patrol vessels remained a chronic problem, while the vessels allotted to them were usually outdated. The Indian Navy vessels frequently arrived at the site of an incident only after the slave ships had departed.[34] And when the Navy gave chase, the slavers were often able to

---

[25] Ibidem, 176–178, 220–221.

[26] J. G. Lorimer, Gazetteer of the Persian Gulf, Oman and Central Arabia (9 vols. London, 1986), V, 2476–2484.

[27] BPP, Slave Trade, XXIV, Class D, 27 [Kemball to Robertson, Karrak, 8 July 1842].

[28] The Indian Navy was originally organized in 1613 by the British East Indian Company and was eventually dissolved in 1863. Between 1687 and 1830, it was called the Bombay Marine. It was different from the Royal Navy, although they often conducted same missions in the Indian Ocean waters.

[29] See, for example, E. Gilbert, Dhows and the Colonial Economy of Zanzibar, 1860–1970 (Oxford, 2004), 60–61; Hopper, The African Presence, 52.

[30] Gilbert, Dhows, 60–61.

[31] C. R. Low, History of the Indian Navy 1613–1863 (2 vols., New Delhi, 1985), II, 577–584.

[32] Low, History, I, 410–473, II, 140–160, 238–294.

[33] E.g. Asia, Pacific and Africa Collections, British Library, London, UK (APAC; formerly known as Oriental and India Office Collections) IOR/R/15/1/143/367 [Extract Para 4 from a Despatch from the Honourable the Court of Directors dated the 1st March No 1 of 1854]; APAC IOR/R/15/1/157/195–7 [Jones to Anderson, Bushire, 26 May 1856]; APAC IOR/R/15/1/168/46–47 [Jones to Jenkins, 30 April 1859].

[34] See, for example, APAC IOR/R/15/1/127/40 [Hennell to Porter, Camp neaer Bushir, 26 June 1851]; APAC IOR/R/15/1/157/227 [Ethersey to Jones, Bassadore, 24 July 1854].

escape using their superior sailing skills, camouflage with different flags, and even some restrictions set by anti-slave trade treaties.[35]

British activities were further impeded by the specific terms in their anti-slave trade treaties, which restricted their activities to slave transports on the sea. This allowed local rulers to legitimately reject the British right of detention and investigation of suspects on their own lands. Loopholes did exist in the treaties, however. The British refused to ignore cases involving people from the Indian subcontinent, whether slave or slaver. These individuals were regarded as being under British Indian jurisdiction. Once officers received information about slave dealings in which people from the Indian subcontinent were involved, they quickly investigated and recorded the details of these cases in order to release those enslaved while they laid a complaint before local rulers if there were local suspects. If there were any Indians who dealt in slaves, officers prepared those cases for legal action. Thus the cases offered here for analysis include the voices of the enslaved from both Africa and South Asia.

QUESTIONS TO CONSIDER

1. Why were the routes and the (ex-)owners the focus in these accounts? Why didn't the officers who wrote these accounts say more about the work the ex-slaves did? Consider this aspect of the reports, given the aims of and the limitations on British anti-slave trade activities.

2. The term "middle passage" is most often used to describe the passage that slaves experienced in being transported from a certain starting point to a particular destination. If one focuses on the individual experiences highlighted in the cases examined here, however, a more complex picture emerges. Locate the place names mentioned in each of the accounts on the map and trace the routes on which each person was transported. Then, consider the validity of understanding of the slave trade as one that consisted of a "middle passage." What alternative language might one use instead of "middle passage"?

3. What are the similarities and differences among the experiences narrated in the accounts? What accounts for these similarities and differences?

4. The preference for children as slaves was especially strong in this region. What reasons might explain this beside the fact that children could be easily assimilated and owners could resell them without experiencing social censure?

5. In all these accounts, recorded by British officers, the religion of the enslaver/ slave traders is noted as Muslim. Yet nothing is said of the religion of the enslaved. Why do you think the British focused so much on the religion of the enslavers and the slave buyers?

6. What are the advantages and the limitations of such documented accounts? Can one harmonize these qualitative accounts with quantitative methods?

7. How do these accounts impact your understanding of the slave trade in the nineteenth-century western Indian Ocean?

---

[35] Hopper, *The African Presence*, 49; H. Suzuki, "Indo-yō Nishi-kaiiki to 'Kindai': Dorei no Ryūtsū wo Jirei ni shite (The western Indian Ocean and "Modern Period": A case study with slave distribution)," *Shigaku Zasshi*, 116, 7 (2007): 19–24.

Case I

Context: In July 1856, the Indian Navy's patrols against slave trade operated around the Arabian Peninsula. At the very beginning of this operation, they caught two ships with slaves and rescued four African boys. Naval officers interviewed them. One of these interviews was reported as follows.

Statement of a Boy named Meerjohu aged 13. seized by the Agent at Lingar[36] as a Slave.

(The boy who is very intelligent) states that he with several at the boys and girls were stolen by the men belonging to the Buggalow[37] that brought them to Raselkhyma.[38] He says that these men had plenty of sweetmeats which they gave them every now and then and they followed these men to get these sweetmeats, until they were a long way from their village, when these men caught them and put them in a Boat and took them on board the Buggalow. This was near Zanzibar; there were a great number on board the Buggalow, and there were more than one hundred landed at Raselkhyma. They were all landed there. Seven, of which he was one, were sold and brought to Linga. Six remained with his master when he left Raselkhyma, and all the others had been sent away to Busra in other Boats.[39]

Bassadore True Copy of Statement
24th July 1856 R. Ethersey

Case 2[40]

Context: In 1841, a British agent of local origin at Masqaṭ became aware that an Indian slave girl had been sold in a town market. He engaged several persons to procure information about her. Based on the information collected, he contacted the buyer (Banjoli Beloochee). The agent took custody of the girl and while she was at his house, he summoned the person who had entrusted her to the broker for sale and arranged for that person to return the money to Banjoli. Even after the money was returned, the buyer Banjoli thought that the girl might still wish to go with him. Thus he asked the native agent to bring her to him. The girl claimed that she did not love Banjoli and that she would not return to him. The native agent then asked her how she came to be removed from her native country and brought to Masqaṭ; he then asked her to "speak the truth." The account below is her reply.

My native country is Yedgeer,[41] under the jurisdiction of Nasir ood Dowla; I and two other girls, each of us eight or nine years old, were one day playing in the street, when two Arabs came to us and asked us to go along with them, promising to give us food and money. One Arab took me along with him, and the other two were thus separated. I was then taken to Hyderabad, and sold to one Hubeeb Ibrahim, from whom I was purchased by an Arab named

---

[36] "Lingar" is Bandar-e Lengeh in Iran.
[37] "Buggalow," or correctly *Baghla*, was the largest type of sailing ships used in the western Indian Ocean. They were built in the Gulf and on the western coast of India. It had two or three masts. See D. A. Agius, *In the Wake of the Dhow: The Arabian Gulf and Oman* (Reading, 2002), 49–53.
[38] "Raselkhyma" is Ra's al-Khaymah in the United Arab Emirates.
[39] APAC IOR/R/15/1/157/229.
[40] *BPP*, Slave Trade, XXV, Class A, 401 [Rubil bin Uslan to Hennell, Ramaẓān 13 1257/27 October 1841].
[41] "Yedgeer" is Yādgīr in Karnātaka, India.

Moobaruk. The Arab brought me down to Bombay, where I stayed for upwards of two months. He then took me to Moculla[42], and after a few days sold me to Unbar, a native of Soor,[43] who carried me to the Island of Muserah[44] and sold me to Meroo, a Latia[45] of Muttrah.[46] I lived with Meroo for two months in Muserah, and then went with him to Muttrah, where I lived in his house for three months; meanwhile I had a quarrel with his wife, in consequence of which Meroo took me back to Muserah. Three or four months after, a servant came to him from his wife, along with whom Meroo sent me to his wife in Muttrah, where, after a few days, he himself returned, and sold me to Peroo, a Latia of Bombay. After four or five months Peroo returned to Bombay, leaving me behind in the house of Purdan Latia, both being servants of Seit Nubeeb Ibrahim, a Latia, residing in Bombay. Five months after, being tired of me, Purdan, two days before the 1st of Ramazan (17th October), took all my things from me, and having given me some tattered clothes, brought me in a boat to Muscat, and entrusted me to Mooseleim bin Budeo, a broker, from whom Banjoli Beloochee purchased me.

CASE 3[47]

Context: Eight days after Case 2 occurred, the same agent again received information that a wheat merchant named Hajee Mahomed Mughrabee held an Indian female slave. He investigated further and realized that she was sold to him by one Unbar. The agent asked Hajee Mahomed to hand her over to him. Hajee Mahomed initially refused, but finally brought her to the agent. When the girl, who was about twelve years old, came to the agent, she was crying and asked him to let her return to Hajee Mahomed. The agent kept her for a while in order to ascertain if she really wanted to return to her master or not. On the other hand, Hajee Mahomed claimed that he had an intention of marrying her, but the agent had received information that he had exposed her for sale. After the girl became calm, she confessed to the agent that she was forced to say that she loved her master, and wished to remain with him. According to the agent, she also told him that she could not bear to see the face of her master. On 24 Ramaẓān (November 9), the agent asked her to tell him all her particulars. The following account is her reply.

My native country is Cawnpore,[48] whence my parents afterwards removed themselves to Calcutta, on account of the scarcity of rain there. One day when I was playing in the street, an Arab came to me, and asked me to go along with him, promising to give me sweetmeats. Having thus wheedled me, he took me along with him to Hyderabad, in the Deccan. When I began to cry on the road, he told me that my parents were at Hyderabad, and that he intended to take me to them. I was at that time seven or eight years old. He then sold me to one Mahomed, with whom I stopped for some time. At that time there were two persons in Hyderabad engaged in the purchase of slaves; one of them, an Abyssinian, by name Zakoot, a servant of a merchant

---

[42] "Moculla" is al-Mukallā in Yemen.

[43] "Soor" is Ṣūr in Oman.

[44] "Muserah" is Maṣīrah in Oman.

[45] "luti" derives from *lūṭī, lūṭīyā, lūṭīwālā*, in Hindu or *luṭaru, luṭaro* in Gujarati, or in Arabic and Persian *lūṭī*, which mean "plunderer," "blackguard," "robber," and "pederasty." See also Yule and Burnell, *Hobson-Jobson*, 520–521, s.v. Looty, Lootiewalla.

[46] "Muttrah" is Maṭrah in Oman.

[47] *BPP*, Slave Trade, XXV, Class A, 401 [Rubil bin Uslan to Hennell, 13 Ramaẓān 1257 / 27 November 1841].

[48] "Cawnpore" is Kānpur in Uttar Pradesh, India.

in Judda[49]; he had married an Indian women in Hyderabad. The other was Shaik Mahomed Ameer, a native of Medina. He had an Abyssinian woman with him; both of them lived together. Zakoot purchased eight girls, including myself, and the Shaik bought two girls and one boy. Both of them then went to Aurungabad,[50] where Zakoot sold two girls to a dancing-woman. They thence proceeded to Bombay, and on their arrival at Panwell[51] they halted in a mosque. Zakoot, accompanied by his wife and two girls, came to Bombay, where, on being questioned regarding his companions, he replied that one of them was his wife, and the remaining two his daughters. He took up his lodgings in a house situated in the market street. Next day Shaik Mahomed Ameer also came to Bombay in a similar manner. Zakoot afterwards brought over to Bombay the remaining slaves, under cover of similar pretences, and sold three of them there. Zakoot and the Shaik then embarked for Muscat, whence they went to Muttrah. Some time after the Shaik proceeded to Bussora,[52] where he sold his three slaves. Zakoot, after selling one slave to his Highness the Imaum, embarked for Bussora, and had only two slaves with him; one of them was purchased by an Indian, and the other, that is myself, by Hajee Ibrahim of Turkey, who kept me in the house of Hajee Suleman, an Abyssinian inhabitant of Surat.[53] Hajee Ibrahim afterwards sold me to Hajee Hoosain, who was a friend of Hajee Suleman, and lived with him. When Hajee Hoosain was preparing himself to embark for Bagdad, Hajee Suleman persuaded me to cry, and express my disinclination to go to Bagdad, on which Hajee Hoossain sold me to Hajee Suleman, who brought me to Muscat, and sold me to Umbar, a servant of Hajee Ibrahim of Turkey, from whom I was afterwards purchased by Hajee Mahomed Mughrubee for 37 rials, through a broker, without being brought to the market.[54]

CASE 4

Context: W. C. Harris, an engineer with the East India Company, interrogated a number of slaves about their life histories during his eighteen-month stay in Ethiopia during the early 1840s. Dibbo, the son of Betta and a native of the village of Suppa in Enarea, narrated the following account.

When about twenty years of age, being one day engaged in tending my father's flocks, an armed band of the Ooma Galla, with whom my tribe had long been in enmity, swept suddenly down, and took myself, with six other youths, prisoners, killing four more who resisted. Having been kept bound hand and foot during five days, I was sold to the Toome Galla, one of the nearest tribes, for thirty amoles (about six shillings and three pence sterling). The bargain was concluded in the Toomee market-place, called Sundáffo,[55] where, in consequence of the dearness of salt, two male slaves are commonly sold for one dollar; and after nightfall the Mahomedan rover who had purchased me, came and took me away. Having been kept bound in his house another week, I was taken two days' journey with a large slave caravan, and sold privately to the Non Galla for a few ells of calico. My companions in captivity were

---

[49] "Judda" is Jiddah in Saudi Arabia.
[50] "Aurungabad" is Aurangābād in Mahārāshtra, India.
[51] "Panwell" is Panvel in Mahārāshtra, India.
[52] "Bussora" is al-Baṣrah in Iraq.
[53] "Surat" is Sūrat in Gujarāt, India.
[54] *BPP*, Slave Trade, XXV, Class A, 401–2 [Rubil bin Uslan to Hennell, 27 Ramaẓān 1257/12 November 1841].
   A shorter version of the report is in *Ibid*, 427 [Reuben Aslan to Hennell, 27 Ramaẓān/12 November 1841].
[55] "Sundáffo" is Sendafa in Oromīya, Ethiopia.

assorted according to their age and size, and walked in double file, the stout and able bodied only, whereof I was one, having their hands tied behind them. In the market-place of Nono, called Mugra,[56] I was, after six weeks' confinement, sold by public auction to the Agamecho Galla for forty pieces of salt (value 8s. 4d.), thence I was taken to the market-place, which is beyond Segualo,[57] on the plain of the Hawash, and sold for seventy pieces of salt to the Soddo Galla, and immediately afterwards to Roqué,[58] the great slave-mart in the Tener[59] district, where I was sold for 100 amoles (20s.). From Roqué, I was driven to Aia Amba,[60] in Shoa, where a Mahomedan subject of Sehela Selassie purchased me in the market for twelve dollars; but after three months, my master falling into disgrace, the whole of his property was confiscated, and I became the slave of the Negus, which I still am, though permitted to reside with my family at Angollolla,[61] and only called upon to plough, reap, and carry wood. Exclusive of halts, the journey from my native village occupied 15 days; I was tolerably fed and not maltreated. All the merchants through whose hands I passed were Mahomedans, and until within a few stages of Alia Amba, I was invariably bound at night, and found no opportunity to escape. Prior to my own enslavement, I had been extensively engaged as a kidnapper; and in this capacity had made party in three great slave hunts into the country of the Doko negroes, beyond Caffa, in the course of which 4,000 individuals of both sexes were secured.[62]

CASE 5

Context: On May 7, 1859, British resident in Mits'iwa (Massawa) received information that the *nakhoda*[63] of English ship, called Soobloo Salam, – who had arrived from Singapore and Malabar at Mits'iwa three days before – had purchased a young girl. The following morning, a young boy escaped from Soobloo Salam and went to the resident's house. After meeting with the resident, this boy revealed that he has been brought from al-Ḥudaydah with another girl; he also found the girl who had just been purchased in Mits'iwa on board. The resident then summoned this *nakhoda* named Hadjee Abdelkursem and examined him before the governor of Mits'iwa. *Nakhoda* confessed that he purchased the slaves. Thus, resident put this *nakhoda* under arrest and seized the ship, and he also liberated the

---

[56] "Mugra" is Mīgra in Oromīya, Ethiopia.

[57] "Segualo" is Segalat' in Āmara, Ethiopia.

[58] "Roqué" is Rogē in Oromīya, Ethiopia.

[59] "Tener" is Yerer in Oromīya, Ethiopia.

[60] "Aia Amba" is Āliyu Āmba in Āmara, Ethiopia.

[61] "Angollolla" is Āngolela in Āmara, Ethiopia.

[62] *BPP*, Slave Trade, XXV, Class A, 440 [Harris to the Secretary of the Bombay Government, 20 July 1842]. W. C. Harris, *The Highlands of Æthiopia* (3 vols. London, 1844), III, 303–305 cited the same story but changed the spelling of several place names. Dibbo's case was moved around the interior of Africa. However, the places to which he was taken were obviously along the caravan route that led to a number of coastal ports including Mits'iwa (Massawa), Tadjoura, and those of the Somali Coast. See *BPP*, Slave Trade, XXV, Class A, 440–441 [Harris to the Secretary of the Bombay Government, 20 July 1842]; A. d'Abbadie, *Géograhie d'Ethiopie : ce que j'ai entendu, faisant suite à ce que j'ai vu* (2 vols., Paris, 1890); R. Pankhurst, "The Trade of Northern Ethiopia in the Nineteenth and early Twentieth Centuries," *Journal of Ethiopian Studies*, 2, 1 (1964): 49–159; R. Pankhurst, "The Trade of Southern and Western Ethiopia and the Indian Ocean Ports in the Nineteenth and Early Twentieth Centuries," *Journal of Ethiopian Studies*, 3, 2 (1964): 37–74.

[63] *Nakhoda*, or *nākhūda, nākhudhā* (several spellings exist in Arabic, in Persian, in Gujarati, and in Swahili), is often translated as "captain." However, his role is not restricted to sailing matters. He managed the cargo, recruited sailors, and performed other duties. See Yule and Burnell, *Hobson-Jobson*, 612–613 s.v. Nacoda, Nacoder.

slaves and placed them under the protection of the English nation. After protecting these three ex-slaves, he interviewed with them.

The Statement of the three liberated Slaves.

The boy named originally Hassen but now Kaman, says that he is a native of Abyssinia in the province of Tigray and was stolen by a Mussulman slave hunter, who sent him to Hodeidah[64] by way of Tajourra[65] where he was sold, and resold lately by Ahkmed Cahatan, his master, to Abdelkooreem the Nakoda of the English ship Soobloo Salam.

One of the girl name was Abbina who was purchased at Hodeidah, states that her country is Metiba in the province of Galla under Abagefar government. She was stolen by Mussulman and sent by way of Tajourra to Hodeidah, where she was sold to a merchant whose name she does not know, and who had sold her to the Nakoda of the English ship who brought her to Massowah.

The third a girl named Tooroonga says that her country is Gomma in the Galla's provinces and she was stolen and sent to Massowah to Ali BaGenit who had sold her to Captain of the English ship, Soobloo Salam; she says that she was brought on board the ship in a evening by the ship's boat.

The age of the boy is about 12 years. The age of the two girls about 9 years.

Massowah 10 May 1837

B. Barroniz[66]

SUGGESTED ADDITIONAL READINGS

Beachey, Ray. *The Slave Trade of Eastern Africa*. London: Rex Collings, 1976.

Campbell, Gwyn (ed.). *The Structure of Slavery in Indian Ocean Africa and Asia*. London and Portland: Frank Cass, 2004.

Christopher, Emma, Cassandra Pybus, and Marcus Rediker (eds.). *Many Middle Passages: Forced Migration and the Making of the Modern World*. Berkeley, Los Angeles, and London: University of California Press, 2007.

Clarence-Smith, William (ed.). *The Economics of the Indian Ocean Slave Trade in the Nineteenth Century*. London: Frank Cass, 1989.

Cooper, Frederick. *Plantation Slavery on the East Coast of Africa*. Portsmouth: Heinemann, 1997.

Gilbert, Erik. *Dhows and the Colonial Economy of Zanzibar, 1860–1970*. Oxford: James Currey, 2004.

Jayasuriya, Shihan de S. and Richard Pankhurst (eds.). *The African Diaspora in the Indian Ocean*. Trenton and Asmara: Africa World Press, 2003.

Kelly, John. *Britain and the Persian Gulf 1795–1880*. Oxford: Oxford University Press, 1968.

Nicholls, Christine. *The Swahili Coast: Politics, Diplomacy and Trade on the East African Littoral, 1798–1856*. London: George Allen and Unwin, 1971.

Sheriff, Abdul. *Slaves, Spices and Ivory in Zanzibar: Integration of an East African Commercial Empire into the World Economy, 1770–1873*. Oxford: James Currey, 1987.

---

[64] "Hodeidah" is al-Ḥudaydah in Saudi Arabia.

[65] "Tajourra" is Tadjoura in Djibouti.

[66] APAC IOR/R/20/A1A/255/111.

28 Gender, Migration, and the End of Slavery in the Region of Kayes, French Soudan

MARIE RODET

French Soudan was a former French colony now known as Mali. From the end of the nineteenth century onward, with the gradual abolition of slavery in this part of West Africa, newly emancipated slaves began to leave their former masters. Some of them left for their region of origin. Others went to colonial towns or founded new villages. It is estimated that after the introduction of legislation permitting them to do so, an average of one-third of the French Soudan slaves left their masters.[1]

The first attempts to restrict the slave trade in this region of West Africa began in 1895 with the banning of the slave trade. Slave caravans crossing the territory of French Soudan were to be seized and slaves sent to the "liberty villages" where they would be issued a liberty certificate after three months of stay. The liberty villages had been founded by the French administration in the first years of the conquest. In the beginning, they hosted the slaves of the defeated enemies of the French army. They also provided a refuge for mistreated slaves, for those threatened with sale by their masters, or for those whose family masters had already sold. Above all, liberty villages were an attempt by the French administration to control increasing slave flights in the region and to create permanent settled communities in deserted areas around colonial posts and along the main conquest and trade routes. They were also a first response to the lack of a labor force. In fact, they enabled the administration to organize a cheap labor supply, as the inhabitants of the liberty villages were the first target for colonial labor requisitions and *corvée* labor.[2]

However, up to 1901, slaves were systematically returned to their masters if the masters claimed them within three months of the date of entry into the liberty village. Slavery abolition politics took a new impulse under the administration of William Ponty, the delegate (representative) in Kayes of the Governor-General from 1899, especially with the promulgation of the Decree of 12 December 1905, abolishing the slave trade in French West Africa. If the Decree as such did not seem to ban domestic slave ownership,[3] circulars of 20 February 1906 and 24 April 1908 clearly invited colonial administrators to ban all forms of slavery.

---

[1] M. Klein, *Slavery and Colonial Rule in French West Africa* (Cambridge, 1998), 197.

[2] D. Bouche, *Les villages de liberté en Afrique noire française 1887–1910* (Paris, 1968).

[3] There were two ways of becoming a slave in Western Sudan: one could be bought or captured as an adult (i.e., "trade slave" or *captif de traite*), or one could be born in the master's household (i.e., "domestic slave," "slave born in the household," or *captif de case*).

At the end of the nineteenth century in the region of Kayes,[4] the economy relied heavily on slave labor. The slave population represented around 40 percent of the total population of the region, but this number could be as high as 60 percent in some areas.[5] Moreover, female slaves formed the majority of the slave population. Women had a greater value than men. Female slaves gave new dependents to their masters, but above all, female labor was predominant in production. Their domestic labor was also essential to the family economy. Their value was therefore attached to their reproductive role, as well as to their productive role. In the region of Kayes, they formed at least 60 percent of the slave population.[6]

Some scholars have argued that it was easier for men than for women to leave their former master, as female slaves often had children born in the community, and were therefore said to be more socially attached.[7] A closer examination of the colonial archives shows, however, that former female slaves in the region of Kayes, alone or with their family, even if they were the wives or the concubines of their masters, did participate in the migratory movements spurred by the abolition of slavery.[8] The two following petitions (and the related exchange of correspondence) are dated 1900 and 1907 and addressed to the colonial administration of the region Kayes. Both allow us to uncover slave women's migratory strategies at that time. Actually, the petitions were written by men, but their analysis can help us recover female slaves' voices in the process of emancipation. We do not hear women speaking directly in these documents because French colonial archives were essentially produced by male colonial civil servants and politicians who, in their project of domination, were little interested in women. When women are mentioned in colonial documents, they are discussed in stereotypical reproductive roles, like wives and mothers;[9] this is one of the reasons why, in the two petitions, the issue of their marital situation is central for the colonial administration. Colonial administrators seem to have been reluctant to disentangle the complex relations between slaves and masters. The colonial administration defended an ambiguous position toward slave women's emancipation. Because slave women were the cornerstones of the economy in the region, colonial administrators preferred not to confront this ambiguous status and therefore the consequences of a true emancipation. They therefore claimed that, as wives and daughters, they had to remain under the control of male guardians. A gender approach to these sources can help us disentangle women's voices in order to build up a history of their mobility.[10] When reading these petitions, we have to ask ourselves what it meant to be a female slave at the time. What were the options available to

---

[4] The region of Kayes is located in the Western part of French Soudan and is bordered by Senegal, Guinea, and Mauritania. Kayes was the first capital city of the colony of French Soudan up to 1904. The region of Kayes refers in the French colonial archives to the *cercles* (districts) of Bafoulabé, Kayes, Kita, Médine, Nioro, and Satadougou.

[5] M. Rodet, "Migrants in French Sudan: Gender Biases in the Historiography," in T. Falola and N. Afolabi (eds.), *Trans-Atlantic Migration: The Paradoxes of Exile* (New York, 2008), 173.

[6] Rodet, "Migrants in French Sudan," 173.

[7] R. Roberts and S. Miers, "Introduction: The End of Slavery in Africa," in S. Miers and R. Roberts (eds.), *Slavery and Colonial Rule in Africa* (London, 1988), 38–40.

[8] Rodet, "Migrants in French Sudan," 170–175.

[9] M. Rodet, "Disrupting Masculinist Discourse on African Migration: The Study of Neglected Forms of Female Migration," in C. Baker and Z. Norridge (eds.), *Crossing Places: New Research in African Studies* (Newcastle, 2007), 30.

[10] To adopt a gender approach is to take into account in the analysis of the text the discourses, performed identities, behaviors, and power relations associated with one sex. The social construction of masculinity and femininity has varied among societies; their meaning has constantly shifted. See N. Vince, M. Rodet, and O. Goerg, "Introduction: Shifting Gendered and Colonial Spaces in Africa," *Stichproben*, Special Issue: Fracturing Binarisms: Gender and Colonialisms in Africa, 12:3 (2007).

them to enhance their position in a society where being a slave or of slave ancestry was a serious stigma? Furthermore, we have to question to what extent slave women's voices were likely to disrupt supposedly fixed relations of gender and power hierarchies. The end of slavery not only disturbed slave and master relationships but also troubled gender relations because of the massive participation of women in the slave exodus.

I present the two petitions in the same order in which they are filed in the archives so as to give the reader a glimpse of the historical work of reconstituting slaves' histories using scattered documents. The first petition is concerned with the efforts by a master to claim his slaves back, whereas the second petition deals with a soldier of slave origin who struggles to assist his family and to create his own household.

THE BEYDY COULOUBALY PETITION

In September 1900, the Delegate of the Governor-General in Kayes received a complaint from Beydy Couloubaly asking for the return of his three wives who sought refuge in the liberty village of Kita. In a preceding letter, the commandant in Kita had declared that these women were free because they had left the liberty village after a three-month stay. He considered henceforth this case as a divorce that had to be brought in front of the colonial court. This petition encourages us to question the colonial use of categories like "wife" and "slave woman," and highlights the "shifting" border between the two at the time in which colonial government was making its first political steps toward slave emancipation. A female slave was a worker and a commodity, but she was also often the concubine of her male master.[11] Slavery for a woman meant that her body became the property of her master; it was subjected to her master's will, unlike a free woman whose sexuality and virginity was tightly controlled.[12] This explains why some masters claimed that their slave women were actually their wives even if they bought them as slaves.

QUESTIONS TO CONSIDER

1. Why did the three women not go to the liberty village first?
2. Why did the administration refuse to give Beydy Couloubaly his "wives" back?
3. Could these women be at the same time the slaves and the wives of Beydy Couloubaly? Why?

ANM 1 E 201 (FA): Political Issues. Correspondence. Cercle (District) of Kayes. 1882–1921.

Letter from Beydy Couloubaly to the Delegate of the Governor General. Médine, 19 September 1900.

Sir,

By sending this letter I beg to inform you that my three escaped wives took refuge at the liberty village of Kita. The named Dadié Bakayoko who I bought from Mamadou Dambélé for 350 francs. This woman has been living with me for thirteen years.

---

[11] E. S. Burrill, "'Wives of Circumstance': Gender and Slave Emancipation in Late Nineteenth-Century Senegal," *Slavery & Abolition*, 29, 1 (2008), 52.

[12] Klein, *Slavery and Colonial Rule*, 247.

Fatimata Couloubaly who I bought for five hundred francs, who has been living with me for five years.

The third one Téné Sidibé who I bought for five hundred frnas [*sic*][13], she stayed with me for about ten years.

The named Dadié Bakayoko the first of my wives got two children from me.

These three women went to do trade in several villages and got captured and dragged to Kita by a fellow who I do not know.

Last July I went to Kita to take them but these women had been staying for more than three months in the liberty village, the Commandant has therefore categorucally [*sic*] refused to give them to me.

I went back another time, but the answer of the Commandant was not more favorable.

I therefore turn to you, Mr. Delegate and I come to beg you to use all of your authority [*sic*] so that these women are given back to me as soon as possible.

Yours sincerely,
Your humble servant.
Beydy Couloubaly.

Archives nationales du Mali, Koulouba, 1 E 203 (fonds ancien): Political Issues. Correspondence. Cercle of Kita. 1883–1908.

Senegal and Dependences. Territory of Upper-Senegal and Middle-Niger. Letter #222. Cercle of Kita. Kita, 2 October 1900. Assistant Administrator Commandant of the Cercle of Kita to the Delegate of the Governor-General in Kayes.

Sir,

In response to your letter n 487 of last 26 September concerning the three wives of the named Beydi Coulbaly [*sic*] I could not do better than sending you a copy of my letter #164 of 2 August to the Commandant of the Cercle[14] of Médine, in response to his letter #232 of 25 July. I would only add that these women have left indeed and they must be, at the moment, back in their village of origin from where, whatever Beydi Coulbaly [*sic*] might say, they had definitely been abducted as captives by the columns of Samory.[15]

Only one of them, having had children, must be considered as free and her case would then fall within the competence of the court of Cercle upon which she depends.[16]

As for the two others they have been well and truly bought by Beidy Coulbaly [*sic*] as captives and cannot be considered as free if Beydi [*sic*] has not made a liberty certificate

---

[13] [*sic*] has been added here and in other parts of the text by the author of the chapter to indicate an incorrect or unusual spelling in the original archival document.

[14] Each French West African colony was administratively divided into districts called *Cercles*. Each *cercle* was run by a commandant of *cercle* and each colony by a governor.

[15] Samory Toure was a military leader from Upper Guinea who successfully conquered West African territories extending from Sierra Leone to Northern Côte d'Ivoire in the second half of the nineteenth century (Klein, *Slavery and Colonial Rule*, 52–53). He financed his warfare by selling slaves. From the 1870s, he resisted French expansion, but he was captured by the French and deported to Gabon in 1898.

[16] French interpretation of customary law on slavery was that any slave woman marrying a free man and bearing him a child had to be considered free. According to local customs, a slave woman could be a concubine but as long as she was not officially married to a free man and therefore freed, she was still considered a slave and her children would also be slaves.

issued for them and if he has not paid any bridewealth to the family. This is at least an uncompromising custom for the Malinkés and Bambaras[17] from the Cercles of Bafoulabé and Kita: The cohabitation between a captive and a free man only became a lawful union, therefore shielding the woman from a possible sale in days of misfortune or when this woman gives birth to children.

In the first petition addressed by Beydi Coulbaly [sic] to Mr. Maubert, the Commandant of the Cercle of Médine, and when he [Beydy Couloubaly] himself came to Kita he never mentioned the abduction of these women; he said before numerous witnesses (the heads of the village of Kita) that these women had escaped. In the aforementioned letter he simply tried to incriminate the non-commissioned officer of the Post. In the petition he addresses to you, he seems to accuse somebody of having captured and dragged these women to Kita; but, as you will see in the copy of my response to the Commandant of the Cercle of Médine, I brought them from the village in Kaarta all the way back to Kita.

I would be very eager to know if Beydi Coulbaly [sic] could be more explicit in his information and if, by an investigation, he could prove that these women had indeed left for trade and had then been victims of violence; in the case he could not prove such a fact and as it would be the second time that such a thing happened to him, I would be pleased if a punishment could be imposed on him since he addressed an ill-founded petition and begged for your authority rather than for your benevolence.

Yours sincerely,
[Illegible Signature].

Upper-Senegal and Middle-Niger. Cercle of Kita. Letter #164. Kita, 2 August 1900. Administrator, Commandant of the Cercle of Kita to Commandant of the Cercle of Médine. Copy.

My dear friend,

I am writing you to acknowledge receipt of your letter # 232 dated 25 July 1900.

Moussa Coulibaly[18] must have mislead you concerning the date on which these women left Médine, since on 6 May, as I was in Diougou in Kaarta, the head of the neighboring village, the one of Labadéri, sent his son to explain that three escaped women from Médine had been staying at his home for one month. I told him to keep them until my arrival in his village.

Due to diverse circumstances, I was unable to go to Labadéri and the three women in question were brought to me to Sakara on 17 May when I went by this village.

On 28 May, when I came back to Kita, I inscribed them, since they claimed to be captives, in the liberty village, I made the date of their inscription go back to 10 April, the approximate date of their arrival in Labadéri. But, Moussa came to me only on 17 July to claim his three escaped captives, that is seven days too late, so that I could not give them back to him.

The date of 15 June mentioned on his pass is when he came to the post to claim his three captives. According to custom, he had to search for them by himself and came on

---

[17] Malinkés and Bambaras are French colonial designations for West African peoples belonging to the larger Mande cultural and linguistic group.

[18] Here you have to understand Beydy Couloubaly. The colonial administration often mistook one person's name for another.

17 July to report that he eventually found them; but the normal prescribed time of three months was over and I could not give freed women back to him.

Today the three women are free and they will soon go back home. I therefore advise Moussa Coulibaly [*sic*], since he pretends to treat them as free women, to approach the Commandants of Cercle in which they will stay. In the settlement of this case, which becomes a simple divorce case, I do not have to interfere further as neither the women in question nor the husband fall within the scope of my authority.

I do not know whether the sergeant school instructor had or did not have one of these women as his mistress. What I can affirm to you is that I was not called as a civil officer to sanction this union. Moreover, when I ordered Moussa Coulibaly [*sic*] to prove his statement, he based his responses on what two old procuring Muslim women from Kita told him. As the custom goes, these women today have sworn on the Koran according to the rites that they had not said anything to Moussa Coulibaly [*sic*].

I would be therefore grateful if you could punish this native for having put forward a fact that he cannot prove.

You will well understand, my dear friend, that only my obligation to obey rules in force prevents me from conforming to the wish indicated in your letter and that I am not worried at all about the supposed alliance with the sergeant school instructor, since the three women who are concerned by the petition of Moussa Coulibaly [*sic*], as I was telling you at the beginning, will have left the Cercle of Kita tomorrow on 3 August.

Sincerely yours…
Signed: Pierre Dupont.

The Amady Penda Petition

This second set of documents deals with the petition addressed by Amady Penda, police guard in Louga[19] in September 1907, to the colonial administration in order to set free his family which, he claimed, was still enslaved in French Soudan. Unfortunately the original petition by Amady Penda was not to be found in the file. We also do not know how the story of Amady Penda ended. But the exchange of correspondence highlights to what extent the struggle for the control over the family life was a very important issue during "emancipation." It shows that (former) slaves were neither without connections and social networks nor without family ties.

DISCUSSION QUESTIONS

1. Why did Amady Penda seek the help of the colonial administration to set his family free?
2. Why did the governor of Senegal disagree with the decision taken by the administrator Bonnathiés to authorize Amady Penda's sister Kouta Bâ to join him in Louga?
3. Why was the colonial administration reluctant to encourage the true emancipation of former slave women?

[19] Louga is a Senegalese town located in the northwest of the country.

4. Why was the bridewealth of Amady Penda's two sisters kept by the master and why did Amady claim it?

Archives nationales du Mali, Koulouba, 2 E 12 (fonds ancien): Petitions from natives and miscellaneous in order to return to their country. Correspondence with Senegal.

Governor of Senegal in Saint-Louis. Petition from Amady Penda. #a168. 15 October 1907.

In response to your letter #646 of last 5 September concerning a petition from Amady Penda, a police guard in Louga, I am writing to you to transmit, as follows, the results of the enquiry that I confided in this matter to the Administrator of the Cercle of Kayes[20].

Kouta Bâ, married to Tiébilé Sidibé, servant of Amady Coumba, declared that she would join her brother, Amady Penda. She has been granted a pass to go to Bakel where she was eager to see her sister, Sadio Ba; from there, she intends to go directly to Louga. Kouta Bâ left Kayes with her two children, Mamadou Sidibé and Fatoumata Sidibé. The preceding facts having occurred while Tiébilé Sidibé was absent in Saint-Louis[21] for two months, we have every reason to expect him to claim his rights as husband and father. Personally I cannot sanction the decision taken by the Administrator Bonnathiés.

Penda Bâ, second sister of the plaintiff is currently married to Mamady Diénéba. She declared that she is entirely free and indicated that she wanted to stay with her husband. With such a definite declaration, the Administrator of Kayes refrained from pushing his intervention any further.

As for the despoilment the plaintiff charged Amady Coumba with, the sisters of Amady Penda have categorically declared they had no complaint to register.

Upper-Senegal and Niger. Cercle of Kayes. Kayes, 4 October 1907. Administrator of the Cercle of Kayes to Acting Lieutenant-Governor of Upper-Senegal and Niger. #602. Petition 'Amady Penda'. One enclosed document.

I am writing to you to acknowledge receipt of your letter #B.705 transmitting a petition formulated by the named Amady Penda, police guard in Louga (Senegal), and to give you the account of the follow-up that this case appeared to have entailed.

In 1906, Amady Penda, at that time spahi in the 1st squad of the Senegalese Spahis,[22] had already made a complaint concerning his family.

By letter #9 dated 6 January 1906 this petition was transmitted to my predecessor by Mr. the lieutenant-governor of the Upper-Senegal and Niger.

---

[20] We suspect here that Mamadou Penda got special consideration for his petition because he was a former soldier and an employee of the French colonial administration.

[21] Saint Louis was the Capital of French West Africa up to 1902 but remained capital of the colony of Senegal up to independence in 1960.

[22] The Senegalese Spahis were a cavalry army corps created in 1902 in French West Africa. French sometimes tried to recruit freemen, but generally accepted that military service was a slave role. Slaves were therefore numerous in entering the colonial army at the time, either because the masters sent them in order to avoid forced recruitment of their own children, or because slaves willingly enlisted and used this opportunity to emancipate themselves from their masters. We suspect here that Mamadou Penda enlisted in the Spahis to escape slavery. Before 1905, enlisted slaves were officially freed by the colonial administration at the end of their service. Former soldiers were also often employed by the colonial administration as police or guards.

From the response made by the administrator of the Cercle – copy enclosed – it results that Amady Penda partially obtained satisfaction.

The sisters of the one lodging the complaint invited at the Cercle came yesterday and made the following statements to me:

1. <u>Kouta</u> Ba, married to Tiébilé Sidibé, non-free who is in the service of Amady Couma, declared that her husband had been to St Louis for two months; she said she would be only too pleased to join her brother.

   I therefore immediately put down the named Kouta Ba and her two children Mamadou Sidibé and Fatoumata Sidibé in the registers of Kayes-Refuge.[23] I then issued a pass as she asked for one to Bakel where she wishes to go in order to see her sister before going to Louga.

2. <u>Penda</u> Ba, married to Mamady Tienéba, declared that her husband had bought her back from Amady Coumba, she was therefore entirely free, she wished to stay with her husband and did not want to go to Louga.

   Regarding the petitions from Amady Penda concerned with the spoliations of which his family would have been victim by Amady Coumba, it is not up to me to give a follow-up, they are first of all expressed in too hazy terms, moreover the two sisters of Amady Penda informed by myself that they had to submit the case to the province court of Kayes, have declared that they did not have any complaint to register. In this case, it is besides a matter of the bridewealth of the two sisters of Amady Penda, which has been kept by Amady Coumba according to the native custom.

Copy. Administrator of the Cercle of Kayes to Acting Lieutenant-Governor of Upper-Senegal in Kayes.

By letter #9 of last 6 January under the stamp of the first Bureau you were kind to transmit to me a request addressed by the trooper Mamadou Penda of the first squadron of the first Senegalese spahis to his captain for investigation in order to have several members of his family who are held in captivity in the village of Kotéra (Cercle of Kayes) allowed to join him in Senegal.

I beg to inform you about the results of the inquiry I carried out.

The father of Mamadou Penda, Samba Bâ, died about ten years ago.

The mother, Penda Bâ, spent her entire life in the village of Kotéra in the service of Mr Amady Coumba, I informed him of the desire expressed by Mamadou Penda to have his mother join him in St Louis: he made no objection to the departure of this woman.

The wife of Mamadou Penda, Fatou [Fati in the original] Madia is currently living in Kotéra in the house of Boubou Kamara, whose servant she has always been. This woman had two daughters from Mamadou Penda who live with her; she showed a very strong desire to join her husband from whom she had been separated for four years. Her owner Boubou Kamara without being absolutely opposed to the departure of this woman explained to me

---

[23] Kayes-Refuge is the name of the former liberty village of Kayes. Following the promulgation of the decree of 1905, the administration could no longer use the appellation of "liberty village," which implied that the administration recognized the existence of a non-free population. It is also from this time that the colonial administration started to use on purpose the word "refugees" or "domestics" rather than "former slaves" because of its reluctance to recognize the difficult issue of slavery and its legacy in the region.

that Fatou Madia however never lived at his place like a servant of the house, that she never provided any work and that not only had he constantly provided for her needs, but he also covered all the expenses for her marriage with Mamadou Penda and raised the two children born of this marriage.[24] He asked me whether I did not reckon under these conditions that he would be entitled to ask Fatou Madia, who wishes to leave him, to reimburse a part of the expenses caused to him by her presence in the house.

The woman Fatou Madia recognized the exactness of the observations of Boubou Kamara. She told me he had always treated her well[25] and that she had even been able to treat herself to the luxury of having a servant[26] and to acquire a cow, a heifer and three donkeys thanks to his liberalities.

She had furthermore recognized that Boubou Kamara had personally paid the total of the head tax for her and her family.[27] In order to testify to her gratitude, Fatou Madia spontaneously offered to abandon the five animals she owns to Boubou Kamara.

The two parties being in agreement, I thought I had to sanction this transaction thanks to which Boubou Kamara will be partially reimbursed for his costs of maintenance.

It has been furthermore agreed that the servant of Fatou Madia would not come with her to Saint-Louis and that she would be free from now on. The woman Fatou Madia has been authorized to get under way to Saint-Louis at the same time as the mother of Mamadou Penda.

I thought I could not grant the same permission to two sisters of Mamadou Penda who are in the following situation:

The first named Kola Bâ lives in the village of Kotéra with her husband Tiélibé Sidibé and her two children and is in the service of Amady Coumba.

The second Penda Bâ who is also in the service of Amady Coumba is married with Mamady Diénéba in Kotéra.

These two women declared to me that they had a happy married life and had no complaint to express against their owner Amady Coumba. They wish however to join Mamadou Penda in Saint-Louis and to abandon their husbands and children if necessary because as according to the native expression: 'They cannot refuse the word of their brother'.

I draw the attention of these two women to the fact that the Koranic law obliged a woman to live with her husband; that they themselves reckoned they had no reason to get a divorce and that in any case I did not have authority to dissolve their marriages.

---

[24] Traditional masters' obligations toward their slaves were those of their daily maintenance. They were also in charge of finding a wife for their male slaves. It is possible, as Boubou Kamara declared, that Fatou Madia never worked for him in the sense that she never worked on his fields, but it is very unlikely that she never provided any housework for him and his family.

[25] It is difficult to know why Fatou Madia admitted she was treated well. One can suspect that she simply considered herself as well treated compared to the slaves of other masters: as she said, her master always provided for her, she did not have to work on his fields, and she could acquire some property thanks to his generosity. It is probably also why she never left her master. Most of the slaves who left at the time did it so because their master mistreated them or were not able to provide them with their daily sustenance. These flights happened especially in times of food shortages. Between 1897 and 1915, the region of Kayes suffered fourteen years of bad harvests and food shortages, with the most severe crises in 1905–07 and 1913–15. The 1913–14 period was the worst. The most important waves of slave exodus happened between 1908 and 1914.

[26] Slaves were allowed to buy slaves for their own use. They could buy and own whatever they wished during their lifetime, but once they died, their masters always inherited their belongings.

[27] Following the French conquest and the introduction of a head tax, paying the head tax also became part of masters' obligations toward their slaves.

Under these conditions I sent them back to take their case to the jurisdiction concerned and have forbidden them to leave their husbands before a court order had authorized them to do so.

The spahi Mamadou Penda got thus satisfaction at least partially; his mother, his wife and his children will join him. Only his sisters have been refused authorization.

Petition of the named Amady Penda. #B.765. 13 September 07. Administrator Kayes.

I am writing to you to send you as enclosed the petition of the police guard Mamady Penda in service in Louga.

This native claims that his two sisters, Penda Ba and Coula Bâ as well as their children are held in captivity at the place of Amady Coumba, in the village of Kotéra, province of Gadiaga. The plaintiff also declares to have been despoiled by Amady Coumba.

I would be most obliged to you if you could examine whether these allegations by the guard Amady Penda are well founded and if you could send me as soon as possible the results of your investigation.

Colony of Senegal. Political Department. #646. Saint-Louis, 5 September 1907. The General Secretary of the colonies Haut-Commandant Acting Lieutenant-governor of Senegal to the governor of Upper-Senegal and Niger. Concerning police guard Amady Penda.

I am writing to you to send you the petition of the police guard Amady Penda who asks that his two sisters, PENDA BA and COULA BA and their children held in captivity at Amady COUMBA's place in Kotera, province of Gadiaga, be returned to him.

Amady PENDA who is the former captive of the same master would have found himself stripped of his trunks [full of his personal belongings] and his animals, which he had left at his sisters' place.

SUGGESTED ADDITIONAL READINGS

Bouche, Denise. *Les villages de liberté en Afrique noire française 1887–1910.* Paris: Mouton, 1968. An English summary of this work can be found at: <http://courses.wcupa.edu/jones/his311/archives/sec/bouche.htm> (accessed August 1, 2011).

Burrill, Emily S. "'Wives of Circumstance': Gender and Slave Emancipation in Late Nineteenth-Century Senegal," *Slavery & Abolition,* 29, 1 (2008): 49–64.

Clark, Andrew F. "Freedom Villages in the Upper Senegal Valley, 1887–1910: A Reassessment," *Slavery and Abolition,* 16, 3 (1995): 311–330.

From Frontier to Backwater. Economy and Society in the Upper Senegal Valley (West Africa), 1850–1920. Lanham, MD and Oxford : University Press of America, 1999.

Klein, Martin A. *Slavery and Colonial Rule in French West Africa.* Cambridge: Cambridge University Press, 1998.

Klein, Martin A. and Richard Roberts. "The Banamba Slave Exodus of 1905 and the Decline of Slavery in the Western Sudan," *Journal of African History,* 21 (1980): 375–394.

Manchuelle, François. *Willing Migrants, Soninke Labor Diasporas, 1848–1960.* Athens: Ohio University Press, 1997.

Meillassoux, Claude. *The Anthropology of Slavery: The Womb of Iron and Gold.* Translated by Alide Dasnois. Chicago: The University of Chicago Press & Athlone Press, 1991.

Miers, Suzanne and Igor Kopytoff, eds. *Slavery in Africa. Historical and Antropological Perspectives.* Madison: The University of Wisconsin Press, 1977.

Robertson, Claire C. and Martin A. Klein, eds. *Women and Slavery in Africa.* Madison: The University Press of Wisconsin, 1983.

Rodet, Marie. "Disrupting Masculinist Discourse on African Migration: The Study of Neglected Forms of Female Migration," *Crossing Places: New Research in African Studies.* Edited by Charlotte Baker and Zoë Norridge (Newcastle: Cambridge Scholars Publishing, 2007), 28–38.

⸻ "Migrants in French Sudan: Gender Biases in the Historiography", *Trans-Atlantic Migration: The Paradoxes of Exile.* Edited by Toyin Falola and Niyi Afolabi (New York: Routledge, 2008), 165–181.

Vince, Natalya, Marie Rodet, and Odile Goerg. "Introduction: Shifting Gendered and Colonial Spaces in Africa," *Stichproben,* Special Issue: Fracturing Binarisms: Gender and Colonialisms in Africa, 12 (2007): 1–11. Available at: http://www.univie.ac.at/ecco/stichproben/nr12.htm (accessed August 1, 2011).

PART SIX

LEGAL RECORDS

29   INTRODUCTION: Voices of Slaves in the Courtroom

Historians have increasingly found evidence from the courtroom to be very valuable, particularly in reconstructing social history. This does not mean that there are no problems with such evidence. Two kinds of problems exist. The first is with the transcript. Rarely are they complete. In many cases, there is only a list of decisions, though even such evidence can be valuable, as Richard Roberts has shown.[1] Even where there is a transcript, the slave's testimony has usually been filtered through translation and summed up by a magistrate or a court clerk. The second problem is the nature of the court. Even where there was a court with the full apparatus of European judicial procedure, as in Lagos or the Gold Coast, the operation of the court was influenced by the strategies of opposed attorneys, the accused, and the different witnesses. The slave witness was usually in an unfamiliar court situation, where his or her interests were secondary to these strategies and where he or she was being pressed in Stickrodt's terms, "to say the 'right' thing."

Still, these witnesses tell interesting stories. Dalu Modu, a slave-trader presented by Bruce L. Mouser in Chapter 30, gives a frank discussion of his relations with the struggling Sierra Leone colony. Three documents give us a picture of slavery in nineteenth-century coastal West Africa. In the case of Abina Mansah, a female slave who ran away from her master when he tried to force her to marry a male retainer, Trevor Getz (Chapter 32) gives a picture of the different actors in a court case. Silke Stickrodt in Chapter 34 gives us the tale of Aballow, also a young female slave, who was central to the trial of a British merchant, who was a major commodity trader, but also dealt with and used the services of domestic slaves. In the Gambia, almost a half-century later, the complaint of two runaway slave women led to the trial of a merchant, who was a British subject and who sexually exploited his female slaves. This case is analyzed by Alice Bellagamba in Chapter 31. Kristin Mann (Chapter 33) presents an account not of slavery, but of the way slavery shaped inheritance law in Lagos even for people freed from slavery in Brazil. Mann has elsewhere used court data for other purposes, particularly in trying to understand the struggle for the control of labor after abolition.[2] Richard Roberts in Chapter 35 presents a case of kidnapping and slavery in colonial Senegal, where there clearly was an underground economy using kidnapped children. Each of these cases is a window on a small piece of African life that is rarely available from other sources.

[1] Richard Roberts, *Litigants and Households: African Disputes and Colonial Courts in the French Soudan, 1895–1912* (Portsmouth, NH, 2005).

[2] Kristin Mann, *Slavery and the Birth of an African City: Lagos, 1760–1900* (Bloomington, IN, 2007).

30 The Expulsion of Dalu Modu

A Muslim Trader in Anti-Slavery Freetown

BRUCE L. MOUSER

Alimaamy Dalu Mohammedu Dumbuya (henceforth Dalu Modu) was a Muslim headman and trader expelled from Freetown in November or December 1806. He and his followers moved across the estuary of the Sierra Leone River to northern Bullom Shore where they settled in a town called Lungi, only a brief distance from Freetown. Three years later, he was interrogated by British officials at Freetown about the circumstances of his expulsion. The interview shows his understanding of servitude within the settlement and provides information about slave trading and selling within a colony formed originally as the "province of freedom." The question-and-answer nature of the document suggests that this was a verbatim transcript of Dala Modu's testimony, and not an analysis.

Governor Thomas Perronet Thompson had requested this legal testimony in 1809 as part of an ongoing claim of malfeasance against Thomas Ludlam who had preceded Thompson as governor of the colony. Founded in 1787, Freetown was envisioned by its early sponsors first as a refuge on the African coast for Black Poor from England and later as a home for blacks from the New World that longed for an African homeland. From 1792 to January 1, 1808, the settlement had been administered by the Sierra Leone Company, which publicly opposed slave trading and portrayed the settlement as an oasis of freedom on the African coast. In 1808, when the British made the slave trade illegal for British subjects and the colony a base in the struggle against the slave trade, Freetown changed from a company-governed settlement to a royal colony. Upon his arrival as the colony's first royal governor, Thompson found sufficient reason to believe that former governor Ludlam had violated recently passed British laws that had ended the slave trade, and Thompson became determined to gather evidence that would be acceptable in a British court, if a case were to be brought against either Ludlam or the Company. This testimony by Dala Modu is one of those pieces of evidence that Thompson collected.

The "evidence" was produced with two purposes in mind. Thompson sought testimony that would discredit the Company and Ludlam. In effect, only two questions were asked: (1) how long did you live in the settlement, and (2) what do you know of buying and selling of slaves within the settlement while Ludlam was its governor. The testimony does not indicate that additional questions were asked to lead the answerer, although that may have occurred and those may have been deleted in this "corrected" version. Nor is it certain that this version contains all that Dala Modu said in his oral deposition. From

Dala Modu's perspective, this may have been his first opportunity to explain his side of his expulsion from the settlement. It also permitted him to describe the differences between African definitions of slavery and subordinate status and British attitudes about slavery and pawnships, indentures, apprenticeships, and subordinate status within its own settlement. Dalu Modu's views were probably shared by most if not all African slave owners who visited the settlement or traded with it.

At the core of the testimony, however, was the question of what had occurred in Freetown when the Royal Squadron Ship *Derwent* brought two captured American slaving vessels containing slaves into that port early in 1808, after the Anti-Slave Trade bill had taken effect on January 1, 1808 and before Thompson arrived to take charge of the colony on July 27, 1808. Although Dala Modu was then living at nearby Lungi on Bullom Shore, he was frequently in the colony and would have been a credible witness to what happened there in 1808. The *Derwent* seizures also had been the first implementation of new laws that made it illegal for British and American citizens to engage in slave trading and authorized royal vessels to seize suspected slave ships. Ludlam was uncertain of what to do with the slaves found on board the vessels. Sending them back to their homes was problematic because many spoke unknown languages, and the task of sorting them out and of sending them back to distant places was great. Ludlam, who then was only acting as temporary governor until Thompson's arrival, chose to distribute the slaves to settlers and others, and to impose a fee of US$20 per slave, which could be recouped through labor and service to those who paid the fee. Thompson considered the "fee" to have been the same as slave trading, little different from a sale of a person for a period of servitude. In the British and the American systems, such a practice might have been interpreted as indenturing, but official indenture contracts were officially registered with respect to longevity and restrictions to protect those being indentured from the dishonesty of those who might take advantage of unwritten or verbal agreements. No official papers, however, had been registered for those slaves taken from vessels captured by the *Derwent*.

For Dala Modu, there were other issues that dominated his testimony. One was the difference between what he perceived as legally acceptable behavior for a European or a settler within the settlement and that permitted for Africans who lived alongside the settlement or who conducted business there. Dala Modu might be "headman" or ruler in his own village, and he might be able to engage in "country councils or courts" within his indigenous system of obligations, but once he crossed over into British territory, he lost those privileges as now a client within another relationship arrangement. In his case, Dala Modu was confused regarding the line that separated the two. Second was the issue of religion, and how that issue played out in Dala Modu's trial. Both sides of the dispute were offended by what transpired in the colony's church during Dala Modu's trial and by the symbols (clothing, manners, and ornaments) exhibited by the other while within the church. A third issue involved property rights and the right to profit as a consequence of improvements and enterprise. African custom demanded compensation for seized property, except in a case of warfare or specific instances of legal (or social) malfeasance. Dala Modu believed that he had been misjudged and that his land and wealth had been seized arbitrarily and with malice. Finally, Dala Modu was caught in an indigenous and African-based system of "landlord/stranger" relationships wherein a "stranger" was always expected to follow regulations stipulated by his "landlord" – in this case that was acceptable to the Sierra Leone Company and its governor. The "landlord/stranger relationship" was a contract drawn between a person who held the right of land use (the landlord) and an outsider (the stranger) who wished to use the land but had no natural right to that use, except the right contractually granted him by a landlord. His own chiefs – those to whom he owed allegiance in his African sociopolitical world – required as well that he adhere strictly to his contract with his British landlord, for they expected the same from "strangers" who lived in their own towns and territories.

The long-term impact of Dala Modu's trial, his expulsion from the colony in 1806, and this testimony or "evidence" provided to colonial authorities were minimal. Ludlam was never brought to trial, and from his center at Lungi, Dala Modu continued to play a prominent role in the colony's commerce until his death in 1841.

QUESTIONS TO CONSIDER

1. How clearly did Dala Modu understand the statuses of free persons and persons in the settlement who were of non-slave but of subordinate status? Do you believe that Dala Modu was confused about this issue? Was he angry about it or thought it unfair to him as an African?

2. From what is reported here, how would you defend Dala Modu against the charges brought against him? Did his argument that conversion to Christianity was an unrealistic and unfair expectation influence your analysis of his testimony?

3. Assume that English was one of several languages spoken and understood by Dala Modu. How important was language (i.e., word meanings and mannerism or body language) in this trial, the charges brought against him, and the understanding of law?

4. What does this testimony tell you about an African perspective of slavery and status of subordination within the African context? How important were "chains" or "irons" in the story? How were you affected by the case of the boy becoming a surrogate for the misdeeds of his father?

The Document

Evidence of Dalu Mohammed[:] Corrected from Minutes of Council, 5 Aug. 1809.[1]
Dalu Mohammed, (called by the Settlers Dalla Mooda)

Q[uestion]. Of what religion are you?
A[nswer]. The Mohammedan.
Witness sworn by the Koran & by Mohammed:

Q. State how long you have lived in this Colony, & what you know of the buying and selling of Slaves in it?
A. I live at Lungea on the Bullom Shore. I left this Colony three years ago, in the fast-moon.[2] At the time the Sierra Leone Company settled here [in 1792], I lived at Wonkapong in the Susoo

---

[1] This is an accurate copy of the testimony found as "corrected from Minutes of Council, 5 Aug. 1809," in the Papers of Thomas Perronet Thompson, file DHT 1/16, Hull University Library, Hull, United Kingdom. Words crossed out in the original are reproduced here with words "struck through." Minutes of Council refers to official records of the Sierra Leone governing body that met regularly in Freetown, and copies of its minutes were sent to London.

[2] Month of Ramadan. Ramadan began on November 12 in 1806.

Country, & came backwards & forwards to make trade.[3] When I first came to the Colony, I heard that no Slave Trade was to go on in it. I went to Mr. Cox,[4] the Sierra Leone Company's Storekeeper, & asked him. Mr. Cox said no Slave Trade was to go on in the Colony. I was making trade with Mr. Cox, & asked him what I was to pay him in? Mr. Cox said, in wood; & rice; & ivory, & stock.[5] Soon afterwards a brig came in with slaves; I went to Mr. Cox's house, & saw a strange boy there. I asked where he came from, & Mr. Cox said he came from the brig. I asked how he got him. Mr. Cox said he bought him[6] of the Captain of the Brig. I said, "*I thought you told me there was to be no Slave Trade.*" Mr. Cox said; "*he had bought the boy but he could not sell him again.*" I asked Mr. Cox if he would take Slaves from *me* in payment? Mr. Cox said that "the country was too near; when the boys began to have sense, they ran away to their own country."[7] "The boy he had bought," he said "could not run away for he came from a far country." This happened before the Timmaneys attacked the Colony [in 1802].

In palavers (councils)[8] in the country among the Native Chiefs, I have heard complaints, that the people [British] at Sierra Leone came & pretended to have no Slave Trade, but if any of the slaves of the Natives ran away, they kept them[9] & made them work worse than Slaves.

I was informed against by a Mulatto in the Colony as having sold some slaves, & was brought to trial in the Court-House, & they could make nothing of it. I had a town of my own [Dalamodiya] outside the wall[10] at that time; & a reward of fifty dollars was offered to anybody that would go into my town to spy, & find a slave or any person in a chain.[11]

---

[3] The Dumbuya family was of Susu descent and was the principal military/commercial lineage within the Bullom state of Sumbuya (capital town of Wonkapong) and acted as protectors for Sumbuya's Baga/Bullom rulers. The Dumbuya lineage operated rice plantations and salt-gathering operations, and traded goods extensively into the interior and along the coast. Dumbuya canoe commerce in rice and cattle (the latter coming from Fuuta Jaloo) reached as far south as Freetown and northward as far as the Rio Nunez. This lineage controlled a significant section of coast near Wonkapong and the Iles de Los.

[4] Thomas Cox was the first mayor of Freetown. In the original handwritten document, names were originally given, and later crossed out and replaced with letters. In this instance, the name Cox was replaced with the letter "O". This transcription uses only the original name.

[5] Stock refers to beef cattle.

[6] It was common practice to purchase slaves in this manner, but the British termed this as a "redemption" of slaves, a purchase that ended their slave status. At the same time, it was expected that the person paying the purchase price for a redeemed slave would be able to receive equal value from that redeemed person in the form of labor or service.

[7] Effectively, once a slave had recovered from the initial confusion of capture, sale, and release at Freetown and once he realized that his native home was close to or nearby Freetown, Cox expected that that slave (now free but tied by service obligations within Freetown) would attempt to flee from the settlement and return to his homeland.

[8] A palaver (from the Portuguese *palavra*, or to talk or speak) generally referred to a lengthy discussion, debate, or conference at which issues of state and commerce might be resolved. Dala Modu also uses the term later in the document to refer to a feud or argument.

[9] Sanctuary for escaping or "runaway" slaves was a major problem for the settlement's governors. The first governor, John Clarkson, had made the pledge of sanctuary, but that policy was abandoned by 1796 when it became clear that it created an obstacle for easy interactions with indigenous traders whose commercial goods were carried by slaves. They feared loss of their slave property. Once the promise of sanctuary had been given, it became difficult, if not impossible, to reverse the perception in the neighborhood of the settlement that the policy remained active, as attested by this testimony from 1809, more than a decade after the policy had been reversed.

[10] Towns along this section of the coast generally were walled for defense. In this instance, Dala Modu may have referred to Freetown's formal boundaries. His town of Dalamodiya was technically alongside the Freetown settlement and not a part of it, but he was still expected to follow Freetown's regulations regarding slave trading.

[11] Slavery was still legal in 1806 within the British Empire, but the Company had stipulated that neither slavery nor slave trading or selling would be permitted within the settlement. The use of a chain would indicate slave or criminal status.

Some time after this, a man was sent to me by a head-man on the Bullom shore named King George,[12] to be kept for trial according to the country-law. I was out of the Colony at the time, & when I came back, I found the man had run away in his irons, & had been taken up the hill. (Fort Thornton).[13] The Governor, Mr. Ludlam,[14] sent for me, & asked me what business I had to have a slave in irons at my place? I told him the man was no slave, but a prisoner for trial by country-law. I said to him; "Governor, you look very sharp after me, why do you not look after your own people? they may have plenty of slaves in their houses, though I must have none in my place." I told the Governor to inquire on the Bullom shore,[15] whether the man was not a prisoner, but the Governor would take no notice of what I said. The Governor asked how I could prove that there were slaves in the Colony? I told him, that "if he would turn out all the people in the Colony before me, I would soon tell him which were the Settlers, & which were the Slaves." The Governor was vexed, & told me, "I wanted to make myself head-man." I replied that "I could not make myself a head-man more than I was already in my own town." The Governor said "he would see about turning out the people"; but he never did it. I told the Governor "if he would only turn the people out for me to see, I would show him 'country-provement' (African manner of proof) by pointing out the Slaves." About the same time I bought slaves from the Colonists myself; at least my women bought them, & paid for them in manillas.[16] I was much astonished that the people that came from another country might do such things, but I could not do it.

After this, Seróchata of Port Logo seized a boy on account of an old palaver (an ancient feud). The boy's father had killed Seróchata's brother. Seróchata gave me the boy to me to keep, & the matter was to be decided by a native council. If Seróchata "had reason," Seróchata was to sell the boy; & if he was in the wrong, the boy was to be given up to his friends. Seróchata "got reason," & and the boy was sold at Bance Island.[17] I was one of the council that sat upon Seróchata, & I thought I was bound to give my judgment according to the laws[18] of my country, without any references[19] to my living in the Colony of Sierra Leone. Mr. Ludlam said "I did it", & he seized my people & put them in prison. Lamina, one of my people, wrote to me that Mr. Ludlum went to them every afternoon to ask them how many slaves their Chief had sold, & said that if they would only tell, they should be let out of prison. I wrote to Lamina to tell him, if he was examined again, to tell all he knew. The next time Lamina was asked he told, that "it _was_ I that settled the palaver [court], & made Seróchata sell the boy"; for Lamina knew that I "was the head of the palaver." The same week that I came back from the native council, Mr. Ludlum sent a white man & a black man, & the black man was Warwick Francis, to me with a large sheet of paper written all over, & they read it to me, & tried to explain it, & told me that if I would acknowledge that I had bought the boy, I should not be brought to trial; but if I would not acknowledge it, I should: & that I must go into the town with all my

[12] George Wilson, ruler of the Kafu Bullom. As ruler, George Wilson also controlled the use of land within territory under his jurisdiction.

[13] Fort Thornton was the term given to the center of Company authority within the settlement.

[14] Marked through in original and name replaced with the letter "H".

[15] Bullom Shore was directly opposite of Freetown on the northern bank of the Sierra Leone River estuary.

[16] Manillas were small but standardized pieces of brass that were used as currency along this section of coast.

[17] Effectively, the "native council" had decided that the boy's freedom was forfeited as a result of his father's actions, and that he would be sold to slave-traders located on Bance Island, not far from the Freetown settlement. Slave trading for British subjects not affiliated with the Sierra Leone Company was still legal until January 1, 1808. Bance Island was operated by the firm of John and Alexander Anderson.

[18] The letter "s" was struck through in this copy.

[19] The letter "s" was struck through in this copy.

people & be christened;[20] & if I would do these two things I should not be brought to trial. I said to Mr. Francis, "I did not understand it before; but now I understand it; if I am to change my religion, I had better go to the Governor tomorrow, & tell him to cut my throat, sooner than my countrymen shall hear it."[21] Before this happened I used to dress in the English manner & follow English fashions; but when they talked about forcing me to be christened, I said "off with my head – before the chiefs in the country hear this thing I am to be christened; I cannot promise this thing; I must go to trial." And the trial was held in the church, & I came there in the full dress of a Mohammedan Chief, with my *grigris* (amulets)[22] about me, & the white turban which is the mark of an Imâm,[23] & which none else may wear on high occasions. (I was not born an Imâm; but I first gained reputation for knowledge of the country-law; & five Kings were gathered together against Yangiakurry,[24] & they promised me that if I could take the place I should be made an Imâm; & I fought against it for five months & an half, & took it, & burnt it, & threw down the wall. And I brought all the captives before the Kings, & put them on one side; & King Sitafa [ruler of Moria] put a sheep-skin on the ground, & made me sit down on it, & called a *garengay* (crier), & took the turban & gave it to the garengay, & the garengay gave it to the *Santighi* (king's private councellor), & the Santighi put it on my head.[25] And all disputes in this part of the country[26] must come before me as Imâm; & I can make head-men in the country, & in council I must sit next to the King, & no man may sit between us.) – And when I was in this church, people asked where[27] I was, for nobody knew me, because I had my dress of a Chief. And I stood by myself, & none of my people were with me. And Mr. Ludlum sat as Judge; & Warwick Francis stood up & said, "When I was in Rokelle, I heard that Dalla Mooda was going to take Maheira."[28] And this was all that I heard against me; & nobody talked much except Mr. Ludlam. And Mr. Ludlam told me that "I had lost reason" (cause was given against me), but I do not know how I lost it. And Mr. Ludlam told me I must go away within three days, & if I stopped any longer I should see something I should not like. I said, "I shall go away tomorrow morning, sooner than see something I shall not like; but if you were my own countrymen, I would not leave my town so quick." And that same night fifty armed men slept in my town. And I slept in my own house, & my wives with me;[29] for

[20] Baptized as a Christian. Dala Modu Dumbuya was a Muslim.

[21] Islamic law forbade conversion to Christianity and stipulated the penalty of death for those who did convert. The custom in Sumbuya and nearby Moria was to slit the throats of rebellious or runaway slaves.

[22] *Grigris* or amulets are protective charms worn by persons in time of war and on other occasions of importance.

[23] The title of Imam is generally restricted to learned scholars or teachers, but in Sumbuya and Moria to the north of Sierra Leone, the title of Imam was given also to town and district headmen and to those who were honored for having given special service to the state. In this case, Dala Modu was given the "mark" of Al Imam or Alimaamy as a result of his military accomplishment.

[24] Yangiakurry (Yangekori) is the name of a region and a town located along the border of Sumbuya and Moria in the Northern Rivers where a famous slave rebellion occurred between 1883 and 1896. Many rebel villages were involved in this rebellion, but the last holdout in the rebellion was Yangiakurry. Dala Modu claimed to have been put in command of regional forces to end the rebellion.

[25] This formal process signified to all persons in the region that Dala Modu had obtained special status and that this status had been sanctified by the rulers.

[26] "This part of the country" refers to the neighborhood of the Sierra Leone settlement.

[27] In this instance, the word "where" may have been a miscopy of the word "who."

[28] Rokelle is the name of a river located south of the Freetown settlement, and Maheira is the name of a town. In this instance, Dala Modu understood the comment to mean that he had intended to wage war or expand his influence southward from the settlement, perhaps to surround it with his command.

[29] Along this coast, it is still common that persons with multiple wives live in compounds, with each wife having a separate dwelling for herself and her children, and for the husband to have a house for himself and his favorite wife or for himself alone.

they were afraid of the armed men.[30] And the armed men, I believe, were sent because they did not think I would leave my town without fighting; for I had made much improvement there, & had houses for myself & for my wives; & my people had houses, & the marks of them are left to this day. And the next day I went to Captain Digby of the King of England's ship the *Argo*; & Captain Digby gave me a boat, & an officer, & people; & my head-men went in the boat which Captain Digby had given me, but I went in my own canoe.[31] And they went over to the Bullom shore. And Mr. Ludlam had told me to take what I liked from my town; because all that was left would be taken for the Sierra Leone Company. And all my houses I left standing, both great & small, & my large house that would have stood forever, it was built so strong. And the next time I came into the Colony, my houses were pulled down, & there was not a stick left.

Before I was tried in the church; I went twice to Mr. [Alexander] Smith[32] because Mr. Smith & the Governor were "close together" (intimate), & asked him to make the Governor understand the case of Seróchata's boy. Mr. Smith said, "it is of no use; I have told you before, that any body might buy slaves in this place to help him, but he cannot sell them."

The Mohammedan Chiefs in the country[33] sent to me to tell me "I was to attend all legal proceedings in the Colony & make my report to them upon the English law, whether it was like the Mohammedan law or not; because they had heard that the English law was written in books, & that no judgment could be given except according to those books." And after I was driven from the Colony, I sent this answer to the Chiefs, & I have a copy of it here written in the Mandingo tongue with Arabic letters, & the English of it is this:

From what I have seen of English law, if a stranger[34] lives among them, they will oppress him; but for their own people that live in the place, there is no law at all that I can see. For I have bought slaves myself in their town, from their own people, & yet every thing that I do, they must look into; but if their own people do it, they do not look after it. When I lived in the country when these people first came here, they said they were come to teach people to make rum, & tobacco, & sugar; but when I came here, I saw nothing of it. And for this I say that the English law is nothing but power; when you have power, there is law for you. I say so because when their Governor sees his own people have slaves, he takes no notice; but because I am one among his people, he imposes on me. And this I take to be very hard; for some people may do a thing, but it is not the same with all.

I heard at on the Bullom shore that Slaves had been taken out of an American Sloop in Sierra Leone for some crime of the master, & that the Slaves had been sold in the Sierra Leone Company's store.[35] And when I heard this, I went to a Timmeney head-man named

---

[30] A note was inserted at the end that read: "It is the custom of the country for each wife to have a distinct house, & the husband also. T.P.T."

[31] Much of commerce along this section of the coast was conducted along a canoe corridor that linked sources of trade goods from the northern rivers to markets at Freetown. Canoes often were large enough to carry a ton or more of rice and even able to transport cattle.

[32] Marked through in original and name replaced with the letter "N".

[33] This refers to those rulers or chiefs to whom Dala Modu owed allegiance.

[34] The word "stranger" in this context was and is used to refer to that outsider who places himself under obligations to the rightful "landlord" who either owns or regulates the use of land. That arrangement between landlord and stranger is known as the "landlord/stranger relationship." Along this coast, that relationship was formal and approached the Western concept of a binding contract to which might be attached taxes, obligations of both parties, definitions of terms, length of service, and so forth, depending on the individuals and interactions involved.

[35] This is likely the only reference in Dala Modu's testimony to circumstances involved with the cargoes of slaves captured by the *Derwent* and "sold" to settlers in early 1808, after the slave trade had been made illegal for all British citizens.

King George, & said, "If these were any black people, I would fight them till they beat me or I beat them; for they have driven me from my houses because they said I sold slaves; & now they are selling them themselves." And King George[36] showed me two boys, & said they were his share, for he had one share, & King Firama had another share, & Papa London had another share, & Mr. Ludlam had another share. And the boys are at King George's place at this time.

George Richards Esqr., the former witness, says he believes the paper brought to Dalu Mohammed in his town by Warwick Francis & others, was a *Writ of Right*[37] from the Court of the Mayor & Aldermen of Freetown.

SUGGESTED ADDITIONAL READINGS

Coleman, Deirdre. *Romantic Colonization and British Anti-Slavery*. Cambridge: Cambridge University Press, 2004.

Howard, Allen M. "Nineteenth-Century Coastal Slave Trading and the British Abolition Campaign in Sierra Leone." *Slavery and Abolition*, 27, 1 (April 2006): 23–49.

"Pawning in Coastal Northwest Sierra Leone, 1870-1910." In *Pawning in Africa: Debt Bondage in Historical Perspective*. Edited by Toyin Falola and Paul E. Lovejoy (Boulder: Westview Press, 1994), 267–283.

Johnson, L. G. *General T. Perronet Thompson*. London: George Allen & Unwin, 1957.

Lovejoy, Paul. "The African Diaspora: Revisionist Interpretations of Ethnicity, Culture and Religion under Slavery," *Studies in the World History of Slavery, Abolition and Emancipation*, 2, 1 (1997): 1–22.

Lovejoy, Paul and David Richardson, "The Business of Slaving: Pawnship in Western Africa, c.1600–1810," *Journal of African History*, 42 (2001): 67–89.

Mouser, Bruce L. "Landlords-Strangers: A Process of Accommodation and Assimilation," *The International Journal of African Historical Studies*, 8 (1975): 425–440.

"Rebellion, Marronage and *Jihād*: Strategies of resistance to slavery on the Sierra Leone Coast, c.1783–1796," *Journal of African History*, 48 (2007): 27–44.

Rodney, Walter. "African Slavery and Other Forms of Social Oppression on the Upper Guinea Coast in the Context of the Atlantic Slave-Trade," *Journal of African History*, 7, 3 (1966): 431–443.

Skinner, David. "Mande Settlement and the Development of Islamic Institutions in Sierra Leone," *The International Journal of African Historical Studies*, 11, 1 (1978): 32–62.

Turner, Michael J. "The Limits of Abolition: Government, Saints and the 'African Question,' c. 1780–1820," *The English Historical Review*, 112, 446 (April, 1997): 319–357.

Walker, James. *Black Loyalists: The Search for a Promised Land in Nova Scotia and Sierra Leone 1783-1870*. New York: Africana, 1976.

---

[36] Chiefs George Wilson, Firama, and Pa London were significant indigenous rulers of regions near the British settlement. It was perhaps only reasonable that Ludlam might have distributed slaves from the captured cargoes to these headmen, for such an act might have been considered as an inexpensive act of diplomacy.

[37] A Writ of Right normally refers a writ (an order) to restore the property belonging to another person. In this case, this definition would not fit well with the intentions of Ludlam when Dala Modu believed he had been given a choice either to stand trial and risk conviction and punishment or to confess and convert to Christianity and escape punishment.

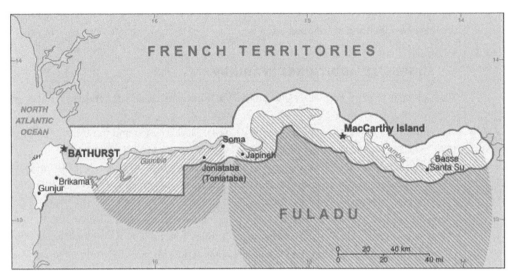

31.1. Map of the Gambia showing the boundary between British and French territories in the 1890s and the areas where the events in the court case took place.

"Being a Slave, I Was Afraid…"

Excerpt from a Case of Slave-Dealing in the Colony
of the Gambia (1893)

ALICE BELLAGAMBA

For most of the nineteenth century, British control of the Gambia River was limited to a number of small enclaves. The two most important ones were Bathurst (founded in 1816 on an island at the river mouth by British merchants and militaries) and MacCarthy Island located in the middle of the river about 300 kilometers from the coast. The latter was acquired in 1823 to defend British commercial interests in the interior of the country.[1] In 1888, both settlements became a Crown Colony. The following year, in 1889, an Anglo-French Convention settled the boundaries of The Gambia, and a strip of land not larger than 47 kilometers and extending for about 400 kilometers inland fell under British control. The establishment of a Protectorate began in 1892 with the appointment of two traveling commissioners, who took up their duties in the first months of 1893.

At the time, slavery and the slave trade were endemic along the river. The metropolitan government in Britain was pressing for the implementation of some abolitionist provisions.[2] Mass liberation, however, was out of the question, as was explained to the

[1] Bathurst's first settlers included British merchants, mulatto traders, and ladies (locally known as señoras) who left Gorée after the end of the Napoleonic wars, when the island was returned to the British after being under French control. The domestic slaves of these merchant traders and ladies (along with a number of Wolof artisans and disbanded black soldiers from the Royal African Corps and the West India regiments) lived in the African section of the town. In addition, there were black troops drafted from Sierra Leone, together with a small number of Liberated Africans, who participated in the building of the town. Liberated Africans were men and women who had been freed from slave-dealers and then brought to Freetown by British naval patrols after Great Britain abolished the slave trade in 1807. More of them came in the 1830s when the government solved Freetown's overcrowding problem by forcibly resettling thousands of men and women in the Gambia. Some were apprenticed to the British merchants in the colony. Others were transferred to MacCarthy Island. Most converted to Christianity and adopted a European lifestyle. J. M. Gray, *A History of The Gambia* (London, 1966), 317–319; P. Curtin, *Economic Change in Precolonial Africa. Senegambia in the Era of the Slave Trade* (Madison, 1975), 136 and ff.

[2] M. Sherwood, *After Abolition. Britain and the Slave Trade since 1907* (London and New York, 2007) reviews British abolitionist policies and their difficult application at home and abroad. R. Roberts and S. Miers,

The record of the court procedure is at the British National Archives (BNA), London, Kew Garden, CO 87/144, Slave dealing case enclosed in Gambia Confidential Dispatch of 2.08.1893, n. 14153. I have used 1893 colonial correspondences and reports to contextualize the events narrated, as well as ethnographic information about Gambian social life to explain the cultural practices mentioned in the document. As the text is fairly long and repetitive, I selected a number of passages with the purpose of disclosing as much as possible about the experiences of the three slave women involved. I use square brackets either to signal the presence of questions and comments made during the court procedure but not written down, or to insert short summaries of the excluded sections.

Secretary of State for the Colonies by the administrator of the protectorate after he, the administrator, had completed his first official tour in the newly annexed territories and introduced the two traveling commissioners to local chiefs and notables. As a consequence of the tour he had realized that:

> The slave question can only be gradually approached and I fear that the traffic must prevail over every effort against it for many years to come. To prevent a panic I was obliged to state that the hoisting of the English flag did not necessarily free at once all the slaves in the territory. I was then annexing but [I had to explain that] if any complaint was made of ill treatment the Travelling Commissioner would enquiry into the circumstances and decide whether the slave was to return to his owner or be sent to Bathurst and liberated. I further stated that any cases of trafficking in slaves in the future would be punished and I hoped all the people would assist in detaining any slaves they saw being carried across the Gambia and communicate with the Travelling Commissioner. I have instructed the Travelling Commisioner not to encourage in any way the slaves to run away from their owner en masse, and to deal with the question very cautiously until the government is more firmly established.[3]

The panic this document refers to is that of slave-owners, who feared losing control of their slave entourages. Slave labor was crucial both to the household economy and the expansion of commercial groundnut cultivation, which had boomed along the river in the second part of the century.[4] Slaves had a different point of view, however. Although the anti-slavery crusade had not been a top priority before 1892 (nor would it be after, when Britain took possession of the Colony and Protectorate), the late-nineteenth-century Bathurst administration had promoted a number of treaties with native chiefs for the protection of trade and the elimination of the slave trade.[5] Reports of British abolitionist stances were spreading in the region thanks to the work of Wesleyan missionaries (whose MacCarthy Island station opened up in 1838) and via the river trading networks. Both slaves and masters had quite a clear idea of what the 1892 British annexation meant to their reciprocal relationship.

In the course of 1893, as soon as the two British traveling commissioners appeared in the areas under their responsibility, a number of enslaved men and women jumped at the opportunity to free themselves. Recently enslaved young men fled in an effort to return to their natal homes or to enter migrant labor circuits spurred by the expansion of commercial agriculture. In pleading their cases to the commissioners, women lamented either

"Introduction: The End of Slavery in Africa," in R. Roberts and S. Miers (eds.), *The End of Slavery in Africa* (Madison, 1988) focuses more specifically on Africa.

[3] BNA, CO 87/143, 24th of May 1893, Protectorate between Bathurst and McCarthy Island, Confidential, Administrator Lewellyn to Secretary of State for Colonies.

[4] See G. E. Brooks, "Peanuts and Colonialism: Consequences of the Commercialization of Peanuts in West Africa, 1830–1870," *Journal of African History*, 16, 1 (1975): 29–54; K. Swindell and A. Jeng, *Migrants, Credit and Climate. The Gambian Groundnut Trade, 1834–1934* (Leiden and Boston, 2006).

[5] For instance, in 1829, a treaty was signed with the rulers of Bundu and Wuli. Other treaties followed but turned into dead letters. British military presence was too limited to ensure their enforcement even in the immediate outskirts of Bathurst and in the other small portions of British territory along the river. In addition, the second half of the century witnessed the outburst of religious conflicts that overthrew most of the local leaders who negotiated with the British in the first place. For a selection of documents and official correspondence relating to this issue, see C. W. Newbury, *British Policy towards West Africa, Select Documents*, vol. I–II (Aldershot, Hampshire, 1992).

mistreatment or forceful separation from their children. These actions often resulted in their receiving a certificate of freedom and assistance to reach Bathurst. This happened to Yahling and Dado, two slave women who in the first part of 1893 asked for the assistance of the south bank commissioner, Mr. Cecil Sitwell. A few months later, the administration accused their owner, Mr. Edwin, of slave-dealing and brought him before the Acting Magistrate of the Colony. Yahling and Dado, together with another slave woman called Maladdoo, testified before the court.

The rest of this introduction provides some of the background necessary to understand the events narrated by these three slave women as they sought to emancipate themselves. A short discussion describing the nature of slavery and slave-dealing in the Gambia immediately before the establishment of the British Protectorate is followed by information about the individuals who appeared before the court. Last but not least, I read the testimonies of Yahling, Dado, and Maladdo in light of the particular vulnerability that enslaved women experienced.

SLAVERY AND SLAVE-DEALING ON THE EVE OF COLONIZATION

Mr. Sitwell's official report for June 1893 – which paved the way for Mr. Edwin's prosecution – provides a fairly detailed picture of the intense slave trade going on along the south bank of the river Gambia. For almost two decades religious conflicts and confrontations between warring factions had ravaged that part of the country and the areas of Fogny, Kiang, and Jarra where Mr. Edwin operated as a slave-trader. Both the court record and Mr. Sitwell's report mention one of the principal protagonists of these marauding activities, Fode Kabba Dumbuyaa, an Islamic reformist and warlord who began to attack south bank communities around 1878. He was eventually defeated by a joint French and British military expedition in 1901.[6]

Sitwell identified a number of villages as slave-trading nodes linking the French territory of the Casamance to the north bank of the Gambia river, where captives were exchanged for horses, guns, and gunpowder. Each of these villages hosted some of Fode Kabba's relatives and trustworthy men. The traffic took place at night and along secondary paths, and equally involved Moors, local traders, and businessmen from the Colony. For the sake of our discussion, the interesting point is that Sitwell collected this information only with the help of some slaves, because chiefs and traders were reticent to offer such intelligence.[7] The British official feared that if too pressed, the latter individuals would rap-

---

[6] For an overview of Islamic wars and their impact on Senegambian societies and economies, see M. Klein, "Social and Economic Factors in the Muslim Revolution in Senegambia," *Journal of African History*, 8, 3 (1972): 419–441. C. Quinn, *Mandinko Kingdoms of the Senegambia* (Madison, 1972) describes the religious and political career of Fode Kabba Dumbuya. In 1892, Fode Kabba retired from British territory and found refuge in the Casamance. His repeated attacks on villages in British territory kept feeding an underground slave trade, which ended in 1901 with his final defeat.

[7] Slaves' living conditions were particularly harsh in Western Kiang where "in nearly every town – Mr. Sitwell wrote – I had a number of slaves begging me to free them, they dare not speak but only made signs that they wanted to come with me." See Gambian National Archives (GNA), Banjul, The Gambia, ARP 28/1, Travelling Commissioner's Report, South Bank, June 1893. I commented on these colonial sources in A. Bellagamba, "Slavery and Emancipation in the Colonial Archives: British Officials, Slave Owners, and Slaves in the Protectorate of the Gambia (1890–1936)," *Canadian Journal of African Studies*, 39, 1 (2005): 5–41.

idly move their slave entourages to the other side of the international boundary, therefore shutting down his limited chances for intervention.

Such difficulties notwithstanding, Sitwell managed to warn two of the major local slave-dealers of the concrete risks of being prosecuted if they were not to stop their activities immediately. What led to the arrest of Mr. Edwin instead of other south bank slave-traders – whose names and locations the British official knew – is not explained in the account of his court case. Certainly, his arrest generated a sensation both in Bathurst and along the river. For the first time, the British administration was taking overt action against the slave-dealing activities of Bathurst merchants and their African associates. Even when their businesses dealt in groundnuts, cloth, and European imported items, all legitimate trade goods, the river trade also included forms of slave-dealing, because slaves were given as collateral or were bartered for weapons and gunpowder.[8] Wealthy urban dwellers kept slaves in their urban premises and used slave labor to cultivate their peri-urban farms.[9] This was the case even though the administration had earlier announced in 1820 that any Bathurst slave "who applied for it, would be issued with a document declaring him to be free."[10] In addition, apprenticeship regulations – originally introduced to smooth the transition to freedom of the slaves owned by the town's first settlers (regulations that were also used in the course of the 1830s to integrate into the town the Liberated Africans brought from Sierra Leone) – simply hid an underground but significant traffic in children.[11] Boys and girls brought into town for training were often so mistreated that in 1884 the administration prescribed the registration of all foreign children below the age of sixteen years and fixed a minimum monthly wage of five shillings for apprentices.[12]

MR. EDWIN AND OTHER FIGURES IN THE STORY

Yahling, Dado, and Maladdo were first-generation slaves while Mr. Edwin was a representative of Bathurst trading community. It is impossible to say whether or not he attended the court case, as he did not testify. Beside second-hand information on his conversations with Mr. Sitwell and the dynamics of his arrest, the record states he had reached the Gambia from Sierra Leone in the 1840s. The evidence is too scarce to assert whether he was of mixed European and African origins – that is the "mulatto" issue of a British merchant or official and a local woman – or if he was a Liberated African resettled in the Gambia.

---

[8] Swindell and Jeng, *Migrants*, 26 and M. Klein, *Slavery and Colonial Rule in French West Africa* (Cambridge, 1998), 38–39.

[9] C. Quinn, *Mandinko*, 91 and 139.

[10] J. M. Gray, *A History*, 317–319. It is worth remembering that John Gray served as Judge of the Supreme Court and then as Governor of the Gambia from 1934 to 1940. His remarks on the early anti-slavery position assumed by the Bathurst administration (even before the 1833 British Parliamentary Act, which made slaveholding illegal for British subjects) are to a certain extent self-apologetic and should be read against the concrete difficulties the British encountered while ruling the settlement. Merchants' interests dominated the political life of the town until the 1880s. Being unable to provide the assistance and protection merchants requested, the government could not push for the enforcement of regulations the merchant oligarchy disliked. F. Mahoney, "Government and Opinion in The Gambia, 1816–1901" (unpublished PhD thesis, University of London, 1963), 127.

[11] Indentured labor was abolished in the late 1830s. New rules for apprenticeship were introduced in 1863, when Islamic conflicts on both banks of the river brought to the fore the issue of hosting refugees on British soil. F. Mahoney, "Government," 79.

[12] *An Ordinance to make better provisions for the introduction into and removal from the settlement of the River Gambia of Alien African Children*, n. 8, 10th September 1884.

At the time of the events described in the court case, Liberated Africans and their descendants – locally known as Aku – had become vocal representatives of Bathurst trading and professional community. As individual merchants or subagents of European commercial firms, they dominated the river trade, and their social networks spread to Freetown, other West African British settlements, and Great Britain, where they traveled for business and education.[13] Mr. Edwin's solicitor, a certain Mr. Gibson, was a fairly prominent personality of the time. Like Mr. Cates, the prosecutor, he belonged to a group of educated Creoles from Freetown who filled up positions in the Gambia administration in the course of the 1860s.[14]

Mr. Sitwell himself did not appear before the court, having this duty entrusted to Joseph Pullen, one of the police constables who accompanied him on tour. Mr. Augustus Gibbs, another representative of the Bathurst police force, testified about having arrested Mr. Edwin, while two clerks – one from the Registry Office and another from the Governor's Office – certified both the defendant's status as a British subject and the fact that the village where he kept Yahling and Dado had been placed under British protection some time before the events, probably in 1892. Both details were relevant, as they established the possibility of prosecuting Mr. Edwin for slave-dealing, as a British subject who had illegally held slaves, and in an area under British jurisdiction.

LIFE IN BONDAGE

Yahling, Dado, and Maladdoo together provided detailed recollections of their life in slavery. Yahling described her status as reasonably tolerable in the hands of her first owner, a lady named Haminah. Domestic slavery could indeed have a benign face that mitigated the intrinsic vulnerability of having being enslaved. It was this possibility that led the colonial administration to slow down the pace of emancipation. Yahling could not remember her home village, but she spoke Jola, her mother tongue.[15] Maladdoo was also Jola, and both women ascribed their enslavement to the military activities of Fode Kabba Dumbuyaa on the south bank.[16]

Maladdoo explained how she resisted by running away with two other men. Eventually she was recaptured and sold several times until she became the slave of Mr. Edwin's wife, Fatou James. Dado had no memories of home, but she believed herself to be of Fula origin, even though she spoke only English and Mandinka. Yahling, Dado, and Maladdoo also spoke about a fourth woman – Horaajah – who did not appear before the court. She was described as a slave "without blessing." This probably refers to either her infertility or to her numerous unsuccessful attempts to escape enslavement.

---

[13] A. Hughes and D. Perfect, *A Political History of The Gambia (1816–1994)* (Rochester, NY, 2006), 23; J. M. Gray, *A History*, 357.

[14] On Zachariah T. Gibson, see A. Hughes and D. Perfect, *A Political*, 82. William Cates had been trained in London and became schoolmaster of Bathurst Anglican School in 1869. Mahoney, "Government," 177.

[15] The Jola (Diola or Jolah as spelt in the document) are one of the ethnic groups of the Lower Gambia and Casamance rivers.

[16] Fode Kabba heavily raided Jola communities on the south bank of the Gambia River and in the Casamance to punish their resistance to conversion. Jola men also served as mercenaries in the Islamic wars of the second half of the nineteenth century – a detail that in some ways balances the stereotype that depicts Jola communities as mere victims of the slave trade. Klein, *Slavery*, 41; H. Gailey, *Historical Dictionary of The Gambia* (Metuchen, NJ, 1975), 76.

At first glance, it seems that recollections spontaneously stream out of the conscious-ness of Yahling, Dado, and Maladdoo, but that is not the case. The interrogatory nature of the court system shaped their narrative, although the questions did not appear in the final report.

Yahling and Dado, in particular, had to repeat the same point time and again so as to clarify what kind of work they did for Mr. Edwin: cultivating rice, spinning cotton, and engaging in domestic chores. We can only imagine what efforts they took to narrate their experiences in such a detailed manner. Mistreatment was one of the reasons slaves could use to plea for their freedom before the British court, and surely the three women received instructions from the prosecutor on what kind of events and situations could impress the court. One, for instance, was the lack of proper food and clothing to which slaves had a right according to local custom. This is why both Yahling and Dado insisted on detailing what Mr. Edwin provided for their and their children's well-being.

Another point is the narrow definition of slavery emerging from the court proce-dure. The definition fit neither of the three women's experiences, nor did it describe the nuances that characterized captivity in the Protectorate and the Colony itself. For the court, the slave was property, sold in exchange for money or goods. The enslaved worked without remuneration and was subject to ill-treatment and abuse. Yahling, however, had not been sold to Mr. Edwin. Rather she was given to him in a nonmonetary exchange. Mr. Edwin had trading relationships with a man named Checoota, whose aunt (his mother's sister) had recently been kidnapped. To obtain her release, Checoota had offered to give Yahling, whom he owned at the time, to Mr. Edwin in exchange for one of Mr. Edwin's slaves, a woman by the name of Hooraajah. Mr. Edwin accepted Yahling from Checootah in exchange for Hoorajah. Cheecoota then used Hooraajah as a ransom payment to obtain the release of his aunt. This is how Yahling became the slave of Mr. Edwin. No money was exchanged as expected by the court when dealing with slavery cases. Further complicat-ing the issue was the fact that both Yahling and Dado earned a little money (even if Mr. Edwin seized it all) by working for people other than Mr. Edwin. Both women mentioned repeated sexual abuse. What strikes one about these witnesses is the way they became aware of their condition. Dado explained to the court that she understood her status as a slave because the freeborn were neither tied nor put in irons as she often was. Yahling described her difficult life with Mr. Edwin, which she contrasted with the treatment she received from her former mistress and master. Cheecota had treated her kindly. She also recalled how she had to ask Cheecota to take her first child because she could not take proper care of the infant while under her new owner. She felt she had no other options than to consign the boy to the care of her former master, whom she considered more lenient than Mr. Edwin. Maladdoo, the third enslaved woman, emphasized her deep feel-ings of impotence. In explaining how Mr. Edwins' wife forcibly separated her from her own child, she stated: "I could not help myself, I am a slave." "It was not with my consent, I cried."

That and other details point to the kind of subjection and humiliations the three women experienced. In the final judgment of the court, Mr. Edwin obtained the benefit of the doubt. He was acquitted. This must have reassured Bathurst slave owners that the colonial administration would move against them only with great caution in spite of its renewed anti-slavery statements. The 1894 anti-slavery ordinance banned the slave trade and the practice of pawnship and provided for the freeing of slaves at the death of their masters and for the free status of children born after its proclamation. Slave men and women, however, could gain their freedom only by proving mistreatment or by paying the ransom fee of 10 pounds for adults and 5 pounds for children.

For Yahling, who had two children, this meant the exorbitant amount of 20 pounds, corresponding to the average annual stipend the government had begun to pay to head chiefs under provisions of the 1894 Protectorate Ordinance. Slavery legally ended only in 1930, when the generation of chiefs and slave owners, with whom the British negotiated the establishment of the Protectorate in the course of the 1890s, had almost completely passed away. Legal abolition did not completely erase the social boundary between former slaves and masters, as slave origins still carry significance in contemporary Gambian social life. After the end of the court case, Yahling, Dado, and Maladdoo probably found employment as domestic servants in the Colony or married and began a new life in Bathurst's poorest neighborhoods together with other rural immigrants in town. Surely, like thousands of other women in bondage, they greatly struggled to carve out a path to emancipation, if not for themselves, at least for their children and grandchildren.

QUESTIONS TO CONSIDER

1. Can you identify the main protagonists of the events and the role they played in the court case? Beside Yahling, Dado, Maladdoo, and Horaajah, what other slaves are mentioned and what is said about their living conditions?

2. What passages of this document illustrate the vulnerability of female slaves in terms of labor, sexual exploitation, and lack of control over their children?

3. Does the document provide any hint about the way slave women negotiated their motherhood? For instance, what did Yahling do to protect her child? And how did Maladdoo describe the way she was separated from her child?

4. Use the court case to elicit the different points of view of masters and slaves on their reciprocal relationships. What did Mr. Edwin think of his slave women? And conversely, how did the latter describe Mr. Edwin before the court?

5. Why, in your opinion, did the court asked both Yahling and Dado if Mr. Edwin compensated them for their work? Was this detail crucial for establishing whether or not they were his slaves?

Cases 9 and 10

Regina vs. James Edwin
　　Charges – Slave-dealing
　　Plea – Not guilty

　　Enclosure n. 2 in dispatch Gambia n. 57, 2nd August 1893
　　Mr. Gibson appear for the Prisoner
　　Mr. Cates opens Case for the Crown

"Yahling Dahbo sworn saith. My name is Yahling Dahbo. I am of the Jola tribe. I was born in Fogni. I was living in my father's place until war drove us away. Foday Cabbah made the war.[17] I was a little girl at the time I was taken captive and taken to Mandingo country. Fodey Cabbah's people sold me. I was young and I did not know the person who sold me. When I knew myself I found myself in the hands of Checoota Haminah[18] at Secoondah.[19] I was a long time with Checoota, more than ten years. Haminah was Checoota's mother, [she] owned me. After Haminah's death, Checoota owned me. I was in Checoota's hands until the Foulahs caught Checoota's mother's sister, she was taken captive by the Foulahs.[20] I remained with Checoota until prisoner gave his girl to Joomany in exchange for me as the girl had no blessing.[21] The girl's name is Hoorajah. I was not present when prisoner asked Joomany to make the exchange but prisoner was sent for to Secoondah. Joomany called me and I went up with my child on my back. I found prisoner sitting in the house with Joomany. Joomany said I called you and then he said go. I went away. The next day prisoner's girl Hoorajah was taken to Foulahs by Kittim Cisey, Joomany's man. Joomany is the prisoner's trader. Joomany brought Hoorajah to Secoondah. Hororajah spent a rainy season at Secoondah. It was then I was sent to Bye.[22]

Court adjourned until Tuesday the 18th July at noon
Tuesday 18th July 1893
Court resumed 12 noon
At the time I was sent to Joomany's house Hoorajah had been at Secoondah a long time.
Mr. Gibson objects to evidence being given about Hoorajah being taken to Fulladou.
Mr. Cates replies. Objection overruled.

I was taken to Bye by a young man named Lamin Binta, Joomany Marrang sent Lamin Binta to take me to Bye.

Before leaving Bye my former owner Checcota had said nothing to me about the transaction, he hid it from me. Lamin Binta took me to the prisoner and said to him "Father, let me bring Yahling to you."

Prisoner said "I hear; it is alright." Lamin did not remain, he returned to Secoondah the same day. After Laming left, prisoner said nothing to me.

[17] This is Fode Kaba Dumbuyaa.
[18] The name of the man was Checoota. Haminah is the name of his mother, which is used to distinguish Checoota from his namesake within the same household or settlement. In another passage of the document, we learn that Checcota's surname was Darammeh. Yahling is instead Darboe, and it may be assumed that she got this surname from her mistress, Checoota's mother, as it was customary to give slaves the surname of either the person or the family who owned them.
[19] Like the majority of the localities mentioned in the court case, Secoondah is a village on the South Bank of the River Gambia between the districts of Kiang and Jarra.
[20] The Foulahs (Fulas) are one of the ethnic groups of the Senegambia. Probably the events narrated took place during one of Mussa Molo Baldeh's 1890s attacks against Fode Kabba's followers in Kiang and Jarra. Mussa Molo was the ruler of Fuladu (a large kingdom including a large portion of contemporary middle and upper Casamance), and his rivalry with Fode Kabba is duly detailed both in oral traditions and colonial sources.
[21] As explained in the introduction, "no blessing" can either mean she was infertile or that she was a rebellious slave, whom the master wished to get rid off because of her continuous flight attempts.
[22] Bye is probably Bai, a wharf and a trading post situated on a stream connected to the Gambia river in proximity of Jappineh, the village of the Jarra chief, where Mr. Edwin's slaves used to seek protection when they feared retaliation from their master. Dado's testimony clarifies this point quite well. To identify this and other localities I used the map from H. F. Reeve, *The Gambia* (New York, 1912).

I was at prisoner as a slave. I used to work for prisoner, rice farming, spinning and cooking food. Prisoner used to cook for himself. He did not plant corn. Dado and I used to work the rice farms.

Year before last and last year we had plenty of rice. When prisoner is at Bye we get no rice to eat but when he is absent we have plenty.[23]

It was year before last I was taken to Bye.[24] I have spent the rainy season at Bye. I found no Constable at Bye. I saw none. I had no time to go about. Even if I wished to go to the well I had to ask permission from prisoner.

When I was taken to Bye I had a boy child at the breast. The boy was taken by Checoota Haminah, my first owner, who claimed him. I met Dado Baso in prisoner's yard.

Whenever I woke up at night to breast feed and I had the child in my arms, the prisoner would take the child from me. This often occurred. This caused me to send to Checoota to come and take the child. I was not better treated after the child was taken away. From the time I got to Bye, prisoner never treated me well. From Bye I was taken to Somah.[25]

I had no child at Bye. It was at Somah I got a child.

Prisoner said nothing to me about Dado Baso. Prisoner never said anything to me as to the relation I have to him. Prisoner called me "Yahling." At Somah I knew Pauly Cisey. He came with the prisoner. Prisoner never flogged me at Bye. At Somah prisoner flogged me once. I was sitting down with the child, the one now in my arms, when the child caught hold of Dado who was passing and he flogged me.

The child now in my arms is the prisoner's. He used to come and meet me at night in bed. We lived in the same house, only a partition between one room. Prisoner never said anything to me before he used to come to me at night. This child is a female. After the child was born, prisoner did nothing. It was Buby's wife who shaved the child's hair.[26] Prisoner never paid me for my services nor made any present. Prisoner had given me only one Buba and 1 pagn.[27] After the child was born, prisoner never gave me a pagn. Pagn I have now was given me by Bubi's wife.[28]

Prisoner said nothing nor made me any promise. It was against my wish that prisoner came to me at night, being a slave, I was afraid.

I had occasion to complain to a white man this year. I knew no one when at Bye, that was the reason I did not run away. Prisoner told me that if any slave runs away and complains to the white man, the white man will ask you for money before freeing you.

---

[23] Rice was a luxury food at the time, commonly available in colonial settlements but not in rural ones. Most of the time people ate millet.

[24] This probably took place in 1891.

[25] This is Soma, another settlement in Jarra, which in the course of the twentieth century became an important administrative and commercial hub linking northern Senegal to the Casamance. At the time of the events, it was a wharf, which traders from Bathurst used as a basis for their commercial activity in the dry season. Mr. Edwin traded both in Bai, in proximity to the chief's village, and in Soma.

[26] Yahling refers to the naming ceremony, which is due to take place seven days after birth. The father is supposed to participate in its organization by providing at least the material assistance necessary for holding the feast. Shaving the hair of the child is one of the phases of the ritual. The newborn is then introduced to the community.

[27] The *buba* is a sort of shirt while the pagn is a piece of indigo-dyed native cloth, measuring about two yards. During the nineteenth century, traders used pagnes as currency. See, for instance, D. Ames, "The Use of Transitional Cloth-Money Token among the Wolof," *American Anthropologist*, 57, 5 (1955): 1016–1024.

[28] This second pagn refers to that usually given at birth so that the woman can use it to carry the child on her back.

I saw the white man at Somah, I went to him to complain that I was a slave not well treated and got nothing to eat. I went alone to the white man. The white man said he would be going to Joniataba that evening.[29]

Prisoner was absent when I went to the white man. I ran away the same evening to Joniataba to meet the white man. Dado and I went to Joniataba together. The next morning prisoner was sent for by the white man – he came – the white man told prisoner that we had come to him and asked what relation we bore to him. He said we were not his slaves, he had never treated us as slaves. The white man told prisoner that he could take me, his wife, to go and cook for him.

The white man said to the prisoner: "Look at the condition of these people they do not eat, see how they are!". We had no clothes. I was just as I am now. The pagn I have now was given to me by others. One Marie gave me the pagn to tie the child on my back and another pagn. When the white man told the prisoner he could take me with him, the prisoner told Abduli and a Joloff woman that the white man can have both of us for if he take me I would give him trouble.

[Question by Mr. Gibson]

I do not know if Abduli is a P.C.[30] I saw him in uniform. I know in Bathurst that he is a P.C. I saw Abduli at Somah. Abduli used to keep company with the prisoner. Prisoner used to give Abduli colah nuts.[31] It was after Abduli and the white man came to Somah that I ran away. I only know that Abduli is a Jolah.[32] I did not see any Constable beside Abduli when we were coming down. Abduli never told me that things would be right but he told me to keep hearth. It was three days before I ran away.

The first time I ever saw Hoorajah was at a Joomany's place.[33] I never knew her before. I did not know where she came from. I did not know who brought her to Joomany's place. Joomany's boy told me Joomany had sent for me. I went and found Prisoner in the house, I do not know when and where he came from. Prisoner did not say anything to me.

Lamin Binta took me to Bye to Prisoner. It was Joomany who took me.[34] I saw Hoorajah at Joomany's place- Hoorajah was taken to Fouladou[35] before I was taken to Bye. I do not know where Hoorajah is now. I did not go with her to Fouladou. I was told that Hoorajah was to be taken to Fouladou. When I was taken to Bye I was not tied, I walked. I was not tied at Bye. I was at Prisoner's as a slave. Nobody has put the word slave into my mouth. Prisoner himself used to tell us that we were his slaves. That is all the reason I have for saying I am a slave. It is

---

[29] Joniataba is instead Toniataba – at the time, a big village not far from Soma.

[30] P.C. is the abbreviation of police constable. Abduli is one of the local names for Joseph Pullen, the police constable who testified before the court about Yahling and Dado's flight.

[31] This is a bitter-tasting nut with an oval shape, widely appreciated for its tonic qualities and which had been a major commodity of West African trade for centuries. See P. Lovejoy, "Kola in the History of West Africa," *Cahier d'Études Africaines*, 77–78 (1980): 97–134.

[32] Abduli was probably a representative of the Bathurst Jola community, which sprang up during the early days of the settlement. See J. Gray, *A History*, 319.

[33] As explained by Yahling in the beginning, Joomany is a subagent for Mr. Edwin. He probably organized the ransom of the relative of Yahling's first master from the hands of the Fulas, as Yahling tries to explain.

[34] Yahling already explained the involvement of both Lamin Binta and Joomany in her transfer to Mr. Edwin's premises in Bye. She is now repeating the same statement.

[35] This is Fuladu. See note 20.

not because I beat[36] that I say that I am a slave. All the world beats. Not because I make rice farms. If you are in the hands of a person, if you are a free born you will know.

Prisoner used to cook for himself. Dado only cooked rice for prisoner. I used to see Prisoner eat rice. Any day, the prisoner gave us food I used to cook for myself and Dado. During prisoner's absence, Alcali Bah[37] used to feed us. At times Alcali Bah would bring food for the prisoner who would give it to us. Prisoner only … a time gave us food. I remember prisoner going to S. Leone. He left one small bag of corn for us. Before Prisoner returned from S. Leone we burnt prisoner's house down. We did not burn it wilfully. The house was burnt with what was in it. On prisoner's return he met me and Dado where he left us. We did not run away. We were afraid that prisoner would punish us. We had nowhere to run to.

Yes, I ran to the white man. If one is in difficulty he will find a way to run. At Bye I knew no one. At Somah I knew my way to Joniataba.[38] Prisoner flogged me once. It was a cane stick prisoner used. He struck me four times and I ran away. He flogged me because the child was crying. Prisoner did not flog me when his house was burnt down but he refused to give me corn and that is worse than flogging. I ran away secretly to the white man. When I ran away I had only my rags. I had nothing. I took all I had, my pagn.

Dado had only her small pagn. That was all she had. Dado did not go naked to the white man. Dado used to go naked while working either at Bye or Somah or elsewhere. I used to go naked. People used to give me charity. I did not go naked to the prisoner. The pagn I had is now worn out.

[Question by Mr. Cates]

Before I left Secoondah I had two pagns. I tied one and covered with the other. When I said I was naked I meant I tied a small pagn but had no pagn to cover. The pagn that Dado had when we went to Joniataba was bought by me from groundnuts picked by Dado. Prisoner had given me all the time I have been with him one buba and one pagn. The handkerchief on my head was given me by Peter Gilphin's mother. The earning I had before I went to prisoner also the necklace I have on.

The flogging I had from prisoner was painful. The marks on my right shoulder are scars from the flogging. Dado used to ran away to Japineh and prisoner used to send people to Jarra King for Dado. If he refused, prisoner used to send pagn to get her back. Dado ran away more than four times. Each time she was brought back, sometimes he flogged Dado, at other times not.

After cutting the rice, it was kept in the house. We were afraid to eat it. We went with Buley's wife to gather beans to cook while cooking the flames were high and caught the roof of the house. The fire was accidental, not wilfully done.

---

[36] This could be a translation or transcription mistake. Yahling probably wanted to say: "It is not because I was beaten." The same is true for the following section. Flogging of women was rather common on the south bank of the River Gambia, as the British commissioner reported to the administrator. See GNA, ARP 28/1, Traveling Commissioner's Report, South Bank, June 1893.

[37] Alcali or Alkaloo is the term to identify the village chief but can be used also as a nickname. So, it is not clear whether or not Yahling refers to the Alkaloo, the village chief, of the settlement where she lived together with Dado.

[38] This means "I knew how to reach Joniataba from Soma."

I had been a slave before but the woman in whose hands I was had treated me not as a slave. Since I have been with prisoner I never had liberty to do as I liked. Prisoner never paid me anything as a reward for my services. Since I have worked for prisoner, I have received nothing whatever for my services. Even my own earning last year prisoner took it from me. It was not my pleasure to work for prisoner for nothing but I could not help it.

[By juror]

Abduli did not come to Bahurst with us. My earnings that prisoner took away from me was what I received from Fattoumata for beating rice for her. Fattoumata gave me the 2 pence and Dado 1 pence. I never communicate to Abduli my position.

[By court]

Prisoner took all the 3 pence. When we went to the white man I did not see any other slave run to the white man.

Dado Bass sworn saith my name is Dado Bass. I know prisoner. I have known him since I was a little child. I do not know the names of my father or mother. I do not know where they are. I say I am a Fulah because I have people saying so a Bye. Prisoner has told me so. When he cursed me he used to say you are a Fulah. I never asked him about my parents. Since I have known myself only the prisoner I know. I knew Comba, she was Hoorajah's mother. I used to work rice farm, make [sic],[39] draw water, beat coos and other small work in the house. Prisoner never paid me for work. He never gave me pagn or equivalent to payments. He used to give me pagn and clothes.[40] Since I left Bye for Somah he never gave me pagn. I went to Somah before last year. Comba died at Bye in prisoner's yard. I was then a young girl and I did not know what work Comba used to do. Prisoner exchanged Hoorajah for Yahling Darbo.

I know Fantah. She has run away. Her surname was Congillah. Fantah was a slave to prisoner. Fantah had two children. One boy and one girl. The boy child is in Bathurst. Prisoner was the father of the two children. Fantah ran away with the girl.

I know Yarrah Darbo. She was also a slave to prisoner. She has run away. She had a girl child. She ran away with the child. I do not know who the father of Yarrah's child was. I know Maladdoo. I knew her at Bye. I know Sally. I knew her at Bye. She was then with her [husband]. The man's name was Mousa. They were at Japineh. Sally never lived with prisoner. When Mousa died Bootoomy took Sally for his wife. When Mousa died he was in debt with Mr. Edwin and could not pay. Bootoomy ran away with Sally to Catabah.[41] Mr. Edwin took Sally at Catabah and carried her at Tendito.[42]

I know Maladdoo. She is a Jolah and is now in Bathurst. Maladdoo lived at Bye, she was a slave at Bye. She used to work for prisoner.

Mr. Gibson objects that evidence cannot be given of any previous misdeeds of the prisoner.

---

[39] The sentence is incomplete in the document. The missing word is probably "cotton." See later in the document.

[40] This statement and the one immediately before could sound contradictory. In the first one, Dado refers to the fact that she was never paid for her work; in the second one, she mentions the custom of masters to clothe their slaves. As she explains, even this depended on the master's will.

[41] This is an area at the border between southern Gambia and the Casamance.

[42] Probably a settlement in Fogny, where Mr. Edwin seems to have traded as well. It is clear from the text that Sally was taken because of the debts of her husband.

Overruled
Court adjourned till Wednesday the 19th July at noon
Wednesday 19th July 1893
Court resumed at noon

She[43] used to work rice farm and make cotton,[44] draw water and beat corn. When we harvested the rice, we used to give it to the prisoner and he used to take a part to Bathurst. When we spun cotton it was taken to me and made into pagns for prisoner not for us. I used to run away if prisoner wanted to punish me. This year I ran to Japineh to Jarra Mansah.[45] After the house was burnt I ran away. I was taken back to prisoner by Booly Cisey.[46]

Hoorajah used to run away to Jatta Mansah's yard. Jarra Mansah is King of Japineh. I remember when Hoorajah stole; she ran away; prisoner sent for her and she was brought back by the town people. I never heard prisoner say anything about Hoorajah. Prisoner said to Mr. Jones that he wanted to change Hoorajah and myself. Mr. Jones told him not to do so for if he parted with the two of us he would have no one to draw water for him. The last time Hoorajah ran away one Fantah was sent to fetch her and he was told to keep her a little time at Japineh. Prisoner went to Secoondah to call Joomany Marrang. Joomany was a trader for prisoner at Secoondah. Prisoner told Joomany to go and take Hoorajah at Japineh and carry her at Secoondah. Joomany carried Hoorajaa to Secoondah. I have not seen Hoorajaa since.

[*Dado explains how she met Yahling in Mr. Edwin compound at Bye. She talks about Maladdoo and her child. She narrates the flight to the British official*]

[*Questions by Mr. Gibson. Presumably he asked if Dado understood English*]

I hear English. I am the only slave that speaks English in Mandingo country.

[*Dado's testimony continues by mentioning a number of Mr. Edwin's slaves and dependants and by talking about Hoorajaa again*]

Yarrah Darbo was in the yard. She used to work. I said she was a slave because where free people were she could not go there. Free people never run away. She herself used to say she was a slave. If Yarra had not said she was a slave I would not have said she was a slave. I know I am a slave because they never tie free people or put them in irons. Prisoner used to tie me and put me in irons. He used to tie my hands with a rope. He used to put me in irons. The irons are now in Booly Cisey's yard. We ran away, to Joniataba. I did not show the white man the iron. Another reason I know I am a slave is that when prisoner was abusing me he would say if I did not know that I was a slave.

[*Dado continues explaining their activities for Mr. Edwin and describing how she knew Maladdoo and others were slaves*]

[Question by court]

In the Mandingo country, free people can work farm, spin cotton. I have never seen them tied. I was not well treated. I do not know if prisoner ever tried to traffic with me.

[43] The use of the pronoun "she" instead of "I" clearly shows that Dado was speaking to the court thanks to the assistance of an interpreter, although she could understand some English, as she explains later on.

[44] Dado probably means that she was spinning and weaving cotton, which was one of slaves' working duties.

[45] Mansa or Mansah is a local term for ruler. In the last part of 1893 – and therefore before the anti-slave trade ordinance of 1894 – the Mansa of Jarrah handed a number of fugitive slaves over to the traveling commissioners. See GNA, ARP 28/1, Traveling Commissioner's Report, South Bank, December.

[46] It is impossible to understand whether Booly Cisey was another slave or one of Mr. Edwin's dependants. Yahling and Dado seemed to have been under his care when the defendant was absent.

Maladdo Mangah sworn saith. My name is Maladdo Mangah. I am a Jolah, I was born at Bouyam at Fogni,[47] in the Jola country. Fodey Cabbah, the marabout who used to catch Jolahs, caught and took me to Cansallah.[48] Foday himself caught me, i.e. by his horseman. From Cansallah I was taken by Demba to the town Katoum.[49] Demba gave me to his mother saying "this is my slave." I ran away to Tendito with two men, the two men were captured. I ran to the bush until night. The men who were in search not finding me set fire to the grass and caught me and took me to Goomba Gay.[50] Goomba gave me in payment of debt to one More Fall. More Fall gave me to Fatou James. Prisoner's wife is Fatou James. More Fall was a trader of Fatou James, I was a long time with Fatou James. I know prisoner. Prisoner took me to Badommy[51] and before the rains were over prisoner took me back to Bye.

I used to work for prisoner. He never paid me. Prisoner never made a bargain with me. It was not my will or pleasure to go with prisoner. I could not help myself. I am a slave. Prisoner held me and my child good. Prisoner never flogged me. He used to give me cola nuts and tobacco. Prisoner once put me in irons and threatened to put me in irons. Prisoner wife put me in irons but not the prisoner. I met Dado. I knew Yahling Dabo. I know Yahling at Bathurst. My own child used to tie Hoorajah on her back. Hoorajah's mother is dead. I do not know where Hoorajah is. I left Hoorajah at Bye, I have a child. She is in the hands of Mr. Edwin. Fatou James took the child to Bathurst saying she was a slave. It was not with my consent. I cried.

[Question by Mr. Gibson]

I did not see the goods that Moro Fall gave for me. Fatou told me that Goomba Gay owed More Fall. Prisoner was present, it was at Tendito. Prisoner said nothing. Fatou James was telling me. Whenever Fatou James wanted me to work and I said I was tired she would drive me saying I was her slave. Prisoner and I were at Bye. Prisoner was also there when Fatou James told me that Goomba Gay owed Moro Fall.

[Question by Mr. Cates]

Fatou James used to say at Bye that Coomba Gay owed Moro Fall. Also at Tendito.

Joseph Pullen sworn saith, my name is Joseph Pullen. I am a P.C. May and June of this year I was up river at that time. I know Bye, I have been there. Constables are there and there is an English Flag there. I know Dado Bass, also Yahling Darbo. I knew them at Somah. I was on duty at Somah. I was with Mr. Sitwell, Travelling Commissioner. I did not see prisoner at Bye, I saw him at Somah. I used to go to his premises only three times to buy colah nuts. I never hear any complaints from any person of prisoner's premises. Yahling Darboe did not complain to me when I went to buy colah nuts. I knew Booly Cisey. I had no talk with either Dado or Yahling. I know one Marie, she is not [sic][52] in Bathurst.

---

[47] This is Buwian, an important trading post in the Fogny area, located on the Bintang Creek, not far from Geregia, which is one of the old Portuguese settlements in the area. Bintang Creek flows from the Casamance to the River Gambia.

[48] Cansallah or Kansala was Fode Kabba's base in the Fogny area.

[49] I could not identify this village, which is presumably located either in the Fogny or in the Kiang area.

[50] Goomba Gay or N'Goumba Gaye was one of Fode Kaba's lieutenants. Guns and gunpowder were major trading items at the time, and, as other warriors of the time, Goomba Gay paid his credit with a slave.

[51] Badommy is presumably Badume in the Kiang area, where Mr. Edwin traded.

[52] This probably means "now."

The first time I spoke with Yahling and Dado it was in prisoner's yard. Our talk was only paying compliments.[53] I used to talk with Marie. The first conversation I had with Yahling was at the White Man's place at Somah. Yahling went to the White man to ask him to free her. Yahling was by herself. The White Man sent her back. It was two days after I saw Yahling with the White Man that went to Joniataba. Yahling and Dado ran and came to the White Man at Joniataba. After the White Man asked what they wanted, they said they wanted to be freed. Prisoner came to Joniataba saying he came for his people. He asked Mr. Sitwell to give Dado Bass and Yahling back. He said Yahling was his wife.[54] Mr. Sitwell told prisoner that you are a Trader and an Englishman. You have no right to buy slaves. I shall take them down to Bathurst. Prisoner said you can give me Yahling. I did not make her a slave. She is my wife. Mr. Sitwell gave Yahling to prisoner to bring her down to Bathurst. Mr. Sitwell said he would not give up Dado but would send her to Bathurst. Prisoner asked me if he carried Yahling if he would not get trouble. I told him I do not know. He then said he would not take her, he would give her back. Prisoner came to Mr. Sitwell and said you can take Yahling, you can take her to Bathurst. Mr. Sitwell sent Yahling and Dado to Joniataba. I never told Yahling that I am her countryman. I knew she was a Jolah. I knew Sajou and Belali. Some slaves used to run to the white man for freedom. White man used to set them free.

[Questions from Mr. Gibson]

Mr. SItwell used to send the slaves to Bathurst. There were some Jolahs when I was at Somah and we used to go about together. They had run away from Foday Cabbah. It is not part of my duty to induce people's slaves to run away. That was the first time I went to Somah. I stayed three days there. I met Prisoner, Marie, Yahling and Dado. Yahling and Dado did not come to me at Marie' house. I am a Jolah. I knew Yahling was a Jolah, we spoke in Jolah. Dado was present. She spoke Mandingo. Yahling and I used only to exchange compliments- some with Dado Bass – I used to converse with Marie. I left for Bye. Four days after I left prisoner's place at Somah, then Yahling went to the White Man. I stayed at Bye one month.

When Yahling came to the White Man I was at Somah. The White Man first saw her. White man called me to ask what she wanted, I asked her. She said she was a slave and had come to ask to be freed. The White Man sent Yahling back. The White Man and I were at Bye 1 month and then went to Jassong, then to Boureng 5 days, hence to Barracunda, hence to Pacally Bah.[55]

It was after I had been to all these places that Yahling and Dado made the second complaint to the White Man. This was at Joniataba. I was present with Yahling and Dado and Booley Cisey. Prisoner and White Man spoke English. Booley Cisey begged the White Man to give the women to prisoner. No one else spoke. After prisoner begged and White Man refused then Booley begged. Prisoner then went away, I spoke with Yahling in the White

---

[53] Paying compliments stands for an exchange of greetings. Whenever somebody enters a compound, as Joseph Pullen did, it is customary to introduce oneself to everybody and chat for a while with the people therein.

[54] Slave masters often reclaimed fugitive slave women by stating before colonial officials – who accepted these explanations – that the women were their wives. See Marie Rodet, Chapter 28 in this volume, as well as E. S. Burrill, "'Wives of Circumstance': Gender and Slave Emancipation in Late Nineteenth-century Senegal," *Slavery & Abolition*, 29, 1 (2008): 49–64.

[55] In other words, they went on tour along the south bank of the river to meet people and explain the novelties of British administration.

Man's house at Joniataba. In the presence of White Man and prisoner, the White Man told me to tell Yahling to go with Mr. Edwin and when Mr. Edwin goes to Bathurst he can bring her. This is all I said.

[Questions by Mr. Cates. *Presumably he asked Joseph Pullen what role he played in the conversation between the British commissioner Mr. Sitwell, the two women and Mr. Edwin*]
I interpreted

Court adjourned till Thursday the 20th at noon
Thursday 20th July 1893
Court resumed at noon
[*Still few details from Joseph Pullen; a clerk from the Registry Office introduces the written deposition of the late John Charles Elliott on Mr. Edwin's origins and activities; then the court ascertain whether Bye – the locality where Yahling and Dado lived in slavery – was or not British territory. A clerk at Governor's office testifies of having personally witnessed the agreement between Bye ruler and Governor and produces a copy of the document*]

<u>Stephen Augustus Gibbs</u> sworn saith. My name is Stephen Augustus Gibbs, I am Corporal of Police. I am corporal 2 or 3 months ago. I knew prisoner. I arrested him at Sanguiah.[56] I had a warrant. I went to Somah first. I met prisoner there. I was accompanied by 2 police constables, Georg MacCarthy and Walter Harvey. Prisoner was in his hut, I found three men with him. They were counting pagns. I was in uniform as also the other 2 police constables. After paying compliments, Prisoner said he wanted to go and keep his pagns as they were not safe where they were. I had not disclosed the object of my visit. He went with the two men. He did not return. I waited for a time then I sent a Mandingo man to go with the Police to see whether Mr. Edwin was. I went myself. I did not see him then I sent [sic] to the town.

Mr. Gibson objects to the above evidence as it refers to another charge which has already been disposed of.
Overruled.

And the Police said they had not seen him. I called on the Alcali[57] of Somah and Booly Cisey. They assisted me to search for Prisoner. In consequence of a report from Alcali of Sanguiah I want to Sanguiah with the warrant. I found prisoner at the Alcali's place. I arrested him. I asked him why he had run away. He said he was afraid. He said he did not buy Yahling Darbo. Someone owed him money and required more goods so Yahling was brought as a pledge to him.[58] This conversation took place on the road from Sanguiah to Somah. The Alcali at Sanguiah and Somah are under British protection.[59] I know Bye. Police Constables are stationed there, at Bye. George MacCarthy went with me to Sanguiah.

---

[56] Sanguiah is probably Sangajor, a settlement south of the Bintang Creek in proximity to Geregia and Buwian.
[57] In this specific case, the headman of Sanguiah, who, instead of providing sanctuary to Mr. Edwin, decided to report his presence to the British.
[58] Pawnship was a widespread practice. Young boys and girls often became collateral for a debt. For another example from the River Gambia, see Bellagamba, Chapter 3 in this volume.
[59] This part of the south bank accepted British protection in 1892 after a British military expedition had pushed Fode Kabba and his men across the Gambia-Casamance border. J. M. Gray, *A History*, 406–407.

[Questions by Mr. Gibson]

I went with warrant to arrest prisoner. I went to Court on the charge for which I went to arrest him. I do not know if the charge was dismissed. I was in the court.

[Reply by Mr. Cates]

I do not know if any case against the prisoner has been dismissed in the Police Court.
Case for the Crown closed.
No witness for the Defence.
Mr. Cates' Address – 2 p.m. to 3 p.m.
Mr Gibson's Address – 3 p.m. till 4 p.m.
Court adjourned till Friday the 21st July 1893
Friday 21st July 1893
Court resumed at noon
Acting Chief Magistrate sums up
Verdict – Jury have a doubt as to the Charge with respect to Yahling Dabo and gave him the benefit of doubt.
As for charge with respect of Dado Bass –
Not Guilty.
Prisoner discharged.

SUGGESTED ADDITIONAL READINGS

ON THE END OF SLAVERY IN BRITISH WEST AFRICA

Miers, Suzanne. *Slavery in the 20th century: The Evolution of a Global Problem.* Walnut Creek, CA: Altamira Press, 2005.

ON SLAVE WOMEN, LIFE IN SLAVERY, AND EMANCIPATION

Klein, Martin and Roberts, Richard. "Gender and Emancipation in French West Africa." In *Gender and Slave Emancipation in the Atlantic World.* Edited by Pamela Scully and Diana Paton (Durham, NC and London: Duke University Press, 2005), 162–180.

Macdougall, Anne. "A Sense of Self. The Life of Fatma Barka," *Canadian Journal of African Studies*, 32, 2 (1998): 285–315.

Miller, Joseph. "Introduction. Women as Slaves and Owners of Slaves. Experiences from Africa, the Indian Ocean World, and the Early Atlantic." In *Women and Slavery. Africa, the Indian Ocean World, and the Medieval North Atlantic.* Edited by G. Campbell, Suzanne Miers, and Joseph Miller (Athens: Ohio University Press, 2007), 1–40.

Wright, Marcia. *Strategies of Slaves and Women: Life-Stories from. East/Central Africa.* New York: Lillian Barber Press, 1993.

32 Interpreting Gold Coast Supreme Court Records, SCT 5/4/19

Regina (Queen) vs. Quamina Eddoo

TREVOR GETZ

THE ARCHIVE AND THE DOCUMENT

The National Archive of Ghana in Accra contains thousands of documents dating from the early years of the Gold Coast Colony and Protectorate, which was formed in 1874. Some of these are the private papers and financial records of formally educated African men of high rank or position. Others are letters written by or for chiefly officeholders. Mostly, however, the documents held in the archive from this period were written by professional European men, especially British colonial officials, missionaries, and merchants. Thus the historical record for this period is overwhelmingly dominated by the voices of the powerful: white, male, high-ranking adults. Is it possible, then, to find among these documents the voices of the least powerful: young, enslaved, African females?

Perhaps some opportunities for hearing the voices of enslaved girls can be found in the Supreme Court Records (prefixed SCT), which contain record books of court cases adjudicated by colonial magistrates in the late nineteenth and twentieth centuries. Following the 1874 legal eradication of slavery in the Gold Coast, a number of cases involving the status and treatment of young females in the Colony were heard in these colonial courts. In many of these cases the testimony of these girls was recorded, providing a rare glimpse into their lives. Unfortunately, however, hearing them is not as simple as merely reading the court records. Literate adult males like lawyers, magistrates, interpreters, and clerks controlled the language and questions in the courtroom as well as how evidence was recorded. As a result, the testimony of enslaved girls and young women is often hidden beneath a welter of more dominant voices of older men – lawyers, defendants, clerks, interpreters, and of course magistrates. The problem for the scholar, therefore, is how to excavate their voices from beneath those of other participants and to understand them in their own right.

In this chapter, these issues are discussed as the framework for understanding a particularly moving document: the testimony of Abina Mansah in the case of Regina vs. Quamina Eddoo. Abina Mansah was both the instigator of this case against her former master and a chief witness. The case was heard in the Cape Coast Judicial Assessor's Court on November 10, 1876. The particulars of the case appear to have been written down by the magistrate, William Melton, in the Judicial Assessor's Record Book as testimony was being given. This record book was subsequently filed away, to enter the archives as file number SCT 5/4/19. It remains there today, but so far as I am able to determine, this is the first time

Abina Mansah's testimony has been reprinted or analyzed at any length. What can her testimony tell us about her life, her experiences, and her way of looking at the world around her? That question is at the heart of this chapter.

CONTEXTUALIZING AND HISTORICIZING THE DOCUMENT

In order to understand a single document like the record of Regina vs. Quamina Eddoo, it is necessary first to try to grasp the wider context from which it was produced. This includes both the general conditions that prevailed at the time and place in which the alleged crime occurred and the specific circumstances and situation in the courtroom on that day. This is sometimes called relating the parts to the whole. The document is a "part," a piece of evidence of what was happing in the "whole" of that historical moment. Historians also sometimes refer to this process "historicizing" the document, or setting it in its own place and time.

If we are to understand Abina Mansah's testimony in its own historical setting, it is important first of all for us to question why this document was produced, and thus why this incident came to court. One starting point for our analysis could be the imposition of British colonial rule, without which this case would never have happened. Following a successful war against the large state of Asante in 1873–74, Britain bound a coalition of weaker local states to itself by treaties and force, thus creating the Gold Coast Colony (the area immediately around Britain's coastal forts) and Protectorate (the treaty-bound states). One consequence of this act was to bring into effect in this region laws from the larger British Empire banning slavery.[1]

The legal necessity of abolishing slavery in the region was confounded, however, by the reality that the local slave-owning class was also the economic and political elite on whom the stability of British rule relied. These wealthy merchants, land owners, and chiefly officeholders were too valuable to be angered by emancipating all of their slaves. Thus the British colonial officials on the Gold Coast sought to engineer a strategy that would satisfy the abolitionist British public while not distressing their slave-owning allies. The two laws that resulted from this compromise – the Anti-Slave Trade Ordinance and the Gold Coast Emancipation Ordinance – were very carefully designed to eliminate the legal category of "slave" but at the same time make no real effort to emancipate the enslaved. Individuals who wished to become liberated had to formally apply for emancipation to British magistrates, thus laying the onus of liberation on the enslaved and their families. Of course, some slaves could just walk away, but the evidence is that this was very difficult, especially for enslaved youths who had been brought into the region from far away.[2] Yet the other

---

[1] Raymond Dumett, "Pressure Groups, Bureaucracy, and the Decision-Making Process: The Case of Slavery, Abolition, and Colonial Expansion in the Gold Coast, 1874," *Journal of Imperial and Commonwealth History*, 9 (1981): 193–215.

[2] For more on emancipation and colonialism in this region, see R. Dumett and M. Johnson, "Britain and the Suppression of Slavery in the Gold Coast Colony, Ashanti, and the Northern Territories," in S. Miers and R. Roberts (eds.), *The End of Slavery in Africa* (Madison, 1988); P. Haenger, *Slaves and Slave Holders on the Gold Coast: Towards an Understanding of Social Bondage in West Africa* (Basel, 2000); G. McSheffrey, "Slavery, Indentured Servitude, Legitimate Trade, and the Impact of Abolition in the Gold Coast, 1874–1910: A Reappraisal," *Journal of African History*, 24 (1983): 349–368; T. Getz, *Slavery and Reform in West Africa: Towards Emancipation in Nineteenth-Century Senegal and the Gold Coast* (Athens, OH, 2004); and K. O. Akurang-Parry, "The Administration of the Abolition Laws, African Response, and Post-proclamation Slavery in the Gold Coast, 1874–1940," *Slavery and Abolition*, 19 (1998): 149–166.

route to emancipation – by appealing to British magistrates – was also difficult. Not only did they not speak English, but they often lived and worked in rural regions far from the courts. Moreover, approaching the magistrates required a bureaucratic procedure that was entirely unfamiliar.

The fact that young children found it more difficult than adults to liberate themselves after 1874 was quickly grasped by wealthy people at the coast, and records from the period show that the demand for child captives, and especially girls, quickly grew in the Gold Coast Colony and Protectorate. But some children *did* manage to approach the courts, often by finding a sympathetic adult to help them. This is what Abina Mansah reports that she did by locating free persons from her community of origin, or "country people," who were living in Cape Coast.

PARTICIPANTS

Acting Judicial Assessor William Melton

Once in the court, both the defendant (master accused of "holding a slave") and the allegedly enslaved witnesses were in the almost total power of a British magistrate. He could assign fines or imprisonment (often with hard labor) for those convicted of "slave-holding" or "importing a slave." He could also choose to either liberate enslaved youths entirely or forcibly "apprentice" them to government agencies or powerful local "patrons" – including their former masters! Thus everyone in the courtroom was in essence trying to convince the magistrate of their case. Fortunately, we know some things about these magistrates.[3] Most were not trained lawyers, but rather middle-class men with training in church and public schools, sometimes a few years at a university, and often several years experience in the civil or colonial service. They also had only a very modest understanding of economic, social, or legal institutions in Gold Coast societies.

This fact had three implications. First, the decisions they made were often based strongly on their own cultural perceptions of right and wrong. As befit middle-class Britons of the period, most of the magistrates were idealistic, evangelical, abolitionist, and most of all paternalistic. They believed in the elimination of slavery as part of a sacred duty to "civilize" Gold Coast society by shaping it more toward the morals of British domestic life. They believed that adult males were meant to rule their families, but were to do so with a sense of responsibility. Slavery was a contravention of this duty, and male slave owners who abused enslaved children or overworked them were seen as having abused their positions.

At the same time, however, British colonial magistrates were concerned about childhood delinquency and generally preferred not to liberate children if they felt they were being decently treated, preferring to see them as legitimate "wards," "apprentices," "foster" children, or even "wives" rather than slaves. Slave owners and their lawyers (who understood this cultural perception) thus sought strategies for convincing magistrates that the children in question were legitimate dependents. The most effective was probably to convince the magistrates that the children were well treated and under the effective authority of a caring father figure. They argued that these types of relationships were common in local Akan-, Ga-, and Ewe-speaking societies. This argument was rendered effective

---

[3] See Trevor Getz, "British Courts, Slave-owners, and Child Slaves in Post-Proclamation Gold Coast, 1874–1899," in G. Campbell, S. Miers, and J. C. Miller (eds.), *Children in Slavery*, Vol. 2 (Athens, OH, 2011)

by the magistrates' limited understandings of "local customs." Magistrates often sought out important local men (many of whom were themselves slave owners) in an attempt to understand local society, and they were sometimes manipulated by them. For example, many magistrates erroneously believed that wives were "bought" by husbands in the Gold Coast, or that family members were "in fact so much property, which [the head of household] can sell, pawn, or give away at his pleasure."[4] Arguably, these practices were becoming more widespread because of the effects of the Atlantic slave trade. However, they were still misreading of local cultural norms.

Second, in order to navigate this confusing welter of British common law, their own moral code, and the dimly understood practices of local societies, magistrates often fell back on a simple formula in deciding cases. In the case of Regina vs. Quamina Eddoo, for example, Acting Judicial Assessor Melton looked for five pieces of evidence in deciding whether an individual was illegally enslaved or had legitimately been made a ward.

1. The exchange of money as proof that Abina Mansah was "bought."
2. Evidence of physical abuse beyond which he deemed appropriate for a father figure to give a child, such as flogging.
3. Evidence that Abina Mansah was called a "slave" (including local terms such as "donko" or "amerfefle")
4. Evidence of labor inappropriate for a child.
5. Evidence that the child was not paid or otherwise compensated as a laborer.

Magistrates like Melton usually began the court cases by asking the allegedly enslaved witnesses to give a narrative of their lives, followed by a series of questions. These were intended to determine whether the child's experience fit a definition of slavery as a condition in which an individual is purchased, put to work in the fields, physically abused, unpaid, and formally labeled a slave. However, this definition, which draws deeply on British moral notions and experience with the type of slavery that had predominated in the British Caribbean, had little relevance to the real experiences of young enslaved girls in the Gold Coast. In many cases, the abuse they faced was predominantly verbal, their labor was centered in or around the house, and they were called by a complex series of titles and names that could not be easily equated to the English term "slave." Nevertheless, they were denied mobility, usually treated very poorly, and their fate was not in their own hands.

Finally, as a result of this formulation, magistrates' decisions were often based not so much on the actual experiences of the allegedly enslaved witnesses, but rather on the ability of one or the other party in the case to convince them whether the conditions under which she or he labored fit this peculiarly constructed definition of slavery. In this contest, slave owners (especially wealthy ones) had the upper hand, not only because they were adults, and thus considered more reputable witnesses, but also because they often had more experiences and knowledge of the magistrates' perspectives. They were sometimes also assisted by formally trained, English-speaking lawyers, like James Brew, who acted as experts not only in British law but also in British cultural attitudes. Finally, they were often well known to the court translators and any local "assessors" on whom the magistrate might call for advice on indigenous culture and law. By contrast, the enslaved children

---

[4] Cruickshank, Brodie, *Eighteen Years on the Gold Coast of West Africa*, 2 vols. (London, 1853), 313, 319. Fairfield Report, 1874, CO 879/33.

neither knew how to speak the cultural language of the court nor even understood properly the definition of slavery being applied.

James Davis, court interpreter

Enslaved children also could not communicate in the spoken language of the court – English. Thus they had to put themselves at the mercy of court translators, many of whom were the sons of powerful men and were therefore closely connected to slaveholders and their lawyers. These translators were often biased, and in some cases took advantage of their position by requesting bribes or favoring friends or political allies. The interpreter in Regina vs. Quamina Eddoo, James Davis, was a well-educated African of mixed parentage and a member of an important merchant family in the region, and might have been expected to act in a similar manner. Yet in this case Davis's bias may have been *in favor of* Abina Mansah, as he helped her bring the case to court. In this instance, Davis filled in as prosecuting attorney on the case as well as acting as interpreter. He appears to have helped her complete a written deposition, and may well have coached her in her testimony as well.

What impact does such assistance appear to have had on this case? As intermediaries, interpreters were wielders of great power. They could selectively interpret or embellish the testimony of witnesses without the magistrate knowing. Sometimes they may have done this on purpose, but probably more often misinterpretations were the result of the difficulty of conveying different conceptions and ideas from one language to another.[5] At the heart of Regina vs. Quamina Eddoo, for example, are definitions of the terms "slave" and "free." We have already seen what these terms appear to have represented to AJA Melton. But how did Abinah Mansah understand her status? Is it possible to determine how much of the language written in the court record was hers, and to what degree it was altered by Davis?

James Hutton Brew, lawyer for the defense

Unlike the witnesses who accused them of enslavement, the (often wealthy) defendants were generally somewhat familiar with court procedures or were able to employ trained lawyers like James Hutton Brew, who represented the defendant Quamina Eddoo and his sister Eccoah in this court case. As a descendant of Irish and African parents, Brew's relationship with the British authorities was somewhat ambivalent. He was often used by colonial officials as a middleman or ambassador to local dignitaries. At the same time, some administrators saw him as being somewhat "uppity" in that he acted and dressed like a European but also espoused the cause of African nationalism. Yet Brew was a master of the tools of speaking to and petitioning colonial administrators. In defending Quamina Eddoo, why did Brew ask Melton to appoint a local jury to help him differentiate between and a slave and a dependent? What advantage would an answer provided by urban, property-owning African and Euro-African jurors have given him with regard to the magistrate, the European William Melton?

---

[5] For an excellent collection of work on interpreters and their roles, see Benjamin N. Lawrance, Emily Lynn Osborn, and Richard L. Roberts (eds.), *Intermediaries, Interpreters, and Clerks: African Employees in the Making of Colonial Africa* (Madison: The University of Wisconsin Press), 2006.

One more warning must be made on reading these documents. Not only translators, but also clerks interfered with the production of enslaved girls' testimonies into the record book. Clerks, usually formally educated locals, were employed by many magistrates to write down testimony. In the process, they often edited testimony both on purpose and because it was difficult to write down everything that happened. In order to understand the text, therefore, we must think about what spin the clerk may have put on events in the courtroom. In the case of Abina Mansah's testimony, it seems that AJA Melton wrote the document himself.

Abina Mansah

Although she is the most important figure for us in this trial, I have left Abina Mansah for last. We know quite a bit about her life before she became the property of Quamina Eddoo. We know that she had been captured or kidnapped in Asante territory, and enslaved at two residences in the Asante Confederation, first in the capital city of Coomassie (Kumasi) at the home of Eddoo Buffoe and then again in the province of Adansi (Adanse). At some point, she was then purchased by a trader named Yowawhah (Yaw Awoah) and traveled with him to the town of Salt Pond, not far from Cape Coast and legally within the borders of the Colony. In Saltpond, Yowawhah then appears to have secretly sold her to Quamina Eddoo, who turned her over to his sister Eccoah. After several weeks, she was told that she was to marry Tandoe, at which point she ran away to her "countrypeople" in Cape Coast. They in turn led her to Davis, who helped her appear before the court.

HEARING ABINA MANSAH

The dominant voice in the courtroom was that of the magistrate. The testimony of the enslaved witnesses, by contrast, was obscured by the act of translation and by the editing of the clerk. It was also shaped by the questions of the magistrate and lawyers, because the witnesses were only allowed to respond to questioning aside from an initial statement, which was probably also shaped by the demands of the magistrate. The question we must ask, therefore, is whether it is possible to hear the voices and perspectives of the enslaved *beneath* all this noise?

How much speculation should one engage in when trying to excavate the voices of the least powerful voices present in a document like this one? Abina Mansah's testimony is an exceptional document. Ironically, it is special particularly *because* of the many misunderstandings between her and AJA Melton. Abina Mansah was almost entirely unfamiliar with the language and arguments required by the court. At the same time, Melton was extraordinarily uncomprehending of her actual experiences of enslavement. As a result, the testimony is a relatively long and complete record of the two clashing perspectives. There are several other factors that make this case unusually suited to interpretation. Melton's written record of the case, while not by any means unbiased, is more complete than those normally written by clerks. Also, the involvement of James Davis and James Hutton Brew meant that many more questions were asked than usual, helping deepen and broaden the testimony.

We must recognize, however, that the exceptionality of this document is, more than anything, a result of the exceptionality of Abina Mansah. Technically, Mansah was merely the star witness in a trial brought by the British Empire (Regina, or Queen Victoria, was the official plaintiff). In actuality, she was the individual responsible for bringing the case to trial. Not only did she run away from her place of enslavement in a foreign land; she sought out aid in the form of James Davis. Once in court, she then forced both Melton and Brew to listen to her carefully formulated and intensely emotional arguments rather than backing down or conforming to their expectations. Perhaps the most important thread running through her testimony, in this regard, involves the question of what it means to be a slave.

Unfortunately, despite Abina Mansah's strenuous efforts, her case may not have had a happy ending. Stymied by the lack of the kind of evidence he was looking for, Melton allowed Brew's motion to bring in a jury. Eleven Western-educated, high-status jurors proved unsympathetic to the young girl, and Quamina Eddoo was found not guilty. It is not entirely clear what happened to Abina Mansah after this. As she was not an adult, she may have been turned over to her former "employer" Yowawah to take back to Adansi, or returned to Quamina Eddoo. Possibly she was able to live with her countrypeople as a free individual. Such details were apparently too unimportant for Melton to record.

QUESTIONS TO CONSIDER

1. What questions does AJA Melton ask to try to determine whether Abina Mansah was "really" a slave? What do these questions tell us about his conception of slavery, of local society, and of human rights?

2. Read through the trial transcript and identify points at which Abina Mansah misunderstands, is unable to answer, or contradicts the questions asked by Melton, Davis, and Brew. Why are these moments so important to our task? What do they tell us about the different ways in which each participant understood slavery?

3. Consider this statement made by Abina Mansah: "If when Yowahwah gave me to defendant to keep the defendant had not given me in marriage to Tandoe I would not have entertained such an idea that I had been sold. *Because defendant gave me in marriage I knew that I had been sold.*"

   a) Why do you think Abina Mansah did not know that Yowahwah had sold her to Quamina Eddoo at first? Why do you think the transaction was hidden from her?

   b) What does this statement suggest Abina Mansah understood as the meaning of her impending marriage? Why did that event make it clear to her that she had been sold to Quamina Eddoo?

4. Abina Mansah gives a whole series of statements that give us clues as to how it felt to be in her position. Interpret these statements in the context they appear in the testimony. What was Abina Mansah trying to tell the magistrate, and what do these statements tell us about her experiences and perspectives?

   a) "When a free person is sitting down at ease the slave is working that is what I know."

   b) "I had been sold and I had no will of my own and I could not look after my body and health."

   c) "As they were in defendant's house long before if the defendant had done anything for them I could not tell *but as for me he did nothing good for me.*"

   d) "I thought I was a slave, because when I went for water or firewood I was not paid."

5. James Davis, who was probably of mixed European and African heritage, acted both as the court interpreter and the prosecutor. Is there any evidence in the transcript that follows that he may have impacted, shaped, or edited Abina Mansah's testimony? Consider especially questions he asks Mansah and the introduction of the deposition he helped her write.

6. Consider the following two items of testimony:

a) Question by prosecutor of Abina Mansah: "On the evening as your master [Yowahwah] took you to the defendant did he say to you 'I shall not take away the cloths on your person because I have known your body, but I will cut my beads' and did he not cut the beads?"

b) Testimony of Abina Mansah: "The defendant's sister said to me, 'You have taken some cloths to go and wash for some person, but will you not cook for your mother.' I thought on this that I had been purchased."

From these questions and the broader testimony, what do you deduce is the significance of the acts of cutting beads and of receiving cloth? Why did Abina Mansah and the prosecutor linger on this matter? Does Melton seem to understand its significance?

SCT 5-4-19 Regina (Queen) v. Quamina Eddoo 10 Nov 1876
Testimony of Abina Mansah

Abina Mansah, having been promised and declared that she would speak the truth says:

Abina Mansah

A man called Yowawhah brought me from Ashantee. I was his wife. He brought me to Salt Pond. Yowawhah went on purchasing goods. On the same day as he finished, he handed me over to defendant to be with him, and said that he was going back and would return.

About ten days after the defendant gave me two cloths and told me that he had given me in marriage to one of his house people, and I remonstrated with defendant. I asked him how it was (that when I had been left by Yowawhah to live with him, and that he would return), that he had given me in marriage to one of his people. On this I thought that I had been sold and I ran away. At the time the defendant said he had given me in marriage to Tandoe. And the defendant said that if I did not consent to be married to Tandoe he would tie me up and flog me. I heard I had country people living at Cape Coast, and for what the defendant said I ran away and came to Cape Coast.

The defendant's sister said to me "You have taken some cloths to go and wash for some person, but will you not cook for your mother." I thought on this that I had been purchased. That also induced me to run away.

(continued)

Prosecutor Davis	On the evening as your master took you to the defendant did he say to you "I shall not take away the cloths on your person because I have known your body, but I will cut my beads and did he not cut the beads?"
	[The form of the question is objected to by Mr. Brew on behalf of the defendant.]
Prosecutor Davis	On the evening as your master took you to defendant what did he say to you?
Abina Mansah	When my master finished buying what he wanted to buy, I carried some of the goods and went with him to his lodgings, and in the evening he handed me to the defendant and said "I should live with the defendant until he returned." That was what he said to me. And after that I thought on what the defendant's sister said to me and I made up my mind to run away as I heard that my country people lived in Cape Coast.
Prosecutor Davis	Anything else?
Abina Mansah	Nothing else.
(Deposition read by the court)	[Prosecutor Davis now asks that Abina Mansah's written deposition be admitted into the evidence. The deposition appears to have contained at least three statements missing in this account:
	1) that Abina Mansah came from Kumasi (thus was imported as a slave)
	2) that she was told she would have to marry Tandoe or she would be flogged.
	3) that she knew she had been sold by Yawawhah
	Davis, who probably helped prepare the deposition, would have been aware of the importance of these statements in proving the case. Abina Mansah probably was not.]
Abina Mansah	When I came to the Court before I said I live at Coomassie in Ashantee.
Prosecutor Davis	What is read to you now, did you not make that statement?
Abina Mansah	I did make that statement. But two persons called Attah and Sanygar of defendant's house said to me that if I did not consent to be married to Tandoe and live with him they would tie me and flog me. I do not know whether it was the defendant that said so or not.

Prosecutor Davis	That part of your statement where you say that Yawawhah would give you to Quamina Eddoo, was it false?
Abina Mansah	Whether the defendant purchased me or not I do not know. If the defendant had not given me in marriage, I could not have formed any idea that he had purchased me.
Prosecutor Davis	Do you see then that you were a slave?
Abina Mansah	Yes, I thought I was a slave, because when I went for water or firewood I was not paid.
AJA Melton	When Yawawhah handed you to defendant, did defendant receive you? Did he take you by the hand? What did he say?
Abina Mansah	He (defendant) did not take me by the hand. He [Yawawhah] said "Go live with this man. I am going to Ashantee [Asante] and will come back."
AJA Melton	Were you placed with any woman to work?
Abina Mansah	He (defendant) gave me to his sister to live with her, because I am a woman. Eccoah is the name of defendant's sister. I was not given to anyone to work.
AJA Melton	How were you employed during the time you were with Eccoah?
Abina Mansah	I swept the house. I go for water and firewood and I cooked and when I cooked I ate some. I went to market to buy vegetables. I did so by the order of Eccoah.
AJA Melton	Did defendant or Eccoah make any agreement with you to pay you any wages for your services?
Abina Mansah	No, I worked for nothing.
AJA Melton	Did Eccoah call you any particular name?
Abina Mansah	No.
AJA Melton	Did you not say when you were before the court before that she called you her slave?

(*continued*)

Abina Mansah	On the occasion when I went and washed some clothes and returned, defendant's sister said to me: "a person like you go out and wash cloths for other persons not for me nor your master," "did you expect other persons to cook for you to eat," [and] "a slave like you."
AJA Melton	When Eccoah said "Your master," what did she mean?
Abina Mansah	I cannot answer.
AJA Melton	During the time you were with Eccoah, did she compel you to do these things against your will?
Abina Mansah	In some instances, she said "do so" and "do that," others I did of my own accord.
AJA Melton	When you were a slave at Adansi, what kind of work did you do there?
Abina Mansah	I did the same work as defendant's sister told me.
AJA Melton	When Yowawhah left you with defendant, did he take away your cloth?
Abina Mansah	No, only the beads below my knee in remembrance.
AJA Melton	You have been a slave in Adansi and know how slaves are treated. Did you experience the same kind of treatment whilst with defendant and his sister?
Abina Mansah	Yes, in the same way that I was treated at Adansi the same way I was treated at Salt Pond.
AJA Melton	Are free persons treated in the same way?
Abina Mansah	No.
AJA Melton	Then not being treated as a free person, what did you consider you were? What did you know that you were?
Abina Mansah	A slave cannot be treated as a free person. [While] I was a slave at Adansi, there is a word by which a person who is a domestic slave and another by which a slave is called, which is "Amerperlay" or slave.
AJA Melton	Were you addressed by that name by Eccoah?

Abina Mansah	On the day that I returned from washing the clothes, she called me "Amerperlay," which in the Kreppee means "slave."
AJA Melton	Had you a will of your own? Could you do as you pleased without the control of Eccoah?
Abina Mansah	What came in my own I did it and what came in my own mind I did it.
AJA Melton	Altogether did Eccoah treat you as a free person or as a slave?
Abina Mansah	She treated me as a slave and called me a slave.
AJA Melton	Did you, when she so called and treated you, believe that Yowahwah would return?
[Here the witness who appears to understand Fantee speaks in that language]	I did not think he would return, because Eccoah scolded me and abused me. I thought then that Yowahwah had sold me and that he would not return.
Abina Mansah	From that time that defendant placed you in his sister's hand, did she commence to treat you as a slave?
James Hutton Brew	Yes. When I was handed to Tandoe to be his wife, he gave the Handkerchief I hold in my hand. Defendant said he was going to have plenty of cloths sewn for me by this. I thought that I had been sold.
Abina Mansah	Were you given to Tandoe to be his wife by the defendant without first asking you, without your consent and against your will?
James Hutton Brew	Defendant asked me if I liked him and I said I did not.
Abina Mansah	Were there any other women in the house of defendant besides yourself?
James Hutton Brew	Yes.
Abina Mansah	Did they do any kind of work also?
James Hutton Brew	Yes.
Abina Mansah	Did they also go for wood and water, marketing and do the same work as you did?
James Hutton Brew	Yes.

(*continued*)

Abina Mansah	Were you not aware that all the people in the house were free?
James Hutton Brew	I did not know.
Abina Mansah	Are you aware that everybody in the Protectorate is freed and that those people you saw in defendant's house are as free as defendant and others?
James Hutton Brew	I did not know that I was free.
Abina Mansah	As to the others you saw in defendant's house?
James Hutton Brew	I did not know this. They the persons whom I saw are all the children of slaves.
Abina Mansah	You say you are not aware that all slaves in the Protectorate have been declared free. What led you then to come and lodge this complaint?
James Hutton Brew	I heard that master (meaning white man) had said we were all free. Yet I had been sold and I had no will of my own and I could not look after my body and health: that I am a slave and I would therefore come and complain.
Abina Mansah	So then you were aware that all the people in defendant's house were free, as you state, with the exception of yourself?
James Hutton Brew	They were not all free, but some were slaves.
Abina Mansah	[Question repeated.]
James Hutton Brew	I know that all are free.
Abina Mansah	You said you performed certain work. Were you fed and clothed if so by whom?
James Hutton Brew	Two cloths were given to me, that is all. I was fed by Eccoah.
Abina Mansah	Did you pay for these and the house you live in?
James Hutton Brew	No.
Abina Mansah	Who put the notion into your head that because you were not paid for the services you rendered you were therefore a slave?

James Hutton Brew	I heard that in this place when a man worked in any way he was paid, but I worked and I was not paid. So I thought I am really purchased.
Abina Mansah	You heard also that people are fed and clothed for nothing and paid besides for nothing?
James Hutton Brew	I heard that also.
Abina Mansah	Question repeated in a different form.
James Hutton Brew	If one did not work he could not get cloth nor food to eat.
Abina Mansah	You heard that if you worked you would be fed and clothed and paid altogether?
James Hutton Brew	I heard that.
Abina Mansah	How long were you in defendant's house before you ran away?
James Hutton Brew	I did not count but I came away in the same month.
Abina Mansah	Whilst you were there did you see [that] those of whom you have spoken were fed clothed and paid by defendant?
James Hutton Brew	They had clothes and food given to them. They were not paid.
Abina Mansah	Were you treated in any way differently from the others or were you all treated alike?
James Hutton Brew	As I was not in the house long I could not tell if he had given them anything before. I did not see him give them anything.
Abina Mansah	As to treatment.
James Hutton Brew	They were all clothed and fed, but not fed [sic … meant "paid" I think].
Abina Mansah	When I came I had two cloths given to me. As they were in defendant's house long before if the defendant had done anything for them I could not tell but as for me he did nothing good for me, not having been in the house long, and I ran away.
Abina Mansah	How were you treated by defendant or his sister that you were induced to run away? Harshly treated by your master the defendant? Were you chastised or merely scolded?

(*continued*)

James Hutton Brew	I did not live in defendant's house as he gave me to his sister. I lived in his sister's house; if defendant's sister told me to do this and that, I got up and went and did it. When I did wrong his sister scolded me but never flogged me.
Abina Mansah	In going for firewood, water, etc., were you compelled to go by any species of coercion or threats or told to do so in the ordinary manner, and you went and did it?
James Hutton Brew	If she says go for firewood, or water or to market, I go. She forces me.
Abina Mansah	Do you mean requested, solicited, or how?
James Hutton Brew	I was asked.
Abina Mansah	Were you threatened with ill-treatment or punishment if you refused to go?
James Hutton Brew	If she said to me "go for firewood" and I said "I won't go," she said "if you don't you will be tied and flogged," and I said "Now all are free. I also am free. I claim freedom." That was why I ran away.
Abina Mansah	How often were you threatened with punishment under such circumstances?
James Hutton Brew	About three times.
Abina Mansah	Was threat of punishment made in the presence of any one besides yourself?
James Hutton Brew	Some children but no elderly person belonging to the house of about from 9 to 13 year of age, all girls, vis: Accosuah, Abina, Adjuah, Ambah (the eldest of all).
Abina Mansah	In whose house were these girls living?
James Hutton Brew	In defendant's sisters house.
Abina Mansah	Is not defendant's sister's house a portion of the house in which defendant lives?
James Hutton Brew	They all lived in one house.
Abina Mansah	You stated how people were treated as slaves at Adansi. State how slaves and free people are there treated.

James Hutton Brew	At Adansi, when a free person is sitting down at ease, the slave is working. [T]hat is what I know.
Abina Mansah	Did free person do no work in this household?
James Hutton Brew	On any day when the freeman liked, he worked. I did the necessary work such as women do. [I]f it was firewood or water or plantains, I went and fetched it.
Abina Mansah	Were you not cuffed and beaten at times?
James Hutton Brew	I was not long at Adansi before I was brought to this place. When I did wrong I was scolded.
Abina Mansah	Were you a slave before you came to Adansi?
James Hutton Brew	I was a slave to Eddoo Buffo.
Abina Mansah	Were you never during that time beaten for misconduct or anything like that?
James Hutton Brew	When I was with Eddo Buffoe and did wrong I was flogged and sometimes I was logged.[6]
Abina Mansah	Did Eccoah treat you differently to what she did the other maid-servants in the house?
James Hutton Brew	She did not treat me in the same manner as she treated those I met in the house. When she gave them cloths she gave me none. [T]hat is all.
Abina Mansah	You said that someone threatened to tie [you] up and flog [you] if she would not marry Tandoe. Who was it? Defendant or Seney Agay or Attah?
James Hutton Brew	Attah and Senegay.
Abina Mansah	You said you made a statement in court in which you declared to as a fact that Yaowahwah sold you to defendant. Do you still say so? Of your own knowledge?

(*continued*)

---

[6] Chained to a log as punishment.

James Hutton Brew	If when Yowahwah gave me to defendant to keep the defendant had not given me in marriage to Tandoe, I would not have entertained such an idea that I had been sold. Because defendant gave me in marriage, I knew that I had been sold.
Abina Mansah	In what way were you given in marriage?
James Hutton Brew	My master said that I should be married to Tandoe and that he would give me plenty of cloths, and I said I did not like him.
Abina Mansah	Defendant was in earnest. Tandoe first gave me this handkerchief, but my master was vexed and asked Tandoe why he gave me this when he was going to give me plenty of cloths.
James Hutton Brew	You said that [on] only one occasion Eccoah called you a slave. Did she say "you are my slave" or that "Eddoo's slave" or simply that you are a slave?
Abina Mansah	
	"You are your master's slave." [W]hen she said this I sat down and
James Hutton Brew	said I did not like this and I made up my mind to come away.
Abina Mansah	You are certain of this?
James Hutton Brew	Yes, Ambah and Adjuah and Accosuah were present.
Abina Mansah	Do you know how much you were sold for?
James Hutton Brew	I do not know.
Abina Mansah	Do you know how slaves are sold and handed over?
James Hutton Brew	I know it.
Abina Mansah	Are any ceremonies observed on such occasions, if so, what?
James Hutton Brew	Yes.
Abina Mansah	Were any of them gone through on your alleged sale to Edoo?
James Hutton Brew	There was no observance kept to show the sale of a slave. [T]he only thing which was done was the cutting of the beads at the time.
Abina Mansah	Is that one of the observances?
	It was one.

SUGGESTED FURTHER READINGS

Akurang-Parry, Kwabena O. "The Administration of the Abolition Laws, African Response, and Post-proclamation Slavery in the Gold Coast, 1874–1940," *Slavery and Abolition*, 19 (1998): 149–166.

Campbell, Gwyn, Suzanne Miers, and Joseph C. Miller (eds.) *Children in Slavery*, Vol. 2. Athens: Ohio University Press, 2011.

Getz, Trevor. "A 'Somewhat Firm Policy': The Role of the Gold Coast Judiciary in Implementing Slave Emancipation, 1874–1900," *Ghana Studies Journal*, 2 (2000): 97–117.

"The Case for Africans: The Role of Slaves and Masters in Emancipation on the Gold Coast, 1874–2000," *Slavery and Abolition*, 21 (2000): 128–145.

Greene, Sandra. *West African Narratives of Slavery: Texts from Nineteenth- and Early Twentieth-Century Ghana*. Bloomington: Indiana University Press, 2011.

Haenger, Peter. *Slaves and Slave Holders on the Gold Coast: Towards an Understanding of Social Bondage in West Africa*. Basel: Schlettwein, 2000.

Miers, Suzanne and Richard Roberts (eds.) *The End of Slavery in Africa*. Madison: University of Wisconsin Press, 1988.

33 A Tale of Slavery and Beyond in a British Colonial Court Record
West Africa and Brazil

KRISTIN MANN

The town of Lagos on the West African coast, located in what is today southwestern Nigeria, developed into a major port in the Atlantic slave trade only at the end of the eighteenth century, late in the history of the ignoble commerce. During the first half of the nineteenth century, however, it became one of the leading centers of the slave trade north of the equator, in part because of a series of wars in the town's interior related to the collapse of the powerful Oyo Empire to the north, which produced a large supply of captives for export. About 60 percent of the approximately 540,000 slaves shipped from the Bight of Benin between 1801 and 1867 were taken to northeastern Brazil. A small number of these slaves managed in time to earn money to manumit themselves, or they were freed by their owners. The ships in which other slaves were forcibly exported were seized by the British Royal Navy Anti-slavery Squadron patrolling the West African coast, and the cargoes of those vessels found to be trading slaves illegally were freed in Sierra Leone. Many of these liberated slaves converted to Christianity, and some of them or their children acquired Western, missionary education.

A succession of slave rebellions in Bahia, in northeastern Brazil, that culminated in the Malê uprising of 1835 led slaveholders and government officials there to fear freed blacks, whom they believed had conspired with slaves in the revolt. Following the Malê rebellion, the government of the province deported a substantial number of freed blacks to West Africa, including Lagos. In succeeding decades, other freed slaves, such as José Marcos and Henriata mentioned in the document later in the chapter, returned from Brazil to the Bight of Benin voluntarily and rebuilt their lives there. By the 1840s, groups of Sierra Leonean recaptives had also begun returning to the region, and after 1851, substantial numbers of them settled in Lagos, including George Wilson, who appeared in the court case reported in this chapter.

In 1851, Great Britain forcibly intervened in domestic politics at Lagos and established a consulate in the town, as part of its efforts to abolish the Atlantic slave trade and encourage the development of new kinds of "legitimate" commerce with West Africa. Then, a decade later, Britain formally annexed the small kingdom against the will of its rulers and imposed direct colonial rule. The new colonial government, which remained small at first and employed only a handful of British officers along with a larger number of educated Africans primarily from Sierra Leone, slowly established executive and judicial branches. In 1876, a major judicial reform abolished the older colonial courts and created a new Supreme Court, to which many indigenous Africans, Brazilian returnees, and Sierra Leonean repatriates, as well as Europeans resident in the colony, took disputes.

While the colonial government introduced much English law into Lagos, the 1876 ordinance that created the Supreme Court specified that disputes among "natives" could be decided on the basis of their own "law and custom," unless it was repugnant to "justice, equity, and good conscience" or incompatible with local statute. Judges often sought to decide cases between indigenous peoples according to local law as the judges understood it. They were less clear, however, about what law to apply to former slaves who had returned from Brazil or Sierra Leone, particularly those who had been influenced by Christianity. It took many decades for a body of precedent to emerge from the colonial courts that established marriage, family, and inheritance law among the colony's heterogeneous population of indigenous Lagosians, former slaves returned from Brazil and Sierra Leone, and immigrants from elsewhere. The questions of marriage and inheritance contested in the case reported later in the chapter had not been settled in 1879.

Despite the centrality of slavery, the slave trade, and anti-slavery in the history of Lagos and the Bight of Benin, relatively few sources exist that illuminate these important subjects, much less preserve the memories and voices of former slaves. In my research on the history of nineteenth-century Lagos, one source more than any other has shed light on the slave experience: the Judges' Notebooks of Civil Cases from the Lagos Supreme Court. By the time of the creation of the Supreme Court, the British government no longer recognized the existence of slavery within the colony. The Civil Court could not recognize and directly enforce obligations of slavery. However, many men and women of slave origin, whether they had been owned in Africa itself or had returned from Brazil or Sierra Leone, took disputes of different kinds to the court. In the process of litigation, they sometimes told stories about their lives and social relationships that illuminate aspects of slavery and the slave trade.

The documents that come down to us in the Judges' Notebooks were written by British judges for use in a particular institutional setting – a colonial high court. The practices and procedures of the court profoundly shaped their contents, which must be read and interpreted carefully against both the conventions of the court and the goals and strategies of the Africans who contested disputes within it. The case reported in this chapter began when two former slaves from Brazil applied to the Supreme Court for Letters of Administration, legal documents needed to administer the estate of José Marcos, another Brazilian freedman who had recently died. The two men, Bernardo Henrico and Fredrico Marcos, had apparently been named as José Marcos's executors in a document alleged to be his will, which was entered in court but is not preserved with the court records and is not available for examination. A legal hearing eventuated a week later when a man, Luiz José Marcos, and a woman, Maria de Seville bon de Jesus, who claimed to be the deceased's children, approached the court and asked to be heard.

The court summoned all interested parties, and on the appointed date the judge began the hearing by inviting first Luiz and then Maria to state their cases. After Luiz had spoken, he was questioned by the judge. Although questions asked on cross-examination are never included in the record, the judge's notes on Luiz's replies are distinguished from his other testimony, and they read, in places, like answers to very specific questions. When the court had finished questioning Luiz, a woman involved in the case, Reita Francisca, was allowed to question him, and his answer to her was also entered separately. A similar process was then followed with Maria and other participants who either wanted to state their claims or had been called by the court to give evidence.

The Supreme Court Ordinance charged judges with taking down in writing, at "every stage" and in "every case," all oral evidence given before the court. Notes on individual cases, such as those reproduced here, often take the form of multiple overlapping narratives written by the judge from what disputants and witnesses said in the courtroom. While the judge's notes are commonly quite detailed, they are not verbatim transcripts. What survives from the courtroom testimony was filtered through the ears, mind, and hand of the judge who, while instructed to write down "all oral evidence," no doubt listened for facts and arguments he deemed relevant to the case and shaped what he wrote accordingly. Silences and omissions potentially have double significance. They may reflect statements left unuttered by claimants or witnesses. Alternatively, they may reveal discourse left unrecorded by the judge. That the judge's notes were written in English also presents challenges. The record in the following case does not indicate that any of the men or women who appeared in the courtroom spoke Portuguese or an African language, but they may have done so. If they did not speak in English, their remarks were translated for the judge by a court interpreter, whose control of language gave him considerable unacknowledged power in legal proceedings. Information preserved in the court records is, therefore, possibly twice removed from what was actually said in the courtroom. It is widely recognized, moreover, that even verbatim transcripts in the original language fail to capture much-telling nonverbal courtroom communication. At the end of their notes on proceedings, judges recorded the decisions they reached in cases.

Despite the interpretive challenges with which British colonial court records present historians, they constitute one of the few sources for Lagos and other British settlements where stories told by persons of slave origin about their lives are documented in significant numbers. These stories were shaped by multiple influences: legal, moral, social, and sometimes political. Approached carefully, the records can yield fragments of memory about slavery and the slave trade, as well as about the experiences of freedmen and women.

QUESTIONS TO CONSIDER

1. What issues are being disputed in this case? Why?
2. Identify those who spoke in court and those who are mentioned in the text but did not appear in the courtroom. What were the relationships among them? How were they related to the deceased? Based on what was said in court, how were these relationships created and sustained?
3. What were the different speakers trying to establish through their remarks in court and why? What were their discursive strategies in the courtroom? Why did they say what they did at specific points in their testimony? (Hint: Compare and contrast what speakers said both in their own testimony and when cross-examined by the judge or another participant. Also compare and contrast what different speakers said.)
4. What roles do marriage and gender play in the case? What about other family relationships? How did the participants think about marriage? What did it mean to them?

5. What can be learned from this document about slavery and the slave trade? What can be learned about the experiences of former slaves? Are the memories and voices of former slaves preserved in the record?

6. What can we infer from the outcome of the case?

THE DOCUMENT

Judge's Notebook of Civil Cases, Supreme Court, Lagos Colony, vol. 2, pp. 114–121.

In the Estate of José Marcos, alias Ojo Ladipe, 2 June 1879.[1]

Bernardo Henrico and Fredrico Marcos applying for Letters of Administration 9 June 1879, Luiz José Marcos and Maria de Seville bon de Jesus enter a caveat.[2]

Luiz José Marcos, bricklayer, Bamgbose Street[3]: I entered the caveat because my father, the deceased, made no will.

Cross-examined by the court: The deceased married Henriata bon de Jesus at a church in Bahia. She came [to Lagos] with him [from Brazil]. I was not born at the time [of their marriage], but she told me. He had no children by her, and she is not now living. My mother was Maria da Conceicao, and my father was not married to her. I was born in Brazil, and the deceased brought me to Lagos with him. My mother still lives near Bahia. Father came to Lagos in June 1867, and besides myself he brought his wife and my sister Maria, who has entered the caveat jointly with me. Her mother was not the same as mine, and she is living now in Bahia. Her name being Rosa. When my father died, I was living with him, but my sister lived with her husband. There was one time I had to remove from the house because I had a young girl my father did not like. I remained away for a month, after which I returned. I was away at no other time. Reita Francisca came from Bahia in the same ship as I did, and on coming to Lagos we all lodged in the same house. I never knew she was my father's wife, but I came to know it after the death of Henriata. She lived with my father up to the time of his death. The deceased used to remonstrate with me sometimes, but we never had any row. I am quite sure that I and my sister never left my father until he died. She married about three years ago and then went to live with her husband. The deceased said nothing to me about making a will or leaving property to Reita Francisca. I am sure the document entered in court was not executed by him, for if it had been I should have been called. The deceased used to have fever and sickness, but it did not prevent his going to farm. The last attack of illness he had lasted only 45 days, and then he died.[4] The day of his death was the 6th of May 1879. I am quite sure that Reita Francisca was never married to my father. Bernardo Henrico and Fredrico Marcos used to come to my father. They were his friends and nothing more.

Cross-examined by Reita Francisca: I spent money on my father in his illness.

Maria de Seville bon de Jesus. I am married according to Mohammedan law to Antonio Grillo who lives at Oko Awo, but I was brought up in the Christian faith. I came to Lagos

---

[1] The names in this document have been changed to protect the identities of the disputants and witnesses.

[2] A caveat was a formal notice filed by an interested party or parties with the court requesting the postponement of a proceeding until they were heard.

[3] Many former slaves who returned to Lagos from Brazil worked as artisans, plying trades learned abroad. Their skilled labor helped shape the face of nineteenth-century Lagos. Bamgbose Street lay in the heart of the quarter of the town settled by the Brazilian freedmen and women.

[4] Establishing who cared for José Marcos during his final illness was important during the hearing, because in local culture such behavior conveyed rights to inherit from a deceased.

with the deceased, who was my father. My mother was Rosa de Jesus, and she was not married to my father. When I was born, both lived in Bahia. The deceased, Henriata, the last witness, and myself all came together to Lagos about twelve years ago. Reita Francisca was a fellow passenger with us, and when we arrived we all lodged in the same house. She never left my father.

Cross-examined by the court: The deceased was married to Henriata. She took care of the last witness and myself up to the day of her death about seven years ago. My father said he had lawfully married her in the Brazils, and she said the same. The deceased used to call George Wilson his relative. Wilson attended him and treated him always very kindly. The deceased never quarreled with me. I went regularly to see him. I never heard of a will. He professed Christianity. Reita Francisca was not married to my father. Bernardo Henrico and Fredrico Marcos were friends of the deceased, not relatives. I do not know Joaquim Paulo or Manuel Gomes Lopez. If the deceased had made a will he would have told me.

Cross-examined by Reita Francisca: When I was married, you made the country custom.[5]

George Wilson, gravedigger, Broad Street:[6] The deceased was my cousin. My mother and his father were brother and sister. Their country was Jana, a Yoruba town. War came and broke up the country. Dahomians caught me, and I was sold, then rescued and taken to Sierra Leone from whence I came to Lagos.[7] At that time, I was twenty-four years old. The deceased was at the time also captured, but he escaped from the Dahomians and returned to the ruined town. Sometime after, war again visited the town, and he was then captured and sold and sent to Brazil.[8] He came from Brazil eleven or twelve years ago...and we recognized each other. We used always to visit each other and when he was ill I looked after him. The name of the deceased was Ojo, but he took the name José Marcos.

Cross-examined by the court: He never told me he had made a will. When he was ill, the deceased said to me 'if I die provide me a good funeral.' He did die, and I provided the coffin and paid the expenses of the grave. When I went one day to see the deceased, he said he knew that the sickness would not leave him and that I must give him a good funeral and take care of Reita Francisca.[9] He said nothing about a will.

---

[5] This statement implied that when Maria, who claimed to be José Marcos's daughter, had married, Reita Francisca had performed the social roles of a mother or senior female relative. It said, in effect, that Reita Francisca had acted as a mother to Maria on the occasion of her marriage.

[6] Broad Street was a major commercial thoroughfare in the quarter of Lagos settled by the Sierra Leonean repatriates who returned to the town.

[7] "Jana" refers to Ijanna, a prosperous town among the Egbado subgroup of the Yoruba-speaking peoples. It lay on the frontier between the southwestern province of the crumbling Oyo Empire and the expanding Fon kingdom of Dahomey to the west. Dahomian warriors attacked Ijanna in 1830 or 1831, and Wilson was probably enslaved at that time. The ship on which he was exported into the Atlantic trade was seized by the Royal Navy Anti-slavery Squadron, and he was freed in Sierra Leone, where he lived for some years before migrating to Lagos.

[8] The Egba, another Yoruba-speaking subgroup, sacked Ijanna in 1832 or 1833, because the town's rulers supported their enemies Ijebu and Ibadan in the Owiwi war. José Marcos was probably enslaved for the second time when Ijanna was overrun by the Egba.

[9] Establishing who had organized and paid for José Marcos's funeral was significant during the hearing, because, like care during a final illness, such behavior legitimized rights to inherit in local culture. The reference to having been asked by José Marcos to "take care of Reita Francisca" underscored George Wilson's kinship with the deceased, because senior male relatives commonly assumed responsibility for widows in local culture.

Joaquim Paulo, farmer, Oke Ile. I am acquainted with the deceased, having known him in Bahia. He died in Lagos two months ago. He never spoke to me about making a will. I never saw the paper marked "A" and never made my mark on it.

Manuel Gomes Lopez, tile maker, Oke Ile.[10] I knew José Marcos in Bahia. Three years before his death, the deceased told me he would make a will and appoint me executor. I refused on the grounds that I did not know the customs of the country.[11] I never saw the paper marked "A" and never marked it.

Reita Francisca, provision seller, Oke Ile: The deceased brought me from Bahia. On arrival he got sick, and I took care of him. He had his own wife, but she died soon after arriving here.[12] At one time when he was ill, I took him to Ojo.[13] Luiz refused to go with me. I brought the deceased back, and he was still ill. He said if he died I should bury him and any debts owing I must pay.[14] He left his house to me, and I was to stay in it as I was the person who had taken care of him during his illness. He further said that the two executors were the persons who had assisted in taking care of him. His wearing apparel was to be given to Mr. Wilson's son. The paper marked 'A' was written one year ago by a clerk. Three of us were present – myself, the deceased, and the clerk.

Joseph Lawrence, writing clerk, Tokunboh Street[15]: On 15 April 1878, the deceased sent for me. He said he was very ill and thought he would die and asked me to make book or paper.[16] He dictated to me. He said in case he died his house in Bamgbose Street should be given to his wife, Reita Francisca. I asked if she was his lawful wife,[17] and he replied she was not but he gave her the house because she took care of him in his illness. [He said] that he had a brother in the interior named Popo-Ola and that if he came to Lagos, his wife Reita Francisca should allow him free lodging. He said Luiz and Maria took no care of him when he was sick, so he would give them nothing. He appointed Bernardo Henrico and Fredrico Marcos to be his executors and said they should have possession of his farm to divide amongst them. He said Joaquim Paulo and Manuel Gomes Lopez would witness the will. I made the document and read it to the deceased. He called Reita Francisca, and I read it before her. He called Joaquim and Lopez. Both came. The deceased talked to them in Portuguese. After that he told me to read the will for them, and I asked the deceased in their presence to make his mark. Joaquim Paulo and Manuel Gomes Lopez made their marks.

---

[10] Tile making was another craft that Brazilian freedmen brought to Lagos and pursued to make their living.

[11] This remark suggests that Manuel Gomes Lopez was either not African-born or had been enslaved outside of Yorubaland.

[12] Subsequent evidence indicates that Henriata in fact died about five years after arriving in Lagos.

[13] There were several southern Yoruba villages known as Ojo, and it is impossible to know to which Reita Francisca took José Marcos or why. They may have gone to seek care from a well-known *babalawo* or indigenous healer.

[14] In Yoruba culture, widows were supposed to pay debts left by their deceased husbands. By stating that José Marcos had asked her to pay his debts after he died, Reita Francisca was asserting that he regarded her as his wife.

[15] Literate clerks commonly hired out their services as letter or document writers. Tokunboh Street ran parallel to Bamgbose Street. Lawrence thus lived near José Marcos.

[16] Lagosians commonly used such language to refer to the creation of a written document.

[17] The phrase "lawful wife" is ambiguous in this context. Lawrence was probably seeking to determine whether José Marcos had married Reita Francisca in a licensed and registered Christian ceremony, which would have given the union a special status in the eyes of missionaries, colonial authorities, and many African converts. However, he may also have been inquiring whether the couple had performed African marriage rites. Not until 1884 did the colonial administration introduce a Marriage Ordinance that prohibited polygyny among men who made Christian marriages and altered the inheritance rights of their wives and children.

The third day, I went to the deceased's house. He asked me if I knew where Luiz was. I said no. Reita Francisca was not there when it was signed.

William Cartright, night watch: The deceased was one of my family. George Wilson's father and my father had the same mother and father. Wilson's father was older than mine. I became acquainted with the deceased shortly before his death through a sister of the deceased now in court. I never knew him in the interior before I went to Sierra Leone.

Laside, seller of small wares, Broad Street: I knew the deceased before he went to Bahia from the interior. I lived in the same house with him. The father of the deceased was the brother of my father, but older. Wilson was the son of my father and my brother. I and the deceased were cousins. I am older than Wilson. The name of the town in which he lived was Jarna.[18] It was broken by war. I escaped to Porto Novo, and Wilson and the deceased were captured. When [the deceased] came from Bahia, he sent to Porto Novo for me, and I came down to Lagos. We were all glad to see each other and recognize ourselves.

Judgement: The Registrar of the Court do administer this estate and the proceeds pay into the court, the peculiar circumstances of this case seeming to me to require that it be dealt with under order 51, sec. 39, Supreme Court Ordinance, No. 4, 1876.[19]

[18] "Jarna" is a further reference to Ijanna.

[19] Order 51, sec. 39, of the Supreme Court Ordinance, No. 4, 1876, reads: "In a case of Intestacy, where the particular circumstances of the case appear to the Court so to require … the Court may … grant Letters of Administration to an Officer of the Court." The judge's ruling in this case specified a process for the administration of the estate, but it unfortunately does not clearly reveal the outcome of the dispute. The judge ordered the Registrar of the Court, an educated African named J. A. O. Payne, to administer the estate and pay the proceeds of it into the court, which suggests that Payne liquidated José Marcos's property. But what did the court then do with the proceeds?

As order 51, sec. 39 of the Supreme Court Ordinance pertains to intestacy, we can infer that the judge decided the alleged will was invalid. That decision must have left Reita Francisca, whom José Marcos had admitted to Jacob Lawrence was not his "lawful wife," with a weak legal claim to inherit, despite any care of him in illness, contributions to his funeral, or posthumous payment of his debts. In local culture, wives did not normally inherit their husbands' residences, and Reita Francisca was clearly not José Marcos's wife under any other law.

Even if the judge accepted that Luiz and Maria were José Marcos's children and not estranged from him at the time of his death, they were illegitimate under English law. In local culture, paternal recognition, not the marital status of the mother, generally determined legitimacy, but I doubt that in 1879 a judge would have extended such consideration to offspring born in Brazil. Luiz's and Maria's legal claims were thus also weak.

Might the judge have recognized George Wilson and possibly also Laside as José Marcos's next of kin and heirs? Perhaps, but the fact that Wilson and Laside remembered their biological relationship to José Marcos differently may have raised doubts in the mind of the judge.

It is possible that the judge reached a decision founded on equity – his sense of what was just and fair. If so, I suspect that the claims of Luiz and Maria superseded those of George Wilson. There was a move in the colonial court toward recognizing the inheritance rights of children over those of siblings or more distant kin, even among indigenous inhabitants who were not Christian. But between the dutiful "informal wife" and the truculent alleged children, whose claims would take precedence? Perhaps the judge divided the proceeds in some way.

A further possibility exists. In 1871, an elderly Brazilian freedwoman had died intestate leaving a valuable house, also on Bamgbose Street. The government sold her property and retained the proceeds. When the woman's sister petitioned the Administrator of the Colony three years later protesting that the estate should have been paid to her, a legal officer advised that the deceased's property was rightfully taken by the government under the English Statute of Distributions in the Estates of Intestate Bastards. Authorities advised that as the old woman had died intestate and was supposed illegitimate, she could not have next of kin unless she had descendants. The sister's claim was dismissed. In that instance, the government acted on the astonishing assumption that the parents of a female slave exported from the Bight of Benin decades before must have been unmarried from the perspective of colonial law.

It may be that in 1879 the judge treated José Marcos as illegitimate, as well. If he then concluded that Luiz and Maria were not the deceased's legitimate descendants, the proceeds of José Marcos's estate may have passed to the government.

SUGGESTED ADDITIONAL READINGS

Adewoye, Omoniyi. *The Judicial System in Southern Nigeria, 1854–1954*. Atlantic Highlands, NJ: Humanities Press, 1977.

Elias, T. Olawale. *Nigerian Land Law and Custom*. London: Routledge and Kegan Paul, 1951.

Fyfe, Christopher. *A History of Sierra Leone*. London: Oxford University Press, 1962.

Kopytoff, Jean Herskovits. *A Preface to Modern Nigeria: The "Sierra Leonians" in Yoruba, 1830–1890*. Madison: University of Wisconsin Press, 1965.

Lindsay, Lisa A. "'To Return to the Bosom of their Fatherland': Brazilian Immigrants in Nineteenth-Century Lagos," *Slavery and Abolition*, 15 (1994): 22–50.

Mann, Kristin. *Slavery and the Birth of an African City: Lagos, 1760–1900*. Bloomington: Indiana University Press, 2007.

Marrying Well: Marriage, Status and Social Change among the Educated Elite in Colonial Lagos. Cambridge: Cambridge University Press, 1985.

Mann, Kristin and Richard Roberts, eds. *Law in Colonial Africa*. Portsmouth, NH: Heinemann Books, 1991.

Reis, João José. *Slave Rebellion in Brazil: The Muslim Uprising of 1835 in Bahia*. Trans. Arthur Brakel. Baltimore: Johns Hopkins University Press, 1993.

Schwartz, Stuart B. *Sugar Plantations in the Formation of Brazilian Society, 1550–1835*. Cambridge: Cambridge University Press, 1985.

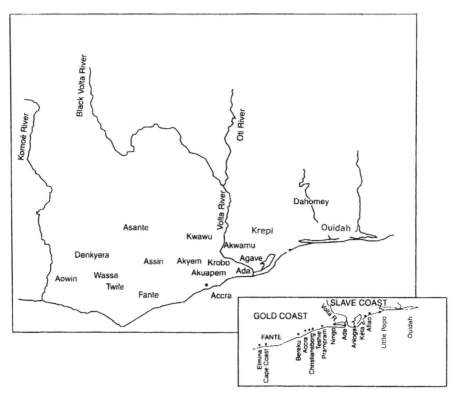

34.1. Map of the Gold and Slave Coasts showing the major towns.
Source: Based on a map in Sandra E. Greene, *Gender, Ethnicity and Social Change on the Upper Slave Coast* (1996) 56.

34   Aballow's Story

The Experience of Slavery in Mid-Nineteenth-Century West Africa, as Told by Herself

SILKE STRICKRODT

In 1851, the acting judicial assessor of the British settlements on the Gold Coast investigated a case of suspected slave-dealing by a European trader. In this investigation, an enslaved woman by the name of Aballow, a number of her fellow slaves, and other Africans appeared as witnesses and testified about her experiences. Their testimonies provide a rare and exceptionally rich account of the career and experiences of a female slave in West Africa in the era of the illegal slave trade. However, questions inevitably arise about this material. How reliable are these testimonies? What do they contribute to increasing our understanding of the experience of slavery and the slave trade? These are the questions I address in this introduction. First I contextualize the documents by explaining the historical circumstances in which they were produced. This is followed by a discussion of two factors that shaped them: the judicial context and the editorial mediation. In the last part, I pose a set of questions concerning the history of slavery and the slave trade about which this investigation can provide some insights.

THE ACTING JUDICIAL ASSESSOR'S INVESTIGATION OF JOHN MARMAN'S AFFAIRS (ACCRA, 1851)

By the mid-1830s, the Atlantic slave trade had been legally prohibited by the European countries and their former colonies in the Americas. However, slave exports continued illegally, particularly from the 'Slave' Coast (extending from the River Volta, in today's Ghana, to Lagos, in today's Nigeria) with its central port at Ouidah (in today's Republic of Benin). British cruisers, among others, strove to suppress the trade by patrolling this coast, arresting suspicious vessels, and sending them for adjudication to the court of mixed commission in Sierra Leone.[1] On the Gold Coast, where the Europeans had been maintaining fortified trading posts for more than 300 years and where there was a strong British presence, slave embarkations had ceased soon after the British abolition of the slave trade in 1808. However, slaves continued to leak from the eastern Gold Coast via canoe transport and overland routes into the western Slave Coast, from where they were shipped to the Americas. From the late 1830s, British impatience with the continuing slave trade led to a number of increasingly aggressive measures. In 1839, the Equipment Act enabled British

---

[1] After 1842, other places also hosted these courts, including Luanda in present-day Angola.

cruisers to arrest Portuguese slave ships that were outfitted for the trade, rather than – as was necessary before – actually carrying slaves. In 1842, the senior officer of the British naval squadron for the suppression of the slave trade on the West African coast threatened to 'knock down' Little Popo (today's Aneho, in Togo), on the western Slave Coast, should any more slaves be exported from there. In 1845, the Palmerston Act unilaterally legitimated the seizure of Brazilian slave ships suspected of the slave trade by the British navy. In 1850, the British took over the Danish settlements in West Africa, thus strengthening their presence on the eastern Gold Coast and western Slave Coast. In 1851, they bombarded Lagos and deposed Oba Kosoko, who had refused to sign an anti-slave trade treaty. In January 1852, the British navy imposed a blockade on the ports on the Slave Coast and prevented all trade. The blockade was lifted only after the local rulers had signed anti-slave trade treaties.

It was in the context of these efforts to suppress the Atlantic slave trade that in November 1851 the British authorities at Accra investigated the affairs of the British trader John Marman.[2] Marman played an important role in the commercial life of the Gold and Slave Coasts, particularly in the development of the export trade in agricultural produce. By the time of the investigation, he had been active on the West African coast for about forty years. Since the early 1830s he had been working as an agent of the English firm of Messrs W. B. Hutton & Sons, beside trading on his own account. He was based at Accra, where he lived with his local African wife, Abenah, but he maintained factories – that is, trading establishments – at various places on the eastern Gold Coast and western Slave Coast, at Winnebah, Prampram, Adafia, Kedzi, and Little Popo. At Marman's subsequent trial in Sierra Leone, one of the European witnesses considered him to be "the father of the palm-oil trade in the Bights about Popo and that neighborhood [i.e., on the western Slave Coast]."[3] Another witness credited him with controlling "two-thirds of the whole business at Accra. He was the most active man [i.e., trader]."[4] The factory at Little Popo had been established by him for Messrs Hutton & Sons in the mid-1830s. It was located in the house of George Lawson, an important African trader, and was managed by Lawson's eldest son, George Latty Lawson. By the mid-1840s, Marman also had a private interest at Little Popo, having married George Latty Lawson's sister Sashey, who traded on his account in a separate establishment.[5] Beside being married to Abenah at Accra and Sashey at Little Popo, Marman also had an English wife, Elizabeth, and children in London.

The investigation of his affairs was prompted by a complaint by Amatey Bouchee, who is identified as "of Moesay" (i.e., Mossi, in today's Burkina Faso) and a "slave of Amadee of the Dutch town of Accra," to the magistrate at Christiansborg (former Danish Accra) that he had not been paid for services rendered to Marman several years earlier.[6] It turned out

---

[2] For a detailed discussion of this investigation and its outcome, see S. Strickrodt, "British Abolitionist Policy on the Ground in West Africa in the Mid-Nineteenth Century," in T. Falola and M. Childs (eds.), *The Changing Worlds of Atlantic Africa: Essays in Honor of Robin Law* (Durham, NC, 2009), 183–200.

[3] British National Archives, Kew (BNA), CO 267/228, Macdonald to Sir J. Packington Bart, Sierra Leone, 21 April 1852, Encl., Chief Justice's notes taken at the trial of Marman indicted for Slave dealing [n. d.], (R. A. Oldfield).

[4] *Ibid.*, (J. Effenhausen).

[5] For more information concerning the Lawsons' role in the political and commercial life of the region, and references to Sashey as "Mrs Marman," see A. Jones and P. Sebald (eds.), *An African Family Archive: The Lawsons of Little Popo/ Aneho (Togo) 1841–1938* (Oxford, 2005).

[6] BNA: CO 96/23, no 87, Hill to Earl Grey, Cape Coast Castle, 24 Nov. 1851, Enc., Cruickshank to Hill, Cape Coast Castle, 24 Nov. 1851 (Amatey Bouchee's deposition, Accra, 12 Nov. 1851).

that these services involved the sending of slaves from Marman's household at Accra to his factory at Little Popo, a port notorious for its role in the "illegal" slave trade. This appeared to implicate Marman in slave-dealing, a serious crime that carried a punishment of up to fourteen years "transportation beyond Seas" or up to five years hard labor.[7] In view of the seriousness of the allegations, the acting judicial assessor of the British settlements on the Gold Coast, Brodie Cruickshank, took charge of the case. Cruickshank's investigation was meticulous, involving the examination of numerous African witnesses. It revealed what Cruickshank regarded as "circumstances of a very criminal nature."[8] Marman's household in Accra comprised a large number of slaves who were employed in "domestic service," apparently including work in his palm oil factory. These slaves were represented by Marman as belonging to his African wife, Abenah, rather than himself, which Cruickshank, however, believed to be a pretence by which Marman tried to evade the laws that prohibited British subjects from holding slaves but that did not contest the right of "natives" to do so. According to Cruickshank, Abenah herself had been a slave who had been purchased by Marman and brought to Accra to live with him. Some of the slaves from his household had been sent from Accra to his factory at Little Popo where, it was suspected, they had been sold, on his instruction, to slave-traders and transported across the Atlantic.

Moreover, Cruickshank discovered that three years earlier, in 1849, Marman had been investigated for similar offenses. This earlier investigation had also been prompted by the complaint of one of Marman's agents, Odattey, about Marman's negligence in paying him for taking slaves from Accra to the western Slave Coast. Odattey had allegedly moved five slaves – four men and one boy. The boy was said to have been taken to Agoué (another notorious slave-trading port about 10 kilometers to the east of Little Popo) and sold into the Atlantic trade. Marman's Accra wife, Abenah, had assumed responsibility for violating the law in this case. She had been fined, the mildness of her punishment being explained by the allowances made by the magistrate because of "her sex and the insufficiency of prison accommodation for females."[9] The fate of the four enslaved men had never been ascertained, although Marman had maintained that two of them had died of illness and that the others were still at his factory in Little Popo. He had been ordered to present the latter to the Christiansborg magistrate, but when he failed to do so the investigation had been allowed to peter out.

These circumstances convinced Cruickshank that the sending of slaves from Marman's Accra household to Little Popo had been "frequent and systematic," and he was determined "to bring the guilt clearly home" (i.e., to Marman) in his investigation. However, in Aballow's case he faced three major obstacles with regard to the successful prosecution. First, he found it difficult to prove the charges he leveled against Marman: that Marman rather than Abenah was responsible for holding Aballow as a slave, that Marman had physically abused her, and that he had then sold or helped sell her. Marman insisted that the handling of his household slaves (including Aballow) was Abenah's responsibility – a strategy he had successfully adopted in the 1849 investigation. A second obstacle was the

---

[7] See Slave Trade Act of 1824 (5 Geo IV c. 113, 24 June 1824): http://www.pdavis.nl/Legislation.htm (accessed 27 April 2009).

[8] BNA, CO 96/23, no. 87, Hill to Earl Grey, Cape Coast Castle, 24 Nov. 1851, Enc., Cruickshank to Hill, Cape Coast Castle, 24 Nov. 1851, p. 1.

[9] BNA, CO 96/23, no. 87, Hill to Earl Grey, Cape Coast Castle, 24 Nov. 1851, Enc., Cruickshank to Hill, Cape Coast Castle, 24 Nov. 1851, p. 34, quoting the records of the police office ([British] Accra, 17 Dec. 1849).

fact that Cruickshank found it impossible to determine the exact time when the alleged offenses had occurred. Dates were important because the relevant piece of legislation, the Slave Trade Act of 1843, which Cruickshank intended to use to prosecute Marman, had only come into effect on November 1, 1843. This Act extended the provisions of the Slave Trade Act of 1824 (which had made illegal the involvement of British citizens and businesses in the slave trade within British territories) to British subjects living outside the British Empire. It effectively prohibited slave-dealing as well as the holding of those slaves acquired after October 1843 by British subjects anywhere in the world.[10] Western dates, however, meant little to most of Cruickshank's African witnesses and they were unable to remember exactly when the alleged offenses occurred.[11]

These problems were compounded by a third obstacle: the complicated judicial situation on the Gold Coast. The British settlements on the Gold Coast were simply trading posts and, legally, British authority reached no further than the walls of their forts. This had several implications for Cruickshank's investigation. The absence of territorial rights beyond the walls of the forts meant that the British authorities on the Gold Coast were unable to try British subjects – such as Marman – for serious crimes but had to refer them to colonial courts – that is, they had to be sent for trial to a British colony, in this case Sierra Leone.[12] The British on the Gold Coast were, however, able to sentence Africans, such as Abenah. This practice of administering justice among the African population in the neighboring towns and villages had its roots in the long history of Afro-European trade relations on the Gold Coast. It had been extended under George Maclean, who had been president of the Council of Merchants at Cape Coast Castle from 1829 to 1843, and had been regularized by the Bond of 1844, a voluntary agreement in which African rulers on the Gold Coast accepted British jurisdiction. The judicial functions assumed by the British became the responsibility of the judicial assessor, a post created in 1843.[13] The justice administered by the judicial assessor on behalf of the African town and villages was not based on British law, however, but on local law and included an acceptance of the institution of slavery. British interference with local African slavery, therefore, was restricted to cases of maltreatment of slaves or the sale or transport of slaves out of British territory or to districts not under the protection of the British government.[14]

Using the 1843 law banning British subjects from dealing in slaves, and the Bond of 1844 prohibiting Africans from abusing their slaves or selling them into districts not under British protection, Cruickshank charged both Marman and Abenah. Marman was indicted on five distinct counts. Four of these involved the sending of five slaves from Accra to Little

---

[10] See Slave Trade Acts of 1824 and 1843 (5 Geo IV c. 113, 24 June 1824 and 6 & 7 Vict c. 98, 24 Aug. 1843): http://www.pdavis.nl/Legislation.htm (accessed 27 April 2009). I am grateful to Robin Law for discussing with me the implications of these Acts for the Marman case and the Gold Coast more generally.

[11] BNA, CO 96/23, no. 87, Hill to Earl Grey, Cape Coast Castle, 24 Nov. 1851, Enc., Cruickshank to Hill, Cape Coast Castle, 24 Nov. 1851, pp. 14–15.

[12] Jurisdiction over British subjects outside British territory was regulated by the Foreign Jurisdiction Act of 1843. See D. C. M. Platt, *The Cinderella Service: British Consuls since 1825* (London, 1971), 146–147; for a copy of the act, see G. E. Metcalfe, *Great Britain and Ghana: Documents of Ghana History 1807–1957* (London, 1964), 191–192.

[13] D. Kimble, *A Political History of Ghana: The Rise of Gold Coast Nationalism 1850–1928* (Oxford, 1963), 193–196; G. E. Metcalfe, *Maclean of the Gold Coast: The Life and Times of George Maclean 1801–1847* (London, 1962), 88–97; 170–178, 296–297.

[14] BNA, CO 96/23, no. 87, Hill to Earl Grey, Cape Coast Castle, 24 Nov. 1851, Enc., Cruickshank to Hill, Cape Coast Castle, 24 Nov. 1851, pp. 9–11.

Popo, and consigning two of these slaves for sale into the Atlantic trade. The fifth charge referred to the case of Aballow, who had been taken in the opposite direction, from Little Popo to Accra. This charge was for

> having brought the person of Aballow in his vessel from Little Popo to British Accra, and having there feloniously consigned her to slavery by giving her as a present to his mistress Ebner [Abenah], and for afterwards aiding and abetting in the barbarous and cruel treatment of the said Aballow, and for being accessory either before or after the act, to the said Aballow being sent from his factory house in British Accra, and sold into slavery in Akim.[15]

Abenah was charged with the offense of "cruelly maltreating her slave [Aballow], and of transporting her for sale to a district of the country where she might be less under the protecting care of the government."[16]

Abenah was found guilty and punished with two years' imprisonment. Marman was sent to Sierra Leone for trial. In Sierra Leone, things became complicated for reasons beyond the scope of this chapter. In the end, the authorities in Sierra Leone decided to commit Marman for trial on only one charge, the transportation of two slaves from Accra to Little Popo and their consignment for sale into the Atlantic slave trade. They did not deal with Aballow's case at all because Abenah had already been found guilty and punished for it. Marman's trial, which took place in March 1852, ended in the verdict of not guilty. To the disappointment of the Gold Coast authorities, Marman returned to the Gold Coast a free man. However, the investigation had ruined his business as well as his reputation and he disappeared from the records a few years later.

ABALLOW'S STORY

Aballow appeared in Cruickshank's investigation as a witness for the prosecution. She was the only one of the six slaves on whose account charges were brought forward. She was also the only one who gave firsthand testimony because only she was successfully traced by Cruickshank and brought to Accra. In her testimony, she gave a summary of her life as a slave, focusing on her experiences in Marman's household.[17] Her account is brief, comprising just 433 words, but poignant. She began by stating that she had been taken away from her country at such a young age that she did not know her origins. She then recorded the way in which she came into Marman's hands, her good looks having attracted his attention while she was in a slave-trader's slave chain at Little Popo and intended for shipment across the Atlantic. Marman purchased her and took her to Accra, where she was given as a present to his wife, Abenah. She was charged with the care of Abenah's (and Marman's) child. Subjected to sexual exploitation by Marman (which resulted in a pregnancy) and to physical abuse, she suffered a miscarriage. She was then sold to Akyem, in the interior, where she married and had two children. She was still living there – probably as a slave – at the time of the investigation. After giving her testimony, she chose to return there.

Aballow's testimony is supplemented by the statements of six other individuals. Three were witnesses for the prosecution: George Latty Lawson, Marman's factor at Little Popo;

---

[15] *Ibid.*, 20–22.

[16] *Ibid.*, 11–12.

[17] BNA, CO 96/23, no. 87, Hill to Earl Grey, Cape Coast Castle, 24 Nov. 1851, Enc., Cruickshank to Hill, Cape Coast Castle, 24 Nov. 1851 (Aballow's deposition, Accra, 12 Nov. 1851).

Yantchey, who had also been a slave of Abenah's and had had a child by Marman, but who had meanwhile left Marman's household; and Ammah, "a native of Dutch Accra" who had taken Aballow to Akyem and sold her there. The other three were witnesses for the defense: Ana Baissa, Coffee Simpessah, and Yammingay, who had all been fellow slaves of Aballow's in Marman's household and who still lived there – still enslaved – at the time of the investigation. The statements of these witnesses are brief, no longer than a paragraph. George Latty Lawson's statement deals with Marman's acquisition of Aballow at Little Popo. Ana Baissa's, Coffee Simpessah's, Yammingay's, and Yantchey's statements concern the physical abuse Aballow suffered in Marman's household at Accra, while Ammah's and Yammingay's testimonies detail her sale to Akyem.

The timing of the events recorded in these testimonies is difficult to determine. As noted previously, the lack of dates presented a major problem for Cruickshank's investigation. This was why the case against Marman fell apart during the trial at Sierra Leone and why he walked free. Nevertheless, from details given in the testimonies it is possible to narrow down the period when these events occurred. The date of her acquisition by Marman can be approximately calculated with the help of information given in George Latty Lawson's statement.[18] According to Lawson, Aballow was acquired at Little Popo from Isidoro de Souza, the eldest son of Francisco Felix de Souza of Ouidah. The time of Isidoro's sojourn at Little Popo is known from external sources. He worked there as his father's agent in the slave trade between 1840 and 1849, returning to Ouidah following his father's death and the destruction of his house at Little Popo by a fire in May 1849.[19] Regarding the date of Aballow's departure from Marman's household, she stated that she was sold to Akyem "about 8 Years ago" – that is, about November 1843. (It is noteworthy that this was just the time when the relevant piece of legislation, the 1843 Slave Trade Act, came into effect. Was the remembered sale date a coincidence or due to Cruickshank's influence?) The combination of the information given by George Latty Lawson and Aballow would mean that the events described in the testimonies occurred between 1840 and 1843. It would also mean that she did not spend a very long time in Marman's household, a few years at most.

It is very tempting to speculate about aspects of Aballow's life, such as her age and her origins. However, there is very little information to go on in these testimonies. Lawson observed that she was "small" at the time Marman acquired her. This description probably referred to her young age rather than (merely) her size. However, at Accra she became pregnant, which means that she was nubile. If we assume that she really did not stay at Accra very long, this would mean that she probably was in her (early) teens when she came into Marman's hands and in her (early) twenties when she gave her testimony.[20]

---

[18] Unfortunately, the Lawson family archive does not help here as the documents preserved in it start only from 1843, with only two exceptions. However, for the period between 1843 and 1850, many visits by Marman to Little Popo and the western Slave Coast are documented (Jones/Sebald, *An African Family Archive*).

[19] R. Law, "Francisco Felix de Souza in West Africa, 1820–1849," in by J. C. Curto and P. E. Lovejoy (eds.), *Enslaving Connections: Changing Cultures of Africa and Brazil during the Era of Slavery* (Amherst, NY, 2004), 187–211; S. Strickrodt, "'Afro-Brazilians' on the Western Slave Coast in the Nineteenth Century," *ibid.*, 213–244.

[20] In his published account of his sojourn on the Gold Coast, Cruickshank notes that the age of marriage for girls there was "about the thirteenth year": *Eighteen Years on the Gold Coast of Africa* (1853, 2nd ed. London, 1966), 193.

With regard to her origins, she was unable to give any information about this because "she [had been] carried away from her native Country at such an early age that she [did] not know the place of her birth."[21] According to Lawson, she had been one in a group of 250 slaves who had been brought "from leeward [that is, from the east] to Papo to be shipped."[22] Most likely, this meant that she had come from Ouidah, Dahomey's port and the center of the illegal slave trade on the Slave Coast. The decentralization of Ouidah's trade after the Equipment Act of 1839 meant that the slave-traders based there sent slaves in canoes along the coastal lagoons in order to be embarked from places to the east and west, as these were less rigorously watched by the cruisers of the British navy's anti-slave trade patrol.[23] However, beyond Ouidah it is difficult, if not impossible, to trace Aballow's movements. Dahomey was one of the biggest suppliers of slaves in the illegal trade, acquiring slaves from a huge area through warfare, raiding, and trade networks with the interior.[24] Neither does her name seem to give more information. These days, "Abalo" is used by the Ewe, Mina, and Fon, groups resident on what used to be the western and central Slave Coast and its immediate interior. Her name means "to move away the bad spirits" and is given to children "who are born with the propensity to attract negative spirits."[25] The question, however, is who gave Aballow this name; was it her original family or (one of) her owners? The latter seems more likely, particularly given the young age at which she was enslaved. Perhaps it was George Latty Lawson's sister Sashey, under whose control the girl came just after she had been acquired by Marman, or Abenah, to whom she was given at Accra. Other evidence arising from the trial verifies that slaves were often given new names by their owners.[26]

THE JUDICIAL CONTEXT AND EDITORIAL MEDIATION

The testimonies of Aballow and the other witnesses make for gripping reading. They are concise, yet rich in detail. As historical sources, however, two factors influence how they should be read: the judicial context in which they were generated and their editorial mediation.

---

[21] BNA, CO 96/23, no. 87, Hill to Earl Grey, Cape Coast Castle, 24 Nov. 1851, Enc., Cruickshank to Hill, Cape Coast Castle, 24 Nov. 1851 (Aballow's deposition, Accra, 12 Nov. 1851).

[22] BNA, CO 96/23, no. 87, Hill to Earl Grey, Cape Coast Castle, 24 Nov. 1851, Enc., Cruickshank to Hill, Cape Coast Castle, 24 Nov. 1851.

[23] This practice was documented by several contemporary observers. For an account of a slave who was transported from Ouidah along the lagoon in order to be embarked elsewhere, see M. G. Baquaqua, *The Biography of Mahommah Gardo Baquaqua; His Passage from Slavery to Freedom in African and America*, ed. by R. Law and P. Lovejoy (Princeton, NJ, 2001), 148–149.

[24] If Aballow had been captured by Dahomey in the 1830s, it is likely that she was of Yoruba or Mahi origin, as these groups were the main targets of Dahomean campaigns. For the 1840s, Le Herissé gives the following lists of Dahomean campaigns: [1841] Houebi (Nagots); [1842] Sakete (Nagots); [1843] cultures d'Atakpame; [1844] Ouece; [1845] Mondjiba (Nagots). See Le Herissé, *L'Ancien royaume du Dahomey: moeurs, religions, histoire* (Paris, 1911), 323. "Nago(t)" means Yoruba.

[25] Mama Zogbé Durchbach, "Bestowing of Names in Ewe Culture," www.mamiwata.com/names.html (accessed April 6, 2009).

[26] An example is one of the slaves who had been sent by Marman to Little Popo, a Krepi woman, and who allegedly been given as a present to Sashey. With reference to her, George Latty Lawson stated that "[h]e did not know her name, but his sister called her Kakaye" (BNA, CO 96/23, no 87, Hill to Earl Grey, Cape Coast Castle, 24 Nov. 1851, Enc., Cruickshank to Hill, Cape Coast Castle, 24 Nov. 1851).

With regard to the judicial context, the fact that these testimonies were produced in a courtroom casts doubt on their reliability.[27] In such a venue, people are under great pressure to say the "right" thing. Rather than stating the truth, even as they understand it, they have their own reasons for saying things, or not saying them, or saying them in a particular way. This is clearly shown in the testimonies, which, while agreeing on the major points of events, show remarkable discrepancies about the details. One sees these discrepancies in the three episodes that became the focus of the investigation: the purchase of Aballow at Little Popo, the flogging she suffered at Accra, and her sale to Akyem.

Aballow mentions three floggings, all of which were inflicted by Abenah. She gives no reason for the first beating, but stated that Marman was away at Little Popo at the time. The second flogging she explained as punishment for having "allowed the Child to sit down among tar." It was this second beating she alleged was ordered by Marman. The third she attributed to Abenah's jealousy after she had become impregnated by Marman. This flogging, meted out while Marman was in the house, is said to have resulted not only in her back being "much cut" but also in a miscarriage. Describing it in detail, she remembered being held over a puncheon by four people, among them Coffee Simpessah, one of the witnesses for the defense.

The other witnesses described just one flogging, and apparently not all of them the same. According to the defense witnesses, Aballow was punished for an injury Abenah's child suffered (involving tar stuck to his bottom) while the infant was in her care. This indicates that they refer to the second flogging. But then their testimonies diverge. Ana Baissa implies that the child's injury was a result of an accident or negligence: "one day [Aballow] allowed [the child] to fall into the tar on the floor." Coffee Simpessah and Yammingay, however, testify that Aballow had willfully hurt the child. According to the former, "[Aballow] took care of her Mistress's child and one day put tar up its fundament." Yammingay stated that "Aballow closed up the Child's fundament with Pitch, which caused the Child to become Sick and Cry." All three of them stated that Abenah reacted by flogging Aballow severely, with Coffee Simpessah and Yammingay implying that this was a mother's passionate reaction to the injury done to her child. According to Yammingay:

> When the Mother Marman's Wife discovered what Aballow had done, she was very angry, and flogged her Severely with a Whip. She (Mrs Marman) used the Whip severely. Aballow's back was cut. The child was sick for some time. It took three days to get the Pitch from the child's bottom by means of Palm Oil [...]

While agreeing that Aballow's back was cut, Yammingay and Coffee Simpessah denied any knowledge of her pregnancy and miscarriage. Ana Baissa implicitly did the same by making no reference to Aballow's health issues after she was beaten. An explanation for this may be that they were referring to the second rather than the third beating; that there may have also been some confusion on Cruickshank's part who questioned them. All three made it clear that Marman played no role in this incident. Yammingay does not mention

---

[27] For an inspiring discussion of court records as historical sources, see K. Mann, "Owners, Slaves and the Struggle for Labour in the Commercial Transition at Lagos," in R. Law (ed.), *From Slave Trade to "Legitimate Commerce": The Commercial Transition in Nineteenth-Century West Africa* (Cambridge, 1995), 144–171; *id.*, "Interpreting Cases, Disentangling Disputes: Court Cases as a Source for Understanding Patron-Client Relationships in Early Colonial Lagos," in: T. Falola and C. Jennings (eds.), *Sources and Methods in African History: Spoken, Written, Unearthed* (Rochester, NY, 2003), 195–218.

him at all, whereas Ana Baissa and Coffee Simpessah positively stated he was away at Little Popo at the time, thus contradicting Aballow's statement that he was there and had even ordered the second flogging.

Yantchey, who was a witness for the prosecution, gave a very different version of events, but given that she refers to the pregnancy/miscarriage, she seems to be referring to the third, not the second, beating. She implied that she had not been present at the flogging but saw Aballow shortly afterward, "laying on the floor with her back much cut and complaining of great pain in her belly." She remembered Aballow telling her not only that the flogging had been attributed to Abenah's jealousy concerning Aballow's pregnancy by Marman (thus confirming Aballow's statement), but also that it had been Marman himself who had meted out the punishment: "[Aballow] said her Mistress, Marman's Wife, had been jealous of her and had caused Captain Marman to flog her and that being pregnant, the flogging had made her miscarry." Furthermore, she testified to seeing "the abortion on the floor." At the end of her statement she again emphasized that she had been told by Aballow that Marman himself had flogged her. This is remarkable, as it differs from Aballow's own testimony. Aballow claimed it was Abenah who beat her. How can this difference be explained? Was it because of a lapse of memory on either Aballow or Yantchey's part? Or was it attributable to personal motives? Did Aballow want to protect Marman and/or incriminate Abenah? Or might Yantchey, who had a child by Marman, have used the opportunity to try to retaliate against him?

Ammah, another witness for the prosecution, also supported the possibility that Aballow was pregnant. He did not witness the flogging of Aballow, but saw "recent sores on her back" when he took her for sale to Akyem. These wounds would have been from the last – that is, the third – flogging. Although he states that he did not know that she had been pregnant, he remembered her being "sickly all the way" and telling him "her belly was sore."

What should we make of these discrepancies? They may seem baffling on the face of it, but – apart from the confusion concerning the various floggings – they result from the two different strategies used by the contesting parties. Cruickshank wanted to build a case against Marman and therefore needed to prove two things: first, that Aballow had been treated cruelly, and second, that Marman had taken an active part in this. This may have been why the witnesses for the prosecution emphasized Marman's role in the abuse as well as Abenah's maliciousness in causing Aballow to be beaten. The strategy of the defense to counter these charges was to show, first, that the treatment of Aballow, while severe, was not cruel, and second, that it had been Abenah's doing rather than that of Marman (this being the strategy that had worked so well in the 1849 investigation). Thus, in the version of the events presented by the defense's witnesses, Marman played no role at all but was away at Little Popo. The responsibility for the flogging was solely Abenah's. Moreover, in the testimonies by Yammingay and Coffee Simpessah, Aballow was represented as a wayward slave whose punishment was justified because of the willful injury of her mistress' child. Their denials of any knowledge of her pregnancy and miscarriage make the punishment appear less cruel, although one must question whether this was done intentionally or was a result of confusion on Cruickshank's part as these accounts do not all seem to refer to the same flogging. Significantly, we never hear Abenah's voice directly – only indirectly through the slaves who were still in her household. Do they portray her more favorably because their deposition was "true" or because they were in her power?

The second episode on which Cruickshank focused his attention had to do with the sale of Aballow to Akyem. The crucial issues here were the reason for which Aballow was sold, the identity of her seller (Marman or Abenah?), and, if it was Abenah, was she responsible for Aballow's sale to Akyem (which, according to Cruickshank, was illegal as it meant selling her "out of the country or to districts not under the protection of the British government")? Or did she merely sell Aballow to Amahsaye (which was not a crime as he lived in Dutch Accra, unless the transfer had been made "by compulsion and for the purpose of punishment"), who then decided on his own to sell her to Akyem with the help of Ammah?

According to Aballow, her sale to Akyem had taken place soon after the flogging that had led to her miscarriage, but after her back had healed. She offered no explanation for the sale but implied it too was connected with Abenah's jealousy. Furthermore, she implicated Marman by noting that the man who organized her sale, Amahsaye, was Marman's servant. Yammingay and Coffee Simpessah, however, clearly represented her sale as a separate punishment for another serious misdemeanor by Aballow: the theft of beads from a woman in Dutch town. In their version, this was the last straw for Abenah, who again became angry and resolved to sell Aballow. They emphasized that the sale was made at Abenah's initiative. Both also emphasized that Marman himself had nothing to do with it but was away at Little Popo at the time. Significantly, Yammingay did not refer to the sale to Akyem but only stated that Aballow had been sent to Amahsaye's house in Dutch Accra. The man who sold Aballow in Akyem, Ammah, testified for the prosecution that Aballow had been brought to him by Amahsaye for sale in Akyem. According to Ammah, he had been told by Amahsaye that Aballow belonged to Abenah, but he did not know whether she had been sold by Abenah to Amahsaye or – implicitly – whether it was Abenah who sent her for sale to Akyem. Again, the discrepancies in these statements illustrate the respective strategies of the prosecution and the defense. The witnesses of the prosecution implicate Marman, emphasize the gratuitous harshness of the punishment (for which no reason is given beyond Abenah's jealousy), and suggest that Marman and/or Abenah illegally sold Aballow out of the territory under British protection. According to the version of the defense's witnesses, however, there was no case to answer: Marman had nothing to do with Aballow's sale, but it was Abenah's responsibility. The sale – which in these accounts is never clearly described as such – occurred within Accra – that is, the territory under British protection – and is portrayed as a means to control an unmanageable slave.

The third episode on which the investigation focused was that of Marman's purchase of Aballow at Little Popo. For this, there are two descriptions, one by Aballow and the other by George Latty Lawson. Aballow simply stated that Marman "bought" her from her owner after he had discovered her in Little Popo and "took a fancy to her." This clearly implicated Marman in slave-dealing, a serious crime if it had happened after November 1, 1843. George Latty Lawson's version of the events was more complicated. According to him, Marman did not acquire Aballow himself; rather he, Lawson, did so for him. Furthermore, she was not bought but exchanged for another slave, and Lawson gave her to Marman as a present for the latter's wife, Abenah, refusing to accept any money for her. This means that Marman was not guilty of dealing: he may have incited Lawson to acquire Aballow, but he did not buy her himself.

How reliable was Lawson's testimony? By the time of the investigation, he had been engaged as Marman's agent at Little Popo for nearly fifteen years and had developed a close relationship with him. At the trial in Sierra Leone, he stated that Marman was to him "more like a father than anything else."[28] As a native of Little Popo, he was not under the jurisdiction of the judicial assessor, but his family's (and particularly his father's) influence at Little Popo depended to a large extent on their good standing with the British.[29] In the early stages of the investigation of the Aballow case, he was trying to protect Marman. However, he was caught committing perjury in his deposition concerning the fate of two slaves whom Marman had sent to Little Popo in 1849. Cruickshank then forced him, under threats of punishment, to admit that he had lied, which seems to have frightened him into becoming a witness for the prosecution.[30]

The second problem concerns the question of editorial mediation. Whose voice, in fact, are we hearing?[31] Is it really Aballow's, or is it that of the acting judicial assessor, Brodie Cruickshank? On the one level, what do we know about the way in which Aballow and the other witnesses were prompted or led by questions, and the way in which their statements were recorded and turned into coherent accounts? Very little indeed. Some of Cruickshank's questions can be deduced from the witnesses' statements. Aballow's poignant statement about her ignorance of her origins was evidently a response to a question asked by Cruickshank concerning her country of origin. Similarly, the emphasis placed by Yammingay and Ana Baissa on the fact that Marman was not present when the incidents occurred was probably prompted by questions by Cruickshank or the defense counsel. The way in which Cruickshank's questions may have obscured rather than clarified what actually happened is illustrated by the confusion in the testimonies concerning the various incidents of flogging.

Another question is the issue of translation. Neither Aballow nor any of the other witnesses spoke English as their mother tongue, and only George Latty Lawson had any proficiency in English. He knew how to write and read it. He was the only person to sign his witness statement, whereas all the others made a cross. Aballow's mother tongue is unknown, but presumably she and the other witnesses gave their statements in Ga, the language spoken in Accra. Or was it Fante, which in this period was widely used as a lingua franca on the Gold Coast? Brodie Cruickshank, who by the time of the investigation had lived on the Gold Coast, specifically in the Fante area to the west of Accra, for more than fifteen years, was fluent in Fante and probably also in Ga.[32]

However, these problems are not unique to this material. All historical sources may be subject to distortion attributable to the context in which they were produced. Furthermore,

---

[28] BNA, CO 267/228, Macdonald to Packington Bart, Sierra Leone, 21 April 1852, Enc., "Chief Justice's notes taken at the trial of Marman indicted for Slave dealing" [n. d.], (G. L. Lawson). The use of the kinship idiom in Lawson's description of his relationship to Marman is intriguing, particularly in the light of Kristin Mann's discussion of a court case at Lagos in 1879. In this case, one client described his relationship to his patron as follows: "He agreed promising to be as a father to us and help us in any difficulty. We were to be his sons and do what he wished us to do [...]" (Mann, "Owners," 161).

[29] For a detailed discussion, see Jones/Sebald, *An African Family Archive*, 22–24.

[30] BNA, CO 96/23, no. 87, Hill to Earl Grey, Cape Coast Castle, 24 Nov. 1851, Enc., Cruickshank to Hill, Cape Coast Castle, 24 Nov. 1851 (G. L. Lawson's deposition, Accra, 12 Nov. 1851).

[31] Cf. R. Law, "Individualising the Atlantic Slave Trade: The Biography of Mohammah Gardo Baquaqua of Djougou," *Transactions of the Royal Historical Society*, 6th series, 12 (2002), 117.

[32] P. Haenger, *Slaves and Slave Holders on the Gold Coast: Towards an Understanding of Social Bondage in West Africa*, ed. by J. J. Schaffer and Paul E. Lovejoy (Basel, 2000), 2. For the subsequent trial in Sierra Leone, Lebrecht Hesse, a member of Accra's merchant elite (and himself a larger holder of slaves) was sent to Freetown as an interpreter. For information concerning Hesse, see Parker, *Making the Town*, 66, 91, 123.

individual accounts of experiences may be shaped by the mediation of editors and/or translators. This is particularly true of subaltern groups such as slaves and women, and especially enslaved women. In this particular case, some degree of control is offered by the plurality of voices, which allows the historian to cross-check the accounts against each other. Therefore, it is possible to reach reasonable conclusions about what Aballow might have experienced.

Aballow's testimony is an important source for the study of slavery and the slave trade in West Africa in the mid-nineteenth century because this is a period for which there is little firsthand information, particularly by enslaved women. Moreover, it is corroborated by collateral testimony. Although (as discussed earlier) the collateral witnesses differ on the details, they do corroborate the general events recorded in Aballow's account, such as her acquisition by Marman at Little Popo, the treatment she suffered in Marman's household, and her subsequent sale. All this makes Aballow's testimony especially valuable as a source for the history of slavery and the slave trade in Africa as described by the enslaved of Africa themselves.

QUESTIONS TO CONSIDER

1. To what extent was it a matter of chance whether or not an enslaved person remained in Africa or was sold into the Atlantic trade?
2. To what extent were Aballow's experiences as an enslaved person specific to her gender?
3. What does the document tell us about the agency of female slaves (in the household)?
4. John Marman was one of the pioneers of the "legitimate" commerce in agricultural produce on the Gold and Slave Coasts. What does the document tell us about the relationship between the Atlantic slave trade and the "legitimate" commerce in this period?
5. Given the influence of the judicial context and the editorial mediation on the testimonies, how far is it possible to reconstruct Aballow's experiences?

THE DOCUMENT. BRITISH NATIONAL ARCHIVES, KEW (UK), CO 96/23, NO 87, HILL TO EARL GREY, CAPE COAST CASTLE, 24 NOVEMBER 1851, ENC., CRUICKSHANK TO HILL, CAPE COAST CASTLE, 24 NOVEMBER 1851.

[Editor's note: The following testimonies were recorded (probably by a clerk) during an investigation, in Accra on November 12, 1851, by the acting judicial assessor of the British Settlements on the Gold Coast, Brodie Cruickshank, of a case of suspected slave-dealing by a British trader, Captain John Marman. A copy of them was included in Cruickshank's report of this investigation to the Governor and Commander of the British Settlements on the Gold Coast. The latter enclosed a copy of this copy in his dispatch to the Colonial Secretary in London. It is this copy, which is twice removed from the original record and preserved in the British National Archives at Kew, that forms the basis of my transcript. Another copy of these testimonies was enclosed in a dispatch of the Governor of the Sierra Leone concerning John Marman's subsequent trial at Freetown in March 1852 and is also preserved at Kew. This is a copy of the copy of Cruickshank's copy of the witness statements, which Governor Hill had sent to Freetown to be used at the trial (and is thus three times removed from the original).]

Deposition taken in reference to the Sale of Aballow.

Aballow being sworn deposes, that she was carried away from her native Country at such an early age that she does not know the place of her birth. Many years ago, she does not recollect how long, Captain Marman was at Papoe [Little Popo] and saw her in the Slave Chain of a Slave dealer with many others. Seeing that she was a handsome girl, he took a fancy to her, and bought her from her Owner.

He gave her into the charge of Sashey, George Latty Lawson's Sister, until he was ready to proceed to Accra,[33] when he carried her away with him to Accra in his Ship.

On Captain Marman's arrival at Accra, he made a present of her to his Wife Ebner [Abenah], with a caution to his Wife to treat her (Deponent) well as he intended to marry her. She was employed to take care of her Mistress's Child; and on one occasion during Captain Marman's absence at Papo, his wife flogged Deponent.

On another occasion Deponent allowed the Child to sit down among tar. Her Mistress was angry with her, and when Captain Marman returned home, she reported to him and he ordered her to be flogged.

Captain Marman was in the habit of having Carnal intercourse with Deponent. She became pregnant by him. Her Mistress, in consequence became jealous, and flogged her severely with a Whip, which caused a miscarriage. This took place in Captain Marman's Factory House. Captain Marman was in the House at the time. Deponent was held by four People over a Puncheon, and her Mistress used the Whip herself. Deponent knows the names of two of the People who held her. They were Amahsaye and Caffee Simpessah. Her back was much cut. Yantchey, Anabaissa, and Yammingay serving in her Mistress's House saw her at the time. When her back got better, she was sent one Evening by Mrs Marman in Company with Yammingay to the House of Amah Saye in the Dutch Town. Amahsaye was a hand Servant in the employment of Captain Marman. He desired Yammingay to return to the Factory House and kept Deponent at his own.

At night Amah Saye gave her in charge to one Ammah to take her to Akim[34] and to sell her. He (Ammah) sold her to a man named Shunti.

Deponent has been detained in Akim since that time and was brought down by order of the British Authorities.

Has a husband in Akim and two Sons and has been treated well. Has no wish to remain at Accra. She was sold to Akim about 8 Years ago.

(sd) Aballow X her mark
Sworn before me at Christiansborg Castle this 12th day of November 1851.
(Signed) B. Cruickshank
J. P. and Acting Judicial Assessor

---

[33] Accra, on the eastern Gold Coast (today's Ghana), consisted of three towns that had grown around three European forts: James Town or English Accra around James Fort, Danish Accra around Christiansborg Castle, which in 1850 had been taken over by the British, and Dutch Accra around Fort Crèvecoeur, which the British were to take over in 1868 (see Parker, *Making the Town*, 8–17). Marman's household was located in English Accra.

[34] Akyem ("Akim") lay to the north and northwest of Accra and comprised three states, the most important of which was Akyem-Abuakwa.

Yammingay a native of Creepee,[35] and Slave of Marman's Wife being sworn, deposes, that she knows Aballow. She was a Slave in the House of her Mistress. Remembers her being flogged, and the cause of it. Aballow closed up the Child's fundament with Pitch, which caused the Child to become Sick and Cry. When the Mother Marman's Wife discovered what Aballow had done, she was very angry, and flogged her Severely with a Whip. She (Mrs Marman) used the Whip severely. Aballow's back was cut. The child was sick for some time. It took three days to get the Pitch from the child's bottom by means of Palm Oil, about a year after this, Aballow stole Beads from a woman in Dutch town.[36] Marman's Wife was again angry with her and determined to sell her. Deponent remembers going with Aballow at 6 o'clock in the Evening from the Factory House to Amahsaye's House in the Dutch Town. Amahsaye received his Instructions from his Mistress, Marman's wife and came down Stairs to the Store and gave Deponent and Aballow a load of Cowries to carry to his House in Dutch Town. They went and she left Aballow with Amahsaye. The Cowries were taken from the Store in the yard where Amahsaye sold Rum. She lived in the same House with Aballow, but knew nothing of her being pregnant, nor of her having had an abortion.

Captain Marman was absent at Papo when Aballow was taken to Amahsaye's House.

(sd) Yammingay X her mark
Sworn before me at Christiansborg Castle
this 12th day of November 1851.
(Signed) B. Cruickshank
J. P. & acting Judicial Assessor

Yantchey a native of Dutch Accra being sworn, deposes that she lived with Aballow in Captain Marman's Factory House. Deponent became pregnant and went to a House in the Dutch Town to be delivered. Captain Marman was the Father of her child. She went to the Factory House one day and saw Aballow laying on the floor with her back much cut and complaining of great pain in her belly. She asked her the reason why she was in such a Condition. She said her Mistress, Marman's Wife, had been jealous of her and had caused Captain Marman to flog her, and that being pregnant the flogging had made her miscarry. Deponent saw the abortion on the floor. Aballow said Captain Marman had flogged her himself.

(sd) Yantchey X her mark
Sworn before me at

[35] Krepi ("Creepee") was the name of a particular Ewe state, also called Peki (in today's Ghana), and situated in the interior of the Slave Coast to the east of the River Volta. However, in the period the term was also used to refer to the Ewe more generally, although individual writers' definitions vary. According to T. E. Bowdich, "Kerrapay" included Anlo, Aflao, Tetetuku, and Tado – that is, Aja as well as Ewe: *Mission from Cape Coast Castle to Ashantee* (1819, reprint, London, 1966), 221–222. G. A. Robertson seems to distinguish "Crepee" from Anlo ("Awoona") and Agotime and says that it "must be an extensive country, as we are led to believe that it is bounded by Mahee and Fakpama [= Atakpame]." According to him, "the Accra traders travel to Crepee, the capital, to exchange European commodities for the manufactures and other articles of that populous district." At another point he notes that "During the Slave-Trade, Little Popo sold a considerable number, who were chiefly Creepees and Mahees": *Notes on Africa particularly those parts which are situated between Cape Verd and the River Congo* (1819/2007), 234–235. J. A. Horton distinguishes "Creepee" from Agotime and describes it as "a large, well-cultivated, and extensive country on the banks of the Volta and interior of Agotime": *West African Countries and Peoples* (1868, reprint, Edinburgh, 1969), 130.

[36] "Dutch town" = Dutch Accra; see note 31.

Christiansborg Castle
this 12th day of November 1851.
(signed) B. Cruickshank
J. P. & acting Judicial Assessor

Ana Baissa, a native of Creepee and Slave of Marman's Wife being sworn, deposes, that she lived in the same House as Aballow at Captain Marman's Factory. Aballow took care of the Child, and one day allowed it to fall into the tar on the floor, for which she was flogged. Amahsaye and Caffee Simpessah were present when she was flogged and held her. Marman's Wife used the Whip herself, and punished Aballow upon the back until she bled. About two months after she heard of her being in Akim. A woman who saw her there told Deponent that Aballow had spoken about her and had sent her Compliments to her. Captain Marman was not at Accra at the time. He had gone to Papo.

(sd) Ana Baissa X her mark
Sworn before me at
Christiansborg Castle
this 12th day of November 1851.
(Signed) B. Cruickshank
J. P. & acting Judicial Assessor

Coffce Simpessah, a native of Moesay,[37] a Slave of Ebner, Marman's Wife being sworn, deposes, that he knows Aballow, Captain Marman brought her from Papo and gave her to his Wife Ebner. She took care of her Mistress's child and one day put tar up its fundament. Her mistress was angry and flogged her severely. Marman's wife used the whip herself. Aballow's back was cut. He does not know that she was pregnant at the time of her being flogged. Amahsaye is dead. Captain Marman was at Papo at the time. She remained in the House for two or three months after this and Stole Beads from a Woman in Dutch Accra. On this account Marman's Wife determined to sell her. Deponent was present and saw her flogged.

(sd) Coffee Simpessah X his mark
Sworn before me at
Christiansborg Castle
this 12th day of November 1851.
(Signed) B. Cruickshank
J. P. & acting Judicial Assessor

George Latty Lawson of Papo, being sworn, deposes, that he had been a Factor at Papo, for Captain Marman for many Years. He remembers upon one occasion, when Captain Marman visited the Factory, that Two Hundred and Fifty Slaves were brought from Leeward to Papo to be shipped. They were in Slave Chains, and belonged to Isidore de Souza. Captain Marman took a fancy to the girl Aballow, who was small at that time, and desired Deponent to try to purchase her for him. Deponent prevailed upon her owner to accept another Slave in her place and gave her to his sister Sashey, Marman's wife, to take

---

[37] Mossi ("Moesay") lies in today's Burkina Faso. For near-contemporary information on its role as a source of slaves, see S. W. Koelle, *Polyglotta Africana*, with an introduction by P. E. H. Hair and an index by D. Dalby (1854, reprint, Graz, 1963), IV.A.1. ("Mose").

care of her until Captain Marman was ready to go to Accra. Captain Marman carried her away in Vessel (he thinks the "Sea Bird") and as he was going, he asked Deponent how much he had to pay for Aballow. Deponent answered that as he (Captain Marman) had taken a fancy to the girl and wished to make her a present of her to his Wife, he would charge him nothing, but give her as a Present. Deponent knows nothing more of her. He is still in Captain Marman's employment at Papo.

Sworn before me at
Christiansborg Castle
this 12th day of November 1851.
(sd) George Latty Lawson
(Signed) B. Cruickshank
J. P. & acting Judicial Assessor

Ammah a native of Dutch Accra being Sworn, deposes, that he knows Aballow. He rembers [sic] Ahmahsaye having sent for him and given ["him" crossed out] Aballow into his charge to take to Akim to be sold. Amahsaye gave him private instructions to sell the Woman in Akim; but he deceived her by making her believe that she was to accompany him to the bush to make Fetish. Does not know why the Woman was sent to Akim. She was sickly all the way and told him her belly was sore. Saw recent sores upon her back and thinks they were about a months old. She told him she had been flogged. When he got three days' journey from Accra, he sold her to a man named Shanti for one ounce twelve ackies of Gold. When Aballow saw that she was sold she wept. He returned to Accra with the money and paid it to Amah Saye.

He had seen Aballow several times before in the English town. She told him, she belonged to Marman's Wife but does not know if her Mistress had sold her to Amahsaye. Knows nothing of her having been pregnant.

(sd) Ammah X his mark
Sworn before me at
Christiansborg Castle
this 12 day of November 1851.
(Signed) B. Cruickshank
J. P. & acting Judicial Assessor

SUGGESTED ADDITIONAL READINGS

Haenger, Peter. *Slaves and Slave Holders on the Gold Coast: Towards an Understanding of Social Bondage in West Africa*, ed. by J. J. Shaffer and P. E. Lovejoy. Basel: Schlettwein, 2000.

Law, Robin. "Individualising the Atlantic Slave Trade: The Biography of Mohammah Gardo Baquaqua of Djougou," *Transactions of the Royal Historical Society*, 6th series, 12 (2002): 113–140.

Miller, Joseph C. "Women as Slaves and Owners of Slaves: Experiences from Africa, the Indian Ocean World, and the Early Atlantic," in *Africa, the Indian Ocean World, and the Medieval North Atlantic*, vol. 1 of *Women and Slavery* (2 vols.). Edited by Gwyn Campbell, Suzanne Miers, and Joseph C. Miller (Athens: Ohio University Press, 2007), 1–40.

Robertson, Claire S. and Martin Klein (eds.) *Women and Slavery in Africa*. Madison: University of Wisconsin Press, 1983.

Robertson, Claire and M. Robinson, "Re-Modeling Slavery as if Women Mattered," in *The Modern Atlantic*, vol. 2 of *Women and Slavery* (2 vols.). Edited by Gwyn Campbell, Suzanne Miers, and Joseph C. Miller (Athens: Ohio University Press, 2008), 253–283.

35

A Case of Kidnapping and Child Trafficking in Senegal, 1916

RICHARD ROBERTS

The effort to curtail slavery, the slave trade, and kidnapping in French West Africa has a long and tortuous history. The French decreed a law in 1831 that criminalized the slave trade and decreed the abolition of slavery in its small West African towns of St. Louis and Gorée in 1848. These laws were often subordinated to the imperatives of colonial rule and the realities of the colonial state's limited power to impose its laws. The gradual end of the trans-Atlantic slave trade increased the supply of slaves in Africa and thus expanded the slave trade. As the pace of the Scramble for Africa heated in the last quarter of the nineteenth century, the primary European powers engaged in the process met in Berlin in 1884–1885 to agree on formulas for claiming territory, avoiding conflicts over contested claims, and for promoting "free trade," at least for Europeans. As part of the broader free-trade ideology, participating powers pledged to prohibit the export slave trade from Africa and to suppress enslavement in Africa. As would be the case for so many of these international instruments, little thought was given to enforcement.

The Berlin Act of 1885 nonetheless linked the rhetoric of anti-slavery and anti-slave trade to colonialism and thus committed its signatories to efforts to suppress both. With greater territorial claims also came greater pressure, mostly from metropolitan humanitarian and missionary societies, to act more aggressively against the slave trade. The leading African colonial powers thus met again in Brussels in 1890 to decide on ways to suppress the slave trade. The signatories to the Brussels Act of 1890 reiterated the principle that the occupation of Africa was part of a broader anti-slavery mission, and they agreed to pass and enforce laws against the capture, transport, and sale of slaves on land and on sea. Various bilateral and multilateral agreements were reinforced regarding international search and seizure of ships transporting slaves on the Atlantic and Indian oceans in particular. The signatories also agreed to restrict the sales of firearms and liquor in Africa, which were believed to be essential to the trade in slaves.[1] Despite increasing rhetoric favoring the suppression of the internal slave trade in the newly conquered regions of West Africa, colonial conquest actually encouraged the slave trade.[2]

---

[1] Suzanne Miers, *Slavery in the Twentieth Century: The Evolution of a Global Problem* (Walnut Creek, 2003), 19–22.

[2] Martin Klein has written extensively on the ways in which the French colonial conquest indirectly and directly fed the slave trade. See Martin Klein, *Slavery and Colonial Rule in French West Africa* (New York,

Africans bought slaves during this period to enlarge the size of their households, to serve as wives and concubines, and to increase their labor supply to produce products for both the African and international markets. The supply of slaves in Africa declined with the final conquest of African states, although it did not dry up completely. Even if armies no longer captured and enslaved their enemies, small bands of kidnappers trolled the vast, poorly controlled regions of the continent and fed the continued demand for slaves in Africa and abroad. The nascent and poorly developed colonial states wanted to avoid inciting revolts and unrest and thus avoided moving too forcefully to abolish slavery and the slave trade.

In 1905, however, slaves in the French Soudan took the initiative and began to leave their masters.[3] Over the next six years, slaves throughout French West Africa left their masters. The slaves' exodus actually pushed the colonial administration to act upon its rhetoric and to decree the end of enslavement and the alienation of any person's liberty. This was the decree of 12 December 1905, which was to play a role in the court case described in this chapter.[4] Martin Klein estimates that upwards of one million slaves left their masters during this period.[5] The colonial state still did not have the capacity to enforce its laws, and the slave trade persisted in some places well into the second half of the twentieth century. There were, however, renewed efforts to end the slave trade and slavery, especially after World War I.

Following World War I, the Versailles Peace Accords led to the establishment of the League of Nations, the Mandate system governing the seized colonies and territories of the defeated powers, and a vague commitment to "secure fair and humane conditions of labor" at home and in the mandated territories, which also meant dealing with the persistence of slavery. Britain, France, and Belgium met outside of Versailles in 1919 at St. Germaine-en-Laye to renegotiate the Berlin and Brussels conventions. Subsumed within these negotiations was the issue of slavery and the slave trade. The St. Germaine-en-Laye convention committed these powers to "secure the complete suppression of slavery in all its forms, and of the slave trade by land and sea."[6] But no enforcement mechanisms were defined.

Under pressure from religious and secular humanitarian groups, the League established a Commission on Slavery, which was to inquire into the "resurgence" of slavery, especially in Africa. In 1922, the Commission requested information from all States Parties to the League to provide information on slavery. This was a request, but it nonetheless sent a bolt of activity from the Ministry of Colonies to the governor-general of French West Africa and from there outward to the lieutenant governors of the various colonies. The minister wanted a report that examined the efforts and status of the campaigns against slavery in the various colonies and the measures, including criminal sentences, which were being undertaken to suppress slavery.[7]

1998), ch. 5; Richard Roberts, *Warriors, Slaves, and Merchants: The State and the Economy in the Middle Niger Valley, 1700–1914* (Stanford, 1987).

3   See Martin Klein and Richard Roberts, "The Banamba Slave Exodus and the End of Slavery in the Western Sudan," *Journal of African History*, 21, 4 (1980): 375–394.

4   For more information on how the colonial court system was structured and how it operated, see Richard Roberts, *Litigants and Households: African Disputes and Colonial Courts in the French Soudan, 1895–1912* (Portsmouth, NH, 2005).

5   Klein, *Slavery and French Colonial Rule*, 172–173.

6   Convention quoted in Miers, *Slavery in the Twentieth Century*, 61.

7   Minister of Colonies to Gov-gen AOF, 27 Oct 1922, Paris, Archives Nationales, Republique du Sénégal (hereafter ANS) 2 K 4. Many thanks to Paul Lovejoy for making available the electronic version of the Martin Klein Collection.

The report indicated that the administration was pleased with itself: "The developments recounted in this report demonstrate that for her part, France has largely fulfilled its obligations imposed on States Parties to the Brussels Act and that its cooperation in the grand work of liberating the African populations has not been the least active nor least fecund [of its fellow signatories]."[8] To further substantiate its efforts to suppress the slave trade, the governor-general of French West Africa included in this file a transcript of a 1916 criminal trial against two Senegalese men accused of buying children kidnapped by Mauretanian traders. The transcript of this trial is included later in the chapter.

The case was heard at the district tribunal of Louga in Senegal. The district tribunal was one of three levels of courts created by Governor-General Ernest Roume in 1903 as part of a thoroughgoing reform of the colonial legal system in French West Africa. The 1903 decree established two sets of courts – one for French citizens and other European nationals and the other for African subjects – that were nonetheless joined at the top by a common appeals court. These two sets of courts closely resembled each other in the kinds of cases they heard; they differed in that the courts for French citizens applied metropolitan civil, commercial, and criminal codes whereas the courts for African subjects applied statute law and African "customs" as long as these customs were not considered repugnant to French civilization. In the case we examine later in the chapter, kidnapping may have been widely practiced in the area, as one of the defendants claimed, but because the French had outlawed new enslavement ("the alienation of a person's liberty"), the case wound up in the district court of Louga, which was charged with hearing criminal cases brought against African subjects.

The senior French administrator of the district presided over the district tribunal. If he was absent, then another, more junior French administrator presided. The French administrator was assisted in his assessment of the case and the relevant African customs by two African assessors selected by the French administration for their knowledge of African customs. All defendants were permitted to have their own advocates, usually a respected community notable or kinsman, but never a defense attorney because lawyers were not permitted in these African tribunals.[9] A court interpreter translated the testimonies from the African languages of the defendants and witnesses – in this case from Wolof to French – and the judge's instructions originally given in French into the African languages. A court secretary transcribed the judge's instructions in the case and the testimonies presented. In this case, the court secretary was another French colonial official, although in principle Africans could have staffed this position. By the time of this case in 1916, however, the numbers of Africans who had sufficient skills to transcribe court testimony in French were still few.

The case examined here was initially brought by the mother (Massouda Fall) of two kidnapped children. As we learn from the court case, Massouda was a wood and charcoal merchant, who lived in Senegal, but was near the Mauretanian town of Mederdra on business when her two sons were kidnapped by a Mauretanian named Amir. At least one of her two kidnapped sons stated that he was actually born in Mederdra, which suggests that Massouda was a regular trader back and forth between Senegal and Mauretania. Amir, the kidnapper, took the children back across the Senegal River to the town of Same in the Gandiolais district, not far from St. Louis. Indeed, the border between Senegal and

---

[8] Report, no title, no date [probably 1923], ANS 2 K 4.

[9] For more detail on the structure and legal procedures in the 1903 legal code, see Roberts, *Litigants and Households*, chapter 3.

Mauretania was defined by the Senegal River and people moved back and forth frequently for commerce, herding, and Islamic learning.[10] Transporting slaves across the Senegal River in both directions seems to have been part of a long-standing trade.

Demand for children as slaves was high. One of Massouda's kidnapped sons worked in the fields and the other joined the ranks of children begging, which was part of a tradition of mendicancy linked to Islamic learning in Senegal.[11] It is not clear that the child sent out to beg did so within this tradition of Islamic learning; it may be that he merely brought back either food or money to his master. Amadou Diop, one of the defendants in the case, told the court that he bought one of the kidnapped boys because his own son had joined the French army and was a soldier, probably posted away, perhaps actually in France, where many African soldiers fought for the French during World War I. One of the most astonishing statements made in court was when one of the accused stated that although he knew that buying a slave was prohibited, everyone in the region did so as well or at least knew about it and thus tolerated both enslavement and slavery. Both of the accused slave buyers stated that they knew other people in the area who bought and owned slaves, but both refused to name them. Both of the accused were sentenced to five years in prison and five additional years of involuntary probation, which was the harshest sentence possible under the law. Both were also fined 1,000 francs each, which was then given to the mother of the kidnapped children. We are not at all sure what happened to the third kidnapped child, who was too young to even remember his family name. No one seemed to claim him.

The third defendant in the case was Faoussa Guèye, the sister-in-law of one of the accused slave owners. Faoussa denied any involvement in the case, but the court produced testimony from several witnesses that corroborated the claim that she had given hospitality to the kidnapper and the kidnapped children as the kidnapper sought buyers. The act of giving hospitality to the kidnapper effectively made Faouossa complicit in the slave trade, and the court sentenced her to six months in prison. Readers should note how quickly the case went to trial: the trial took place five days after Massouda Fall brought her complaint before the district officer regarding her kidnapped sons.

The court transcript provides us with testimony from the kidnapped children. Testimony from children caught up in the slave trade is rare. But the testimony also shows the limitations of children as witnesses. The ten-year-old is by far the best witness, but even his testimony is limited and his sense of time somewhat distorted. His older brother had a better sense of chronology, but could not remember the sequence of events. In contrast, the youngest child knew virtually nothing about the circumstances of his kidnapping or his family's name. Because of their need to have protectors and people to care for them, kidnapped children were attractive slaves. They rarely ran away and could often be easily disguised as children of their masters or as adopted children. Kidnapping was one of the earliest forms of enslavement and it continues to this day.[12]

[10] David Robinson, *Paths of Accommodation: Muslim Societies and French Colonial Authorities in Senegal and Mauritania, 1880–1920* (Athens, OH, 2000); and James L. A. Webb, Jr, *Desert Frontier: Ecological and Economic Change along the Western Sahel, 1600–1850* (Madison, 1995).

[11] See, for example, Rudolph Ware, "Njàngaan: The Daily Regime of Qur'anic Students in 20th Century Senegal," *International Journal of African Historical Studies*, 37, 3 (2004): 515–538.

[12] According to UNICEF, 1.2 million children are trafficked each year. See especially United Nations, General Assembly Document A/HRC/10/16, 20 February 2009, Joy Ngozi Ezeilo, Special Rapporteur on trafficking in persons, "Promotion and Protection of all Human Rights, Civil, Political, Economic, Social and Cultural Rights, Including the Right to Development." http://www2.ohchr.org/english/issues/trafficking/docs/HRC-10-16.pdf

QUESTIONS TO CONSIDER

1. Why would anyone (male or female) want to acquire a kidnapped child? What value did children provide to the people who bought them?
2. In this document, the two defendants, N'Diouga Guèye and Amadou Diop, claimed that in buying kidnapped children, they were doing what everyone in the village did. If everyone was buying kidnapped children, as they claimed, were Guèye and Diop justified in buying kidnapped children because it was customary to do so?
3. What was the significance of having a long-standing practice, such as acquiring kidnapped children, made illegal? How did what Guèye and Diop define as African customs fit together with emerging ideas of international human rights?
4. What is the meaning of the term "trafficking" and when does trading something become trafficking?

DOCUMENT

Colony of Senegal
Case number 41: Case of Trafficking
Defendants: N'Diouga Guèye, Amadou Diop, Faoussa Guèye

NATIVE JUSTICE

District of Louga, Senegal

Public trial of 23 June 1916 at 3 PM held at the District Tribunal of Louga. The judges were Mr. Grandry, adjunct administrator of the colonies, replacing the district officer, who was unable to attend because of sickness; Ibrahima N'Diaye, official assessor, Muslim social status; Malic Sall, supplementary assessor, Muslim social status, replacing Alasaane Gissé, official assessor, who was away on a trip. Acting as secretary to the court was Mr. Portes, adjunct employee of the Native Affairs Department.

Defendants were N'Diouga Guèye, Muslim social status and living in Same, district of Gandiolais, of the Wolof ethnic group, held in custody since 19 June 1916; and Amadou Diop, Muslim social status, born and living in Diaji, district of Gandiolais, of the Wolof ethnic group, held in custody since 22 June 1916.

Assisting in the proceedings is the interpreter, Massamba Aram Diop, aged twenty-three years.

The President of the court alerted the defendants that they had the right to choose their own advocate for the defense from among their relatives or from among the local notables of their homes, whose status will then be recognized by the court. The first defendant, N'Diouga Guèye, declared that he chooses Guibril M'Baye, his brother-in-law and a notable from the village of Same. The second defendant declared that he did not want to be assisted by an advocate. After swearing in Guibril M'Baye, he will assist the first defendant until the end of the trial.

Exposé of the Facts:

The woman Massouda [Fall], lives in Louga, went on 18 June 1916 to district headquarters to complain that two of her children, who were kidnapped in Mauretania, had been bought in Senegal. She affirmed that she saw the youngest of her two children in the village of Same in N'Diouga Guèye's concession.

The provincial chief of Gandiolais sub-district began an inquiry and discovered that N'Diouga Guèye had purchased the child, who was around four years old and named Gora, in April 1916. When the child was placed before Massouda, she did not recognize the child as her own. The chief then set out to discover whose child this was. A second child was found at Same, aged around twelve. He stated that his name was Guibril Guèye and he was immediately recognized by his mother as her own child. He affirmed that N'Diouga Guèye had bought him several years ago. He also stated that his older brother, kidnapped at the same time as he, could be found in the village of Diad, part of Gandiolais in a concession belonging to Amadou Diop. Faced with the evidence, the chief immediately arrested N'Diouga Guèye. The young Guibril Guèye then accompanied a police sergeant on horseback to that village, where the sergeant then arrested Amadou Diop and took the child that Guibril had identified.

The two defendants were taken into preventive detention and the district officer called for a court hearing regarding this case dealing a serious felony. The President of the court invited all the witnesses to tell only the truth and to avoid the punishment that false testimony would bring.

First Witness: Massouda Fall, resident of Louga, aged around 35 years, charcoal and wood merchant, Muslim social status and neither a relative or servant of the defendants.

> I was living in Mauretania in the neighborhood of Méderdra with my two children over there [in the courtroom]. Around the time of Tabaski (December) 1913, the two [children] disappeared. I went in search of them. Then, just by luck one fine day, when I was in the district of Tivaouane, I came face to face with my youngest son in the village of Same in the sub-district of Gandiolais. I took my son a short distance away and he told me that was living with a man named N'Diouga Guèye. I immediately went to [the district headquarters in] Louga and filed a complaint. These are truly my two sons who are present, and moreover, they have recognized me. Questioned, the two children affirm that Massouda is their mother.

Second Witness: Guibril Guèye, about ten years old, son of Massouda, born in Mauretania in the neighborhood of Méderdra and currently living in Same.

> I was kidnapped at the same time as my brother, several years ago, but I do not know exactly when. It was a Mauretanian named Amir who one day during the absence of my mother, asked my brother and me to give something to drink to his camels. Arriving at a stream, the Mauretanian ordered us to follow him and we could not refuse. We walked for a long time over many months and finally we arrived at a village, which I later learned was called Same. There the Mauretanian made us enter the house of Guibril M'Baye, where the three wives of Guibril brought us food each in turn. The day after our arrival, the Mauretanian returned with a Wolof and ordered my brother to follow that man and to go begging for him. My brother left and I did not see him again for a long time. I stayed for three days in that house and then the Mauretanian took me to N'Diouga Guèye, with whom I lived since. It was sometime later that I met [as part of his itinerant begging]- my older brother while he was in the fields [working] and heard from his mouth that he lived in the village of Diad with Amadou Diop.

Third Witness: Momar M'Baye about thirteen years old and brother of the previous witness:

> I was stolen with my younger brother it must be now about two and a half years ago, but I can not be sure. We stayed several months with the Mauretanian who kidnapped us, he was called Amar and he was accompanied by Illy Ould Sidy Bayar of the tribe of the Ooumlailen; we stayed in a camp called Riobane. I don't know the name of the village where we stopped and where I was sold. I do not remember the name of the woman who brought us food, but I only stayed 24 hours in that house with my brother.

Fourth Witness: Gora, about four years old, who could not remember his family name.
I remember that I lived with the Maures who then left me with N'Diouga Guèye.

Fifth Witness: Guibril M'Baye, Muslim social status, Wolof ethnic group, born in Danguène and living in Same, and the brother-in-law of the accused N'Diouga Guèye.

> My name has been mixed up with this case, but I know absolutely nothing about it. At the time when these alleged events took place, I was away on a voyage. When I returned, my first wife, Faoussa, who ran my household in my absence, told me that she had given hospitality to a Mauretanian and these children. She let him stay in one of my houses. Since then I learned, as did all the people of my village, that these children had been kidnapped and sold. Moreover, N'Diouga Guèye, my brother-in-law, told me that he had bought these children.

Question from the Judges: Why didn't you report this matter to the your provincial chief?
Response: I didn't think about it.
Q: While your wife Faoussa put up the Mauretanian and the children [in your house], did she know that the Mauretanian was trying to sell the children?
R: I don't know.
Q: The accused N'Diouga Guèye has chosen you as his advocate. Do you accept this role?
R: Yes, but as I said before I do not know anything about this case.

Sixth Witness: Faoussa Guèye, Muslim social status, Wolof ethnic group, born and living in Same; also wife of Guibril M'Baye and sister-in-law of the accused N'Diouga Guèye.
Q: About two and half years ago around the time of Tabaski, while your husband was away on a voyage, did you lodge a Mauretanian with two children in your house?
R: No, I don't know anything that occurred in my husband's concession.
Q: However, your husband just told us that when he returned from his voyage, you alerted him to the fact that you had extended hospitality [to the Mauretanian and the children]. Is this not so?
R: No, I never said that.
Q: When your husband leaves the concession, who is left in charge?
R: Everyone.
Q: This is false. Following local customs, in the absence of the household head of a concession, the first wife is left in charge.
R: Yes, the first wife is supposed to supervise the household, but when my husband was away, there was another wife of my husband, who was much older than I. She has since died.
Q: for Guibril M'Baye: Is this true?
R: This is false. Faoussa has always been my first wife and she has always been in charge of the household during my absence.

Q: for Faoussa Guèye: Are you lying when you state that you did not supervise the household in the absence of your husband and in affirming that you do not know that the Mauretanian and the children lived in your house? Furthermore, do you deny that you were the one who alerted your husband to the fact that those travelers stayed in your concession?

R: I affirm that I never saw them.

Q: The young Guibril Guèye, who was purchased by your brother-in-law, [has told the court that] he recognizes you perfectly and he affirmed that you personally brought him food before he was sold.

R: In a large concession [like mine], each wife of the same husband is in charge of the cooking for any travelers who happen to be in her house.

Q: Therefore, do you recollect that you provided for the Mauretanian and the children?

R: No, that is false.

Q: However, at this time, the accused N'Diouga Guèye told us that the child in question was in Guibril M'Baye's concession for three days during which he negotiated the price with the Mauretanian.

R: It is possible that they were in my husband's concession, but I never saw them.

Having heard the witnesses, the court began its interrogation of the accused, starting with N'Diouga Guèye.

Q: Do you remember having bought two young children, the first a few years ago and the second more recently?

R: Yes, I bought the first one seven years ago and the second one in April 1916. I paid 160 francs for the first one and 150 for the second.

Q: Do you not know that the purchase of a human being is against the law?

R: Yes, I know, but I do as everyone else does.

Q: Do you know other people who have bought people?

R: Yes.

Q: Who are they?

R: I know them, but I will not say their names. Everyone in Gandiolais is familiar with this trade.

Q: You refuse to tell us the names of the natives who have committed the same felony as you?

R: Yes, I refuse to say anything even if kill me.

Q: Where did you conclude the first purchase?

R: A Mauretanian found me working in my fields and proposed to sell me a child. We discussed the matter and agreed to the price of 160 francs. I took possession of the child in one of the houses of Guibril M'Baye's concession. Guibril is my brother-in-law and he was away on a voyage at that time.

Q: Who supervised the household in his absence?

R: His wife, Faoussa.

Q: How did you get the money to pay for these purchases?

R: I paid with the money from the sale of my harvests.

Q: Faoussa then witnessed that you bought the child?

R: Certainly. As did everyone else. Moreover, she asked me what I paid for the child.

Q: to Faoussa: How do you respond to this statement?

R: My brother-in-law is lying.

Q: to N'Diouga Guèye: Do you maintain your statement?

R: I swear to all that I have said. Why would I now tell lies? Faoussa was aware of everything and in addition, she was the one who told her husband when he returned from his voyage.

Q: to Faoussa: Your husband, the young Guibril, and your brother-in-law N'Diouga Guèye have all affirmed that you were aware of the transaction that took place. Moreover, the facts demonstrate that you alone gave hospitality to the Mauretanian and to the children as household head in the absence of your husband. You have therefore aided following the transaction in hiding the children that were sold.

R: I had no part in any of those things.

Q: to N'Diouga Guèye: Could you please inform the court as to the provenance of the children that you bought and the identity of the Mauretanians who sold them?

R: No, I have no information on those subjects.

Q: Have you seen again the Mauretanians who sold you the children?

R: No.

Q: Do you have anything to add to your defense?

R: Nothing. One can do whatever they want, it is all the same to me.

Q: to Guibril M'Baye: You have accepted to act on behalf of the accused and to defend your relative. Do you have anything to add on his behalf?

R: No. He committed a fault and has to suffer the consequences. It has nothing to do with me.

Questions for the Second Accused: Amadou Diop.

Q: Do you remember having bought the young Momar M'Baye?

R: Yes. I bought him from a Mauretanian during the winter of 1913. I paid 400 francs for him. The Mauretanian found me in Diadj. He spent a day in my concession and once we agreed on the price, I accompanied him to Same where he gave me the child. I bought that child to replace my son, who is a soldier. I know very well that I have done wrong and that the purchase of people is prohibited, but like everybody else does in Gandiolais, it did not bother me [to purchase the child].

Q: How did you get the money for the purchase of the child?

R: The money came from the sale of my peanut harvest.

Q: You have said that everyone buys children. Do you know the names of those who have done so?

R: Yes, but I will never tell you their names.

Q: Do you refuse to inform the court?

R: Yes. You can do whatever you want to me, even kill me. I will never talk.

Q: Do you know where the Mauretanians found the children?

R: No, they have never returned to Gandiolais since the sales.

Q: to N'Diouga Guèye: You stated in your disposition that the first purchase took place seven years ago. However, Amadou Diop states that it occurred only two or three years ago and that the young Momar M'Baye confirms that date.

R: That is correct. I initially said seven years because I did not believe that the children would be here to contradict my testimony.

Q: Did you set out to mislead the court?

R: Yes (the accused laughed raucously).

Q: to Amadou Diop: Do you have anything to add on your behalf?

R: No. I was caught. Do with me what you want because I don't care (the accused laughs).

Having explained the case and evaluated the evidence, the president of the court requests each of the assessors to give his opinion on the guilt or innocence of the accused and what punishment to render. Each made his opinion clear.

The court renders the following judgment: following the discussions, the proof that the named N'Diouga Guèye and Amadou Diop, the former at the end of 1913 and in April 1916, and the latter at the end of 1913, in the village of Same did conclude a transaction that had as its goal the alienation of the liberty of those named Guibril Guèye, Gora, and Momar M'Baye. These facts constitute a felony identified and punishable by articles 1 and 3 of the decree [12] December 1905. In consideration also of the fact that the accused did not manifest any regret or repentance for their acts and that neither was willing to expose other acts of trafficking in Gandiolais; and in consideration of the fact that at the moment of this court's hearing that another child that Mauretanian [kidnappers] sought to sell in Gandiolais was strangled as the kidnappers fled and died a few days later. It is therefore important to seriously repress such felonies.

In consideration also of the crime of complicity that could be imposed on the woman Faoussa Guèye, who, despite her protestations that she knew nothing of the transactions with the Mauretanian, but according to witnesses did indeed host the Mauretanian during his stay at the end of 1913 and watched over the two children and that she, as a consequence of her actions, aided the authors of their actions, the court has decided to include her in this trial.

The court condemns N'Diouga Guèye and Amadou Diop each to five years in prison and each a thousand franc fine. The court also declares that both are deprived of their rights [to return home] according to article 48 of the penal code for a duration of ten years. The place where they will reside for the next five years will be determined upon their release from prison.

The fines from each guilty party will be given to the woman Massouda, mother of the two children as compensation for damages.

The court condemns Faoussa Guèye to six months prison.

The court alerted the condemned parties to their rights to produce additional evidence to be presented before the court of homologation where they had the right to be defended by a defense attorney.

Judgment ratified by the court of homologation, 23 August 1916.

President of the Court:

Signed Grandry

SUGGESTED ADDITIONAL READINGS

Gallagher, Anne T. *The International Law of Human Trafficking.* New York, 2010.

Klein, Martin. *Slavery and Colonial Rule in French West Africa.* New York, 1998.

Lawrance, Benjamin N. and Richard Roberts, eds. *Trafficking in Women and Children in Africa: Colonial and Postcolonial Perspectives.* Athens, OH, 2012.

Miers, Suzanne. *Slavery in the Twentieth Century: The Evolution of a Global Problem.* Walnut Creek, 2003.

Roberts, Richard. *Litigants and Households: African Disputes and Colonial Courts in the French Soudan, 1895–1912.* Portsmouth, NH, 2005.

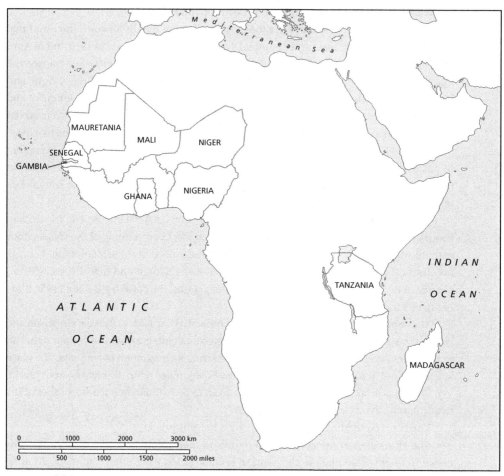

36.1. Map showing the countries featured in Parts Seven, Eight, and Nine.
Source: Based on a map published by *Africa Today*. 1990. Revised Edition.

PART SEVEN

RECORDED ENCOUNTERS WITH THE ENSLAVED: CHRISTIAN WORKERS IN AFRICA

INTRODUCTION: Missionary Records

Missionary societies operating in mid- to late-nineteenth-century Africa sought first and foremost to convert African men and women to Christianity. However, their understandings of this religion were also deeply infused with cultural values, assumptions, and concerns specific to their home communities. Among the assumptions held by European missionaries was the inherent sinfulness of the long-standing universal institution of slavery and the practice of human sacrifice. Slavery remained a general phenomenon in mid- to late-nineteenth-century Africa and was widely condemned by missionary workers. Human sacrifice, however, was not so common. In areas where Islam was well established, for example, the killing of individuals to accompany the dead into the spiritual world had long been condemned and therefore did not take place. Even where it did exist, missionary opposition to slavery and human sacrifice rarely led to its abolition. European religious workers simply did not have the power to prohibit the continued existence of these practices in the communities where they worked. They were, more often than not, guests who could exhort and attempt to persuade, but they had little power to force their values upon their hosts. They did, however, use the power of the pen to condemn these and other practices and to publicize their existence in publications read by audiences in Europe. These audiences, in turn, used their influence to pressure colonial government authorities (who themselves often agreed with missionary concerns anyway) to make it a priority to include prohibition against slavery and other such practices in the treaties that their governments signed with local African authorities. The existence of these shared concerns and the collaborations between missionaries and European colonial offices are among the themes that emerge in the missionary documents presented here. Perhaps even more important for our purposes is that missionary records are especially useful for hearing the voices of the enslaved. In the accounts discussed here by Sandra E. Greene (Chapter 37), Hilary Jones (Chapter 38), Ute Röschenthaler (Chapter 39), and Klara Boyer-Rossol (Chapter 40), one can read firsthand testimonies offered by the formerly enslaved about their experiences in bondage. Included as well in some of these sources are life histories and missionary recorded information about the political and social contexts in which the enslaved and formerly enslaved lived their lives. Emphasized in all the analyses of the sources discussed here – no matter their content – is that missionary accounts must be read with care. Often the accounts penned by European missionaries were based on misunderstandings. Cultural differences and linguistic barriers undermined in some instances the very accuracy of their reports. Nevertheless, missionary accounts are quite valuable for detailing the experiences and concerns of individual slaves and the enslaved more generally, even though the missionary voice is the predominant one heard in these accounts.

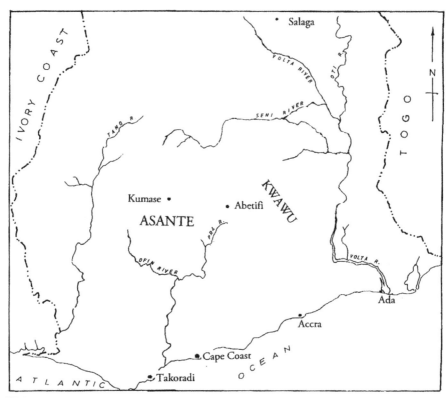

37.1. Map showing the location of Asante and Kwawu.
Source: Based on a map by Phil Bartle, www.scn.org/rdi/kw-map3.htm

37 Experiencing Fear and Despair

The Enslaved and Human Sacrifice in Nineteenth-Century Southern Ghana

SANDRA E. GREENE

The killing of innocent individuals so they could serve their social superiors in the afterlife is a topic that has attracted for centuries the attention of Europeans writing about western Africa. The earliest accounts date to the late seventeenth century, when Dutch scholar Olfert Dapper described the practice, sometimes in graphic detail, and then used it as proof of "African barbarity." In the eighteenth century, English apologists for the slave trade claimed that the purchase of west African war captives for enslavement in the Americas should be seen as a humanitarian act because these same individuals would have otherwise become the victims of human sacrifice in Africa. And at the end of the nineteenth century, a number of French and British writers justified colonial wars of conquest as the only means to put an end to the practice of using innocent human beings for sacrificial offerings. More recent scholarly studies on ritual killing in western Africa have attempted to blunt the negative impact of these obviously self-serving descriptions by emphasizing the limited extent to which human sacrifice was practiced or by noting its benign character where it can be confirmed to have existed. But as Law indicates:

> The weakness of this approach [is] that it sees the problem of human sacrifice in essentially moral terms. Human sacrifice is seen as self-evidently wicked, and therefore not congruent with the essentially sympathetic picture of pre-colonial West African societies which these authors seek to project.[1]

How then should we understand this practice? What exactly do we mean by human sacrifice? Would one consider convicted criminals sentenced to death, but held for execution at annual religious ceremonies (as was known to have occurred in Asante, Dahomey, and Benin), to be victims of human sacrifices? Or were they simply criminals executed at an event that served the multiple purposes of demonstrating state power through mass execution, and renewing the religious foundations of the state? Should one confine the definition of human sacrificial victims to those who were executed only because of their social status as dependents (slaves and wives)? What of those few reported instances in which individuals voluntarily agreed to be executed in order to continue to serve their masters in the afterlife? Would they too be considered victims? How did the practice of human sacrifice change over time, and under what circumstances? Did the Atlantic slave trade

[1] Robin Law, "Human Sacrifice in Pre-colonial West Africa," *African Affairs*, 84, 334 (1985), 53–87.

devalue life so much that the practice became rampant in slave-exporting states? Did the closure of the trade create such a surplus of indigenous slaves that it was this that created the conditions for an increase in human sacrifice? Or were reports of mass ritual killings simply propaganda, generated by European observers to serve their own interests? These questions have generated considerable interest among scholars and stimulated rousing debates about an institution that still remains a sensitive topic among historians of precolonial Africa.[2]

The purpose of this essay, however, is not to rehearse the varied approaches taken by scholars of Africa on this topic. Instead, the emphasis is on providing the reader with the information they need to understand and interpret two unique documents. The first, written in 1886 by the German-Swiss Basel missionary G. Schmid, recounts the experiences of Amma Tanowa, a young woman who was enslaved in northern Ghana and then sold into a community to the south. After serving her master for some time, Amma ran away and sought asylum with Schmid at the Basel Mission station in the Kwawu town of Abetifi. Although it is unclear what her daily life was like as a slave, she willingly shared with her missionary amanuensis the events that compelled her to flee: immediately after the death of her master, Amma witnessed the bloody execution of three of her fellow female slaves as sacrifices to accompany her recently deceased master into the spiritual world. She then barely managed to escape the same fate herself. Twice she fled; twice she was captured. Only on the third try did she manage to reach Kwawu, which she had heard had banned human sacrifice.

The second is an excerpt from the life history of Aaron Kuku. Enslaved as a child in an Asante village between 1871 and 1874 after being captured in war,[3] Kuku recalled a number of his experiences during this period. But those he remembered with the greatest emotion some fifty years later involved his direct experience with the practice of human sacrifice. After he heard that his father had been executed in the Asante capital, Kuku attempted to take his own life. And after learning some years later that he himself had also been identified as a possible sacrificial victim, he suffered an emotional breakdown. Both these accounts provide unprecedented insights into the thoughts and feelings of two individuals who faced the prospect of death by ritual killing.[4] They also raise a number of questions.

---

[2] See, for example, Clifford Williams, "Asante: Human Sacrifice or Capital Punishment? An Assessment of the Period, 1897–1874," *International Journal of African Historical Studies*, 21, 3 (1988), 433–441; Ivor Wilks, "Asante: Human Sacrifice or Capital Punishment? A Rejoinder," *International Journal of African Historical Studies*, 21, 3 (1988), 443–452; Thomas C. McCaskie, "Death and the Asantehene: A Historical Meditation," *Journal of African History*, 30, 3 (1989), 417–444; and Olatunji Ojo, "Slavery and Human Sacrifice in Yorubaland: Ondo, c. 1870–94," *Journal of African History*, 46, 3 (2005), 379–404.

[3] The war in which Kuku was captured occurred as a result of an invasion of the polities located immediately east of the Volta River by the state of Asante. See Marion Johnson, "Ashanti East of the Volta," *Transactions of the Historical Society of Ghana*, VIII (1965), 33–59, and Donna J. E. Maier, "Asante War Aims in the 1869 Invasion of Ewe," in Enid Schildkrout (ed.), *The Golden Stool: Studies of the Asante Center and Periphery* (New York: 1987), 232–244.

[4] That Amma's and Kuku's fears were certainly not unique is evident from accounts discussed by Basel missionaries stationed in Akropong in the polity of Akuapem. See Peter Haenger, *Slaves and Slave Holders on the Gold Coast: Towards an Understanding of Social Bondage in West Africa.* Edited by J. J. Shaffer and Paul E. Lovejoy (Basel, 2000), 41, 44, 46 (fn. 70), 57–58, 79, and 101. See also Gareth Austen, *Labour, Land and Capital in Ghana: From Slavery to Free labour in Asante, 1807–1956* (Rochester, 2005), 38, 187–188, and 227. In one instance, the Basel missionaries thought a woman was actually lying about being the intended victim of ritual sacrifice to gain their support for other reasons. See Haenger, *Slaves*, 80–81. Austen sites a similar case in his study of slavery in Asante. See Austen, *Labour*, 197–198.

Slaves were not the only individuals who could potentially suffer such a fate. Convicted criminals and war prisoners were held by the Asante state in specific villages until needed for execution at annual religious rituals; select wives and servants were sometimes dispatched in many communities throughout nineteenth-century southern Ghana to serve a deceased husband or master, an esteemed relative, or political leader. Thus fear of being the victim of a ritual sacrifice was hardly unique to the enslaved, nor was this the only source of dread in their lives. Like others during this period, the enslaved were also apprehensive about the ordinary difficulties anyone might face: an intractable illness, the possibility of being attacked by bandits or creditors while traveling for purposes of trade, the sudden or unexpected outbreak of war. Given this, it seems appropriate to ask whether or not fear of execution for ritual purposes was any greater among slaves, servants, and war prisoners than the fears shared by much of the rest of the population in nineteenth-century southern Ghana. How significant was this fear even among slaves in comparison with the known dread they experienced from the possibility of being sold unwittingly to a new master who had unknown proclivities for kindness or cruelty? How do we account more specifically for Amma's and Kuku's fears? Were they terrified by the prospects of death by ritual sacrificial or were their fears rooted more simply in the shock of knowing that their friends and relatives had, and they too could meet an untimely death? These two accounts provide few answers to these questions. They do, however, tell us a great deal about the worlds of the enslaved in southern Ghana and the lived experiences of those who faced the possibility of being offered as a human sacrifice.

In both accounts, we see that slaves were able to rely on communication networks that stretched far beyond the localities in which they were enslaved. Kuku heard that his father, along with many of the other prisoners of war taken in the 1869–71 war, had been executed in Kumase, the Asante capital, some distance from where he himself was enslaved.[5] Amma, who was enslaved in a polity located between the slave market town of Salaga and Kwawu, fled to the latter in 1886 based on information she had received about the absence of ritual sacrifice in that particular polity. Given her tremendous reluctance to place herself under the authority of the local Kwawu leader in Abetifi, Kwamo Udo, it is likely that what she really heard was that the Basel missionaries in Kwawu, who had been stationed there since 1876,[6] could offer her protection. The British had abolished slavery in 1874 and had been campaigning against the practice of human sacrifice since at least 1817.[7] The British outlawed the ritual in 1844 among the coastal Fanti communities over which they assumed protective rights. The outlawing of ritual sacrifice in Kwawu did not occur, however, until 1888 when Kwawu came under British colonial jurisdiction, two years before Amma fled to Abetifi.[8] Even then enforcement was voluntary given the quite limited ability

---

[5]   Kuku remembered the name of the Asante village in which he was enslaved as Konya. The community that most closely resembles this place in name and location is a village called Kona, c. 15 miles south of the Asante polity of Nsuta.

[6]   On the history of the Basel Mission in Abetifi, see Kofi Nkansa-Kyeremateng, *One Hundred Years of the Presbyterian Church in Kwahu, 1876–1976* (Accra, 1976). See also Stephan F. Miescher, *Making Men in Ghana* (Bloomington, 2005), 5–6.

[7]   Edmund Collins, "The Panic Element in Nineteenth Century British Relations with Ashanti," *Transactions of the Historical Society of Ghana*, V: 2 (1962), 98.

[8]   Kwawu willingly sought British protection, according to K. Nkansa-Kyeremateng, because as a conquered territory of Asante since 1818, it had been "bled-white ... of troops and supplies ... [and by] Antwi Akomea, the Asante envoy in Kwawu ... for his personal aggrandisement." Once Asante was defeated by the British

of the British government to enforce the ban. Thus, it was understood by most that one could only gain access to the protection offered by the British if one sought the direct intervention of Europeans (who were frequently equated with the extension of British influence no matter their nationality or their reason for being in the region).

Concerns about the fate of lost family members and the importance of kinship ties are also evident in the two accounts. According to Basel missionary Schmid, who recorded Amma's account of her travail as a slave, she was first captured as a child with her siblings and sold in the market town of Salaga. When her master died, she along with several other women – described as her sisters – were slated for execution to serve as his attendants in the spiritual world. But were the "sisters" who were captured with her when she was initially enslaved the same "sisters" who were executed before her eyes? Other accounts by those enslaved in both southern and northern Ghana indicate that absolutely no effort was made on the part of the buyers and sellers of slaves to keep families together. Was Amma's experience unique? Or did she call the other women with whom she was enslaved "sisters" as a means of recreating the bonds of kinship that had been torn asunder by her enslavement?

As a child forcibly separated from his parents and siblings, Kuku remembers clearly the despair he felt. He attributed his suicide attempt shortly after his enslavement to the news of the death of his father and sister and being separated from his mother. But he also recalls the consideration shown to him by his master. Kuku remembered, for example, that his master expressed concern that he be allowed to finish his meal before being taken before the chief of the village. Similar consideration on the part of his master is mentioned when he attempted suicide. His master searched for him for a long time, assuming he was either lost or hurt, not that he had run away. When his master found him, it was he who carried Kuku home and then made sure he was given the best of care so that his wounds healed completely. Kuku describes this same kind of consideration shown to him by the political leader of the community in which he was enslaved. In conversation with that leader, Kuku was told that an incident in which he was earlier involved, and about which Kuku was clearly confused, was actually an instance in which Kuku was almost used in a human sacrificial ritual. By revealing this incident, the chief was indicating to Kuku that he no longer needed fear such a fate even though Kuku, at the time, felt only debilitating despair at hearing of the death he had managed unwittingly to escape. In recalling both his master's actions and the chief's words of assurances, did Kuku signal that as an enslaved person he had begun to accommodate himself to his situation, in part, by transposing an absent father-son relationship onto the bonds of slave and master? Perhaps.

What is most apparent is the tremendous emotional impact that being designated as a sacrificial victim had on Amma and Kuku. Both had already managed to survive war, capture, and sale, and both had also already adjusted themselves culturally and linguistically to being a slave in a foreign community. With the news of their likely death, feelings of fear and despair overwhelmed them. One suffered an emotional breakdown; the other fled in terror. Were such responses typical? Did others simply resign themselves to

---

in 1874, Kwawu requested the British flag but did not receive it until 1888. J. Nkansa-Kyeremateng, *Kwahu Handbook* (Bepong-Kwawu, 2000), 71. For more on Asante-Kwawu relations during this period, see Thomas J. Lewin, *Asante before the British: The Prempean Years, 1875–1900* (Lawrence, 1978), 103–104, 149, and 163.

the inevitable? We may never know, but these accounts provide some insight into how two individuals in southern Ghana experienced the vicissitudes of life as a slave in the late nineteenth century.

Equally important for understanding these two accounts is the fact that they are far from transparent in their presentation of the actual voices of the enslaved. Amma Tonawa's and Aaron Kuku's experiences were either recounted by others or were dictated to an amanuensis who then structured and edited the accounts according to their own concerns. In fact, we do not hear Amma Tonawa speak at all. Her three escape attempts and the harrowing journey she made to Kwawu that was written onto her body in the form of wounds and tattered clothing, the nightmares she experienced after having seen three other women described as her "sisters" killed to accompany her master: all are described instead by the Missionary Schmid. Kuku's voice is similarly muted. The account excerpted here is from the narrative he dictated about his own life to fellow Ewe Christian and German-trained minister, Samuel Quist in 1939. Using this oral account, Quist then wrote a biography of Kuku in the Ewe language, which never saw publication[9] but which came into the hands of the German missionary, Paul Wiegräbe. Posted to the then British mandated territory of Togoland between 1926 and 1931 to assist the Ewe Evangelical Church in producing Ewe language materials for the church and its schools, Wiegräbe edited Quist's biography. He then translated it from Ewe into German and published it under his own name in the Bremen Mission's monthly periodical.[10]

Given the way in which these accounts were produced, and the obvious distance created between ourselves as readers and the voices of the enslaved, one might ask to what extent we can really hear the voices of Amma Tonawa and Aaron Kuku? Did the missionaries who recorded, edited, and published these two histories neglect other concerns to focus exclusively on the fear of being a human sacrificial victim because it served particularly well their own purposes as Christian missionaries? If so, does that really matter, given the otherwise extremely limited opportunities we have to hear about the felt experiences of the enslaved? I think not. Accordingly, I offer these two accounts as rare depictions of the way the enslaved in nineteenth-century southern Ghana experienced the practice of human sacrifice.

QUESTIONS TO CONSIDER

1. What do these two accounts together say about the experience of enslavement in western Africa?
2. How typical or atypical do you think their experiences were?
3. To what extent can we actually disentangle the voices of Amma Tonawa and Aaron Kuku from the opinions and concerns of the missionaries who recorded their accounts?
4. To what extent can these accounts be taken at face value given their propaganda value for the missionaries who collected, edited and published them?

[9] The manuscript is currently held at the Staatarchiv, Bremen: 7, 1025–30/1, and is entitled S. Quist, *Nyanyuiegblola Aaron Kuku fe agbenonutinya. Enlola enye Osofo*. (Kplalime, September 1929). For a translation of this text, see Sandra E. Greene, *West African Narratives of Slavery: Texts from Late Nineteenth- and Early Twentieth Century Ghana* (Bloomington, 2011).

[10] It appeared as Paul Wiegräbe, "Aus dem Leben des Afrikanischen Evangelisten Aaron Kuku," *Monatsblatt der Norddeutschen MIssionsgesellschaft*, 91 (1930), 51–57, 67–71, 186–189, 214–217.

1. What do Kuku's war experiences say about the goals of individual west African soldiers in combat?
2. What was the cause of Kuku's suicide attempt? Was it the news he received about his family as he reported? If so, why would he also talk about his failure to properly handle the tapping of the palm tree?
3. Why would Kuku – a convert to Christianity at the time his experiences were recorded – remember his master in such favorable terms?

ON AMMA TONOWA'S NARRATIVE

1. Why was the political leader of Abetifi prepared to allow Amma to stay?
2. Why did this same political leader want Amma at first to stay with the royal family rather than with the missionaries?
3. In being willing to pay Amma's sale price to the Kwawu chief so that she could stay with them, were the missionaries engaging themselves in the slave trade and thus helping keep alive this activity? What alternatives might the missionaries have pursued?

FROM THE LIFE OF THE AFRICAN EVANGELIST AARON KUKU, TOLD BY HIMSELF

Paul Wiegräbe
Translation by Sean Franzel

My name Kuku, "the dead one" is a so-called child's death name. The first child of my mother died; when she gave birth to me, she said: "I have simply borne 'a dead one.'" By this she wished to say: "this boy will also surely die soon." At the same time, this ugly name should have also prevented the evil spirits from killing the little child....[11] My year of birth must have been around the year 1860, because during the large Asante war, I was 8–9 years old.[12] I had three living siblings ...

The Time of the Asante War (1869–1870)

I was about 8 years old when everyone began speaking of the Asantes, who [after invading the area] were to have already reached Peki. Indeed, refugees had already begun coming to us. Then, one day at midday we heard the racket of flintlocks coming from the way to

[11] This practice of giving "death" or "ugly" names to children was based on a belief that the spirit of a dead child could return to its mother and be born again. That spirit might decide or be called back to the spiritual world by the inhabitants of that world, however, and thus would make the mother suffer by dying again. To prevent this, parents who had suffered the death of one child might give the next child born to them an ugly name to repel or fool those in the spirit world, making them believe that the child was not worth much and thus not worth calling back to the spiritual world.

[12] Statements about his age and the dates of particular events occur throughout this narrative. It is wholly unclear, however, if it was Kuku who provided this information. Kuku – who had only six days of formal education – may have been able to recall his approximate age based on his memory of what he was able to do at the time of the Asante invasion. But this calculation of his age could have also been the work of Samuel Quist, who in 1929 recorded Kuku's life history and clearly shaped it to conform to the format typical of biographies used in the Ewe-language schools in southeastern Ghana.

Fodome.[13] My father and the other men only had their bush knives with them and ran with them from the fields to the battle. My mother took two children by the hand and one on her back and fled with the others to Leklebi-Kame. There, our father met us along with the other men in the night. They couldn't fight off the enemies, and in this way, we became homeless refugees. We fled from one location to another. The Asantes always forced us to change locations. At that time, my mother gave a boy the gift of life, but the entire disturbance caused the child to die by the third day without having received a name. (At that time, children were not named according to the days of the week, as is the case today.) When we turned towards Likpe, the Asantes caught up with us. Our parents tied the two youngest children on their backs and fled, but by then, the first bullets had begun flying between us. I threw myself to the ground and laid myself on one of the cloths that I had taken out of one of the discarded sacks of clothing.... Then one of the enemies found the clothing sack, and when he saw me, he threw away the sack and wanted to take me prisoner. As I fled, I wounded my head. The man ran behind me. Although he was wounded at the knee, he grabbed my hand and ran with me up the mountain.... They then brought me to Vli and then to Kpakpa. There I saw my father, my siblings, and many relatives again, who had also been taken prisoner.... Through Wusuta and the great Volta river we now arrived in Kwawuland and had almost reached the home of the Asantes.... There the Asante king received the message that his troops no longer had any food. For this reason, we had to bring them provisions quickly. But the war was soon over. They fought once more in Agu and in Avatimeland, then all returned back to Asante.

The War Report to the King

When all warriors had returned, a day was chosen on which they all gathered in the capital Kumase in order to report to the king about the course of the war.[14] In addition, all captives had to be brought along as well. However, the man who captured me did not take me there. I was too small. When the people came back from the festival I asked them intently if anyone had seen my father. Each person replied only: "He is on his way;" but he did not come. I later heard, they had killed all older prisoners in Kumase as sacrifices for the gods. My father was amongst them.

Now on that day, my master told me that I should go to his palm forest and smoke out the oil palms that he had felled and drilled to get their wine.[15] But I was so sad and cried

---

[13] Kuku's village, Petewu, was part of the Liati District, and was located c. 7 kilometers south of the separate political community of Fodome.

[14] As indicated in accounts by a number of Europeans who witnessed this event, there were several gatherings, beginning first in July. On that day some 2,000 prisoners were marched through Kumase. Two months later, on September 2, more booty (goods and slaves) was paraded through the streets by 10,000 soldiers. Reports to the king about the commanders and soldiers who had died in the war occurred on September 4. On September 7, the actual report to the Asante king was given by the commander of the forces that had fought in the war. The days that followed were set aside for the mourning of the dead. It was during this period that prisoners were executed to accompany the deceased commanders as servants in the spiritual world. According to Ramseyer and Kühne, "one hundred and thirty-six high chiefs had fallen in this war, which gives some idea of the sacrifice of human life that followed. For each of the six [chiefs] belonging to Coomassie [i.e., Kumase] thirty of their people were killed, thirty for Sokora, and so on." F. A. Ramseyer and J. Kühne, *Four Years in Asantee* (New York, 1875), 130, 135–138.

[15] Oil-palms produce a nut that is processed to produce palm oil, a substance used locally in food preparation and for fuel in oil lamps. By this date, in 1870, there was also considerable demand in Europe for palm

so violently about all the news from Kumase that I did not pay attention and the oil trees burned entirely instead of just smoking out the holes where the wine was to flow. I ran away, sought a vine plant, and tried to hang myself. My master looked for me for a long time. Finally he saw me and carried me home. It took quite some time before I came to myself again. My entire throat was a single wound. The people said that I had done this to myself. All sorts of good remedies soon allowed the wounds to heal... Something that had especially moved me to my suicide attempt that day was the message that my little sister had died on that day in Kumase. All of this sadness shook me severely.

How I nearly was killed

The chief of our land was on a trip to Kumase.[16] It had to do with conflicts over the throne.[17] The message arrived while he was resting in our village that one of his generals had died. At this point, according to old customs, he had to sacrifice a person for the soul of the deceased. However, there was nobody there who had been sentenced to death, for these people were normally taken for this purpose. The chief did not know what he should do. Someone then said to him: "There is still a prisoner of war here in the village!"[18] By this they meant me. I had just returned from picking Kola nuts with my master. We were eating. I had just taken a piece of food onto my plate when someone cried "Ago" ("I am coming") and I had already been grabbed by the arm so that my food fell to the floor. My master asked: "What's going on here? Can't he eat a little first?" However, the men handcuffed me, led me away, tied my arms and legs and bound me to a weaving stool. I sat there from 12 noon until the next morning at eight-o-clock. Then they let me go, laid a cord around my waist, and lead me to the chief. I was forced to carry a bowl with a heavy cannon ball on my head. I was sentenced to death without knowing it. Soon we reached the chief. Shots were being fired constantly, as was normal at such burials. The executioner said to the chief: "Everything is finished. Here he is!" With these words he came to me holding his large executioner's knife in the hand. He wanted to kill me! Then someone cried out: "Stop!

oil as well as palm kernel oil as a lubricant. When used for palm wine extraction, the tapper used a process that is still used today: "the tapper will first fell the tree.... They then cut a hole just below the crown of the fallen tree, creating a well in its trunk. At the bottom of this well they punch a small hole right through the tree. A collecting pot is then placed underneath. The hole is fired to encourage the free flow of liquid from the tree. This is done using a large staff of tightly wrapped palm fronds, slowly burning at one end ... finally, large leaves are placed over the top of the well to stop rain and insects from entering. When the tapper returns to collect the wine he will bore a new section inside the well. Fire is used once more and the process begins all over again. The tree is tapped continually until it produces no more wine." http://www. winesoftheworld.com/news/static/article_268.asp

16 Kumase was the capital of Asante, a state that has been the subject of many historical studies. See Ivor G. Wilks, *Asante in the Nineteenth Century: The Structure and Evolution of a Political Order* (Cambridge, 1975); Thomas J. Lewin, *Asante before the British: The Prempean Years, 1875–1900* (Lawrence, 1978); and Thomas C. McCaskie, *Sate and Society in Pre-colonial Asante* (Cambridge, 1995).

17 It appears that the dispute in question was not about succession to a political office, as indicated here, however. Instead, it probably involved differences within the governing council of Asante over whether or not to free the European prisoners who had been captured in the war that had also brought Kuku and thousands of others prisoners to Asante, and whether or not to free them without being paid a ransom. Fighting broke out in Kumase in March of 1872. See Wilks, *Asante*, 500–501. The death of the military commander mentioned here was probably unrelated to events in Kumase.

18 It was common practice in Asante to use prisoners of war and criminals condemned to death for ritual sacrifices. Some were even settled in villages as a reserve body of potential sacrificial victims to be used years later for this purpose. See R. S. Rattray, *Ashanti Law and Constitution* (New York, 1911/1969), 442–443.

look over here!" Oh no! A woman was led forth, and she was even with child. She had had a fight with another woman and had sworn that she wanted to prove the guilt of her adversary through a "judgment of God". However, she was found to be guilty and was therefore sentenced to death. The chief cried: "kill her!" O dear, and she fell straight to the ground. The people broke her neck, bound a rope to her foot, and dragged her away. (Otherwise it is not allowed for the Asantes to kill a woman in such a condition).[19] At this point they unbound me. In a wonderful way I had avoided death. I didn't even know it at that point! God is great! ...

A long time after this event the chief called me to him one day and asked: "Can you still remember that man who came after you?" I said yes. He continued: "We wanted to kill you then, and we took that woman in your place." At that point a light went on; I began to shake and nearly fainted. The chief said: "It's over! Don't have any more fear!" But I was shattered for three whole days; it was as if I were sick.

THE MORTAL FEAR OF A SLAVE WOMAN

G. Schmid
Translation by Timothy Haupt

Already some time ago, in October 1886, Brother G. Schmid from Abetifi wrote the following to our station in the country of Okwawu [Kwawu] on the Gold Coast:

I would like to share with you the story, at least as much of it as I have heard, of a roughly 30 year old Donko negress,[20] who has lived in our house for the past four weeks. In her childhood, she, along with all of her siblings, was taken captive and sold in Salaga.[21] Her master lived a 5–7 day trip from here and died a little while ago. Three of her siblings were decapitated before her eyes so that they could accompany the deceased master into the Kingdom of the Dead.[22] She too was supposed to be a death offering but she fled by night toward Okwawu, for she had previously heard that people lived here, who did not kill slaves. People were, of course, immediately sent out to capture her, yet she knew to elude her pursuers. A slave of the local chief, Kwamo Ado, was hunting in that region at the same time and happened upon our Amma Tanowa. When the people searching for her also happened to meet and interrogate this slave of Kwamo Ado, he revealed to them her

---

[19] Descriptions of the crimes that might result in capital punishment are described in Rattray, *Ashanti Law*, passim and Wilks, *Asante*, passim. Of all the crimes mentioned, the only ones that seems to have been serious enough to warrant a pregnant woman's death was murder or the swearing of an important oath. Rattray, *Ashanti Law*, 302 confirms that pregnant women were also never executed, but usually held until they gave birth. After delivering, both the woman and the child were killed. The fact this woman was killed using the bloodless form of breaking her neck rather than decapitation was probably the result of her pregnant state.

[20] *Translator's note:* Instances of the term *Neger* – here *Donkonegerin* – are translated as "negro," or in the latter case with a feminine inflection, "negress." *Editor's note:* "Donko" is the term used to refer to slaves that were non-Asante in origin. By the late nineteenth century, it was usually used to refer to slaves from what is now northern Ghana. See Rattray, *Ashanti Law*, 35–36.

[21] Salaga was a large market town controlled in the mid-late nineteenth century by Asante. On the history of this town, see Wilks, *Asante*, passim; and Paul Lovejoy, "International Trade in West Africa in the Nineteenth Century: Salaga and Kano as "Ports of Trade," in Toyin Falola (ed.), *Ghana in Africa and the World: Essays in Honor of Adu Boahen* (Trenton, 2003), 477–511.

[22] Why decapitation? See Robin Law, "'My Head Belongs to the King': On the Political and Ritual Significance of Decapitation in Pre-colonial Dahomey," *Journal of African History*, 30: 3 (1989), 399–415.

whereabouts, in order to earn the bounty established for such cases. Amma Tanowa was bound and brought back to the village of her master; yet she was able to escape again and actually made it to Okwawu this time. She was once again recognized here by Kwamo Ado's slave and was captured, though she was not brought to him, but rather to an elder of this city. She fled in the night and came to our station[23]. Her feet were in a deplorable condition, blood ran from between her toes; she could hardly cover her nakedness with a short scrap, her body was thoroughly covered with dust and dirt. As soon as the chief heard that she was at the station, he sent 3 men and the slave that had caught her to bring her back to the city; it was heartbreaking to see her defend her life and freedom; I attempted to quiet her and said that so long as she was with us, nothing evil could befall her. In response to the inquiry as to why the chief had sent for the woman, the people told me that she had been found on his land and that he therefore has the first claim to her. The woman, however, assured us that he would send her back in order to obtain the bounty from her master and that she would then certainly be killed. I, for my part, would not have defied the chief but the Christian with whom the woman had been staying did not hand her over.[24] A few days later, the Christian went to Mpraëso and the woman came and implored us to take her in but not to confess to it such that she would be brought to the city; we of course did not refuse her hospitality. Before all else, we gave her water and soap so that she could for once wash herself properly; afterwards, we gave her fat to rub into her skin, just as our natives are accustomed to doing it after every bath and finally we gave her a new shawl. The woman was beside herself; she prostrated herself flat on the floor to thank us, which was for us an

---

[23] The location of the Basel Mission station in Abetifi was just outside of town. As was typical of the Basel missionaries who operated in southern Ghana, they often established separate communities for themselves and their Christian converts that were known as Salems. See Stephen Miescher, *Making Men in Ghana* (Bloomington, 2005), 5–6 and Paul Jenkins, "The Basel Mission in West Africa and the Idea of the Christian Village Community," in Godwin Shiri (ed.), *Wholeness in Christ: The Legacy of the Basel Mission in India* (Balmatta, Mangalore, 1985), 13–25.

[24] Schmid's comment that he would not have defied the chief as did the local Kwawu Christian can be explained by Basel Mission policy and the political circumstances that brought the Mission to Abetifi in the first place. As indicated by Peter Haenger, the Basel Mission in Switzerland instructed its overseas missionaries on the Gold Coast "to admonish and encourage the converted [Christian] slave of heathen masters to be at all times loyally devoted to and love their heathen masters as well as to fulfill their duties industriously in every matter." They did so, in part, because their mission activities could operate only with the permission of the local political authorities. If they encouraged slaves (whether Christian or traditional belief practitioners) to defy their masters, they would have faced unrelenting hostility from the local political authorities and many of the town's inhabitants. On this point, see Peter A. Schweizer, *Survivors on the Gold Coast: The Basel Missionaries in Colonial Ghana* (Accra, 2000), 40. Only the British colonial government had the authority, backed by its military forces, to defy local norms that saw slaves as accepted symbols of social and economic status, and as integral (if not subordinate) members of one's extended family. Even then, when the British abolished slavery in 1874, they did so with the proviso that they would hear petitions from aggrieved slaves only if there was abuse involved. Otherwise slaves were expected to obey their masters and masters were expected to treat their slaves as family members. Basel Mission work in Abetifi began in 1876, ten years before they were faced with the question of how to deal with Amma Tanowa's case. Abetifi was their first successful mission effort in the state of Kwawu. By the end of 1886, they had stations in eight other Kwawu towns. See K. Nkansa-Kyeremateng, *Kwawu Handbook*, 87. African Christians were often much more vocal in their opposition to slavery as an institution. Perhaps the best known of these local African Christian anti-slavery advocates was David Asante. On Basil Mission policy and African Christian anti-slavery efforts, see Haenger, *Slaves*, 23–24; 134–140. On the history of the Basel Mission in Abetifi, see K. Nkansa-Kyeremateng, *The Story of Kwawu* (Accra, 1990), 67–69. On David Asante in particular, see Sonia Abun-Nasr, *Afrikaner und Missionar: Lebensgeschichte von David Asante* (Basel, 2003).

unbearable sight. She wished only to receive food from us on her knees, whereby she turned her head entirely to the side. Only after having stayed with us several days could one get anything out of her; indeed, in all of those around her she saw a thief, a murderer. She spent a week with us in this fashion. We occupied her with cutting bushes in the immediate vicinity of the house and saw how she breathed easier day after day. Nevertheless, she locked herself in her room before nightfall. Quite early on the 23rd of July, King Kwamo Ado[25] arrived with all of his chiefs or elders and had me called to exchange a word with him. We all knew what it was about. After several ceremonial expressions serving as an introduction, he brought forth his request that I give him Amma Tanowa, which I emphatically refused. I asked him first how he justified his claims to the woman; he said that the woman had been captured on his land and therefore belongs to him, just as with the ivory that is found on his land. Now, I explained to him, a human ought not to be treated as a "thing;" the woman ran away twice and sought her refuge here and found it, she is free! With this word, however, I touched upon a very sensitive spot; the negotiation back and forth became so lively that one could not even understand one's own speech. A slave should win his freedom through escape? That would be something entirely new and outrageous in Okwawu. How then does the maxim I express that I do not want to mix myself up in her private or public affairs relate to what I now say of the emancipation of slaves! It was of course easy for me to refute him in that I explained to him that this case was a very particular one and has nothing to do with the emancipation of slaves. The woman comes from an entirely foreign country that does not stand under your embassy; she was sentenced to a sacrificial death and saved her life twice by fleeing and we see it as our duty to protect her and to assure that she is not again taken to a place where she is at no point certain of her life. He acknowledged that I was right and thanked me also when I added that none of his slaves, who were also abundantly present in his party, nor any other slave of a man from Okwawu ought now think that he need only to flee to us and we will protect him from his master; I would send every one back to his lord and master without further ado, except when the latter wished to kill him; in this case only would I have to take in a slave from Okwawu, not only in order to save his life, but also preserve them from sin and responsibility, who would bring it on themselves through the slaying of an innocent person. Everyone, even the King, is responsible to God for all their actions. Now, Kwamo Ado explained to me, given that we preach the word of God in Okwawu, no one else will be killed and he will also see to it that no harm will come to the woman. To which I responded that if he leaves her with us we would serve as the best guarantee of this and if her earlier master should send for her, I will surely know how to deal with him. Now he urged me quite insistently and obsequiously to not insist that the woman remain with us; I should turn her over to him; he would certainly see to it that no evil would befall her; he would not send her back, but rather satisfy the man with a sum of money and that we could inquire about her at any point; he would also give her permission to come to the station whenever she pleased. Further, he claimed, if I insist on my demand, he will surely have difficulties with those people from whom the woman escaped; his people often go to Salaga and must make their way through that region. If someone there hears that he withheld one of their slaves, then

---

[25] Kwamo Ado was not the king of Kwawu, but served under the Kwawu paramount chief as the chief of Abetifi. He was a signatory to the 1888 treaty that the Kwawu chiefs signed, recognizing their status as a protection of Great Britain. See Nkansa-Kyeremateng, *The Story*, 40–41.

they will take his people captive and he will not be able to prevent it. He promised me that he would send her previous master compensation for his loss and that he would treat her well. To this we could not object for any good reason. I said to him that he gave his word before all of his elders and that a man keeps to his word or as they express it more concretely in the adage: "a man does not spit and then slurp the saliva back up with the tongue again." So I went for the woman who was cutting grass behind the house and handed her over to the king: it was a heartbreaking scene that so consumed my wife that she lied down two hours later and was not able to leave her bed for the next 10 days.[26] In her fever she heard the wailing and crying of the poor woman and at night she dreamt of her or exhausted herself with horrid visions. Later I visited the Chief and said to him that my wife has been sick ever since and feels quite unwell because he took the woman from her. That troubled him and he said to his elders that sat around him: "The white woman has too tender of a heart!" Already on the next day he sent Amma Tanowa to visit my wife; we questioned her as to how she was; she did not have anything to complain about. Later, we saw her more often; every time we went to the city. A few days later, I heard that the chief sent 18 Dollars, which is 90 Fr., to the earlier master of Amma Tanowa in order to satisfy him; was it true? The price for a powerful slave woman is 10–13 pounds sterling, thus 250–325 Fr., that for a male slave only 150–200 Fr. For slave women there is the prospect that she will yet bear children and these are valuable in Okwawu and are hocked for 50–100 Fr. already at a tender age. Many children have been offered us already for this price, with whom we could fill our schools; but without a preliminary payment of 2–4 pounds one cannot receive a heathen child or only for a very short time when the people see that we do not fulfill their expectations (i.e. complete payment).

Amma Tanowa was thankful; one afternoon she brought a bundle of firewood that she gathered in the bush and said to my wife that she was giving this to her. My wife said later that she never would have believed that even her Tanowa would be able to give something, being such a frail creature; but love is generative. Four weeks ago she appeared again on Sunday evening as we returned from the street sermon; she appeared quite haggard and one could hardly get a word out of her; we gave her some of our evening meal but she did not want to touch it. Different demands revealed that she was again horrifically afraid to be sent back to her old master. She had bumped into the fufu[27] of the King's wife and hurt the same on her hand; later the King then said that she [Amma] had intended to kill his wife. He said this jokingly but Amma Tanowa no longer understood jokes after having experienced what she had; the negro adage expressed her situation: "Whoever is once bitten by a snake is afraid of an earthworm." While it was yet night, Kwamo Ado sent two men for her; we however requested that she be allowed to spend the night at our home. On the following morning we brought her into the city ourselves in order to make an appeal on her behalf that she not have to pay for having come to us. We found the King in a good mood;

---

[26] The principle role of European women married to Basel missionaries stationed on the Gold Coast was as wife to her husband, mother to both her own children and the local African children adopted by the mission (enslaved girls and those born with physical deformities), senior "sister" to the younger married women associated with the Mission, and midwife. See Waltraud Haas, "The Nineteenth Century Basel Mission and Its Women Missionaries" and "On being a Woman in the Nineteenth Century Basel Mission," in Waltrad Hass and Ken Phin Pang (eds.), *Mission History from the Woman's Point of View* (Basel, 1989), 12–40.

[27] *Footnote in original text*: A porridge that in West Africa is generally made from boiled yams that are pounded to a paste.

he assured us repeatedly that he had nothing against Amma and also that he had not even considered the idea to send her back again. But we said to him that the poor creature will never be well disposed and even if he treats her very well, her fear will never permit her to rest; it is therefore best if he would allow her to come again with us and to stay with us entirely. Yes, he said, if I pay him what he sent to her master for her; I asked how much that amounted to, he said, 18 Dollars = 90 Fr. I agreed and the deal was immediately sealed with a calabash of palm wine, from which he and his people along with me and my wife had to drink. Given that I did not have so much money on hand at that moment, I had to convince him to wait.[28] Amma Tanowa was permitted, however, to return to the station with my wife immediately, while I made house visits until Wednesday. After 14 days, Kwamo Ado came with his entourage in order to pick up his money; I was after a long while again not well and had an intense headache. Further, I had to speak more that day than I would have liked to. For that reason, I quickly settled matters with the chief on the veranda, but gave him 6 Shilling = 6 Mark[29] too much by mistake, which I did not notice until the following morning. I excused myself for not being well; he asked me what the matter was and I said to him: your adage expresses well my situation today: "when a tongue must meet a thousand tongues, it falls into exhaustion." In response, he left me with these words: Then just go and rest. The next day, after I had noticed my mistake, I went to him and requested that he give me back the 6 Shilling; if he would count the money one more time he would realize that it is over by that much. He said that he believed me and would not want any of my money to be found in his house; he immediately gave me the money back. I am firmly convinced that he noticed the breach of contract that very night and that he would have never brought the money back himself; for, as pertains to counting money, our people are not exactly on the "left" and would be able to use twice as much; furthermore, I was thankful that he quickly corrected the situation. As far as Tanowa is concerned, she is staying with us and feels secure; we let her dig wild sugar cane and plant corn, which she enjoys. As long as she was not certain, though, that we had paid Kwamo Ado the money, she did not entirely trust the situation. One evening she went to one of our presbyters and complained of her distress; she said that she is terrified as soon as she falls asleep, it is always as if someone grasps her arm and calls: Kyere no, Kyere no! (Grab her, grab her!) Only after repeated assurance that she is entirely free and Kwamo Ado has received his money, does she become quieter again.

Thus there occurs in our solitude now and again something that is entirely new for us.

SUGGESTED ADDITIONAL READINGS

DEBATES ABOUT THE NATURE OF HUMAN SACRIFICE IN WEST AFRICA

Law, Robin. "Human Sacrifice in Pre-colonial West Africa," *African Affairs*, 84, 334 (1985): 53–87.

---

[28] *Footnote in original text*: Incidentally, the slave woman was not bought free with *mission funds*. (Emphasis in the original.)

[29] A mix of currencies circulated in the nineteenth-century Gold Coast. Gold dust was the traditional currency in Akan-speaking areas like Kwawu, but other currencies were used in areas that had trade relations with this region: cowries were used in what is now northern Ghana and in the districts east of the Volta, for example. Prices during the period were cited in British currency (pounds, shillings, and pence), in German marks, and in U.S. dollars, depending on the location and the individuals involved in business. See Austin, *Labour*, 128–134, on slave prices, the gold and cowrie currencies used, and their equivalencies.

McCaskie, Thomas C. "Death and the Asantehene: A Historical Meditation," *Journal of African History*, 30, 3 (1989): 417–444.

Wilks, Ivor. "Asante: Human Sacrifice or Capital Punishment? A Rejoinder," *International Journal of African Historical Studies*, 21, 3 (1988): 443–452.

Williams, Clifford. "Asante: Human Sacrifice or Capital Punishment? An Assessment of the Period, 1897–1874," *International Journal of African Historical Studies*, 21, 3 (1988): 433–441.

ON SLAVERY AS AN INSTITUTION AMONG THE AKAN (INCLUDING THE KWAWU AND ASANTE) OF WEST AFRICA

Austin, Gareth. *Labour, Land and Capital in Ghana: From Slavery to Free Labour in Asante, 1807–1956*. Rochester: Rochester University Press, 2005. See, in particular, chapters 6–10.

Rattray, R. S. *Ashanti Law and Constitution*. New York: Negro Universities Press, 1911/1969. See in particular chapter V.

ON THE ACQUISITION OF THE ENSLAVED BY THE AKAN (INCLUDING THE KWAWU AND ASANTE) THROUGH TRADE AND WAR

Johnson, Marion. "Slaves of Salaga," *Journal of African History*, 27 (1986): 341–362.

Lovejoy, Paul E. *Caravans of Kola*. Zaria, Nigeria: Ahmadu Bello University Press, Ltd., 1980. See especially chapter 2.

Maier, Donna J. E. "Military Acquisition of Slaves in Asante," in *West African Economic and Social History: Studies in Memory of Marion Johnson*. Edited by David Henige and T. C. McCaskie (Madison: African Studies Program, University of Wisconsin, 1990), 119–133.

ON THE BASEL AND BREMEN MISSIONS' APPROACH TO THE ISSUE OF SLAVERY IN WEST AFRICA

Debrunner, Hans W. *A Church between Colonial Powers: A Study of the Church in Togo*. London: Lutterworth Press, 1965. See especially chapter 6.

Haenger, Peter. *Slaves and Slaveholders on the Gold Coast: Towards an Understanding of Social Bondage in West Africa*. Basel: P. Schlettwein Publishers, 2000.

Ustorf, Werner. *Bremen Missionaries in Togo and Ghana, 1847–1900*. Legon, Ghana: Legon Theological Studies, Asempa Publishers, 2002. See especially chapter 4, section 4.2.1.

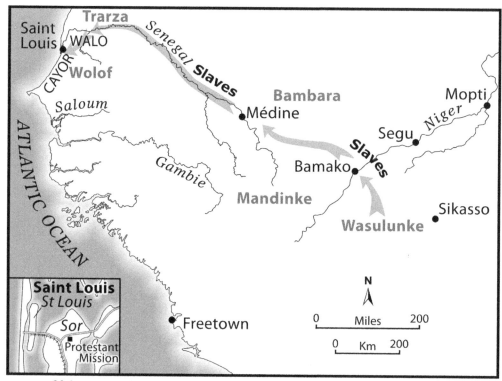

38.1. The location of the Protestant Mission in St. Louis.

The Testimony of Lamine Filalou

A Young Man's Experience of Enslavement and His Struggle
for Freedom in French West Africa

HILARY JONES

In the last quarter of the nineteenth century and the first decade of the twentieth century, a number of enslaved men and women in Senegal, Guinea, and the French Soudan
sought freedom in the town of Saint Louis, Senegal's colonial capital.[1] In 1848, the revolutionary government in Paris proclaimed an end to slavery "on French soil." But French
abolition was more concerned with the French colonies of the Caribbean than her African
possessions, which consisted only of the Atlantic coast towns of Saint Louis and Gorée and
a few river trading posts along the Senegal. Nevertheless, the 1848 proclamation abolished
slavery in the two towns, though not elsewhere. It was only in the late nineteenth century,
when military conquest resulted in the consolidation of colonial rule, that French administrators turned their attention to the problem of slavery in the interior.

In 1874, Prosper Darrigrand arrived in Senegal as a lawyer with the colonial judiciary.
Darrigrand prosecuted a number of individuals suspected of slave trading in Saint Louis.
Disturbed by slave trading in Senegalese villages outside of Saint Louis but under French
control, he turned his attention to prosecuting Senegalese subjects of France suspected
of trading slaves. Although Darrigrand's position put him at odds with the governor and
other colonial officials, the courts in Saint Louis began to enforce existing laws regarding runaway slaves more strictly. During this decade, anti-slavery activists in metropolitan France also pressured Paris to enforce abolition in her African territories. In 1878, a
Protestant missionary in Senegal wrote an article about slavery and slave trading in the
colony for a Protestant publication. The article was reprinted by several other papers and
was sent to Victor Schoelcher, the most prominent abolitionist in France. Schoelcher, a
prolific author instrumental in drafting the 1848 emancipation decree, used his position
as a newly elected Senator in the French National Assembly to criticize colonial officials
in Senegal for not enforcing anti-slavery laws in the colony and to argue for more serious
enforcement of existing anti-slavery laws.[2]

---

[1] Senegal and the French Soudan were the earliest colonies to comprise French West Africa. Military conquest spread from the French capital of Saint Louis (Senegal), which existed as a trade post for French
merchants in the Atlantic slave trade of the eighteenth century and the legitimate trade that followed in
the first half of the nineteenth century. The French Soudan is known today as Mali. The French military
gained control of much of the interior of West Africa during the 1880s and 1890s.

[2] Victor Schoelcher (1804–93) became France's most prominent abolitionist in the nineteenth century.
Schoelcher wrote a number of works arguing for an end to slave labor and the benefits of free wage labor

Although colonial officials remained ambivalent about attacking slavery outside of the towns, by the 1880s the governor and his top officials (aided by pressure from the Ministry of the Navy in charge of colonies) took more serious steps to enforce the 1848 principle.[3] Existing laws held that escaped slaves who claimed physical mistreatment or had fled enslavement from enemies of France could obtain a certificate of emancipation after registering with the judiciary and waiting three months in Saint Louis. In 1883, Governor Servatius decreed that escaped slaves had only to report to judicial authorities and could receive their certificates without any other formalities. These measures led to an increase in the number of certificates of liberty awarded to escaped slaves seeking freedom in Senegal's colonial capital. Martin Klein found that emancipation petitions increased from fewer than 100 a year between 1857 and 1862 to between 350 and 674 from 1875 to 1881. From 1881 to 1889, the number of slaves who received a certificate of freedom in Senegal rose from 1,058 to 2,198 a year.[4] Yet, the emancipation process proved costly for the fledgling colonial administration. Colonial officials feared that liberating slaves would create a population of "criminals and vagabonds" in the towns. In addition, anti-slavery laws presented problems for the expansion of French rule in the interior where local officers sought to maintain good relations with African rulers and heads of household who were slave owners. French military officers needed local collaborators to push forward their plans and maintain security in the conquest.

By the 1860s, Christian missionaries realized the difficulty of proselytizing in a region with such strong ties to Islam and turned to evangelism among former slaves as the most effective means of gaining converts. Roman Catholic missionaries established a "Christian village" within their Church in Saint Louis comprised primarily of former slaves. In 1864, the Paris Evangelical Missionary Society, a Protestant order, sent missionaries to Sedhiou, in the Casamance region of southern Senegal, with the intention of redeeming slaves to create a Christian community in an area where slave trading was common. Three years later, the Church abandoned the mission because of lack of personnel. In 1870, the Paris Evangelical Mission Society opened a Church in Saint Louis but again suffered from lack of financial support from the metropolitan Church, lack of supplies, and loss of French personnel. Faced with a fledgling enterprise, the Paris mission named Pastor Taylor to head the station in Saint Louis. Born in Sierra Leone of Nigerian parents and a one-time trader in the Gambia, Taylor served as head pastor of the mission until 1890. Taylor came from the Krio ethnic group, a population of liberated slaves who settled in Freetown after being freed by the British navy.[5] The navy transported captives to Freetown where they settled with the assistance of Protestant missionaries and British officials who encouraged

---

for production in France's Caribbean colonies. Schoelcher remained well informed about developments in Senegal, and when he entered politics in the 1870s, he used his position to advocate for reform to anti-slavery measures in France's African territories. See Nelly Schmidt, *Victor Schoelcher et l'abolition de l'esclavage* (Fayard, 1994).

[3] Jauréguiberry, a Protestant who served as governor of Senegal (1861–63) and once referred to slavery in the country as "hereditary serfdom," put pressure on successive governors to enforce anti-slavery laws when he became Minister of the Navy in 1880. See Martin Klein, *Slavery and Colonial Rule in French West Africa* (Cambridge, 1998), 62.

[4] Klein, *Slavery*, 73.

[5] The term "Krio" corresponds to the term "Creole" but comes from Pidgin English spoken by African settlers in Freetown. In the nineteenth century, this group was alternatively called liberated Africans or re-captives to specify their status as former slaves and captives who had been freed.

them to pursue trade with the local population. Taylor would surely have been steeped in Protestant Christianity prior to his arrival in Senegal.

Taylor transformed the Church's mission in Senegal by capitalizing on the growing population of escaped slaves seeking certificates of liberty in Saint Louis. He kept in touch with abolitionists in France who were well informed on the problem of slavery in Senegal and solicited financial support from a group of Protestants in Bordeaux. The Protestants of Bordeaux and Switzerland who supported this plan created an organization called the Society for Fugitive Slaves from Saint Louis. Their donations allowed the mission to feed, clothe, and house escaped slaves who arrived in the town. In 1883, Taylor received a concession of eight hectares from the governor in the suburb of Sor to provide housing and land to cultivate crops for subsistence and market trade. Taylor built a church and school on the land to promote Christianity and train young people in trades such as dressmaking and watch and shoe repair. Missionary pastors considered education in skilled trades necessary for transforming former slaves into a viable African working class and religious instruction necessary for instilling Christian morality and work habits. Taylor called the mission station Bethesda – a Biblical reference to the healing waters of Jerusalem where Jesus was said to cure the infirm.

The 1880s proved a time of growth for the mission. During this decade, the mission claimed to have "liberated" 200 slaves. The majority of escaped slaves came to the mission from the French Soudan (known today as Mali) and spoke Bambara, a Mande language spoken widely across West Africa. The concentration of Bambara-speakers in the predominately Wolof-speaking region of Senegal led pastors to refer to their mission as a Bambara village.[6] Most stayed temporarily until they could reunite with family or strike out on their own. Others joined the *tirailleurs Sénégalais* or the Senegalese riflemen, a cadre of African soldiers recruited by the French. Some married, learned skills, and settled at the mission station on the outskirts of the colonial capital. While missionaries hoped that former slaves would embrace Christianity, pastors routinely complained that most of the former slaves in the village continued to celebrate "pagan" healing and religious traditions as well as Islam.

In 1909, the mission closed the refuge for escaped slaves. The Church decided that it no longer needed to provide sanctuary for former slaves once anti-slavery measures enacted by the colonial government began to take effect. In 1903, French West Africa issued new laws and decrees making possible emancipation and cracking down on the slave trade. As a result, the number of slaves seeking refuge in Saint Louis declined dramatically as most opted to return to their home country or settle elsewhere in the interior. Perhaps more tellingly, the mission closed because of its lack of success in gaining converts. The final report authored by the head pastor noted that it no longer made sense to continue the mission given the lack of success that missionaries had in achieving lasting and meaningful conversion. After 1909, Protestants in Senegal turned their attention away from Saint Louis.

---

[6] The term "Bambara" refers to Mande-speaking people that trace their lineage to the Bambara kingdom of Segu on the lower Niger River. In the late eighteenth century, Segu engaged in slave raiding for political and military expansion. The Bambara-speakers who entered the mission came primarily from Mande-speaking regions outside of Segu. But the first slaves "liberated" by Taylor came from the Wolof state of Cayor in Senegal. Although some former slaves were Wolof-speakers, in Saint Louis the term "Bambara" came to refer to slaves and former slaves who settled in Sor on farms of elite slave owners of the town.

The Paris Evangelical Mission Society abandoned the fugitive slave mission and turned its resources to establishing a new church in Dakar to serve French settlers and merchants arriving in the new administrative and commercial capital.

Slave testimonies contained in missionary reports offer valuable insight into the first-hand experience of slavery through the voice of the enslaved themselves. At the same time, missionary sources present particular problems that researchers must be aware of. The authors of mission reports wrote specifically for the congregation at home, who provided financial support for the running of the mission. Individual testimony contained in mission records, therefore, may contain elaboration, exuberances, and fantastic tales in order to reach supporters at home on an emotional level. For instance, Filalou's account of cutting a piece of the ear of a freeman's child (or more commonly his camel) may seem illogical on the surface. Yet, the practice of ear cutting in nineteenth-century Mauritania was not uncommon. Ear cutting resulted in physical damage that caused blood to flow. Symbolic of killing, such an act required compensation according to Islamic law. Turning over one's slave to the injured party served as a means of restitution. If neither party could settle the matter, as we learn occurred in this case, it was not implausible for a judge to order the killing of the slave who did the cutting in order to rectify the symbolic killing of drawing blood intentionally. For the enslaved, resorting to ear cutting indicated mistreatment by one's master, an act that brought dishonor upon one's owner. The act itself required great risk, but the possibility of mitigating cruel treatment and subjugation at the hands of a harsh master brought a certain reward. Lamine's account of ear cutting offers us insight on how West Africans enslaved in Muslim societies of the Sahel experienced and understood Islamic law regarding the treatment of slaves by their masters.

When reading testimonies in mission reports, it can be difficult to distinguish between the missionary voice and the voice of the escaped slave. Written documentation of oral testimony lends itself to misunderstandings. Missionary interpretations often reflect inherent biases or incorrect assumptions. In Lamine's testimony we learn that his father died when Lamine was young and that authority over the family fell to his brother. Was this "brother" the child of his mother and father, a distant relation, or simply someone with high authority in the village? Does the statement that sending the children to work in the fields acted as an "indirect way of reducing one to slavery" reflect a misunderstanding by missionary observers of the role that the family unit played in the agricultural production of West African societies? Could it have been added to equate the problem of slavery with putting children to work in the fields for readers in metropolitan France, who might be sympathetic to the plight of children in societies where plantation slavery had existed? The Wasalunke had no permanent state structures. They also adhered to a system of patrilineal descent where children "belonged" to their father's lineage and authority rested with the eldest male in the household. In such societies, kin could be enslaved by other kin. But when a male head of household died, widows and their children were particularly vulnerable to the authority of senior men of their husband's lineage. For women, the fear of enslavement corresponded to the problem of being kinless in her husband's village at a time of great insecurity.

Finally, Pastor Taylor and his supporters in France and Switzerland intended the mission to become a Protestant enclave in a predominantly Muslim region of sub-Saharan Africa. Yet annual reports of the mission tell us that Mande language, customs, and religious and healing traditions persisted at the settlement. Instead Bethesda became an enclave of Bambara people in a predominantly Wolof region of Senegal. In the 1890s, the neighborhood around the mission station became home to Muslim Mande-speakers fleeing wars of expansion launched by the Mandinka state-builder Samori Toure. Lamine's story indicates that he was "discovered" and brought to the mission by another member of the Protestant community, Moussa Sidibé. Also a native of Wasulu, Sidibé gave testimony published in the mission's annual report. He recalled becoming a captive when his chief went to war with a rival chief and lost. Sidibé knew of the possibility of escaping to Saint Louis but feared the rumors that his Moor masters perpetuated of white sorcerers at the coast who cannibalized Africans. Lamine's account of meeting Sidibé when he arrived in the capital provides insight into the transmission of information among escaped slaves. Perhaps knowledge of a Bambara community in Saint Louis encouraged other escaped slaves to seek freedom and find refuge in the Protestant settlement.

Mission reports contain a number of contradictions and ambiguities. Missionaries often acted in collaboration with the colonial administration. At the same time, they fiercely guarded their autonomy. Supporters of colonialism justified foreign occupation on the basis that it would contribute to ending slavery and spread what they perceived as superior democratic and universal values of the West. Missionaries envisioned the spread of Christianity as central to colonialism's "civilizing mission." In their view, former slaves provided a critical mass of possible converts. Yet testimonies contained in mission reports suggest that escaped slaves had a more ambivalent attitude to the church. Mission accounts are often the only documents that remain of the experiences of escaped slaves themselves. By listening closely to the words contained in these reports and charting the trajectory of escaped slaves such as Lamine Filalou, we learn more about strategies for resistance, the search for family, and African Diaspora formations within Africa as a result of forced migration and the struggles of men and women to define freedom on their own terms. Bambara-speaking men and women escaped slavery in the interior and created their own Mande community outside of their homeland. Reading these testimonies allows us to recreate the biographies of individuals who might otherwise remain lost to history.

QUESTIONS TO CONSIDER

1. Lamine makes an extensive journey from his home village in Wasulu, near present-day Guinea, to Bamako, Mauritania and then Saint Louis, Senegal, where he obtains freedom. What insight does this testimony offer on Lamine's feelings of displacement from home and the challenges of living among foreigners such as the Trarza Moors?

2. Gender and age figure prominently in this testimony. What difference did it make that Lamine was a young boy when he was captured and sold into slavery? Do you see his gender and age as an advantage or disadvantage in his struggle to obtain freedom?

3. We learn of the trials and tribulations that Lamine Filalou experienced as a slave owned by a Trarza Moor. Yet we also learn that in Trarza society, slaves had the right to change masters who treated them badly – a common principle of Islamic law that prohibits masters from mistreating their slaves. Why do you think Lamine chose to pursue this option, even though it did not guarantee his freedom? Did his actions make his situation better or worse?

4. Can you distinguish between the missionary voice and the voice of Lamine Filalou himself? Why would Lamine Filalou choose to tell his experience of enslavement to the missionary reporter in this way? Why would the missionary choose to record it in this way?

5. What do you think of Pastor Taylor's role as the head of this fledgling mission enterprise? Why was he chosen as the head of the mission and how might his background as a descendant of "liberated" Africans from Freetown, Sierra Leone, have strengthened his connection to escaped slaves seeking freedom in Saint Louis?

6. Can you imagine what the experience of being forcibly taken so far from home, multiple captivity, and escape must have been like for a young West African man separated from his kinsmen and his native country? How might Lamine's discovery of a Bambara-speaking community on the outskirts of Senegal's colonial capital have provided a sense of security and protection in a new and unfamiliar environment?

THE STORY OF LAMINE FILALOU

Lamine is a native of Wasoulous country.[7] He lived with his father and his mother and three older brothers in the village of Téguénédougou; he was still young when his father died.[8] So his [so called] brother took control of the management of the family's affairs and would have required the two oldest of the children to go to work in the fields, which is an indirect way of reducing someone to slavery.[9] After having first refused, the older of Lamine's brothers, on the advice of the elders of the village, agreed with his uncle's wishes [to become head of the family] but the uncle died soon after. The mother fearing for her other children, fled with them to a village far enough away, but the brother didn't waste time coming to get them and he and his relatives claimed them as their captives. The chief of the village sided with the widow and the kidnapper's claim was dismissed. Soon after, when the young Lamine was sent to the market in a neighboring place, he was seized upon, tied up by men that his brother sent to ambush him and march him away to Bamako on the Niger where his mother and brother soon arrived in the same situation as he. They were all sold to different owners and separated, since then for always. Lamine fell in the hands of a Trarza Moor who soon resold him to another Moor, who gave him some camels to take care of and protect.[10] His

---

[7] Histoire de Lamine Filalou, *Asile des Esclave Fugitives*, Annual Report, 15 April 1883 to 15 April 1884, IFAN Library, Dakar.

[8] Wasoulous country is a reference to Wasulu, an autonomous area located in the lightly wooded savanna region of today's southern Mali, northern Ivory Coast, and eastern Guinea. Reports of runaway slaves in Senegal commonly mention Wasulu as a place of origin. The Wasulunke speak Bambara and to colonial officials they resembled other Bambara. In the nineteenth century, the Bambara kingdom of Segu raided Wasulu for slaves. After 1870, the Wasulunke found themselves surrounded by powerful slave-raiding states (Segu, Sikasso, Futa Jallon, and Samori's empire). In 1882, Wasulu voluntarily submitted to Mandinka state-builder Samori Toure. Lamine probably became enslaved during the period of instability between 1870 and 1882 when Wasulunke were faced with the danger of being enslaved by their more powerful neighbors who shipped them westward.

[9] This expression most likely refers to a classificatory brother – a so-called brother but not a real one.

[10] People of Mauritania are commonly referred to as Moor (Maure in French). Moor refers to the Arab-Berber population who lived in nomadic groups in today's Mauritania. As Saharan people, the Moors have a long history of Islam and of traveling trans-Saharan trade routes. The Trarza Moors ruled the north bank of the lower and middle Senegal River.

life was excessively hard; deprivations and bad treatment were his daily lot. What was worse after one of the camels disappeared having been lost or stolen, he was beaten either with a baton or a cord. One day for no reason his master pushed him down on the ground, his face in the dust, with his arms behind his back all in raising his legs, he tied his hands and feet together; this poor boy endured such bad tortures that even the neighbors interceded, but in vain. Lamine was often tied up for hours and even days in the hot sun without even a taste of water to quench his thirst. One time, after having been untied he remained absolutely inert for a considerable amount of time because he had been tied up tightly and for a long time. At that moment he resolved to change masters and he took advantage of a strange custom that reigned among the Moors. When a slave wants to change masters, he looks for someone who appears less worse off than him and if he succeeds in taking off with a knife a small bit of the ear of the child of the man for whom he would like to become a slave, the father of the injured child must accept him as his slave. The slave is his by law.

Lamine resorted to this means: unfortunately the new master did not care about having Lamine. He said to the other [Lamine's former master]: "You are a preacher, I don't want to deprive you of a slave, but give me his equivalent in merchandise and I will leave him for you." Lamine's former owner responded "no keep him I don't have anything to pay for him." With that the parties could not come to an agreement so they went to find the judge who, after hearing them, turned first to one then to the other, giving his sentence in the following terms: "You, you do not want this slave who has become yours because of the treatment that he put your son through; you, his former master, you neither want to take back your slave or pay for his value: well! Then the slave must be killed!" Then and there, poor Lamine was tied to a stake and was going to be hit with a gunshot when his former master threw himself on him, held him in his arms in crying: "Don't kill him or else kill him with me! If he is killed and I survive, he will take the place that is destined for me in paradise and I will go in his place to hell. If we die together, we will both go together in the sky, but I like better to pay and I will pay all that is reasonable."

And so it was done, but one understands that life was far from being easier for poor Lamine. After having looked in vain to sell him to make amends, no one wanted to buy this slave, his master – we are going to write to his executioner – made him undergo the following punishment, which appeared as a religious sign that M. Taylor has not yet succeeded in clarifying. The master solidly tied his slave to a piece of wood of the same height as him, then he struck him with blows to the head just until it was horribly swollen, nothing but a frightful sore; the poor injured Lamine was well cared for; when he healed, his master managed to sell him without difficulty.

After some time his owner brought him to Cayor to look for salt.[11] Lamine accompanied him. When he was careless in asking his master for a taste of tobacco, his master was so infuriated that he set about insulting his captive and insulting Lamine's father and his mother by

---

[11] Kajoor, often spelled Cayor, is the name of a Wolof state in Senegal. In the nineteenth century, Cayor was the center of a thriving salt trade. Salt mined in northern Cayor was sold to merchants, like the Trarza Moors, who transported salt by donkey and camel caravan for sale in the interior. Cayor was also a principal slave market. Typically, slaves were sold from the regions of eastern Guinea and southern Mali and transported by land to the Sahara, towns on the southern border of the desert, or Senegal. Mauritanian traders commonly sold slaves at slave markets in Cayor to slave-traders who sold them again for labor in Senegal's peanut basin or along the Dakar to Saint Louis railroad that linked Saint Louis to Dakar. Lamine went to Cayor with his master to buy salt, but while there he may have encountered slaves as well as individuals in this commercial hub, who knew about the possibility for emancipation in Saint Louis.

some hateful words. This, a black man can never tolerate. Lamine promised himself to run away and did so that night as soon as his master was soundly asleep. He got a hold of a *toubé* (*toubé* are a kind of men's drawers with lots of pleats which serve as pants and which are a sign of authority) allowing him to be free to go anywhere. In a few hours he was in Leybar from where he came to Saint Louis.[12] He was free and discovered by Moussa Sidibé, one of our future evangelists, who brought him to M. Taylor and he was instructed in the Gospel and he became a member of the Church. He asked M. Taylor for baptism saying "It must be that powerful God has changed my heart, because I became a reasonable man and I don't recognize myself any longer. When I was with the Moors I only thought of stealing, brigandage, and cheating as I saw my masters doing. I became mean and cruel and now all that has passed. I can not stand those things. Don't you see that God has changed me?"

This brave Lamine finally had a broken heart. He was supposed to marry one of our freed women, but it was called off at the last moment. He courageously dealt with the ordeal and one sees in it a kind of blessing: he understood that he still lacked certain things to be a good husband and he is in the process of making real efforts to correct it.

Signed: L. Jacques

SUGGESTED ADDITIONAL READINGS

Barry, Boubacar. *Senegambia and the Atlantic Slave Trade*, translated by Ayi Kwei Armah. Cambridge: Cambridge University Press, 1998.

Bouche, Denise. *Les villages de liberté en Afrique noire française, 1887-1910*. La Haye: Mouton, 1968.

Clarke, Peter B. *West Africa and Christianity*. London: Edward Arnold, 1986.

Falola, Toyin. "Mission and Colonial Documents." In *Writing African History*. Edited by John Edward Philips (Rochester, NY: University of Rochester Press, 2005), 266–286.

Klein, Martin. *Slavery and Colonial Rule in French West Africa*. Cambridge: Cambridge University Press, 1998.

McDougall, E. Ann. "Salt, Saharans and the Trans-Saharan Slave Trade: Nineteenth Century Developments," *Slavery and Abolition* 13, 2 (1992): 61–88.

Robinson, David. *Muslim Societies in African History*. Cambridge: Cambridge University Press, 2004.

---

[12] Leybar is a region located at the mouth of the Senegal River and the Atlantic Ocean. It was known for its salt flats and was a stop on a trade route commonly traveled by Mauritanian traders.

39 The Blood Men of Old Calabar – a Slave Revolt of the Nineteenth Century?

UTE RÖSCHENTHALER

Old Calabar was one of the major precolonial trading ports of West Africa, now located in the southeastern corner of Nigeria. Literature on the history of this town describes the Blood Men as slaves who organized a revolt against their Efik masters that first occurred at the mid-nineteenth century. Missionaries of the Presbyterian Church of Scotland, who had just begun operating in the area, witnessed the events and provided several accounts about them, on which all subsequent historical interpretations have been based.

This chapter presents two passages from missionary texts, which not only describe the first public appearances of the Blood Men but also offer intimate insights into the social life of Old Calabar. The first account is from the diary of Hugh Goldie. Written in December 1850, it recounts the first armed insurgence of the Blood Men. The second is from an entry in missionary Anderson's diary and a letter of missionary Goldie, both from January 1852 and published together under the title *"The death of King Archibong: More than twenty persons killed by the poison nut."*[1]

To supplement the missionaries' point of view, and to show how Nigerian historians and intellectuals have created their own understanding of the history of the Blood Men, I have also included here two short texts published by contemporary Efik historians: Chief Ekei Essien Oku and Noah Monday Efiong. Both know of and quote from the nineteenth-century missionary sources, but they provide an interpretation of the causes of the movement that focuses more on the solidarity bonds linking masters and slaves than

---

[1] The Calabar missionaries' diaries are published in the *Missionary Record of the United Presbyterian Church*, Edinburgh, Scotland, with introduction and subheadings by the publishers marked in italics. Summaries of the movement are also found in Hope Masterton Waddell's and Hugh Goldie's books or memoirs on Calabar published many years later: H. M. Waddell, *Twenty-Nine Years in the West Indies and Central Africa: A Review of Missionary Work and Adventure 1829–1858* (London, 1863); H. Goldie, *Calabar and Its Mission* (Edinburgh, 1890).

This chapter is based on archival studies and field research in southwest Cameroon and southeast Nigeria. Between 1987 and 1988, research was supported by the *Nachwuchsförderung des Landes Berlin* and the German Academic Exchange Service, between 1998 and 2001 by the German Research Council in cooperation with the Goethe University of Frankfurt, and in 2008 by the Cluster of Excellence "The Formation of Normative Orders" at the Goethe University Frankfurt, Germany. I am also particularly grateful to the many informants in Cameroon and Nigeria who took the time to patiently discuss their culture with me.

on slaves' aspirations for freedom.[2] Chief Ekei Essien Oku first worked as a teacher and then trained as a librarian in the United Kingdom. Back home she became the first female Chief Librarian in Nigeria in 1964. Her book, *The Kings & Chiefs of Old Calabar (1785-1925)*, published in 1989, focuses on the lives of the Efik chiefs and kings. She writes on the Blood Men in the context of King Archibong I's achievements. Noah Monday Efiong studied history at the University of Calabar in Nigeria and at Howard University in the United States, where he received his PhD in the 1970s. His book, *Old Calabar: The City States and the Europeans 1800-1885*, is based on his dissertation. His chapter on the missionaries' influence also deals with the slave revolt.

For the missionaries, the movement gave voice to slaves' requests for freedom, although the missionaries themselves admitted not having fully understood what was going on. A careful reading of their two accounts reveals that slaves operated in support of their deceased master's family when they felt it was necessary to find those responsible for his death, and that local politics played an important role as well. By taking cues from such details in the missionary accounts, Chief Ekei Essien Oku and Noah Monday Efiong suggest instead that the slaves were rather supporting their masters in their political rivalries and intrigues and keen on revenging their death.

HISTORICAL BACKGROUND

In 1846, the Presbyterian Church of Scotland opened the first Christian mission at Calabar. Hope Masterton Waddell, who had already spent many years in Jamaica, became the leading figure in the Calabar mission. Fellow missionaries Hugh Goldie, William Anderson, and Mr. Edgerly helped him expand his religious work. For the first time, Europeans were bold enough to live onshore with local people. The missionaries obtained land to build on a hill that was said to be inhabited by ghosts – the roaming and angry spirits of people who had died by accident or as witches and had therefore not received a funeral.

Calabar is situated at the mouth of the Cross River near the Atlantic coast in the Bight of Biafra. In the mid-nineteenth century it consisted of several "towns" or villages inhabited by Efik, Efut, and Qua-Ejagham people. These settlements were also called Old Calabar to distinguish them from New Calabar further west at the mouth of the Niger River near Port Harcourt. The Efik quickly became the middlemen in the trade between the Europeans and the hinterland of Calabar. When the Efik arrived from the Ibibio country, they founded several settlements or villages. Creek Town was one of the oldest Efik settlements further up the river. Then Old Town was founded, and the most recent was Duke Town (Figure 39.1) with its offshoot Henshaw Town settlement, nearest to the Atlantic. Duke Town population grew steadily from 2,000 in 1805 to 6,000 in 1846, with ten times as many in the farming

---

[2] The missionaries give the most detailed accounts of the movement of the Blood Men. Nigerian historians and Efik local historians usually write about the history of Calabar referring to the events on the basis of the missionaries' books. Some of the most important histories of Calabar written by Efik historians are: E. U. Aye, *Old Calabar through the Centuries* (Calabar, 1967); A. Eyo, "Efik Political Agents of Old Calabar, 1891-1924," in S. O. Jaja, Erim O. E., and Bassey W. Andah (eds.), *Old Calabar Revisited* (Enugu, 1990), 46–62; Ekpo Eyo (ed.), *The Story of Old Calabar: A Guide to the National Museum at the Old Residency* (Calabar, 1986); M. E. Noah, *Old Calabar: The City States and the Europeans, 1800-1885* (Uyo, 1980); Nyon Asuquo, *Reflection on Nation Building: An Old Calabar Perspective (1900-1976)* (Calabar, 1989); Ekei Essien Oku, *The Kings & Chiefs of Old Calabar (1785-1925)* (Calabar, 1989); K. O. Dike, *Trade and Politics in the Niger Delta, 1830-1885* (Oxford, 1956).

39.1. Cameroons River (Cross River) from above Akwa [Duke] Town.
Source: Photograph from Mary Kingsley, *Travels in West Africa* (1897), 413.

areas to the north and east. Much of this increase was attributable to the settlement of large numbers of slaves in Akpabuyo, east of Duke Town, where they worked on farms.[3]

Local chiefs, also called kings in analogy to European rulers, were rich merchants dealing with European traders of various nationalities who anchored at the Cross River to buy mainly slaves and palm oil in exchange for cloth, beads, metal bars and rods, and other fashionable items. The people spoke Pidgin with the traders and the missionaries, but the latter soon learned the Efik language into which they translated the Bible.

By the eighteenth century, two wards had emerged as politically dominant in Duke Town: Eyamba and Duke. Competition for the two leading positions of the *Obong* (chief or king of Duke Town) and of the *Eyamba* (chief of the men's *Ekpe* leopard spirit association[4]) was confined to these two wards because their mercantile prominence had allowed them to obtain large numbers of slaves or retainers (Figures 39.2 and 39.3).

In an official letter to British officials, the "kings" of Calabar had asked for missionaries to come to their town. They assumed that with the help of the missionaries, they would be instructed in economics to carry out trade more efficiently. One of the traders had explained to them that "a missionary was a juju man," which means somebody who can influence of how things are done.[5] The missionaries, however, instead of teaching them business, had come to disseminate the word of God. They began to teach them Christian values and the importance of stopping the trade in slaves and human sacrifices. In spite of the 1807 British Abolition of the Atlantic slave trade, many slaves continued to be secretly sold to Portuguese traders all through the nineteenth century. Slaves reached Old Calabar from the hinterland of the Cross River region, from the Igboland, and from the Cameroon

---

[3] A. J. H. Latham, *Old Calabar 1600–1891: The Impact of the International Economy upon a Traditional Society* (Oxford, 1973), 91. For early sources, see also S. Behrendt and E. Graham, "African Merchants, Notables and the Slave Trade at Old Calabar, 1720: Evidence from the National Archives of Scotland," *History in Africa*, 30 (2003), 37–61.

[4] *Ekpe* was (and still is) an association of prominent political and economic leaders that worked with the Calabar rulers to enforce local laws.

[5] Waddell, *Twenty-Nine Years*, 272.

39.2. A Calabar chief.
Source: Photograph from Mary Kingsley, *West African Studies* (London: Macmillan 1899, 2nd ed. 1901), opposite 122.

Grassfields. Some of them lived with the Efik as domestic servants, but the majority stayed on the plantations of the Efik east and north of Calabar in order to produce foodstuffs to feed the growing town of Calabar and the slaves on the ships. They also processed palm oil and kernels for sale. Still others worked as crew members on the large canoes of their masters (Figure 39.4). When the missionaries arrived, the Efik were wealthy enough to bury many of their slaves in a potlatch-like destruction at the occasion of the burial of an important big man or trader, or his mother. So a good number of slaves went with their master

39.3. King Duke of Calabar in full dress.
Source: Photograph from Mary Kingsley, *Travels in West Africa* (1897), 37.

into the grave.[6] In a few years, in early 1850, the missionaries successfully convinced the kings of Calabar to sign a treaty in which they agreed to stop such human sacrifices. The rules were issued and sanctioned by *Ekpe* – called *Egbo* by missionaries and traders. This treaty was one of the first achievements of the missionaries. As a result, slaves could no

---

[6]   All the sources mention that the slaves had used the opportunity to announce that they did not wish to be sacrificed by their masters at will. Robin Law in his article on human sacrifice, however, also mentions the possibility that slaves and wives of a respected man followed him voluntarily into the grave, a deed that was regarded as a great honor to be permitted to do, see "Human Sacrifice in Pre-colonial West Africa", *African Affairs*, 84 (1985), 53–87. Clearly they would not have received such elaborate funeral ceremonies themselves, locally considered very important.

39.4. Long dugout canoe on the Cross River, usually rowed by slaves.
Source: Photograph from Charles Partridge, *Cross River Natives* (London: Hutchinson & Co, 1905), opposite 179.

longer be placed in the graves together with their masters or otherwise sacrificed to the local deities – at least officially.

In 1850, four years after the arrival of the missionaries, the slaves in the plantations organized themselves into a group, called the Blood Men. The event that prompted their formation was the death of three Efik rulers of Duke Town, all in a short span of time, between 1834 and 1852. The first was Duke Ephraim, also called Great Duke Ephraim IV, from the so-called Duke family or ward of Duke Town. He ruled Duke Town from 1814 until 1834, and was said to have had numerous wives. He still traded in slaves, but also sold palm oil at the same time. The Liverpool trader Sir John Tobin was his good trading friend who brought him a solid brass chair as a present in 1826. Tobin's ships carried the majority of the trade in palm oil from Calabar amounting to 2,000 tons a year. He had also begun to transform Akpabuyo, the vast land east of Calabar, into an Efik colony where he settled the majority of his slaves. These slaves worked on his farms and produced food for themselves and the inhabitants of Calabar. Missionaries' accounts call these farms "the plantations" or "Qua plantations." Duke Ephraim was followed on the throne of Duke Town by King Eyamba V, who ruled from 1834 to 1847 and came from the Eyamba family ward. He was so wealthy that he ordered an entire palace – called the Eyamba's iron palace – along with the workers to erect it, from England. Wealth depended as much on the possession of material goods as on the number of dependants: wives, children, and slaves. His successor was King Archibong I (from the Archibong family, closely linked to the Duke family), who ruled from 1849 to 1852.

The slave revolt started in 1850 and was begun by those working on the plantations of the deceased Duke Town ruler Duke Ephraim. The slaves resumed it in 1852 at the death of King Archibong I and continued thereafter, as the Blood Men periodically rampaged through the town, until the beginning of British colonial rule in 1884.

What was the cause of their revolt? At this point, we only know that it started after the treaty against human sacrifices had just been signed in early 1850. In December of the same year, as a consequence of the Blood Men's insurrection, another treaty guaranteed both the established social and political order of the Efik society and the rights of the slaves as human beings, who were not to be killed for sacrifice. In 1852, the Blood Men appeared again in Duke Town: King Archibong had fallen ill and died shortly later. People interpreted his illness and death as resulting from the witchcraft of malevolent members of his family entourage. As a consequence, his family members and relatives were expected to prove their innocence by taking the so-called *esere* bean as an ordeal.[7] This is narrated in the second missionary account, which shows how the missionaries tried to convince the dying King of the uselessness of this "superstition." It also describes the intervention of the British consul in support of the traders who feared the destruction of their property by the angry slaves.

SLAVES, THE *EKPE* CULT ASSOCIATION, AND WITCHCRAFT

According to the missionaries, the Blood Men were not only fighting against being sacrificed but also to escape the oppression of the *Ekpe* association, which the Efik to this day consider their "traditional" form of government.

Ekpe was, and to some extent still is, the executive institution instructed to enforce the Calabar rulers' laws. In 1850, the use of the *esere* bean was placed under the authority of the *Ekpe* society to prevent it being invoked too often.[8] The association enabled members to collect debts, punish lawbreakers, announce laws of the council, and perform at other member's funeral ceremonies. Above all, it was a social meeting place where members sat together according to their rank in the association, discussed the latest news about trade, and celebrated their achievements. Higher grades and full knowledge of *Ekpe* secrets were reserved for members of the leading Efik families.

Slaves were at first excluded from participation but later, when some of them became wealthy enough to pay the fees, they were allowed to enter the lower grades and purchase expensive prestigious titles, as were some of the European traders. *Ekpe* had a considerable impact on the daily social life of Calabar (and its hinterland). It was an executive institution that was mainly involved in locating individuals who had transgressed one of its laws. One of these rules was that when *Ekpe* was celebrating or treating a case, nonmembers were not allowed to leave their houses. They had to wait until the *Ekpe* meeting had ended. This was not particularly directed against women or slaves, as the missionaries thought, but against traders who were not members of *Ekpe*. Rather it allowed women and slaves to stay indoors instead of having to go out on errands or to work on their farms.

Death of old age was believed to be the only natural way of dying. All other deaths were considered to be caused by evil spirits or witchcraft – the use of spiritual means to harm another – of relatives or neighbors. To find out who had caused the death by using witchcraft, an *abia idiong*, a diviner, was called to perform his ordeal. He was paid for his services to determine the innocence or guilt of all those persons who were accused by the family of the deceased. Explanations for witchcraft beliefs usually focus on social tensions between related individuals who are supposed to support and love each other. It does not generally occur between individuals who have no previous social involvement or nothing to do with one other. The missionaries felt that the majority of those who died of the ordeal were women. Evaluation of the early reports shows, however, that more or less

---

[7] *Esere* or Calabar bean, with its Latin name *Physostigma Venenosum*, was ground up and mixed in water. Whoever was accused of having practiced witchcraft was to drink the concoction.

[8] According to Waddell, *Twenty-Nine years*, 480.

the same number of men and women were accused. The men were from the same patri-lineage (uncles, brothers, nephews) of the deceased, and the women were mostly wives from another family. Women frequently accused other women. Slaves could also support accusations.[9]

At the death of King Eyamba in 1834, about fifty members of his family seemed to have taken the *esere* bean ordeal, of which forty died, including all his wives and many relations. Mr. Young, a leading political figure of Eyamba ward, made the accusations. As a result, the Duke ward was weakened, his successors died by the ordeal, and King Eyamba V of the Eyamba ward gained the office of the *Obong* and the *Eyamba*.

Nothing much is known about the death of his follower, but when Archibong I died in 1852, witchcraft accusations were used again as a political tool. Archibong's mother accused three women in the family and several of Archibong's wives. All died from the ordeal. Mr. Young fled, which meant a loss of prestige for him, so that Duke ward candidate, Duke Ephraim, became *Obong*, and not Mr. Young. Duke Ephraim was followed by Archibong II of Duke ward. Eyamba ward was so weakened that they had no candidate for twenty years. Only in 1878 was the poison ordeal abolished by a treaty with the British under Archibong III who was Elder of the Presbyterian Church and an active politician. He died the following year. At times of difficult political succession, the leading wards used a common form of accusation to solve conflicts, one that associated witchcraft with political and economic success. Usually witchcraft increases with economic decline, although in Calabar there was no sign of recession at the time.[10]

A number of authors (the missionaries mainly, but also the Efik and other historians who read the missionary sources) have taken the side of the most vulnerable sections of Calabar society, namely women and slaves. According to these authors, slaves had established the Blood Men and taken the opportunity to liberate themselves and fight for their civil liberties against the atrocities of the *Ekpe* society and the dominance of their masters who sacrificed them at will. Others say, and sometimes also Waddell and Goldie mention this in their accounts, that the slaves sought to revenge the death of their "father" or master, and that they had come to punish those who had caused his death by practicing witchcraft against him.[11] Still others underline that the slaves were rather instrumentalized by their masters so that they would support them in their political rivalries and intrigues. In this perspective, the slave's first concern was to prevent the death of their master, and if he died, to revenge him. Their next concern might have been to reduce the risk of being sacrificed at their masters' death. As an agreement against human sacrifice had just been signed, the missionaries overlooked this motivation in their explanation of the revolt.

As a matter of fact, the slaves' opinions do not emerge from any of the four accounts. Their voices are never quoted and they are treated as a homogenous and cohesive social group without mentioning that their association with particular Efik wards could create substantial differences within the slaves' community. Surely, not all joined the Blood Men

---

[9] A. J. H. Latham, "Witchcraft Accusations and Economic Tension in Pre-colonial Old Calabar," *Journal of African History*, 13 (1972), 249-260; G. I. Jones, "A Boundary to Accusations," in M. Douglas (ed.), *Witchcraft: Confessions and Accusations* (London 1970), 321–331.

[10] This argument is elaborated by Latham, "Witchcraft Accusations," and supported by G. I. Jones, "A Boundary to Accusations," 325.

[11] Missionary Waddell notes in his book, *Twenty-Nine years*, 496–497, that the Blood Men who appeared in February 1952 after the death of King Archibong I came to "avenge the death of their 'father.'" After a funeral, commemorative places were constructed for the kings, the roof and sides of which were covered with the skulls of the victims who had died in the course of the deceased's death.

and those who did belonged to different Efik families to whom they remained loyal. Some were domestic slaves living in town, others were slaves living on the farms, leading a more or less independent life from their masters in town, and still, others were hard-laboring canoe boys. A number of slaves had become wealthy traders and active in politics themselves. Did they operate as a coherent, monolithic group? For whose interests did they work? Their own? Their masters?

The sources themselves, as indicated, are ambiguous. They can be read in multiple ways. How would you interpret the actions of the Blood Men after reading these missionary narratives?

DISCUSSION QUESTIONS

1. Can you reconstruct the sequence of events by using the missionaries' accounts? How are the same events described by the two Efik historians? What are the similarities and differences between the four accounts?
2. Who were the main persons responsible for the Old Calabar disorders? Compare the perspective of the missionaries with that of the Efik historians. Did the missionaries themselves play a role in the unfolding of the events?
3. What reasons can be given for the slaves' coming in arms from the plantations to the town of Calabar? What speaks in favor of the different possible reasons and what speaks against them?
4. What do we learn about the conditions of slaves in Old Calabar from these different accounts?
5. What differentiated a slave from a freeborn?
6. Why had the poisonous nut to be taken?
7. What could be the reason that so many women were killed by the poison ordeal?
8. Why did the British consul or governor not subdue the revolt himself and send the slaves back to the plantations?

THE DOCUMENTS

1. "Old Calabar. Negotiations between the slaves in the plantations and the chiefs of Duke Town," in *Missionary Record of the United Presbyterian Church August 1851*, 117–120.

The following details go to show that the suppression of the slave trade and the establishment of commerce will ere long abolish the internal slavery of Africa. It would seem that the slaves are becoming numerous at the plantations, which are at some distance from the towns, and that these are beginning to assert their right to be treated as men. The Rev. Mr. Goldie says –

The enslaved desiring to be free, 12th December 1850. A dispute has arisen between the chiefs of Duke Town and some people in the plantations. The people belonged to the late Duke Ephraim; but knowing their strength, they refused to remain slaves to any one. It appears that several of them were seized by the head men of Duke Town for some reason or other; upon which the rest of them, by a covenant of blood,[12] bound themselves to stand by

---

[12] Blood brotherhood has been frequently practiced in the entire area. For example, it is known among Igbo trading partners who undergo the ritual whereby they mix some of their blood, which they drink or rub into their skin, and take an oath that they will always help and never betray each other until they die.

each other, and in retaliation plundered a plantation belonging to King Archibong's mother. The men put in chains were released, and the plunder taken from the plantation restored; but, in order to a full settlement of the matter, the people demand that they be not troubled by any, as they are resolved to be treated as freemen, and that the Duke Town chiefs abandon the practice of killing for the dead. The former demand, the chiefs have not power to refuse, and the latter is granted beforehand, the plantation people having been ignorant of the abolition of the custom; but, in order of the confirmation of this treaty, they require that the chiefs come out to the plantation and chop doctor, that is, go through the ceremony of taking a solemn oath.[13] This last demand the chiefs feel to be an encroachment on their dignity, and are very unwilling to submit to it, insisting that the people of the plantation come to them. Iron Bar has been sent on an embassage to endeavour to prevail on them to do so; with what success remains to be seen.[14]

Threatening appearances, Mr. Goldie says, under date *25th December*, The dispute with the plantation people is settled; but this agreement does not seem to have been lasting; for he says in another communication – *Friday 31st January*, A considerable number of the slaves in the plantation, who have banded themselves together, for their mutual protection, came into town to-day. They were all armed – most of them having their faces smeared with black and red colours, and many wearing war-caps, that they might appear, I suppose, as terrible as possible; and certainly the chiefs did not venture to raise a hand against them. A number of them had been in on the previous week, ostensibly to inquire after Archibong's health, and stated, that if he died they would cut off the head of the doctor-man who attended him, and big palaver would arise. There is not much the matter with Archibong, but he believes himself under the influence of witchcraft; and today the insurgents denounced about forty individuals who had, no doubt, been named by some *abiidiong* as practicing against the king, and threatened vengeance if they did not desist.[15] Most of those denounced are women, very likely because they can be more safely dealt with, and the poison nut will doubtless be administered should Archibong continue to entertain his suspicion. The slaves, I dare say, made the demonstration chiefly to show their strength and to overawe the town.

War-steamer sent for – Wednesday, 5th Feb. – H.M. [Her Majesty's] Steamer Archer, Commander Strange, came up the river this evening in consequence of an application of

---

[13] When Goldie writes that the chiefs have no power to refuse to stop the killing of slaves for funerals, he refers to the treaty signed by the Efik chiefs in early 1850 in which they agreed to abolish human sacrifices. "Chop doctor" or "chop nut" is a term in Pidgin English, which refers to the taking of an oath which is fortified by an ordeal that shows whether the truth was sworn. "Chop nut" specifically refers to the ordeal of eating of the poisonous *esere* bean or also the drinking of a liquid prepared from it. The oath taking is usually accompanied by the words: "If I am guilty of having caused this problem (by using witchcraft), then the ordeal should kill me, but if I am innocent, then the ordeal will reveal the truth. The guilty ones die and the innocent ones vomit the concoction."

[14] Iron Bar is the name of a trader from the Duke ward, who was of slave descent but had become wealthy and influential as a member of the Duke Town council, especially after the death of Duke Ephraim, whose right-hand man he had been. From the 1850s onward, other wealthy slaves became council members, too, and were allowed to acquire *Ekpe* titles. Iron Bar died in 1851, and then his brothers took over; cf. Latham, *Old Calabar*, 97, 102.

[15] "Abiidiong" should be *abia idiong*, which is a diviner (literally a practitioner of divination) who belongs to a guild or society of diviners who are paid to find out where problems come from, particularly at the death of people. In parts of the Ibibio hinterland, they have possibly also been involved in selling the accused persons as slaves instead of executing the accused witches. *Abia ebok* is a healer who uses medicinal herbs to cure people; cf. M. Abasiattai, "Ibibio Traditional Religion and Cosmology," in M. Abasiattai (ed.), *The Ibibio: An Introduction to the Land, the People and Their Culture* (Calabar, 1991), 108.

the captains of the merchant ships, who are afraid that the people in the plantations may proceed to serious lengths.

Thursday, 6th. This morning Captain Strange and two of his officers called at the mission-house. Captain S. was lieutenant of Wilberforce in the disastrous Niger expedition.[16] He said he had been instructed by the senior officer on the station to visit us, and render any assistance in his power should we require it, and kindly offered us sanctuary in his ship if we felt alarm at the demonstration of the plantation people. We thanked him for his kindness, but said that we felt no alarm. It is said that the slaves who have asserted their independence, look upon the white men as their friends; and the insurrection is by their chiefs attributed to the measures forced on them by the whites, especially the prohibition of the slave-trade and the abolition of the rite of human sacrifice.

In the evening, H.M. Steamer the Jackall, came up the river with governor Becroft.[17]

Friday, 7th. Governor Becroft, the captains of the steamers and of the merchant vessels, had a meeting with the chiefs of Duke Town to-day. After hearing what they had to say, it was resolved to send for the leaders of the insurrection and hear from them what their grievances and claims were.

Terms of peace. Wednesday, 12th. This morning Governor Becroft and Captain Strange had a meeting with some of the plantation people who have come into the town in obedience to the Governor's summons, in presence of the chiefs. The men stated that the object they had in view in binding themselves together by a covenant of blood, was to preserve themselves from the oppression of the chiefs. If they committed crime, they refused not to die; but they refused to be destroyed at the pleasure of their masters. The Egbo law that was made awhile ago, prohibiting sacrifices, was mentioned to them. They said, they had heard of it, but appeared to place little dependence upon it; and we hear that one of their grievances is, that that law has been violated, and that, apart from this rite, in one or two cases lately, slaves have been causelessly destroyed. Indeed, so long as the power of life and death remains in the hands of the masters, such cases will occur; and nothing is easier than for a master to evade the Egbo law above referred to, by merely alleging that the slaves destroyed were guilty of crime, there being no check upon the supremacy of his authority. Captain Strange threatened to take Archibong prisoner if any injury was done to British property or life; but as the principal men had not come in, the conference was adjourned.

Saturday, 15th. The leaders have now come in, the Consul had a long palaver with them this morning. They said they had come into the town armed because of the chiefs destroying slaves without cause; but their spokesman, on its being put to him, said that he had seen no instance of this. They bound themselves by chopping doctor not to come armed into the town, nor to receive any more runaway slaves from the town, and to allow the execution of

---

[16] This refers to the 1841 expedition of several British steamers, among them the Wilberforce, up the River Niger to the confluence of the Chaddah River, for the exploration of trade opportunities for palm oil with inland people in the hope to transport this good on steamers instead of canoes. During the expedition, 53 of the 303 crew members died of fever or accidents; cf. Latham, *Old Calabar*, 62.

[17] John Becroft (also often spelled Beecroft) was appointed as Consul in 1849 and considerably raised British power in the Bights of Benin and Biafra. He acquainted Africans with the British rule long before the partition of Africa and the coming of European colonial government in 1884, when Nigeria became a British colony. He acquired considerable power for himself, often met with fierce resistance from the local people, protected the British trade interests in the region, and so was often called "the Governor." Many of the Efik traders of Old Calabar were his personal friends. For more information, see Dike, *Trade and Politics*, 129–152, and Latham, *Old Calabar*, 134–135.

Egbo law. If they became aware of any breach of the law prohibiting human sacrifice, they were to inform the ship-captains or the missionaries, who would write to the Consul....

An arrangement was come to last Saturday [8th February 1851], when seven articles of agreement, or treaty, were signed by Duke town gentlemen, and about twenty of the plantation representatives. Article 1st provides – That Egbo law of the country is to be respected and adhered to. Art. 2d – That no more bodies of armed men are to come into Duke town. Art. 3d – That no slave who has a master alive shall chop blood[18] with other slaves, without his master's consent. Art. 4th – That should any slave belonging to any person in town runs away to the plantation, he is to be given up when demanded. Art. 5th – That any combination among slaves for interfering with the *correction* of any domestic servant by his or her master is to be considered illegal. Art. 6th – That the law (made a year ago) for the abolition of human sacrifices be confirmed, and that the said law is not interpreted so as to interfere with the criminal law of the country. Art. 7th – That should any article of the present treaty, or the law for abolishing human sacrifices, be infringed, the injured party is to apply for redress to her Majesty's consul through any British resident on the spot....

2. "The death of King Archibong: More than twenty persons killed by the poison nut," in *Missionary Record of the United Presbyterian Church August 1852*, 134–137.

We take the account of the horrid scenes which followed the death of King Archibong, from the narrative of Mr Anderson, inserting two extracts from a letter of Mr Goldie: –

But passing other matters, I shall come to the principal event which we have at present to record, viz., the death of King Archibong. He was very unwell a year ago, and I believe never fully recovered. When we arrived last month, he seemed pretty well, and in good spirits. On the evening of January 31st, when Mr Goldie and I took our usual round to announce the approach of Sabbath, we found him very ill. He had had fever for three or four days. He said that he could not be at the meeting on the morrow, but that we must come down and hold it as usual. When we saw him the next morning (the Sabbath), he was evidently worse. We then began to apprehend danger. His mother had arrived from the plantation, and was beside him. Her name is Obuma, but she is frequently styled by the white people, Mrs. Archibong. She is wholly devoted to the superstitions of her country. *Idiong*, or the carcasses of sacrificed animals were to be seen in all quarters.[19] The atmosphere was quite polluted with their pestilential effluvia. Here was a goat's head, there one of its legs, yonder another of them; while within two yards of his sickbed was a putrefying fowl, tied (probably while it was alive) to a stick. Mr Goldie on that morning, as at our subsequent visits, spoke to him of the Saviour, and prayed with him or for him in the Calabar tongue. On the Monday when Mr Goldie was speaking to him and the folly of *idiong*, and urging him to commit himself to Christ, he called on one of the gentlemen, and repeating what Mr Goldie had just said about their own foolish condences, he declared most seriously that they were 'Ikemeke', i.e., unfit to benefit, worthless. We called on the Tuesday, and found him sinking. About noon on Wednesday the 4th instant he died.

---

[18] The Pidgin term "chop blood" means to form an alliance by blood brotherhood; see also note 12 to this chapter. As will become clear later in the chapter, however, often the masters also joined their slaves' covenant.

[19] The Efik term *idiong* refers to a conjuring or a charm, and also to a soothsayer who can apply charms to protect his patient. He can also divine the person who placed a bad charm or has bewitched the patient. See also note 15 to this chapter.

A large number of Persons killed by the Poison Nut – [Mr Anderson writes:] A work of slaughter forthwith commenced. His mother, Obuma, took four of the family connections, one man and three women, to Mr Young, and charged them with having killed her son by means of *ifod*, otherwise called *freemason*; in Jamaica it is called *obeah*; witchcraft is, I suppose the nearest approach we can make to the meaning of the word in English.[20] They were subjected to the ordeal of the poison nut, *and all died*. Mr Goldie and I having got a hint about the *chop nut*, took the round of the town to see how matters were looking. Mr Young looked as innocent as an infant, and protested so strongly that no *esere* had been administered, that for my part I thought he was speaking the truth. We are certain now however that he was deceiving us. On the same night the king's mother caused several of his wives to take the nut. The greater part of those who took the poison died under its influence. It is reported that Mrs Archibong broke the Egbo law made two years ago, by killing several slaves; but there are so many conflicting statements that we hardly know what to believe and what to disbelieve. If she had broken that law, I feel convinced that she has *now* some powerful enemies among the Egbo gentlemen, who would rejoice to see her brought down, and if they can convict her of the crime led to her charge by common report, she will not escape Egbo's vengeance.

On the day after Archibong's death (Thursday the 5th), large bodies of armed men began to pour in from the plantations. They came with the avowed purpose of ascertaining who had killed Archibong.[21] We have since learned that they came into the town on the invitation of the king's mother, who, it appears, offered them great rewards, provided they would procure the destruction of the *Young* family by denouncing its members, as the murderers of Archibong by having *freemasoned* him, and by demanding that their guilt or innocence be manifested by their submitting to the ordeal of the nut. On the Friday, a large meeting was held in the market-place. All the gentlemen of the town were present with their retainers – there must have been from 1000 to 1200 armed men from the plantations, and there were 200 to 300 spectators, chiefly women. There could not be fewer than 1500 on the ground, probably a good many more. It was one of the most sorrow-inspiring spectacles I have ever seen. The professed purpose of the assemblage was to ascertain who had killed the king. Mr Goldie and I went down twice to see what was going on. We could do nothing more than to speak a few words to the gentlemen, and protest against more killing. We could not arrest the progress of events, but we felt it our duty to watch, and to show that we were watching, the proceedings of the day. We stopped both times as long as the scorching sun would allow us. We saw four poor women eat the fatal nut. Three of them seemed very indifferent about the matter. While chewing the poison, they were laughing and talking to those around them. The fourth, she was quite young, seemed very thoughtful. It would have afforded us no pleasure to see the approach of death's agonies – our hearts had a sufficient load to bear without that addition. We withdrew from the scene. It was no long ere we were informed that two of the victims were dead. The other two rejected the poison.

With regard to the scenes of this dreadful day, Mr Goldie says: – Others were put to death in the same manner on that day. The chiefs assured us that the people had come in

---

[20] *Ifod* is the Efik word for what is usually translated as witchcraft. *Freemason* (or to *freemason* somebody, i.e., to bewitch somebody) is the Pidgin word for witchcraft used in Old Calabar, and derives from the contact with the traders and may refer to the secretive aspects of both crafts: that of the fraternity and that of the witches.

[21] Note the discrepancy between this statement and what the missionaries said in the beginning, namely that the slaves were fighting for their rights to be considered free men.

on hearing of the king's death, but with no bad intentions. Returning shortly after, I saw they were busy with something, but from the crowd filling the market-place, could not see what it was. I pressed forward to where the chiefs sat, and asked Mr Young what the people were doing. He said it was not his palaver. Gathering from this that they were about some deed of blood, I pushed into the centre of the crowd, and found several poor women seated on the ground, to whom they were about to administer the nut. My presence was most unwelcome, and I was called on frequently to withdraw, but I stood for a considerable time beside the women, attempting to gain a hearing from the surrounding multitude in vain. The noise was so great that I could make myself heard only by two or three about me, who were deaf to all remonstrances, insisting that I had no business there. I took two nuts from the hands of one of the women, but they were quickly taken from me, and handed to her again. Two of the ship captains then came up, and endeavoured to prevent the scene of murder, but in vain. Seeing I could do nothing, I withdrew, having again charged the chiefs with the deeds of murder, Mr Young, as usual, disclaiming all part in them, and Duke Ephraim full of wrath that we should presume to interfere by a single word in the matter.[22] In a short time, Mr Anderson and I went down again to watch the proceedings, and I found them busy at the work of death. Pressing into the centre, we saw four of the women eating the nut, the others having been already disposed of, and an individual grinding a quantity on a stone, to administer to them, I suppose, as a daught. Several of the victims are already dead. All those yet subjected to the ordeal are women, and several more are threatened, some of them being of the principal women of the town.

Mr Young and other Chiefs denounced by the Plantation people – It appeared evident that the plantation people were dictating to the town gentlemen, and that the town gentlemen were not at all sorry to comply with their demands, and to give the nut to as many as they chose, so long as they themselves were not pinched. Matters went on smoothly enough between the parties, till an old lady of the powerful *Ephraim* family was denounced. She availed herself of her privilege to nominate another individual to chop nut with her. She nominated *Mr Young*, her age and family connections giving her a standing in the country equal to his.[23] Notwithstanding his doctrine that the nut cannot harm the innocent – false doctrine, and that he and others knew very well – he refused to submit to the ordeal. He managed to get the meeting adjourned for that day, and in the evening he decamped. I am informed that he spent the night on board one of the ships. On the next day he escaped to Creek Town, and he is there now. He has a brother, the individual who once confessed to me that he had a principal hand in the slaughter of fifteen of Eyamba's wives, who has also made his escape to Creek Town. The plantation slaves intended to have a fearful reckoning with a bloody house. Here we see the hand of God dealing out retribution, and the wicked snared in the pit which they themselves had digged. Early on Saturday morning, Mr Young's daughter (an adopted daughter, I believe), who is also one of Eyamba's widows, came to the mission-house for protection. What a change! Our house has often been a sanctuary for the *slave*; it is now resorted to as a refuge by the *free*. On Saturday the 7th, business was resumed.

---

[22] The Duke Ephraim V succeeded King Archibong I after the appearance of the Blood Men following his death in 1952.

[23] From this can be gathered that the Ephraim family with Eyamba and that of Archibong to which Mr. Young belongs are the two rival parties for kingship in Duke Town at the time. The slaves should not be all lumped together: each of the Duke Town families had their own plantation slaves who would support them whenever necessary. So, not all slaves were uniting to fight for a common objective.

The assembly is again convened. Fresh bands of armed savages have poured in from the plantations. The town is at their mercy. They seem inclined to subject all the free people of the town to the ordeal. Some one demands that if Mr Young and his family must chop nut, Mrs Archibong must do so too. The armed bands, a strong body of whom the old lady herself had encouraged to come into the town, see no harm in this demand, and the cry becomes general. "*Let Obuma chop nut – make her do it.*" She, like her worthy half-brother or cousin, Mr Young, declines the trial. It is proposed to use compulsion with her, but she, we are informed by those on whom we can depend, lays a train communicating with a good many barrels of powder, with the determination to blow herself and all around her to pieces, if any attempt be made to force her to chop the deadly nut. Here again we behold *retribution*.

The killing continued – Saturday, 7th – Mr Goldie says: – Mr A. and I, on going down to the market-place, found it crowded with the plantation people, who had, in truth, complete possession of the town. Not one of the chiefs were present, though we afterwards heard that Duke Ephraim had been forced to appear in the market-place. Ephraim John Duke, a young man who formerly attended school, told me as I stood by the group of victims yesterday in the market-place, that the people were demanding of his mother to take the nut. I told him to send her up to the mission-house, which, however, he did not do.[24] It appears that his wife was sitting among the victims at the time he was speaking to me, though he made no reference to her; and that she died in an hour or two after. Poor John is one of the people banded together by the covenant of blood, and so he had to shoulder his gun and march along with them, taking part in the execution of his own wife, and not daring to utter a word.

In the evening, called on two or three of the town's people who were making themselves active in this horrid work; but they all maintained that those who died were justly punished, for had they been innocent the nut would not have injured them; and one of them stated that it was Archibong's own persuasion that he was under the influence of witchcraft. On going in to see Archibong's mother, we found a cloth hung up before the apartment in which the body is interred, and a covering spread over the grave, on which were seated several of the king's wives in complete darkness.[25] We were guided to a small room adjoining, where sat Archibong's mother with several other women in gloom as if of midnight. She evidently did not at all like what we said to her respecting the poisoning.

Seeing on Saturday that Duke Town was in a state of anarchy – the king dead – the premier fled – and no acknowledged head in the place, Mr Goldie and I wrote to King Eyo requesting him to interpose, and if possible to prevent the further destruction of life. He wrote us, in reply, that Duke Town people had not informed him of what was going on, but that he would send his brother, John Eyo, to stop any more chopping nut, and to make the plantation people go away. On the following day, Sabbath the 8th, John Eyo came down with the Creek Town insignia of official *Egbo* authority; and 'Egbo' himself came down from Old

---

[24] When individuals were escaping from the poison ordeal or were worried about taking it, this was interpreted as a sign of guilt or bad conscience. They could escape, of course, but this suspicion was not forgotten and taken up again afterward whenever another case came up. Therefore, sending victims to the mission-house was only an option when immediate death was to be prevented. People somehow believed that the ordeal was just, and those who died were real witches.

[25] The actual burial obviously went unnoticed or was uncommented on by the missionaries. One would have expected that they at least comment that human sacrifices were no longer carried out. Possibly the missionaries assumed that because of the numerous presence of the Blood Men, sacrifice of slaves with their master was unthinkable.

Town. But neither the ordinary mortal, nor the mysterious personage from *the bush*, could quell or control the tumult. Both returned to their homes in the afternoon.[26]

Arrival of King Eyo – Quiet restored – On Monday the 9th, King Eyo himself came down, and to our great joy succeeded in restoring order. On the Saturday when we wrote to him, we wrote also to Mr Waddell and to Mr Edgerley, proposing that they should join us here on the Monday morning in a special meeting for prayer in behalf of poor destructed Duke Town. They reached this place at nearly the same time with King Eyo. After he had taken his chair in the market-place, all four of us went down to pay our respects to him, and Mr Goldie and I thanked him for his attention to our request. We intimated that if he needed us in any way, we were at his service. We then left him to transact his business, and we came up to hold our meeting. I believe we helped him better by our prayers on his behalf and on behalf of the country, than we could have done otherwise. After meeting, Mr Waddell and I went down to see what was going on, and we found that King Eyo had managed the business of restoring peace and order, at least for the time being, that all parties were about to *chop doctor* – take oath – that there was to be no more nut chopping, and that the plantation people were to go to their homes. King Eyo must have performed his part of the business with great skill and prudence. Had he not done so, his presence in Duke Town would have increased rather than hushed the storm. Duke Town is again without a head, and I suppose that for a season, every man will just do what is right in his own eyes. I earnestly wish, and have some small expectation, that the occurrences mentioned above will lead to the total abolition of the ordeal of the poison nut. I have no doubt that many thousands of lives have been destroyed by it in this country. This is probably the first time that the head men have themselves been required to make trial of it. If they be wise, it will be the last. The question has perhaps occurred to you. Seeing that *women* are so much undervalued in Old Calabar, how has that old lady, Obuma, so much influence? There are some excellent remarks on the chief points involved in the question in Kitto's daily Bible Illustrations, forty-fourth week, fifth day, – article, "The Queen". Here, as in the lands of the Bible, the king's *wives* may be, and are, of little importance in the country, while his *mother* occupies a very high place. It is perhaps worthy of remark at present, that what we call *murder* by the poison nut, is not considered to be such in this country. To administer it here is quite legal, so that no proceedings can be instituted against those who have at this time employed it. In so doing, they broke no *Egbo* law.[27] I trust that an *Egbo* law will soon be passed prohibiting its use in all time coming.

We are again turned adrift as to our Sabbath-day meetings in Duke Town. We feel now, more than ever, the necessity of our having a place of meeting of our own, unconnected with any party or family in the country.

Various reports are in circulation respecting the numbers who have been destroyed by the *esere*. It is impossible to ascertain the truth on such a point. From what I have learned, I should suppose the number of victims to have been between twenty and twenty-five.

Note – a letter just received from Mr Anderson, dated 21st April, states that order has been restored, and that Duke Ephraim has been elected King.

---

[26] *Egbo* is the Pidgin term for the men's *Ekpe* society. "Egbo himself" is not really seen by people; it can only be heard. The missionary probably means that the masked dancer of *Ekpe* with his messenger, his leader, singers, and musicians came down to Duke Town, being a sign of the power of the *Ekpe*.

[27] The missionaries were aware that there were two different views or normative orders at work. They understood that the local people explained the premature death by the agency of malevolent witches, and that it was logic for them to punish them. Therefore, in their own opinion, the local people did not violate an agreement.

3. The text by Efik historian Ekei Essien Oku gives a different view of the events and reasons for the slave revolt. She argues that the Blood Men were acting in support of their masters. It is taken from her book, *The Kings and Chiefs of Old Calabar (1785–1925)*, Calabar: Tidings Press, 1989, pp. 58–62. Under the heading "Birth of the Blood Men," she writes:

Extensive plantations lay in the hinterland of Efik territory both in Calabar and Creek Town. These plantations were worked by slave labour and the coastal community depended on them for their food supply. From the 1850s, the plantations, notably Akpabuyo, became strongholds of fugitives and runaway slaves who were trying to escape the atrocities of the Ekpe confraternity.[28] They began to band themselves together by a covenant of blood for mutual protection and were thence known by the name 'Blood Men' (Nka Iyip). Their objective was to resist the oppressions of the Duke Town gentry, and to preserve themselves from being killed on all occasions according to old customs. They knew of the law abolishing human sacrifices and also that this was still secretly violated. They therefore resolved to stand by each other in self-defence. It was reported that King Archibong I and other free men in Duke Town joined the Blood Men for their own ends. This proves that their combination was not so much that of slaves against masters as that of self preservation and that their avowed objective was not regarded by the rulers as contrary to the order and peace of the country. This said Hope Waddell (1863:476), "was the origin of the Blood Society which attained much strength as to rival and defy the Egbo association …"

The first clash between the two orders i.e. Ekpe and the Blood Men was provoked by the arrest by Ekpe Law, of some Blood Men who had come into town in 1851. The slaves retaliated by ravaging the plantations and also threatening to destroy the town if their imprisoned colleagues were not released. The insurgents were joined by many free men of Duke Town including those whom the small clique of Ekpe dictators oppressed. Although the rebellion united many diverse interests it was predominantly a slave revolt and it was of such magnitude that the supercargoes were afraid for themselves and their properties. They summoned Consul Beecroft and the warships from Fernando Po. Dike comments that Beecroft knew Old Calabar and its institutions more intimately than those of Bonny and had no prejudice against Calabar rulers such as he entertained for King Pebble of Bonny who was himself also having problems of slave revolts.[29] He, Beecroft, was of the view that whatever the grievances of the insurgents, they must seek redress along constitutional lines. He did not therefore seek to abolish Ekpe authority as he had done in the case of King Pebble but as the treaty which

---

[28] Domestic slaves were much more concerned by the actions of the *Ekpe* society – which proclaimed laws and also sanctioned them – than those on the plantation who lived further away and more or less in peace, although the sources also mention that slaves had fled from town to the plantations. Whenever the *Ekpe* society held important meetings – and one day of the four-day week (which was widespread before the missionaries introduced the seven-day week) was reserved for such meetings anyway – nonmembers such as slaves, women, and foreigners who wanted to trade had to stay indoors. The missionaries had arranged with the Efik chiefs that they and their servants were made an exception to this *Ekpe* rule and allowed to walk around in the streets on *Ekpe* days.

[29] The Nigerian historian Kenneth Dike explains that the slave revolts of Bonny were different from those at Old Calabar. At Bonny, he writes, it consisted of ex-slaves who were powerful and wealthy merchant-princes debarred from enjoying political positions. Dike, taking over Waddell's opinion, holds that in the revolt at Calabar slaves were fighting for their freedom. He presents the Blood Men as an association comparable to *Ekpe*, which succeeded to undermine the power of *Ekpe* (cf. Dike, *Trade and Politics*, 154–157), whereas the critical reading of the four documents suggests that the problem were rather the political rivalries of the Duke Town families.

was concluded through his mediation between masters and insurgents showed, he thought to reform existing authority rather than destroy it.[30] ...

[D]efending his action, Beecroft stated that he treated the Blood Men "not as slaves nor the higher powers as slave masters but the whole as a community, a part complaining truly of a barbarous and inhuman custom held by the more powerful division."[31] ...

The fact that the slaves continued to strengthen their numbers was proof that they did not believe in the good faith of their masters and that all that was achieved was merely a truce. They therefore used their combinations whenever their hard-won liberties were threatened, or as occasion dictated. One such occasion was when Archibong I fell ill.

Hope Waddell records that his men who had joined the Blood Men in large numbers came into town to save his life. They resolved that if he should die, his Abia Ibok (doctor) and all suspected parties should also die.

But as nothing happened, they retired to the plantation. When, however, the king eventually died on the 4th of February, 1852, and succession disputes commenced, the Blood Men were summoned into town by Archibong's mother, Obuma. Latham recorded that she offered the men 100.000 copper rods if they would force the leaders of Eyamba ward to submit to the Esere Ordeal.[32] This would be a way of avenging the massacre of important Duke House leaders on the occasion of Great Duke's death in 1834. And so the new treaty was set aside and numerous people were killed. Mr Young was required to submit himself to the ordeal but promising to do so in the public square the following day, provided Obuma joined him, he escaped with his brother Ntiero to Creek Town. Obuma of course would not go through the test and threatened to blow up the town with a keg of gunpowder if anyone attempted to force her.

Blood Men were also called upon by Duke Ward when Mr Young insisted on being conferred with the title of Iyamba VI and prepared to have himself proclaimed.[33] Having no money with which to counter the men, he gave up the attempt.

It is said that Archibong II also used the Blood Men to fortify his position especially as he did not possess the Iyamba title unlike some of the earlier kings.

The last appearance of these men in Duke Town was in 1872, when King Archibong II died and in 1861 at Creek Town when Eyo III died.

Although King Archibong I's reign was a brief one yet it was a significant period in that it saw the promulgation of the treaty against inhumanity to slaves.

4. This text is taken from the book of the Efik historian Monday Efiong Noah: *Old Calabar: The City States and the Europeans: 1800–1885,* Uyo: Scholars Press, 1980, pp. 110–115. In chapter V "The Church of Scotland Mission: 1846–1885" he writes under the subheading "Political and Social Revolution" and argues that the Blood Men should be understood as a group of slaves who operated as an unruly mob with not very clearly articulated social, political and economic grievances.

---

[30] The author refers to the treaty that Consul Becroft made with the Efik chiefs in 1851, which the missionaries have also mentioned earlier. It says that *Ekpe* law should be respected, that slaves should not come with arms into town, that they should not engage in blood brotherhood or otherwise rise against their masters, and that the law against human sacrifice was herewith confirmed.

[31] Ekei Essien Oku quotes Becroft according to Dike, *Trade and Politics,* 158.

[32] Ekei Essien Oku refers to the same poison ordeal described by the missionaries.

[33] *Iyamba* is the title that the chief of the *Ekpe* society holds. Together with the title of king (*Obong,* chief), it had become the most prestigious of all titles among the Efik. Both came into existence with the social, economic, and political changes brought about by the increasing trade.

If the Sabbath preaching of the missionaries appealed to no other class of people, they certainly had the strongest appeal among the slaves. The first sign of this appeal seemed to have occurred in 1847 after the death of King Eyamba V when several of his domestic slaves fled his house denouncing their allegiance to Eyamba's heir. Some of them fled to the mission houses, others to the plantations. In the course of the years, the numbers of those runaway slaves in the Qua plantation increased, and they banded themselves in a covenant of blood and became known as the Bloodmen, from the manner of their oath. The Bloodmen tried to found their own system of government by organizing their own branch of the *Ekpe* society, but they were not allowed to do so by the urban authorities.[34] Barred from forming their own separate government, the Bloodmen then proceeded to use their superior members in winning concessions from former masters. They declared themselves as a special group not to be bound by *Ekpe* laws and, among other things, they insisted that substitutionary punishment be abolished.

The phenomenon of Bloodmen in Calabar history is very difficult to analyse in lucid terms. They might be characterised social bandits of which Robin Hood would be the archetype.[35] …

Even though most of the members of this group were members of the servile class, some of them had ingratiated themselves with the nobles and some of the nobles had fraternized with the group. This is born out by the fact that when King Archibong was unwell, the Bloodmen came into town to save his life and resolved that "if he died, his native doctor should die too, and other suspected parties."[36] In fact, Archibong himself was reported to have joined their covenant to secure their allegiance. In Duke Town, a 'gentleman' of servile origin was reported to have had some dispute with a 'gentlewoman' who was a freeborn. The woman sent to the farm for her son who came and flogged the 'gentleman' because he was of servile origin though wealthy. This reveals that membership of the organization did not always coincide with the actual stratificational practice of the rich versus the poor.

It must be pointed out, however, that the nobles were not blind to the threat implicit in the rise of the Bloodmen. At the same time, it would be wrong to imply that the existence of this group was an index that the city government was growing more corrupt and decrepit. Rather it seems that traditional mechanisms of civil control were now incapable of dealing with a huge rural population in which traditional social relationships were rent by an increasingly desperate economic situation.

Regarded from this point of view, the Bloodmen could be described as the city mob, for it should be understood this group lived in the plantations, the city remained their theatre of action. What is certain is that their activities could be regarded as an inchoate protest against injustices, economic, social and political.[37] …

---

[34] The "Qua plantation" refers to the same plantation area earlier called Akpabuyo, to the east of Calabar. In the entire Cross River region, people were of the opinion that they would never show the secrets of the *Ekpe* society to the slaves or their descendants, and until today to own an *Ekpe* association is a sign of freeborn status. This does not mean that slaves could not become members; some even purchased the high titles. Owning high titles did not, however, necessarily mean that the slaves that bought them underwent all the accompanying initiations.

[35] Noah borrows the term "social bandits" from Eric Hobsbawm who understands banditry as a "primitive form of social protest"; cf. E. Hobsbawm, *Primitive Rebels: Studies in Archaic Forms of Social Movement in the 19th and 20th Centuries* (New York, 1959), 13.

[36] Here, Noah refers to Waddell, *Twenty-Nine Years*, 476.

[37] "City mob" is also a term Noah has borrowed from Hobsbawm's *Primitive Rebels*, 7, mentioned previously.

By 1851, the Bloodmen had emerged as the most threatening force in Old Calabar. It would seem that King Eyo was correct when he argued with Hope Waddell that if he relaxed his control and allowed indiscriminate changes in the name of reform, there would be chaos, in which both, the state, the traders and the mission would suffer. When the Bloodmen appeared in the city in 1851, the supercargoes were so frightened and so concerned about their property ashore that one of them was quoted to have told King Eyo that he would not hate to see "the heads of a hundred of these fellows cut off." Another supercargo recommended that "they ought to be shot down like dogs". But the Bloodmen were in town on the invitation of the ailing King Archibong and quickly went back to the plantation on his instructions.[38]

Since the supercargoes had sent for Consul Beecroft and the man-of-war to help the chiefs in suppressing the armed band, the consul invited the leaders of the group to Duke Town in order to listen to their complaints. But on the first day of the meeting, the leaders of the Bloodmen failed to attend. Beecroft held conferences with King Archibong and intimated that it had been rumoured that the principal men of the town were behind the appearance of the Bloodmen, but the chiefs all flatly denied the charge. In order to make this order more effective and to assure the Bloodmen that the order came from the Consul, Beecroft dispatched a special messenger the next moment, giving the messenger his own ring to help him establish his credibility before the Bloodmen.

Meanwhile, Beecroft sent for King Eyo, who denied any knowledge of the affair, but assured the Consul that "he had taken the necessary precautions to make a law, that the first slave of his that was found chopping blood from another slave should suffer death."[39] But the Consul expressed doubts about the effectiveness of such precautionary measures as the King might take because if the insurgents were united, any law (by the king) would be useless.

On March 15, the Consul was able to assemble the ring leaders of the Blood Brotherhood in a meeting with the Kings, Chiefs and the supercargoes. When asked to state their grievances, the group was not unanimous in its statement. Some said that their reason for coming to the city armed was to intimidate the nobles to stop human sacrifices. But when the Consul asked them whether they were not aware that human sacrifices had been abolished by law, the group told him that they did not believe it. Hennie Henshaw Duke, the delegate from the Qua plantations, denied any knowledge of such atrocities even though he admitted partaking in the blood ceremony. Not being able to obtain any substantial evidence from the delegates of the Bloodmen, the Consul then drew up a treaty prohibiting such combines which would injure the trade of the river. *Ekpe* laws were to be tightened to prevent any repetition of acts of lawlessness.[40] ...

---

[38] Here, Noah quotes Waddell, *Twenty-Nine Years*, 477, again. Goldie and Anderson did not mention such statements. Waddell included them in his book, which was published after his retirement some twenty years later. Noah uses the words "city" and "state" conceptualizing Calabar at that time as a city-state, which is quite a euphemism.

[39] This shows how seriously the movement was taken. Noah took the information in this and the previous paragraphs from an official communication by Consul John Becroft with the Foreign Office.

[40] Becroft intended to protect the interests of the British traders who feared for their property. The Foreign Office in London reacted with questioning how the consul could suggest reinforcing traditional institutions such as the *Ekpe* society, which it had earlier condemned as a hindrance. According to the Foreign Office, the British government should not interfere in problems of the local people with their slaves, the more so as these slaves were fighting for freedom, and the law would only encourage the nobles to be more reactionary.

By 1864, Consul Burton estimated that their number might have exceeded 20,000, but he was still of the opinion that much of the social upheaval that had afflicted Calabar was caused by the missionaries. Burton condemned the standpoint of the missionaries who, he said, take it as their duty to oppose the customs of the people: "their sacrifices, their wars, their polygamy and their system of slavery. He will strain any point beyond the limits of the most elastic conscience to protect, shelter, and to secure the escape of a fugitive servile."[41] It seems, however, that the most devastating conduct of the Bloodmen was carried out in 1856 when the mob surged the streets looting shops and farms. Some of them were caught by their former masters and locked up. In consequence, the rest of the Bloodmen plundered the farms of the nobles who had arrested their fellow members and "not till the former were released did the latter restore their booty."[42]

In 1858, When King Eyo Honesty II died, the Bloodmen appeared in Creek Town and retired to the plantations only after Creek Town nobles had assured them that the King's death did not warrant their presence. In 1861, on the death of King Eyo Honesty III, the Bloodmen compelled the King's brother, Ekpo Eyo, and several other people to take a certain oath (*esere* bean) to prove their innocence in the King's death. The Bloodmen continued as an active organization up to and beyond 1871 and successfully defied *Ekpe* authority each time they were in town. It was only after 1884 when the British government had declared the Protectorate of Southern Provinces and had taken over the administration of Southern Nigeria that the activities of the Bloodmen were brought to an end.

SUGGESTED ADDITIONAL READINGS

Forde, Daryll (ed.). *The Efik Traders of Old Calabar*. London: Oxford University Press, 1956.

Goldie, Hugh. *Calabar and Its Mission*. Edinburgh: Oliphant, Anderson & Ferrier, 1890.

Latham, Anthony J. H. "Witchcraft Accusations and Economic Tension in Pre-colonial Old Calabar," *Journal of African History*, 13 (1972): 249–260.

Old Calabar 1600–1891: The Impact of the International Economy upon a Traditional Society. Oxford: Clarendon Press, 1973.

Lovejoy, Paul and David Richardson. "Trust, Pawnship, and Atlantic History: The Institutional Foundations of the Old Calabar Slave Trade," *The American Historical Review*, 104, 2 (1999): 333–355.

Nair, Kannan K. "King and Missionary in Efik Politics, 1846–1858," *Journal of African Studies*, 4, 3 (1977): 243–280.

Röschenthaler, Ute. "'A New York City of Ibibioland'? Local Historiography and Power Conflict in Calabar," in *A Place in the World: New Local Historiographies from Africa and South-Asia*. Edited by Axel Harneit-Sievers (Leiden: Brill, 2002), 87–109.

"Translocal Cultures: The Slave Trade and Cultural Transfer in the Cross River Region," *Social Anthropology*, 14, 1 (2006): 71–91.

---

[41] In 1855, T. J. Hutchinson succeeded Beecroft as consul, who in turn was succeeded by Captain R. F. Burton in 1861. Noah took the quote from an official communication of Burton with the Foreign Office in 1864.

[42] Noah here quotes Waddell, *Twenty-Nine Years*, 76.

Makua Life Histories

Testimonies on Slavery and the Slave Trade in Nineteenth-Century Madagascar

KLARA BOYER-ROSSOL

I n Madagascar, the history of slavery and the slave trade has long been treated with silence. Studies of memory made during the last twenty years have not been translated into action and the evocation of this history remains taboo. In some regions, including in the West, descendants of slaves are still seen as lacking ancestors, deprived of a history of descent and thus of family memories. The Makua seem to be an exception. Settled in western Madagascar, they descend from slaves imported during the nineteenth century. The Makua was the only group of former slaves that has been considered as an ethnic group[1] in Madagascar. Recognition of this can be explained by their origins outside the island. Makua oral traditions continue to transmit the memory of ancestors coming from "beyond the seas." Testimonies of enslaved persons have also come to us from life histories collected by Norwegian missionaries who settled at the end of the nineteenth century in the west of Madagascar. Makua life histories were oral testimonies of the trade and of slavery, which have never been used.[2] The main thread of these histories is the major stages of this crossing, which reflect the process of enslavement. They give us crucial information on the slave experience, which is not remembered in Makua oral tradition.[3] I am presenting two life histories, translated from Norwegian into French and then into English,[4] that put into perspective familial oral traditions I collected in 2004 and 2008.

---

[1] The term ethnicity is defined here as a large group, whose members recognize themselves as sharing ancestors and a common culture, and knowing a territorial anchoring. During the French colonial period, the Makoa appeared in the administration's reports, as one of the "ethnic" or "racial" identified in the districts of the West. In Madagascar, which is now called "ethnic group" ("foko" in Malagasy) means rather regional entities (such as the Merina in Highlands or Sakalava in the West) and does not apply to the Makoa, which group identity is no longer asserted.

[2] K. Boyer-Rossol, "De Morima à Morondava: itineraries [itinéraires] d'ancêtres venus 'de au-delà des mers.' Contribution à l'étude de la formation du groupe makoa (côte ouest de Madagascar au XIXe siècle)," in D. Nativel and F. Rajaonah (eds.) *Madagascar et l'Afrique* (Paris, 2007), 183–217.

[3] Oral traditions are silent about the experience of slavery. This conscious forgetting is part of the construction of Makua memories.

[4] These tales are from a work by L. Aas, *Oplevelser og indtryk Fra mit missionarsarbeid pä Madagaskars vestkyst. Første del 1880–1889* (Stavanger, 1919), 2 volumes, 166–181 and 182–194. Josef's story was translated into Malagasy by S. Ramaka, "Kalamba Mahihitse Josefa," in his *Mpamangy* (1944), 88–91. I have used the original versions, which were translated into French by a Norwegian student, Christoff Hoff Hansen, who I thank warmly.

THE SLAVE TRADE AND SLAVERY SEEN THROUGH MAKUA ORAL TRADITIONS

The Makua are the largest group in Mozambique – about 4 million in a population of 19 million. The slaves imported to Madagascar were not all Makua, but in Sakalava country on the west coast, this term is used for all slaves imported from Africa. In the Highlands, they were called *Masombika* because they came from Mozambique.[5] In Madagascar, such ethnic or geographic terms appeared during the first half of the nineteenth century. In this period, the Merina[6] sovereigns of the highlands, whose capital was at Antananarivo, conquered most of the island. In the west, several pockets of resistance remained, but the old Sakalava kingdoms were in decline. From the seventeenth century, the Sakalava kings developed their power by monopolizing trade with Europeans. The activity of the Sakalava ports increased with the development of trade, especially the slave trade. In exchange for manufactures and firearms, they provided Europeans with slaves raided from the interior.[7] At the end of the eighteenth and the beginning of the nineteenth century, Sakalava sea raids even reached the Mozambican coast.[8] These ended near 1820, when the Sakalava faced Merina expansion, which increased after 1820. Militarily strong, the Merina quickly occupied the Sakalava west, put garrisons along the coast, and controlled the ports. In the second part of the nineteenth century, except the area around Morondava, the west coast alongside the Mozambique Channel, including the Fiherana, North Menabe and Ambongo, remained independent. Apart from these regions, the Big Island was ruled by Merina kings and queens from Tananarive. Madagascar seemed to be a united kingdom, recognized by European states like Great Britain, which in 1817 imposed on the Merina a treaty renouncing the slave trade. The island, which had for several centuries exported slaves, then began to import them from East Africa. Exports and imports coexisted throughout the century, but imports intensified even though the trade was considered illegal. The island became the center for a trade in which many slaves were re-exported, disguised as indentured laborers, to other islands in the Indian Ocean.[9] In Madagascar, most of the trade was directed to ports in the west that were not under the authority of the government of Antananarivo. Morondava, one of the oldest Sakalava ports, was an important trade port and the location of a Merina military post. Many Merina officers were involved in the trade. Creole traders from Reunion were denounced for their involvement in the trade by the Norwegian missionaries, who arrived in Morondava in 1876. The illegal trade became so

---

[5] Alpers describes a similar process of ethnogenesis in Mauritius, where East African slaves were known as "Mozambiques." E. A. Alpers, "Becoming Mozambique : Diaspora and Identity," unpublished paper presented to the Harriet Tubman Seminar, Department of History, York University, November 15, 1999.

[6] The term Merina was first appointed to people of Imerina Region Central Highlands of Madagascar and especially that around Antananarivo. At the end of the eighteenth century, the emergence of a united kingdom in this region is at the origin of a collective Merina identity. Today, Merina are 3, 5 million people out of a population of the island of 21 million people. For the construction of identity Merina, refer to the work of Pier Larson, *History and Memory in the age of enslavement. Becoming Merina in Highland Madagascar, 1770-1822*, Portsmouth, New Hampshire, Heinemann, 2000, p. 23.

[7] J. Lombard, *Le royaume sakalava du Menabe. Essai d'analyse d'un système politique à Madagascar* (Paris, 1988), 46.

[8] E. A. Alpers, "Madagascar and Mozambique in the Nineteenth Century: the Era of the Sakalava raids (1800–1820)," on microfiche by L'O.R.S.T.R.A.M (1977), 36–53. Also available in the University of Madagascar library collection, Omaly Sy Anio, 5–6.

[9] According to Campbell, between 1821 and 1890, at least 650,000 slaves were imported to Madagascar, of which perhaps 10% were re-exported, mostly to Reunion and Mayotte. Gwyn Campbell, "Madagascar and the Slave Trade, 1810-1895," *Journal of African History*, 22 (1981), 203-227.

large that many became convinced that only the liberation of all African slaves would end it. Different measures taken by the government under British pressure culminated in June 1877 in the collective emancipation of *Masombika* by Queen Ranavalona II. The 1877 liberation did not completely stop the trade, but it seems to have been effective in areas under Merina control like Morondava. Elsewhere in the west, in regions still independent where laws promulgated by Tananarive were not applied, Makua remained enslaved until 1896, when the definitive abolition of slavery in Madagascar was decreed by French colonizers.

There was a tendency for freed Makua slaves to regroup in new villages. At Morondava, the Makua village, Bemokijy, founded about 1880, was once called Morimabe (Big Morima). Makua oral traditions say that their ancestors were captured at Morima, somewhere in Africa, over the seas.[10] The story of capture suggests an earlier status; they were not born slaves, but became so in crossing the Mozambique channel. Thus, the centrality of the crossing in Makua oral history makes it possible for them to attach themselves to free origins. In the corpus of Makua oral traditions I have collected, the first part of the tale, a part of the traditions of origin is devoted to the journey of the ancestor. My research has been to first reconstruct the historical process of Makua journey, from Mozambique to Madagascar. The Mozambique channel also seems to be a frontier in the historiography: research in Portuguese and English is concerned almost exclusively with the African coast, but Makua oral sources create a bridge between the two sides of the Mozambique channel. The intersection of direct oral sources (testimonies) and indirect oral sources (traditions) enables us to reconstitute the different steps in the crossing by African slaves. In the Indian Ocean, the voice of enslaved persons comes to us essentially through testimonies collected by European functionaries during the height of abolitionist efforts.[11] Beside the different levels of mediation of these voices, they are submitted in pieces, in official transcripts or question-and-answer interrogations.[12] These testimonies, shaped by closed questions, describe brief episodes extracted from the larger story (which remains in the shadows). In contrast, the life histories present the lives of former slaves from birth in their country of origin until their death. These life histories often link oral sources to written missionary sources. The life histories of former slaves are often presented by missionaries – for example, by the Jesuits of Bagomoyo in East Africa and in Madagascar by Protestants in the Highlands.[13] The Makua life histories, which I am presenting here, were collected during the 1880s by the missionary Aas from the Norwegian Mission at Morondava in Western Madagascar.

[10] According to Schrive and Guenier: "Morima is understood as the east coast of Africa, including Mozambique or even the continent of Africa in general." M. Schrive and N. J. Guenier, "Histoire du peuple. Souvenirs sur the esclavage des Makoa du Nord de Madagascar," *Etudes Océan Indien*, 15 (1992), 196 n. 22.

[11] Alpers and Hopper underline the limits of such sources, the tales being very brief and made up of many layers of mediation, a result of the very approximate translation of these testimonies. E. A Alpers et M. S. Hopper, "Parler en son nom? Comprendre les témoignages d'esclaves africains originaires de l'océan indien (1850-1930)," *Annales HSS* (2008), 801.

[12] Interrogation of indentured children on January 13, 1880, by the Commandant of Mayotte. CAOM. mad.c.269 d. 601. See K. Boyer-Rossol "De Morima à Morondava: itinéraires d'ancêtres venus de l'au-delà des mers. Contribution à l'étude de la formation du groupe makoa (côte ouest de Madagascar au XIXe siècle)," in D. Nativel and F. Rajaonah (eds.) *Madagascar et l'Afrique* (Paris, 2007), 183–217. See also the attached documents.

[13] For example, the life history of Isambo from the manuscripts of Walen. See N. J. Guernier, F. Noiret, and S. Raharinjanahary, "L'histoire de l'asservissement et de la redemption d'Isambo ou Aogosta Herman Franke, 1877-1893, d'après les manuscrits Walen," in *Hommage à Bruno Hübsch* (Lyon, 2006), 69–178.

THE NORWEGIAN MISSION IN WEST MADAGASCAR

The Norwegian Missionary Society, founded in 1842 by the Lutherans, sent its first missionaries to Antananarivo in 1866, four years after the reopening of the Kingdom of Madagascar to Christian missionaries. Between 1835 and 1861, the kingdom was closed and missionaries persecuted. In 1869, Queen Ranavalona II converted to Protestant Christianity and it became the state religion. Madagascar then became a vast field for evangelization contested by different missions. With the London Missionary Society influential in the highlands, the Norwegians, turned toward Sakalava areas in the west, only partly occupied by the Merina.

In 1874, the Norwegian Mission of the west founded its first station at Tulear, situated in southwest Sakalava. The Norwegians extended themselves northward to Morondava, building mission stations near Merina posts. Morondava was under the authority of the government of Antananarivo, represented by a governor, whose authority was scarcely extended outside the city. Even areas near the Merina garrisons were not safe. Western Madagascar was thus a difficult field for evangelization. In addition to the different climate and malaria, which decimated missionary families, the mission had to deal with Sakalava revolts against the Merina and the resultant pillage and raids.

Created in 1876, Morondava was one of five mission stations. It was constructed in a village, which came to be known as Betania, on a peninsula facing the port of Morondava, which had been a place where slaves were landed. The Norwegian missionaries denounced the illegal trade and attacked slavery, which flourished in an unstable region prone to slave raids. Although under Merina authority, the illegal trade persisted with the help of corrupt officers, provincial governors, and Creole traders. The trade even intensified between 1860 and 1870, the period when the ancestors of the Makua of Morondava arrived. We can date these arrivals from oral traditions and genealogies.

On June 20, 1877, the collective enfranchisement of the Masombika was announced. When Pastor L. Aas arrived in 1880, the newly liberated Makua were concentrated in villages several kilometers from the city on land provided for them by the queen's government. A mission station was founded there at Betela. With the Sakalava hostile to the evangelical message, the Norwegians concentrated on the Makua. The massive conversion of the Makua only reinforced Sakalava rejection of the evangelical message. Christianity was perceived as a religion of slaves, which was reinforced by Christian opposition to the ancestral cult and the success of Protestantism as the official religion of the Merina rulers.[14] Aas, who spent twenty-seven years in Madagascar, returning only occasionally to Norway, spent all these years as head of the mission in Morondava. During his first stay, from 1880 to 1889, he was surrounded by former slaves, either those who came from the Highlands or Makua, from whom he collected life histories.

LIFE HISTORIES OF JOSEF (KALAMBA) AND MIKAL

Context of writing the life histories

In his book, Aas devotes three chapters to the first Christians and native evangelists, symbols of the success of the mission in western Madagascar. Aas seems to have been asked to

---

[14] On these relations, see Archives Royales de Madagascar, Series III CC, and the church archives, Archives de Stavanger, Fonds AAs.

write something on the first evangelists and teachers, who could be presented as Christian models. Written in Norwegian, the book was directed at a public for which Madagascar seemed like a land of adventure plunged in paganism. Aas wanted to promote evangelization and to attract attention to the financial difficulties of the mission. The book was written after his definitive return to Norway.

The two life histories I have chosen were in a chapter on the training of the first evangelists in the first volume, devoted to the period from 1880 to 1889. They seem to have been written from several oral recitations, collected and transcribed during the decade when Aas trained about fifteen converts to become evangelists and teachers. Some were Sakalava, but most were from Highlands or Makua. Most of the first native Christians were not from Sakalava country. The Makua are still known as allies of foreigners, missionaries, and sometimes even the colonial administration. They brought precious assistance to the development of the Norwegian mission during a period of instability. With the area around the mission unsafe, Makua auxiliaries accompanied the missionaries in their exploration of neighboring areas, during which the former were often armed. During the 1880s, brigandage increased with the return of forced labour and recruitment by the government of Tananarive for the malagasy army during the first Franco-Merina war (1883–85). Many slaves were freed to become soldiers. The Masombika had been freed, but they were not allowed to leave the country and, as subjects of the queen, were available for forced labor. Provincial governors regularly pointed this out to Aas, who often had to suspend evangelization during labor levies. As Aas wrote, "Evangelisation was often interrupted. One day, the governor sent us a message indicating that all members of the Church should come to help construction of his new house and the cultivation of his rice fields. Then, I received another message from the governor asking us to send men from the Church to help unload a steamship loaded with military supplies."[15]

As co-religionists of the Merina sovereign, the Norwegians were very conciliatory toward the government of Tananarive. They supported the Kingdom of Antananarivo against the French, who were traditionally allied to the Sakalava kings who did not recognized the authority of Antananarivo. Power struggles were particularly manifest during this period. The new Makua converts exploited these power struggles to advance socially. The first Christians and the first to be literate were also the first salaried employees of the mission.[16] Payment in money was not insignificant in a society where the monetary economy was only beginning. Money given or loaned by the mission seemed like an instrument of emancipation; the evangelist Rainivony, a former malagasy slave, was able to purchase the freedom of himself and his family.[17] The Makua auxiliaries invested their income in improving their lands and in buying cattle, necessary for ancestral rites. Josef's account tells us that he was able to take advantage of mission education to become a teacher in a Makua village. His grandson also told us that he inherited from his ancestors land near the village. Comparing the life histories and Makua oral traditions raises the question of chronology. The bearers of oral traditions are the grandchildren and great-grandchildren of the ancestors who came from "beyond the seas" between 1860 and 1880. Only one old

---

[15] Aas, *Oplevelser*, 130.

[16] There is extensive correspondence with the auxiliaries in the Fonds Aas at the Norwegian Missionary Archives in Stavanger.

[17] Aas personally loaned Rainivony money for his redemption. Another evangelist, Rabe, served twelve years at the mission and with the money he saved was able to purchase his freedom. Aas, *ibid.*, 129–138.

man told us that his father came as a slave. We are therefore dealing with a history of a recent slave trade. The life histories of Josef and Mikal trace their journey in slavery from Mozambique to Madagascar, probably dating to the late 1860s. Pastor Aas collected these testimonies about twenty years after their arrival.

Of all the portraits of the first evangelists drawn up by Aas – seven in chapter 7 of volume 1 and seven more in chapter 6 of volume 2 – those of Josef and Mikal appear the most successful. They are the only ones that are full life histories with a proper structure and internal coherence, which suggests careful rewriting. The others in volume 1 reflect the subtitle, "Some images of life." The writing is disjointed and reflects no chronological order, the author only evoking some events or character traits of persons, chosen to illustrate their quality as model Christians. The last two portraits, those of Josef and Mikal, neatly display the richness of the testimonies. They are presented as a subchapter with photographs. They open with their birth and end with death, covering a period of fifty to seventy years.[18]

These life histories are integrated in a work that traces the story of the missionary, who was born in Norway in a modest and pious family. Aas uses the first-person narration throughout his work, introducing the third-person narration only in transmitting the life histories of his auxiliaries. The voices of Josef and Mikal are reintroduced through citations given within quotation marks. This raises the question of language. The work was written in Norwegian, but the testimonies were collected in Malagasy. Pastor Aas's notes, written over the years, were probably transcribed into malagasy.[19] Thus, we have a compilation of oral texts, collected over a decade, written down and then reconstituted as a life history. In evaluating the transformation of testimony into a biographic tale, we must take into account translation, which involves interpretation and reformulation, the author's voice masking that of the witness.[20] The account is shaped by the author, who has known the persons and participated in the events described. He cites his own writings and those of other Norwegian missionaries and their wives. We can ask what the scientific value of this is. We can also ask whether Aas is a missionary-ethnographer like other members of the Norwegian mission such as Lars Vig.[21] Vig also uses Malagasy autobiographies, but he was interested in malagasy custom and beliefs. By comparison, Aas does not present detailed description or analyses of malagasy customs. His approach is more that of a compiler of testimonies. The life histories Aas collected are not the object of his writing, but rather are used to illustrate the author's own life. They are presented in very personal terms. He speaks of the ties uniting his auxiliaries. Speaking of Mikal, we writes: "There are probably none of our brown and black friends in Sakalava country with whom I have shared as much sorrow and joy as with Mikal." Aas had baptized Mikal, a decisive step in the journey of this former slave because he then chose his new name. These ties were like ties of kinship, the missionary becoming a spiritual father of the converts, who he trained as teachers and evangelists. These narratives often display a swing of emotions:

> I remember the day when [Mikal] was still alive, when he offered his hand to my wife and
> myself to say good-bye: "Good-bye, father and mother, now we are on a beach beside a

---

[18] Josef lived around fifty years (1850–1903) and Mikal sixty-five (1850–1915).

[19] I could not consult the "Kopibok" of Pastor Aas in the Stavangar archives because it is in poor condition.

[20] Aas shows a certain distance from Josef's oral account. For example, he uses terms he considers more appropriate to describe events. Thus, the "army" of the Portuguese becomes a "troop."

[21] Sophie Blanchy, "Les archives lutherienne norvégiennes de Stavanger," *Terrain et archives*, November 15, 2006, or online at: http://lodel.imageson.org/terrainarchiv/document244.html (accessed August 4, 2011).

river with all of our memories before us; but our hope is that with Jesus, we will meet again beside the marvelous river of paradise on a blessed beach."

The numerous biblical references indicate that these narratives are part of missionary history. From a symbolic perspective, the portrait of Josef is that of the former slave become a model Christian, an example of the "work of Christ,"[22] and by extension, the Norwegian mission. If these tales appear particularly rich as sources for itineraries in the trade and in slavery, it is because this journey illustrates the spiritual path of these new converts.

THE NARRATIVES OF KALAMBA AND MIKAL: ITINERARIES OF THE SLAVE TRADE AND SLAVERY

Makua life histories present the major steps of the story: infancy in northwest Mozambique, capture, journey from the interior to slave trade port, crossing the Mozambique channel, arrival in western Madagascar, purchase and servitude, journeys within the region (flight) to Morondava, and liberation in June 20, 1877. The episode of capture is determinant because it illustrates forced migration. In Makua oral traditions, the organizers of this capture are presented as outside the captive's society. Traditions speak of Indians or Sakalava[23] having kidnapped Makua using ruses. There are, for example, stories of potential victims being attracted by the smell of meat being grilled on festive occasions and then captured. The life histories also report deception, but the persons involved were Makua, and sometimes even family members. Josef was delivered to the traders by his own parents.

Makua oral traditions leave out the journey from the interior to the coast and do not speak of June 20, 1877. More generally, Makua oral traditions remain silent about the experience of slavery. This silence is broken by the voices of the ancestors. Josef and Mikal speak about the servile experience, which extends more than twenty years. Because these narratives are part of missionary literature in an abolitionist context, they stress the suffering of the slaves. Physical and psychic violence is omnipresent in these tales, from the interior (Josef speaks of atrocities committed on the Asiko), the use of terror as in the myth of cannibalism, and the traumatizing experience of crossing the sea to the cruelty of masters, whether Arab, African, Malagasy, or European. African captives were deported from a society being ravaged by internal wars and slave raids. They were brought to the declining Sakalava kingdom, where they experienced domination maintained by the use of violence.

Josef tried several times to flee his masters, but did not succeed. His testimony shatters the myth of the mildness of Malagasy slavery. He is constantly exposed to death. The episode of the ordeal displays institutionalized violence. He is threatened with death by the same government that liberated him. The true liberation at the end of this journey was his baptism. Symbol of rebirth, Kalamba chose the name of Josef, the only identity that was not assigned to him. The change of name from Kalamba to Mahihitse, his slave name to Josef is representative of the changes of identity in this journey, identities that do not exclude but, on the contrary, coexist.[24] The title of this narrative, "Josef," is revealing. Aas is

---

[22] "If someone asks what changed such a miserable appearance into a child of peace, I respond 'It is the work of Christ.'" Aas, *Oplevelser*, 179.

[23] Sakalava raided the north coast of Mozambique during the first two decades of the nineteenth century, but the ancestors of the makua oral traditions bearers I interwied, were deported from Mozambique to Madagascar in a later period, during the second part of the XIXe century.

[24] S. Ramaka, who translated the original text from Norwegian to Malagasy, used the title "Kalambe Mahihitse Josef." The author of this chapter has this translation on file.

presenting the life history of one of the mission's first Christians, which influences how we see his itinerary. Seen in the perspective of a spiritual journey, the major steps are capture in Africa, deportation to Madagascar, enslavement, the search for God in the reading of the Bible, and liberation by conversion and baptism.[25] The journey is thus presented as a beneficial experience. Mikal "recalled to the Makua (who were now freed slaves) the affection the Lord had shown them in leading them to Madagascar to receive the <u>Gospel of Jesus Christ</u> while their poor families still in the country of origin had not heard of the Salvation of Christ."[26]

It is difficult to present slavery and the slave trade as "blessings" to those who lived it. Mikal is trying to calm the ardor of the Makua of Morondava to return to their country of origin. Missionary sources suggest the desire of the Makua to return. They even solicited through the first evangelists, Josef and Mikal, the intercession of the mission to support their request. It seems that the missionaries did not really respond to their attempt, there being no trace of correspondence on the matter. It was impossible for the Merina authorities to accede to such a request. After the liberation of Makombika in 1878, a new edict prohibited the freed slaves from leaving the kingdom. One of the other Makua evangelists, Samuel, confided to Jacobsen his nostalgia for his homeland, but this was not cited by Aas. It was only mentioned.[27] Thus, behind these Makua life histories, the trace of other voices comes to us, voices that speak of their desire to reverse the crossing, to return "over the seas."

QUESTIONS TO CONSIDER

1. What are the major stages in the process of enslavement? Put the two documents in perspective and define the general texture of the tales.
2. What do these tales tell us about the servile experience and the different forms of resistance?
3. What do the voices of these enslaved persons tell us? Distinguish between that which comes from the author's pen and that which comes from the oral testimony of the persons themselves – for example, the presentation of text in a direct style, the testimony of the author, and the testimony of the enslaved persons.

THE LIFE HISTORIES OF JOSEF AND MIKAL

Josef[28]

His native country was the area where the highlands begin, far from the Mozambique Channel. His father was named Anarabia and his mother Ameniko. At the time of their removal from this place, they had four children, three boys and a girl. They were pagan; they

---

[25] Jacobsen, another missionary, reported of another convert: "I have already heard how slaves were trapped over there in Africa, the voyage to the coast, then how he was sold to several masters, finally how he sought God and became a Christian." Letter from Jacobsen, written in 1880 and cited in Aas, *Oplevelser*, 162.

[26] Aas, *Oplevelser*, 189.

[27] According to Jacobsen, Samuel said: "He missed Africa very much, as much as other Makua did. We could write a lot on this subject and their attempts to return to their native country." Aas, *Oplevelser*, 162.

[28] This is taken from Aas, *Oplevelser*, 166–181. Because of the length of the text, we have shortened it, selecting the most pertinent passages. Bracketed ellipses indicate that a passage was removed from the text. Terms in parentheses were so indicated in the Norwegian text.

did not know the true God. There was a great circumcision celebration and several fathers were there with their children and Josef's older brother was also there. It was about 30 or 40 kilometers from their house and his father had strictly forbidden Josef's brother to go there, but he went with another boy, walking stealthily. En route, they were captured by bandits. His parents tried several times to recover their oldest son, but the brigands would not free him without having a slave in his place. His parents were not willing to lose their oldest son. "Because," they said, "it is he who will bury us when we die and make sacrifices for us to the gods of our ancestors." They sent a message to the bandits, but without results.

Then, his mother had the idea of putting another of their children, the youngest, in his place, which the father approved. They thus asked the bandits to exchange the biggest boy for the youngest, which was accepted. Josef – Kalamba was then his name – was chosen by his parents to be sent to the bandits in place of his older brother, but no one wanted to take him to the bandits. His parents then sent him to his grandmother, who lived far away. His grand-mother sent him out to play with other children and trap birds on the slopes of a mountain. While the children were playing, a strong strapping man named Neoala, sent by Josef's parents, arrived and seized him, put him on his shoulders and took him to the bandits. No one paid any attention to the cries and supplications of the child.

"When I arrived near the brigand camp, there was a large crowd assembled," Josef explains. "A group that I knew from the village of my parents was there also, and all were armed. They sent a message to the bandits who dispatched an armed force with my older brother to negotiate the exchange. I cried and my older brother also cried when he saw that I was to take his place, but tears had no influence here. The exchange was carried out, they shook hands,[29] and then returned to the house with my older brother while I was led to the bandit's camp."

He spent two weeks with the bandits. He met a boy who was taken prisoner with his older brother. He was chained, while Josef, who was only a child of probably seven or eight, had to guard the house and the chained boy. After two weeks Josef was sold to a local king who gave him to a wife in his royal palace. This woman was to raise him and keep him as her son. He was with her for about four months, until a large force (he called it an army) sent by the Portuguese came to capture slaves. When they approached the royal palace, the king sent them a message: "We do not want to fight you; we wish peace and will give you this slave, 'Kalamba,' if you leave us alone."

The slave hunters took Kalamba and continued to ravage and pillage village by village, assembling a large number of people. The boy already mentioned, chained under the surveillance of Kalamba, was exchanged for another boy just as Josef was traded for his older brother, and Josef never saw him again. The assembled humans (slaves) were tied to each other and moved like a herd of sheep, while they left Kalamba, who had become known to them and for whom they had a little pity, to march alongside like an errand boy. He had to look for water and food like a servant.

He told the most horrible stories of the march with these men. For example, there was an episode during their war against the tribe of "Asiko." One day they arrived at a city which resisted so fiercely that the band sent to capture it was repelled. A stronger force was then sent with orders to kill all of the inhabitants except the children, who were to be captured as

---

[29] He means that Josef shook hands with his brother. The author has simply shifted to the third-person singular.

slaves. The "Asiko" were defeated and killed one after another after the most horrible torture. They cut the ear of the first and asked him to eat it. Before he could do so, he was killed and after him the others. Only one, who had been shot and who they believed dead, succeeded in fleeing. He remained as if dead until they moved away a little and then he fled, which led these barbarians to take many of the bodies and cut them up, spreading their intestines on the field while saying "We will do this to anyone who tries to flee." Thus they continued across the region. They tied the lips of some, children were cut up and they said "This is what we will do to those who resist us."

Then, they burned a house full of slaves from a nearby village saying that they did not want slaves from such a resisting population. "After this terrible and frightening spectacle and after gathering slaves elsewhere, they left," he said "with us for a long and difficult trip during which some died of hunger, thirst and fatigue. Finally, the slave hunters stopped and asked who could no longer continue. Some responded that they couldn't. They were gathered with small children who had become difficult and four or five of them were put on top of each other and killed with knives. After several were killed in this way, the head of the procession asked if there were others who wanted to die this way."

After eight days of difficult march, they arrived at the city of the slave hunters and told the chief or king, Moloko of their exploits and the results of the voyage [30] "And here," they said, is a boy given to us by a king who wanted forgiveness and peace, welcome him as if he was one of your own.

"Yes," answered Moloko. "I wish to sacrifice him in gratitude for our victory. I wish to spread the blood of this boy on the fetish to thank it for our continuous victory. I will give his body to my hunting dogs so that they will be sanctified and satisfied by this boy."

"Oh King," said the slave hunter, "we have begun to like Kalamba and don't want him to be sacrificed. If you do not want to keep him for yourself, we ask that you return him." "Yes then, take him as yours," said king Moloko. Then, they took him to Sarangaen (a port) Sangotse in southern Mozambique,[31] where he was sold and deported in a boat full of slaves: men, women and children.

The suffering on this voyage was terrible, he said, because they lacked food and water. Some slaves jumped into the sea to kill themselves not only because they suffered from lack of food but because of the rumor that the Malagasy ate people. Evil persons in the crew amused themselves by spreading rumors that fat slaves were sold at a high price, but no one was interested in skinny ones. The crew was Makua, which meant that the slaves could speak to the crew without the Arab proprietor and captain understanding them, but at the same time, the crew spoke enough Malagasy to communicate with the Arabs.[32]

After five days, they reached Maintirano, on the west coast of Madagascar where the slave trade flourished. Maintirano was a center of the slave trade. There, Kalamba was sold to an Arab named Ranapake,[33] who gave him the new name Mahihitse, which means

---

[30] *Muluku* means God in Makua.

[31] Angoche, south of Mozambique Island, was a preferred port for slaves being sent to Madagascar.

[32] These Makua slaves sailors spoke some malagasy and could also speak the language of the Est African slaves. The malagasy appears as a maritime lingua franca, whereas this kind of emakhuwa spoken between the two ranks of the Mozambique Channel, appears as a servile language. It is significant all the same that the Makua crew, slaves themselves, scared the captives in making them believe that they were going to be eaten by the Malagasy. The Makua sailors involved in keeping the captives in fear and aloneness, while appearing as the only intermediaries with the foreign country.

[33] This is a Malagasy name.

wise.[34] He remained eight years with this master and he suffered a lot because Ranapake treated his slaves harshly.

One night, two of the slaves, Mahihitse (Kalamba) and another, who later became a Christian at Morondava under the name Obeda, fled. After three days, they reached Tsiribihy[35] where King Itoera[36] received them, but after a month, sold them to an Arab named Bakary. The sale was decided by the king without telling them and Bakary came immediately to say he had bought them from King Itoera and asked if they would be loyal to him. They both responded unhappily that they had suffered for so long with Arabs that they hoped he would sell them to someone else. When Bakary heard that, he led them to the seashore saying that he was looking for something, but when they arrived at the shore, they understood that Bakary had sold them to a French man, the old L.L., who was the most important merchant on the West coast. He was about to leave with a boat loaded with slaves for Morombe,[37] somewhat south of Sakalava country, from which they would be transported elsewhere in the world.[38] The two were immediately put into chains. As the winds were not favorable and the captain fell sick, they remained chained on the boat for three days.

One night while the guard slept, they succeeded in freeing themselves from their chains. They tried to slip away noiselessly, but in a careless moment, the item they used to detach the chains fell in the water. The noise woke the guard, who said "ino ety? (What's that?)." "A piece of wood has fallen in the water," Mahihitsy said to him. The guard fell asleep again and they fled by swimming. It was far and they had to swim against the current of the Menabe river outside Tsimanandrafoza,[39] which was against them. It was with difficulty that they reached the shore.

[…] Our two friends ended up at Ambiky with King Itoera, who sent a message to L.L. saying that these two slaves had returned to Ambiky. When they heard that L.L. was returning, they fled to King Tsiately.[40]

[…] L.L. was very angry because Itoera had let the slaves escape. Itoera then sent a message with one of his men, who went to Tsiately with a pound of gold to recover his slaves.

They were now put back in chains and brought to Morondava where L.L. took them on and put them to work. Mahihitse and another, who has also become a Christian named Jeremias, were to take a boat, while Obeda had another job. On the coast, near Maintirano, they were shipwrecked and the Sakalava stole everything on the boat, even taking their clothes.[41] They were completely nude. They were tired and hungry when they reached

---

[34] It also means intelligent.

[35] Tsiribihy designates the Tsiribihina River in the region of Menabe, the site of Sakalava royal capitals.

[36] Toera was the last Sakalava king to resist the French, who eventually beheaded him. He reigned in North Menabe, just south of Maintirano. Slaves often fled to nearby kings, who gave them a sort of protection. Only the reigning king had the right of life or death over his subjects. These flights led to a change of master, not of status.

[37] This is in southwest Madagascar.

[38] Not only was Morombe involved in regional trade, but this Sakalava port was involved in international trade networks. In the nineteenth century, the export and import trades coexisted, the two currents linked together. In this case, Makua slaves, who had already spent ten years in Madagascar, were to be re-exported elsewhere.

[39] Tsimanandrafozana was an old Sakalava port in northern Menabe, a short distance from Toera's royal capital. The two captives then tried to go upriver toward the interior.

[40] A Sakalava king near Toera.

[41] Kalamba, in his servile activities, reverses the route he took as a chained captive. This shows the internalization of the slave condition. Kalamba does not seem to have used these sea voyages to try again to escape.

Maintirano where they learned that L.L. was dead and that M.L.L. had inherited them. With M.L.L., Mahihitse was to endure a harsh test. One day, [...] jealous people accused him, telling M.L.L., that Mahitse had a large knife, with which he wanted to kill M.L.L. Without interrogating him, M.L.L. sent a message to the Hova (Merina) of the customs station to take Mahihitse in chains to the Hova fortress of Andakabe.[42] For a long time, he had scars on his arms and feet because the rope was so tight. The Hovas knew well how to immobilize someone. They tied the knots so tightly it caused suffering. And when an unfortunate complained of the pain and cried, the officers and soldiers coolly told him: "Don't cry, it is the government's will,"[43] and they tightened even more until he became blue and bloody.

The inquiry at Andakabe was odd. The Governor, the old Rainitsianoro told him: "We will shoot at you from a short distance with a revolver that has eight bullets, and if no bullet touches you, you will be innocent, but if you are wounded or if you die, you will be guilty."

Mahihitse (Kalamba) responded: "I have neither a defence nor a father or mother who can take care of me. Do with me as you wish, but I am innocent of the charges against me." They responded that they would await the master's order before executing the decision. His master came the next day and when asked by Rainitsianoro what he should do with his slave Mahihitse, he replied that Mahihitse was in their power, but that it was unacceptable for them to release a slave who wanted to kill his master.[44] With such a response, there was no solution but to condemn him to death. Mahihitse understood everything while he was in his cell. The guard told him that they said "Tomorrow, you will be killed." But that night, while the guard slept, he fled, but he could not leave the fort without passing through a cactus enclosure, which gravely wounded his naked body.

He eventually reached a person named Piera (Piera also later became a Christian), who hid him in a sugar plantation near the present site of Bethel.[45] Later, he left and went a half-day north to Ambato, where Obeda took him to his master, who in seeing him, said: "The Hovas have not killed you. I also do not wish to do so. Obeda, give him work." But then the Hova order freeing the Makua slaves was announced and Mahihitse was free! Ranavalona's 1877 order on the liberation of African slaves was observed, at least in Hova districts.

The missionaries Jakobsen and Rostvig had just begun their work at Morondava and tell the story that one day, Mahihitse saw Rostvig listening to a Hova reading the Bible and Rostvig asked Mahihitse if he understood what was being read. "No, how can I understand when no one is teaching me," was Mahihitse's response.[46]

[...]

In my years at Morondava, from 1880, I do not think he ever missed a service without good reason. The day of Pentecost, 1 June 1879, he was baptized and chose Josef as his Christian name.

Back home, we learned from Brother Aarnes and our native Pastor Petro of Bethel that Josef had become so sick that he was withdrawn from Antsakamirohake, where he was teacher and evangelist the last three years and brought to Bethel.[47] My wife and I thought

---

[42] Hova is another term for the Merina, who had occupied Morondava and erected a customs post there.

[43] These soldiers were obedient to the queen and the government in Tananarive.

[44] There are several levels of power: the Tananarive government, the Sakalava king, and the master.

[45] Makua oral traditions preserve the name of Piera as one of the founders of a village near the missionary station of Bethel.

[46] In the Acts of the Apostles, this was the Ethiopian's response to Philip. Kalamba thus takes on the role of the African disciple.

[47] Bethel was the name of a new mission station east of Morondava and surrounded by Makua villages.

that we would never again see him alive. When we reached Morondava, we tried to see if Josef was among the many Christians and pagans who came to meet us, but we did not see him. We saw him when we reached Bethel where he was fighting with his last enemy – death. He was so thin that he resembled a skeleton, but peace radiated from his face. At our arrival, many Christians gathered together to comfort him with a song. He asked us to pray for the love and force of God for him in order to triumph with Jesus Christ. We prayed for that.

This happened the third Sunday of Advent. He remained in bed suffering until January 5. Then he was able to return. During my last visit, he could no longer speak, but he pointed to heaven to indicate his hope in God and his wish to be received on high. He went to sleep like a child and was buried at Betania on 6 January 1903. He was about 50 years old.

It was strange the Day of Epiphany to see a large funeral cortege fill the church at Bethel and come to see the body of our deceased friend – his visage was covered with divine peace and to hear first what was said by Brother Aarnes. I gave the funeral oration, which I did in commenting on the words of Our Lord: "The death of saints is dear to the Lord," (Salame 116, 15).

The Evangelist Mikal

The evangelist Mikal was one of the best-known persons among native Christians in Sakalava country.[48] He was born in Matatani[49] in the high lands of Africa, two and a half days journey from the Mozambique channel. His father was named Anambatry and his mother Tschemo.[50] They had two children, a boy and a girl. Tamaman was the name of the son. Their father had only one wife, though he was chief of a tribe that ruled many people. He had a great reputation and as a non-believer probably followed the laws of his fathers. No one had yet spoken to him of the one true God. Anambatry, who was also a diligent farmer, injured his foot one day while planting. He developed gangrene and died. His daughter also died. Tschemo was all alone with her son Tamaman. About a year later, slave hunters came and ravaged the area, taking many people. Tschemo fled with her son and went to live near the sea, but after half a year, she was dead as an effect of the flight and the boy was taken in by a relative. Soon after, he was stolen when someone who claimed to be a good friend of his father and mother took him to a nearby city for a "visit." There the boy was sold to a Portuguese slave trader, who quickly sold to an Arab slave ship owner before his family could get together and reclaim him. The slave ship was at Sangotsy, south of Mozambique city, full of slaves and ready to leave the next day. He described the suffering of crossing the Mozambique channel as unspeakable. They were almost nude and lacked water and food. They arrived at Baly, south of Mojanga, after four men died of hunger and thirst.[51]

At Baly, he remained for a year with an Arab. Then the Arab took him to Maintirano to sell him, but the prospective purchaser did not have the sum he wanted and he took him to Morondava where he was sold for 30 dollars to a powerful Sakalava man. The latter then sold him for 40 cattle, a high price for a slave. This is because he was no longer a boy, but a man in the prime of youth. He remained for five years at Maharivo, but then he was sold at Morondava, where after a year, he was liberated by the decision of Queen Ranavalona to free all African slaves.

---

[48] The term "native" can be confusing because Mikal was not born in Madagascar, but in Mozambique.
[49] Matatani is in northern Mozambique, south of Mozambique Island.
[50] This is a Malagasy rendering of their names.
[51] Baly was an important Sakalava slave trade port in the northwest, outside the area of Merina control.

Because he had passed from one master to another as a slave, he felt at home in Sakalava customs and above all, he had adopted their pagan beliefs. From his arrival at Maharivo, he was considered a priest and a respectable pagan doctor.[52] At Morondava, he became a district chief and had the authority of a judge in the Malagasy system. I saw this as a good thing when the parish grew to have an important man in the church so we could say to Christians to hold *kabary*[53] with him rather than with pagan big men.

[...]

Because of his advanced age – he was almost 40 years old – it was difficult for him to get the knowledge he sought, but through perseverance he improved himself so much that I was able on 1 January 1883 to accept him for sacred baptism in the church with two of his children.[54] At baptism, he chose the name of Mikal and for his children, the names of Daniel and Elisabeth.

[...]

The conversion of Mikal to Christianity brought a great change to the pagans in his entourage. Several of them asked to whom they should now address themselves as they felt abandoned by their *Ombiasy* or priest for offerings. "Turn toward those to whom I address myself, turn to the living God," was Mikal's response. Many took his advice and he was thus a large part of the missionary work at Morondava, perhaps more than any other man, particularly at Bethel, where he lived the most.

[...]

Mikal was in some ways the opposite of Josef. While Josef was a quiet Christian, Mikal was always less calm and perhaps gave to those who knew him the impression of being proud, which is the reason I was always firm with him. This boisterous manner changed with the years and now he completely gives the impression of being a humble Christian.

[...]

After a while, he had the esteem and confidence of the church. He was chosen as an evangelist and remained in that position until his death. Mme. Fagereng[55] wrote about him: "Mikal died several months ago. He worked until a lung infection took him from us. His eldest son Daniel died a little bit earlier. I hope that they will both have a place in the home of the Father up there."

Yes, when he was 70, Mikal had finished his work. We will miss him. He died 10 November 1915. There is probably no person among our brown and black friends with whom I have shared as much sorrow and joy as with Mikal. That is why it was strange to say *au revoir* on the beach where the Morondava River ends. I remember the day while he was still living when he gave his hand to my wife and myself to say good-bye. He said: "Good-bye father and mother. We are now on the beach beside the river with all of our memories facing us; but it is our hope that with Jesus, we will meet again beside the marvelous river of paradise on the blessed beach."

---

[52] Mikal was considered as an *ombiasy*, a diviner-healer.

[53] *Kabary* were meetings held by traditional chiefs to regulate conflicts in the community. The word means discourse.

[54] Baptism appears to have been the result of a long personal journey, which included apprenticeship in the Bible and renewal of his vow to become Christian. Protestant missionaries were stricter than the Catholics in the amount of knowledge of the faith expected of new converts.

[55] Wife of a missionary.

SUGGESTED ADDITIONAL READINGS

Alpers E. A. et M. S. Hopper. "Parler en son nom? Comprendre les témoignages d'esclaves africains originaires de l'océan indien (1850-1930)," *Annales HSS* (2008) : 799-828.

Boyer-Rossol K. "De Morima à Morondava : itinéraires d'ancêtres venus de l'au-delà des mers. Contribution à l'étude de la formation du groupe makoa (côte ouest de Madagascar au XIXᵉ siècle)." In *Madagascar et l'Afrique*. Edited by D. Nativel and F. Rajaonah (Paris: Karthala, 2007), 183-217.

Campbell G., "Madagascar and the Slave Trade, 1810-1895," *Journal of African History*, 22, (1981): 203-227.

Gueunier, N. J., F. Noiret, and S. Raharinjanahary. "Esclavage et liberté sur les Hautes Terres à la fin du XIXe siècle. L'histoire de l'asservissement et de la rédemption d'Isambo ou Aogosta Herman Franke, 1877-1893, d'après les manuscrits Walen." In *Hommage à Bruno Hübsch*. Edited by C. R. Ratongavao (Lyon: Profac, 2006), 69-178.

Schrive M., and N.-J. Gueunier. "Histoire du peuple. Souvenirs sur l'esclavage des Makoa du Nord de Madagascar," *Etudes Océan Indien*, 15 (1992): 177-197.

PART EIGHT

DOCUMENTS FROM MUSLIM AFRICA

41   INTRODUCTION: Islamic Sources

Islam arrived in Africa soon after its establishment in seventh-century Arabia. For more than a thousand years, it has been slowly expanding, bringing with it Islamic law and Arabic literacy. Consequently, there is a rich variety of sources in Arabic or in African languages written in Arabic script. Some of these sources have long been used by historians of Africa – for example, the writings of Arabic travelers and geographers, and chronicles collected by explorers and colonial officials. Muslim scholars and state-builders also left large numbers of documents. From the 1960s, there were efforts by historians to search for or uncover more documents. From the turn of the twenty-first century, the quest for documents has shifted to the Sahara, where many noble families had thousands of documents stored in trunks or leather sacks. For example, the Ahmed Baba Institute in Timbuktu, the largest of many Saharan research centers, has 30,000 of these documents.[1]

Two of the documents presented in this part of the volume were the first fruits of this research in recently uncovered documents. They are not the writings of scholars or statesmen, but rather documents that tell us something about everyday life in the Sahara. They are unusual in that each in its way contains a slave voice. Ghislaine Lydon in Chapter 43 gives us a legal case in which a slave was able to get protection from the law and, remarkably, the person who brought the case that protected him was a woman. Islam brought with it the rule of law, which was particularly important in an area like the Sahara, where political authority was widely diffused. Law regulated not only relations between people from different areas, but also between different social strata, and in this case provided some protection for a slave who had been mistreated. Bruce Hall and Yacine Daddi Addoun (Chapter 42) provide us with another kind of documentation, letters exchanged by a merchant family and a slave who traded on their behalf. Anjay was trusted enough to be given important commercial missions, but the language he used in dealing with his masters suggests limitations to his autonomy.

There is a lot of Arabic documentation in colonial archives, such as legal judgments of Muslim judges and correspondence between European and Muslim authorities. Elisabeth McMahon in Chapter 44 presents slave wills she found in probate records on the island of Pemba in the Sultanate of Zanzibar. These wills were written in Arabic by a paid scribe and were usually signed with a thumbprint. According to the 1897 Zanzibar Abolition of Slavery decree, masters no longer had rights to the possessions of slaves, but some continued to claim such rights. The wills slaves left illustrate strategies designed to increase their autonomy and protect the rights of their heirs.

[1] John Hunwick and Alida Jay Boye, *The Hidden Treasures of Timbuktu* (London, 2008).

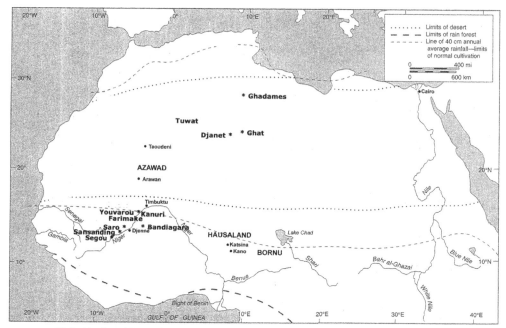

42.1. North and West Africa with major towns.

42 | The Arabic Letters of Ghadames Slaves in the Niger Bend, 1860–1900

BRUCE S. HALL AND YACINE DADDI ADDOUN

In this chapter, ten letters are presented that were either written by slaves, or addressed to slaves, in their role as commercial agents in the Niger Bend region of West Africa during the second half of the nineteenth century. It is a correspondence centered around two literate Muslim slaves who belonged to the same master, and who referred to themselves as brothers. The older of the two was named Ṣanbu ʿĪsā and the younger Anjay ʿĪsā. Both carried the name of their master, a man from the northern Saharan oasis of Ghadames (in present-day western Libya), who was known as ʿĪsā b. Ḥmīda b. Muḥammad b. Mūsā b. Muʿizz al-Shaʿwānī al-Ghadāmisī.[1] The master ʿĪsā b. Ḥmīda was the head of a family-based commercial network that connected the Sahara desert with the Sudanic region of the Niger Valley in present-day Mali. He established a household in the town of Timbuktu (Mali) in the 1850s, from where he organized trade that linked the Saharan sellers of products such as salt, tobacco, and textiles with the Sudanic commerce in gold, foodstuffs, textiles, kola nuts, ostrich feathers, and slaves. What makes these letters so remarkable is less the content of the individual letters themselves, which are often focused on matters of accounting and market conditions, than the evidence that they provide of literate slaves playing a crucial role as agents in the commercial networks of precolonial West Africa.[2] These letters open a window on relatively autonomous and high-status slaves living in the circum-Saharan world of the nineteenth century. Sources of this kind will allow us to add new stories to the history of slavery in Africa.

The most striking thing about this correspondence, and the aspect that first caught our attention while looking through nineteenth-century documents concerning slavery held at the important archive of Arabic-language manuscripts in Timbuktu,[3] was the degree of

[1] ʿĪsā's nisba "al-Shaʿwānī" suggests that he, or his ancestors, were not from the town of Ghadames itself, but from a smaller town called Shaʿwā (in present-day Libya), approximately 150 km to the north east of Ghadames. The earliest dated letter that mentions ʿĪsā in Timbuktu is from 1851 (Institut des Hautes Etudes et de Recherche Islamique Ahmad Baba, Timbuktu, Mali [IHERIAB], ms. 8244).

[2] James Richardson noticed that slaves in the Saharan towns of Ghadames and Ghat (Libya) were sometimes sent south across the desert to act as commercial agents for their masters. See his *Travels in the Great Desert of Sahara, in the Years of 1845 and 1846* (London, 1851), 260. Charles Monteil remarked on a similar phenomenon in which slaves played an important role in commercial networks based in Djenné (Mali). See his *Une cite soudanaise: Djenné, métropole du delta central du Niger* (Paris, 1932), 261–262.

[3] The archive is part of research institute in Timbuktu called the Institut des Hautes Etudes et de Recherche Islamique Ahmad Baba (IHERIAB), which was formerly known as the Centre de Documentation et de la Recherche Ahmad Baba (CEDRAB). We first came across examples of letters from this correspondence in

rhetorical respect accorded to the slave Anjay ʿĪsā by his interlocutors. In one of his letters to Anjay, his master ʿĪsā b. Ḥmīda begins as follows: "From ʿĪsā b. Ḥmīda with full and generous greetings (bi-ʾl-salām al-atamm al-akram) to his slave (ghulām) Anjay…"[4] In correspondence from his master's sons, written in the 1880s and 1890s, we find repeated usage of the following salutary formula at the beginning of the letters: "From Aḥmad al-Bakkāy b. ʿĪsā b. Ḥmīda to his brother and friend, and only then his slave (ghulām) Anjay, greetings to you and your family."[5] The language of greeting is even more familiar in some of the correspondence with Anjay's business associates in the Niger Bend region. One example is as follows: "Full greetings and general respects from Bāba b. al-Shaykh Kumu to his beloved, and his brother, Anjay…"[6] In this last letter, and in others like it, there is no mention of Anjay's status as a slave, although this might be understood from the fact that no father or lineage is invoked after his name. Finally, Anjay is represented as a paragon of virtue in letters written by other slaves. For example, in a letter written by a certain al-Barka, who describes himself as the slave of Shaʿbān the cutler,[7] we have the following elaborate greeting at the beginning:

> From the beloved and respectful brother al-Barka, slave (ghulām) of Shaʿbān the cutler, to his beloved, excellent, honored brother – the most blessed (al-abrak), the most refined (al-adīb), the most distinguished (al-nabīh), the most highly esteemed (al-aʿazz), he who has surpassed his mates, a shining light for the people of his time; may God help us and him – Unghī [Anjay] ʿĪsā. Greetings to you and to everyone with you.[8]

The tone here goes far beyond the formula of greetings and praises. There is no mention of Anjay's status as a slave. However, the use of the language of "brotherhood" suggests that the writer, who identifies himself as a slave (ghulām), shared the same social status as Anjay.

These letters march us down the stairs of social status in the Ghadames commercial network. They are simultaneously friendly and familiar, frequently using the language of consanguinity, while also reinscribing the servile status of those who are identified as slaves. It may be possible to see in some of these letters indications of the personal qualities of the recipients, at least in the minds of the letter writers. So for example, it seems clear that al-Barka holds Anjay in high personal esteem. The language used seems to be much more than formulaic flattery, although it is also that. However, in using the familial language of "brotherhood," while at the same time identifying himself as a slave, al-Barka displays a level of social familiarity that one would not find in letters written between social unequals. Likewise, in the letters written by Anjay's master, the relatively simple greetings indicate the social status difference between writer and addressee. The letters written by ʿĪsā's sons maintain the distinction of social status by calling Anjay the slave of their father,

2001 while we were both at the Institute. There are more than 1,000 letters from the Ghadames commercial network held at IHERIAB, and hundreds more in private libraries. All manuscripts referred to in this chapter are from IHERIAB.

4   Letter from ʿĪsā b. Ḥmīda to Anjay ʿĪsā (IHERIAB ms. 5453).
5   Letter from Aḥmad al-Bakkāy b. ʿĪsā to Anjay ʿĪsā (IHERIAB ms. 11690); there are many examples of this formula used in letters written by Aḥmad al-Bakkāy b. ʿĪsā.
6   IHERIAB ms. 10333.
7   It may be that the scribe is the one who is describing him in this way. See later discussion.
8   IHERIAB ms. 10471.

while at the same time they indicate a respect for Anjay's age as an older person whom they had grown up around.

It is possible that the self-identification as slaves came not from the slaves themselves, but from a scribe who wrote some of the letters. The nineteenth-century Niger Bend was a partially literate society, and many people were able to read and write in Arabic to some extent. But even if this region had a relatively high level of literacy compared to most other parts of sub-Saharan Africa at that time, there was still a significant demand for scribes, letter writers, and letter readers who provided their services to the majority of the population that was either not literate at all or limited in this respect. These skills were especially in demand in the market towns of the region where long-distance communication was so important to the functioning of commercial networks.[9] The handwriting of al-Barka's letter to Anjay suggests that the writer was not al-Barka himself, but a copyist. One letter written by another slave belonging to ʿĪsā b. Ḥmīda named Ibrāhīm ʿĪsā credits the actual writing of the letter to a scribe named Muḥammad Yintāwū, whose name is sometimes written "Ṣintāwu" in other letters, and who is frequently greeted in this correspondence. Judging from the handwriting, the same few scribes did much of the actual letter writing for some of these slaves.[10]

But it is clear that Ṣanbu ʿĪsā and Anjay ʿĪsā wrote their own letters, at least some of the time. In the case of Ṣanbu there is a clear difference in handwriting, language style, and uses of colloquial Arabic expressions in the letters that he wrote himself and those that were written by scribes. Ṣanbu's written Arabic was much less literary than that of the scribes. Anjay, on the other hand, was a more sophisticated writer of literary Arabic, and his letters do not betray colloquial expressions in the same way that Ṣanbu's writing does. When he died in Timbuktu in the first decade of the twentieth century, the executers of his possessions listed thirteen Arabic books that were found in his house. While such a collection is hardly unusual or outstanding for its time and place, it does indicate that Anjay had a level of sophistication in the areas of Islamic law, Arabic grammar, and devotional literature.[11] That a slave would possess these texts is surprising and suggests a level of education well beyond what we would expect slaves to possess.

The literacy and education of certain slaves made them valuable to their masters. It seems likely that the slaves were educated as children so that they could work as commercial agents when they became older. Masters encouraged their slaves to marry and have children because it bound slaves more closely into the affairs of their masters' family, and because it led to the biological reproduction of their workforce. Ṣanbu and Anjay both married and established families in Timbuktu (Ṣanbu's wife was named Kani, Anjay's wife was named Bintu).[12] The Arabic word that we have been translating as "slave" is "ghulām." The other term of self-identification that appears in one of the letters presented later in the chapter is "surriya," which we have translated as "concubine," from a letter from Yājīda,

---

[9] Ghislaine Lydon, *On Trans-Saharan Trails: Islamic Law, Trade Networks, and Cross-Cultural Exchange in Nineteenth-Century Western Africa* (Cambridge, 2009), 353.

[10] An example of a letter where the scribe is named and credited is a letter from Ibrāhīm ʿĪsā to Anjay ʿĪsā (IHERIAB ms. 8593).

[11] Inventory executed by Shaykh Sīdī Aḥmad al-Bakkāy in the presence of Sīdī Ḥamād b. Sīdī ʿArwah, no date (IHERIAB ms. 10741).

[12] Letter from Sanbu ʿĪsā to Anjay ʿĪsā (IHERIAB ms. 10577); letter from Ghalu Bubu to Anjay ʿĪsā (IHERIAB ms. 9311[30]).

who identifies herself as a sister of Anjay and concubine of ʿĪsā. These are not ambiguous or euphemistic words, but they do imply a level of relationship with the master that is greater than the bare legal terms for slave such as "ʿabd" ("slave"), "mamlūk" ("person owned"), "ama" ("slave girl"), "khadīm" ("servant"), and so forth. "Ghulām" signals a level of acculturation into the master's society and culture, and in this way it may be equated with second-generation slaves, or even with groups of people called slaves in many West African societies who, by virtue of having been born into the status of slavery, were not supposed to be sold.[13] Masters were reluctant to allow these valuable slaves to be manumitted. Even when they were freed, as Anjay was as an elderly man, freed slaves continued to work on behalf of their masters in the same kinds of commercial affairs.

The letters we present in this chapter allow us to further understand some of the complex meanings given to these terms of social inferiority and slavery in a nineteenth-century circum-Saharan trading network. Only some of the letters are dated. However, the correspondence took place in the period between 1854 and 1900. One letter was written from the Saharan town of Ghāt (in present-day southwestern Libya), while others were written from Timbuktu and different commercial towns along the Niger Valley to the southwest such as Youvarou and Sansanding.[14] This was a period of political instability in the Niger Bend, in the aftermath of the wars in the 1860s between the Futanke forces led by al-Ḥājj ʿUmar Tall, the forces of the Fulbe of Macina and the Arabophone Kunta. Insecurity was a major concern for traders throughout this period, and the letters indicate that at times transportation arteries were blocked by military forces. It was only when French colonial forces definitively established themselves beginning in the late 1890s that a certain amount of security returned to the area.

QUESTIONS TO CONSIDER

1. What does the respectful language used in so many letters between master and slave tell us about the personal relationships between these individuals?

[13] Ghislaine Lydon points out that the term "ghulām" refers to slave boys between the age of ten and fourteen. She also notes that it was a common epithet for "male slaves or freed slaves working as commercial agents and couriers for merchants of Ghadāmis and Ghāt." "Slavery, Exchange and Islamic Law: A Glimpse from the Archives of Mali and Mauritania," *African Economic History* 33 (2005), 122–123. The same term was used in medieval North Africa. According to S.D. Goitein, there is some ambiguity in understanding its precise meaning because it could refer to a slave, or to a manumitted slave. It was a polite form of address that made it possible to avoid the use of the legal term for slave (ʿabd). Goitein, *A Mediterranean Society: The Jewish Communities of the Arab World as Portrayed in the Documents of the Cairo Geniza*. Vol. 1 (Berkeley, 1967), 131. John Ralph Willis cites a North African text defining the *ghulām* that equates them with sexually exploited "beardless youths" ("The Ideology of Enslavement in Islam," John Ralph Willis [ed.], *Slaves and Slavery in Muslim Africa. Volume I. Islam and the Ideology of Enslavement*, ed. John Ralph Willis [London, 1985], 11). There is no hint in the letters from Timbuktu that the term has any sexual connotation in this context. In the Songhay-speaking societies of the Niger Bend, these people were called "hosso" or "gaa-bibi," and they formed a quasi-caste of low-status people. Horace Miner, *The Primitive City of Timbuktoo* (New York, 1965), 54–62. Jean-Pierre Olivier de Sardan, *Les sociétés songhay-zarma (Niger-Mali): chefs, guerriers, esclaves paysans* (Paris, 1984), 40–43; Boubou Hama, *L'histoire traditionnelle d'un peuple: les Zarma-Songhay* (Paris, 1967), 16. Paul Lovejoy points out that this injunction against selling second-generation slaves was often overcome in practice. "Slavery in the Sokoto Caliphate," in Paul Lovejoy (ed.), *The Ideology of Slavery in Africa* (Beverly Hills, 1981), 222; Lovejoy, *Transformations in Slavery: A History of Slavery in Africa*. 2nd edition (Cambridge, 2000), 115–116.

[14] These are the spellings used for these towns in contemporary Mali. Youvarou is spelled "Yuwar" in the Arabic letters, and Sansanding is spelled "s-n-s-n-d." Sansanding is spelled "Sinsani" by Richard Roberts, based on contemporary pronunciation. *Warriors, Merchants and Slaves: The State and the Economy in the Middle Niger Valley, 1700–1914* (Stanford, 1987).

2. How should we understand the social position of slaves in this commercial network in which a degree of intimacy and confidence characterized relations between masters and slaves?
3. Why is the social status of slaves reiterated in these letters by slaves and masters?
4. What do the letters tell us about the importance of slaves in commercial networks in West Africa and the Sahara?
5. Why would slaves be useful agents in long-distance trading networks?
6. What role, if any, did shared Muslim identity play in the relationship between slaves and masters?

DOCUMENTS

1. Letter from Ṣanbu ʿĪsā to ʿĪsā b. Ḥmīda[15]

This is a letter written by the slave Ṣanbu ʿĪsā to his master ʿĪsā b. Ḥmīda in 1865. It is written from the town of Sansanding on the Niger River east of Segou, at a time of significant conflict in the region between Futanke forces after the death of their leader al-Ḥajj ʿUmar Tal in 1864, on one hand, and those of Masina and the Kunta on the other. The main interest of this letter is that it provides an example of the commercial correspondence in which these slaves were involved. In this case, Ṣanbu acts as the commercial agent of his master in Sansanding. He has come from the north with salt to sell. He buys cloth, gold, and grain with the money he earns from selling the salt. He says that he could not find slaves for a good price. The currencies used in these transactions are cowry shells and gold. It is difficult to follow the different denominations of cowry shells because Ṣanbu refers to different systems of counting (the footnotes explain the different systems). Ṣanbu also reports on the general market conditions in Sansanding. One important thing to notice in the letter is the use of "commercial houses," which acted as a form of bank, where money could be deposited and later transferred to people in different locations. The precise structure of the particular commercial house mentioned in this letter is not made clear. In general, commercial networks used a variety of means including debt swapping, bills of exchange, and credit to avoid the dangers of theft that were especially acute in the context of the Niger Bend in the second half of the nineteenth century. When somebody died, as is mentioned in this letter, there were often disputes over settling his debts. In this case, Ṣanbu mentions that a certain person died and that his slave was to be seized in an effort to reimburse his creditors.[16]

Praise be to God and may God bless he who was the last prophet.

This letter is from Ṣanbu to his master Sīdi ʿĪsā b. Ḥmīda al-Ghadāmisī.[17] Thousands and thousands of greetings to you and may God Almighty's blessings and mercy be upon you. You asked about us and we ask likewise about you. We are well and in good health and we hope that you are also well.

The reason for this letter is that ʿUthmān[18] has left twenty units[19] of grain with Yarūsāgh in Kārib Tamā.[20] I sent it on the 27th of the month of Shaʿbān [25 January 1865], but we heard

---

[15] IHERIAB ms. 5451.

[16] On this issue, see Lydon, *On Trans-Saharan Trails*, 312–339.

[17] "Sīdi" is an honorific meaning "master."

[18] ʿUthmān is another slave owned by ʿĪsā, who was involved in this network.

[19] The precise weight of a unit is not known to us. This appears to be equivalent to a sack of grain.

[20] This is an unknown location.

that he was not able to go that way [because of insecurity] so he instead headed for Djenné, which he reached without trouble. I also sold nine blocks of water-damaged salt for 64,000 cowries, and I gave the money in trust to the commercial house (*dār*). I also sold four blocks of salt for 24,000 cowries, and I bought two long strips of cloth (*durrā'atayn*)[21] for 26,000 cowries. I made four blankets (*awāq*) from each one, and the thread and the tailoring to do this cost 10,000 cowries.

I bought the 20 units of grain that I sent with Yarūsāgh for a value of 17 blocks of salt.[22] This accounts for thirty blocks. After that, I sold 48 blocks for 120 mithqāls of gold,[23] which means that each block was exchanged for 2 1/2 mithqāls of gold. After that I bought 50 units of grain. This is all that I have right now, in addition to the remaining value of the salt and the cowries. When al-Bajāwī arrived,[24] he found only four blocks of salt and the grain left with me, which I exchanged for 300 cowry [piles].[25] Altogether, this made 20 cowry baskets (*qashāsha*), each of which contains 250 cowry [piles] per basket (*qashāsha*).[26] The remaining salt with me that belongs to al-Sharīf was 102 blocks, which I sold for 2 1/2 mithqāls per block. I have the gold with me now.

You asked about the prices of commodities in Sansanding: One block of salt sells for two mithqāls of gold, or 10,000 cowries. Labor is 2,700 cowries. Grain is 400 cowries for a basket (*qashāsha*).[27] There are no slaves (*khadim*) that can be bought profitably here. Cotton strips (*tāri*) are cheap, but honey is expensive. Shea butter is expensive, baobab flower is not available, and tamarind is expensive. Grain is expensive throughout the country but there are no

---

[21] This word usually refers to the long, sleeveless garments, often called *boubous*, worn by men in this part of West Africa. In this context however, it appears to be strips of cloth, because the next sentence indicates that they were sown together into large blankets.

[22] We will see later in the letter that one block of salt is worth 6,000 cowries. At the ratio of 20:17, one unit of grain sells for 5,100 cowries.

[23] The mithqāl was the weight unit of gold in West Africa. However, its precise weight varied considerably in different times and places. In the second half of the nineteenth century in the Niger Bend, one mithqāl was equivalent to approximately four grams of gold. See Marion Johnson, "The Nineteenth-Century Gold 'Mithqal' in West and North Africa," *Journal of African History*, 9, 4 (1968), 557; John Hunwick, "Islamic Financial Institutions: Theoretical Structures and Aspects of Their Application in Sub-Saharan Africa," in Endre Stiansen and Jane I. Guyer (eds.), *Credit, Currencies and Culture: African Financial Institutions in Historical Perspective* (Uppsala, 1999), 85.

[24] This is an unknown location.

[25] This is very confusing for the uninitiated. He appears to be talking about a different denomination of cowries here. Ṣanbu first indicated earlier that he had sold the blocks of salt for 6,000 cowries each. When he first discusses this, he uses a system of counting based on denominations of single cowries. But there was another system of counting cowries in towns such as Sansanding in which cowries were counted by piles, in which each pile contained a standard number of cowries (60, 80, or 100 cowries depending on the particular local system). These piles were called "hundreds" even if they had less than 100 cowries in the pile. When Ṣanbu switches to this denomination of cowries as he does here, he is referring to 300 piles ("hundreds") of cowries for four blocks of salt. If each pile has 80 cowries, as was the common denomination in Bamana-speaking areas of the Niger Valley, that means he received the same 6,000 cowries for each block (300 ÷ 4 = 75 × 80 = 6,000). See Marion Johnson, "The Cowry Currencies of West Africa, Part I," *Journal of African History*, 11, 1 (1970), 38.

[26] The term "qashāsha" is derived from a word for "straw" or "rush," and it means "sweeper, broom, rake" in different contexts. Here, it refers to a basket or sack made from rushes. This basket contained a standard 20,000 cowries, which weighed between 50 to 100 pounds depending on the type of cowry shell. When Ṣanbu explains that each basket contains 250 cowries, he means 250 piles of 80 cowries each. This equals 20,000 individual cowries (250 × 80 = 20,000). See Marion Johnson, "The Cowry," 41.

[27] There is something missing from this price. If it is in the second denomination of cowries, in piles ("hundreds"), it would mean that a sack of grain costs 32,000 cowries in Sansanding (400 × 80 = 32,000). We have already learned at the beginning of the letter that a unit (*farda*) of grain costs 5,100 cowries.

people who are more dishonest than the people of Sansanding. They gouge prices all the time because they do not believe in God or shaykhs.

L-T-W-N and Ḥamad have left for Saro,[28] and ʿAbd al-Salām left Sansanding headed south. You asked about the news from Djenné: The road is blocked and this has caused prices to rise. Grain is 140 cowries per measure (*sāʿ*) and rice is 200 cowries per measure (*sāʿ*).[29] As for salt, we know its value already. Today, I am worried because you said in your letter that you wanted honey, baobab flour, shea butter and tamarind. I have sent word that I am looking to purchase those products.

The slave girl (*ama*) of Brāhīm, son of what's-his-name al-Arawānī, went to Segou[30] even though I told her, and she knows very well, that she will have no better luck there. As for the slaves of the Whites[31] who died in Segou, they ran away and left Segou. Masʿūd has passed away, may God have mercy upon him, and the only thing that he left was a young slave (*ghulām*). Three people here asked about his debts and I said that we would seize the slave. They said that no one had seized him yet, that he is currently at the mercy of God and His Prophet.

Greetings from us to all of the members of the household in His name. Greetings to [Maḍīḍan] Mattīḍan b. Aḥmad. Goodbye. Written on the 11th of Dhū ʾl-Ḥijja, 1281 [7 May 1865].

2. Letter from Ṣanbu ʿĪsā to ʿĪsā b. Ḥmīda[32]

The second letter was written by Ṣanbu ʿĪsā to his master ʿĪsā b. Ḥmīda. This letter is not dated, although judging from the discussion of military maneuvers, it was probably written at around the same time as the first letter, in the mid-1860s. It refers to the disappearance and death of the Futanke leader al-Ḥājj ʿUmar in 1864. The letter is interesting because it shows another aspect of Ṣanbu's role as commercial agent for his master, that of creditor and debt collector. We will see in another letter presented later in the chapter that this could be the cause of conflict between master and slave. This letter appears to have been written by a scribe on Ṣanbu's behalf. The spelling of names and the expressions are different from the first letter, which was also almost certainly written by a scribe.

Praise be to God and may God bless he who was the last prophet.

This is from the slave (*ʿabīd*) Samba,[33] slave (*ghulām*) of ʿĪsā b. Ḥmīda al-Ghadāmishī[34] to his master, the elegant (*al-ẓarīf*), the superior (*al-fāʾiq*), the peer of the good and the great alike, the above-mentioned ʿĪsā. Thousands and thousands of greetings to you and may you

---

[28] It is written "Sār." Saro is the region between the Niger and the Bani rivers, east of Sansanding and west of Djenné.

[29] The *sāʿ* is a measure of grain equivalent to a handful. The derivative term "saawal" is used in Songhay and Fulfulbe to mean the same thing. According to Major Dixon Denham writing in 1822 in Marzuq, One *sāʿ* was equal to 1/96th of a sack. Edward W. Bovill, ed. *Mission to the Niger. Vol. II, The Bornu Mission, 1822–25* (Cambridge, 1966), 284.

[30] This is written "Sīk."

[31] "Bīḍān" means "Whites" and is a term used to refer to the Maures or Arabs of what is today Mauritania and Northern Mali.

[32] IHERIAB ms. 8297.

[33] Spelled "Samba" instead of the normal "Ṣanbu."

[34] The *nisba* is spelled incorrectly as "Ghadāmishī" instead of "Ghadāmisī." Among other things, this is evidence of a different scribe.

have God Almighty's mercy and blessings. Greetings also to all the people whether known to me or not.

Now then, the reason for my letter is to inform you that I have still not been able to collect the debt that is preventing me from leaving and coming to you. The debt is 10 *bīsāti al-maḥmūdhiyya*[35] for ʿAlāmūsu, as well as some salt. If it were not for that debt, you would have seen me already. I wanted to leave because I don't have any more business here other than the debts. What is preventing boats from moving are the Dajjāliyīn[36] who have blocked the way by assembling in the town of Yafuka,[37] where travelers cross the river. That hinders the boats from coming your way.

As for the news of the country that you asked about: The Shaykh went to the town of Wanza and he stayed there with the army. As for Sidiyya, he entered Kunāri.[38] Ibn al-Dajjāl went up to the land of stones (*arḍ al-ḥijāra*), and they did not find him.[39] He was not found in Djenné either. He was not found and our horses did not enter (that country), but we pray to God on his behalf.

Our greetings to the children of my master, both the boys and girls, and to Muḥammad al-Sināwi,[40] and to the great jurisconsult Matīdan. This is the end. You asked about us and we are well and in good health. We ask for your prayers. Goodbye.

3. Letter from Anjay ʿĪsā to ʿĪsā b. Ḥmīda[41]

The third letter was written by the other main slave in this correspondence, Anjay ʿĪsā, who, like Ṣanbu, was a slave of ʿĪsā b. Ḥmīda. In this letter written to his master, Anjay details commercial information and reports on his purchases and sales from the town of Youvarou, on the Niger River just north of Lake Debo. The town is known as Yuwar in Arabic writings from Timbuktu. More than just the reporting of prices and accounting of merchandise, we also see part of a conflict between master and slave over Anjay's conduct and the accusation that he has disobeyed the orders of his master. What is especially interesting in this letter is the way that Anjay argues, how he compares himself to a mouse, and how he makes reference to his piety in defending himself. The letter is not dated, but it does refer to political and military disorder that is hindering trade. This may mean that the letter was written in the 1860s, like the letters presented earlier.

Praise be to the Unique God and may God bless the best of His creation.

This is from Anjay[42] to his noble master ʿĪsā b. Ḥmīda al-Ghadāmisī. Greetings to you and those who are with you.

---

[35] We do not know what this refers to. One possibility is that it is a set of women's wraps ("baysa" in Hassaniya Arabic).

[36] The term "Ibn Dajjāl" means "swindler, cheat, charlatan." It is derived from the Arabic name for the antichrist, Dajjāl. It was often used by opponents to refer to the Futanke forces of al-Ḥājj ʿUmar Tal and his successors.

[37] We do now know where this is.

[38] Kanuri is a region east of the Niger River to the north of Mopti and south of Lake Debo.

[39] This appears to be a reference to the death of al-Ḥājj ʿUmar Tal (if this is indeed who Ibn al-Dajjāl refers to). He was killed in 1864 in a cave on the Bandiagara escarpment, which is what "land of the stones" refers to.

[40] This is a variation on the spelling of Muḥammad Sinṭāwu, a scribe used often by the Ghadames network.

[41] IHERIAB ms. 8308.

[42] Anjay's name is written as "Unkī." The spelling may indicate that the letter was composed by a scribe.

Now then, I write to tell you that, God willing, you will find 30 cotton bands (*tārī*) brought to you by Saddi Maflūṭ. They will be folded in a mat and marked by two circles, one inside the other, plus the foot of a bird just like the mark[43] from twine made from palm frond fiber (*koroŋgoy*).[44] He is also bringing with him one rod (*'ūdu*) of kola nuts,[45] which contains 1500 nuts. As for the cotton bands, they are in the middle of the two veils (*disa*),[46] and their price is 11,000 cowries. The cotton bands cost 100,000 *salāmiyya* [of salt] and 2000 cowries.[47] As for the price of the 1500 cotton bands, it was 93,000 cowries. Inside of the cotton bands you will also find 8 garments (*libās*) – they are for your beloved al-Madani.[48]

I also received your first letter and the second one which arrived on the same day that I wrote you my letter. I read both of them and I understood their content. You said in the two letters that you had ordered me to return to you and not to remain here. I have not deviated from this for even one day. I do not disobey your commands and your orders because I do not wish to disobey them even for a single moment. Everything that you reproached me for is because of a delay caused by circumstances, not my personal choice. There is no quick business in the town of Youvarou.[49] Salt is not sold quickly and gold is not found easily. But you are absent and I am present here. It is those who are here on the ground who can see and know what those who are not here cannot see and cannot possibly know. This is the difference between you and me. I have no personal business in remaining here other than your service and business. Since we have come to the town of Youvarou not one of us has slept securely in our houses; instead we have spent our nights beside the river guarding our goods from our enemies. None of [the foreigners] who are in the town of Youvarou sleep in their houses because they must spend their nights beside the river. We have spent three consecutive nights outside in this way. In these conditions, the heart does not rest peacefully. It is better to do that than to do something else.

I asked Saddi to delay his trip here for a few days so that I could put together a little bit of gold and send it to you with him, but he said that he could not stay here any longer. God willing, you will see all the gold that I acquired in these last days.

As for the fact that he said that I had sold on credit: I did this only for one half load (*'adīla*)[50] of tobacco, which I sold for 100,000 cowries on credit. This was a mistake on my part, but it was decreed by God Almighty and I did not do it by my own will. God willing, I will come to you without further delay. Do not listen to everything that people say to you until you see me, God willing. To you, I am like the mouse that is in the house of the people: He does not abandon these people of the house. You and I are like that. So rest your heart in peace about me. From me you will see only things that please you, God willing. I swore

[43] These marks are drawn. This is a mark of three lines, shaped like a capital "H" on its side.
[44] This is a Songhay word.
[45] "gūriya," spelled "jūriya."
[46] We have read this as the Songhay word for veil (*disa*). But it may refer to a more generic kind of textile, or even to a hiding place (from the Hassaniya Arabic "dsiisa").
[47] "100,000 salāmiyya" appears to be a measure of salt, construed here as a barter, plus 2,000 cowries of currency. This at least is how John Hunwick interprets "salāmiyya;" see Hunwick, "Islamic Financial Institutions," 98.
[48] This is a woman's name in the Niger Bend. (Though in this case it refers to a male, as evidenced by the term *ḥabībuk*: your beloved.)
[49] This is called "Yuwar" in this and other documents from Timbutku. It is a town on the Niger near Lake Debo.
[50] The 'adīla refers to a half camel load in much of the Sahara, including Ghadames. In Mauritania, the term referred to a large salt bar. Here, it refers to a half camel load of tobacco. See Lydon, *On Trans-Saharan Trails*, 210.

an oath to God Almighty to never betray you. Even if people tell you that I am stealing your money, I will walk to you on my two feet, God willing. I will walk to you myself and you will do with me what you want. I prefer this to betraying you.

As for the boats, they were held up by the emir ʿAliyu b. Awda.[51] He decreed that nobody should travel before he crossed the river. Al-Kāhiya Burāhīm[52] also sent a letter to Baba Saʿīdu saying that he should not let anyone travel to Timbuktu before ʿAliyu b. Awda has crossed the river. These two people prevented travelers from coming to you. Goodbye.

4. Letter from Aḥmad al-Bakkāy b. ʿĪsā to Anjay ʿĪsā[53]

The next letter was sent to Anjay ʿĪsā by one of ʿĪsā b. Ḥmīda's sons, named Aḥmad al-Bakkāy. There is no date on this letter but it must have been written later than the letters presented earlier in the chapter. It is a simple request that Anjay carry out certain commercial tasks and it demonstrates that Anjay continued to fulfill his role as commercial agent for ʿĪsā's children, even after ʿĪsā died, sometime before 1878.[54]

Praise be to God and may God bless he who was the last prophet.

This is from Aḥmad al-Bakkāy b. ʿĪsā b. Ḥmīda to his brother and beloved, and only then his slave (*ghulām*) Anjay. Greetings to you and may you have God's mercy and blessings. How are you? How is your family? We hope that you are just as we are and that you are satisfied with that.

Now then, know that I wrote to you previously asking you to come over to me quickly and leave what you have with you in the custody of my shaykh Baba b. Sinṭāwu. We ask him, and likewise God Almighty, for his continuing love for me and for the blessings which he transmitted to me. If this is not possible, then leave it with whomever you have confidence in, and may God bless you. Do what I have told you quickly and without delay or interpretation. You must know that I see what you do not see. Goodbye.

In addition, bring along with you the blankets (*khash*) that you think will be profitable for us to sell here along with the trunk which does not have a key. Put parts of K-L-ʿ and the new books which are valuable in the trunk. Bring whatever you can from there. Goodbye.

Appoint someone who can recognize and differentiate between these things for you and pay him very well. Greetings to my brother and Shaykh Baba b. Sinṭāwu and to my brother al-Bashīr b. Ṭālib and to everyone else who asks about us.

5. Letter from Aḥmad al-Bakkāy to Anjay ʿĪsā[55]

The next letter was also addressed to Anjay ʿĪsā by Aḥmad al-Bakkāy b. ʿĪsā. Although there is commercial information in this letter, it is mainly about Aḥmad al-Bakkāy's son, who has been sent to study under the teacher, scribe, and jurisconsult Baba b. Sinṭāwu. Aḥmad

---

[51] He was the Futanke emir of the region of Farimake, which is west of Lake Debo. He is also known as ʿAli Awdi.

[52] This is the emir (kāhiya) of Timbuktu who died in 1884. See Elias Saad, *Social History of Timbuktu: The role of Muslim scholars and notable, 1400–1900* (Cambridge, 1983), 220.

[53] IHERIAB ms. 10332.

[54] The date of the death of ʿĪsā b. Ḥmīda al-Ghadamisī is taken from a document assigning the custody of his children in Ghadamis and Timbuktu to his two eldest sons, Muḥammad al-Ṣāliḥ and Aḥmad al-Bakkāy. (Cf. IHERIAB ms. 12367).

[55] IHERIAB ms. 8339.

al-Bakkāy instructs Anjay to discipline the child and to ensure that he follows his lessons. This letter highlights the complex position of Anjay in this network. He is a senior, perhaps fatherly figure for the younger Aḥmad al-Bakkāy, who is entrusted with the education of his own son, yet he is still apparently a slave.

Praise be to God and may God bless he who was the last prophet.

Full and generous greetings from Aḥmad al-Bakkāy b. ʿĪsā to his brother Anjay. Greetings to you. You will see my son ʿĪsā[56] coming to you. Put him in the Quranic school (*maḥaḍra*) of my shaykh Baba b. Sinṭāwu and support him as much as you can. Hit him and imprison him, and do whatever is possible and even that which is impossible until he obeys God and obeys you. Do not neglect him.

He is bringing with him 20 units so give two of them to my shaykh. The first one is tobacco and the second one is corn.

Many greetings to you and greetings to my shaykh Baba b. Sinṭāwu. You will see my son and the son of your pupil (*talmīdh*)[57] coming to you. Struggle hard with him. May God bless you and reward you. You will find him to be lower than you deserve [and not well prepared for his studies] but bear with him. Many greetings. Goodbye.

6. Letter from al-Mukhtār b. al-Ḥājj ʿAlī b. al-Ḥājj Muḥammd ʿAmmūsh al-Balīlī to Ṣanbu ʿĪsā and Anjay ʿĪsā[58]

The sixth letter was written in 1884 from the Saharan oasis of Ghāt, located in present-day southwestern Libya. It was written by someone connected to ʿĪsā b. Ḥmīda's firm, perhaps even a son, and addressed to the two slaves Ṣanbu and Anjay. The author complains that he has been kept out of the loop on commercial opportunities in Timbuktu and he asks repeatedly for news of different people he knows. He says in this letter that one must correspond with the slaves if one is to be kept up to date with business on the southern side of the desert. This suggests just how important these slaves were to the larger commercial network.

Praise be to God and may God bless our master Muḥammad and his family and his companions.

This letter is from al-Mukhtār b. al-Ḥājj ʿAlī, son of the late al-Ḥājj Muḥammad ʿAmmūsh al-Balīlī, to our dear and honorable Ṣanbu, slave of ʿĪsā b. Ḥmīda, and to Anjay,[59] slave of ʿĪsā b. Ḥmīda and all of the children. Greetings to you and may you have God's mercy and blessings. You asked about us and we are well. We hope that, God willing, it is the same for you. The only goodness we are lacking here is to see your face dear to us. May God bring us together soon, He is the All-Hearing, the All-Responsive.

The reason for this letter is because Muḥammad b. ʿĪsā and I have come to Ghāt and we were told that if we want to know what is happening in Timbuktu, we must correspond with the slaves in order to gather news. How can we respond to you unless you send us all the news? And you, O Ṣanbu, this matter is shameful to you. You know everything, and now

---

[56] This is written as "your son," but it clearly refers to Aḥmad al-Bakkāy's son.
[57] He is referring to himself here, indicating that he had been a student of Baba b. Sinṭāwu.
[58] IHERIAB ms. 8246.
[59] Spelled "N-J-Y."

you are the equivalent of our father. Indeed you have al-Ḥājj Muḥammad there with you in Timbuktu if God guides you, send news with him. Eight years have now passed and we have not had a letter in response from al-Bakkāy. You must absolutely give us all the news from these people. Give the servant (waṣīf) al-Ḥājj, ʿAwn Allāh a letter containing all the news of our father, and what has become of al-Bakkāy, and what Bana-kayār and Bou Naʿām have done with the house. Give us all the news about any matter which might materialize for our brothers in Timbuktu and we will respond accordingly. This is our news. Goodbye. Written on 18 Safar 1302 [6 December 1884].

7. Letter from ʿAbd al-Raḥmān Yāmina to ʿĪsā b. Ḥmīda al-Ghadāmisī[60]

The next letter was carried by Ṣanbu to his master ʿĪsā b. Ḥmīda. It was not written by a slave, nor sent to a slave. We have included it here because it reveals that the status of being a slave, even a relatively high-status slave such as Ṣanbu and Anjay, rendered one uniquely vulnerable. This was not in any sense a theoretical vulnerability. In this letter, after detailing some of the commercial goods he is transferring to ʿĪsā with Ṣanbu, he explains that he is sending two slaves who must be sold into the Saharan slave trade. One slave, named Kunma, who presumably traveled with Ṣanbu and the letter, is to be sold to the merchants from Tuwat in the Algerian Sahara because he knows too much about the internal workings of the master's family. We assume that this fate was unknown to Kunma. We can only guess at exactly what this means, but marital infidelity seems a likely reason. That he could be sold to Saharan merchants from Tuwat because he posed a potential threat to his master's honor reminds us of how precarious the position of slaves was. It is interesting, however, that the writer felt compelled to at least explain what must have been, at some level, a difficult commission for ʿĪsā to carry out.

Praise be to God alone and May God bless the one after whom there is no prophet.

Now then, generous greetings from the servant of his Lord, ʿAbd al-Raḥmān Yāmina to he who is honored by the Most honorable, he whom peace never leaves, master of his companions, light of his age, the most obedient in this generosity, ʿĪsā b. Ḥmīda al-Ghadāmisī. After our greetings to you, may God have mercy on you and bless you. You asked about us and we are well, praise be to God. Perhaps you are likewise.

The reason for our letter to you is to tell you that you will see with the slaves, brought to you by your slave (ghulām) Ṣanbu, in loyalty to God and under His protection, 30 units of food, 8 of which are unadulterated rice while the rest are white corn. In this, there are two or three units of personal property, which God only knows the value of.

You will also receive one container of kola nuts, which holds 2200 nuts, that belongs to Nana Zawja.[61] After that, know that one unit of this number is marked by a white rag tied to the container of the kola nuts which belongs to Zawja. From God and then from you, we want you to use the kola nuts to buy sheep. Zawja tells you that when you sell her merchandise, you should ask for a silver Maria Theresa dollar and lace; also selling 5000… [unreadable] which you should count in the money of Zawja. Exchange what remains for good salt. After this, you will see in the aforementioned merchandise a little bit of honey and that belongs to me, ʿAbd al-Raḥmān, so put it together with the food.

---

[60] IHERIAB ms. 8261.

[61] The letter refers to Zawja as a proper name, although the word means "wife."

After that we want from God and His Prophet, and only then from you, for you to sell one of the slaves named Kunma when he arrives. Sell him to the people of Tuwat so that he will go to their country.[62] You must sell him because otherwise he will reveal the secrets of his master's family. This is the reason that I ask you to sell him may God reward you. In addition, you will receive one female slave. Sell this slave girl together with the aforementioned slave for a single price when the notables from Tuwat come to you. Exchange them for tobacco, or, if the notables from Tuwat do not come, wait for the Azalaï[63] to arrive and exchange them and the food and honey for salt. May God preserve your life.

Know that we want from God, and only then from you, that we all join together in the matter of your merchandise and the matter of the food. I will bring it with me or send somebody with it very quickly without delay, God willing. I ask you to look for 10 measures of wheat which we will put in a container. Praise be to God who has reunited you and your slave [the letter carrier]. Goodbye.

8. Letter from Ṣanbu ʿĪsā to Anjay ʿĪsā[64]

The eighth letter was written by the slave Ṣanbu to his "brother" and fellow slave Anjay. Whether they were actually brothers is not clear. Ṣanbu was older than Anjay and his written Arabic was much weaker. This letter appears to have been written by a scribe. There are a few items mentioned in this letter that we are unable to understand and translate. However, it provides a window into the ways in which even slaves participated in joint commercial ventures among themselves. Notice that the amount of money at stake in these transactions is much less than in earlier letters where the goods were being sold on behalf of the master ʿĪsā b. Ḥmīda. This letter also mentions the larger families that these slaves established in Timbuktu, and provides further evidence (after the previous letter) that women were also investors in this commerce.

Praise be to God alone and may God bless the best of His creation.

This letter is from the big brother Ṣanbu ʿĪsā to his cultured (al-adīb) and distinguished (al-nabīh) younger brother Anjay, slave (ghulām) of ʿĪsā. Greetings to you and to everyone with you.

Now then, I write to tell you that we arrived safely and in good health but since we have arrived here I have fallen ill and I have not gotten better. I am so sick that I have not even been able to pay a visit to Shaykh ʿAbidīn, and I have not sold a thing since coming here. That's why I was not able to send you the ṣibrī[65] that you commissioned. The man for whom I came to this place has left for Suraya,[66] but he informed his people about my arrival and instructed them to make me wait until he returned. I will wait for him until he comes back, but I decided that if I feel healthy enough, I will go and travel to him, God willing.

Tell my creditor not to be alarmed about my health. God will solve what is between us

---

[62] Tuwat is an oasis complex in southern Algeria. Merchants from Tuwat were prominent in the Saharan trade from Timbuktu.

[63] The Azalaï is the annual salt caravan from Taoudeni to Timbuktu and other sites where salt is in demand.

[64] IHERIAB ms. 10577.

[65] This probably refers to nitron, although it is possible that it is the Songhay word "siibi," which means "men's pants."

[66] It is not clear where this is. It seems unlikely that this is the Saraya in present-day Guinea.

without fatigue or effort. Tell my wife Kani, after giving her my greetings, and my greetings to Baniya and his brother ʿUthman as well, that she should not neglect the few things that I brought to her, and should hold on to them. I have not been able to sell any of the string of beads which I brought with me. The scribe Muhammad Yintawu sends you his greetings.

I was able to sell the entrusted (*amāna*) *Būbu*[67] for 60,000 cowries and then I bought 15 silver *ḍiyār*[68] and sent him with Bukayyil al-Aʿrab. The price of porterage and the rent is 2,000, which I paid. I also sent with him 8 other *ḍiyārs* to give to al-ʿArbi b. Tata, as the price for the kola nuts. So now you know about them. Goodbye. Four [*ḍiyārs*] are big and four are thin.

9. Letter from Yājīda, the concubine of ʿĪsā, to Anjay ʿĪsā[69]

The next letter was written by a female slave named Yājida, who calls herself a concubine of ʿĪsā. The handwriting of the letter indicates that she used a scribe to compose it. Nonetheless, it is the sole example of a female slave letter in this correspondence that we are aware of. Like the other letters, the subject here is commercial. Whether or not female slaves like Yājida commonly participated in commercial ventures as partners in larger ventures or, as in this case, on their own using slave agents like Anjay and Ṣanbu is difficult to know. There are relatively few letters of this kind that we have found, although it is also true that women commonly appear as commercial partners. This letter does certainly raise the intriguing prospect that more research might reveal a much greater role for slave women in commerce.

Praise be to God and may God bless the one after whom there is no prophet.

Please accept full and generous greetings from Yājīda, concubine (*surriya*) of ʿĪsā, to her beloved and distinguished brother Anjay ʿĪsā. After invoking God, I write to inform you that you will receive from Tafa two units, one of hulled rice and the second of tobacco, and two strips of cotton (*tāri*) equal to 20 lengths (*dhirāʿ*), and 5 *lūb*[70] turbans (*ʿamāʾim*) marked with an "X." When they reach you, may God's blessings be upon you, send them to me quickly in less than three day and no more than five days. I have also sent one blanket (*kāsha*)[71] made from wool at the house of Fāṭim Gh-Th-M. Take possession of it and buy it for me in exchange for tobacco (*tabāk*).[72] We send our greetings to you, to everyone with you, to those who are related to you and to all of the people, even those we don't know. Know that I did not remain during this period of time in J-N-B-L only because I am waiting for Kīrtī Yukuru, who has not come yet from her travels to Djanet.[73]

As for the blanket that I mentioned to you already in the letter, do not ask where it is. Just send me its price with the writer of the letter. Also, the first writer of the letter had (mistakenly) revised the word "tārī" (cotton strips) as "kharīj" the first two times, holding the same mark as the first one…

---

[67] This is the name of an enslaved person.
[68] It is not clear what this refers to.
[69] IHERIAB ms. 10444.
[70] It is not clear what this refers to.
[71] The word "kasha" is used especially in Morocco. Marcel Beaussier, *Dictionaire pratique arabe-français* (Alger, 1958), 867.
[72] In Hassaniyya Arabic, this refers to leaf tobacco. It is not clear if that is what is intended here or if it is a more general meaning.
[73] Djanet, if this is what is meant here, is a town to the west of Ghāt, in present-day southeastern Algeria.

10. Letter from al-Khalīfa b. ʿĪsā to Anjay ʿĪsā[74]

The final letter is from al-Khalīfa, one of ʿĪsā b. Ḥmīda's sons, to Anjay. This letter does not concern commercial affairs, but it was written because of a conflict between al-Khalīfa and one of his brothers. What is especially interesting is that al-Khalīfa mentions the issue of Anjay's manumission, denying that he acted to prevent it from happening. There are other letters that refer to this issue as well. We know that at some point Anjay was manumitted. One might have expected this to have happened at his master's death, but that does not appear to have been the case. Even after ʿĪsā b. Ḥmīda's death, the language of slavery continued to be used in correspondence with Anjay. There is a larger story behind this letter but we do not know the details of it at this time. However, this letter demonstrates that the issue of manumission was one that was clearly discussed between masters and slaves.

In the name of God. Praise be to God and may God bless His chosen one. That's enough.

Now then, full and generous greetings from al-Khalīfa b. ʿĪsā to his father Jī [Anjay]. I inform you that I am in good health. You should know that I am in disagreement with my elder brother Sīdi, son of my father the master, who claims that I said to you (pl.) that he stole 600,000 cowries of my money. If I had said it, then you would know about it; if not, then you would know it too. Write a quick response to us [about this].

Sīdi also claimed that I said that I had not given you permission to be manumitted and to be free. If I had said it [and had given you permission to be manumitted], then you would have known about it, and our jurisconsult (*faqīh*) Baba Ṣantāwu would have known too. I also inform you that Sīdi wrote a letter to the jurisconsult and judge Aḥmad Bāba,[75] so I am asking for news of the letter which was sent to him. How is it? And I also inform you Jī [Anjay] that Sīdi said that you have not written him a letter since you have been staying there.

Endeavor to send a letter to Sīdi and I will send him a letter out of my desire to make peace and perform good deeds. Do not believe what you hear from others unless you see it for yourself and it comes from me. I told you one evening a long time ago that a wedge will be driven between Sīdi and me one day, and that day has arrived. Pass our greetings to our jurisconsult Bāba Ṣintāwū and ask him to please include us in his prayers at all times. We also send our greetings to Bintu and to Tasyīn and to ʿĪsā Bakkayu. We also send our greetings to our mother Musūd and we ask her to include us in her prayers.

SUGGESTED ADDITIONAL READINGS

Baier, Steven. *An Economic History of Central Niger* (Oxford, 1980).

Boahen, A. Adu. *Britain, the Sahara, and the Western Sudan, 1788-1861* (Oxford, 1964).

Harmann, Ulrich. "The Dead Ostrich: Life and Trade in Ghadames (Libya) in the Nineteenth Century," *Die Welt des Islams*, 38 (1998): 9–98.

Hogendorn, Jan and Marion Johnson. *The Shell Money of the Slave Trade* (Cambridge, 1986).

Hunwick, John. "Islamic Financial Institutions: Theoretical Structures and Aspects of Their Application in Sub-Saharan Africa," in Endre Stiansen and Jane I. Guyer (eds.),

---

[74] IHERIAB ms. 5510.

[75] This is Aḥmad Baba b. Abī ʾl-ʿAbbās, the qāḍī of Timbuktu beginning in 1894 at the beginning of French colonial rule. He died in 1931.

Credit, Currencies and Culture: African Financial Institutions in Historical Perspective (Uppsala, 1999), 72–99.

Johnson, Marion. "The Cowry Currencies of West Africa, Part I," *Journal of African History*, 11, 1 (1970): 17–49.

Lovejoy, Paul. *Caravans of Kola: The Hausa Kola Trade, 1700–1900* (Oxford, 1980).

Salt of the Desert Sun: A History of Salt Production and Trade in the Central Sudan (Cambridge, 1986).

Lydon, Ghislaine. *On Trans-Saharan Trails: Islamic Law, Trade Networks, and Cross-Cultural Exchange in Nineteenth-Century Western Africa* (Cambridge, 2009).

Schroeter, Daniel J. *Merchants of Essaouia: Urban Society and Imperialism in Southwestern Morocco, 1844–1886* (Cambridge, 1988).

Walz, Terence. *Trade between Egypt and Bilād al-Sūdān, 1700–1820* (Cairo, 1978).

Wright, John L. *The Trans-Saharan Slave Trade* (London, 2007).

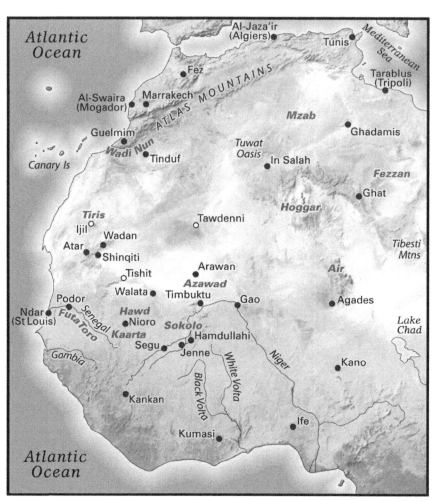

43.1. Northwest Africa with major towns.

The "Hidden Transcripts" and Legal Rights of Slaves in the Muslim World

A Legal Case from Nineteenth-Century Mauritania

GHISLAINE LYDON

Until the second half of the twentieth century, slavery and the trade in slaves were part of everyday life among many societies of western Africa. After the abolition of the trans-Atlantic slave trade by European powers in the nineteenth century, the practice of slavery in Africa might have increased to some extent because of the drop in the price of enslaved peoples resulting from the shift in the international demand for slaves. Two main types of caravans circulated within and across the Sahara Desert in the nineteenth century, the larger of which transported enslaved Africans as well as all kinds of international merchandise (such as carpets and prayer rugs, cloth and clothing, teapots and other metal utensils, books, weapons, spices, sugar, tea, cereals, and perfumes) destined for the markets of Africa and the Middle East. Such caravans traveled the longest distances across and within the desert regions of northern and western Africa (up to fifty days one way); these trans-Saharan caravans were truly international in scope. The second type of caravan was more regional, traveling shorter distances between markets to transport local goods, such as slabs of rock salt mined in several Saharan salt quarries, to markets on the southern desert edge to be exchanged for subsistence goods, such as cereals, nuts, and spices, as well as textiles and enslaved Africans from all over the regions of western Africa.

African Muslim communities tended to follow Islamic legal rules to organize and legislate their civil, criminal, and commercial affairs. The *shari'a* (the divine law of Muslims) contains explicit rules governing the lives of both free and enslaved people, including the rights to property of enslaved caravan workers and enslaved literate trade agents. Because being Muslim often entailed being literate in the Arabic language, many Muslims recorded their commercial and legal transactions in writing. Thankfully for historians of Africa, many Muslim families held on to their family archives across the generations, preserving papers in private libraries or simply in storage boxes.

This chapter examines a legal debate surrounding the ownership and treatment of an enslaved caravan worker. The details of this unusual case, which sheds light on the local determinants of slavery, were recorded in a legal document found in a private family archive[1] in the oasis town of Tishit (also spelled Tichitt), located in the heart of the Saharan

---

[1] The archive where this document is preserved is typical of the kind of family treasures found in the Saharan regions and cities of West Africa such as Timbuktu. In the past, Muslims from the area were highly literate in Arabic, the language of their holy book, the Qur'an. They expended considerable energy and resources to access writing paper in order to document their economic transactions and legal matters as well as

country known today as the Islamic Republic of Mauritania, a region formally part of the French colonial empire. The town once was an active center of both regional and international caravan trade. The document dates from the 1830s and deals with a legal trial involving an enslaved caravan worker who was originally from the northern town of Shinqiti (also spelled Chinguetti). This slave was loaned out by an uncle to his nephew, along with a number of camels, to work on a salt caravan bound for Tishit. Upon the caravan's arrival in Tishit, the two men had a fight during which the slave was severely beaten and subsequently chained. Miraculously, he managed to free himself from the chains, run away, and find refuge in a noblewoman's house. Meanwhile, word got out among both the enslaved and free residents of Tishit about this remarkable slave's heroic actions.

Despite the fact that it was penned by a member of the slave-owning elite, the legal document contains some of the voices of the slaves involved in the case. In this sense it offers exceptional glimpses into the "hidden transcripts" of the enslaved, to borrow an expression coined by James Scott.[2] At the same time, the document conveys something of the mentality of Muslim slave owners and the Islamic legal culture that framed their everyday affairs. Detailing a complex trial between the owner and would-be owner of the slave, the document also cites the slave's remarks concerning his keeper and includes hearsay evidence of another slave. This document sheds light on the following four subjects: (1) the trans-Saharan slave-trading world and the use of slaves as caravan workers; (2) Islamic law and the rights of slaves; (3) the public space accorded to the enslaved in various cultural settings; and (4) the voices of the enslaved or "hidden transcripts" that can be gleaned from legal documents.

QUESTIONS TO CONSIDER

1. The practice of Islam is in many ways defined by the legal and moral codes embodied in the Qur'an, the holy book of Muslims. How is the writer's religious faith apparent throughout the legal document?

2. Muslim names tend to be very long because they are genealogical in structure. In Arabic, *ibn* (also spelled *b.*) means "son of." For example, the name appearing in the third line of the text means that Al-Sharif Muhammad is the son of Fadil al-Sharif. From the lines that follow, can you figure out what would be the equivalent for "daughter of"?

3. What examples of the trade in slaves are revealed in this document? Do these differ from your understanding of the history of the slave trade? If so, how?

4. Imagine what could have caused the altercation between the male slave and the nephew, his keeper. What did the nephew claim took place and how did the justices of Tishit receive his testimony?

5. The text between the lines 20 and 25 is critical for understanding how the news of the male slave's exploit spread across town. Who was responsible for spreading the news? How are the voices of the enslaved recorded? How does this document inform about the power of the enslaved community to affect change?

engage in religious and scholarly pursuits. Saharan libraries contain manuscripts of all kinds, such as religious, scientific, and legal, and general documentation, such correspondence, trade records, and legal writings of the kind discussed in this chapter.

[2] Scott, *Domination and the Art of Resistance: Hidden Transcripts* (New Haven, 1990).

6. Maya bint al-Mukhtar ibn al-Amin appears to be a strong, wealthy, and notable woman of Tishit, who took on the cause of the male slave. Paying particular attention to her words expressed in lines 24 to 27, consider this woman's motivations in protecting the slave.

7. In order to keep custody of the runaway slave, Maya agreed to exchange him for another slave. Why do you think she was so eager to hold on to this particular slave? What does this transaction tell you about the economy of nineteenth-century slave societies?

8. The judges and town council of Tishit took several actions to protect the rights of both the slave, his original master in Shinqiti, and Maya bint al-Mukhtar ibn al-Amin who took possession of the slave man. What are some of these actions and how do they reflect a sense of law and order prevailing in nineteenth-century Tishit? Would you say that in this Muslim society, the rights of all – free and enslaved – were protected?

9. Was the local authority (the judges and the town council) the only body engaged in placing judgment in this case? Indeed, how did the community of Tishit react to these events?

10. In your opinion, who is the true hero of this story?

THE DOCUMENT[3]

1. Praise be to God, the one who revealed the truth and commanded it to be followed.[4]

2. He who forbade tyranny and ordered it to be committed to writing.

3. And so, al-Sharif Muhammad ibn Fadil al-Sharif [a local Muslim judge of Tishit] pleaded to me, the writer named below,

4. as their representative, the case of Maya bint al-Mukhtar ibn al-Amin and Ibrahim ibn Hamin

5. al-Ghalawi of Shinqiti. He claimed that Ibrahim [the uncle] entrusted to his nephew [the son of his brother]

6. his young camels carrying his salt and his male slave to work for him [on a caravan] headed to the town of Tishit. So when

7. he arrived there, a fight (*niza'*) erupted between him and the slave whom he accused of stealing.

8. So he treated him with contempt, he frightened him and he put a shackle (*kabl*)[5] on his two legs. He remained in this way until

---

3 Legal Report 1249/1833–4 (SS28) Sharifna wuld Shaykhna Family Archive (Tishit, Mauritania).

4 Paraphrased from Qur'an 007.157: "Those who follow the messenger, the unlettered (illiterate) Prophet, whom they find mentioned in their own scriptures, the Torah and the Gospel. *He commands them (to do) what is just and forbids them (to do) what is evil. He allows as lawful what is good and prohibits what is bad.* And he relieves them of their heavy burdens and the shackles (*aghlal*) that were upon them. Then those who believe in him, and honor him, and help him, and follow the light which is sent down with him: they are the successful." My translations of the Qur'an are primarily based on A. Yusuf Ali (ed.), *The Holy Qur'an: Translation and Commentary* (Brentwood, 1983). This reference obviously was not random on the part of the author considering the discussion of the shackling of a slave that follows. I thank Ahmed Alwishah for making me aware of the reference to this verse.

5 *Kabl* (plur. *kubul*) means leg iron, chain, shackle, fetter. It is a synonym of *qaid* (plur. *quyud*), used further in the document, and of *aghlal* (in the plural form) repeatedly used in the Qur'an in 007.157 (as quoted in

9. he broke the shackle, he became a runaway (*abaqa*)[6] and he set himself free. Until he [the nephew] learned about his whereabouts and he requested his return

10. from them [he asked that Maya and the people sheltering the slave return the slave to him]. But they declined his request unjustly (*zulman*). And so when he [the nephew] became despaired from waiting for him [the slave] to leave their home [and return to him],

11. they [the people sheltering the slave] decided to exchange him for another slave. And he (the nephew) agreed to this

12. unwillingly (*kurhan*). Then he came to me with the [exchanged] slave and he narrated the story to me. At that point, I took

13. the slave by the hand to the judges (*al-qudah*) and the town council (*al-jama'a*) among whom was Sid Ahmad ibn Sidi al-Mukhtar.

14. I confiscated the slave from him and I handed the slave over to them. And they disapproved of all of the nephew's actions

15. from the first to the last one. So the judge and his council formulated a ruling (*ijtahada*)[7] on the best resolution [in this case] which was

16. to release the slave back to him for [a fine of] 70 slabs of rock salt (*'adila*). They handed over [the verdict] to the nephew

17. and I [the judge and writer of the report] arrived. The nephew requested his slave [i.e. his uncle's slave] and al-Sharif Muhammad answered him and he refused to acknowledge (*ankara*)

18. the piece of writing[8] relating the slave's refusal [to return to] his[9] nephew, why he relinquished him and that

19. they [Maya and her people] requested that he agree to the exchange [of one slave for another] unwillingly after renouncing [to his claim]. Al-Sharif [Muhammad] asserted that

20. what [the nephew claimed] took place between him and the slave did not in fact happen, that the slave ran away from him (*abaqa al-'abd minhu*). News of [the slave's] story

21. spread and a slave woman (*ama*) came upon the shackle (*al-qaid*) that had been placed on the slave, [she heard about] his detention,[10] and [she went to]

22. Maya bint al-Mukhtar and informed her about the slave and that he [reportedly] said that

the previous fn); 034.033: "... and We will put shackles on the necks of those who disbelieved; they shall not be requited but what they did" and 076.004: "Surely We have prepared for the unbelievers chains and shackles and a burning fire."

[6] The verb *abaqa*, meaning to escape, run away, applies specifically to the action of a slave running away from his/her master. From it is derived the word for runaway (*abiq*; plur. *ubbaq*). See J. M. Cowan (ed.), *The Hans Wehr Dictionary of Modern Written Arabic* (Urbana, 1994), 2. See also Catherine Taine-Cheikh, *Dictionnaire Hassaniyya Français*, vol. I (Paris, 1988), 5.

[7] From the Arabic word *ijtihad*, which is the act of formulating an independent judgment on a legal question by reasoning based on interpretation and application of the sources of Islamic law.

[8] This is an indication that the nephew's transaction with Maya was the subject of a written contractual agreement.

[9] The preposition here is referring to the uncle, Ibrahim ibn Hamin.

[10] In Hasaniya, the Arabic-Berber language spoken in parts of western Africa (namely Mauritania, Mali, Senegal, Morocco, and Algeria) the noun *ghafal* means detention or to be locked up, whereas in classical Arabic it means carelessness or negligence. I take the author's intended meaning to be closer to the local language.

23. he never wants to be reunited with your nephew ever again. Upon [hearing] this, Maya sent for

Page Two

24. your nephew and she informed him about what the slave woman[11] had said to her and about the shackle and the detention and she said to

25. him that: "If you want your slave, take him and so here he is. We will deliver him to you.

26. God Willing. But if you think that this is not the right thing to do and instead you choose to exchange him for another slave,

27. then exchange him and therefore choose the exchange." And so she paid to him a slave [she acquired the runaway slave by exchanging him for another slave] and he looked him over and he agreed [to the transaction]

28. and he was satisfied willingly (*tawu'an*) and in full accord (*istis'an*) and without undermining [the agreement] and [in acknowledgement of] his previous action.

29. And he went away with the slave and he was satisfied. But then after that, Maya began fearing

30. that bad words would follow her [i.e., she started to worry about how her actions might damage her reputation] and she requested from him [the nephew] that the exchange be revoked (*iqala* in Islamic law is the revocation or annulment of a sale or transaction) but he refused to agree to [the revocation of the sale]. So

31. the slave remained in her possession until the legal witnesses came to her

32. on behalf of Ibrahim [ibn Hamin, the uncle and rightful owner of the slave in Shinqiti] to say that he had not agreed to his nephew's transaction concerning

33. his slave and that his slave remained his property. And so when Maya investigated this matter

34. she repealed [the exchange]. So she relinquished the slave and she referred the case to the judges and the

35. town council. They then cleared her of [all liability towards] the slave, but they gave her [temporary] custody of slave for safekeeping (*'ala wajh al-amana*)

36. until the matter was resolved and [they ordered her] to keep track of everything that she spends

37. on the slave, including what she paid in doctor's fees and so forth

38. including all expenditures [because] at that point he is homeless and because there is no one to care for him because he is

39. sick at the moment and there is no one who will buy him. And when their requests were fulfilled by both parties,

40. I first requested from Ibrahim [the slave's original owner in Shinqiti] evidence documenting the stated cause of the slave's refusal

41. to return to his nephew [illegible]. Then I asked al-Sharif [Muhammad] for a statement

42. for his plea to overturn the settlement agreement made by the judges and the town council.

43. So he came to me with a piece of paper written by the judge (*qartas bikhat al-qadi*) 'Abd Al-Qadar ibn Abubakkar ibn al-Shaykh

---

[11] It is apparent at this point that the slave woman (*ama*) in question did not belong to Maya.

44. al-Zali'[the judge of Shinqiti] including a statement about what Maya had heard, and that Ibrahim disapproved

Page Three

45. of the actions of his nephew towards his slave, and that she had raised the issue of the slave in the presence

46. of a large crowd of people which included the slave and [missing word], and Ahmad al-Sharif

47. and al-Sharif ibn Muhammad ibn al-Imam[12] and al-Imam Ahmad al-Sharif

48. Bu'Asriya ibn Ahmad ibn al-Sharif Muhammad and others from among the noble people

49. about the settlement. They freed Maya from being liable for the slave [i.e. they took him into custody]. After that they deliberated

50. about what was the most appropriate resolution for the slave and for the one absent [i.e. the uncle and owner]. They decided that the best resolution for the two parties

51. was for him [the slave] to remain with Maya until they settled the matter and that she calculate her expenditures

52. and what she spent on doctor's fees and so forth for he is sick at the moment.

53. And the judge and a majority of the town council withdrew [the fine] at that point. So I asked al-Sharif [Muhammad]

54. for the written proof from the judge [from Shinqiti] so he [the nephew] presented himself with Muhammad

55. Ibn Ambake al-Sharif and al-Imam Ahmad who testified to the validity of

56. the paper written by the judge. I presented the witnesses for Ibrahim

57. and I reprimanded him for both of them. A resolution of the abuses against them did not arise

58. because it was appealed in the presence of 'Abd ibn al-Hasan, that the legal decision

59. of the town council and their judge was unfavorable. And I said that the judgment

60. of the judge and the town council carried forth and was legally binding

61. unless evidence to dispute it was brought forward. So he failed to present a convincing rebuttal

62. of their ruling and the two agreed that they would not accept

63. any legal reasoning except [if pronounced] by Muhammad ibn Hamallah

64. ibn al-Shawwaf. We asked him and we asked Muhammad ibn Ambake

Page Four

65. Ibn Al-Talib Ahmad about [their legal opinion regarding] the action of the judge and the town council

66. concerning Ibrahim's slave, and the two agreed that the best resolution of the matter

[12] This was the imam of Tishit, son of the previous imam who died in 1245 (1829–30), according to the Tishit Chronicle.

67. of the slave [should involve] their action. Then, after all this was established

68. [the two witnesses] Sidi Baba and Al-Hajj Al-Siba'i both testified that

69. his nephew had lied about the incident and about the slave refusing to have anything to do with him and about being obstinate ('anada) about it.

70. It was ruled that Maya was to be exonerated [of the liability of] of the slave who was to be returned [to his rightful owner]

71. [and] she should be reimbursed for the money she spent taking care of him, including doctor's fees, and for the price of her slave [whom she had given in exchange]

72. or [the equivalent in value of the price of] a camel. This was ruled in the year

73. 1249 (1833–4). 'Umar ibn 'Abdallah

74. Ibn Abu Bakr nicknamed Ankak in any case.

75. Amen

LOWER PARAGRAPH

1. Praise God and as for the handwriting on these two sheets of paper it is by the handwriting of the abovementioned legal arbitrator (*al-muhakkam*)

2. whose writing was authenticated [by witnesses]. A second issue concerning Maya that Ghaly [this is the name of the slave she gave in exchange for the male runaway slave] was handed over to her and we discharged

3. Muhammad ibn Hamad [the nephew].[13] I am writing for him [Ibrahim] (a document to certify) that she [Maya] hired 'Aly to transport her rock salt [to Ibrahim]

4. for the price of the slave. And when he took it in his possession [illegible] until [illegible]

5. Muhammad ibn Fadil reaches you or he receives his letter certifying

6. to the authenticity of the attribution of the handwriting of the arbitrator and the validity of the agent and in safety

7. 'Aly, the abovementioned young boy, on the abovementioned date by Muhammad ibn Muhammad Al-Saghir ibn Anbuja. May God be satisfied with him and his disciples.

SUGGESTED ADDITIONAL READINGS

Austen, Ralph and Dennis Cordell. "Trade, Transportation, and Expanding Economic Networks: Saharan Caravan Commerce in the Era of European Expansion, 1500–1900." In *Black Business and Economic Power*. Edited by Alusine Jalloh and Toyin Falola (Rochester: Rochester University Press, 2002).

Hall, Bruce. *A History of Race in Muslim West Africa, 1600–1960*. Cambridge: Cambridge University Press, 2011.

Klein, Martin. *Slavery and Colonial Rule in French West Africa*. Cambridge: Cambridge University Press, 1998.

Lovejoy, Paul E. (ed.), *Slavery on the Frontiers of Islam*. Princeton: Markus Wiener, 2004.

---

[13] Note that this is the first time the nephew's name is mentioned in the document.

Lydon, Ghislaine. "Slavery, Exchange, and Islamic Law: A Glimpse from the Archives of Mali and Mauritania." *African Economic History*, 33 (2005): 117–48.

"Islamic Legal Culture and Slave Ownership in Nineteenth-Century Sahara." *International Journal of African Historical Studies*, 40, 3 (2007): 391–439.

Manning, Patrick. *Slavery and African Life: Occidental, Oriental, and African Slave Trades.* Cambridge: Cambridge University Press, 1990.

McDougall, Ann E. "Salt, Saharans and the Trans-Saharan Slave Trade: Nineteenth-Century Developments." In *The Human Commodity: Perspectives on the Trans-Saharan Slave Trade.* Edited by E. Savage (London: Frank Cass and Co., 1992), 61–88.

Sikainga, Ahmed. "Slavery and Muslim Jurisprudence in Morocco." In *Slavery and Colonial Rule in Africa.* Edited by Susanne Miers and Martin Klein (London: Frank Cass and Co., 1999), 57–72.

Willis, John Ralph (ed.). *Slaves and Slavery in Muslim Africa, vol. II, The Servile Estate.* London: Frank Cass and Co., 1985.

Wright, John. *The Trans-Saharan Slave Trade.* New York: Routledge, 2007.

44 Slave Wills along the Swahili Coast

ELISABETH McMAHON

Pemba is a small island located in the Indian Ocean off the coast of eastern Africa and was part of a British protectorate during the early twentieth century. During the nineteenth and early twentieth centuries, cloves and coconuts, which are tree crops, were the main produce of the island. Slaves were brought from the mainland, primarily the regions of present-day Tanzania and Malawi, to keep the areas around the clove trees weeded and to help pick cloves during the harvests. The work and lives of slaves on Pemba ranged widely from working in the household and being treated as a member of the family to working in the *shamba* (farms) on the island. The colonial government often portrayed slavery on Pemba as relatively benign, although officials did record instances of terrible cruelty by masters.

In 1897, the government ordered all slaves except concubines be allowed to ask for their freedom if they so desired. Slaves had to travel to the Slavery Commissioner court, which could often take a full day of walking. This meant that slaves could ask for their freedom but it was not easy because if they traveled all day to get to the court and the court was closed, they had nowhere to sleep and no food to eat while they waited for the court to reopen. Also, once slaves left their masters, they had to prove to the government that they had somewhere else to work and slaves lost all security that they would be cared for if they were sick, which happened often. Pemba is a tropical location, and malaria, smallpox, and other diseases were commonplace during the time. It is no wonder then that only 10 percent to 25 percent of slaves ever applied for their freedom. In 1909, the colonial government officially abolished slavery on the island, yet some people still called themselves slaves and were treated as such for several more decades.

Pemba and its more famous sister island of Zanzibar are mostly Islamic. Islam dominated people's lives, and masters generally converted their slaves to Islam. While for some this conversion may have been titular, many took the new religion to heart. It was often these slaves who continued to work for their former masters after the emancipation order. In 1912, a colonial official was discussing slavery with an elderly former slave. The official asked the man where he was from and he replied that he came from the area around modern-day Malawi. The official then asked him if he intended to go back to his home area and was surprised to receive the answer "return to those pagans? No way."[1] The ex-slave's

---

[1] J. E. E. Craster, *Pemba, the Spice Island of Zanzibar* (London, 1913), 95.

home community was not Muslim and therefore was not "civilized" in the eyes of the slave. This one moment in time indicates how important Islam became to former slaves and why most slaves living on Pemba did not return home after emancipation.

According to customary understandings of Islamic law on Pemba, when Muslims die, their bodies should be bathed, shrouded, and buried in a grave. Funeral costs are to be paid from the estate of the deceased. Expenditures to cover all other debts incurred by the deceased must be delayed until after the burial expenses are met. Even if the Muslim dies without having left a will, their body should be handled with respect.[2] Yet, this was specific only to those individuals who were recognized in the community as Muslims. Descriptions of Zanzibar from Europeans visiting the island in the nineteenth century always mentioned the "rotting corpses of slaves" on the beaches, although most slave owners considered it a duty to bury their slaves.[3] By the twentieth century, such sights no longer occurred, but the legacy of slaves not receiving a proper burial or any of the rites of an Islamic burial may have lingered.

The four documents presented here constitute a small sample of the probate records and wills of former slaves on the island of Pemba. While the wills themselves are brief, they offer important insights into the religious beliefs and communal networks of former slaves. Moreover, they allow us to see how former slaves negotiated their ongoing relationships with their former masters and each other. As stipulated by local Islamic law, each of the four wills contain instructions to guide the funeral rites and how to distribute the property of the deceased. Only after the funeral occurred would division of the estate begin.

The rules of division are detailed and based on three forms of relationship: blood (*nasab*), marriage (*sabab*), and patronage (*al-wila* or *wala*). All blood relatives would be considered for the purposes of inheritance but not all relatives through marriage would receive part of the estate. Only the spouses of the deceased, who could prove they had a valid marriage at the time of death, counted. Slaves married to free people were not counted in Zanzibar as having a valid marriage for the purposes of inheritance.[4] The last category of relationship, *wala*, was very important for former slaves. When an owner manumitted his slave, it created a bond between them that was "similar to *nasab*" (blood). While this did not allow former slaves to claim an inheritance from their former masters, it did entitle former masters and their agnate heirs to any remaining portion of the estates of former slaves.[5] However, in some cases, *wala* was used to keep a slave from devolving property onto his heirs. In some rural parts of the eastern African coast, Islamic judges still upheld *wala* into the 1920s, allowing a master to inherit all of his former slaves' land.[6] The argumentation given for these cases was that the slaves were not freed by their masters but by decree of the government, therefore according to Islamic law they were still slaves and must follow the legal precedents that technically any property "owned" by a slave belonged to the master. This remained a problem for slaves well after emancipation.[7]

---

[2]   L. Bakhtiar, *Encyclopedia of Islamic Law: A Compendium of the Major Schools* (Chicago, 1996), 286.

[3]   F. B. Pearce, *Zanzibar: The Island Metropolis of Eastern Africa* (London, 1920), 189.

[4]   E. McMahon, "'A solitary tree builds not': *Heshima*, community and shifting identity in post-emancipation Pemba Island," *International Journal of African Historical Studies*, 39, 2 (2006), 197–219.

[5]   See Bakhtiar, *Encyclopedia*, 289 and J. N. D. Anderson, *Islamic Law in Africa* (London, 1955), 378 for Zanzibar-specific cases.

[6]   Anderson, *Islamic*, 118.

[7]   Zanzibar National Archives (ZNA), Zanzibar Town AC8/7 Letter from the Friends' Industrial Mission Pemba to the Vice Consul of Pemba dated 19 January 1904.

QUESTIONS TO CONSIDER

1. Why might slaves find it important to write a will? What does this tell us about their position in their communities?
2. Why would former slaves leave property to their master? What are the different possible explanations for this choice?
3. How was kinship constructed between people?
4. What does it tell us about slavery on Pemba island that former slaves could own so much property by 1910 when slavery was only fully abolished in 1909?

DOCUMENT 1

AK1/46
Baraka Mnyasa[8]
Male
Native of Pemba
Death: 21st May 1910

Will
Will of Baraka Mnyasa

1) To buy *saada*[9] and other expenses of burial.
2) Food to be given to the mourners worth Rs 20/-[10]
3) For washing Rs 4/-
4) For digging grave Rs 4/-
5) Reading Koran[11] on his grave
6) To fast for a period of a month
7) Rs 5/- to be given to the relation who [unreadable]
8) To be *wasir*[12]: Hamid bin Suleiman and Said bin Masood and Hashim bin Amur, to do everything as pay debts. In absence of any wasir one is sufficient. To be given Rs 20/- for their work.
9) To be given to my wife Halima binti Makame 9 coconut trees in shamba[13] Kingoni and 50 clove trees in shamba Nyagole.

Dated 39th el-Haj 1327[14]

---

[8] Mnyasa is an ethnic group from modern-day Malawi. This suggests the person is a former slave. He could, however, have been a migrant laborer brought to the island after emancipation.

[9] Swahili for "assistance"; it means to pay for help in preparing the burial.

[10] Rs is short for rupees. This was the currency used in Pemba at the time. A monthly wage of a laborer in 1910 was anywhere between 6 and 15 rupees per month.

[11] This is the Swahili spelling of the word "Qur'an."

[12] In this instance, a *wasir* is an administrator of the estate.

[13] *Shamba* means piece of land in Swahili. However, it does not describe the size, so a *shamba* could have 9 trees or 900 trees planted on it. The main cash crops on the island were coconuts and cloves, both of which grow on trees. The name following the word *shamba* is the name of the land.

[14] January 21, 1910. Land was not considered to hold much value, only the producing coconut and clove trees held value. The way a person claimed land as belonging to themselves was to plant permanent tree crops such as cloves and coconuts. However, the land under trees usually was sold with the trees. Exceptions existed; for example, trees planted in cemeteries could be considered as owned separately from the land.

<u>Probate Record</u>

Left several properties one with 105 clove trees and one with 9 clove trees (valued at 315/- & 27/- respectively)

Also one property was sold for 100/- by "the heirs".

Later listing of properties follows:

Shamba 105 cloves – 315/-

Shamba 50 cloves – 150/-

Shamba 8 coconut – 16/-

Shamba 20 coconut – 40/- (question mark next to this one)

House 15/-

Total estate 536/-

Debts: 5/-, 1/-, 3/-

Witnesses were brought in about the estate

[unreadable first name] b. Hamadi of Ole[15] testifies:
I knew Baraka Mnyasa

(1) Shamba Tundadowa has coconut and clove trees
(2) Shamba Kichaw has coconut and clove trees
(3) Shamba Nyajali has clove trees only

As for the price I say that the (1) shamba would fetch at the least Rs 150/-. He has no brother to my mind. I saw some 60 pishi[16] rice in the house. I know [unreadable sentence then a list of names] and went away running at this moment I saw them and some others. The deceased has 3 shops. He had good many things in the house. He had plenty [unreadable]. All these were sold by Nasib H. Seif bin Najim of Ole.

Seif bin Najim of Ole testifies:

The deceased was living in my shamba in his own house. Then after 2 years he was sick. He wrote the will by his own will. When he died there were myself, Abdallah bin Masoud el Barwani, Siwa bin Ali Swahili, Ahmed bin Musa Swahili, Makume bin Kombo Tumbatu, Nasib H Seif bin Njim and Faraji and others. Afterwards we all sat outside in the baraza[17] waiting for the executors. One of the executors, named Hamis b. Suliman came and went inside the house. Then he, Siwa, Kisuka and Hawifu [unreadable] came out and went into W.C. with a hoe. They dug the ground and took something which I presume to be money. They went to the house of [unreadable]. I asked Siwa and Kisuka how much money they had found. They told me Rs 80/- and that they had given to Hamis.

When I had asked Baraka he had told me that he had given all the money to Hamis amounting to Rs 450/- being Rs 300/- for feast (mourning) Rs 150/- for [unreadable] to be bought for him. In the next morning the sheha[18]… came to one and told that Baraka was

---

[15] This witness appears to be an appraiser. The probate courts always sent an appraiser to value the property because the court received a fee based on the value of the property. Ole is a town in Pemba.

[16] A *pishi* is between 4 and 5 pounds, depending on the size of the container used for measuring.

[17] A *baraza* is the stone bench built onto the front of houses in the Zanzibar islands. It is customary that men would sit outside on the *baraza* because women sit inside the house.

[18] A *sheha* is much like a village mayor but without any power to make decisions. The *sheha* reported to the probate court any deaths in their communities and the potential value of the estate.

dead in my shamba and showed me hole which had been dug. Hamis bin Suliman brought Rs 20/- and the burial expense was done. The sheha asked me what was left by deceased and I told that he had shambas. I gave the names of shambas and some details. I recognized in the will the hand writing as to that of Saleh bin Amur b. Saleah Mauri. I am certain that the deceased had a wife but not a brother. I heard that Rs 20/- were offered to one man to say that he was the brother to the deceased by one Sudi bin Farazi H. Barwani, but afterwards nothing was given to him.

Uledi b. Mnyasa of Ole testifies:
I am brother to the deceased by being slave of the same master. I am not brother by mother or father. I told you that I was brother to the deceased only because I was offered Rs 20/-, 1 (English pound) and cloves 20.[19] Swedi bin Feruzi and Hamis bin Suliman forced with the above agreement to say so. I told what they wished. I do not know when Baraka died. I did not go to see Baraka. I was sick. If I had been well I would not go. I am ignorant and beg your pardon. I made a great mistake and hope to be pardoned. I will [unreadable] to say more. I will come when the govt. wants me and I will always say the same which I have said above. If I am given any money I will bring here in the court without failure.

DOCUMENT 2

AK1/58
Mabruk Wadi Sunizani
Male
Native of Pemba
Death: July 1910

Will
1) For digging grave and washing his body and other expenses Rs 5/-
2) Rs 50/ to be sent to Mecca.[20]
3) Reading Koran on his grave.
4) For mourners for food, and obligation that the mourners should say "Loa-hi-la-haits allah" seventy thousand times.[21]
5) All these above expenses to be met out of 1/3 of his property.
6) 1/3 of his property to be given to his master Hasan bin Jaffer or Hasan's children.
7) 1/3 for the heirs
8) to wasirs, Hasan bin Jaffer, Ali bin Fakhi Swahili and Ali bin Salim bin Mohamed Amuri and for their wages Rs 15 to be given to them.

Probate Record
Heirs: Wife, Binti Dawenga living at Zanzibar

---

[19] He means a plot of land with twenty clove trees on it.
[20] This means that 50 rupees are to be spent sending a person on the pilgrimage to Mecca. It is the duty of all good Muslims to go on the pilgrimage once in their life. If a person died and had not gone on the pilgrimage, they could pay for someone to do it in their name.
[21] This phrase translates as "there is no God but God (Allah)."

Shamba

70 cloves	210/-
30 small cloves	30/-
2 houses	20/-
Household value	15/-
Total value	275/-

DOCUMENT 3

AK1/76
Kichipele Mrashi
Female
Native of Pemba
Death: 10 Oct 1910
Heir: Husband, Idi bin Khalfan bin Nasor

Will
Will of Kichyeli Mrashi binti Amur[22]

1) For washing Rs 2/-
2) For digging grave Rs 5/-
3) For reading Koran and [unreadable] Rs 120/- for 3 days
4) For reading Koran on the grave Rs 20/-
5) 27 clove trees to be sold to defray all these expenses
6) Rs 10/- to be given to Maua binti Nasor bin Khalef Rekeshi
7) To be wasirs: Nasor bin Khalef Rekeshi and Omar bin Omar Genzuani for their wages Rs 20/-. In the absence of one the other is sufficient.

Written 11th Ramadhan 1324[23]

Translation of a document attached to the will:
Mrashi binti Khombo gives freedom to her slave Mapili binti Akida and gives her 7 clove trees and 5 cocoanuts and 1 mango tree in the shamba Kekewani situate at Wawi in Pemba, bounded on the east by Binti isa Fathilii, on the north by Heirs of Mohamed bin Salim, on the west by Mrashi and on the south by that of Suliman bin Said Hatherui.
Dated: 23 Shaban 1324[24]

Translation of a document attached to the will:
Mrashi mother of Suliman bin Amur gives as gift to her husband Fundi Idi slave of Khalfan bin Nassor Korbi 13 clove trees, 11 cocoanut trees and a house in the shamba Kekewani.

Probate Record
Shamba 46 cloves = 118/-
26 coconuts = 52/-
2 houses = 20/-
Household things = 19/-

[22] "Bin" means "son of" and "binti" means "daughter of."
[23] October 29, 1906.
[24] October 12, 1906.

Shamba in Vitongoji bush[25] = 17/-
Shamba in Vitongoji bush = 9/-
Shamba in Vitongoji bush = 34/-
3 mango trees [no value given]
Total estate 289/-

Juma Heri and Hamadi Heri came to claim share in the estate as brothers of deceased. Told to prove in a court of law.

Household things
    Visyi = 2–8–0[26]
    Panga[27] = 1-0-0
    Choka Mulote[28] = 1-0-0
    2 beds = 2–8-0
    1 bed = 1-0-0
    1 box = 10-0-0

DOCUMENT 4

AK1/3310
Hashima binti Baraka Mgɪndo
Female
Native of Pemba
Died 27 August, 1934

Will
    1. Funeral at the discretion [unreadable]
    2. Rs 100/- feast at the closing of mourning
    3. Rs 5/- to be paid to the washer of her dead body
    4. Rs 10/- to be paid to the digger of her grave
    5. 20 clove trees in shamba Mgeni-Haji to be given to Said bin Suleiman
    6. Rs 60/- to be given to Biubwa binti Swedi
    7. Rs 100/- remuneration to Hidaya binti Chande

The above deceased has directed in her Will that 20 clove trees in Shamba Mgeni-Maji be given to her master Said bin Suleiman bin Abdulla El-Marhubi for the debt owed by her. It is reported to me that the said Said bin Suleiman El-Marhubi died before the death of the above deceased at Zanzibar leaving 3 sons, 1 daughter and a widow residing in Zanzibar.

Probate Record
Heir: husband Awali bin Baraka
Beit El-Mal[29]

---

[25] Vitongoji is a location on the eastern side of the island, composed mostly of sandy soils – called "bush land."
[26] The value here is given in rupees and pice, so two rupees and eight pice.
[27] Machete is a large knife used for cutting vegetation.
[28] An axe.
[29] The *beit-el-mal* was the fund for the poor, upkeep of mosques, and the like. It was basically a religiously prescribed social welfare fund.

Estate divided equally between husband and Beit el-mal but then it states "I allow Beit-el-mal's share to husband"

Shambas 2–660/-, 117/-

One mud house 22–50

She had a variety of shambas, a "mud house" at Zanzibar valued at 100/-, house effects of 15/- for a total value of 758/-

-a total of 4 shambas, although one of them was worth 430/-, another one had a house on it – total land and house valued at 93/-

She was owed debts by Ali bin Said El-Kharusi of 49–50 and Mkono bin Mwinyi of 12/-

The executor of her will was Khamis bin Magera el Mnyasa.

SUGGESTED ADDITIONAL READINGS

Cooper, Frederick. *Plantation Slavery on the East Coast of Africa*. New Haven: Yale University Press, 1977.

   From Slaves to Squatters: Plantation Labor and Agriculture in Zanzibar and Coastal Kenya, 1890–1925. New Haven: Yale University Press, 1980.

Deutsch, Jan- Georg. *Emancipation without Abolition in German East Africa c.1884–1914*. Athens: Ohio University Press, 2006.

Fair, Laura. *Pastimes and Politics: Culture, Community, and Identity in Post-Abolition Urban Zanzibar, 1890–1945*. Athens: Ohio University Press, 2001.

Glassman, Jonathan. *Feasts and Riot: Revelry, Rebellion, and Popular Consciousness on the Swahili Coast, 1856–1888*. Portsmouth: Heinemann Books, 1995.

Lodhi, A. Y. *The Institution of Slavery in Zanzibar and Pemba*. Uppsala: Scandinavian Institute of African Studies, 1973.

Mirza, Sarah, and Margaret Strobel, eds. *Three Swahili Women: Life Histories from Mombasa, Kenya*. Bloomington: Indiana University Press, 1989.

Romero, Patricia. *Lamu: History, Society, and Family in an East African Port City*. Princeton: Markus Wiener, 1997.

Strobel, Margaret. *Muslim Women in Mombasa, 1890–1975*. New Haven: Yale University Press, 1979.

Wright, Marcia. *Strategies of Slaves and Women: Life-stories from East/Central Africa*. New York: L. Barber Press, 1993.

PART NINE

LIVING WITH THE PAST

45 INTRODUCTION: Contemporary African Societies and the Legacy of Slavery

I n the past decade, research on the legacy of slavery has expanded significantly. A new field of investigation, which focuses on current relationships between the descendants of slaves and masters and the different ways they look at their shared past, has emerged at the intersection of social and cultural anthropology and African history. The contributions of Benedetta Rossi (Chapter 47) and Paolo Gaibazzi (Chapter 46) are excellent examples of this trend. Rossi introduces sources from the Hausa and Tuareg groups of the Ader region (Republic of Niger), while Gaibazzi focuses on two slave descendants' narratives from the Soninke communities of the Upper River Gambia.

The aftermath of slavery is a sensitive topic. Both authors base their analysis on long-term ethnographic fieldwork. Confronted with enduring social and political discrimination, Rossi's and Gaibazzi's informants have not been in a position to express their indignation, although they consider what happened to their ancestors extremely unjust. While in other African contexts slave descendants have begun to use contemporary movements for greater democratization to contest their past and present subjection, the slave descendants of Ader and The Gambia still feels held back by their ancestry.

Rossi and Gaibazzi explain how masters strove to maintain their privileges after the legal ending of slavery in the colonial period. In both contexts, former masters have subjected slave descendants to belittling discourses about their social role, and they continue making humiliating references to their ancestry. Rossi's and Gaibazzi's informants give voice to the rage resulting from this ongoing discrimination, but they also express the dignity with which slaves of the past, and slave descendants today, cope with their marginality. The fact that slave ancestry can be a resource for maintaining feelings of solidarity between slave descendants and the former master class is another interesting point addressed in these testimonies. Not all slave descendants see their ancestry as a social hindrance. Some can become extremely defensive when their reciprocal relationships with the descendants of masters are put into question. Nor do all descendants of yesterday's masters look down upon people of slave ancestry. Respect, affection, and mutuality shape the interactions between these two contemporary social categories as much as hierarchy and rank.

46 Two Soninke "Slave" Descendants and Their Family Biographies

PAOLO GAIBAZZI

Baba and Tamba[1] are two Soninke[2] (or Serahule) elders living in the Upper River Region, Eastern Gambia. In narrating their family history,[3] they shed light on the course of emancipation, which in this area of West Africa lasted from the end of the nineteenth until at least the middle of the twentieth century. Although in this region slavery began to be abolished in 1906 and ceased to have legal validity in 1930,[4] actual changes in social relations took longer to sediment, as Baba's and Tamba's recollections indicate. Both speak of negotiations and resistances, openings and closures, changes and legacies accompanying the end of slave trading and slave ownership under the aegis of British colonialism. They do so from a particular perspective; in their village they are called *komo* (sing. *kome*). Before abolition, this term identified Soninke slaves who often lived in their masters' compounds and worked for them. After abolition, the *komo* became free persons able to decide their own destiny and that of their children, and yet this label has continued to be used to identify people descending from the slaves of the past.

Being *komo* today means belonging to a status group integrated at the bottom of the Soninke social hierarchy, in which "nobles" control political and religious offices and free-born "casted artisans" (leatherworks, blacksmiths, bards, etc.) feature as clients.[5]

---

[1] In order to protect the identity of the narrators and the people they mention, pseudonyms or only initials of names and places were used. I carried out interviews with the two narrators between October 2007 and January 2008, thanks to the collaboration of Musa Sumbundu. Translations into English were carried out by Musa Sumbundu, Facuru Silla, and myself.

[2] The literature usually refers to this ethnic group as Soninke. In the Gambia, the term Serahule (Seranxulle in Soninke language) is often employed by other ethnic groups. The Soninke themselves are prone to using that ethnonym, while "Soninke" can be used to refer to families (pl. Soninko) of noble origins (*hooro*). To avoid confusion and help the reader compare the case with the literature, I will use the term Soninke for ethnicity and language only, while the nobles will be *hooro*.

[3] The term "family" is used to indicate the patrilineal and patrilocal "extended family" known as *xabila* among the Soninke; such families live in one or more joint households or compounds (*ka*). In this particular case, Baba's and Tamba's families have only a compound each.

[4] The first ordinance against the traffic in slaves was promulgated in 1894 immediately after the Proclamation of the British Protectorate of the Gambia. The 1906 ordinance followed the annexation of the Upper River province to the British Protectorate in 1901. It promulgated the ban on the traffic in slaves, regulated slave ownership, and envisaged ways in which slaves could ransom themselves. The 1930 ordinance finally declared all forms of trade and possession of slaves illegal. From that date on, slavery ceased to be a legal institution.

[5] Nobles are called *hooro* (sing. *hoore*), while artisans are called *nyamaxalo* (sing. *nyamaxala*) and are divided into mostly endogamous subgroups: leatherworkers (*garanko*), smiths (*tago*), woodworkers and

Baba and Tamba narrate not only the difficulties in coping with the ongoing significance of servile status, but also the peculiar ways in which this status was produced and maintained during abolition. Although their grandfathers were neither bought nor caught, when they migrated and settled in the upper river valley at the end of the nineteenth and beginning of the twentieth century, they had little choice but to integrate in the *kome* group.[6] This subaltern integration notwithstanding, Baba's father and Tamba's grandfather became wealthy farmers and traders, taking advantage of the booming commercial peanut agriculture in the upper Gambia during the first part of the twentieth century. As they acquired wealth and prestige, they found themselves coming to terms with, and testing, the boundaries of slavery during a period in which the status of *kome* was undergoing rapid change.

The setting of these family biographies is a Soninke village established "only" at the turn of the twentieth century on the south bank of the Upper River Gambia by Soninke farmers and traders coming from Bundu, a region in Eastern Senegal. Even though the Soninke were fleeing from raids and political turmoil,[7] they maintained a degree of social cohesion during the exodus and even took along some, albeit not many, slaves. The Gambia was not new to them. During the era of the Atlantic slave trade, the Soninke had traded in slaves along the river, and continued to sell them during the nineteenth century. After the advent of legitimate trade in the early and middle part of the century, many other Soninke came to the Gambia to farm peanuts, which soon became the major export commodity of the Gambian valley.[8]

After the annexation of the Upper River province to the Gambia Protectorate in 1901, Soninke villages as well as other rural communities along the river resisted the end of slavery, though they avoided overt challenges to the colonial state. Upheavals and flights of former slaves did occur, but a common pattern was negotiation.

Ties of interdependence were not severed in most cases, particularly in the case of vulnerable slaves. Patron-client relationships with former masters provided social security and gave access to local resources, such as land. The true impact of abolition on the upper-river Soninke villages was probably felt only in the 1930s. Slaves progressively

---

basket weavers (*saako*), praise-singers or bards (*jaaru*), Islamic bards (*finanu*), and oral "genealogists" (*geseru*). Pre-abolition slavery took many forms, and second-generation slaves usually enjoyed better conditions and more rights compared to trade slaves. For a description of Soninke social structure, see E. Pollet and G. Winter, *La société Soninké (Dyahunu, Mali)* (Bruxelles, 1971).

[6] As is made clear later in the chapter, slave ownership is transmitted through the mother; therefore, children of immigrant men who married slave women or women of slave descent were considered slave or slave descendants.

[7] Bundu is an area between the upper valley of the Gambia and that of the Senegal River. Before French colonization, it was a kingdom ruled by a Muslim dynasty of Fula origins. As from the 1850s, succession struggles, Islamic armed movements, and French colonization greatly affected the stability of the kingdom, disrupting trade and threatening the security of its inhabitants. See M. Gomez, *Pragmatism in the age of Jihad: The Precolonial State of Bundu* (Cambridge, 1992).

[8] In 1807, British abolition of the Atlantic slave trade inaugurated the transition to "legitimate trade," which included several indigenous commodities (gold, leather, beeswax, gum Arabic, etc.). By the 1850s, peanuts had become the main export product of the Gambian valley. Some indigenous slave traders, including the Soninke, invested or converted into peanut cultivation, contributing to the spread of commercial agriculture and paving the way for successive waves of seasonal agricultural migrants. Peanut cultivation was not based on large plantations; it was integrated into household production. See K. Swindell and A. Jeng, *Migrants, Credit and Climate: The Gambian Groundnut Trade, 1834–1934* (Leiden, Boston, 2006), 68–93.

managed to carve out social autonomy and control over their labor. However, it seems that in 1950s it was still not uncommon for some *komo* to work on their former masters' fields one day a week or during specific periods.[9]

The *komo* have not disappeared. Their descendants are still known as such and they are considered one status group like the nobles and the casted artisans; accordingly, they can only marry among themselves. The only exception to this marriage rule is that *kome* women can marry freeborn men; as Baba explains in his narrative, these women are required to undergo a purification rite to remove the stigma of their slave origins and thus bear freeborn children. Were the stigma not removed, the children would inherit it because, before legal abolition, ownership in slaves followed matrilineal descent.

Genealogies of slave descent, and thus of master-slave relations, are often remembered in detail.[10] Today, former slaves and former masters are tied by customary relations, as is the case among other status groups: the *komo* are frequently called upon to perform particular *kome* tasks at ceremonies, such as fetching firewood (the men) and cooking the communal meals (the women). In turn, some *komo* can ask for financial assistance from their former masters in case of need, as Tamba explains. These customary relations are ambivalent: they are often portrayed as a matter of politically neutral tradition between groups, while they are predicated on the memory of former master-slave relations between families. Tamba seems to sustain this perspective, but it is also the case that some freeborn adopt discriminatory attitudes toward the *komo*, considering them shameless dependents who belong to a sort of second-class humanity. In addition to stigmas, the *komo* have suffered from marginalization in social, religious, and political life.

Given the persistence of slave descent, it is not surprising that Baba's and Tamba's narratives pay some attention to how their ancestors settled in the village and were integrated into village society. Baba's grandfather arrived in the upper river valley in the late nineteenth century, when colonial rule had not been established yet. He came to look for economic opportunities and joined the army of Musa Molo Balde, the then-ruler and one of the most important warlords of the time. Baba and Tamba's village was situated in his kingdom, known as Fuladu.[11] Having earned the trust of the king on the field of battle, Baba's grandfather received a woman in marriage from him and settled in this village. By the turn of the century, colonial pacification had put a halt to raids and wars, so he became a farmer.

Musa's grandfather arrived later, probably during the second decade of the twentieth century. This was a period of economic expansion, when farmers eagerly took to growing and selling peanuts to European traders and their agents. The recently established Soninke villages of the upper river region welcomed migrants and settlers

---

[9] During the transition period, the workload was reduced to one day a week – Saturday or Sunday – sometimes two. It is difficult, however, to know the frequency and extension of such practice.

[10] The Soninke are a patrilineal society; the children of a married couple belong to the lineage of the father and acquire his patronym. After abolition, when the *komo* gained control over their families and their descendants, they also founded patrilineages.

[11] In 1861, the kingdom of Fuladu was established by Alpha Molo Balde with the support of the Muslim state of Futa Jallon. Conquest continued under his son, Musa Molo, who took over in 1881. At its apex, Fulladu comprised much of the south banks of the Upper Gambia River valley. In spite of the religious motivations behind the Fulladu conquest, Musa, like many of the Senegambian warlords, engaged in violent reprisals and frequent raids on neighboring populations and dissidents. A. Bellagamba, *Ethnographie, histoire, et colonialisme en Gambie* (Paris, 2002).

coming to expand commercial agricultural production. Thousands of young men (known as *navetans* in Senegal and "strange farmers" in the Gambia) from surrounding regions reached the Gambia during the rainy and harvest seasons (June–December) to work on a share-cropping basis with their landlord/host.[12] When the season was over, they sold their produce, paid their seed debt back to the landlord, and bought goods before returning to their homes. Some of these migrants, however, decided to marry and settle down. Musa's grandfather – Yugo – was one of them.

How were newcomers integrated in local communities? Strangers had to negotiate their inclusion into village society, and local elites had to deal with the great diversity of the migrant population and with a changing sociopolitical order. The idiom of slavery mediated the integration of some of immigrants, especially those who lacked substantial socioeconomic resources. Baba and Tamba are not so explicit about their ancestors' entry into slavery, which they contest anyway. However, Baba is clear about one thing: when the villagers did not know where the person came from (i.e., his social origins), they gave him a slave woman. Marriage was one of the main doors into "slavery." Immigrants did not become "slaves" themselves, but because slave descent follows the maternal line, their children belonged to the mother's master, or at least inherited the status of *kome*. Former slave owners were often the hosts of seasonal migrants; by procuring wives for their stranger, they could enlarge their slave entourages or extend their influence to him and his children. Even for those who got married elsewhere and brought their wives along like Baba's grandfather, misrecognition of their social origins left little choice but for them to be positioned within the *kome* group, the only place where they could possibly find marriage partners for their children.

In retrospect, it seems surprising that migrants agreed to marry *komo*. Tamba suggests that deception could have been used to subordinate newcomers. More frequently it was poverty and indebtedness that left migrants with little choice but to rely on a patron or host to acquire a wife. Marriage in this part of the world is a complex, expensive activity, implying lengthy negotiations between the two kin groups, something that was out of reach for an individual migrant isolated from his extended family, lacking sufficient resources and significant status markers (e.g., Islamic education) to claim freeborn origins. It must be said that some of these immigrants were indeed former slaves, either fleeing their masters after abolition in French territories or coming to the Gambia as seasonal migrants.[13]

However degrading being or becoming *kome* might be, inclusion in Soninke society had some advantages. The Soninke were and are experienced farmers and successful traders who enjoyed a certain degree of prosperity in the region. Baba's father, Mari Penda, may have especially benefited from Soninke trading networks ranging from Guinea-Bissau to Eastern Mali.[14] Mari Penda became one of the richest and best-known traders in his village

---

[12] Hospitality is an ancient and important institution in West Africa and West African mobility. Hosts offered food and shelter, and acted as representatives or brokers on behalf of their guests in their local communities. Host-guest arrangements became important in the "strange farmer" migration, enabling hosts to cope with labor shortages and migrants to have land and seeds in addition to food and shelter. Migrants worked three to four mornings a week for their landlord. See P. David, *Les navétanes: histoire des migrants saisonniers de l'arachide en Sénégambie des origines à nos jours* (Dakar, 1980); Swindell and Jeng, *Migrants*, 56–66.

[13] Cf. F. Manchuelle, *Willing Migrants: Soninke Labor Diasporas, 1848–1960* (Athens and London, 1997), 84–86.

[14] For an account of Soninke and other trading diasporas, see P. D. Curtin, *Economic Change in Precolonial Africa: Senegambia in the Era of the Slave Trade* (Madison, 1975); A. Bathily, *Les portes de l'or: le royaume de Galam, Sénégal, de l'ère musulmane au temps des négriers, VIIIe–XVIIIe siècle* (Paris, 1989).

and the surrounding area, and became friends with Tamba's grandfather, Yugo, another successful peanut farmer and wealthy cattle owner. Tamba emphasizes hard work as key to his grandfather's success, and it is possible that the example of self-made men in peanut agriculture enticed other young men into settling down to try to achieve similar results.

The transformation of slavery during this time did create room for upward mobility for wealthy strangers and descendants of slaves, although there were limitations. Baba's and Tamba's children never worked for any villager, or indeed for anybody else. This may have constituted an advantage compared to other settlers and *komo* residing in the same village. Mari Penda is described as a respected and generous patron; he married four wives and managed to marry some of his daughters to prominent nobles. Concessions about who could have access to an Islamic education also benefited his sons. Indeed, Islamic faith and Islam's alleged egalitarianism are cited by both Mari Penda and Yugo, like several past and present *komo*, as a superseding moral order that would trivialize the label of *kome* attached to them. Having been excluded from religious office and higher Islamic education, however, they would hardly have the authority, let alone the willingness, to critique the foundations and ongoing significance of slave descent on religious grounds.[15]

In contrast to Mari Penda, Yugo faced more difficult times, and at one point he moved out the village to avoid discriminations and tensions. Even if slavery was progressively outlawed, local elites were not willing to concede too much ground. The issue of status and descent could be used to exclude lower classes from political and religious office, and generally to buttress claims about their inferiority. Above all, refusing to give a freeborn woman to "strangers" and descendants of slaves must be read also as a statement about status inequality and as an example of the attempt by the freeborn to subordinate people over whom they wielded less and less control, and who could threaten their primacy by acquiring wealth.

Baba clearly feels discriminated by this practice. Having lived for so many years in other West African countries (like other Soninke migrants of his generation),[16] he has experienced relationships that were less determined by status.[17] By becoming a successful trader, he has contributed to his father's pleas for full emancipation. "Nobody can call them *komo*," I was repeatedly told by villagers – an acknowledgment of his family's acquired status and their painstaking process of redeeming traces of servile origin, which the narrative

---

[15] The issue of slavery in African Islam is a complex one. Even though the Quran acknowledges the legal status of slavery, slavery among Muslims is usually discouraged in Islamic jurisprudence. Many Soninke informants also state that, in theory, all Muslims are equal. However, in West African history, Islam has also legitimized the status quo and sanctioned discipline even during the abolition process. Contemporary reformist currents inspired to the Middle East tend to downplay the division in status groups, but this does not always translate into practice. Cf. M. Klein, *Slavery and Colonial Rule in French West Africa* (Cambridge, 1998), 229-231; R. Roberts and P. Zachernuk, "Introduction," *Canadian Journal of African Studies*, 34, 3 – Special Issue: On Slavery and Islam in African History: A Tribute to Martin Klein (2000), 497-511; R. Dilley, *Islamic and Caste Knowledge Practices among the Haalpulaar'en in Senegal: Between Mosque and Termite Mound* (Edinburgh, 2004), esp. chapters 1 and 8.

[16] In the second half of the twentieth century, migrations from the upper Gambia and Senegal valleys boomed. Soninke migrants went to West Africa, working as traders and intermediaries in the diamond and African art industries, and in the commerce of other goods. Migration to Europe and North America soon developed as well. The Soninke of the upper Senegal River valley are well known for their migration to France, cf. among others: S. Bredeloup, *La diams'pora du fleuve Sénégal: sociologie des migrations africaines* (Toulouse; Paris, 2007); M. Timera, *Les Soninké en France* (Paris, 1996).

[17] It is worth remarking that status distinctions have been also maintained and reproduced in the Diaspora. For a contemporary case study on the significance of "slavery" among Soninke migrants, see Y. Sy, "L'esclavage chez les Soninkés: du village à Paris," *Journal des Africanistes*, 70, 1-2 (2000), 43-69.

relates in some detail. Redemption has not, however, translated into a change of status: Baba's family still faces a barrier if they want to marry freeborn women. Thus the issue of origins continues to haunt Baba; he even went on a sort of "roots trip" to Mali to ascertain his grandfather's noble origins. Interviewing him about his family biography gave him the opportunity, perhaps compelled him, to rethink these topics. "Slavery" remains a delicate issue in his village. The word *kome* might offend people if not properly handled; yet public dissent on the issue of slave ancestry might prompt freeborn to firmly reassert status distinctions. Digging into family biographies is fraught with ambivalences – ethical and methodological. Slave descendants may understandably avoid recounting old conflicts and their present echoes. Or they may omit those parts of their past that refer to, and reinstate, their status. Such difficulties make us appreciate the testimonies of Baba and Tamba. One might argue that Tamba gives a rather positive account of "slavery" before and after abolition precisely to avoid overexposure. Tamba has not had much opportunity to travel and accumulate wealth like Baba: relationships with his former masters have played an important role in his life. In contemporary Soninke society, indeed in the Gambia, there are different understandings of what *kome* was and still is. Like Baba, Tamba gives us a glimpse of this plurality, opting for a vision that emphasizes tradition and interdependence rather than opposition. Far from being uncritical, his words invite the reader to reflect on the spaces of accommodation and maneuver that his position allows.

QUESTIONS TO CONSIDER

1. Baba's father and Tamba's grandfather arrived as strangers and became wealthy people in their village. What relations did they establish with the villagers? How did the village elite view them?
2. Baba and Tamba say that their ancestors were freeborn and later became "slaves" or equivalent to "slaves." Did Baba's father and Tamba's grandfather claim free origins vis-à-vis their community? Did they try to contest or overcome their slave origins? If they did not, how did they motivate their strategy?
3. The issue of slavery is also relevant to Baba and Tamba today. Compare and contrast their opinions and experiences of "slavery."

BABA[18]

[My ancestors arrived here] step by step. They left Segu and went to Wagadu[19] – they stayed long in Wagadu. When Wagadu was not good anymore, they left Wagadu and went to Kanta.

---

[18] The following accounts stem out of semistructured interviews. Baba and Tamba were asked to tell how their ancestors arrived and got settled in the village. As they narrated their family biographies, more prompts and questions followed on how the ancestors and their descendants fared in village life and established matrimonial ties with villagers. Only the most salient parts of their narratives are reported here. Square brackets indicate editorial changes – additions, summaries or deletions from the original version – in order to ease the reading of the texts.

[19] Segu is a region and city in central Mali, while Wagadu is a region in eastern Mali, home to the famous Ghana Empire, which waned by the thirteenth century. In the following lines Baba seems to make reference the legend of Wagadu, a widespread trope among the Soninke to explain how their ancestors scattered and moved south and west. Even though he relates only essential elements of the legend, it is interesting to note here that Baba places his family history within such a storyline, perhaps to claim pure Soninke origins, or simply to provide a more general historical account as elders sometimes do.

When Kanta was ruined, our forebears met in the bush, and asked each other: "How is it over there?" They replied "Over there is destroyed." That is why the Soninke say *"Kanta kare"*[20] to mean something disastrous happened. When they left Segu, they came to Bundu.[21] Their stay in Bundu lasted long till war reached them. In Bundu, they scattered, and some went to Tambacounda [...] In Tamba, they scattered again ...

[Then they crossed the Gambia river and came here] [...] When our ancestor came, he settled at S. family's compound. That was our first compound. Our grandfather was over there, in the compound of T. S. When our grandfather died he left only my father in that house ... my father and his two sisters remained there. One married in Kumbija, the other in Kunda. The former married in the S. family, the latter in the S. family[22] [...] Thanks and praise to Almighty, [my father] alone entrusted himself to the village head.[23] He alone: no elder brother, no younger brother. He was the only one in that house. There was no maternal uncle, no younger brother. Allah helped him so that he got *barake*:[24] he acquired cattle, he acquired donkeys, his luck began to work. He was travelling to Kayes.[25] He was returning with cotton wrappers; sometimes he was coming with one hundred pieces. When weeding in the fields was over [around October], he was going to trade the remaining wrappers to Fogny, Gambia Fogny.[26] He was going, and going, and going ... when harvest time approached [November–December], he processed peanuts and sold them. Sometimes he was going to Guinea with 300 CFA;[27] he was going on foot up to Futa [Jallon]. [One of the leatherworkers in the village] used to make sandals for him [...] Sometimes then he was going to Futa Jallon. He was travelling on foot. He was going to buy cloth and some goods worth 300 or 400 [Francs]. At times he bought two cows. If he had bought two hundred wrappers, he would sometimes pay

---

[20] *Kanta kare* (Kanta is destroyed) is an idiomatic phrase originating from the legend of Wagadu: the drought and destruction of Kanta spurred the Soninke exodus. The phrase is now uttered when something catastrophic occurs.

[21] Here Baba switches to a different narrative plot, referring to the much more recent emigration of Soninke from Bundu (second half of nineteenth century). Tambacounda is a Senegalese city close to the eastern border of The Gambia.

[22] The families Baba cites are *kome* families in the two Soninke villages of the Upper River Region he mentions (Kunda is a pseudonym); it appears that his grandfather, or at least his children, were classified accordingly in society. From other interviews, it seems in fact that his grandfather's wife was considered as being of servile descent (see also the discussion later in the chapter).

[23] Entrusting (*xalifa*) usually refers to an asymmetrical relationship between individuals, like the host-guest one. Entrusting somebody with oneself is a way of granting protection and services while recognizing the superiority of the other party. In the narrative, this could mean that Baba's father, having remained alone, accepted his subordinate place in society in exchange for protection. On the other hand, all strangers, regardless of their status, had to submit to the village head upon settlement, not least to acquire land. It is therefore difficult to ascertain the political significance of Baba's statement. Cf. A. Bellagamba, "Entrustment and Its Changing Political Meanings in Fuladu, the Gambia (1880–1994)," *Africa*, 74, 3 (2004), 383–410.

[24] *Barake* (from Arabic *baraka*) means blessing or state of grace of divine origin. It is an important feature of Sufi Islam, and it especially mediated by parents and saintly figures (*marabouts*). In this particular context, the power of blessing becomes evident in the way Mari Penda is able to amass wealth in a steady and enduring manner. On the issue of "blessing" in the regional context, cf. D. Cruise O'Brien, *The Mourides of Senegal: The Political and Economic Organization of an Islamic Brotherhood* (Oxford, 1971); S. Bava, "De la ‹‹baraka aux affaires››: ethos économico-réligieu et transnationalité chez les migrants sénégalais mourides," *Revue Européenne des Migrations Internationales*, 19, 2 (2003), 69–84.

[25] Kayes is the name of a city and region in Western Mali, not far from the border with Senegal.

[26] A region in the lower southern Gambian valley.

[27] This is probably an anachronism, for the CFA currency (*Colonies françaises d'Afrique* – French Colonies of Africa) was only introduced in 1945 in French colonies. Before then, the currency in use was the French Franc.

people to bring the goods. He used to say that the baggage was too heavy to offload. If they offloaded it [from their heads], they could not find anyone to help them to take it up again. Futa is bush like, there are not many people there […] He had a stick with which he used to walk. When he was tired of travelling, he would place this stick under the load to hold it up. He would take his head out from underneath it as the stick was enough to hold the load in place. He would come with his load up to this village here. By the time he reached here, those sandals were all pierced. In those days there was no vehicle, only foot transport.

He got his wealth this way, thanks to God. He told us all about that. He used to get wealth in that way. As he amassed it this way, his wealth began to be abundant, cattle increased in number. The herd began to come into the village, so he called the village head and told him "give me a place to clear for myself. My cattle and I would settle outside the village so as not to give people a hard time." The village head said "That is true! […] You are welcome, there is no problem." Things went on till he came to clear this place. When he finished, he dug a well; they say "Mari's well." […]

So, this is the way [my family] settled here, and I have said it to you. *Alhamdulillah,*[28] little by little "we refill the river."[29] It did not happen only because of our father alone! But today, *Alhamdulillah,* we moved on from the condition we were as Allah has made our fortune easier.

My father was going like that until he married my mother in Kayes. The person who used to host him there was a ruler. His name was Sidi Jallo […] His name was Sidi, his surname was Jallo. My father used to lodge at his house. My mother grew in this man's house.[30] My father asked "Who is responsible for this girl?" The man said "It's me." "Won't you give her to me?" He said "Fine." [The woman] and he came together, and they stayed at Badjakunda [north bank Gambia]. When they left Badjakunda, *Alhamdulillah,* they came to this village. He stayed first at S. family's compound […] That is why, the S. and ourselves are inseparable now.[31]

Our history proper says that we come from Mali. That is the history I know […] Because you are a person who comes here from Mali, if they do not know you, they will give a slave woman to you. They will say "You are a slave." They don't know. Our grandfather who came from Segu was the first one to build a two-storey building there. But he was not a slave. Our sister went up to that place. I myself passed by there on my way to Ivory Coast where [my brother] was. I stopped, washed and had food, till the evening when I boarded a [rural taxi] to go to Kallake. I left Kallake for Sinkuran. I toured all around to inquire, even went to ask the village head. I asked the elders who know about the past. They said we are not slaves.

Our father told us that if he looked for any woman to marry, he would make sure that she is redeemed from slavery. He used to say "If she has not been redeemed yet, I will not die leaving the family dirty/impure." When any noble man who wants to marry one of our daughters, there is no need for redemption. There is no redemption, there is no "purification ceremony."[32] If we give them our daughters, nobody will consider them slaves.

---

[28] Arabic: thanks and praise to the Almighty.

[29] This is an idiomatic sentence, meaning: one generation is succeeding to the other.

[30] It is not clear which position this woman occupied in Sidi Jallo's house; she might be "adopted" or be a relative integrated in the man's family.

[31] There appears to have been a preexisting host-guest relationship between S. and Baba's family (not the same S. family that hosted his grandfather). That is why the S., as the custom requires, probably offered to host the bride coming from outside the village before the wedding had to take place.

[32] In the text, redemption is referred to as *bagandinde* (lit. taking out). It refers to the practice of buying one's freedom out of slavery, whether for one self (*dubgandi*) or for someone else. Even if legal slavery

This village is deceptive. If they don't know you, if you come and just stay once, they will say "give him a slave woman." Since they don't know where you come from … there are many free-born [turned slaves] in this village. They will say to them "those are *komo*." If they don't understand your place of origin, it won't work.[33] However, the place where our noble families come from – Loni – is the place where we used to be together. […] In that time, the Soninke and us left Loni. There were lots of lineages: Jabbi, Janka, Tunkara, Dukure…. You know the Bambara refer to the Konte who are slaves as Jarra. They call the free-born Konte. As for the Dambele, their free-born counterparts are called Trawally. Their slaves are called Dambele. But here they do not differentiate.[34][…] The noble counterparts of the Dambele, in Kulari and Badjakunda, are called Trawally. Those Trawally are not slaves. Those were pure nobles. They are not calling them Dambele […] My father gave his first child, a daughter, in marriage to the great *marabout* of Kunda village, known by the name of Al Haji F. [who has the same patronym as ours]. Our father's first daughter married him.[35] His family and us are the same thing. We don't differentiate among us: [families sharing our patronym] are in Garawol and in Dembakunda – some are there too. Some are here, some are in Garawol.

[The reason why they placed some of the people with our patronym below] is Islamic knowledge. Some were Islamic scholars, some others did not learn. They called the latter slaves. It is lack of education which brought this [difference] about: some had not learned.[36] At least that was their idea, because they did not know. It is quite possible that those were instead *hooro*. Because they didn't know, they sorted it out that way. But you cannot know the way a person took to come here! You cannot know the way your companions came! You cannot know the condition that they left behind!

Our grandmother was a Fula woman. They called her Penda Balde. That is not a *kome*; she is a *hoore*. She was the daughter of Musa Molo Balde's sister.[37] That is our grandmother. Is that a kome? No, that's not […] Our grandfather and Musa Molo were carrying out raids and

was formally abolished in 1930, redemption is still necessary to break up the original bond linking former slave and former master. It usually involves a payment, sometimes just a gift, to the former master; sometimes the latter grants redemption for free, his verbal approval being sufficient. "Purification ceremony" or *yankinde* (lit. washing) refers to the practice of bathing the bride during the wedding night before she is taken to the husband's compound. Here, Baba is referring to a particular case of *yankinde*. When the bride was or is a descendant of slaves and the groom is a freeborn, the *yankinde* is loaded with symbolic and practical meanings. It removes the impurity of the slave status, so that the children born of that wedlock will be free.

[33] "The place where one comes from" is not merely a geographical location; knowing the geographical location implies knowing about the village families and their interrelations, that is, the social position and status of the migrant.

[34] The Bambara are an ethnic group. Among the Soninke, too, patronymic differentiation can be an index of status, a way to tell the freeborn apart from those who fell into slavery. This principle is not universal, however, and does not apply to all patronymics, as Baba remarks. In some villages, Trawally and Dambele are interchangeable patronymics and both belong to the *kome*. Note that the different families belonging to different status groups can share the same patronymic.

[35] This seems quite indicative of Baba's family's strategies of upward mobility through marriage allegiances, for they gave their first, thus the most prestigious, daughter to an important noble family. Note, however, that the opposite does not apply: no *hoore* woman is given to them.

[36] Islamic knowledge was mainly confined to the *hoore*, and scholars (the *moodi*) were a subsection of this group. Therefore, as mentioned earlier, it constituted a criterion for reckoning the migrant's status. On the issue of status groups and Islam, cf. Dilley, *Islamic*, 27–56.

[37] Musa Molo Balde was said to be of servile descent, but because of his power he married across the social hierarchy and his descendants are today considered a noble lineage. Musa Molo was also famous for his large entourage of slaves, made up especially of slave women and concubines. It also appears that he, and Baldekunda after him, incorporated outsiders and slaves into his kin group.

waging war up to Tambasansang, that Tambasansang which is here in the Gambia.[38] They would leave Tamba to go up to Fogny, then they would leave Fogny and come back here. All of this to make war. Since Musa trusted my grandfather, he gave him his sister's daughter, Penda Balde. That is why my father was called Mari Penda.[39]

Our father was a very careful man … this village is not good. He said "the snake that hides is the one that sees its grandchildren [i.e., will live long], but a snake that exposes itself does not live long enough to see her grandchildren. She is killed early in her life." When my father wanted to marry a *hoore* woman, my grandfather refused. He said that he would give him too much exposure, which was dangerous. He satisfied himself with redeemed slaves. He said they were the same as noble women. He said: "since it is not the case that *komo* cannot enter paradise,[40] it is fine to be a *kome*. If any one calls you *kome*, answer positively. Nothing is wrong with that. Paradise is said to be for good people. There is no mention of nobility and slavery in the business of paradise." That was his advice for us.

I was taught by D., the father of S.[41] One day as we were reading, one boy […] called me, "Baba, the *kome* boy." Our teacher heard him and immediately rebuked him. He asked, "Is he your father's *kome* or your mother's *kome*? Don't ever call this boy *kome* again. He is not one." […] Our father advised us to be quiet about [the issue of slavery] […] He was alone here. He had no family support. He was all alone and he had the Quranic scholars as his friends. He was rich though. When his livestock increased in number, he opted to transfer to the outskirts of the village. He went to clear that place. He had a big orchard […] but he did not show off his wealth and kept a low profile. He acknowledged the superiority of the nobles. [That] is good. Let nobody have too much courage here. Just keep a low profile […]. [The nobles] only challenge you when you show yourself up to be rich.

Even when my father killed a cow for sale, he initially gave it out on loan and wrote the names of the debtors. He finally tore the paper and said that it was for charity.[42] [There was one] of the butchers in the village who gave meat on credit. When the payment was due, he went to the debtors' houses very early in the morning asking for his money. But he only asked for his money during the trading season.[43] My father never waited for that. He just tore up the list of debtors and declared the debt charity. Thus they left him alone because of his generosity. He was very rich. He had a lot of cattle. He had about 160 cows. During the rainy season, he killed a cow on every Friday. He also cooked a lot of food for the poor and Quranic students to eat as charity. Charity is good. It is very useful. Let nobody beat you in giving charity. Give as much as you can, you will not regret. Our father was alone in this compound. Look at it now. Isn't it as big as a village? […] My father [did not desire to leave this place]. We don't

---

[38] Tambasansang is a chiefly town in Fuladu West.

[39] It is very common across Senegambia to use the mother's name as a suffix of people's own name in order to distinguish people with the same name within the same family.

[40] Baba is referring to a widespread credo about slaves: that someone cannot enter paradise as a captive.

[41] He refers to Quranic education taking place at the scholar's compound. The period of reference is between 1941 and 1946.

[42] In this context, charity is *sadaka* (not to be mistaken for *zakat* or tithe), voluntary alms accruing divine rewards to Muslims. Almsgiving is also a way through which people get a reputation as good, generous Muslims. Cf. B. Soares, *Islam and the Prayer Economy: History and Authority in a Malian Town* (Edinburgh, 2005), 165.

[43] The trading season corresponds to the dry months of the year, extending from the end of the rains and the harvests (November–December) to June, when the first rains fall again. In colonial days, peasants sold their produce during the dry season and then bought goods for consumption or for trade, or, as in this case, to pay debts (see also Baba's narration of his father's commercial activity earlier in the chapter).

want to leave either. We are satisfied here. We don't even want a farm house elsewhere. This place is good for us. We have not been disturbed here. You only think of leaving when you don't like it here. [...] [The places we Soninke migrate to] are different. There, we are all one.[44] We are the same brothers there. Whoever is wealthy, others leaned on you. A noble can ask a leatherworker for support and vice versa. Here it is difficult but there is no problem abroad. There is no low and high position there. Just like [one of my sons] is there right now. He is stronger [financially] there than other *kome* and *hoore* as well. Everyone seeks support from him. [...] [But] it can't work here. We are different from them. The elders here will not allow that. [...] Here ... you are at home as a *kome*. Another is in his house as a *hoore*. That's all.

TAMBA

Our elder was Tamba but he was better known as Yugo [...] He hailed from Gidimaxa.[45] He came here as a strange farmer. He spent two rainy seasons here, but he fell out with the *hooro*. He then transferred to Basse.[46] He settled in Basse where he cleared a big area and farmed there. After some time he moved to a small Fula village near here, called Sare. He spent two years at Sare and returned to [the outskirts of] Basse, a village called Kabakama. When he returned to Basse, he stayed there. My father was tending the cattle for him. Our mother was his first wife. She took care of the cattle too. The cattle multiplied until the calves reached the good number of 170. [...] One-hundred-and-seventy! ... and those were only the bulls and cows excluding the suckling calves. After a long time, our grandfather died and Mari Penda[47] [...] came for us and brought us to [this village]. That was when they dug this Mari's well. He built houses; when he finished the buildings, he brought us from Kabakama. When we came here, that brother of mine living close to the gate [...] was the first to be born here. Our family gave some of our sisters in marriage to the people of Bajakunda in the person of Y. S., some to the people of Allunhare, another one to the people of Kabakama. J. is in Allunhare. She is in Allunhare is the oldest among those who are there. She was the one you were talking about; the old woman. She has two other younger sisters there and seven younger brothers.[48]

When he farmed, he used his earnings to buy cattle. He went to buy the cattle from French Fuladu.[49] He would buy about 10 cows. At that time, cows were not expensive. He did that on a yearly basis. That was how he had a lot of cattle. [He] never returned [to his homeland]. His sister followed him here and he was very happy to see her. He gave her out in marriage in this village. She is married to the S. family. Another sister of his, K., also came and he married her to the K. family. They have many children now, they belong to the S. and S. [...] But our descendants in K. have all died [...] Yugo only got to know these people here. They only became connected through marriage[50] [...]

---

[44] Remember that Baba had firsthand knowledge of migration, as he was himself a migrant in Sierra Leone.

[45] Gidimaxa is a region on the northern banks of the Upper Senegal River, in the Mali-Mauritania-Senegal borderland.

[46] The main commercial town on the upper river.

[47] Baba's father.

[48] In sum, Yugo's daughters were given in marriage to other *kome* families in Soninke villages, which placed him at the same level in society. This positioning becomes clearer when Tamba later explains the village's marriage policy.

[49] French Fuladu included most of the Casamance region of present Senegal.

[50] These are all *kome* families in Tamba's village. Once established here, Yugo positioned himself within the *kome* group through marriage exchanges. This also qualifies the earlier comment on Yugo's daughters

The nobles initially welcomed him but after a while when he began to be rich, they became jealous and "fought" him and he left. He left their village to them and went to clear land in Kabakama. He had been here for only two years as a guest farmer. As he was a serious man, a hard worker, he quickly made it. He was not a lazy man. You see from that workshop to the Mosque up to the Fatoto road, he cleared the whole of that area [...] He did it with his wife, Fatu Jobe [...] [The father of this woman] came from the Wolof countries[51] [...] he came with his children. There were grown up daughters among them. Our grandfather married one of them and they became family members. But I don't remember who their hosts were. They have all died.

When Yugo became wealthy, he clashed with Jewuru, the would-be district chief, as it was rumoured that he wanted to be chief as well.[52] Jewuru called and asked Yugo about that. He replied that he was not interested in power. He was satisfied with his authority over his family. He reassured Jewuru that he was not vying for power. He was a powerful man but the autochthones were not comfortable with him. Our grandfather had six horses and he rode the sixth one himself. Jewuru too had six horses and he rode the sixth one himself. Jewuru, Yugo, [other two men] were the heroes in those days; they were afraid of one another and they watched one another closely as they all knew what the other was capable of. But they discriminated against Yugo as a stranger; but he believed that a good man is not a stranger anywhere. Everywhere is home for a good man. Thus, he made himself feel at home and went about his business surmounting all obstacles. There was no one like our grandfather in this community. [Anybody can confirm this].

Basse was a small place when Yugo moved there. It was not big. There were [European companies and Lebanese traders]. He had friends among them and they visited each other. Occasionally, he gave them a seven-year old bull to slaughter for their entertainment. He was generous; there was no man like him on this land. He did not want people to know his real name. He was humble. It was only after his death that he became popular. His real name was Musa. We were all named after him.

[At the time he came from Gidimaxa] he came with many young men, all strange farmers looking for hosts. There were 12 of them; all had hosts except our grandfather. He sat under the fig tree waiting for his luck. One man finally took him and he said to him "as you have taken me as your guest worker, you are going to make all other men women in this village". He worked like a mad man. Even at night when the moon was bright, he worked on the farm. He took his cooking pot to the farm. He cooked there and ate there [...]

[The reason we turned into *komo*] is that he wanted a woman to marry. [He saw one woman] and enquired about her. They said "Eh, that one is a [freeborn]." He replied "I am one too." They did not trust him. He said: "Fuck off! Take your woman and keep the money I have spent on her so far."[53] Then Fatu came with her father, and he wanted her. His host told him

---

betrothed to other *kome* families in Soninke villages. For further details, see later in the narrative, when Tamba explains how his grandfather acquired his wife.

[51] The Wolof countries are in northwestern Senegal.

[52] The period is around the early 1920s. Jewuru Krubally, the would-be chief in question, succeeded to Mansajang Balde as the chief of the Fulladu East in 1924 and ruled until 1962. The Kruballys were recent immigrants too, showing that new settlers could climb the political hierarchy at the district level. Yugo's wealth and connections were probably seen with suspicion by Jewuru.

[53] In other words, Yugo advanced some money for the bridewealth of this woman, but he was then told that he could not marry her because his origins were not ascertained.

that he could get her. Those [the Jobe] were *hooro* too but they changed them all into *komo* here. [...] The *finanu*[54] were her masters. That's a difficult story.

How that too happened? Your wife gets ill and others are jealous and do not help you. Then a good friend of yours – Ibrahima's friend – gives you his "daughter" to cook for you until your wife gets well. She does that until you finally marry her and your sick wife dies. Then they say you are a slave.[55] Fatu's father quarrelled with the villagers about that. He said, "you'd better look at me! Slavery and love are different." He insulted them and they all ran away, sneaking around the village platform. It was not good for the one he insulted as his mouth was washed with charms.[56]... His friend did not benefit him, he didn't really. [...]

That's how things went. We were here like that. They called us slaves of the *garanko* and they called them the slaves of the *finanu*.[57] We ourselves were *hooro*. [They called us] Samangare, also known as Tunkara. Those days, my brothers and I were young. We did not know much. There was slavery around. That does not exist anymore. But for us, we never mind, we think slavery is nothing bad. The only slaves are those who don't know God. For all those who pray, we consider them nobles. We shall not quarrel over that. All those who say *Allahu Akbar*[58] have equal status. That's what our grandfather said. He said there is one God; not two. He gives and takes life. When something happened to you, don't accuse anyone. Just attribute it to God. That was his belief. He said God is not interested in envy [...]

Many other *komo* resist slavery but our family do not. We accept it. We don't mind. It does not prevent us from praying and doing all our religious services. We still go to our *garanke* masters to beg them. If they are not useless people, they give us. They dare not refuse. They are the offspring of my masters. They owe it to us. That is the way it is.[59] [...] In my

---

[54] The *Fina* are a subcaste of the *nyaxamalo*, bards or praise-singers of the Islamic scholars (see also a discussion earlier in the chapter).

[55] The story is not entirely clear, nor was it in the original recording. Regardless of the actual dynamic, the bottom line of the story is that people or guests could fall into slavery through deception and in moments of hardship, when they had to rely on others. Such an interpretation, however, remains speculative. The "you" of Tamba's narrative appears to be Ibrahima, the father of Fatu. It seems that, having Ibrahima's wife fell ill, he needed some help with household chores. A friend offered to him a girl as a helper, but it is not clear whether this man was his patron/host in the *fina* compound or another person. Later in the narrative Tamba uses the word "friend" to refer to his former masters, so that friend here could be actually the host or patron of Ibrahima, a *fina* man. If this were the case, the girl would probably be a slave girl addressed as a "daughter," as was common for children of slaves, especially when raised in the owner's compound. Ibrahima then probably falls in love with the girl and marries her, but he does not pay any bridewealth to her family or owner. This means that his children do not legally belong to him, but to the girl's owner or family. This is the way slaves marry, so Ibrahima is considered as a slave; in addition, he has probably married a slave and had a woman paid on his behalf, just like a slave.

[56] Charms (commonly known as *juju or gri-gri*) are "magical" items made by *marabouts* (Islamic clerics) and other specialists. They usually involve bits of papers with Quranic, or at least Arabic, writings on them. They take many forms and have different effects; usually people carry them on their bodies or wash with it when it is given in liquid form [*nasi*]. The one described seems to be a liquid used to wash the mouth in order to empower or give material effect to the words pronounced thereafter. On esoteric practices and charms, see Soares, *Islam*.

[57] There is a temporal mismatch with respect to the story just narrated. Tamba does not tell us how his family became slaves of the leatherworkers. This seems to occur only later, when his father marries a *kome* woman belonging to the leatherworkers.

[58] Arabic: Allah is the Greatest. In other words, by stating one's faith in Islam, one becomes equal to all other Muslims.

[59] Begging is the clearest marker of *kome* status in this context. Nobles deem begging extremely shameful, a sign of *kome*'s dependency and inferiority. But Tamba gives us a more balanced view: to beg is to rightfully demand one's share on account of the work and services done for the master or for his family, in the present and in the past.

generation, we never worked for our masters [...] your good friend, you call him your master [*kama*]. You serve him and he patronizes you. That is the type of slavery we have now. [...] My master paid the whole cost of my marriage. He took my wife from Kumbija and gave her to me[60] [...] I did some work for my master because he helped me a lot. I did it in appreciation of his deeds. He was my big man. But he didn't even want me to work for him. When I told him, he refused to let me do it. I surprised him. I mobilized friends, young men, and we went to his farm without his knowledge and we weeded for one afternoon. If we become close friends, we have to benefit one another. I do something for you and you reciprocate to show appreciation. That is our definition of slavery. Isn't it like that?

SUGGESTED ADDITIONAL READINGS

ON SONINKE SLAVERY AND MIGRATION

Manchuelle, François. "Slavery, Emancipation and Labour Migration in West Africa: The Case of the Soninke," *Journal of African History*, 30 (1989): 89–106.

Manchuelle, Francçois. *Willing Migrants: Soninke Labor Diasporas, 1848–1960*. Athens and London: Ohio University Press and J. Currey Publishers, 1997.

Sy, Yaya. "L'esclavage chez les Soninkés: du village à Paris," *Journal des Africanistes*, 70 (2000): 43–69.

ON SLAVERY AND EMANCIPATION IN THE SENEGAMBIA

Bellagamba, Alice. "Slavery and Emancipation in the Colonial Archives: British Officials, Slave-Owners and Slaves in the Protectorate of the Gambia (ca.1890–1936)," *Canadian Journal of African Studies*, 39 (2005): 5–41.

Klein, Martin. *Slavery and Colonial Rule in French West Africa*. Cambridge and New York: Cambridge University Press, 1998.

Moitt, Bernard. "Slavery and Emancipation in Senegal's Peanut Basin: The Nineteenth and Twentieth Centuries," *International Journal of African Historical Studies*, 22 (1989): 27–50.

Searing, James. *"God Alone Is King." Islam and Emancipation in Senegal*. Oxford: James Currey, 2002.

Swindell, Kenneth and Jeng, Alieu. *Migrants, Credit and Climate: The Gambian Groundnut Trade, 1834–1934*. Leiden and Boston: Brill, 2006. See especially chapter 4.

Weil, Peter. "Slavery, Groundnuts and the European Capitalism in the Wuli Kingdom of Senegambia 1820–1930," *Research in Economic Anthropology*, 6 (1984): 77–119.

---

[60] This is a clear example of ongoing relationships between former masters and former slaves. By paying for Musa's marriage, the leatherworker fulfills his role as master; as a consequence, Musa complies with his role as *kome*.

Without History? Interrogating "Slave" Memories in Ader (Niger)

BENEDETTA ROSSI

This chapter makes available four testimonies of slave descendants focused on how slaves lived their lives in the second half of the nineteenth century in the Ader region of the Republic of Niger. Memories of slavery today vary across groups and individuals. This is partly because slaves did not have one social status, but many: the testimonies represent the perspectives of groups and individuals whose ancestors were positioned differently in Ader's society. It is also because memory is mediated by present circumstances. While today slavery has disappeared, discrimination on the basis of slave descent persists. The speakers' lives have been marked by slavery as an inherited status. Some did not cut ties with their former masters, and may owe to this the social mobility they were able to achieve. Others feel that although they severed relations with their masters' descendants, economic vulnerability forces them to accept new forms of dependence. Although these testimonies inevitably reflect the concerns of their authors, they provide a valuable complement to the texts of colonial administrators and the narratives of elites. They break the silence of the slave constituency, which has long been characterized as "without history." Their integration with other available records yields a more complete picture of regional history and the experience of enslavement. The four testimonies are preceded by sections introducing the regional context and discussing the methodological considerations that went into their collection and analysis.

TRANSFORMATIONS OF SLAVERY IN ADER

The Ader region lies at the boundary between the southern edge of the Sahara and the northern border of Hausaland. Its society is composed of Hausa and Tuareg groups that, in the second half of the nineteenth century, were integrated into two interethnic hierarchies headed by the warrior elites (*imajeghen*) of the Iwellemmedăn Kel Denneg in Northern Ader and the Kel Gress in Southern Ader.[1] Ader's social hierarchy followed the ranked divisions of Tuareg society, at the bottom of which were liberated slaves and slaves. The former were classified among the free, but carried the indelible mark of enslavement. Slaves were internally diversified and stratified. Tuareg hierarchies encompassed Hausa society, and the Hausa system of status and rank remained relevant to intra-Hausa relations. Free

---

[1] See F. Nicolas, *Tamesna: Les Ioullemeden de l'Est ou Tuareg Kel Dinnik* (Paris, 1950), 58.

Hausa households also owned slaves. Before 1900, slaves could be acquired in multiple ways. Not all free groups engaged in slave raiding. Religious specialists (Tuareg: *ineslemen*; Hausa: *malamai*; also generally known as *marabouts*) assisted particular warrior elites and were compensated in goods and slaves. As reported in the following quote, the accumulation of slaves at the top of social hierarchies was facilitated by established forms of gift giving to political elites.

> *Abzinawa*[2] youths would kidnap people also to prove that they were ready to get the turban [i.e., ready for transition into adulthood]. A youth may have had animals and slaves, already. He was given weapons and a horse or camel. He and his best friend, to prove that they could wear the turban, had to kidnap animals or people. When they sold them, they got married with the money they earned. Not all *imajeghen* kidnapped and raided. [Some] only bought slaves, or obtained them in several ways. After a war, they would receive them as a share of the booty. Or they got them from rich people in the area. They would call upon rich people they knew, saying that they had a youth who wished to get married, asking them to send something. Their rich friends sent one or two heads of cattle, or whatever else they could. This is how they found the money to arrange marriages. Slaves were not only taken in wars. They were also inherited from rich people. If a rich man died, he left an inheritance: lands, animals, slaves. Before parting his inheritance amongst his descendants, he had to give something to the chiefs of the region. For example, a certain man from a village around here ... when he died, he had more than 100 slaves. He left 60 slaves to the chief (*sarki*) – 30 males, 30 females. He collected his slaves thanks to his business in tobacco and cloth. He was a Bahaushe [sing m. for Hausa], so he did not raid, but had inherited and bought slaves. The Hausa also got Buzu[3] slaves because the Tuareg obliged rich Hausa people to buy slaves from them after raids, threatening to take their belongings if they refused.[4]

Slave labor maintained and transformed the productive property (herds, land) of slave owners and was used in the organization of caravan trade.[5] Some slaves lived attached to their master's family, women taking care of domestic chores and men primarily involved in herding and caravan trade.[6] Others lived in relatively autonomous hamlets scattered in areas controlled by their masters (see testimonies 1, 2, 4). These semiautonomous slave communities were particularly common at the desert's edge, where they functioned as outposts for their masters' operations and as reservoirs of labor and resources.[7] Their

---

[2] In Hausa, *Abzinawa* (sing. *Baabzine*) refers to people from the Air region (*Abzin*). But in Ader today this term is used broadly to translate the Tamasheq *imajeghen*, indicating the warrior elites of Tuareg society, irrespective of their provenance. In this and most other quotes, *Abzinawa* should be understood as referring to the warrior elites of the Kel Gress and Kel Denneg.

[3] The terms Buzu, Buzaye, or Bugaje refer to Tuareg slaves and slave descendants. It is sometimes applied to all Tuareg with derogatory connotations.

[4] Interview with Alhassan, Keita, September 25, 2005.

[5] See J. Nicolaisen, *Structures politiques et sociales des Touareg de l'Air et de l'Ahaggar* (Niamey, 1962), 102–103; P. Bonte, "Esclavage et relations de dépendance chez les Touareg Kel Gress," in C. Meillassoux (ed.), *L'esclavage en Afrique précoloniale* (Paris, 1975), 145.

[6] Yet, in Ader the sexual division of labor was not stringent for slaves.

[7] P. Lovejoy and S. Baier, "The Desert Side Economy of the Central Sudan," *International Journal of African Historical Studies*, 8, 4 (1975), 551–581; P. Lovejoy and S. Baier, "The Tuareg of the Central Sudan: Gradations in Servility at the Desert's Edge (Niger and Nigeria)," in I. Kopytoff and S. Miers (eds.), *Slavery in Africa: Historical and Anthropological Perspectives* (Madison, 1977), 391–411.

settlements were interspersed among villages of manumitted slaves and free Hausa villages. Unlike slaves living with their masters, slaves who lived in separate villages had to provide for their own subsistence. They held usufruct rights on the animals they herded and the lands they farmed.

The function of these slave villages at the desert's edge differs from the better-studied case of slave compounds working on plantations further south.[8] There were no plantations in the arid and rocky surroundings of northern Ader. Slaves here functioned as surplus labor that could be accessed when needed, and they also could be sold or exchanged for cereals or other goods. From the masters' perspective, these communities made possible the accumulation of wealth (herds, farming produce, and slaves themselves) while retaining a nomadic lifestyle. From the slaves' perspectives, they – and the resources they used – were protected from attacks of other warrior groups. Unlike domestic slaves, they were able to lead quasi-autonomous lifestyles. Rarity of interactions with masters resulted in greater freedom to manage one's time, but it also reduced the masters' obligations toward them and exposed them to rougher treatment, including the possibility of sale and forced family separation.

Slave revolts do not appear to have occurred (see testimony 4). Particularly harsh conditions of enslavement led to escape and/or institutionalized ways to change master.[9] Perhaps paradoxically, fear of enslavement by capture strengthened the voluntary acceptance of dependence from benign masters. Constant threat of enslavement did not result in struggles for autonomy, but in increased tolerance toward the security of dependence, ultimately reinforcing slavery as an institution. Even escape was limited, as the desert (or semi-desert) is a hostile environment for fugitives, particularly when moving away from a region controlled by one's masters and into areas controlled by enemies. Risk of recapture was high.[10] Slaves did not necessarily show solidarity toward each other: slave villages competed over access to resources, and loyalty to one's master constituted the main avenue of social mobility.

Social mobility, and eventually emancipation, tended to take different forms for female and male slaves. For females, it occurred primarily through concubinage and/or marriage. A female slave's offspring belonged to his/her mother's master and had free status. The genitor role of the male slave was downplayed culturally, reflecting his incapacity to assume legal fatherhood.[11] A free man wanting to take another person's slave as concubine was obliged to pay her ransom first. If she gave birth to his child, he would have to free

---

[8] P. Lovejoy, "Plantations in the Economy of the Sokoto Caliphate," *Journal of African History*, 19, 3 (1978), 341–368; M. F. Smith, *Baba of Karo: A Woman of The Muslim Hausa* (New Haven, 1954).

[9] It was dishonorable for a master to mistreat his/her slave, and a mistreated slave could change master by scraping or cutting a small part of the ear of another free man's camel. This is a widely reported custom among different Tuareg groups. See, for example, Nicolaisen, *Structures politiques et sociales*, 101–102. In Hausa society a wronged slave could, apparently, return to the market and find a new owner; I. Hamza, "Slavery and Plantation Society at Dorayi in Kano Emirate," in P. Lovejoy (ed.), *Slavery on the Frontiers of Islam* (Princeton, 2004), 139.

[10] If found, fugitive slaves could be re-enslaved or returned to their masters. According to one testimony, Tuareg chiefs had a habit of returning fugitive slaves to each other: "The Tuareg of the Air and those of the Azawagh had agreed amongst themselves that if they found slaves they would bring them back to original patrons." Interview, group of elders, Seyte, March 9, 2005. The expressions "Tuareg of Air" and "Tuareg of Azawagh" refer, respectively, to the Kel Gress and Kel Denneg.

[11] E. Bernus and S. Bernus, "L'évolution de la condition servile chez les Touaregs saheliens," in C. Meillassoux (ed.), *L'esclavage en Afrique précoloniale* (Paris, 1972), 37.

her or marry her. Marriage with a female slave did not contradict endogamic principles that prevailed among Tuareg elites. Because the master had full rights over his slaves, this type of marriage reinforced the groom's patrilineage, as the offspring would belong exclusively to his lineage. By limiting the potential redistribution of the surplus extracted from different categories of dependents, endogamy was essential to the retention of privileges in the hands of few elite families.[12]

Male slaves could become free through ransom or manumission. Ransom took different forms, but before abolition it was rare for a slave to be able to accumulate the money necessary to buy back his own or his relatives' freedom. It was more common for free people to ransom members of their family who had been enslaved or buy them back:

> If the *Abzinawa* had taken your son away, and he was sold in some market, you could go to that market and find those who bought him, and try to buy him back. They would accept, because the same could happen to them one day. This is how we would find the child and come back with him.[13]

After colonial and national abolition, many people of slave descent have been choosing to ransom themselves and their dependents from the descendants of their former masters. This practice is particularly common among descendants of slaves of religious groups, ransom being sometimes presented as a religious obligation (see testimony 4). In the second half of the nineteenth century, the Kel Gress emancipated large slave constituencies and turned them into tributary farmers.[14] Retrospectively, it is difficult to discern the relative role played by internal change from the consequences of colonial conquest for the progressive emancipation of slaves.

In their first few years of rule following the occupation of Ader in 1900, French military officers did not oppose slavery and related practices. The first *Commandants de Cercle* commonly returned fugitive or stolen slaves to people whom they saw as rightful owners. In 1905, France abolished the legal status of slavery in its West African territories, but the position of local administrators remained ambivalent. Officially, the representatives of the French Republic condemned slavery. On the other hand, they feared the political instability that, in their view, could result from the sudden achievement of freedom by the part of ex-slaves and captives.[15] The main consequences of colonization for slave status in Ader followed not so much from legal abolition, which was not enforced in practice, but from the colonial repression of former rulers, particularly the Kel Denneg. The Kel Gress surrendered early, eager to resume the trade activities that were at the basis of their wealth and power. The Kel Denneg, on the other hand, resisted until most of them were killed in Tanout in 1917, at the height of the French repression of Tuareg resistance. Automatically, most of their former slaves acquired independence.

Throughout the 1920s, increasing numbers of former slaves started migrating seasonally to Northern Nigeria and earning cash with which they paid taxes back home and

---

[12] On the Kel Gress, see Bonte, "Esclavage," 53 and 69.

[13] Interview with anonymous speakers, June 10, 2005.

[14] P. Bonte, "Structure de classe et structures sociales chez les Kel Gress," *Revue de l'Occident Musulman et de la Méditerranée*, 21 (1976), 145; B. Rossi, "Tuareg Trajectories of Slavery: Preliminary Reflections on a Changing Field," in A. Fisher and I. Kohl (eds.), *Tuareg Society within a Globalized World: Saharan Life in Transition* (New York, 2010), 89–106.

[15] M. Klein, *Slavery and Colonial Rule in French West Africa* (Cambridge, 1998), 134.

met the needs of their families. Those who did not migrate could work for a new patron in the local economy, but conditions of labor did not differ substantially from what they had experienced as slaves. They were often paid in kind, and relations with new patrons hindered their freedom to move independently. Forced labor recruitment and military conscription hit servile and low-status groups harshly, as local elites charged with recruitment only mobilized the most vulnerable people. In these circumstances, those who could migrated permanently or seasonally. Departures expanded in years of heightened colonial recruitment and drought. This phenomenon attracted the attention of the French administration, which feared losing taxes and manpower. Eventually in the mid-1930s, central government in Dakar introduced incentives aimed at encouraging migrants to return or remain. But labor migration continued to be practiced in large numbers.[16]

At the *Cercle* level, colonial debates on the "slavery question" hinged on the classification of various forms of dependence. Until well into the 1940s, it was common to distinguish between the slave trade and domestic slavery, classifying the latter as a mild form of dependence that, it was argued, should be tolerated in order to safeguard the social order. The specter of anarchy was raised whenever measures that would facilitate emancipation were discussed. The moral corruption of slave populations, supposedly prone to theft and incapable of self-government, was invoked to defend the exceptional maintenance of the harshest disciplinary measures of the *Code de l'Indigénat* even after their abrogation in most regions of French West Africa. International pressure and enquiries into the conditions of labor and the resilience of slavery forced local administrators to pay constant attention to the evolution of the "slavery problem" in order to avoid scandals. In the late 1940s, following a series of studies that revealed the endurance of domestic slavery and unpaid labor, efforts were made to introduce contracts to regulate local labor relations between former masters and slaves. But the majority of works carried out by the poorest people continued to be remunerated casually and in kind: herders, guardians, occasional manual workers, poor women helping with food preparation and cleaning – all of these categories of workers did not receive a salary or fixed cash payment. This situation did not change substantially after independence. All money came into Ader from the outside, through trade and migrant earnings. People who could not travel far or support themselves through their own means or the help of relatives accepted to work for someone else in exchange for food and protection. For many slave descendants, legal abolition remained a dead letter.

The image of wealthier people feeding poorer villagers in exchange for work looked like a vestige of slavery to activists and researchers unfamiliar with the local economy. They blamed local mores, but overlooked the complex economic and environmental causes accounting for the slow pace of the evolution of a free labor market in Ader. Institutions governed by "modern" employment criteria (the colonial administration first, international development projects later) continued to fabricate ideological justifications for avoiding to pay standard wages to local labor. Economic vulnerability and exploitation still affect a large portion of Ader's population. While these conditions result in the reproduction of social dependence, it would be misleading to interpret them narrowly as vestiges of precolonial slavery.

---

[16] B. Rossi, "Slavery and Migration: Social and Physical Mobility in Ader (Niger)," in B. Rossi (ed.), *Reconfiguring Slavery: West African Trajectories* (Liverpool, 2009), 182–206.

WITHOUT HISTORY? SOME METHODOLOGICAL AND ETHICAL CONSIDERATIONS ON "SLAVE" TESTIMONIES AS SOURCES

I started working in northeastern Ader in 1995. Since then, I conducted a total of about three years of field-based research focused on contemporary social, economic, and political dynamics, before starting to work on oral history in 2005. The testimonies that follow are taken from 170 interviews made between January 2005 and December 2008 by myself, mostly together with my senior research assistant. These were semistructured discussions with one or more (usually no more than five) persons. My inquiries were never focused solely on slavery, but slavery turned out to be a major institution, frequently mentioned also when discussing other subjects. With key informants, I conducted repeated interviews. When possible, I allowed interviewee(s) to take the discussion in any direction they deemed relevant. In the absence of written records, my primary methods for validating information have been triangulation and integration with other types of data (e.g., genealogical information). Oral history testimonies are complex texts that contain mixed information. Their factual accuracy cannot always be established, but attempts to do so rest on accumulation (how many sources concur on a particular version), triangulation (comparison across different perspectives), and contextualization (how far different perspectives reflect their holders' positions in social fields governed by unequal power relations). Another research question consists of inquiring into why certain statements are generally held to be true, or why certain people are seen as "holders of historical truth" more than others. The deconstruction of "truth effects" should be a major concern when working on slave memory.

Slaves, and their descendants, are often considered liars. If they are seen as knowledgeable at all, such knowledge tends to be underrated as "second class." Biased perceptions of the intellectual status of slaves are as common among the subjects of research as they are among researchers. It is a widespread contention that slaves are "without history," or alternatively, that they internalize their masters' views of history, and therefore interpret the past through borrowed memories.[17] Ader is no exception to this. In a comparative article on Hausa and Tuareg conceptions of the past in Ader, Pierre Bonte and Nicole Echard – two of the main students of this region – write: "*les classes sociales dominées sont-elles réellement "sans histoire"? La réponse est clairement affirmative en ce qui concerne les iklan.*"[18]

Struggling with this perspective, I found that many slave descendants had distinctive memories of the past. But "slave memories" also exhibit considerable internal differences. In Ader, slave descendants do not hold a uniform view of their past. Moreover, like anywhere else, there are *different types* of historical discourse, access to which is dependent on social status. This means that certain historical registers and/or tropes are commonly associated with particular status groups. For example, when I started collecting oral testimonies, I noticed that some elders stated at the outset that they could only speak of events that went back to their grandfathers, and they did not know anything about earlier periods. I realized that these statements were made primarily by slave descendants. They could be

---

[17] For examples on African contexts, see M. Klein, "Studying the History of Those Who Would Rather Forget," *History in Africa*, 16 (1989), 211–212; M. De Bruijn and L. Pelckmans, "Facing Dilemmas: Former Fulbe Slaves in Modern Mali," *Canadian Journal of African Studies*, 39, 1 (2005), 72.

[18] P. Bonte and N. Echard, "Histoire et histoires. Conception du passé chez les Hausa et les Twareg Kel Gress de l'Ader (République du Niger)," *Cahiers d'Etudes Africaines*, 61–62, XVI (1976), 269.

interpreted quite literally as recognitions that their memories were truncated at a certain time, possibly corresponding to the moment when their forebears had been enslaved or forcibly separated from their (slave) parents. A kidnapped child often had no chance to learn the historical traditions of his/her society of origin, and thus would have been unable to transmit this information to his descendants.

In spite of their initial *recusatio*, the accounts of slave descendants did not differ sub-stantially from those of elders of free descent. My oral history work suggests that memory retains some accuracy[19] over three generations: the interviewee's, his/her parents, and his/her grandparents. Informants who had lived with their parents or grandparents could remember details about the life of their relatives, which they themselves had witnessed or heard about directly from their elders. This finding set a chronological limit to my inquiries approximately at the end of the nineteenth century. Up to the end of the nine-teenth century, memories differed across groups. Instead, testimonies on earlier periods fused into a shared repertoire of stereotyped traditions about ancient conquerors (e.g., Askia Mohamed, Sarkin Darei, the Kanta of Kebbi, Agabba) and distant origins (e.g., from Mecca, or from Instambul).[20] People of slave descent often knew the feats of ancient heroes believed to have ruled parts of Ader in "a very distant past," but this information is taught at school, broadcasted in vernacular languages on the radio, and circulated in the form of a popular genre of Hausa songs. It constitutes a regional folk-history that cuts across age and status, and positions Ader in national history and culture. This type of regional historical tradition unifies rather than divides Ader inhabitants of free and slave descent by creating a sense of shared regional identity.

Other types of historical discourse have the opposite function of establishing social distinctions between stratified social constituencies. Hence, a different historical regis-ter is used to convey the pedigree of particular elite families. I was sometimes explicitly directed to individual elite elders when I inquired into what is seen as "their" *tarihi*.[21] On some occasions, former dependents would be able to recite the *tarihi* of their masters, but their version usually differed from versions provided by the masters themselves.[22] People of liberated-slave status would sometimes appropriate their ex-masters' past and mold their

[19] By this I mean factual accuracy in the recollection of particular events, the occurrence of which could be confirmed through comparison with post-1900 colonial archives (especially *Rapports de Tournée* and the *Journal du Cercle*, where daily happenings at the *Cercle* level were recorded) and through extensive trian-gulation of interviews within a sample of roughly forty villages.

[20] In Ader, there is a relatively stable set of traditions of foreign origins that connect certain high-status groups to the history of Agadez, Istamboul, Ghat, Songhay, Mecca, and others. These traditions are pre-sented and discussed in the work of Djibo Hamani and Nicole Echard; see D. Hamani, *Contribution à l'étude de l'histoire des états Hausa: l'Adar précolonial, République du Niger* (Niamey, 1975); N. Echard, *L'Expérience du passé. Histoire de la société paysanne Hausa de l'Ader.* Etudes Nigériennes no. 36 (Paris, 1975a); N. Echard, *Répertoire historique des communautés rurales de la région de Tawa, République du Niger* (Niamey, 1975b).

[21] In the Hausa of Ader, the word *tarihi* has two meanings. It refers to "history" in a generic sense, and to the traditions of origin of particular groups. While this latter sense tends to imply written Arabic form, if one asks elders of these groups for "their *tarihi*," they will recite orally a particular story that is broadly known in the region as the particular heritage of their lineage.

[22] Further triangulation and, when possible, confrontation with archival material suggested that slave mem-ory of their masters' *tarihi* was almost invariably inaccurate about genealogical detail and succession to chiefly positions. On the other hand, slave testimonies were often more reliable on – for example, the nature of the interaction between their masters' group and French officials, whereas the masters' descen-dants tended to aggrandize the behavior of their forebears.

own history on their masters' *tarihi*, claiming that they had never been enslaved. These accounts are characterized by a brusque transition between relatively recent memories and a highly stereotyped *tarihi*. Claims to exclusive ownership of a *tarihi* or to the *tarihi* of higher-status groups constitute strategies in contemporary power struggles. They tell us less about the past than about the nature of today's power relations.

The notion that slaves are "without history" has no analytical coherence unless it is appropriately qualified in relation to different *types of knowledge* of the past. In Ader, and possibly elsewhere, symbolic capital is derived from possession of historical knowledge. Different narrative registers and types of discourses of the past have different potentials to accrue prestige to groups or individuals perceived as the rightful deployers of particular historical genres. This is altogether a different question from a historian's concern with how memory can be used to achieve a fuller insight into a past that, today, is primarily accessible through the colonial perspective alone. If we are concerned with recording a variety of experiences, the recollections of people of slave and free descent have equal importance, and even truncated memories constitute evidence of loss through violence that "bears witness to desubjectification."[23] But the majority of slave descendants today are often three generations (or more) removed from their ancestors' enslavement, and their recollections are not shallower than those of people of free descent. Indeed, those slave descendants who cannot attempt to pass as free lack a *tarihi* and the higher social status that goes with possessing one. But the analytical status of the *tarihi* of certain elite groups, like that of regional folk-histories, is questionable. In Ader, it is difficult to check the accuracy of these traditions. From a researcher's perspective, lacking a *tarihi* cannot be equated to "lacking history." The idea that slaves are "without history" belongs to the ideological denigration of slave status and exposes some historians' uncritical acceptance of the social construction of slave inferiority.

CONCLUSION

The four testimonies presented in this chapter have been collected from elderly descendants of slaves who lived in separate settlements characterized by homogenous "slave" status and attached to particular masters' families or individuals. This group has a collective history *as slaves*. Younger people across status respect them for their knowledge. However, this respect accrues to them as individuals, and contrasts with the generalized stigma placed on slave descent in Ader society. This stigma accounts for the fact that, generally, slave descendants do not wish to reveal their history. They are, in Martin Klein's words, "those who would rather forget."[24] In some West African societies, remembering slavery evokes a sense of shame for victims of past abuses. Slave intellectual production exists in a hegemonic context that devalues it. This devaluation results from the naturalization of hierarchy by those in power, who justify enslavement by turning it into a natural, and therefore indelible, flaw in the moral constitution of the slave person.[25] A common trait of these contexts is that they put a premium on silence and passing as a strategy of status mobility. Many slave descendants would rather avoid discrimination by attempting to pass

---

[23] G. Agamben, *Remnants of Auschwitz. The Witness and the Archive* (New York, 2002), 151.
[24] Klein, "Studying the History."
[25] R. Botte and J. Schmitz, "Paradoxes Identitaires," *Cahiers d'Etudes Africaines*, 34, 133–135 (1994), 9, 11.

as non-slave than by mobilizing politically. While this is not generally true of all slave socie-ties, it applies to Ader and to other West African examples, where the ideology of hierarchy that underpinned social relations remained meaningful while the most brutal aspects of slavery vanished.

In recognition of the interviewees' efforts to bury a stigmatizing past, I have anony-mized information that could connect the following testimonies to particular persons or groups. If integrated with other sources, these accounts can help us reconstruct the history of slavery in Ader. They reveal the perspectives of slave descendants, whose forebears' his-torical experience has been silenced because slave status marginalized them as producers of knowledge. In the first part of this introduction, I relied on these and similar sources for advancing a particular interpretation of Ader's past. Yet, these perspectives are posi-tioned,[26] not in the sense that they give access to a supposedly unified "slave past," but that the present condition of speakers as well as the circumstances of the interview influence the narrative's content. The first testimony joins the accounts of a descendant of masters with that of a descendant of his father's slaves. The elderly slave descendant is also a village chief. His status is complex, for he partly owes his current authority to his past dependence, as it is his former master who facilitated his appointment as chief. The second testimony is by a Tuareg elder of slave descent who owes his prestige to his own achievements and rec-ognized wisdom. Many people who know him ignore that he is the half-brother of a Hausa elder of free status. Kinship ties cutting across the slave-free divide raise questions on the conceptual compartmentalization between "slave" and "free" memories. The elder who gave me the third testimony, whose father had been a slave of an important Tuareg chief, derives a sense of pride from his past tie to the powerful warriors that other testimonies portray as cruel slavers. Finally, the last testimony conveys the contrasting experiences of two generations of slave descendants. Having started his life a slave, the father was able to ransom himself, travel independently, and make autonomous experiences (as a forced laborer and a seasonal migrant doing the humblest types of works). The son expresses a sense of powerlessness: in spite of his many achievements, his family is still too vulnerable to deny ongoing relations with former masters. Together, these four testimonies show that it is equally misleading to think that "slaves lack history"; that all slave descendants share a common memory of the past; or indeed that descendants of slaves and descendants of freeborn are separated by a sharp dividing line.

QUESTIONS TO CONSIDER

1. How do Ader slave descendants describe their relationship with former masters? Do they emphasize conflict or consensus?
2. The first testimony contains the statements of a descendant of slaves and a descendant of masters. Do their representations of the past differ? If so, why?
3. What criteria does the second testimony use to describe different types of slaves? Which type of slaves does the speaker descend from? How, in your opinion, does he relate to other descendants of slaves and freeborn today?
4. How does the third testimony characterize the Tuareg chiefs (*imajeghen*) of the past?

[26] D. Haraway, "Situated Knowledges: The Science Question in Feminism and the Privilege of Partial Perspective," *Feminist Studies*, 14, 3 (1988), 575–599.

5. The fourth testimony contains the statements of two generations of slave descendants. Do father and son represent the past differently? Do you think their attitude toward the present also differs?

6. Why did Rossi choose to anonymize the testimonies? Do you agree with her choice? Why?

THE UNBROKEN TIE: CHANGE AND CONTINUITY IN DEPENDENT RELATIONS (DESCENDANT OF SLAVES AND *INESLEMEN* MASTERS, APRIL 11, 2005)

Different groups of slave descendants are more or less open about their slave origins. The least secretive are the ones living in close proximity to former masters, because such proximity is a constant reminder of their status. In a region where all mention of slavery is taboo, the explicitness of these situations sheds light on the conditions of continued dependence. These conditions do not necessarily involve a denial of slave historical memory. An elderly dependent descended from the slaves of a particular family may assist his younger patron in recollecting the past. This knowledge is both a source of respect for the elder and, at the same time, a service that he finds hard to refuse. On one occasion, I had arranged a meeting with a descendant of slave owners to learn about the history of his family. I did not expect to discuss slavery. While I had not interviewed him formally before, I knew him and his family well, as I was a close friend of some of his relatives. Like other high-status Tuareg, he lived in a large compound at some distance from the closest village nearby. When I reached him, he informed me that he had invited the village chief to join us, because of the chief's old age (the chief was in his late seventies, while my host was in his late forties). The elder had been a slave of his family and had always lived next to them. The elder, my host said, might have helped us in our discussions, on aspects of the past that he ignored. When the elder reached us, the younger man introduced him to me as "village chief" (*hakimi*) and stated that, because of his old age, the chief's knowledge of the past was greater than his own. He then explained the relation between them, and how slavery functioned in the past. At the meeting, they both spoke.

Younger host:

When [my family] came to Ader from the north, they had some slaves with them, maybe ten men and ten women, not many. They mostly bought the rest of the slaves at markets, and slowly these slaves formed the villages around them. As today one can buy cows at a market, then one could buy slaves. My ancestors would also do religious work for the *imajeghen*, who gave them slaves in return.

Sometimes, masters and slaves lived in the same village. My ancestors were not nomads, they lived together with the slaves. The slaves would do herding, would pound cereals, and do a little farming for them.

The [*imajeghen*] would not touch them, their slaves, or their animals, for they were their *marabouts*. Even if one of their slaves was captured in war and told the [*imajeghen*] that he was [their slave], they would not touch him.

Because slaves were very numerous, they could not all be used as servants. Some left and formed their communities. The nobles were few. They married some of their female slaves, and that's how they grew, but at the same time they 'mixed'. Our social group would have died out if it did not marry female slaves. Now there are no more slaves, they are all free.

Elder:

> When slaves went to live independently they paid a *zakat*, the 10% of the farming pro-
> duce. Those who lived attached to their masters did not pay anything. It was like this: if one
> lives on his master's farm, he does not owe a zakat. But if he does not live with his master
> (*ubangiji*), he has his own things. For this to happen, he must part from the master, form his
> own farm (*gandu*), have his own animals, if what he has is enough to pay the zakat, he must
> put aside the sum requested for the zakat.

> If a slave dies, all his property goes to his master. If he marries, the master pays his
> bridewealth. If there is a slave village and the master does not live in the village, the relation
> remains. Even if he is not there, he keeps an eye on what is going on. If his slaves need some-
> thing, the master will give them, and vice-versa.

The discussion moved on to the relations between the villages that existed before the
arrival of the French. My host said that the chief would be much better informed than he
on this, as he was a lot older, and he left me alone with the elderly chief for a while. In this
time, the elder distinguished between more recent villages and older 'mother villages'. This
discussion was inseparable from an assessment of the relative status of villages founded by
slave or free people, and mixed villages. He then mentioned two chiefs who, according to
him, had been important at the beginning of colonialism. One was the chief of the group
of the former masters, whom the French found at their arrival. Later, there was Abdo, the
first man of slave status to have acquired the administrative role of village chief (in a nearby
village). At this point we heard our host who was coming back, and the elder went on:

At the arrival of the French, the [masters] were chiefs everywhere in this area, there was no
other chief but them in this land.

The discussion continued without further reference to slavery. I happened to interview descendants of slaves and masters (together) twice. On both occasions, the man of
the masters' class spoke primarily about his family's origins, while the elderly slave descendant elucidated local history in early colonial times. "Slave memory" was respected and
seen as particularly accurate for factual circumstances. In addition to the information they
convey, these encounters attest to complex social dynamics. Today the aforementioned
elder is a village chief. This position gives him authority in a village inhabited mainly by
other slave descendants. It also gives him a role of responsibility in the local administration. Former masters are still attached to a past code of honor, which makes them scorn the
lifestyle of villagers and the bureaucratic nature of contemporary power. They choose to
keep status and relinquish a power that would constrain their freedom to dispose of their
time as they please. Today, however, they cannot circumvent local administration entirely,
and having a former dependent as village chief is a convenient arrangement. Thanks to
the patronage of the descendants of the old masters class, the former slave is now a village
chief. He acquired authority by embracing, rather than denying, dependence. Both parties
straddle a line between past status and modern power, between hierarchy and citizenship.
The ambivalence of this situation is apparent in the conversation. In contrast with the following texts, the language of obligation here is substituted by a language of accommodation and cooperation. For instance, there is no mention of ransom, which would suggest
willingness to break the tie of dependence; and the elder refers to masters by the respectful
term "ubangiji," meaning "master" or "owner" and an epithet of Allah. However, while the

host is away, Abdo is put at the same level as the chief of the former masters' family. Abdo, one of the first slaves to be recognized as village chief, is often quoted in the testimonies of slave descendants. The salience of Abdo's role in the imagination of slave descendants contrasts with his absence from colonial archives and the historical narratives of elites.

THE PERMEABLE BOUNDARY BETWEEN SLAVERY AND FREEDOM (DESCENDANT OF SLAVES OF *IMAJEGHEN*, OCTOBER 29, 2005)

The following testimony is from an elder of slave descent of unusual lucidity (hereafter Anafaran), whose intellectual qualities owed him region-wide reputation and respect. His first language is Tamasheq, but he can speak Hausa and Arabic, and apparently read the Quran. The way in which I was introduced to him vividly illustrates the fluidity of social relations in practice, as opposed to an ideology of hierarchy that portrays social strata as bounded and impermeable. I used to visit an elder who was one of my closest acquaintances in a village that I shall call Akaran. With him, I discussed the history of particular Hausa groups settled in Ader. One day, I asked him if he knew any elder as experienced as him in a nearby area that I intended to visit. Without hesitation, he recommended Anafaran in a village that I call Wallayan. I discovered later that these two elders were half-brothers, from different fathers and the same (slave) mother who married her second (Hausa, free) husband after parting from her first (Tuareg, slave) husband. Her two sons grew up with different statuses: one was a free man who belonged to one of the Hausa subgroups that until recently practiced traditional animist religion; the other, whose father had been a slave, grew up a slave descendant. The two elderly half-brothers' histories were so closely intertwined as to make the notion of a "slave history" untenable. Having said this, Anafaran's status gave him access to detailed information on slaves' past living conditions, rights, and obligations toward the masters. The testimony below contains some valuable details, most of which were confirmed by other sources.

Before the arrival of the White we lived in Akaran. I do not know where we came from before then. In Akaran we lived in three neighborhoods. In those times, in Akaran there were also two free Hausa groups. The chief of one of these groups was like a village chief (*hakimi*) and a representative at the same time, he was responsible for collecting the bags of cereals that were given as tribute to the *Abzinawa* in a number of villages. We worked for these Hausa, even though we were the slaves of certain Kel Denneg [...]. There were several Tuareg chiefs, but the most powerful of all was Mahaman Tambari. [...] When the *imajeghen* went to Akaran, they stayed at the house of the Hausa chief. Some slaves followed the *imajeghen*, who moved around all the time. But we stayed, we did not follow them.

Then, we moved to Wallayan, and went to Akaran as seasonal migrants. The *imajeghen* never lived in Wallayan. We were almost independent from them, we saw them rarely. We went to Akaran as seasonal migrants, and the *imajeghen* always knew where we were, but we did not have to ask them for permission to go. When we were in Akaran, we had our families and animals with us. Someone may have asked us to keep their animals, but herding other people's livestock was not our main activity there. The *imajeghen*'s animals were kept by the slaves who followed them around, not by us. The *imajeghen* had two types of slaves. Those who followed them around, and those who lived in villages. The latter were more independent, but were also poorer and had less to eat, they were more vulnerable. Those who were with their masters [*bayun murfu*] had no freedom whatsoever, but were always taken in charge. We were the 'far ones'. This group does not have a generic name, slaves in this group are called their tribes' names, if they have one. Slaves in this group were in charge of themselves. They ate what their fields produced, and bought their clothes by selling their own animals, when they had to. They had few rights and obligations toward the *imajeghen*.

The condition of the '*bayun murfu*' was the following: their children did not inherit. They always lived attached to their masters. They married mostly with other slaves of their masters. When they married outside the group of their master's slaves, the bride's master was contacted, by her father if he was there. Then the bride's master would inform the master of the husband that one of his male slaves wanted to marry one of his female slaves. Then, they would agree on the arrangements. The master of the groom had to pay the bridewealth for his slave's future wife. The bridewealth went to the master, not the father. The husband, who was a slave, would spend the night at the camp of his wife's master, with his wife, and the day in the camp of his own master. But when the marriage was between two slaves of one master, usually there was no bridewealth involved. When bridewealth was paid, the amount was undetermined. When distant slaves wanted to get married, the *tambari* of the groom only had to give him his authorization, but would not contribute to the bridewealth. [...]

Our parents were the first generation to go on long distance migration [*bida*]. They started going to Agadez, Kaduna, Jos, Maradi … they went on foot. Before our parents, we did not migrate, but we accompanied the animals toward In Gall at the beginning of the rains.

Our parents did not buy the land they cultivated. It was the land of their *imajeghen*, they could cultivate it without problem. The *imajeghen* did not want the land, but they wanted a part of the harvest. This part was not fixed. After the harvest they would come to our parents' village, and our parents gave them what they could. They did not give directly to the *imajeghen*. The Kel Denneg would send a blacksmith to collect part of the harvest from them. Now we do not give anything to the *imajeghen*. Since the White chased them away, we stopped giving. But when the White arrived we started giving to the *chef du canton*. The taxes paid to the *chef du canton* are more than what we used to give to the *imajeghen*. The *imajeghen* used to send a representative who was not tough, and took little. But the representatives of the *Chefs du Canton* were a lot firmer.

[...]

Not all slaves were treated in the same way and had the same status. The slaves captured in war, they had to pay ransom [*fansa*]. But the greatest part of the slaves were the so called 'slaves of famine' [or 'slaves of hunger', Hausa: *bayun yunwa*], people who put themselves under the protection of someone powerful after famines, because of need. The *imajeghen* did not take ransom from the 'slaves of famine', because they had not been captured in war, they were not domestic slaves [*bayun murfu*], and they had not been bought at the market. They were slaves of famine [*bayun yunwa*]. Ransom is only required from slaves captured in war and bought. [...] The *jajaye* had 'slaves of famine' [*bayun yunwa*], but they told their slaves that if they could they should ransom themselves, and they have a habit of taking ransom from them. [Anafaran recites words in Arabic, perhaps a Quranic surah, then adds:] In taking them in charge at the time of famine, the *jajaye* did something that deserves Allah's reward. But in asking them to pay ransom, they do something against Allah's will.[27]

---

[27] It is difficult to convey the strength of this authoritative judgment. What is implied by this statement and the way in which it was delivered is that it is only God's law that counts for Anafaran, and his age and experience put him above human hierarchies.

THE AMBIGUITY OF MEMORIES OF DEPENDENCE (DESCENDANTS OF SLAVES OF *IMAJEGHEN*, OCTOBER 4, 2005)

I traveled far into northern Ader to collect this testimony from a very old and sick man whom I shall call Imboukan, who lived in a small village that could not be reached by car. I had learned about this man from an acquaintance who originally came from a nearby village and worked as intermediary *(dillali)* in cattle markets. I only interviewed Imboukan once, under exceptional conditions. Both Imboukan and I could understand Hausa, but our social distance was replicated in the interview setting through the mediating role of my senior assistant and Imboukan's classificatory "grandson." I asked questions in French to my assistant, who translated them into Hausa to the younger man, who in turn translated them in Tamasheq to the elder. These "steps" gave Imboukan and myself time to reflect on what we would say and "study" one another. While these circumstances may appear extreme and therefore not likely to yield valuable results, our efforts to trace and reach Imboukan attested to our respect for his experience and encouraged him to collaborate with us. In what follows, I only reproduce those sections of the interview that concern slavery. Imboukan descended from slaves who lived close to some of the most famous Kel Denneg chiefs. His testimony conveys admiration for his former masters rather than resentment. Imboukan knows that we looked for him because of his proximity to some of the most powerful *imajeghen* of Ader, and he exhibits the pride characteristic of a servus caesaris.

I must be 98 years old. [...] I always lived here. Until the arrival of the White, this was the camp of the *imajeghen*. It is here that Al Fourer lived. My parents told me that these chiefs all used to come here, before they moved to their current residence. They were here with their slaves. They did not do anything, and the slaves did everything for them, except farming. The *imajeghen* had absolute power over the entire area. They had no representatives. They exacted no tributes. They took what they needed, at any time. You understand? They did not take anything in person. They sent their slaves to take bags of millet. Only the sight of one of their slaves gave fear to the villagers. As soon as a *baabzine* entered a village, the villagers would rush to find what they had of most valuable to give him. They feared them. The *imajeghen* didn't do anything, slaves did everything for them, and they just sat. The White abolished slavery, and it was particularly when Kountche came into power that everybody was equal, there was no more question of slavery. The Buzaye fear two things, after God: the *imajeghen* and the White.

The *imajeghen* stayed in tents. When they moved around, they would get off their camels, and people would build tents for them. They stayed as long as they wanted and were fed and served. [...] Slaves were sold in markets like animals. They could also be sold at home: someone could come to the place of a *baabzine* and ask him to buy slaves, and he would sell them. Everybody except a slave could buy slaves. I do not know the price. But the *imajeghen* were sometimes more pressed to sell quickly and leave the market than to bargain over the price. They obtained slaves for nothing, so the price was not stable, it varied a lot, it is impossible to quantify.

The *imajeghen* had groups of religious specialists always with them, who did religious work for them, gave them the authorization to make attacks on the basis of their religious knowledge, and received slaves in exchange.

[...]

The French had sent Amajalla to summon the *imajeghen*. Amajalla was a Black working for the White as interpreter and soldier. He was an ex slave of the Kel Denneg. Amajalla was killed in Fachi, close to Chimborien. The killing of Amajalla took place before the killing of Afadandan.

Amajalla was a soldier in the colonial army *(goumier)* who was killed in 1917 by *imajeghen* related to Al Fourer (or Elkhurer), a dissident chief, when Amajalla brought his former master a convocation from the District Officer. This event is mentioned in colonial archives, but there is no reference to Amajalla's slave status, which gives a different meaning to this episode. Amajalla was killed not just to insult the French, who in the eyes of the former Kel Denneg chiefs were illegitimate occupants; but also to punish him for having had the audacity, as a (former) slave, to bring an order to his masters. It is also noteworthy that the speaker mentions the killing of Amajalla alongside the killing of Afadandan, who was the Chef du Canton, and therefore the most important customary authority recognized by the colonial administration. As in the case of Abdo (testimony 1), the testimonies of slave descendants aggrandize the roles of slave historical figures, otherwise marginalized in colonial archives.

THE PRIDE AND FRUSTRATIONS OF FREEDOM: NEGOTIATING SLAVE DESCENT ACROSS GENERATIONS (DESCENDANTS OF SLAVES OF *INESLEMEN*, MARCH 3, MAY 4, OCTOBER 28, 2005)

I collected this long testimony from an elder (hereafter Mousa) and his son (hereafter Mohamed), both of whom I have known since my first trip to Ader in 1995. I worked in this village many times, often in close association with Mohamed and his wives. The friendship that ties me to the speakers explains the frankness of some statements, which openly describe the stigma of inherited slave status and resentment for past enslavement. This testimony (which includes passages from three separate interviews) exposes some particularly humiliating aspects of slave life: the denial of the slave family, the derogatory names given to slave children, the ongoing psychological pressure to ransom oneself and one's wife, the shame attached to slave descent, and the frustration of having to continue honoring relations with former masters because of economic vulnerability. These interviews were the first occasion when I asked Mousa if he could talk to me about how slavery functioned in the past. Our friendship made it a sensitive topic. They knew I was aware of their status, as Mohamed had been one of the few local persons to self-identify as a "Buzu" when talking to me, in a context that left no doubts that he implied slave descent. But we had not discussed slavery before. At the meetings, they gave me a vivid picture of their historical experience. Toward the end of the testimony, Mousa returns to the topics he most enjoys talking about: his work in colonial (forced labor) projects and his migrations. These memories convey the sense of pride that Mousa derives from his experiences away from slavery, when he used his ingenuity to learn new skills after the tie to his master had been formally severed. But the sense of accomplishment that concludes Mousa's speech contrasts with Mohamed's frustration in the face of continued, if muted, dependence and poverty.

Father:

In the past, we only ate milk and meat. We also collected wild herbs and grains. We ate what animals like monkeys eat on the trees. We did not know agriculture, and did not eat cereals. In the rainy season, we stayed here. After the rains, we left with the animals, then we returned back here. This village was the camp from which people left and to which they returned. If someone died in transhumance, his corpse would be brought here on a camel, he would be buried here. In those times, there were few other villages around here. Even Tahoua was a village of a few straw huts and only *buzaye* lived there.

We lived with the masters, who weren't many, as their slaves. The masters didn't do anything, and we did everything for them, we kept the animals and gathered wild plants.

The *Abzinawa* and the [*malamai*] were together, they formed a united front. The *Abzinawa* would tell the [*malamai*] what they intended to do, and the *malamai* would pray for them and recite powerful verses. For example, if the Tuareg went to a foreign region, the *malamai* would arrange for them not to be seen, to be invisible. They could make special prayers and foretell the future.

We never paid a *zakat*, partly because there were no cereals, but primarily because we did not own anything, we could not give anything because we had no ownership over anything at all. We could not even marry. After the arrival of the French, if we wanted to become independent we could try to pay a sum to the master, and the master would have to free us. Money was rare, back then, so one would give animals. But before the French, ransom was not possible because we had nothing, we could not earn anything either. There were no marriages between the [masters] and us. But if the [masters] liked a woman, they could just take her, and her children would be free and of the masters' status. A freeborn woman could not marry a slave man.

Before the arrival of the French no one migrated. Life was different, and a slave had no independence. A slave was like one of the animals of his master. He could not move without his master's agreement. It was like this: every master family had a main camp. Next to this camp, all his people (relatives and slaves) were buried. Even if they died far away, their corpse would be transported back on a camel and buried here. It was the same place and the same ritual for masters and slaves. There were two main migratory circuits. Before leaving, the *Abzinawa* would beat the drum in different camps, as a sign of departure. The rhythm would be different from that of a war. At the beginning of the rains, masters and slaves went northwards, toward the Azawagh. Then they started returning southwards, and in the dry season they went toward the valleys […], but they never went beyond Madaoua at the border of Hausaland. At any time, there were different groups in circulation, and some people (elders, children, and few youths who were tired of traveling around) who stayed in the main camp. At any time, some people could return, stay a few days, go back… But, before the arrival of the French, a slave could not move around – anyway, why would he move around? There were no markets, no need for money. People had animals, drank milk, did transhumance. Clothes and necessities were mostly provided by masters.

Slaves would not marry between them. The master would tell them to take this one or that one and that's it. A slave could disagree and eventually get with someone else.

Son: You see those heads of cattle on that field? A couple gets together and breeds, then they sort of hang together – that's how it was.

Father: This happened between the slaves of one master. They did not see the slaves of other masters often. Sometimes a slave woman would be pregnant, the master would give her to a male slave, just to find a father for the kid. Children born from slaves did not belong to their father. There may or may not be a naming ceremony, depending on the master's will. Anyway, it is masters who named slave children. Some named them real names, but most of them gave them names which were very different from their own. They named them after plants or animals, or gave them funny Tamasheq names. Or the name of the day when he was born. Slaves would be called names like these:[28]

> Akkozkoz: [imitating the cry of roosters]
> Eggur: castrated animal
> Aggaruf: small plant with thorns
> Amajalla: can't be bothered, he is useless
> Amatteya: the one who does not die
> Anafaran: the chosen one
> Imboran: good farmer

As surname they used the name of a maternal uncle, because the father was uncertain, marriages were promiscuous. A master could dispose of the children of his female slaves, and their [slave] father had no rights upon them. Slave couples got together almost secretly, without testimonies or formalities. It is after the arrival of the French, that some slaves started taking the courage to tell their masters that they would like to marry a certain woman. The master could agree or not. If he agreed, the master could help to arrange the marriage and find something as bridewealth. Because they were working for the master but were not paid, they expected the master to cover their needs. But if the master did not help, the slave could migrate to find some money to pay for his bridewealth. After the arrival of the White, he could leave without his master's authorization. That's because masters would be afraid to forbid their slaves to travel.

[I ask if slaves ever revolted]. In any case, I never heard that slaves revolted in this region. The *Abzinawa* were not many, but they were a lot stronger then us in war. Their weapons were superior, and Allah guided their blows – they never missed, they killed, they were strong and protected. When the *Abzinawa* went on a war, sometimes their dependents, slaves and freed slaves, fought next to them. [...]

Different types of slaves were treated differently. [...] The masters were a lot kinder with the slaves who were always with them, they treated them like relatives and looked after them. Those who lived detached got almost nothing, while at the same time they did not gain much more freedom. Not all the slaves who used to be close to their masters ransomed themselves. Some remained with their masters, as they gained protection and food and it was easier than being on their own. If they were well treated, they could have chosen to remain attached to their masters. An old master is obliged to feed his slaves. Even I, after my mother and father, the first person I prefer staying with is my master.

[I ask 'why?' He replies]: food.

I ransomed myself. I gave two oxen, and received a paper as guarantee. My son ransomed his second wife when he married her, because otherwise her children would belong to her master. I never heard that a master turned down ransom. When the development project came and people from this village got food for work to work on the worksites, many people, men and women, saved money so that they could ransom themselves. Today, if a male slave marries a free woman, the kids are free, only the father is slave. If a man marries a slave woman, her kids belong to her master, unless her husband ransoms her first. This is why my son ransomed his wife. [...]

---

[28] These translations were provided by the interviewees.

People still have to pay ransom because if someone wants to go to Mecca, he must have ransomed himself.[29] Religion demands the payment of ransom. And even if it is outlaw in the government, the laws of the Quran are more important than the government's laws. And if ransom has not been paid, a slave can expect from his master that he pay for his ceremonies. And his master will expect that his slave work for him.

Abdo was my grandfather. [...] He was the only one brave enough to talk to the White. The Tuareg feared them and escaped or hid when they came. Abdo asked the *imajeghen* and the *malamai* to see the White and accept to make peace with them, but they refused and left. Abdo went to see the White and made peace with them. [...] But before this, there were no markets for us, and no money. The White brought onions and sweet potatoes. We began to use a currency, which the White brought, called '*jamil*', which consisted in small coins of bronze, that looked like the 25 fcfa coin. At the time of the White, we built the dam of Adouna. In the past there were lakes which did not dry even in the hot season, and that's where we brought the animals. People did not travel far until the arrival of the White. Only after they arrived, we started to move around. This is how we began to farm... two men from this village had traveled all the way to Kano, and observed farming practices. They saw millet and sorghum, and they took some back. They copied more or less what they had seen, but they were not skilled farmers and only produced five bundles[30]. As back then people were not used to eating cereals, the five bundles lasted them a whole year! They ate just a bit of cereals together with other things. They had no granaries either. So they dug a whole in the earth, washed it with water, put the cereals inside, and covered it with earth again, leaving a sign to mark the place. When they wanted to take cereals, they would dig them out.

I was very brave to remain in [this village]. Many times my old masters sent people to take me and bring me where they are now, because I was their slave. But I always refused. They wanted me to go with them, but I refused. [...]

I did the work for the French airport in Tahoua. It was like when the development project was here and worked with my son, directing him – something like that. I had many important friends in Tahoua, but I never learned French because I did not think, at the time, that it would become the language of power. Otherwise, I would have learned it and I, too, would have become someone important. Afterwards I even looked for the friends I had met in Tahoua, but they would not let me trace them. I also built the road between Niamey and Tahoua. They did not pay me. I was a great traveler! I went to Bilma to take salt, and to Zaria. My generation was the first generation which went '*en exode*'. I was amongst those who worked for the French to build the city of Tahoua. The French had African captains working for them, so I did not work directly with the French. The Afro-French chiefs I knew in Tahoua were: Anza, Tunne, Labo, Moga, Balgagi.... They spoke French, but not Hausa, so they had no common language with workers. The French would kill a bull and feed workers with that meat ...

I did limestone work, too. The French dug limestone toward the river, and people worked there to dig out limestone and roast it and turn it into 'dust' and put it in leather bags, which

---

[29] See interview with intellectual of free descent: "Today, most of the slaves are free. But they still try to redeem themselves, to pay '*fansa*' – which is a religious obligation if someone wants to go to Mecca. Because the pilgrimage of a slave who has not freed himself from his master is null, according to religion. Likewise, a rich man wanting to marry a slave woman would have to pay to free her first, because religiously that will make her children free." Interview with Ibrahim, Ibohamane, April 28, 2005.

[30] In Ader one 'bundle' (Fr. *botte*, Hausa: *damma*) yields roughly 8 kilograms of cereals.

the French collected. In those times, this was forced labor – they used force to bring people to the worksites.

Now many old masters are not powerful anymore. The sources of their wealth were animals and milk, which allowed them to support their dependents. But now it's the time of money and *tuwo*.[31] Now, the old masters are our younger brothers. We may even send each other reciprocal gifts to commemorate our past relation. Our old masters can remember about us and send us clothes or sugar. There is no more slavery. Thanks to the White, we have entered the market.

Son: Everybody today wants freedom. Not a single slave would rather remain a slave than be free. No-one wants to know that people look at you and whisper 'you know, *c'est un esclave*', that's why people still pay ransom.

[I say, but it seems that there are some benefits in the relations with the former masters].

Son (stretching his arms forward): I have two arms. Give me one job, any job that I can do, and I will not look for the former masters again. And even if an old woman cannot work, she can still go to her relatives, rather than her masters, if they have a job and can support her.

SUGGESTED ADDITIONAL READINGS

ON SLAVERY IN HAUSA AND TUAREG SOCIETIES

Bernus, Edmond and Bernus, Suzanne. "L'Evolution de la Condition Servile chez les Touaregs Saheliens." In *L'esclavage en Afrique précoloniale*. Edited by Claude Meillassoux (Paris: Maspero, 1975), 27–47.

Bonte, Pierre. "Esclavage et Relations de Dépendance chez les Touareg Kel Gress." In *L'esclavage en Afrique précoloniale*. Edited by Claude Meillassoux (Paris: Maspero, 1975), 49–75.

Lovejoy, Paul and Baier, Stephen. "The Tuareg of the Central Sudan: Gradations in Servility at the Desert's Edge (Niger and Nigeria)." In *Slavery in Africa: Historical and Anthropological Perspectives*. Edited by Igor Kopytoff and Suzanne Miers (Madison: University of Wisconsin Press, 1977), 391–411.

Rossi, Benedetta, ed. *Reconfiguring Slavery: West African Trajectories*. Liverpool: Liverpool University Press, 2009.

Smith, Mary F. *Baba of Karo: A Woman of The Muslim Hausa*. London: Faber and Faber, 1954.

ON THE HISTORY OF ADER

Echard, Nicole. *L'Experience du Passé. Histoire de la Société Paysanne Hausa de l'Ader*. Etudes Nigeriennes no. 36. Paris: Copedith, 1975.

Hamani, Djibo. *L'Adar Précolonial (République du Niger): Contribution à l'étude de l'histoire des états Hausa*. Paris: L'Harmattan, 1975/2006.

Nicolas, Francis. *Tamesna: Les Ioullemeden de l'Est ou Tuareg Kel Dinnik*. Paris: Imprimerie Nationale, 1950.

ON THE HISTORY OF NIGER

Fuglestad, Finn. *A History of Niger 1850–1960*. Cambridge: Cambridge University Press, 1983.

---

[31] *Tuwo* is a typical Hausa dish, a type of millet-based *polenta*.

INDEX

Note: All names associated with or listed in the primary sources in this volume appear in the index as they are found in those sources. Exceptions to this rule include the names of westerners, and those with western first, middle or surnames. Those names are listed by their surnames.

Made in the USA
Columbia, SC
17 July 2021